# MOTOCOURSE™

## THE WORLD'S LEADING GRAND PRIX & SUPERBIKE ANNUAL

icon
PUBLISHING LIMITED

# RIDE
## WITH US!

FIM-LIVE.COM    FIM-STORE.COM    FIM-TV.COM

FÉDÉRATION INTERNATIONALE
DE MOTOCYCLISME

# CONTENTS

## MOTOCOURSE 2010–2011

is published by:
Icon Publishing Limited
Regent Lodge
4 Hanley Road
Malvern
Worcestershire
WR14 4PQ
United Kingdom

Tel: +44 (0)1684 564511

Email: info@motocourse.com
Website: www.motocourse.com

Printed in the United Kingdom by
Butler Tanner and Dennis Ltd
Caxton Road, Frome
Somerset BA11 1NF

ISBN: 978-1905334-58-2

## DISTRIBUTORS

Gardners Books
1 Whittle Drive, Eastbourne,
East Sussex BN23 6QH
Tel: +44 (0)1323 521555
email: sales@gardners.com

Chaters Wholesale Ltd
10B Doman Road
Camberley
Surrey GU15 3DF
Telephone: +44 (0)1276 686639
Fax: +44 (0)1276 686538
email: ray@chaters.com

NORTH AMERICA
Quayside Distribution Services
400 First Avenue North, Suite 300
Minneapolis, MN 55401 USA
Telephone: 612 344 8100
Fax: 612 344 8691

*Dust jacket:* FIAT Yamaha's Jorge
Lorenzo, who won nine races on
his way to the 2010 MotoGP World
Championship.

*Title page:* Max Biaggi took the
Superbike World Championship on
his Aprilia.
*Photo:* Gold & Goose

## Acknowledgements

The Editor and staff of MOTOCOURSE wish to thank the following for their assistance in compiling the 2010–2011 edition: Henny Ray Abrams, Katie Baines, Majo Botella, Jerry Burgess, Paul Butler, Peter Clifford, Maria Garcia, Maria Guidotti, Tom Jojic, Isabelle Lariviere (FIM), Elisa Pavan, David Pato, Julian Ryder, Stuart Shenton, Mike Trimby, Mike Webb, Steve Westlake and Günther Wiesinger; the riders and technicians quoted in this book; Alpinestars, Marlboro and Repsol hospitality staff; and numerous colleagues and friends.

Photographs published in MOTOCOURSE 2010–2011 have been contributed by:
**Chief photographers:** Gold & Goose.
**Other photographs contributed by:** AMA Pro Series, Gavan Caldwell, Clive Challinor, Dave Collister, Tom Hnatiw, Neil Spalding, Mark Walters

publisher
**STEVE SMALL**
steve.small@iconpublishinglimited.com

commercial director
**BRYN WILLIAMS**
bryn.williams@iconpublishinglimited.com

editor
**MICHAEL SCOTT**

text editor
**IAN PENBERTHY**

results and statistics
**PETER McLAREN**

chief photographers
**GOLD & GOOSE**
David Goldman
Gareth Harford
Patrik Lundin
tel +44 (0)20 8444 2448

MotoGP and circuit illustrations
**ADRIAN DEAN**
f1artwork@blueyonder.co.uk

www.motocourse.com

# FOREWORD by JORGE LORENZO

I THINK a lot of people will understand when I say this is a dream come true. It is a literal fact. This is the greatest prize anyone can win on a motorcycle, and it has been my dream and my ambition for as long as I can remember.

MOTOCOURSE has been grand prix racing's annual 'bible' for 35 years – since before I was born! And if you look back, you will see that a lot of champions say that. It's an obvious thing, a bit of a cliché. All the same, I feel privileged to share that powerful feeling, and to join that elite group on my own account. I am 23 years old, and I hope to add more championships in the future.

I am really a lucky guy. I have been given the best chances to achieve my dream. I have not suffered serious injuries. I have had some of the best support to help me find the right direction and to keep improving, to keep learning.

I have also worked hard. I concentrate on trying to become a better rider, and also a more balanced person, to be calm and to have respect for others – for my rivals on the track and for everybody in any walk of life. Of course, my work is not yet finished, but we have passed an important milestone.

I am proud of my season. I was able to win seven of the first ten races, and to be second in the other three. I set a new record, finishing on the rostrum for the first 12 races. I think the pressure I created at the start of the year was crucial. My main rivals felt that pressure, and it had a big effect.

I need to thank my very experienced chief mechanic Ramon Forcada and his pit crew, the designers, engineers and managers at Yamaha: I am very pleased I will stay with this team and factory for at least two more seasons. And many others for their support: my family and friends, and especially the fans who help make racing feel so important.

I am a new-millennium World Champion – I think the first who can say "Follow me on Twitter". The support of the fans means a lot to me. I hope all the other riders will also get behind me next year.

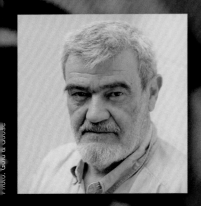

EDITOR'S INTRODUCTION

# A RE-BALANCING OF POWER

THE dust had hardly settled on Spain's amazing year of glory when the new season began at Valencia. That is how it works now. Out with the old, in with the new. Rossi on Ducati, Stoner on Honda, the sights readjust from last Sunday to next November.

It had been an extraordinary year, with an extraordinary new champion. Stoner undid his own challenge, Pedrosa's effort came too late, and ended prematurely. But Rossi, fresh off two more titles in a row but turning 31 before the first race at Qatar and then hurting his shoulder a few days after it ... he was systematically undone by a Lorenzo at full strength. His career-first bone-breaking crash at Mugello was the result of a bad mistake, under pressure. Rossi the perfectionist let his tyres cool off too much while going for bragging rights in free practice.

With the power of a Greek tragedy, racing's all-time superstar fought back, and ended as hero, if not champion. But beneath the spectacle of a natural king fighting to re-assert his supremacy, the plot had many undercurrents. Rossi was plotting his defiant move to Ducati. He will see out his glittering career fulfilling an all-Italian dream that has already galvanised the nation. And Stoner had decided to go to Honda, where a determined development push has turned the unloved RS212-V into the fastest package in the pits.

Other major developments were in progress. Moto2 made such a vigorous debut that questions of whether a production-based control-engine series was worthy of a World Championship title were swept away in a mael-strom of manic motorcycle racing. Moto2 was menacing, and marvellous. A reaffirmation that, as Mick Doohan once said, Sunday's GP "is only a motorbike race". And that is as it should be.

These base-line racers, however, are the precursors of something much more significant: rules were ratified this year for 1000cc production-based MotoGP bikes – a char-ter for Moto2 teams to move up and boost the failing grids of the big class.

Just one thing first. We have to get 2011 out of the way.

Racing only fairly narrowly survived the financial depre-dations of a second impoverished year in succession. More than ever, MotoGP and World Superbikes are competing for a shrinking pool of money. It will not get any easier next year.

But there is a bright side.

Next year will be the last of the 800s, and these unloved prototypes have reached a stage of development where the gaps between the different bikes have been ironed out. There was plenty of good close battling in 2010 – not al-ways for the lead, but good racing nonetheless, belying the bikes' killjoy reputation.

With Simoncelli and Spies joining factory ranks, and the four incumbent aliens all as other-worldly as ever; with Dovizioso up to speed and crazy Toni Elias back, the qual-ity of racing will help MotoGP survive the thin times much better than any rules Dorna or the MSMA could dream up.

Michael Scott – Wimbledon, November 2010

The emperor's new clothes. Rossi wore black for his first ride on his new Ducati.
*Photo: Gold & Goose*

# FIM WORLD CHAMPIONSHIP 2010
# TOP TEN RIDERS
## THE EDITOR'S CHOICE

Rider Portraits by Gold & Goose

# 1 JORGE LORENZO

IT'S hard to decide what was most impressive about Lorenzo during 2010. Was it his results? Nine wins, 16 rostrums, never lower than fourth – and only fell off three times. Was it his record points – 383 was ten more than Rossi in 2008? His partnership with crew chief Ramon Forcada? Always quick to adapt to new tracks or changed conditions, they never missed by much.

We believe, however, that it is his maturity. Most conspicuously, he has added patience and careful measure to the ability to run fast laps – seven times on pole. He showed this several times in his racecraft and, as in his 250 days, a punishing ability to become faster in the closing laps.

"I used to be known as a crazy rider," he said at Valencia, and this was certainly true. Against this, he has become perhaps not the sanest, but certainly the calmest.

Some pundits point to the absence of injured Rossi, suggesting that somehow this undermines Lorenzo's title. But Rossi had crashed while already suffering at the hands of his increasingly unwelcome team-mate.

Lorenzo deserved the championship. And he will be hard to beat in 2011.

# 2 VALENTINO ROSSI

THERE was no doubt about it. Rossi was on the ropes in 2010. Already chafing at the ever growing threat from team-mate Lorenzo – riding his, Rossi's bike, the Italian scuppered his season shortly after inheriting a win in the opening round. A motocross accident left Rossi with a partially dislocated and definitely deranged right shoulder. Rather than mending in six weeks or so as expected, it got no better, requiring surgery after the season.

His broken leg at Mugello, although far more frightening, was less troublesome. But it disrupted his training routine, and for the rest of the year he was less than fully fit, and always with some degree of pain and discomfort from his right shoulder.

He showed his greatness (Again!) by the way he bounced back. Where another rider might have quit early to have the operation, he did much more than soldier on over the gruelling closing stages, with five races in six weeks – including a numerologically apposite 46th win with Yamaha at Malaysia. And that brutal battle with Jorge at Motegi.

And now a new chapter will open, with Ducati. Is there no end to his talents?

## 3 DANI PEDROSA

DANI seemed to cross some sort of a barrier in 2010. He ended the year more highly regarded as a racer, and as a fighter.

It took one or two hard battles to do it – as at Jerez with Lorenzo. Dani came off second best, but still was praised in his home country, rather extravagantly perhaps by one writer, because he had shown the spirit of "a warrior, and a god".

Dani was fighting another battle at the time, with his Honda. Elusive front-end grip and general stability remained a problem through the early races, with Pedrosa pressing on regardless. He claimed five rostrums in the first eight races, and two of them were wins, equalling his previous best result for a season.

By now, however, the Honda was improving rapidly, both in the chassis and in the electronics. He crashed out of the lead at Laguna, but was straight back on the rostrum for the next race, following that with two back-to-back wins – a real first.

By the time his Honda bit him at Motegi, Pedrosa was the strongest rider in the pack, and closing (admittedly from rather a distance) on overall points leader Lorenzo.

A best season, by far.

## 4 CASEY STONER

THE way Casey rode most of the time should put him higher on this list. On his day, he was uncatchable; his fourth successive home GP win is a classic example. But he crashed out of five races.

At first, this was because of a chassis and front suspension that didn't marry up to his individual style, which in turn combines extreme aggression with very sensitive throttle control. The Ducati pit finally got a handle on this in the latter part of the year. Casey kept crashing, but now it was for a different reason. With the championship gone, he was pressing on, win or bust: "I'm not going out there to finish third."

Stoner is a refreshing character in racing. More at ease as he grows older, he has a powerful and often dangerous smile, and likes to speak his mind. Although diplomatic to his employers and sponsors, he is happy to give full vent to his opinions on other riders – especially those who follow him in practice to improve their lap times.

The Ducati is a rather special, personal bike. Stoner now goes to the other end of the spectrum: the committee-built Honda. Test results were ominous for his rivals.

## 5 TONI ELIAS

THE way things were in the Socialist Workers Paradise of Moto2, it took something really special to stand out. Toni Elias had that ingredient, on a serial basis. The engaging Spaniard's first world championship was well deserved.

As a former MotoGP winner, beating Rossi no less, Elias was expected to do well in the junior class. He added a powerful motivation to succeed: it might give him a route back up to the big class.

But he had a lot against him. He was injured at the start of the season after a collision with a slow rider during a mixed 125/Moto2 test session in Spain (who thought that a good idea?), and stricken with fever and illness in the middle of it.

Through it all, he put up a series of indomitable performances and claimed seven wins, four of them in succession. No one else was anywhere near as consistent. Elias scored points in the first 15 races, and only spoiled his perfect record with a couple of rather headstrong crashes in the last two races.

He will get the reward: he returns to MotoGP on an LCR Honda in 2011. It will be interesting to see what lessons he brings back with him.

## 6 BEN SPIES

THE maiden World Superbike champion came into MotoGP racing carrying a lot of expectations. He made good on pretty much all of them. A first-season win was not to happen, but he managed pretty much everything else of importance: qualifying on the front row, and then on pole at Indianapolis; a rostrum at Silverstone and then second at Indy.

All this while learning not only a new motorcycle, but also new circuits. In a generally calm and measured way, he would be unobtrusively fast in qualifying, often lose places in the early laps, then by the end give demonstrations of well-planned overtaking moves as he climbed back through the midfield towards the front.

Obviously absorbed in his task, Spies sometimes could seem distant. But then he was on an express train, and for 2011 it has taken him to central station, to climb on the factory Yamaha so recently vacated by Rossi.

There are parts of his racing armoury that need polishing up, particularly an ability to go faster in the early laps. Nothing about the quiet Texan's progress so far suggests he will not be able to learn this.

DOVI was somewhat disappointing in 2009, his first year on a factory bike, his second in MotoGP. The 2010 season started only a little better. The Italian with the mournful eyes had begun by threatening, in so many words, to oust Pedrosa from the top Honda position after being faster in testing. Then while he racked up a series of rostrums, somehow he seemed to lack the finishing touches.

Funnily enough, it was only when Pedrosa went missing injured that Dovi began to shine – hounding Stoner all the way in Japan, and similarly Rossi in Malaysia. But like Pedrosa, he was undone by an assembly fault at the next race, and although third again at the following race, he never did regain that lost momentum.

By then, he had done enough, contractually, to win another chance on the factory Honda. In terms of natural justice, also he had done enough, but only just.

In 2011, he (like Pedrosa) is in serious danger of being completely overshadowed by new team-mate Stoner. He has another chance to show that while possibly a slow learner, he is a very thorough one.

We shall see if there is more to Dovizioso.

# 8 NICKY HAYDEN

NICKY bounced back from his tricky first year with Ducati, racking up a set of solid fourth-place finishes at the start of the season while team-mate Stoner fizzed and sparkled.

Then the American ran somewhat into the doldrums, often at odds with the settings of his Desmosedici, clearly a tricky bike that Stoner found no easier to fine tune, and he found himself in some undignified battles in the wrong half of the top ten.

By the end of the year, he'd recovered some pride, working hard constantly to overcome erratic practice performances and focus on race day. And all the while he preserved his good humour and rightfully popular persona.

In this way, by sheer dogged persistence, he finally did make it to the rostrum in Aragon, for just one visit, putting an impressively forceful pass on Lorenzo to get there. But he acquitted himself well also when fighting with Rossi for third in Australia. He missed it, but lots of other good riders have been beaten by Valentino.

Hayden has won the world championship in the past, with solid workmanlike riding and sheer dogged effort. He will be lucky if he gets the same chance again.

# 9 MARCO SIMONCELLI

IT'S not easy climbing off a lithe 250 two-stroke on to an 800cc MotoGP four-stroke, as 2010's crop of high-level rookies demonstrated. Alvaro Bautista made a good fist, too, but nobody came close to the big-hair, big-voice and big-character Simoncelli.

He arrived slow and dangerous at the tests, suffering a major crash, and similarly was at sea for the early races. But, in his bull-in-a-china-shop fashion, he was learning fast, and by the time the season wore to a close, he was making his presence seriously felt among the faster riders. Rossi was one who found him hard to pass.

'Super-Sic' describes his racing technique thus: "I don't give my rivals any presents." Nowhere was this better displayed than at the last race at Valencia, when Lorenzo passed him twice in one lap, only to be passed straight back; then on the third attempt, Simoncelli closed the door so firmly that the champion almost crashed. He had got in front of him after qualifying on the front row of the grid for the first time.

For 2011, the Italian gets a factory Honda. He will certainly be ready to wring its neck. Of course, there's more to becoming a great rider than that. But it's not a bad start.

# 10 MARC MARQUEZ

JUST 17, Marquez ran a remarkably dominant campaign. He'd have won the title much earlier but for a crash triggered by technical failure at Jerez, and being knocked off on the first corner at Aragon.

Victory at round four at Mugello was his first GP win, but he picked up the habit quickly, taking the next four in a row, before a mid-season flutter.

Then he was back to the same form, ending up with a total of ten wins, after starting from pole on 12 occasions. Most were dominant, moving clearly away in the later laps. He'd learned to ride so fast, he explained, after a couple of years on the KTM, which had been slower, so you had to try harder. Now on a Derbi, it was easy.

Loris Capirossi was also 17, but 98 days younger when he became the youngest ever world champion in 1990. Marquez is the second youngest.

But at that time, Capirossi was a wild and impetuous rider (to some extent, he still is). Marquez could hardly have been less so. His race tactics showed calm and maturity, so too did his general approach to the whole task.

We may have been watching the start of something very big.

# MOTO-GEDDON: THE YEAR OF ALMIGHTY CHANGE

Thinning grids, disappearing teams and sponsors. Could life become any more difficult in GP racing? Or could there really be light at the end of the tunnel? MICHAEL SCOTT considers the possibility...

*Above:* Sparse grids and spare seats – at least at Indy. Spies leads the charge of the light brigade.

*Right:* There's always one. This year it was Lorenzo.

*Photos:* Gold & Goose

WITH the world still in financial doldrums, why should it be any different in motorbike racing? No matter what the level, everyone was feeling the pinch. Even the last remaining handful of high rolling sponsor spenders – think Marlboro, Repsol and once-a-year BMW – had to tighten their snakeskin belts.

The crisis triggered drastic action over 2009 and 2010, from a knee-jerk flurry of cost-saving measures of dubious value to a total rethink of the basis of racing. This seismic shift towards a humbler, but more numerous future will take time, but it got well under way in 2010. Now we all have to get through 2011 in much the same enfeebled condition as this year before we can see the fruits of the radical new regulations in 2012.

MotoGP had a number of great strengths in place in 2010: lively TV and trackside appeal, several top-class venues eager to host the races and an established seniority in its Latin-European homeland. And the trump card: Valentino Rossi. This one-man cast-iron guarantee of continued high visibility even had an extra afterglow, in the form of intriguing new challenges to the ageing king of the jungle.

Two things were lacking, and they went hand in hand: sponsors and riders. The MotoGP grid shrank to alarmingly low levels – a permanent staff of 17, with no wild-cards. Three races (Britain, the Netherlands and Australia) could muster only 15 starters, a quorum for world championship points all round. In Germany, there were only 13, but it was a restart and four riders had gone missing in action at the first attempt. The lowest ever, by the way, was six, in Argentina in 1961; the highest, 97 in the Isle of Man TT of 1969.

Tumbling motorcycle sales put all the factories in the same sort of tight spot, to varying degrees, while the lack of credible new sponsorship had been a problem long before the financial crisis struck. That just made it worse. For all Dorna's VIP Village and high-end entertainment aspirations, the big players just weren't coming to the casino.

Thus, in a way, the worldwide banking crisis at the end of 2008 merely accentuated what was already happening; and accelerated what has been a radical response – nothing less than a fundamental rethink of the basis of grand prix racing.

To some extent, the world championships have always been beholden to the factories – the only people equipped to build and keep building the sort of pur-sang out-and-out specialised racing prototypes that we expect to see at grand prix level. Even when it was only MV Agusta playing that game, the old order was respected.

It stayed the same through the ages, right up to and beyond the sea-change shift of MotoGP in 2002. When numbers started to dwindle, with the loss of Aprilia, Team Roberts and Kawasaki, and the 'here today, gone tomorrow' Ilmor, Dorna's Carmelo Ezpeleta turned to the remaining factories for support. He sought a solution whereby they might lease more bikes or even just engine packages at prices that independent teams could afford.

The factories failed to deliver; proposed prices were way too high. A solution had to be sought elsewhere.

Effectively, the factories – or their MSMA organisation – had thrown up their hands in baffled surrender. This weakening of position triggered a restructuring of the management system, which is due to come into force in 2012. Ezpeleta seized back future control of the technical regulations from the MSMA (it retains only the power of veto, which must be by unanimous decision).

More immediately, he forced ahead with an idea he'd mooted the year before: of beefing up the MotoGP grid with an underclass of low-cost back-of-the-field bikes. He mollified the MSMA with the notion that their prototypes would remain sacrosanct and unbeatable. And proceeded, at the same time, with the great Moto2 experiment.

This now comes into focus as a trial run. At least the handing over of engines on a plate, solving the sourcing problem at a stroke, would establish the strength of the infrastructure – especially specialised chassis constructors – required to create this new sub-prototype class.

The response was more overwhelming than merely heartening. Fifteen different types of chassis (a couple of them admittedly renamed variations) lined up on a Moto2 grid that bulged out to 40 or more, and will continue to do so in 2011, in spite of attempts to put up the barriers at a more manageable 36. And this in spite of the teams in the feeder class suffering at least as badly, and often a lot worse than in MotoGP from the chill financial climate. Several teams struggled and two went bust during 2010; there is likely to be more of the same in 2011.

Engines for the new 'Claiming Rule Teams' won't be quite as simple to get hold of as in Moto2, but there are a number of possibilities, using production sourced engines as a basis. The chassis technology obviously also is available, as Moto2 has shown. Less clear are the details of exactly how the so-called Claiming Rule will work. Current plans moot a 20,000-euro claiming fee for a team to buy another's engine after a race, giving the teams a fine balance between expensive horsepower and the need for a realistic budget. And a warning, announced after an August GP Commission meeting at Brno, that the commission has the right to promote a Claiming Rule Team to the more stringent status of a factory team by simple majority, "due to the performance of the team". In other words, better not go too fast.

Technical rules for this 2012 sea-change are the same for both types:

Capacity: **up to 1000cc**

Maximum number of cylinders: **four**

Maximum bore: **81mm**

Minimum weight: **150kg (up to 800cc) and 153kg (over 800cc)**

Maximum number of engines available for use by each rider: **six (Claiming Rule Teams, 12)**

Fuel tank capacity: **21 litres (Claiming Rule Teams, 24)**

That only leaves us, in 2011, to put up with one more year of thin grids on obsolescent and expensive 800s. Thankfully, the quality of riders suggests that it might be a lot more fun than one might be entitled to expect.

And if in the future, grand prix racing does veer increasingly towards production-based components, that is in itself an integral part of its very roots.

## FUELS RUSH IN

The concession of twice as many engines for CRTs should release horsepower without unleashing spiralling costs. But the extra three litres of fuel could be as significant. Of all the restrictive rules introduced over the past ten years, the diminished fuel allowance has had more effect on racing than control tyres and reduced engine capacities put together. And not for the better.

The 800s ushered in a notoriously processional period of bike GP racing. Where the wheel-spinning 990s offered riders different possible riding techniques and corner lines, the 800s were exactingly accurate one-line motorcycles that tended to string out along that line during the course of a race, everyone circulating close to his ideal lap time. We saw more of it in 2010, although thankfully a narrowing of performance gaps and a feistier group of riders did shake things up now and then.

The main culprit was said to be the increasingly sophisticated electronics, and to an extent this was true. But electronics, an intrinsic part of modern engineering, can be programmed to perform all sorts of tasks. The reason for them being set to cut wheelspin and measure the power out so carefully was not to help the riders, but to limit fuel consumption.

The same will be true of the 2012 1000cc prototypes, or even more true: the engine capacity has risen by a full 25 per cent; the fuel allocation has remained the same. The extra three litres available to the CRT bikes – an increase of less than 15 per cent – will make only a little difference.

Without doubt, turning grand prix racing into part economy run has seriously damaged the spectacle. Perversely, it has also been an interesting and very valuable avenue of research and development for factory engineers. Lessons learned are directly applicable to production motorcycles: in this instance, racing really has improved the breed, making it highly worthwhile at an important level. It's a pity about the lost spectacle.

The other great limiting rule, new for 2010, had little or no effect on the racing, much to some people's relief, but as yet only an adverse effect on expense, in spite of being intended as a cost-cutting measure. It is the statute of engine limita-

### ENGINE USE TABLE

| | Scrapped | In Use | Unused |
|---|---|---|---|
| **HONDA** | | | |
| Dani Pedrosa | 0 | 5 | 1 |
| Andrea Dovizioso | 0 | 6 | 0 |
| Marco Simoncelli | 0 | 6 | 0 |
| Marco Melandri | 0 | 6 | 0 |
| Randy de Puniet | 1 | 5 | 0 |
| Hiro Aoyama | 2 | 4 | 0 |
| | | | |
| **YAMAHA** | | | |
| Valentino Rossi | 1 | 5 | 0 |
| Jorge Lorenzo | 2 | 4 | 0 |
| Ben Spies | 0 | 6 | 0 |
| Colin Edwards | 1 | 5 | 0 |
| | | | |
| **DUCATI** | | | |
| Casey Stoner | 3 | 3 | 0 |
| Nicky Hayden | 2 | 4 | 0 |
| Mika Kallio/Carlos Checa | 2 | 4 | 0 |
| Aleix Espargaro | 2 | 4 | 0 |
| Hector Barbera | 2 | 3 | 1 |
| | | | |
| **SUZUKI** (nine engines) | | | |
| Loris Capirossi | 2 | 4 | 3 |
| Alvaro Bautista | 2 | 6 | 1 |

same company denied the use of expensive metal coatings, treatments or components (team chief Nakajima insisted the unit cost was as before), other companies told a different story. More highly specialised surface treatments and racing parts – especially pistons and con-rods – had hiked costs significantly. Ducati insiders spoke of another resultant cost – more test days, test riders and test miles, dedicated purely to endurance testing components.

Perhaps the most expensive research has now been done and cost savings will accumulate in the years to come. But engineers agree that the techniques have little relevance to the real world of motorcycling, where targets are more like 100,000km of reliable use, rather than just 2,000.

## TWO-STROKES – THE LAST CADENZA

The final passing of the two-stroke racing grand prix motorcycle gained formal sanction during 2010 with the creation of 250 four-stroke Moto3 for 2012. The death throes had been protracted enough for there to be no element of surprise, nor any outcry. Mourning for the lost strokers had already taken place when the 250s were killed off; GP racing had moved on and was fully occupied with the new excitement of Moto2.

Yet there is a large body of opinion to whom the jettisoning of this type of engine is a betrayal not only of the past, but also the future, and a craven abandonment of any role in potentially valuable engine research.

For well-rehearsed reasons, the two-stroke is an ideal motorcycle power unit: compact, simple, light and very responsive. Modern oils and injection techniques have taken the smoke out of the exhausts and rebalanced the air pollution equation. Environmentally, there are further persuasive arguments. There is a great deal less pollution at all stages: manufacture, maintenance and disposal.

Yet this engine type has been hounded out of fashion and out of the showrooms. And now also out of the GPs.

MotoGP did not lead the two-stroke's fall from grace, but it has followed willingly. At the same time, restrictive and cost-saving technical rules banning direct injection effectively closed further development of the racing two-stroke: the current 125s are the end of the line and have changed little over the past few years.

There are still engineers who believe so strongly in the two-stroke's many merits, compared with the complicated four-stroke, that research and development continues. Sadly, there will be no place for these developments to be tested and displayed anywhere in the MotoGP paddock.

The new class also breaks another link with history. The 125s are the last of the original world championship classes to survive since inception in 1949. The 500s have gone to MotoGP, 250s to Moto2, 350s to oblivion. Goodbye, 125s.

## THE BOOK OF NUMBERS

*Above:* Racing by numbers. Terol's ad logo overpowers his rainbow number 40. And Number 2 behind is actually number 7. Probably. Rules change for next year.

*Top:* The 2011 season started 48 hours after the last race of 2010. Hayden was back on his Ducati.
*Photos: Gold & Goose*

tions: just six sealed units for each rider all year. Unless you are Suzuki, which was granted a special concession for nine.

There were fears that an engine transgression, punished by a start from the pit lane ten seconds behind the rest, might affect the outcome of the world championship. As it turned out, nobody did incur that penalty. All engines went the distance, in spite of some worrying moments, as when Lorenzo's number-two motor, only raced twice, blew up spectacularly in practice at the Sachsenring, triggering two more crashes on spilled oil. (Lorenzo escaped reprimand for not getting straight off the track, but the lesson should have been learned by all.)

All agreed that there had been a significant saving on the actual numbers of engine units built – perhaps halved for a two-rider team from as many as 35 engines a year. But costs had shot up in other areas. Yamaha admitted perhaps a 20-per-cent increase in development costs to convert its 600km engine into a safe 2,000km runner; and while the

It was back in 1992 that grand prix racing abandoned the long-established colour coding of racing numbers to distinguish the different classes – the 500s were black on yellow, for example; 125s white on black. From now, any colour would do.

This was a sop to the big sponsors, whose own carefully researched brand images didn't necessarily sit well with a splash of yellow or green. And over the years, a combination of fashion and advertising had led to increasing latitude in interpretation. It is, for example, quite hard to pick out the numbers on the Aspar 125s, even when they are parked alongside one another, let alone when moving.

In welcome news for TV and trackside spectators, the GP Commission closed the year with firm rules for the return of clearly legible racing numbers, to be displayed on the centre of the front of the fairing, in an easily readable font, and on a sufficiently contrasting single-colour background

Not all changes are for the worse.

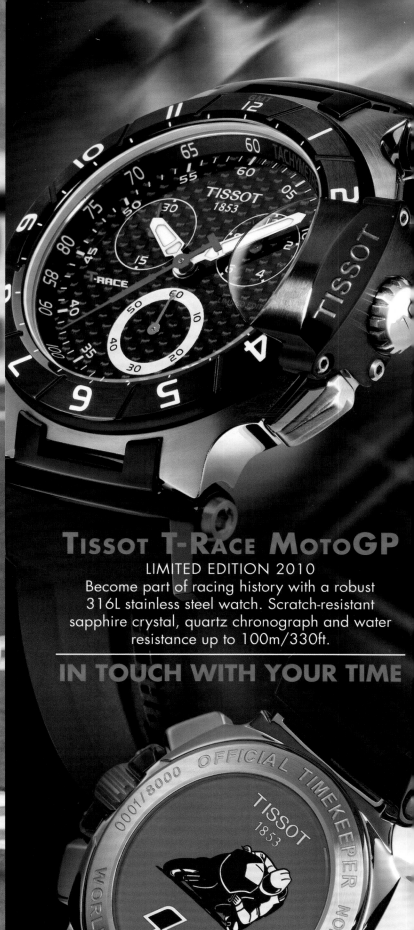

# THE RISE OF SPAIN:
# FROM TORRAS TO LORENZO

In 2010, Spain utterly dominated the motorcycle world championships. DENNIS NOYES, himself a former Spanish champion, looks at the long history behind the current success on two wheels...

*Above:* Centre of attention. Jorge Lorenzo became Spain's first world champion since 1999.
*Photo: Gold & Goose*

*Opposite, from top:* Ricardo Tormo (Bultaco) in action at Brno in 1978, his first 125 season; Victor Palomo, the exception, who won races in both 350cc and 750cc classes in the 1970s; Angel Nieto looked tough and was tough, king of the smaller classes; Nieto in action on the 125cc Bultaco in 1976.
*Photos: Motocourse Archive*

DURING the 2010 season, Spanish riders won 36 of 52 races in the three solo classes, an impressive 69 per cent of all races run. It wasn't quite enough to surpass the record set by British riders in 1967, when, racing in five solo classes, they won 37 of the 50 races (74 per cent). Spanish riders, however, did win all three championships. They took the top three places in 125cc (while running up an ongoing total of 26 consecutive wins in the smallest class), won the first ever Moto2 title and, more importantly, between World Champion Jorge Lorenzo and runner-up Dani Pedrosa, won 13 of the 18 races in the premier class. This kind of success, from a country that hadn't a single GP win until the 20th year of the FIM world championships and that did not win a 500 race until 1992, is the result of sedulous preparation at national championship level, and the passion of a nation where motorcycle racing is an elite sport and its best riders are true national heroes.

When the promoters of the United States Grand Prix played the wrong national anthem, the Italian, after Jorge Lorenzo won in 2010, it came during an extraordinary streak of Spanish wins in MotoGP that eventually would reach 11 in a row. After about ten seconds, they switched to the Spanish anthem, which became ubiquitous at grands prix in 2010.

And I thought, as I saw Lorenzo's perplexed look and Rossi's impish smile, that Spain had certainly come a long, long way in grand prix racing since the days when the Spanish national anthem was the musical background only for 'support class' podiums – often for 50cc and 125cc, but only very briefly, during 1969 and 1970, for the occasional 250 podium. From the death of Santiago Herrero in 1970 to Sito

Pons's win at Jarama in 1984, Spanish riders were not winners in 250, although Victor Palomo, an atypical Spaniard in so many ways, did win a 350cc GP in 1974 at Montjuich. But never, until that day at Assen in 1992, the sunny weekend when Doohan crashed and Criville won, was the stirring and officially wordless anthem ever associated with premier-class ceremonies (wordless, because the Spanish, due to their smouldering differences, still cannot agree on any lyrics).

It was during that ten-second blunder, very uncomfortable for Lorenzo, and very amusing for Rossi and Stoner (who, if he had won, perhaps would have been regaled with *Waltzing Matilda*, as was Chris Vermeulen when he won in Superbikes at Laguna Seca in 2004), that I suddenly thought of Chris Carter, the first editor of *MOTOCOURSE* and for so many years the voice that came down from the sky over major British road races.

It was back in 1975 or 1976 at Anderstorp, because I can almost smell the pines as I remember this, and I was a young GP journalist working for Spain's *Motociclismo*. I always was assigned to the July and August races when the regular GP reporter was off at the beach. So, without really knowing any relevant riders other than Angel Nieto and Victor Palomo, I decided to attempt a trade. I summoned my courage to approach Mr Carter, whom I perceived as the pre-eminent GP journalist in the three-sided Quonset hut that the Anderstorp promoters called a media centre, and suggested to him that we exchange information. I would tell him the news from Nieto and Palomo if he would help me out with Read and Sheene. The reply I have never forgotten because

it established the exchange rate of the day. "I'll agree to a better trade," said Carter loudly. "If you promise to tell me nothing of your Spaniards, I will supply you with some snippets from the garages of *Messieurs* Sheene and Read."

That was Chris being Chris. He really did care what was going on with the factory Derbi rider and the hard-riding Yamaha privateer, but it was his way of putting a 'Spam' in his place. ('Spam' was Chris's name for what he decided I was – a Spanish American.)

So when they didn't play the Spanish anthem at Laguna, it was news, whereas back in those pre-Criville days, the very idea of Spanish music being played after a 500cc race would have been unthinkable.

There was some indignation back in Spain, where the playing of 'Rossi's anthem' after Lorenzo's win was considered a lack of respect rather than just a Laguna Seca gaffe. But Spanish fans have waited 11 years since Criville's 500 title for a second premier-class crown, and they expect what is due them without any funny business.

In 2010, Spanish riders won it all, first and second in all three FIM grand prix classes, an unprecedented feat that may never be repeated. But Spain's current hegemony is no coincidence. It all started a long, long time ago, and for any attempt to understand this Spanish wildfire of success we must look back to a time when British and Italian riders were supreme, and when four-stroke MV 500s were still unchallenged by Japanese two-strokes.

The first Spanish victory was back in 1968, when Salvador Canellas won his home GP at Montjuich Park on a Bultaco TSS 125. In those days, Spain was still under a dictatorship and something of a political pariah. The government had completely closed the Spanish market to Japanese imports to protect the domestic industry.

Today, 42 years after Canellas brought that little single-cylinder Bultaco (number 24, Toni Elias's number) home first, thanks to Phil Read and Bill Ivy breaking their V4 125cc Yamahas while scrapping for the lead, Spanish riders have overwhelmed their opponents in all three GP classes.

How did this come about?

The small, but vibrant motorcycle industry that was protected by trade embargoes produced a fierce rivalry between the likes of Montesa, Bultaco, OSSA, Derbi and Lube, and that created opportunities for Spanish riders at national level. When first Montesa, and then Bultaco and Derbi looked beyond their borders to the challenge of the FIM grand prix series, the very best Spanish riders got their chances in the smaller classes. Beyond the Spanish factories, only the Italian builders considered hiring Spanish riders: the Japanese manufacturers refused to acknowledge the riders of a country that enforced protectionist commercial policies.

Otherwise, Nieto and Ricardo Tormo would probably have found their way up the rungs and would have had their chance on Japanese 500s, just as Barry Sheene, Nieto's contemporary, deservedly did. Instead, unless they could finance themselves as privateers (like the late Victor Palomo, who raced virtually in exile and won the 1976 Formula 750 European title on a Yamaha TZ750), Spain's best riders were obliged to focus on the smaller classes and to ride single-cylinder Spanish bikes.

Although Canellas took that first win for Spain on a

Bultaco in 1968, and Nieto the first title on a Derbi in 1969, there are many old-timers in Spain who would argue that the greatest Spanish rider of all time never won a grand prix.

It was in 1965 that Ramon Torras was killed when he hit a tree at Comarruga with his Bultaco TSS 250, back in the day when the Spanish championship was run through village streets. Already that young season, Torras had shown his potential by taking third in both the 250cc and 125cc events at the West German GP (Nürburgring-Sud), backing that up with a second place, between the factory Yamahas of Read and Michael Duff, at the Spanish GP (Montjuich). It is not a lack of respect for Spain's first world champion, Angel Nieto, that prolongs the legend of Torras.

Likewise, those of us who were following the world championship in the late 1960s believe that the man who should have been Spain's first 250 champion was Santiago Herrero, who died on the Isle of Man in 1970 when his OSSA single went down at the 13th milestone. No disrespect to Sito Pons, the man who finally won the 250 title in 1988, but there were great riders before, and Spain is a country that remembers.

No one who ever saw Torras or Herrero ride doubts that they were great and fearless riders, at a time when racing was so terribly dangerous that the occasional fatality was considered completely normal.

I mention all this to belie the notion that Spain has only recently begun to produce great riders. I could name a dozen from the 1970s who were very good, but who never enjoyed their day in the sun outside their homeland.

Perhaps it is because Spanish riders first distinguished themselves in the smaller classes that the

tradition of starting with 125s continued, when the trend in other countries was to get young riders on to 600cc Supersports as soon as possible. The 125cc class continued throughout the 1990s, and to this day it is the only starting point for all but the tallest and heaviest (Ruben Xaus, for example) of Spanish riders. Traditionally, the best Spanish riders move from the nationals into the 125 world championship instead of moving on or even starting, as is often the case, in the USA and Great Britain, with Supersports.

During the late 1970s and right up until the turn of the century, it seemed that Spain was on the wrong track, or on a dead-end road. After Kenny Roberts revolutionised the way 500s were ridden, the accepted style became that used by ex-dirt trackers from the United States and Australia. The advice to rising stars with 500 aspirations was to avoid the '250 style' based on high corner speed, and to learn to 'back 'em in and fire 'em out'.

With this model and with the fierce power characteristics of the 500s, the change of style, and the need for rear-wheel steering and dirt-track techniques became a self-fulfilling prophecy.

And this meant that the road to 500s was blocked not just for Spanish riders, but also for most European riders. Except for the Lucchinelli-Uncini blip on the chart in 1981 and 1982, every 500 world champion from 1978 through until Spain's Alex Criville in 1999 was a tail-slider.

At the end of the 1986 season, current *MOTO-COURSE* editor Michael Scott wrote of Frenchman Christian Sarron's aspiration to win on a 500 in the dry: "To do that, he and everybody else will need to know how to steer a motorcycle by spinning the rear

wheel. There is no going back, and riders who cannot make the jump will have to stay in the smaller classes, where fluent riding style still wins races. In the 500cc class, the old order has changed for ever."

And that was certainly what we all believed, and something that could become true again if the MotoGP 1000cc bikes of 2011 were stripped of their intrusive electronic rider aids.

Long before traction control, upcoming Spanish riders who managed a track pass for their national GP watched in awe as Roberts, and those who followed over the years, lit up the rear tyres out of Jarama's Bugatti Hairpin and fired out sideways, smoking the rubber uphill towards the Monza right-hander. I remember standing on the outside of Bugatti in 1978 and watching Roberts do just that. It was about that time that he became known as 'The Martian'. The late Italian photographer Franco Villani explained to me, "In Italy, we call Roberts a Martian because he is small, dressed all in yellow and comes from another planet." That was planet dirt track.

As grand prix racing entered the 1980s, European riders, flummoxed by this new and counter-intuitive riding style, seemed destined for the smaller classes, and Spanish riders were relegated even further to the smallest, 50cc (becoming 80cc in 1984) and 125cc.

## The Pons-Cobas factor

I recall a long talk with Antonio Cobas in the late 1970s. He understood exactly what Rainey, Lawson, Gardner and Doohan were doing to get the 500cc two-strokes turned and launched spinning off the corners, sacrificing corner speed, but gaining time by

getting better acceleration. He smiled and made a pronouncement: "The 500 and the way it has to be ridden constitute an aberration."

Until traction caught up with available power, he reckoned, it would take the peculiar skills of dirt-track racers to win in 500. The way the dirt-trackers rode was "more chaos than science," he felt. At the time, he said this, in the spring of 1988, he was working for Sito Pons's Campsa Honda team, at the beginning of what would become the most exciting battle for the 250 title that Spanish fans had ever seen.

Pons and Cobas contributed between them so much to the current state of motorcycle racing in Spain that it would be impossible to chronicle here their joint and individual accomplishments.

Cobas started in automobile racing, and his dream was to build his own Formula One car, but his genius was recognised quickly in Spanish motorcycle racing. His multi-tubular Siroko-Rotax 250 evolved into the aluminium twin-spar 250s that would soon become almost universal in racing. Working out of a private team, Campsa Honda, he introduced sophisticated electronic data acquisition in GP motorcycle racing when the factories were only beginning to go down that path.

With Pons, Spain moved into a 'post Nieto' period. Like his contemporary, Carlos Cardus, and the slightly younger Juan Garriga, Pons set his sights immediately on the 250 class, while Jorge 'Aspar' Martinez was, like Nieto and Ricardo Tormo before him, signed to ride factory bikes in the smaller classes.

And like current Spanish star Dani Pedrosa, Pons made his mark in a highly publicised talent search. The 1979 Copa Streaker, a Bultaco promotional

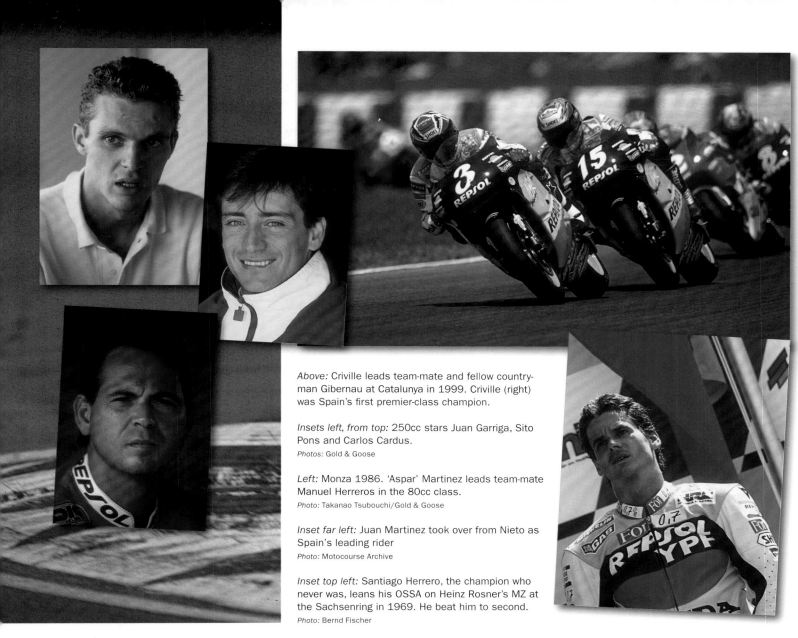

*Above:* Criville leads team-mate and fellow country-man Gibernau at Catalunya in 1999. Criville (right) was Spain's first premier-class champion.

*Insets left, from top:* 250cc stars Juan Garriga, Sito Pons and Carlos Cardus.
*Photos:* Gold & Goose

*Left:* Monza 1986. 'Aspar' Martinez leads team-mate Manuel Herreros in the 80cc class.
*Photo:* Takanao Tsubouchi/Gold & Goose

*Inset far left:* Juan Martinez took over from Nieto as Spain's leading rider
*Photo:* Motocourse Archive

*Inset top left:* Santiago Herrero, the champion who never was, leans his OSSA on Heinz Rosner's MZ at the Sachsenring in 1969. He beat him to second.
*Photo:* Bernd Fischer

championship, employed the Bultaco M204A 125cc single. This was the last great initiative by Bultaco before financial and union problems set in, leading to eventual closure. The purpose of the Copa Streaker was glorious: "To discover the next generation of world champions." And it was a glorious success: Pons (two 250 titles) won, followed by Jorge 'Aspar' Martinez (three 80cc and one 125cc titles) and Carlos Cardus (runner-up in 250 in 1990).

Pons won the 1988 250 world championship after a year-long battle with arch rival Juan Garriga, a battle that polarised Spanish fans, dividing them into 'Ponsistas' and 'Garriguistas'. More importantly, that season changed the way Spanish riders and fans thought about the place of Spain in grand prix racing. No longer limited to 80cc and 125cc, the next step would be the big one to the 500 class.

Suddenly, winning in the smaller classes, including 250, was no longer enough. In 1989, Sito Pons won the 250 title again easily, overshadowing the championships won by Alex Criville (125) and Manuel 'Champi' Herreros, the last ever 80cc champion. That year, the 500cc title was taken for the second season in a row by American Eddie Lawson. The only Spanish riders to score points in the 500 class in 1989 were privateers Fernando Gonzalez de Nicolas (eighth at the largely boycotted Grand Prix of the Nations in Misano) and the late Juan Lopez Mella (once 14th and twice 15th).

Now Pons, who had already ridden for a single season in 1985 on an uncompetitive Suzuki RG500, converted his Campsa Honda Pons 250 team, complete with Antonio Cobas as technical director and his top mechanics (including Ramon Forcada, currently

crew chief for Jorge Lorenzo), into the Campsa Honda Pons 500 team, with himself as sole rider. Juan Garriga also made the move to 500 with his own Ducados Yamaha team.

Spanish fans were excited, but Spanish journalists feared that the country's two best riders would fare no better than Christian Sarron, the 1984 250 champion who had won a 500cc race in the wet in 1985 and had continued to run near the front over the next five seasons, even racking up a string of five consecutive pole positions in 1988 and a career-best third overall finish in 1989. But, like so many riders up from the 250 class, he flew over the bars with predictable regularity.

Garriga proved the better 500 rider over Pons, but neither scored a podium in 1990 and 1991. Pons had already decided to retire after a series of crashes had seen him tenth in 1990 and 14th in 1991 (Garriga, who would carry on for another season with Yamaha in 1992, was sixth and seventh in his first two 500 seasons).

Team owner Pons replaced himself with Alex Criville and unprecedented success came quickly, almost too quickly. In round three of the 1992 series, Criville took his and Spain's first ever 500cc podium, and in mid-summer he won at Assen.

It was a fortuitous win: Rainey had flown home after the first day of practice, suffering from injuries from the previous GP; Doohan had crashed in practice, the crash that caused him to miss three races and lose the title; and then Schwantz and Lawson took each other out early in the race. But the Spanish rookie beat Kocinski and Barros by less than a second, and suddenly Spanish fans and journalists got the faith.

All of this came just as Dorna Promocion del Deporte S.A., in 1992, had obtained from the FIM the TV rights and, in 1993, all commercial rights to the FIM Roadracing World Championship Grand Prix (as the series was cumbersomely titled before Dorna introduced the MotoGP brand). Only a Spanish company could have believed strongly enough in the future of grand prix motorcycle racing to outbid such formidable rivals as The Flammini Group, Mark McCormick's IMG and even Bernie Ecclestone's TWP. (Complicated shenanigans involving IRTA, the major tobacco sponsors and TWP meant that Dorna did not acquire full commercial rights until 1993.)

Although playing a waiting game, big Spanish sponsors like Repsol and Telefónica were now interested, especially since Dorna's new TV contract with TVE included aggressive promotion and increased hours of prime-time coverage.

The images of Criville and Pons atop the Assen podium, seen live on TVE, and on the sports pages and even the front pages of Spanish newspapers, changed the way the nation thought about the 500 class. When I say "the nation", I don't mean just racing fans. In Spain, GP motorcycle racing is so important that it has been declared "of general interest" by the national legislature, meaning, among other things, that GP motorcycle racing cannot be limited to pay-to-view or any limited-access TV network. Criville's win was front-page news, and winning in 500 became a Spanish obsession.

Criville's second year in 500 was still solid, although without further wins (two podiums and eighth overall), but it was enough for Honda to hire the Spaniard to team with Mick Doohan and Shinichi Itoh. Pons re-

sponded to the loss of Criville by hiring Alberto Puig, a former trials rider (national junior trials champion). Puig, tutored by Pons and Cobas, finished fifth overall, a place ahead of Criville in 1994.

## The Spanish championship opens to the world

Meanwhile, back in Spain, another talent search was taking place. The Open Ducados 250, as the premier class of the Spanish championship, was run under slightly restrictive (no factory bikes) rules for the purpose of developing a new generation of stars. Fourteen years after the Copa Streaker produced Pons, 'Aspar' and Cardus, the Open Ducados polished the talents of Sete Gibernau and future 500 world champion Kenny Roberts Junior.

Dorna encouraged the Spanish Federation to open the national series to foreign riders. The focus of the CEV, once a series that only allowed riders born in Spain to score points, changed, and top riders from around the world came to regard it as a showplace for talent. In 1993, German Dirk Raudies, already a grand prix star, gained both the Spanish 125 and World 125 titles, Britain's Steve Borley won in Supersport, and Kenny Roberts Junior battled eventual champion Luis d'Antin and Sete Gibernau (runner-up) for 250 honours.

By the start of 1995, future champion Emilio Alzamora was a rising star in 125cc, finishing overall fourth, ahead of four-times world champion 'Aspar', but the focus was now on the big class.

Although Criville had scored that maiden 500 win for Spain at Assen in 1992, the win by Alberto Puig at the Spanish Grand Prix at Jerez, before a huge crowd, at the first European round of the 1995 season was monumental. A famous Saturday-night exchange between Puig and then Pons team manager Manolo Burillo has been immortalised in legend:
Puig: "If I win tomorrow, will Spain collapse."
Burillo: "If you win tomorrow, the world will collapse."

He won and Spain, though not the world, did 'collapse' in the Spanish sense, with wall-to-wall TV and radio coverage, congratulations from the King and statesmen, and pandemonium in the hillsides of Jerez de la Frontera.

Perhaps the devastating crash that Puig suffered at Le Mans in 1995 changed the future of road racing in Spain more that most observers could imagine. Perhaps Puig, a hard, hard rider and the first Spaniard ever to win a 500GP in Spain that day Doohan crashed out of the lead, would have gone on to great things. The terrible crash eventually ended his career after a series of operations as he battled first to avoid amputation of his left leg and then, in a Quixotic attempt, to continue racing. He did achieve one final

podium appearance (at Paul Ricard in 1996), but he was forced to retire.

After working briefly as a TV pit commentator and retaining an association with Team Pons in an advisory capacity, Puig got the call in 1999 from Dorna CEO Carmelo Ezpeleta to take complete responsibility for the Telefónica MoviStar Activa Cup, the Dorna organised talent search that discovered Dani Pedrosa.

Pedrosa was not the fastest rider and, had someone other than Puig been running it, probably would not have been selected. Puig saw something special in the smallest rider in the series and included him in the three-rider team that he managed in the 2000 Spanish 125 series. Again, Pedrosa was not dominant, finishing fourth overall and behind both his team-mates, but Puig took Pedrosa into the 2001 125 World Championship on the Telefonica MoviStar Junior team that was led by Toni Elias, and was rewarded by two podium finishes and eighth overall. Pedrosa would go on to third in 2002 and then win the 2003 125 title, followed by back-to-back 2005 and 2006 250 titles.

Pedrosa replaced Elias as Puig's protégé, but the Spanish team director also took briefly under his wing a promising young Australian, Casey Stoner, who had won the British Aprilia 125 Cup in 2000 when just 14. Stoner, living in a motorhome with his parents, raced the final two rounds of the Spanish 125 series

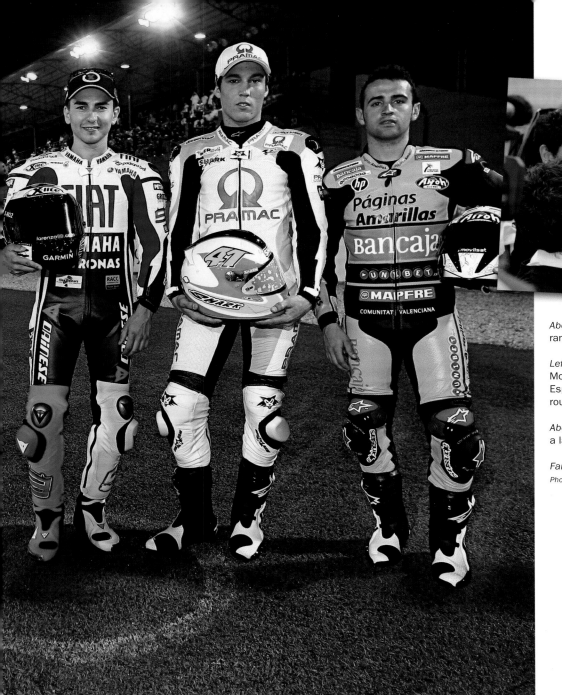

*Above:* Maiden Moto2 winner Toni Elias joined the ranks of Spanish world champions.

*Left:* Spaniards ahoy – almost one third of the MotoGP grid. From left: Bautista, Pedrosa, Lorenzo, Espargaro and Barbera pose before the opening round at Qatar.

*Above far left:* Spain will collapse! Alberto Puig took a landmark win in the 1995 Spanish Grand Prix.

*Far left:* Puig with his protégé, Dani Pedrosa.
*Photos:* Gold & Goose

and Puig befriended the family, letting them park on the grounds of his family home near Barcelona and slotting Stoner into the Telefónica MoviStar 125 team in the 2002 CEV. That season, he was second in the 125 class in two major national championships, the Spanish and the British, the difference being that while in the UK, the 125s were a support class, in Spain they had become the main event, given live TV time over Supersport 600 and Extreme 1000cc.

With Spain also the first country in the world to run a Moto2 championship, this national series that once ran all its races through village streets is now the place where GP teams look first for young talent. A visitor to CEV will see why. The series runs only seven rounds, but all are at FIM homologated circuits with safety standards far more stringent than those of any other national series. The races are televised live on Spain's leading channel (currently TVE), and the riders taking part in the three classes (125cc, Moto2 and Extreme/Superstock 1000cc), though still mostly Spanish, came in 2010 from 12 other countries. In fact, in the two 'direct-transfer' classes to the GPs, 20 of the 35 riders scoring 125 points and eight of the 28 in Moto2 were not Spanish.

As far back as 1996, Valentino Rossi honed his skills racing against the likes of Jorge Martinez. It was in the CEV that Stoner first met up on track with Pedrosa, Elias, Alex de Angelis, Jorge Lorenzo, Hector

Barbera, Chaz Davies, Marco Simoncelli and Alvaro Bautista, in 125s back in 2000 and 2001.

The importance of the CEV is probably best seen in the following statement:

Presently over 70 per cent of the riders currently participating in the three classes of GP racing spent at least a single season racing in the CEV, and that included 12 of the 17 current MotoGP regulars.

From 2003, the year that the Dorna-era CEV developed stars began to win titles, the supply has been constant. Not all have been Spanish, but if we only take world champions from Spain over the last seven years, all graduates from the CEV, the list is impressive: Pedrosa, Alvaro Bautista, Julian Simon, Marc Marquez in 125cc; Pedrosa and Lorenzo in 250cc, and now Lorenzo in MotoGP in the same year that Marquez and Elias took the 125cc and Moto2 titles – with Spanish riders taking runner-up spots in all three classes as well.

And there is depth to Spain's road racing dominance. The one-day European Championships held at Albacete, Spain (admittedly a bit of an ambush for non-Spanish riders) on 24th October, matching the best European riders in three principal classes, 125cc, Supersport and Superstock 1000cc, produced a Spanish runaway, with local riders not only winning all three races and titles, but with riders who currently participate in the CEV taking all three

podium places in 125cc and the top four places in 1000cc Superstock. Spain does not even run a Supersport class anymore, but even that was won by a Spanish CEV rider on a bike that had not been raced since 2009.

Just as Great Britain has become the FIM's major supplier of World Superbike talent, so Spain has at least momentarily displaced Australia, the United States and Italy as the nation producing more future grand prix winners. Thanks to the open doors, not all of them are Spanish, though.

Juan Moreta, president of the Spanish Federation did not create this situation (Dorna did), but he has continued it. Moreta, asked why Spain is so strong in road racing, replied, "I don't like to criticise other federations, but I believe that what we have done right is to treat the national championship not as a business, but as a training ground for grand prix riders. We offer a GP-type format, run on tracks that meet the highest level of FIM safety homologation, and we welcome riders from all countries to compete. The purpose is not to make the CEV the base for a profitable career at national level, but a series where riders can develop their talent and move up. Our first priority is always safety. Too many young riders end their careers on unsafe tracks. In the CEV, our riders usually walk away from crashes."

Like Ramon Torras in Comarruga, 1965.

# FULL CIRCLE

Will 2012's new 1000cc category see a return of production-based engines to the top level of motorcycle racing? NEIL SPALDING analyses the new sanction and reviews the bikes of 2010...

WHEN the world championships were re-launched with the four-stroke renaissance of MotoGP in 2002, everyone knew it would take more than a Superbike engine in a GP chassis to get to the top. It's taken a while, but a lot of lessons have been learned. For then again, maybe this is exactly what MotoGP needs.

MotoGP, all of motorcycle racing actually, is at a crossroads. The money that funded the golden age of the 990s and 800s has gone. MotoGP bikes have to become cheaper to make and to operate, but they must stay fast. That isn't an easy trick.

MotoGP's technical rules are set by agreement between the MSMA, the manufacturers' association, and Dorna. In exchange for authority over the rules, MSMA members undertake to provide sufficient motorcycles to make up the grid. With Kawasaki gone in 2009, as well as Aprilia, Team Roberts, Ilmor and WCM in the years before, it has become increasingly difficult for the few remaining manufacturers to supply a big enough grid. The situation is made worse when the bikes are so complex that only factory machines have a chance of success.

These agreements are contracted in five-year 'packages'. The current package finishes at the end

of 2011. Dorna's solution for the next five years is to create a second tier within MotoGP, one that doesn't need the resources of a factory to be competitive. Given the need to boost the grid, the factories have conceded that cheaper engines are needed, possibly including modified street engines. To keep the engines cheap, opposing teams will be able to claim them after a race for 20,000 euros. Hence the name 'Claiming Rule Teams'.

Even before the world championship was founded in 1949, top-level racing was no stranger to production-based motorcycles, often racing alongside full factory prototypes. After the Second World War, along with a ban on supercharging, the separate class structure by engine capacity was established, and by 1960 we had classes for 50, 125, 250, 350 and 500cc. Each class included factory-level prototypes, but more than anything, it had tuned road-based engines in real race chassis. In the smaller classes, you could buy your 'converted' street bike. Yamaha sold as production racers TZ125s, 250s and 350s, all using original road crankcases with uprated engine internals and cooling systems. In Yamaha's case, the frame was the same, just a few lugs missing, and a race seat and tank added.

The advent of 'superbikes', very powerful large-capacity road bikes, led to a series of races where modified versions could race each other. The World Superbike series was eventually formed in 1988. At the same time, Dorna was soon to take over GP racing and signed a contract with the FIM for a race series for 'prototype' machines.

The result was two promoters chasing one group of sponsors and fans. There has been inevitable friction over the years. The trouble is in the definitions: what comprises a 'prototype' machine and what comprises 'production'? The MotoGP move to four-strokes meant the problem snowballed. Now we have 1000cc Superbikes using standard production crankcases, cranks and main frames in one camp and 800cc MotoGP prototypes in the other. MotoGP electronics are at least a generation ahead, but both types are very well equipped.

The need to economise is not self-generated. Racing is part of the world economy, and the last ten years of credit fuelled super boom led to rapid expansion in racing, not only in international series, but also in national championships. Now, with an ongoing credit crunch, everyone has had to look to ways of reducing costs. AMA's sale of racing operations to

18,500rpm. An engine with the same bore size and BMEP, with the crank stroked to 48.5mm to take the capacity up to 1000cc, will make that same 212 horsepower at 14,800rpm. Simple mathematics will mean a lot more torque will be available, but the jury is out on whether much more can actually be used. The lower rpm should result in a massive reduction in the loads on the rest of the engine, however, and would make the necessary durability much easier (and therefore cheaper) to achieve.

Retaining the 21-litre fuel limit means that each bike will still need the super-sophisticated electronic control systems developed over the last four years. These throttle systems keep the works bikes rideable. Finding ways to make an engine run really lean, yet still able to respond to the throttle has been one of the most important parts of the R&D side of MotoGP. The technology is directly applicable to the future of street riding. From a racing perspective, it rewards the best possible engineering solution, and from a safety perspective, it is a real limiter on how fast the bikes can go. Unfortunately, the only way to save fuel is to stop excess wheel spin, so we aren't going to see a return to the slipping and sliding of the early 990s.

Manufacturers are specifically banned from the second tier, where the Claiming Rule Teams have a different challenge. They have the same 1000cc/81mm limitation, but they can use 12 engines per year and 24 litres of fuel each race. Having extra engines lowers the specification and cost of each powerplant, and the extra fuel means that ECUs can be simpler and hopefully cheaper. The biggest potential saving comes from the possibility to use production parts.

These rules represent a complete U-turn, opening racing to bikes built in exactly the same vein as the WCMs that the FIM went to a lot of trouble to ban eight years ago.

Initially, the allowance of 12 engines looks quite generous, but with a claiming rule of 20,000 euros, you probably would not want your engines to cost much more than 30,000 euros each, and a substantial part of the engine may be based on production parts. Let's consider one of the most likely donor engines, the BMW S1000RR. This has set the production bike world alight with its small size and substantial power output. In tuned form, this engine is probably capable of delivering sufficient power for MotoGP, but then you have to consider what other features are required to do well at that level.

The BMW road engine has a forward rotating crankshaft with the big ends set at 180 degrees and a chain-driven cam drive. The standard bore is 80mm and the stroke is 49.7mm; that's a bore/stroke ratio of 1.61 – probably quite close to the last of the pre-Rossi Yamaha M1s of 2003. The BMW has a red line of 14,200rpm, although Superstock versions rev to

the Daytona Motorsport Group was the first of these changes. DMG's American Superbikes essentially became 1000cc Supersport. In the UK, the BSB organisers are experimenting with 'EVO' – a standard-engine variation on Superbike rules.

The revaluation of the Japanese yen is also relevant. Before the crash in 2008, the yen-to-euro rate was 170; now (late 2010), it is around 115. That means the cost of a Japanese factory lease bike at, say, 300 million yen has increased from 1.76 million euros to 2.65 million, at a time when sponsorship income is falling.

Dorna's June proposal was a determined attempt to cut costs. The new 1000cc category had a maximum bore of 81mm and no more than four cylinders for prototypes, plus the Claiming Rule Team sanction, with slightly looser technical requirements. Production parts are not mentioned, but they are not banned. The only specific 'prototype' requirement is that the rolling chassis should not be from a bike homologated for road use. Superbike regulations require the opposite, insisting on a minimum production run of 1,000. Current Japanese thinking is that if a bike hasn't met homologation standards for production racing, then it is acceptable as a prototype.

The idea of changing technical regulations every five years is to keep the competition fresh and the R&D ideas flowing. But MotoGP cannot escape the current economic realities, or the political and

financial realities of the existence of two series. The change in specifications has been tailored to comply.

The last year has seen engines originally designed to last 500 or 600km reworked to do more than 2,000km. But these engines are still based on the ultra-high revving 800cc engines originally designed four years ago. High revs are the enemy of engine life; it would be easier for endurance to have a larger engine capacity to allow the same power at lower revs. Introducing durability as a core design element should also ultimately reduce costs.

One of the most expensive parts of any engine is the cylinder head. Cam profiles, porting, valve gear – all are very highly specialised parts. The theory behind the new rules is based on being able to use the current cylinder head design, but on top of a bigger-capacity, slower revving cylinder. Piston speed and acceleration are the usual limitation on rpm, but the supporting structures also have to be highly developed to live at high rpm. Bearings, rods and oil systems all are on the limit as the revs rise.

The new rule takes the largest bore size on the current MotoGP grid of 81mm (believed to be the Ducati) for the maximum. The effect, if the cylinder head stays the same, is that the breathing ability stays the same. For example, a theoretical 800cc four with an 81mm bore and a stroke of 38.8mm, given a BMEP of 12.8, will make 212 crankshaft horsepower at

14,700rpm and BMW believes the valve gear to be good for 15,000rpm. That puts into perspective the 16,000rpm to which Yamaha was able to push its 2004 bike; it might have needed a new cam chain every night, but it managed to win the championship.

But the differences between top road sports and MotoGP engines are significant. The Yamaha is a good example. The company developed its reverse rotating 'cross-plane' crank for maximum agility and traction. It wanted to combine the advantages of an in-line four with those of the V4s of the opposition, which were narrower for better manoeuvrability and also seemed better able to put their power down.

Reversing crank rotation reduced overall gyroscopic effects, improving agility in spite of the width. The reversed torque reaction also effectively pitched 4kg of weight to the front under acceleration. A less-productive side effect was the requirement of an extra set of gears for the reverse rotation, costing perhaps as much as 5bhp.

The biggest physical difference between a production engine and a MotoGP engine is size. Having a motor small enough to move around the bike, if only at the design stage, is key to weight distribution. MotoGP engines don't have to survive 50,000 road miles, and the design focus is on minimising size. The other main technical differences are the sophistication and adjustability of the electronic throttle controls, and the way that a lot of power can be found from a very limited fuel allowance.

## HOW TO MAKE A CRT MOTOR

The bulk of the costs of any engine lie in the initial design and development. Short-circuiting that process is endemic; very few engine designs these days are truly 'all new'. So there is no need to saddle ourselves with the costs of 'inventing' an all-new design.

We want to make power, we have more fuel than our opposition and we need to keep costs down. We need the best possible handling and mass centralisation. The BMW stands out among current production engines as being particularly carefully designed. It was beaten in World Superbike by the Aprilia, but that's largely down to each factory's motorcycle racing experience.

Set-up costs will be substantial – say around half a million euros, but once the CNC or Rapid Core casting programs are all in place, each home re-engineered engine should fall into the 30,000-euro bracket.

BMW's S1000RR is notably small and has a particularly well-designed cylinder head. The bore is already 80mm, so a boost to 81mm isn't going to make any dramatic differences. Competitive power should be 'do-able' at 16,000rpm. That will require some careful cam design, however, and some changes to valves and valve springs.

If funding is available for a custom-made cylinder head, an off-the-shelf pneumatic valve-spring system from a company such as DelWest would be relatively inexpensive. That would provide a lot of freedom in

cam profile design and potentially enormous benefits in performance.

The current in-line four of choice is the Yamaha M1. Its design solutions address most of the problems. Kawasaki found this out to its cost. The factory tried practically everything, but it was only with the 2009 Hayate machine that it succeeded. That bike had a reverse rotating, cross-plane crank design.

Could the same changes be made with the BMW?

CNC machining and Rapid Core castings aren't as costly as once thought, so with a decent design, a set of crankcases shouldn't cost more than around 5,000 euros. For once, the recession is motorcycling's friend, as these costs go down. We can add a cassette gearbox to the BMW design without too much drama. Then the crankshaft. Using maximum bore, we will need to shorten the stroke, helping to keep piston speeds down and reliability up, if only a little. So we need a new crank, with a slightly shorter stroke, and we need to reverse its rotation and make it into a cross-plane design at the same time.

It's just a question of how to engineer it. The design eliminates 95 per cent of the inertia torque fluctuations felt at the tyre, but that doesn't mean the actual forces have been eliminated. Instead the re-timed firing intervals mean that the forces counteract one another. This exerts a very powerful twisting force within the crankshaft, so it must be strengthened. The BMW's production main bearing and big-end journals are 34mm in diameter. On Yamaha's R1, the road-

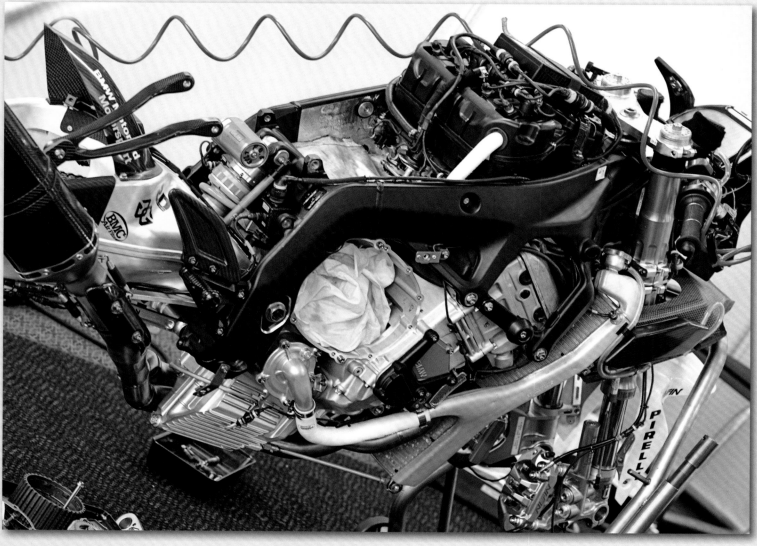

*Above:* Like all the MotoGP bikes, Honda's 990cc RC211V was equipped with a cassette gearbox.

*Left:* FTR Moto's debut frame was very successful, especially in the hands of Andrea Iannone. It would be a good starting point for a CRT frame.

*Below left:* Inmotec engine, Aragon MotoGP 2010.

*Below far left:* BMW's S1000RR is very small and well packaged, the cylinder head particularly so.

*Photos:* Neil Spalding

going cross-plane engine, the main bearing journals went up from 32mm to 36mm, just to make sure it could cope with containing the forces. For our CRT MotoGP engine, we had better add that to the list.

With a new crankshaft, we might as well go the whole hog, to take advantage of the handling benefits of reversing its rotation. The BMW primary drive is taken off the second crank web, direct to a spur gear behind the clutch basket. If, when we designed our new crankshaft, we moved the gear to an end crank web, we would need a jack-shaft to take the power back to the primary gear. In the process, we would reverse engine rotation and provide the balance shaft the revised engine requires. The shaft would also drive a race-size alternator, making BMW's crank-end alternator redundant and the engine that bit narrower.

New camshafts will be required for the revised firing intervals, while the 16,000rpm target is well into cam-chain trouble territory. To use the BMW head, the drive needs to stay on the right-hand end of the crank. Gear drive offers more accurate cam timing at high rpm and is also far more reliable.

It's worth noting that the Yamaha M1 cam drive isn't on the end of the crank like the BMW chain. Yamaha pursued the narrowest possible engine, and the cam drive gear train runs up the back of its engine. Driving the cams from the centre reduces their natural tendency to twist.

A comprehensive re-engineering of the BMW S1000RR makes an engine very similar to Kawasaki's last MotoGP bike. A few last changes would include a deep sump like that used by BMW on its Superbikes, and the relocation of the front engine mounts. The stock BMW locates the engine at the cylinder head. It's one of the things that probably makes the frame a bit too stiff for Superbike racing. With new cases, additional mountings would be placed on the cylinder, allowing the longer mounts that the factories have adopted to improve the controlled flex that assists high lean angle grip.

Now we just need someone to build us a chassis...

# MOTOGP – BIKE BY BIKE

## DUCATI DESMOSEDICI GP10
..........................................................................................

DUCATI'S second year with its unique carbon-fibre 'stressed-airbox' frame was more than a little up and down, literally. Testing went well, with a new Big Bang engine and new forks. The engine improved corner traction, while a different throttle 'feel' and better rear grip changed the balance of the bike. New 48mm through-rod Öhlins forks were fitted in the search for additional braking stability. Testing also included several different carbon swing-arms. One in particular, the most laterally flexible, proved popular.

Come the first race and it all changed. Casey crashed from the front. He was going very quickly indeed, so at the time the crash was put down to that. It clearly affected his confidence, however. After a similar crash at Le Mans, it was clear that changes were needed.

For Mugello, the old 42mm 'non-through-rod' TTX Öhlins were fitted. These gave a different feel during braking and allowed more front-end flex at high angles of lean. The bike stayed wheels-down, but Stoner still wasn't happy. At Brno, Öhlin issued its prototype 2011 forks: 48mm units combining the best of both TTX and through-rod technology. Stoner tried them at Indianapolis, and crashed again. By Misano, there were many more experiments: new flexy top triple clamp, and all three types of fork. Just before qualifying, however, tungsten rods were tied to the radiator, which altered the weight balance without changing anything else.

The next race was at Aragon, and new settings were put in that had been tried by the factory test team. And they worked. Shortening the swing-arm, and moving out the headstock and forks to the maximum effectively pushed the engine weight backwards. Ducati then adjusted Stoner's seating position forwards by the same amount. It seems the difference was in the way that Casey could move and load the front end going into corners.

Now the rest struggled to keep the Australian in sight, and the same happened in Japan and Australia. It seemed that his left wrist hadn't ever recovered fully from the scaphoid operation two years before, and the adjustments allowed him to balance his weight more accurately into corners.

Ducati also refined its aerodynamics. Hayden started out using 2009's fairing at any track where top speed was an issue; it definitely helped. By mid-season, small wings with 'winglet' end-plates had been added to the 2010 fairing flanks. The wings reduced lift, putting 10kg more weight on the front at top speed. The winglets improved cooling by directing air past the lower edge of the radiator exhaust duct. In the cool, blustery conditions of Phillip Island and Estoril, the bikes ran fine wingless and were less susceptible to cross-winds.

*Left:* Ducati experimented with two tungsten bars to change the weight distribution of Stoner's bike at Misano.

*Below:* Flexy triple clamps were also tried in Italy, but hardly again until post-season tests.

*Bottom:* Nicky Hayden's bike stripped at Brno, the carbon 'stressed-airbox' frame being hidden under the cooling and electronic systems.

*Photos: Neil Spalding*

## HONDA RC212V

HONDA struggled to get the best out of the control tyres. It's a completely different racing concept from before: the tyres are no longer tailored to the chassis, so the chassis has to be tailored to the tyres.

In 2010, HRC gave a spectacular demonstration of chassis rigidity tuning. It used a lot of design cues from Yamaha in its 2010 design, the main one being the 'open backed' main frame. This dispensed with the cross-member behind the engine. As the missing strut had carried the suspension mounting, the crankcases gained a cast-on protrusion to locate the top of the Öhlins unit.

The pre-season test bike was so weak around the headstock that it suffered with classic wobble and weave. Pedrosa had major stability problems until after the first race, yet still rode heroically fast. The most likely explanation is a deliberate ploy to force development by taking an extreme position in the initial design. By the first race at Qatar, Honda was reacting: Pedrosa had five distinct chassis options, using a combination of different-thickness aluminium and bonded-on carbon fibre to deliver varying levels of stiffness. By Jerez, it was obvious that Pedrosa was going to stick with a frame that had the cross-member replaced; thus his engines had to be modified by sawing off the cast-on shock mounts.

Honda's strategy was to bring a new aluminium chassis, then strengthen it as necessary with up to three stages of carbon reinforcement; then another new aluminium structure would arrive, and the process would be repeated. At Silverstone, Dovi had what Honda saw as the final developments of both swing-arm and frame. Simoncelli briefly tried the combination, but reverted to a previous version for the rest of the year. Honda tried another open-backed frame for Pedrosa at the Brno test, but he was still not satisfied, and couldn't have raced it anyway because half of his engines would not have fitted.

Honda also made big electronic advances. The Repsol bikes used 'Torducters' mounted on the outside of the countershaft sprockets to accurately measure the power delivered by the throttle system and engine, and to adjust it in real time. This allowed the Hondas to put down the best power of all the bikes out of the corners; it was the most important modification of the year.

Honda did not make life easy for itself: Yamaha inspired frames, new Öhlins suspension, much more complex ride-by-wire systems... But the manufacturer has only one more year in which to break its 800cc MotoGP duck. The pressure is very much on.

*Above:* Honda even glued a serial number on the carbon-fibre stiffening bonded to the aluminium chassis.
*Photo:* Neil Spalding

*Right:* Dovizioso used a thumb operated rear brake. It made the left fork leg a complicated place for mechanics.

*Top:* Pedrosa's bike stripped at Brno. Note the frame cross-member under the rear exhausts, unique to the Spaniard.
*Photo:* Gold & Goose

Left: Suzuki started the year with frames modified for additional flex around the steering head. It took until the middle of the year to debut improved versions.
Photo: Gold & Goose

Below left: Bautista used the latest swing-arm all year.

Below: Suzuki lost two engines for each rider due to quality problems with an outside supplier.
Photos: Neil Spalding

## SUZUKI GSV-R

SUZUKI always seems to be a year behind. It finally worked out that the modifications to engine position – to make the bike pitch more to suit the Bridgestones better – were also making the bike less flexible laterally. Raising the front of the engine had critically shortened the front engine mounts, reducing their ability to flex and affecting the bike at full lean.

During pre-season tests in Malaysia, holes were machined at the back of the steering head. This helped, and these frames were used during the first part of the year. It took until July, however, for new pieces to become available. At the same Malaysian test, new swing-arms were tried. Bautista adopted the new design, but after trying to use it for several races, Capirossi reverted to the older version.

Two new frame designs arrived, both using CNC machined sections for the first time. These allowed Suzuki to control the amount of flex in the chassis by manipulating the thickness of the various sections. Capirossi started using one version, cosmetically the same as the old frame, in July. A new version that was quite different in external appearance arrived for the Brno test and was immediately adopted by Bautista.

By July, however, Suzuki's season had dissolved for other reasons. An outside supplier had got something wrong in the spec of a few engine components; Suzuki was not saying whom or what, but we believe it was a problem with the oil supply. As soon as it knew it had a problem, each rider had two of his engines withdrawn. This left Suzuki with only four engines for the year. At the Brno MSMA meeting, the manufacturer was granted three additional engines each. Bautista had full use of all nine engines, but Capirossi's crew tried to get him to the end of the year on the original allocation. This included competing in five races on one engine.

## YAMAHA M1

YAMAHA started the year with by far the most sophisticated electronics, as well as the best handling. It is a measure of the different philosophies of the companies in MotoGP that Yamaha simply never appeared to have a problem getting its bikes to work on Bridgestone's control tyres. It made a few tweaks to the rigidity of its swing arm and changed the rear section of the main frame to create a more flexible mid-section of the bike. It all seemed relatively easy, while others struggled.

It is obvious that Yamaha's view of engines is slightly different, too. It builds engines that go fast, but it also prioritises the engine's effect on the handling of its bikes. There is a reason why Yamaha's crankshaft turns backwards, why it has a cross-plane design and why it is so small. They were design decisions related to handling and grip. The design dates from a time when engine life simply wasn't an issue: Yamaha has a five-station engine truck in the paddock for a reason. Its philosophy was: as long as it doesn't fail on track, then it's okay.

Thus the new engine rules came as a shock. Yamaha identified high piston temperatures as one cause of short engine life. Ignition timing, fuelling and high rpm all affect that, and all three were changed. It was noticeable that Yamaha's engines didn't have the acceleration in 2010. That was down to far more conservative ignition timing and an engine re-tuned for mid-range; 200mm-longer secondary exhaust pipes indicated a peak torque figure possibly 2,000rpm lower than 2009.

Fuel range suddenly became a problem. The bikes were run as close as possible to the safe limit for finishing the race: i.e., as rich as they dared, with Rossi actually running out on the slow-down laps at Qatar and Misano.

Top newcomer Ben Spies and team-mate Colin Edwards used the 2009 frames and swing-arms for the whole of the season. The difference was very small, a reduction in the section of the frame around the swing-arm pivot area, and did not affect the geometry. For engines, they typically lagged one level of development behind the Fiat Yamaha bikes, but that difference wasn't very great.

*Above:* Yamaha still led the class on electronics at the start of the year. Note the twin gyroscopes.

*Left:* Yamaha added 200mm to the secondary exhaust pipes.

*Top:* Jorge Lorenzo and his crew chief, Ramon Forcada, made their bike work the best of all the Yamahas every time it mattered. The bike itself was little changed from 2009, careful evolution being all that was required.

*Photos:* Neil Spalding

Toni Elias, 2010 Moto2 champion, speeds under the Dunlop Bridge at Le Mans.

*Photo:* Gold & Goose

# GRAND RACING FOR AN AGE OF AUSTERITY

The new Moto2 world championship offers big thrills with no frills, but is it good for GP racing? MAT OXLEY seeks the answer...

*Above:* Toni Elias leads the pack at the start of the Czech Republic Moto2 race at Brno.

*Inset, top left:* The heart of the matter – the Honda CBR600 powerplant.

*Inset, top right:* All you need is your own chassis. One of the Marc VDS team's Suters (Faubel's bike) stripped down.

*Opposite:* Dunlop supplied control tyres for all competitors.

Photos: Gold & Goose

THE inaugural Moto2 season may have looked to fans like the wildest racing ever seen in grands prix, but it was much more than that. Moto2 is a historic race series that marked a fundamental shift of philosophy in a sport that had operated with the same basic mindset since 1949.

For the previous six decades, for the most part, grand prix racing had worked the same way. The factories fielded a handful of very special motorcycles, conceived, designed, built and maintained by the cleverest engineers, and ridden by the best riders the factories could afford. The rest of the grid was made up of lesser machinery, looked after by engineers with fewer resources and ridden by (usually, but not always) riders with less talent. In other words, grand prix racing had always been elitist.

Moto2 changes all that; it brings the walls tumbling down, replacing elitism with equality. The class that replaced the 60-year-old 250 category is nothing less than a revolution. The big men at the top of MotoGP may be anything but socialists, but they have turned GP racing's intermediate class into a socialist experiment, distributing identical engines, tyres, electronics and slipper clutches to all riders.

Perhaps it's no coincidence that most Moto2 races look like some kind of racetrack re-enactment of the storming of the Bastille: noisy, chaotic, frightening to behold and bloody; for if there is equality in Moto2, there's certainly no fraternity.

Without doubt, the new class gives most TV viewers and trackside spectators what they want: hugely unpredictable,

edge-of-the-seat thrills and spills. For fans who want the lead to change at every other corner and the final result to be in doubt until the chequered flag, Moto2 is racing just like it should be.

The starts of most Moto2 races were even more harum-scarum than the finishes – fans holding their breath as the packed grid of 40 riders charged into the first turn, where, often as not, carnage ensued. To fans accustomed to half-empty MotoGP and 250 grids, Moto2 looks like some kind of wildly brave cavalry charge: into the valley rode the 600s.

Equal machinery demands that riders take extra risks to find any advantage, so it is inevitable that there are a lot of crashes in Moto2. It seems like every race and practice session is a frenzy of fishtailing rear ends, cartwheeling motorcycles and shaking fists. All of 2010's accidents would have been nothing to worry about, however – too much derring-do and a few broken bones – if it hadn't been for the death of Qatar Moto2 winner Shoya Tomizawa at Misano.

Some fans – call them purists, if you like – aren't quite so convinced by Moto2. They scoff at the notion of a one-make world championship, and they miss the high technology of no-compromise GP bikes. Legendary two-stroke engineer Harald Bartol summed it up for many when he described a 250 race bike as a race horse and a Moto2 bike as a donkey. He is certainly right from a performance perspective, because Moto2 is considerably slower than the class it replaced. Despite a 30-horsepower advantage, the 600s are more than two seconds slower than the 250s at several tracks, and three seconds slower at Losail.

Purists also suspect the new class to be the thin end of the wedge – the transformation of a once elitist sport into low-brow entertainment, a motorsport *Gladiators*, a two-wheeled NASCAR. Of course, their suspicions are absolutely correct: MotoGP is a 21st-century business like any other: the bottom line and the comfort of the sport's private-equity masters are the primary concerns.

Some of these (mostly older) fans now wonder whether Bernie Ecclestone's famous (and perhaps apocryphal) criticism of motorcycle racing – that there is too much overtaking – might not be quite as ridiculous as it once sounded. Sometimes it seems like there is just too much going on in Moto2, the lead often swapping several times in a corner as riders duck and dive in an attempt to find an advantage amid the chaos.

If the majority of fans love Moto2, some riders and engineers are more sceptical of its merits. Moto2 changes everything for the riders. For the real talents, it makes life much, much harder – they find themselves assailed on all sides by out-of-control rivals willing to hurl their machines into corners, regardless of the consequences. In the past, the golden boys who had shone in the 125 class were equipped with factory 250s that put them on a gilded path to the elite class. With superior machinery, the chosen ones were lifted clear of the rabble, so they could hone their craft in the slipstream of the more experienced factory riders.

Not anymore. Now they are thrown into a nest of vipers where they must fight with all their might to survive, with nothing more than the same weapon as the next man. Moto2 is survival of the fittest.

Some paddock people believe this to be a bad thing. They think that this no-frills, big-thrills class doesn't hone talent, so it won't turn up-and-coming youngsters into fully formed GP racers.

Alongside equality, Moto2's other founding principle is low cost, which inevitably means low technology. In the past, factory 250 riders learned everything they would ever need to know about machine set-up, but Moto2's sealed engines and low-tech electronics (with no traction control) provide little in the way of education.

"With Moto2, everything is simpler," said Jorge Martinez, owner of the Mapfre Aspar team. "But now in MotoGP, the rider needs a lot of experience with electronics, so I think Moto2 riders will need to go to computer school before they get into MotoGP." The same may apply to Moto2 engineers.

Not everyone shares Martinez's opinion. Other experts believe that the lack of high-tech distractions might be a positive for riders, rather than a negative. Many crew chiefs know very well that some riders can't help but lose themselves in a confusing labyrinth of set-up options in a vain effort to find that vital two-tenths of a second, when instead they should be working on their riding skill to find the extra speed.

"I think it's a good thing that riders can concentrate on developing riding, rather than getting too mixed up in the technical stuff," says Pete Benson, Scott Redding's crew chief in the Marc VDS Moto2 team.

Former 500 world champion Kevin Schwantz recalled how his early days of racing a very un-racy Yamaha XJ600 helped turn him into a rider who could get the best out of anything. "I think that's a lot of what made me as good a racer as I was, just having to figure out how to ride around problems," he said. He showed his support for Moto2 by entering his own team, with rider Roger Lee Hayden, at the Indianapolis Grand Prix.

Redding concurred with Schwantz and refuted suggestions that Moto2 dumbs down riding skills – the bikes may be easy to ride, but that only forces the most talented riders to dig even deeper to find an advantage. "Sometimes the chatter you get is horrific," said the Briton. "So the riders are developing different styles and skills to cure these things,

ALONG with control engines, control tyres are a major feature of the 'equality' philosophy of Moto2, ensuring that each rider has exactly the same choice. At every race, the allocation per rider is 16 slick tyres, and Dunlop was awarded a three-year contract to supply them, from 2010 to 2012. Since the company had supplied tyres for the previous 250 class, and continues to do so for the 125s, it was not surprising that it sought to take on that role.

The wheel sizes specified by the regulations are 3.75x17in front and 6.00x17in rear, from which Dunlop determined the tyre sizes: 125/75R and 195/75R respectively.

For each race, riders are provided with a choice of two different compound specifications ('A' and 'B') front and rear. In some cases (such as Australia's Phillip Island), where a circuit has more left turns than right, or vice versa, dual tyres are required, a different compound being used on one side of the tyre compared to the other to ensure optimum performance. Some tracks even require asymmetric carcass construction, but even symmetrical tyres are tailored specifically to each circuit.

**Slick tyres are allocated to each rider in the following manner:**

Front: four of specification 'A' and three of specification 'B'.

Rear: Five of specification 'A' and four of specification 'B'.

In addition, when necessary, three sets of wet tyres in one specification are provided. However, if all practice sessions and the race itself are declared wet by race control, an additional set of wet tyres is allocated.

During the 17-race 2010 Moto2 world championship, six front and nine rear tyre specifications were used by Dunlop, its engineers making the choice dependent on the severity and layout of the individual race circuit.

*Above:* Top men in Moto2 on the podium at Jerez. *(L to R)* The ill-fated Tomizawa, Elias and Luthi.

*Top:* The emerging Scott Redding leads Iannone, eventual winner de Angelis and di Meglio at Phillip Island.

*Above right:* Luthi at speed.

*Right:* Iannone ran away from the pack in Mugello.

*Top right:* Eskil Suter, who supplied more than a dozen Moto2 bikes.

*Above far right:* Mamoru Moriwaki, title winning Moto2 constructor.

*Photos: Gold & Goose*

like feathering the clutch into corners. No one does that in MotoGP, except Rossi."

Thomas Luthi denied accusations that there is no science to getting the best out of a Moto2 bike. "The set-up work is just different, that's all," said the 2005 125 world champion, who was a Moto2 front-runner in 2010. "It's more detailed work, concentrated on the chassis, geometry, suspension and so on, because we cannot work on the engine or the gearbox. In 250s, you took the whole bike and made a good mix of engine, chassis and electronics. In Moto2, you focus only on the things you can change."

On track, the winning secret in Moto2 is pure and simple: corner speed. "The engines are very, very slow, so you need to do everything you can to get more rpm,' said Toni Elias, Moto2's first world champion. "You need to be very fast through the corners so you can be quick down the straights."

When Elias first rode a Moto2 bike in November 2009, just two days after his last outing in a MotoGP race for the San Carlo Honda squad, he joked that it felt like "someone has stolen the engine". Other riders, however, declare that they enjoy riding the 600s, despite the relative lack of pace.

"I love riding my Moto2 bike," added Luthi. "I like the four-stroke style, the sliding, the engine-braking; you have to work more on the bike. The 250s were proper race bikes, light, a lot of power and more difficult to ride, but Moto2 bikes are definitely fun. But they do feel heavy, and not fast and not aggressive, so they are really rideable for everyone. I'd love to have 20 horsepower more; that would be a lot of fun."

Most racers like to fight, to do battle with their rivals, which is another reason why men like Luthi get a kick out

of Moto2. But actually making a consistent mark in Moto2 is something else. During its inaugural year, the class was uniquely topsy-turvy, with even the best riders struggling to record consistent results. Luthi was a case in point – third in Spain, 19th in France, second at Catalunya, 11th at Brno, third at Misano, tenth in Aragon.

The reason for the chaotic nature of the results is straight-forward. Equality of machinery equals equality of lap times, which means a large number of riders circulating within several hundredths of each other. (At Le Mans, the quickest 29 qualifiers were covered by one second.) The machinery is so similar that the tiniest difference in chassis character or riding technique can change everything from one track to the next, so a rider who qualifies on the front row at one race may only make the fifth row at the next. And if a rider doesn't qualify on the first three rows, he has little chance of a good result because he will be stuck mid-pack, riding defensive lines, unable to run his true race pace. The tightness of the pack also magnifies the significance of qualifying – one tiny mistake can relegate a rider several rows. Thus one minor error on Saturday afternoon can ruin the whole weekend.

"If you're on the first two or three rows, you're okay," said Redding. "But after that you get idiots who can't do the pace themselves, but can get on to the back of you because the bikes are all the same. You need to be up front to try to get away, like [Andrea] Iannone did at a few races. Once you're in the middle of the battle, it's hard to get anywhere. Iannone risks everything the first few laps. He puts in five or six really hot laps and makes a gap, while everyone else is battling among themselves."

Luthi struggled on occasion because, he said, he is a racer, not a qualifier. "Sometimes I had bad qualifying sessions because I am not the kind of rider who can close his eyes and do one very fast qualifying lap," he explained. "I'm more the kind of rider who does the lap time he can do all through the race, so that makes it difficult for me to go out and close my eyes in qualifying. But I have to work on this, because if you are not in the leading group in Moto2, the riding can be a bit crazy."

Only a very few riders were able to be anything like consistent during 2010. Even champion Elias sometimes struggled to magic that extra hundredth of a second – at Silverstone, he qualified 18th, and at Aragon he was 12th on the grid – though in the races he was very rarely far from the front. A previous winner of 125, 250 and MotoGP races, he was always expected to do well because he has an adaptable talent. Perhaps it was the Spaniard's unique riding technique that worked so well in Moto2 – his wild hang-off style is reminiscent of old-school proddie racers, leaning way off the inside in an effort to bend the bike to his will.

There were other riders who grabbed the new class by the scruff of the neck and got the maximum out of the motorcycles, most notably Iannone, the stand-out Moto2 star of 2010. The former 125GP winner was the first to magic a runaway win out of the new class, escaping from the pack at Mugello by as much as a second a lap. He did the same at Assen and Aragon, and he may have done it again at Catalunya and Misano if he hadn't been penalised for overtaking under yellow flags and jumping the start. Iannone was certainly keen, his ballet-smooth cornering lines matched by a willingness to slug it out with his rivals in the first laps.

Former 125 winner Iannone adapted brilliantly from a 70kg/50-horsepower 125 to a 135kg/130-horsepower 600, as did reigning 125 world champion Julian Simon, who also managed more consistency than most. There were more riders who blew hot and cold, like Frenchman Jules Cluzel, who won at Silverstone, but more often than not finished outside the top ten. The same went for Yuki Takahashi, who won at Catalunya, but otherwise was seldom near the front.

Then there were the riders who had been following the gilded 250 path to MotoGP, who sank without trace in Moto2. Raffaele de Rosa and former 125 world champion

Mike di Meglio had shown their talent during 2009, taking podium finishes on good 250s. Both struggled to make the top ten in Moto2.

If all Moto2 riders aren't created equal, the machines are, in theory at least. With no scope to find any significant performance advantage via engine and electronics, the new class is a huge challenge for chassis manufacturers. A dozen companies – some well known, others unknown – jumped at the chance to get involved, fully aware that their expertise would be the most crucial element of performance.

Some of these companies were famous decades ago, before the factories assumed responsibility for designing the whole motorcycle. Back in the days of Barry Sheene, outfits like Harris Performance were brought in to build chassis or modify chassis for the big factories. But not since the days of the Harris and ROC 500s of the early 1990s had these companies played any great part in GP racing. Moto2 is a huge boost for this largely dormant cottage industry.

Harris built chassis for the Jack and Jones team – owned by Hollywood heart-throb Antonio Banderas – but apart from Kenny Noyes's pole position at Le Mans, the British firm enjoyed little success. The big winners were legendary Japanese concern Moriwaki, British company FTR and well-known Swiss specialist Suter Racing Technology.

The season started with 14 different chassis makers on the grid and a variety of designs. Harris, FTR, Suter, Bimota, Tech 3, Moriwaki, Burning Blood, TSR/Motobi, Speed Up/FTR, ICP, Force GP210 and ADV conformed by creating mini-MotoGP aluminium beam chassis, constructed from a mix of extrusions, pressings and machined sections. There were only two dissenters – the Italian RSV concern and reborn East German brand MZ, both of whom built tubular-steel units. These were much less successful – by Le Mans, the three riders using RSV chassis had switched to Suter and FTR. MZ struggled all year due to an overweight frame and underweight budget.

Some teams were cheeky, rechristening chassis made by other manufacturers to suggest that the work was all their own. The Italian Speed Up team called its FTR a Speed Up, when in fact Speed Up only made the bodywork; likewise, the Spanish Blusens squad called its Japanese-made Burning Blood chassis a BQR; and Italian JiR named its Japanese-built TSR a Motobi.

Redding believed the FTR, the TSR and the Kalex were the most effective in 2010. "They are the full-gas chassis," said the former 125 winner, who rode a Suter. "The Suter and the Moriwaki are good average bikes, nothing special. We struggle with rear grip and chatter. The FTR seems really good on holding the line, and on rear traction and drive, which is important for the straights."

Moriwaki (seven wins), Suter (four wins) and FTR (four wins) were the most successful brands; all three companies worked hard to stay ahead with regular tweaks and updates. Moriwaki's upgrades adjusted swing-arm rigidity to cure chatter (a common problem, usually blamed on the control tyres and clutch) and increase grip.

Elias attributed his success to a radical revamp at July's German GP. "In my whole career, I've never made such big changes at a race as we made at the Sachsenring," he said. "We changed castor angle, geometry, weight distribution and fitted a new swing-arm in order to put more load on the rear for more traction." Germany was the first of five consecutive wins that put Elias on the road to the title.

Suter – who equipped almost a third of the bikes on the grid – offered a mid-season chassis update to increase rigidity for more edge grip. "We designed our chassis for a lot of grip because we expected more grip from the tyres," explained former 250 rider Eskil Suter, whose initial offering won in cooler conditions, as at Silverstone and Losail. "We realised we needed better performance in lower-grip situations, especially in the heat."

FTR introduced a shorter swing-arm – for more traction

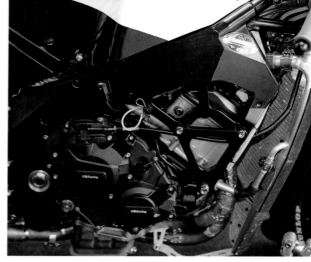

There was a plethora of chassis in the Moto2 class.
*Top row (left to right)*: Moriwaki, Promo Harris, Aspar, FTR.
*Above (left to right)*: JIR, MZ, Tech 3.
Photos: Gold & Goose

– at Jerez, a revised steering stem at Catalunya and a reinforced chassis – for more feedback – at Sepang. But the British company's innovative stemless steering head (designed to increase airflow into the airbox) went unused.

Other chassis makers made dramatic improvements by modifying frames at the races. Tech 3 transformed its Moto2 bike from also-ran to winner overnight at Catalunya. Rider feedback indicated that the Tech 3 frame was suffering catastrophic torsional flex, so the team welded large alloy plates across the engine hangers. Two days later, Takahashi won the bike's first and only victory.

The Moto2 paddock was certainly a busy place, with teams working frantically to gain even the slightest technical advantage. Inevitably, considering the tight technical rules, there were rumours that some teams' working practices were less honourable than others.

"As soon as you've got production-based racing, there's always rumours," said MotoGP technical controller Mike Webb, whose job it is to keep an eye open for cheats. "I hear constant gossip about who's doing this and who's doing that, but I'm reasonably comfortable that we've got good controls in place."

There were reports that rogue electronics boffins were lurking in the paddock, trying to sell teams illegal devices – called down-converters – that would corrupt the engine's pulses to the ECU to allow an engine to exceed the 16,000rpm limit.

Webb insists that he has that angle covered: "We get data from every Moto2 bike, every day. That's our big weapon, getting raw data from all bikes which can't be erased or hidden. I compare all the bikes, so if someone's got a speed or acceleration advantage, I can see it straight away. All the data is downloaded and then we overlay it."

Webb's Moto2 police also patrolled the pit lane, sniffing tyres during qualifying following rumours that some teams were using compound softener to increase grip.

No surprises that there were mutterings about Iannone's machine after he dramatically outpaced his rivals at several races. "There are always rumours when one rider is really fast," added Webb. "So we checked and rechecked Ian-

none's acceleration, top speed and so on, and they were exactly the same as everyone else's. There was only one place he was making up time: in the corners."

To ensure fairness, Webb is allowed to change ECUs and slipper clutches at random during any race weekend. Engines are also sealed to prevent tuning and are rebuilt every three races, with riders receiving reconditioned engines, distributed at random. This system kept most riders happy, although some did suffer from below-par performance. Luthi struggled through three mid-season races with a slow engine, his team unprepared to pay the sizeable fee required to request a new unit. "For three races, I couldn't even stay in the slipstream of other riders," said Luthi.

No one knew how much power the engines made; that was a secret known only to Honda and Geo Technology, the company (owned by former Honda engineer Osamu Goto) that maintains them, for an impressively fat fee of 55,000 euros per rider. Most engineers guess that engine output is around 130 horsepower, considerably lower than a good World Supersport engine. There were no apologies for the low state of tune – longer life equals lower costs.

But for whom? If Moto2 was created to drastically reduce team budgets, it isn't succeeding. Several former 250 team owners insist that Moto2 is barely cheaper than 250s, even though the machinery costs a lot less than the ludicrously expensive Aprilias that dominated the final years of 250s. Outgoings have been reduced, but so too has income. The driving force behind Moto2 was to make life easier for the smaller, hardest pressed teams, but Martinez believes it is the richer teams who have benefited most, at least from a financial standpoint.

"For the big teams who used to lease factory 250s, Moto2 is cheaper," explained Martinez. "But for the other teams who used to buy the 250LE model from Aprilia, then Moto2 is more expensive."

Most private teams seem to think the costs of the two categories are similar, although there is one big plus point to Moto2. "The costs are more or less the same: about one million euro for one rider," revealed a well-established team manager who wanted to remain anonymous. "We spend a

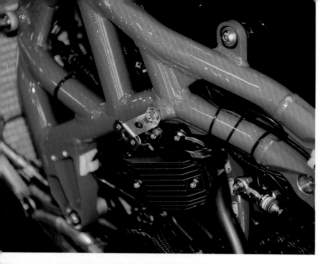

bit less, but we don't see much of the money that comes the other way because 55,000 euros goes to Geo for the engines, 40,000 euros go to Dunlop for the tyres and so on. I believe the engine maintenance costs should be half what they are. From a cost perspective, the advantage is that the budget is fixed, crashes aside, which obviously it wasn't if you were running your own 250s. But the biggest advantage is that we now have a chance to be up front, which we didn't have when we were running old-spec 250s against the latest factory bikes. So that's the bottom line: we have the chance to fight up front. The rest is the same as it was in 250. Oh, and Moto2 is very good business for Geo."

Nevertheless, the class is popular with teams anxious to get in on the action – an amazing 36 teams applied to field 61 riders for the 2011 series. Lack of space – on track and in the paddock – forced IRTA to turn away many of them.

Moto2 certainly isn't cheap enough to have saved teams who were already struggling to stay afloat in the stormy financial conditions. The well-established Scot outfit sank during July after a grim budget struggle. The Italian team's final days were messy, with mechanics going on strike at Mugello, forcing rider Alex de Angelis to call in his brother and a friend to help him out during practice. Unemployed after the Catalan GP, de Angelis found a job subbing for injured MotoGP rider Hiroshi Aoyama. Then when Aoyama returned, he found a ride with the JiR team (and subsequently took a victory at Phillip Island), which had earlier and acrimoniously split with Mattia Pasini, who later rode for the Italtrans and Kiefer Moto2 teams. There were a lot of musical chairs as some teams went broke and others lost patience, either with riders who failed to make an impact on this cut-throat class or with those who failed to bring enough sponsorship with them.

The new category has much going for it, but is far from perfect. Certainly, the concept of a one-make world championship feels all wrong, but Moto2 may be opened up to all four-cylinder 600 street engines from 2013. Some purists will still argue that a street-powered racer isn't a GP bike, but they would be forgetting other times of austerity, when street power filled the gaps left by exotic machines that had priced themselves off the racetrack.

*Above:* Ex-F1 engineer Osamu Goto, boss of Geo, Moto2's engine supplier.

*Left:* Looking for cheats: tech chief Mike Webb.

*Photos:* Gold & Goose

### 250cc v Moto2 lap records

| Track | 250 Record | Moto2 Record | Difference |
|---|---|---|---|
| Losail | 1m 59.4s | 2m 02.5 | +3.1s |
| Jerez | 1m 43.3s | 1m 44.7 | +1.4s |
| Le Mans | 1m 39.6s | 1m 39.1 | -0.5s |
| Mugello | 1m 53.6s | 1m 55.6 | +2.0s |
| Assen | 1m 40.3s | 1m 38.9 | -1.4s |
| Catalunya | 1m 45.9s | 1m 47.5 | +1.6s |
| Sachsenring | 1m 24.5s | 1m 25.6 | +1.1s |
| Brno | 2m 02.2s | 2m 04.3 | +2.1s |
| Indianapolis | 1m 44.3s | 1m 46.6s | +2.3s |
| Misano | 1m 38.9s | 1m 39.4 | +0.5s |
| Motegi | 1m 51.4s | 1m 53.6 | +2.2s |
| Sepang | 2m 07.6s | 2m 08.7s | +1.1s |
| Phillip Island | 1m 32.7s | 1m 34.8s | +2.1s |
| Estoril | 1m 40.5s | 1m 45.5s | +5.0s |
| Valencia | 1m 35.6s | 1m 36.6s | +1.0s |

# A FEW MORE RULES

Ever-fatter rule books and ever-tighter controls are meant to make racing closer, cheaper and greener. But do more rules mean more cheating, innocent or otherwise? Are eco-claims just window dressing? Is the pen mightier than the spanner? KEVIN CAMERON asks the questions...

*Above:* One size fits all ... Honda's Moto2 engine, here in a Moriwaki chassis, was restricted and monitored in every aspect.

*Above right:* Pens or spanners? Öhlins man takes notes.

*Right:* Standardisation meant Moto2 competitors took whatever engine they were given.

*Photos:* Gold & Goose

THE original rules, whose reign in motorcycle GP racing began in 1949, served well through their simplicity for almost 60 years. With periodic small adjustments, they essentially specified an engine displacement, atmospheric induction and petrol fuel. In our own era, this is no longer deemed adequate, and regulations proliferate, specifying, forbidding and adjusting what racers may do in regular bulletins. In the case of the new Moto2 class that replaced the long-running GP 250s, nearly everything about the 'spec' engine and how it is to be used is dictated by rule. Does this simplify or complicate? Is the idea of simplicity in rules making obsolete?

During the 2010 season, there were murmurings that one or more Moto2 teams had somehow hacked the system and broken into the mustn't-touch Engine Control Units (ECUs) of their production-based Honda 600cc engines to achieve an illegal 500rpm-higher rev limit. The claim was that some device had been buried inside the wiring harness that adjusted the tachometer's signal downward in frequency by three per cent.

Whether this rumor was true or false, realists expected this, for that is exactly how popular devices for re-tuning stock production motorcycle engines work. They fox the sensors that supply data to the ECU. As an example, let us suppose that we have put a sportier set of cams into our sportbike's engine, which flow a bit more air on top-end and a bit less on the bottom. In the old days, we'd simply have reached into our boxes of carburettor tuning parts and dealt with this problem directly. But we have no such tuning parts for altering the ECUs of electronic fuel injection systems, which are often built with safeguards specifically to prevent any alteration or reprogramming.

Instead, we adjust the signal coming from the intake air temperature sensor. If the ECU 'thinks' the air is colder, it supplies more fuel, and vice-versa. In this way, such widely sold devices as DynoJet's Power Commander II can alter ECU response without any need to to touch the ECU itself.

When the motorcycle manufacturer responds by narrowing the permitted limits of fuel delivery in software, the aftermarket industry instead may decide to alter fuel flow by changing the fuel pressure. There is always another way.

Just like the perpetual contest between armour and shell, the battle between ECU engineers and the aftermarket is never won by either side, because each side has an unending flow of ideas for frustrating the ambitions of the other.

It might be thought that factory engineers would outwit the aftermarket's non-degreed tinkerers to gain the upper hand, but we must consider a human byproduct of the Cold War. Governments paid the most highly-qualified researchers well to devise such things as data encryption systems, advanced schemes for defeating infrared-seeking missiles or devices that, when externally affixed to submarine cables, enabled interested parties in Langley, Virginia to listen to the conversations of Soviet military planners. Hundreds of billions were spent. Today, numbers of experienced engineers from such programmes are quietly retired. They are bored. Give them an interesting problem and who knows what will result?

It is a regrettable trend in current racing rules writing to replace the usual physical problems (aerodynamic drag, piston

peak acceleration stress, etc) with social ones in the form of rules – such as that the Young's Modulus of brake caliper material may not exceed X. With the best intentions, rules are written in the hope of reducing the cost of racing, of making racing appear socially responsible or of altering racing to make it more saleable.

When I was briefly an FIM tech inspector, I had to slide the official ground-clearance 'rake' under each sidecar outfit to be sure it was not lower than X height. This was a well-intentioned idea to save the teams from entering the ascending cost spiral of ground-effects development that has afflicted car racing for 40 years. But because the rule said only that the rake must pass under the vehicle at tech, I was presented with the comic spectacle of arriving teams furiously screwing their ride-height adjusters up, and the departing teams just as furiously screwing them back down after my 'verification'. They clearly thought the rule – and my 'enforcement' of it – funny.

An equally amusing result can flow from literal interpretation of a poorly written rule. In 1989, male-slider forks were just entering service in Superbike racing, but the rule regarding them said, "Front forks may be altered or replaced, but if replaced, the diameter of the fork tubes must be equal to or greater than that of the original parts."

Officialdom at the US round of World Superbike was ready to disqualify half the starting field, based on a protest under this rule. But what are fork tubes? The official view seemed to be that "They are the shiny things with chromium plating on them."

But for the rule to make sense, as opposed to being just an arbitrary requirement, it had to protect racers against collapse of aftermarket forks that might be weaker than the stock parts. The place where fork collapse is most likely is in the upper tube, just below the lower fork crown. In a male-slider fork, the upper tube is substantially larger than the upper tube in a conventional fork – in fact, that was the very reason for the design's adoption – and it is much stiffer. But in the protest, the diameters quoted compared the upper tube of the conventional fork with the lower tube of the male-slider fork – with a one-millimeter-diameter difference in favour of the conventional fork.

Officials on that occasion wisely decided to rule in a way that reflected credit upon the FIM, rather than making them appear legalistic dunderheads, so the protest was rejected. Extra rules – especially poorly written ones like this – waste time by encouraging 'office racing'. Rules should be interpreted in the light of their functional purpose.

The central nature of riders and teams is that they want to win. Rules that threaten this result will be examined just as carefully as if they were physical impediments, such as chatter or valve float. Back in the days of the F750 class, a few extra ccs of fuel tank capacity could make a big difference to one's chances. Accordingly, on occasion teams either fitted discardable seat tanks or used an air hose to improve their chances. A little showmanship from the rider, such as exuberantly punching the soft aluminium tank on the way to the podium during the cool-off lap, would not be thought out of place.

Riders clearly see the starts of Moto2 events as absolutely crucial to success. If you are not in the front group at the end of lap one, your chances are limited. Moto2 has replaced 250GP as the last rung in the ladder to MotoGP – and a career at the top. This brings heavy determination to the starting line – think of the personalities in MotoGP. The flag moves and they're off. Because Moto2 engines are certified to have identical performance, what Paul Butler feared from launch-control systems back in 2006 is now reality – all 42 starters accelerate equally to arrive at turn one together, where there isn't room for them all. The flow of bikes suggests the laminar-to-turbulent flow transition. You see non-streamline motion develop, and a moment later bikes are sliding off the track, taking down others.

If you are part of that raft of fallers, do you just mutter a quiet "Damn!", then stick out your chin pluckily and resolve to do better next time? Or do you resolve to tackle the underlying problem? We'll fix it. Then let's win some races.

I hear the moral appeal coming – this is only a sport, we are gentlemen, the rule of law must prevail in human endeavour.

In Moto2, the moral appeal has already been made repeatedly. Race Direction takes the riders aside and urges them to co-operate to get through turn one, thereby making unworkable regulations workable. Shall we call this voluntary co-operation 'spec riding'? And like the progressive failure of piston rings, does this just move the problem on from turn one to turn two? Is it realistic to ask such co-operation from persons so focused on competition?

Think of fuel. For years, race organisers offered a fuel for sale, some teams brought their own and others carried a supply of toluene to raise octane number if knock was encountered. Then management perceived a public-relations advantage in 'green initiatives', first by limiting fuel to low-lead in 1993 and then adopting lead-free fuel in 1998. To recover some of the anti-knock margin lost by the removal of the potent lead anti-knock additive, the fuel blenders first

*Above:* Mechanics work on Stoner's Duke. The search for advantage is endless.

*Centre, top:* When laminar flow becomes turbulent: equal performance meant plenty of first-corner crashes in Moto2. Pesek, Cardus, Olive and Faubel come to grief at the Sachsenring.

*Centre right:* Fuel levels played a crucial part in MotoGP in 2010.

*Top right:* Endless changes, endless notes.

*Bottom right:* The new engine restrictions had to be relaxed to help Suzuki escape penalties.

Photos: Gold & Goose

provided 'chemistry set' fuels, consisting mainly of toluene, the four 'good' octane compounds and triptane for their knock-resistance; the ether MTBE for its alcohol-like refrigerative effect; and volatile iso-pentane for cold starting and throttle response. These are all constituents found in motor petrols.

This was seen as too far removed from 'natural' petrols, so rules were written to require a broader range of hydrocarbons, to mimic actual casing-head distillate. Limits were set on levels of oxygen, nitrogen, benzene, dienes, lead and other organo-metallics. Now the cost of the necessary verifications considerably exceeded that of the fuel. Would riders actually be excluded from the results based upon 0.001-per-cent excess of any of the above? Must we wait to announce the actual winner until after the fuel analysis is complete? Such detailed requirements become administrative monsters.

The genie was out of the bottle, and soon 'petrols' appeared that had been dosed with high-energy compounds originally developed as fuels for long-range military aircraft or cruise missiles. Can you say 'tetrahydromethylcyclopentadiene'? There were also wonderful combustion accelerants, additives developed for supersonic-combustion ramjets.

What to do? Adoption of a spec fuel appears to solve all this, but at the cost of eliminating potential team sponsors. Would we prefer to be hanged or shot?

Sometimes rules are made that make no sense and that therefore erode respect for those in control. Such rules can make it appear that the arduous climb to the top has distanced higher management from the realities they direct.

At Daytona in 1976, the 200-mile race was shortened to 180 miles as a 'green' response to the first oil shock. We in racing are doing our bit! That saved about 1.4 gallons per bike, or a total of 112 gallons if all 80 starters finished. But the chartered 747 aircraft that carried Dutch fans to Daytona burned 60,000 gallons of fuel on its way there and back – 500 times as much. Clearly, the way to achieve significant fuel savings in racing is to urge spectators to stay at home.

In MotoGP, rules-makers exert steady pressure on fuel

consumption, despite the fact that the 2002 switch from two-stroke to four-stroke was itself an instant 'green' reduction of 25–30 per cent in specific fuel consumption. The class began with a 24-litre tank in 2002, adopted 22 litres in 2005, and then 21 litres in 2007 with the switch to 800cc displacement. For a 75-mile (121km) race, this is a progression from 12 miles per US gallon (5.04km/litre) to 13 (5.5km/litre) and then 13.5 (5.76km/litre), an overall improvement of 12.5 per cent.

As all who must deal with this know, the effect has been to make racing into something of a fuel economy run. R&D must now split its resources between achieving winning lap times and finding ways to make the fuel allowance go the distance. Segments of the Press inveigh against the electronics now used in racing, but much of that is devoted to dealing with fuel limits. Riders have lost races when fuel-management equipment or software has malfunctioned, and many have reported that their bikes "went flat" or "went lean", losing performance when fuel use compelled the on-board computer to begin conserving it. This is not stimulating new fuel saving technology for motorcycles. It is just an application of off-the-shelf technology now used in every modern petrol-fuelled economy car. During part-throttle operation, the mixture is leaned down from the normal best-power mixture and the ignition timing is advanced to compensate for the lower flame speed of lean combustion. The rider – and often the stopwatch – feel this difference.

The same segment of opinion that deplores MotoGP electronics is often the very one seeking a nostalgic return to the sideways 'cowboy riding' of the middle years of the 500 two-stroke era (and, if they were candid, to the 'exciting' slides and crashes that resulted). However, sliding and spinning are wasteful of fuel, and therefore are effectively forbidden by the 21-litre fuel rule – and doubly will be so from 2012, when the 25-per-cent-larger 1-litre engines return. Why reverse course to larger engines, but with a reduced fuel allowance? What is the goal?

One of the most promising new means of improving fuel

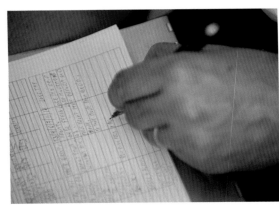

economy in four-stroke spark-ignition engines is GDI, or Gasoline Direct Injection, with a demonstrated potential to cut fuel use by 20 per cent. So far, GDI has been too slow to be of use in MotoGP, but that will surely change. Now a 10-bar fuel pressure rule has been adopted for MotoGP that absolutely rules out GDI. Is fuel consumption important in fact, or is it only a theme for optional use in image management? Engines of smaller displacement would cut real fuel use by any desired amount. Where is the sense? Rules must inspire respect by their sense, or they appear to be just obscure means to undeclared ends.

In the US, and perhaps elsewhere, a view is emerging that, to survive, motorcycle racing must engage and defeat mass-audience competitors, such as televised ball sports or crime dramas. Racing can, it is argued, gain audience only by mimicking their intense start-to-finish action. In this view, new kinds of rules can reshape racing into a more marketable dense pack of closely duelling riders, with never-ending changes of lead. The outcome of racing is difficult enough for riders and teams to control, but ambitious rules makers seem sure that the pen is mightier than the spanner.

The simple clarity of grand prix motorcycle road racing has always been its presentation of the fastest riders in the world, competing on the fastest machines in the world. Inspiration from crime dramas is unlikely to improve on that.

# 2010 MOTOGP REVIEW

**Teams and Riders**

MATTHEW BIRT

**Bike Specifications**

NEIL SPALDING

**Bike Illustrations**

ADRIAN DEAN

Photo: Gold & Goose

# FIAT YAMAHA TEAM

## TEAM STAFF

Masao FURUSAWA: Executive Officer, Yamaha
Engineering Operations
Lin JARVIS: Managing Director, Yamaha Motor Racing
Masahiko NAKAJIMA: Team Director
William FAVERO: Communications Manager
Katie BAINES: Press Officer
Roberto BRIVIO: Team Co-ordinator

## VALENTINO ROSSI PIT CREW

Davide BRIVIO: Team Manager
Jeremy BURGESS: Crew Chief
*Mechanics*
Bernard ANSIAU
Alex BRIGGS
Brent STEPHENS
Gary COLEMAN (assistant/logistics)
Hiroya ATSUMI: Yamaha Engineer
Matteo FLAMIGNI: Telemetry

## JORGE LORENZO PIT CREW

Wilco ZEELENBERG: Team Manager
Ramon FORCADA: Crew Chief
*Mechanics*
Walter CRIPPA
Javier ULLATE
Valentino NEGRI
Juan Llansa HERNANDEZ (assistant/logistics)
Takashi MORIYAMA: Yamaha Engineer
Davide MARELLI: Telemetry

### VALENTINO ROSSI
Born: 16 February, 1979 – Urbino, Italy
GP Starts: 241 (181 MotoGP/500cc, 30 250cc, 30 125cc)
GP Wins: 105 (79 MotoGP/500cc, 14 250cc, 12 125cc)
World Championships: 9 (6 MotoGP, 1 500cc, 1 250cc, 1 125cc)

### JORGE LORENZO
Born: 4 May, 1987 – Palma de Mallorca, Spain
GP Starts: 146 (52 MotoGP, 48 250cc, 46 125cc)
GP Wins: 35 (14 MotoGP, 17 250cc, 4 125cc)
World Championships: 3 (1 MotoGP, 2 250cc)

YAMAHA'S total domination of the MotoGP world championship showed no signs of relenting in 2010 as the all-conquering Japanese factory claimed the triple crown of rider, team and constructor titles for the third season in succession. But the team that overpowered rivals Ducati and Honda once again was barely recognisable at year's end.

Gone was talisman Valentino Rossi, who had single-handedly stopped Yamaha's rapid descent into obscurity in 2004 when he instigated a seismic shift in power from Honda.

Rossi's acceptance of a multi-million-pound two-year offer to join Ducati rocked Yamaha to its core, particularly as he had incessantly declared his intention to undertake what most thought would be a routine renewal of his current Yamaha deal. This married well with Yamaha's desire to use Rossi as a brand ambassador into retirement, his marketing and commercial value far outweighing anything his rivals could offer.

But talks over a new two-year deal fizzled out, and Rossi's move to Ducati was finally confirmed officially immediately after the Czech Republic race in Brno.

What was evident was that Rossi would lay waste

# YAMAHA M1

Sponsors and Technical Suppliers: Petronas · Packard Bell · Semakin Di Depan · Yamalube · Bridgestone · Alpinestars · Fastweb · Termignoni · Exedy · DID · NGK · Magneti Marelli · Beta · 2D · Iveco · Fructis · Flex · Adidas

*Engine:* 800cc, across-the-frame in-line 4, reverse rotating cross-plane crankshaft, DOHC, 4 valves per cylinder, Pneumatic Valve Return System
    *Power:* Around 220bhp at approx 18,000rpm

*Ancillaries:* Magneti Marelli electronics, NGK sparking plugs, full electronic ride by wire · *Lubrication:* Yamalube · *Fuel:* 21 litres; Petronas

*Transmission:* Gear primary drive, multi-plate dry slipper clutch, six-speed constant-mesh cassette-style gearbox, DID chain

*Suspension:* Front, Öhlins TTxTR25 48mm forks · Rear, Öhlins TTxTR 44 shock with linkage

*Wheels:* Front, 16.5in Marchesini · Rear, 16.5in Marchesini · *Tyres:* Bridgestone

*Brakes:* Front, Brembo carbon-carbon 320mm · Rear, Yamaha steel

WATURU YOSHIKAWA
Born: 26 September, 1968 – Tokyo, Japan
GP Starts: 2 MotoGP

Left: Masao Furusawa, his final year.

Below centre: Team photo with special livery for the USA.

Bottom: Lin Jarvis continued as MD.

Photos: Gold & Goose

RAMON FORCADA

JERRY BURGESS

WILCO ZEELENBERG

DAVIDE BRIVIO

to Yamaha's factory garage, much as he had done when he had left Honda, departing in somewhat acrimonious fashion at the end of 2003.

Rossi having spent his entire MotoGP career under the expert technical stewardship of Aussie Jerry Burgess, it was taken as read that their formidable partnership would continue out of the red corner in Bologna. In mid-September, it was confirmed that all of Rossi's crew would go with him.

His decision had other far-reaching consequences. Davide Brivio had taken exclusive command of Rossi's side of the garage when it was divided in 2008 because the Italian and Lorenzo were running different tyre brands. The wall never came down. Brivio also quit on the eve of the final round in Valencia. He didn't defect to Ducati, but it seemed certain that he would assume more of a personal managerial role with Rossi in the future.

The human loss was a bitter pill, but the move had financial implications for Yamaha, too, with Fiat ending its long association. Telefónica MoviStar, Petronas and AirAsia were all touted as potential replacements.

Not only was the on-track messiah leaving, but also Yamaha would lose the huge influence of Masao Furusawa early in 2011. As executive officer, engineering operations for Yamaha Motor Company, he had been instrumental in all of Rossi's success, galvanising an engineering department he had revamped personally for 2004 to make sure the YZR-M1 was capable of winning.

Furusawa had no choice but to leave, having reached retirement age. Rossi cited his departure from active duty as a fundamental reason behind his decision to move to Ducati, although most suspected it was his increasing discomfort with the rise to prominence of Jorge Lorenzo.

Masahiko Nakajima, who was Fiat Yamaha team director, was expected to take over Furusawa's role, while Lin Jarvis remained a prominent figure as managing director for Yamaha Motor Racing. Massimo Meregalli was handed the role of team director, to be reunited with Texan Ben Spies when he had run Yamaha's World Superbike squad when Spies became the first rookie champion in 2009.

He would work with Dutchman Wilco Zeelenberg, who enjoyed a phenomenal first season at the helm of Lorenzo's squad, having been brought in to replace Daniele Romagnoli.

The off-track upheaval aside, 2010 did prove that Yamaha was capable of winning without the inspirational Rossi.

The Italian's final season at Yamaha was a physical and mentally painful experience. Having dominated winter testing, he triumphed in the season's first race at Qatar. But a motocross training accident in late April left him with serious tendon damage in

his right shoulder. The injury troubled him for the rest of the year, and at one stage he seriously contemplated withdrawing early to undergo surgery.

He was also badly injured for the first time in his glittering career when he suffered a compound fracture of his right tibia and fibula in a sickening highside during practice for his home race in Mugello. He missed four races, and while he recovered, his title chances suffered irreparable damage as Lorenzo went on a Rossi-like winning spree. A less-than-fully-fit Rossi, though, was still a marvel to watch on occasion. His epic fight with Lorenzo to claim third in

Japan was only surpassed by an unforgettable ride from 11th to win in Malaysia, undoubtedly stealing some of Lorenzo's thunder on the day he became only the second Spaniard in history to win the world title. He ended with ten podiums, and in the ten races since he returned from the leg break, he never finished outside of the top six.

If Rossi wasn't winning for Yamaha, Lorenzo was proving a more than able substitute. Maturing under the influence of crew chief Ramon Forcada, he came of age in 2010 with an immaculate campaign.

Lorenzo was aggrieved at Rossi for his insistence that the dividing wall remained, and tension between the two escalated pre-season when Yamaha agreed to ban data sharing between the pair. This was another direct request from Rossi. But Lorenzo turned his frustration into a golden run of six wins in seven races at the pivotal mid-season stage, which pushed him to the brink of the title even before the summer break.

He took Rossi's throne in Malaysia and ended the season with nine wins. Perhaps an even more remarkable statistic, though, was the fact that he never finished below fourth, fell off only three times, and scored a record number of points, having finished in all 18 races.

# REPSOL HONDA TEAM

## TEAM STAFF

Shuhei NAKAMOTO: HRC Vice President
Kazuhiko YAMANO: Team Director
Shinichi KOKUBU: Technical Director
Koshiyuki YAMAJI: Team Manager
Roger VAN DER BORGHT: Co-ordinator
Katsura SHIBASAKI: Parts Control

## ANDREA DOVIZIOSO PIT CREW

Gianni BERTI: Team Manager
Ramon AURIN: Chief Mechanic
*Mechanics*
Mark LLOYD · Katzuhiko IMAI
David GUITTEREZ · Keina TAKAYANAGI
Yuji KIKUCHI
Carlo LUZZI: Telemetry
Teruaki MATSUBARA: HRC Engineer
Pete BERGVALL: Öhlins Technician

## DANI PEDROSA PIT CREW

Alberto PUIG: Team Manager
Mike LEITNER: Chief Mechanic
*Mechanics*
Mark BARNETT: Engine Technician
Jordi PRADES · Christophe LEONCE
Masashi OGO · John EYRE
Jose Manuel ALLENDE: Telemetry
Takeo YOKOYAMA: HRC Engineer
Paul TREVATHAN: Öhlins Technician

### DANI PEDROSA
Born: 29 September, 1985 – Sabadell, Spain
GP Starts: 162 (84 MotoGP, 32 250cc, 46 125cc)
GP Wins: 35 (12 MotoGP, 15 250cc, 8 125cc)
World Championships: 3 (2 250cc, 1 125cc)

### ANDREA DOVIZIOSO
Born: 23 March, 1986 – Forli, Italy
GP Starts: 151 (53 MotoGP, 49 250cc, 49 125cc)
GP Wins: 10 (1 MotoGP, 4 250cc, 5 125cc)
World Championships: 1 125cc

Photos: Gold & Goose

HONDA'S 2010 campaign is likely to be remembered as much for political turmoil and spectacular own goals off track as it will be for being the Japanese factory's most successful in the 800cc MotoGP era.

Dani Pedrosa won four races – Honda's best tally since 2006 – and the 2010 factory RC212V was easily the fastest and most reliable bike on the grid as HRC breezed through the six-engine restriction.

Sponsored by Repsol for the 16th successive season, the team was led again by HRC vice-president Shuhei Nakamoto, who was in his second season at the helm following his move from Honda's

Formula One team when it disbanded at the end of 2008.

Working directly below him was Mick Doohan's former mechanic, Kazuhiko Yamano, in his second season as team director. Toshiyuki Yamaji was the new team manager, but Nakamoto was influential in two significant management changes for 2010. It was obvious that he had used 2009 to get a grasp on the strengths and weaknesses of the team that had won only one world title since 2003.

His first move was to appoint former Ducati boss Livio Suppo as head of marketing. Nakamoto was concerned that Honda had relied too heavily on its

# HONDA RC212V

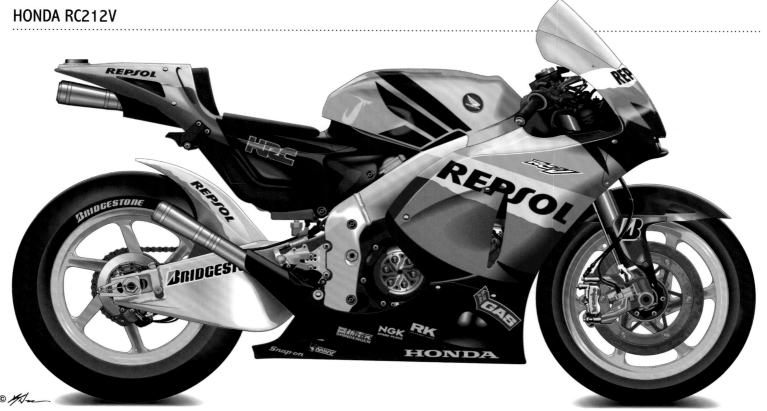

**Sponsors and Technical Suppliers:** One HEART · Bridgestone · Alpinestars · GAS · Kopron · MIVV · NGK · RK Chains · Shindengen · Snap-on

**Engine:** 800cc, 76-degree V4, 360-degree crank (tbc), PVRS. **Power:** More than 225ps

**Ancillaries:** HRC Electronics and ride by wire throttle and fuel injection system with torducter, NGK sparking plugs

**Lubrication:** Repsol · **Fuel:** 21 litres; Repsol

**Transmission:** Gear primary drive, multi-plate dry slipper clutch, six-speed constant-mesh cassette-style gearbox, RK chain

**Suspension:** Front, Öhlins TTxTR25 48mm forks · Rear, gas shock with linkage

**Wheels:** Front, 16.5in Marchesini. · Rear, 16.5in Marchesini · **Tyres:** Bridgestone

**Brakes:** Front, Brembo carbon-carbon 314/320mm · Rear, HRC steel 218mm

longstanding relationship with Repsol, and that it lacked the number of associate sponsors that had invested in Ducati and Yamaha.

Another key appointment was Shinichi Kokubu, who took on the newly created role of HRC technical director. He was formerly the RC212V project leader and had made only brief visits to the paddock. For 2010, he was very hands-on, present at every race, with Nakamoto wanting to establish a clearer chain of communication between staff on the ground and engineers in Japan. He oversaw six HRC engineers who were permanently deployed in the paddock, including electronics specialists Cristian Battaglia and Andrea Zugna, lured from Yamaha in what was seen as a major coup at the end of 2009.

It was clear from an early stage, though, that Suppo's remit wouldn't be restricted to the task of attracting fresh investment. There had been several reports that he had left Ducati at Casey Stoner's behest because of a serious deterioration in their relationship in 2009. That theory was quickly dispelled, and Suppo's close relationship with the Australian made for fairly routine negotiations that saw the 2007 champion agree to leave Ducati for Honda after the second round of the series.

Suppo would also become a central figure in one of the season's major political dramas, which saw Honda only confirm its 2011 plans at the very end of the year.

The controversy focused on Honda's contractual obligations to Italian rider Andrea Dovizioso. Having signed Stoner early, and with Pedrosa never likely to be released because he is intrinsically linked with the Spanish sponsor (he signed for two more years), Honda found itself in a major quandary. For Dovizioso had a clause in his contract that stated that if he were in the top five in the championship at the end of July, he could automatically invoke a new contract in the Repsol squad.

This prompted Honda to formulate plans for a three-rider 'super-team' comprising Stoner, Pedrosa and Dovizioso. Suppo was charged with finding additional investment to fund the project.

Talks with Red Bull and other potential partners never came to fruition, and with Dovizioso rightfully insisting that his contract be honoured, Honda had no choice but to confirm a three-rider factory team in Repsol colours. The team was expected to be structured with Stoner in a separate garage.

At one stage, Suppo's presence appeared to threaten even Repsol's involvement. When it emerged that he could undertake a sporting director role in 2011, the plan didn't sit well with Pedrosa or the management of the Spanish fuel giant, who were reluctant to have the Italian meddling in the operation of the team.

In addition to the political turmoil, prospects on the track were marred on occasion by embarrassing technical blunders.

Once again, Pedrosa worked with crew chief Mike Leitner, and a permanent fixture at the Spaniard's side, both in and out of the garage, was team manager, personal manager and mentor Alberto Puig.

Pedrosa was enjoying his best season in MotoGP when his slender world title hopes completely evaporated in front of an army of red-faced HRC staff at the Twin Ring Motegi. After winning his first ever back-to-back MotoGP races, the Spaniard was starting to exert serious pressure on runaway leader Lorenzo, but a jammed throttle – later attributed to an assembly fault – left Pedrosa with both title hopes and left collarbone shattered.

Dovizioso's personal aspirations were also dismantled by a technical malfunction. His crew was managed by Gianni Berti once more, with crew chief Ramon Aurin overseeing his RC212V for the first season after HRC stalwart Pete Benson had been axed at the end of 2009.

Four podiums in the first five races were signs of huge improvement, and he was challenging for third in the championship when a detached steering damper mount forced him out of the Australian Grand Prix at Phillip Island and left him fifth overall.

# DUCATI MARLBORO TEAM

## TEAM STAFF

Claudio DOMENICALI: Managing Director
Alessandro CICOGNANI: MotoGP Project Director
Vittoriano GUARESCHI: Team Manager
Christhian PUPULIN: Technical Co-ordinator
Francesco RAPISARDA: Communications Director
Federica DE ZOTTIS: Press Officer
Amedeo COSTA: Team Co-ordinator
Paola BRAIATO: Administration, Logistics and Hospitality
Luigi MITOLO: Assistant Technical Co-ordinator
Debora CONTI: MotoGP Assistant Press Officer
Davide BARALDINI: Warehouse and Components

## CASEY STONER PIT CREW

Cristian GABARRINI: Race Engineer
Bruno LEONI: Chief Mechanic
*Mechanics*
Roberto CLERICI
Andrea BRUNETTI
Lorenzo GAGNI
Filipo BRUNETTI
Gabriele CONTI: Electronics Engineer

## NICKY HAYDEN PIT CREW

Juan MARTINEZ: Race Engineer
Davide MANFREDI: Chief Mechanic
*Mechanics*
Massimo MIRANO
Pedro Calvet CARAL
Lorenzo CANESTRARI
Leonardo GENA

### CASEY STONER
Born: 16 October, 1985 – Southport, Australia
GP Starts: 144 (83 MotoGP, 31 250cc, 30 125cc)
GP Wins: 30 (23 MotoGP, 5 250cc, 2 125cc)
World Championships: 1 MotoGP

### NICKY HAYDEN
Born: 30 July, 1981 – Owensboro, USA
GP Starts: 134 MotoGP
GP Wins: 3 MotoGP
World Championships: 1 MotoGP

ASIDE from the euphoria of finally succeeding in capturing Valentino Rossi's prized signature, Ducati's 2010 season will be remembered as one of serious underachievement by the official factory squad.

Since Casey Stoner's embarrassingly easy romp to success in the inaugural 800cc world championship back in 2007, Ducati has found it difficult to resist the subsequent Japanese revival, led overwhelmingly by Yamaha.

The GP10 contender was supposedly the most manageable Desmosedici ever to have rolled out of Bologna. Equipped with a smoother and tamer Big Bang engine, it would actually be the least successful, with Casey Stoner winning only three races in a short end-of-season revival.

Ducati's senior management had something of a different look to it for 2010, although the most highly ranked figures in Italy remained unchanged. Gabriele Del Torchio continued as CEO, while Claudio Domenicali was general manager. Both made fleeting visits to the paddock, Del Torchio notably present in Brno in mid-August to wallow in the glory of Rossi's announcement that he'd quit Yamaha to sign for Ducati. It was a dream marriage of the two-wheeled Italian icons, but Del Torchio had been

# DUCATI Desmosedici GP10

*Sponsors and Technical Suppliers:* Generali · Enel · Riello ups · Bridgestone · Shell Advance · Alfa Romeo · Bosch · Ditec · Guabello · Puma
Tata Consultancy Services · Toshiba

*Engine:* 800cc, 90-degree V4, irregular-fire crank, DOHC, 4 valves per cylinder, Desmodromic valve gear, variable-length inlet tracts
    *Power:* Around 225bhp, revs up to 18,500rpm

*Ancillaries:* Magneti Marelli electronics, NGK sparking plugs, full electronic ride by wire · *Lubrication:* Shell Advance · *Fuel:* 21 litres; Shell

*Transmission:* Gear primary drive, multi-plate dry slipper clutch, six-speed constant-mesh cassette-style gearbox, RK chain

*Suspension:* Front, Öhlins TTx20 42mm Forks/TTxTR25 48mm forks · Rear, Öhlins TTxTR44 shock with linkage

*Wheels:* Front, 16.5in Marchesini · Rear, 16.5in Marchesini · *Tyres:* Bridgestone

*Brakes:* Front, Brembo carbon-carbon 320mm · Rear, steel 200mm

*Left:* Red rose of Aragon: the Ducati team after the first win.

*Below:* New project director Alessandro Cicognani.
*Photos:* Gold & Goose

left red-faced in early August when inadvertently he let slip during an interview that the deal had been made. It was the world's worst kept secret, but his revelation still pre-empted any official announcement and reportedly infuriated the Japanese management at Yamaha.

Once again, Filippo Preziosi was Ducati's gifted and understated technical director, who also played a central role in the Rossi discussions.

The hands-on management in the paddock had changed, though, following the departure of long-serving Livio Suppo at the end of 2009. Alessandro Cicognani took on the MotoGP project director role, while the team manager was Vittoriano Guareschi, who on occasion also continued in his role of test and development rider.

Guareschi was more of a riding and technical consultant than a team manager, although his close relationship with Rossi had eased discussions. It wasn't common knowledge that he and Rossi had forged a close relationship nearly two decades earlier, in 1993, when they had been team-mates at Cagiva while racing in the Italian 125 Sport Production series.

Frequently trackside studying Stoner and Nicky Hayden, Guareschi was also keenly observing the opposition to try to understand where Ducati could improve. His intimate knowledge of the Desmosedici, since its inception in 2003 as a brutal 990cc package, meant that he was trusted implicitly by Stoner and Hayden. Both knew that he could communicate to Bologna what they were feeling and thinking on the bike. Preziosi had another pair of eyes and ears at the track, too, with Cristhian Pupulin continuing as technical co-ordinator.

Despite a wealth of talent working behind the scenes, Ducati couldn't replicate past glory, and Stoner was unable to sustain a title challenge beyond the third round.

Once again, the Australian was under the wing of crew chief Cristian Gabarrini, ably assisted by electronics engineer Gabriele Conti and chief mechanic Bruno Leoni. He crashed out of the lead in the opening race in Qatar and then again at round three at Le Mans. By the end of the season, he'd racked up an unenviable list of five race crashes.

Some in the paddock had even begun to doubt whether Ducati would win a race at all in 2010, until Stoner ended the 11-month winless streak with a virtuoso performance at the Motorland Aragon in September. He would win again in Japan before executing a stunning fourth straight win on home soil at Phillip Island.

By that stage of the season, the GP world had been aware of his move to Honda for 2011 for some months. News had leaked as early as the opening race that he was close to signing for the Japanese

manufacturer. When his father and manager, Colin Stoner, arrived at the second round in Jerez for more talks, it was evident that the Australian was contemplating a move. Indeed, no sooner had the ink dried on Livio Suppo's HRC contract, than rumours emerged that he had been poached with the prime intention of formulating a bid to lure Stoner to Honda.

The deal was wrapped up quickly, and finally announced between the Catalunya and Sachsenring races. Like Rossi's move to Ducati, Stoner would take his entire crew with him for 2011.

Ducati had spoken to Jorge Lorenzo before pulling off the coup of landing Rossi, the signing of the legendary nine-times world champion an ample cushion to soften the blow of losing Stoner.

Hayden's second season at Ducati showed marked improvement on the rodeo ride he had experienced during 2009. The immensely popular American had mastered the nuances of the Ducati and he was a prominent rather than peripheral figure in 2010.

Working again with Spanish crew chief Juan Martinez, Hayden scored ten top-six finishes, including a third at the Motorland Aragon. On four other occasions, he was agonisingly close to the rostrum, and his vast improvement meant that he had a safe seat. His new two-year deal was confirmed on home soil at Indianapolis in late August. It sees him paired with Rossi again for the first time since his rookie year in 2003, when the pair were together at Repsol Honda.

*Above:* Vito Guareschi doubled as test rider and team manager.

*Left:* Ducati's gifted engineering guru, Filippo Preziosi.

*Bottom:* Stoner jokes with his crew.
*Photos:* Gold & Goose

## MONSTER TECH 3 YAMAHA

### TEAM STAFF

Hervé PONCHARAL: Team Manager

Gérard VALLEE: Team Co-ordinator

Laurence LASSERRE: Team Assistant

Eric REBMANN: Parts Manager

Olivier BOUTRON: Fuel/Tyres

Paola DOS SANTOS: Press and Communications

### COLIN EDWARDS PIT CREW

Guy COULON: Crew Chief

*Mechanics*

Jerôme PONCHARAL

Josian RUSTIQUE

Laurent DUCLOYER

Andrew GRIFFITH: Telemetry

### BEN SPIES PIT CREW

Tom HOUSEWORTH: Crew Chief

*Mechanics*

Gregory WOOD

Julien LAJUNIE

Sebastien LATORT

Nicolas GOYON: Telemetry

#### COLIN EDWARDS
Born: 27 February, 1974 – Houston, Texas, USA
GP Starts: 137 MotoGP
World Championships: 2 World Superbike

#### BEN SPIES
Born: 11 July, 1984 – Memphis, Tennessee, USA
GP Starts: 21 MotoGP
World Championships: 1 World Superbike

FOR the third successive season, Hervé Poncharal's Tech 3 Yamaha squad was the top non-factory team in MotoGP, its prominence in 2010 owing much to the affirmation of Ben Spies as a genuine world-class talent.

The France-based squad was in its third decade of grand prix racing, and the arrival of American Spies heralded a rare change in personnel for Poncharal, who had always been reluctant to meddle with his loyal crew.

To accommodate Spies, who was contracted directly to Yamaha and paid by the Japanese factory, the trade-off was that the American was given *carte blanche* to cherry-pick his own crew. A stipulation of his MotoGP move after a record breaking surge to the 2009 World Superbike crown was that long serving crew chief Tom Houseworth and mechanic Greg 'Woody' Wood would follow. Spies placed such value on the American duo that he paid their salaries out of his own pocket, the pair being employed by Speez Racing, of which his mother, Mary, was the majority shareholder.

Their arrival meant that Gary Reynders, who had previously been crew chief for Colin Edwards and James Toseland, and Benoit Bruneau were ousted. Both were given identical roles with Tech 3's new

## YAMAHA M1 YZR

**Sponsors and Technical Suppliers:** Monster · Leon Vince · Motul · DeWalt · Bridgestone · Antoniolupi · Packard Bell · LighTech

**Engine:** 800cc, across-the-frame in-line 4, reverse rotating cross-plane crankshaft, DOHC, 4 valves per cylinder, pneumatic valve return system
**Power:** Around 220bhp at approx 18,000rpm

**Ancillaries:** Magneti Marelli electronics, NGK sparking plugs, full electronic ride by wire · **Lubrication:** Yamalube · **Fuel:** 21 litres

**Transmission:** Gear primary drive, multi-plate dry slipper clutch, six-speed constant-mesh cassette-style gearbox, DID chain

**Suspension:** Front, Öhlins TTxTR25 48mm forks · Rear, Öhlins TTxTR 44 shock with linkage

**Wheels:** Front, 16.5in Marchesini · Rear, 16.5in Marchesini · **Tyres:** Bridgestone

**Brakes:** Front, Brembo carbon-carbon 320mm · Rear, Yamaha steel

*Above:* Team principal Hervé Poncharal.

*Left:* Guy Coulon.

*Far left:* Edwards stays on board for 2011.

*Below:* Ben Spies.

Photos: Gold & Goose

Moto2 venture, where they worked with Japanese rider Yuki Takahashi.

Spies had signed a two-year deal at the end of 2009, and he quickly laid out his master plan. Tech 3 was merely a stepping stone in his meteoric rise to the top, and he fully expected to be in Yamaha's factory team in 2011. Rossi's subsequent departure to Ducati paved the way, and his promotion was confirmed at his home race in Indianapolis in late August. Inevitably, his crew would follow.

Nobody could argue that Spies's promotion wasn't thoroughly merited. His fifth place in Qatar immediately beat James Toseland's best result in 35 races for Tech 3, and frequently he was the top non-factory rider. He scored a brilliant debut podium at Silverstone, pressurising compatriot Nicky Hayden into a vital last-lap error, and claimed another personal milestone in Indianapolis, blitzing to pole before scoring a career-best second in the race.

He scored 12 top-six finishes and claimed the coveted Rookie of the Year crown at Phillip Island with a fifth place, which also secured him the honour of finishing top non-factory rider.

On the other side of the garage was the venerable Colin Edwards, who was in his third year with Tech 3, and many thought it his last. The 36-year-old was again in tandem with vastly experienced crew chief Guy Coulon, who would divide his time in 2010 between overseeing Edwards's eighth MotoGP campaign and masterminding Tech 3 Racing's assault on the inaugural Moto2 series.

Coulon and Nicolas Goyon were vital elements in the Moto2 project, the latter also multi-tasking, as his primary role was as Spies's data engineer.

Edwards had finished fifth overall in 2009, but in 2010, his fortunes plummeted and he became only a bit-part player. For the most part, he was completely overshadowed by Spies and didn't score a top six until round 14, at the rescheduled Twin Ring Motegi race in Japan.

At the mid-season stage, Edwards appeared weary of MotoGP, frustrated at riding with barely no prospect of a podium. He spoke at length with Ducati's World Superbike squad and even flew to Bologna en route to the Sachsenring MotoGP in mid-July for negotiations. But the deal was dead in the water barely six weeks later, when Ducati announced its factory involvement in WSB would cease at the end of 2010.

Edwards signed a new contract with Tech 3 at the Motorland Aragon race, the Texan confessing that he did intend 2011 to be his swansong.

The unenviable task of filling the large void created by Spies will fall to British rider Cal Crutchlow. He was made an offer in Brno and finally signed in Misano, his close links to Monster helping negotiations run smoothly.

Crutchlow was desperate to bring his German crew chief, Marcus Eschenbacher, with him from Yamaha's World Superbike squad, but the team appointed Daniele Romagnoli in his place. The Italian had been Edwards's crew chief in Yamaha's factory team and had managed Jorge Lorenzo's squad in 2008 and 2009.

GREG WOOD

TOM HOUSEWORTH

## RIZLA SUZUKI

### TEAM STAFF

Shinichi SAHARA: Project Manager
Paul DENNING: Team Manager
Takayuki NAKAMOTO: Engine Development and Control
Tetsuya SASAKI: Chassis Development
Tex GEISSLER: ECU Control Assistance
Erkki SIUKOLA: ECU Control Assistance
Richard FRANCIS: Sub-Assemblies Manager
Russell JORDAN: Parts and Logistics
Charlie MOODY: Operations Manager
Dirk DEBUS: 2D Electronics
Yukihiko KUBO: Bridgestone Tyres
Graeme IRVINE: Öhlins Suspension
Eugenio GANDOLFI: Brembo Brakes
Tim WALPOLE: Press and PR Manager
Helen TAYLOR: Team Administrator

### ALVARO BAUTISTA PIT CREW

Tom O'KANE: Crew Chief
Simon WESTWOOD: Crew Leader
*Mechanics*
Ray HUGHES
Tsutomo MATSUGANO
Mark FLEMING (driver/mechanic)
Renato PENNACCHIO: Telemetry

### LORIS CAPIROSSI PIT CREW

Stuart SHENTON: Crew Chief
Ian GILPIN: Crew Leader
*Mechanics*
George DZIEDZIC
Jeffrey OH
Jez WILSON (driver/mechanic)
Gary McLAREN: Telemetry

**ALVARO BAUTISTA**
Born: 21 November, 1984 – Talavera de la Reina, Spain
GP Starts: 133 (17 MotoGP, 49 250cc, 67 125cc)
GP Wins: 16 (8 250cc, 8 125cc)
World Championships: 1 125cc

**LORIS CAPIROSSI**
Born: 4 April, 1973 – Bologna, Italy
GP Starts: 315 (204 MotoGP/500cc, 84 250cc, 27 125cc)
GP Wins: 29 (9 MotoGP/500cc, 12 250cc, 8 125cc)
World Championships: 3 (1 250cc, 2 125cc)

SUZUKI'S abject failure to capitalise on a strong debut 800cc campaign in 2007 would have dire consequences by the end of a 2010 season that had done little to restore the Japanese factory's diminishing reputation as a major player in world racing.

Another season of massive underachievement on track came against a backdrop of plummeting sales. Suzuki suffered a hammering in the market, and the two combined to have a devastating effect on the Rizla backed team and MotoGP in general.

It was in June that Suzuki first communicated to Dorna that it intended to enter the 2011 champion-ship with just one rider. Project manager Shinichi Sahara confirmed that in Misano in early September; barely a month later, half of Suzuki's loyal crew had been informed that their services would no longer be required.

Dorna and its fellow members in the all-powerful MSMA felt the terms of their current five-year agreement, which runs out at the end of 2011, clearly stipulated that Suzuki was obliged to run a two-rider effort. Suzuki vehemently disagreed. While it acknowledged that it was obliged to participate in 2011, its level of involvement meant it could down-scale to one rider and still fulfil its commitment.

## SUZUKI GSV-R

*Sponsors and Technical Suppliers:* Bridgestone · Motul · Akrapovic · Troy Lee Designs · 2D · Marchesini · RK · Mitsubishi · Beta · NGK · Tras
Puig Racing Screens · NRS · Dread · Draggin Jeans · DG · DAF · Blue Chip

*Engine:* 800cc, 75-degree V4, 360-degree crank, Pneumatic Valve Return System. *Power:* Around 21bhp

*Ancillaries:* Mitsubishi Electronics, NGK sparking plugs, electronic ride by wire · *Lubrication:* Motul · *Fuel:* 21 litres

*Transmission:* Gear primary drive, multi-plate dry slipper clutch, six-speed constant-mesh cassette-style gearbox, DID chain

*Suspension:* Front, Öhlins TTx20 42mm forks · Rear, Öhlins TTx44TR shock with linkage

*Wheels:* Front; 16.5in Marchesini · Front, 16.5in Marchesini · *Tyres:* Bridgestone

*Brakes:* Front, Brembo carbon-carbon 305mm or 314mm · Rear, steel

*Left:* Capirossi and Bautista wore special helmets at Valencia.

*Below left, top:* Stuart Shenton.

*Below left, bottom:* Paul Denning.

*Below:* Bautista's side of the garage.

Photos: Gold & Goose

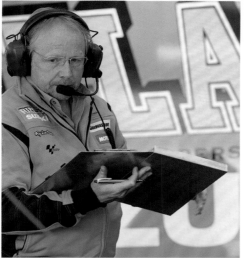

Dorna boss Carmelo Ezpeleta threatened legal action to ensure he didn't lose another bike on a painfully thin grid. One major issue, though, was the precedent set by Kawasaki in 2009, which pulled out at the start of the year. A compromise was that Kawasaki supplied one factory ZX-RR under the Hayate banner, which Dorna sanctioned, despite Kawasaki having minimal input.

Ezpeleta perhaps had good reason to be aggrieved at Suzuki's stubborn stance, having given the manufacturer his unwavering support. Firstly, Suzuki received special exemption from the rookie rule, which barred any factory team from signing a new rider, hence the deal to hire highly rated Spaniard Alvaro Bautista. And when Suzuki embarrassingly failed to meet with the cost saving engine restrictions because of reliability, Bautista and Capirossi were permitted to use an extra three engines, taking their total to nine each.

Another blow for Suzuki was that its 2011 effort would have to be entirely self-funded. Despite a lack of on-track success, Suzuki had managed to keep title sponsor Rizla on board, and 2010 had been the start of a new two-year deal. By the end of the season, though, patience at Imperial Tobacco Group Plc had started to wear thin. Although contracted for 2011, there were break clauses on both sides, but continuation seemed likely.

Sahara had planned for a two-rider effort until the last minute in case of a dramatic change of heart by Suzuki Motor Corporation management, and British team boss Paul Denning had conducted several rider negotiations through the period of uncertainty. Denning was in charge for a fifth successive season, but undoubtedly one of his toughest tasks since taking the reins from Garry Taylor was to inform several crew members in Sepang that Suzuki's intention was to downsize.

Among those released was Suzuki stalwart and vastly experienced crew chief Stuart Shenton, who had worked in the team since 1992, now running Capirossi. Being on Bautista's crew, though, didn't automatically mean an escape from the axe. The team headquarters at Verwood in Dorset, England, meant that all non-British staff on Bautista's side were released, the UK staff on Capirossi's side being transferred accordingly. Most of the crew told that they were free to seek alternative employment were on Capirossi's side, with Bautista already under contract for 2011.

An indifferent campaign from seasoned rider Capirossi did little to convince Suzuki management that it was worth pouring millions of pounds into the GSV-R project. His third season at Suzuki was also his worst, the veteran Italian finishing only 16th in the championship with a best result of seventh

place in Catalunya. Also his hopes of celebrating his milestone 200th MotoGP appearance were cruelly ended in painful fashion, a second corner collision with Nicky Hayden leaving him with a serious right hand injury that forced his withdrawal from the inaugural Motorland Aragon clash. Then he missed the Australian round in Phillip Island through an injury sustained in qualifying.

Bautista was placed under the wing of crew chief Tom O'Kane, who previously had overseen Chris Vermeulen's spell at Suzuki. The Spaniard's season was largely dictated by a nasty shoulder injury he had suffered in a motocross training accident in May. When fit, he showed potential in abundance, scoring fifth places in Catalunya and Sepang.

What was notable about both races was that they were in extreme heat, but for the most part the GSV-R remained a 'Jekyll-and-Hyde' machine, and in cooler conditions it struggled.

Before Suzuki announced its one-rider decision, numerous riders had been in discussion for 2011. It was apparent early in the season that Capirossi had surrendered in his battle to make the GSV-R competitive, and a leading contender was Randy de Puniet. Toni Elias and Hiroshi Aoyama were also mentioned, but talks could never develop to a serious stage while Denning and Sahara were unable to make any concrete offers.

# SAN CARLO HONDA

## TEAM STAFF

Fausto GRESINI: Chairman and Managing Director
Carlo MERLINI: Sales and Marketing Director
Aldo GANDOLFO: Press and Media Relations
Fulvia CASTELLI: Logistics

## MARCO MELANDRI PIT CREW

Antonio JIMINEZ: Chief Mechanic
*Mechanics*
Andrea BONASSOLI
Ryoichi MORI
Alberto PRESUTTI
Diego GUBELLINI: Telemetry

## MARCO SIMONCELLI PIT CREW

Aligi DEGANELLO: Chief Mechanic
*Mechanics*
Ivan BRANDI
Federico VICINO
Marco Rosa GASTALDO
Elvio DEGANELLO: Telemetry

Michel MASINI: Spare Parts
Renzo PINI: Pit assistant

### MARCO MELANDRI
Born: 7 August, 1982 – Ravenna, Italy
GP Starts: 207 (131 MotoGP, 47 250cc, 29 125cc)
GP Wins: 22 (5 MotoGP, 10 250cc, 7 125cc)
World Championships: 1 250cc

### MARCO SIMONCELLI
Born: 20 January, 1987 – Cattolica, Italy
GP Starts: 132 (18 MotoGP, 64 250cc, 50 125cc)
GP Wins: 14 (12 250cc, 2 125cc)
World Championships: 1 250cc

*Photos: Gold & Goose*

IF 2010 was supposed to herald a revival in fortunes for Fausto Gresini's satellite Honda squad, ultimately the season proved one of immense disappointment. And the year would signal the end of a career in MotoGP for a rider once capable of fighting it out with Valentino Rossi.

For the second time in three years, the Rimini-based squad failed to score a podium finish, although Simoncelli nearly made it at Estoril.

A decent 2009 had saved neither Toni Elias nor Alex de Angelis from the axe as Gresini turned to the old and new generation of Italian talent.

Marco Melandri had gone to hell and back in a shocking stint at Ducati at 2008 and then seen the factory Kawasaki team fold around his ears before he'd even raced a ZX-RR in 2009. So after campaigning the uncompetitive Hayate, a rebranded Kawasaki in 2009, he made a return to familiar territory with Gresini.

He'd enjoyed the best spell of his MotoGP career with the team, winning five races in a three-year tenure and taking runner-up spot in 2005. That was the last time both he and the Gresini squad had truly shone.

Melandri was reunited with Spanish crew chief Antonio Jimenez, but his bitter experience at Ducati

# HONDA RC212V

*Sponsors and Technical Suppliers:* San Carlo · Castrol · Bridgestone · Agos Ducato · Airdale · Domino · Berner · Power Cotton Joy · Generazione Vincente
Pascucchi · Pink · Rifle · Termagnoni · ZeroRH+ · Antarex · Bike Lift · Nissin · Thermal Technology · Dread · Honda Italia

*Engine:* 800cc, 76-degree V4, 360-degree crank (tbc), PVRS. *Power:* More than 210ps

*Ancillaries:* HRC Electronics and ride by wire throttle and fuel injection system, NGK sparking plugs · *Lubrication:* Castrol · *Fuel:* 21 litres

*Dimensions:* 2,050mm length, 1,440mm wheelbase, 1,130mm height, 645mm width

*Transmission:* Gear primary drive, multi-plate dry slipper clutch, six-speed constant-mesh cassette-style gearbox, RK chain

*Suspension:* Front, Öhlins TTxTR25 48mm forks · Rear, gas shock with linkage (Melandri for the middle of the season: Front, 47mm Showa forks; Rear Showa gas shock with linkage)

*Wheels:* Front; 16.5in Marchesini · Rear; 16.5in Marchesini · *Tyres:* Bridgestone · *Brakes:* Front, Nissin carbon-carbon 314/320mm · Rear, HRC steel 218mm

and subsequent turmoil at Kawasaki seemed to have scarred him permanently, both on and off the track. Such was his struggle to re-acquaint himself with the RC212V that Honda adopted an unusually lenient policy.

With HRC blessing, Jimenez modified the chassis and swing-arm ahead of the Le Mans race. The DIY alterations, which also included a switch back to the Showa suspension that HRC had ditched at the end of 2009, sparked a brief recovery, with Melandri claiming a top six in France that he followed with fifth on home soil in Mugello. But any shoots of regrowth were dealt a huge blow when he dislocated his shoulder in practice at Assen in late June.

As Melandri's frustrations grew, he was chased by BMW and Yamaha in World Superbikes, and decided between the two as he flew home from Indianapolis. He opted for Yamaha, and the deal was finalised on Sunday night in Misano.

The 2010 season was the 14th in grand prix racing for Gresini, although the close links he had forged with Honda had diminished somewhat since the departure of Sete Gibernau in 2005. A closer relationship re-emerged in 2010, thanks to the arrival of mop-headed former 250cc world champion Marco Simoncelli.

The Italian was courted strongly by Yamaha and Ducati, but, desperate to strengthen its talent pool, HRC hired him for an exorbitant fee. Gresini was the chief benefactor, the rookie rule meaning that Simoncelli could only ride for a satellite team.

Crucially, given the increasingly unstable economic climate, Gresini wouldn't have to pay Simoncelli: his contract was held directly by Japan. And the arrival of the talented and outspoken Italian also helped to persuade Italian snack food manufacturer San Carlo to extend its title sponsorship deal.

Simoncelli's Derbi 250 crew chief, Aligi Deganello, moved to Gresini, as did his brother, Elvio, as telemetry engineer, which helped ease Simoncelli's move.

Initially, he failed to justify his big reputation, two bone crunching crashes in pre-season testing in Sepang jolting his confidence. It took him eight races to claim a top six in Germany, which he equalled in Japan, Australia and Valencia. His best result was a fourth place in Portugal, but he really looked the part in the early stages of the Valencia Grand Prix when he ran wheel-to wheel with the leaders.

For 2011 though, Simoncelli's support from HRC will increase drastically. As per the terms of his HRC contract, he will be a fully fledged factory rider, starting with an identical RC212V to those of Casey Stoner, Dani Pedrosa and Andrea Dovizioso. Despite the increased level of technical support, Simoncelli would remain with Gresini's satellite squad.

Gresini was told to keep his second slot open possibly for Dovizioso, as a major political row engulfed the factory team for much of 2010. But his second bike was eventually taken by Hiroshi Aoyama in a deal announced at Valencia with HRC keen to retain the services of a Japanese rider.

*Above:* Simoncelli's pit crew in action.

*Top:* Simoncelli and crew chief Deganello make a contrast.

*Top left:* Melandri had a disappointing campaign back in the team.

*Left:* Simoncelli made the Honda look tiny.

*Below:* Fausto Gresini, a long-time ally of HRC.

*Photos:* Gold & Goose

One notable absentee from the Gresini garage was long serving technical director Fabrizio Cecchini. He didn't stray too far though and masterminded one of the big success stories of 2010.

Cecchini was put in charge of Gresini's assault on the new Moto2 class. Working closely with Japanese chassis designer Moriwaki, he played a pivotal role in the development of the project. His technical expertise was invaluable in guiding Toni Elias to a historic inaugural success with seven wins that saw the Spaniard wrap up the title at Sepang, with three races remaining.

## PRAMAC DUCATI

### TEAM STAFF

Paolo CAMPINOTI: Team Principal
Fabiano STERLACCHINI: Technical Director
Felix RODRIGUEZ: Team Co-ordinator
Matteo VITELLO: Communications Manager
Francesco NAPOLI: Press Officer
Sara TICCI: PR and Travel Co-ordinator
Vincenzo CAPUANO: Hospitality Manager

### MIKA KALLIO PIT CREW

Fabio STERLACCHINI: Track Engineer
Michele ANDREINI: Chief Technician
*Mechanics*
Paul RUIZ
Pedro RIVERA
Christian AIELO: Tyre Technician
Dario MASSARIN: Electronics Engineer

### ALEIX ESPARGARO PIT CREW

Marco RIGAMONTI: Track Engineer
Michele PERUGINI: Chief Technician
*Mechanics*
Mark ELDER
Guglielmi ANDREINI
Francesco GALINDA: Tyre Technician
Alberto GIRIBUOLA: Electronics Engineer

**MIKA KALLIO**
Born: 8 November, 1982 – Valkeakoski, Finland
GP Starts: 147 (32 MotoGP, 33 250cc, 82 125cc)
GP Wins: 12 (5 250cc, 7 125cc)

**ALEIX ESPARGARO**
Born: 30 July, 1989 – Granollers, Spain
GP Starts: 89 (22 MotoGP, 44 250cc, 23 125cc)

DUCATI has always prided itself on the close association between its factory effort and the satellite Pramac squad, which it has supported in various guises since 2005. So it was perplexing to contemplate again in 2010 why the fortunes of the two camps differed so wildly.

Once more, it was largely an uphill struggle for Pramac, run by the ambitious Paolo Campinoti, the squad failing to register a single top-six finish in the 2010 season

The season started full of promise, not least because of a new mantra that would see the squad branded The Green Energy Team. This venture, used cleverly to market Pramac's eco-friendly employment of power-generation equipment, would promote the use of solar and wind power as part of the team's drive to make its paddock activities more environmentally friendly.

The team also used electric paddock bikes, but ironically the project was launched in a blaze of publicity under the floodlights at Losail in Qatar, where 5.4-million Watts are required to power nearly 4,000 lights for the night race.

Pramac's roots in MotoGP could be traced back to 2002, when it entered the fray; in 2004, it pioneered the split-garage format with Max Biaggi and Makoto Tamada that is now commonplace in racing.

For 2010, Finnish rider Mika Kallio had been

## DUCATI Desmosedici GP10

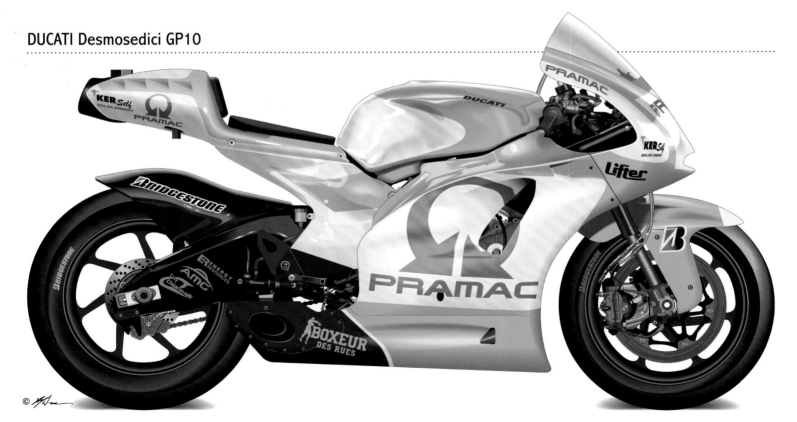

*Sponsors and Technical Suppliers:* Pramac · Bridgestone · ENI · Kerself · ER Energy Resources · Boxeur · Midac · Lifter · Iboni · SC · Puma · Bel-Ray · Flex · Beta
Regina Chains · Termo Race · Speedfiber · Age Consulting · Chicco Doro · AMG · Cima · Meco Alta Spa · Axio · Gefco · Deltacom

*Engine:* 800cc, 90-degree V4, 360-degree crank, DOHC, 4 valves per cylinder, Desmodromic valve gear, variable-length inlet tracts
    *Power:* Around 225bhp, revs up to 18,500rpm

*Ancillaries:* Magneti Marelli electronics, NGK sparking plugs, full electronic ride by wire · *Lubrication:* Shell · *Fuel:* 21 litres; Shell

*Transmission:* Gear primary drive, multi-plate dry slipper clutch, six-speed constant-mesh cassette-style gearbox, RK chain

*Suspension:* Front, Öhlins TTxTR25 48mm forks · Rear, Öhlins TTxTR 44mm shock with linkage

*Wheels:* Front, 16.5in Marchesini. · Rear, 16.5in Marchesini · *Tyres:* Bridgestone

*Brakes:* Front, Brembo carbon-carbon 320mm · Rear, steel 200mm

**CARLOS CHECA**
Born: 15 October, 1972 – Sant Fruitos, Spain
GP Starts: 222 (194 MotoGP/500cc, 27 250cc, 1 125cc)
GP Wins: 2 500cc

retained after a promising rookie campaign, while Aleix Espargaro was rewarded with a full-time GP10 ride, having produced some eye-catching performances as an injury stand-in during 2009.

Kallio was arguably one of the biggest let-downs of the year, and he failed miserably to benefit from the continued input of Pramac stalwart Fabiano Sterlacchini. He doubled as Kallio's crew chief and overall technical director, so he could offer some of his vast knowledge to nurture Espargaro's rookie campaign. Kallio's best of seventh came at the second round, but a torrid period followed, and he made only one more visit to the top ten with ninth at Laguna Seca.

That result came in the midst of a truly shocking period, during which he crashed in Sachsenring, and then in three successive races at Brno, Indianapolis and Misano. Amid a flurry of rumours about his personal life, Kallio informed Campinoti during the re-scheduled Japanese Grand Prix that he wanted to be released early from his contract.

A vicious practice high-side at Le Mans had left him with a lingering and painful left shoulder injury. It was somewhat overlooked in comparison to a similar injury that blighted Valentino Rossi's year, but was no less restrictive and distracting.

He was granted permission to undergo surgery after Phillip Island, and his absence paved the way for a shock return to MotoGP by Spanish veteran Carlos Checa. A successful campaign for the Althea Ducati squad in World Superbikes had seen Checa back in MotoGP just over two weeks beyond his 38th birthday, for the Estoril and Valencia races. He soon found out just how tough and unforgiving the MotoGP class is however, retiring with arm-pump problems from the Estoril race.

Espargaro showed glimpses of the potential that had rightfully earned him his crack at the big time.

But as is so often the case, when he was required to deliver on a consistent basis, he found it hard to replicate the form he'd shown when he had nothing to lose.

Elder brother of rising 125cc star Pol Espargaro, he worked with crew chief Marco Rigamonti, and his squad was boosted by the arrival of American mechanic Mark Elder from the factory team.

Two eighth places in Mugello and Phillip Island were Espargaro's best results, and his MotoGP experience would be a brief affair. Rumours emerged as early as June that Loris Capirossi would make a surprise return to Ducati – he had left the factory team at the end of 2007 following a hammering at the hands of Casey Stoner. His signing hardly seemed to sit well with Ducati's philosophy of unearthing future talent in its satellite team, but at 37 he concluded a two-year deal in Sepang.

Espargaro's seat had seemed safe until it became apparent that Campinoti needed investment to safeguard his two-rider establishment. For a while, it looked like a deal with Max Neukirchner was on the cards. Talks were still progressing in early October, with the German reportedly bringing substantial financial support.

It was a dream scenario too for Dorna, which has yearned for a German rider to be in MotoGP for one its key global markets. Just a week later, though, in Sepang, the deal was dead and buried. This prompted widespread rumours in Malaysia that Campinoti had informed Dorna of his intention to slash his involvement to just one machine.

Those rumours were quickly mothballed, Dorna boss Carmelo Ezpeleta reportedly stepping in to help manoeuvre a deal to bring in de Puniet, after his place at LCR Honda went to Elias.

Espargaro followed Kallio's lead by signing a Moto2 deal for 2011.

*Above:* Aleix Espargaro failed to fulfil his early promise. He's in Moto2 in 2011.

*Top:* Espargaro and crew at Valencia.

*Above centre:* Paulo Campinoti, ambitious team principal.

*Left:* Kallio on the grid with Fabio Sterlacchini *(left)*.
Photos: Gold & Goose

# LCR HONDA

## TEAM STAFF

Lucio CECCHINELLO: Team Owner and Manager
Oscar HARO: PR
Elisa PAVAN: Press Relations and Logistics

## RANDY DE PUNIET PIT CREW

Christophe BOURGIGNON: Chief Engineer
*Mechanics*
Joan CASAS
Casanovas XAVIER
Chris RICHARDSON
Brian HARDEN: Telemetry
Tomonori SATO: HRC engineer
Ugo GELMI: Tyres
Steve JENKNER: Bridgestone technician

### RANDY DE PUNIET
Born: 14 February, 1981 – Maisons Laffitte, France
GP Starts: 200 (87 MotoGP 80 250cc, 33 125cc)
GP Wins: 5 250cc

### ROGER LEE HAYDEN
Born: 30 March, 1983 – Owensboro, USA
GP Starts: 3 (2 MotoGP, 1 Moto2)

NOBODY seized upon Honda's policy of starting out with all six RC212V machines running almost identical technical specifications better than Lucio Cecchinello's Monaco-based squad. Previously, there had been a clear distinction between the Repsol factory bikes and those leased. But as Cecchinello embarked on his fifth campaign in MotoGP and 15th in GP racing, the technical chasm had narrowed considerably.

With French rider Randy de Puniet on board for a third successive season, LCR's fortunes soared in the opening seven races. The immense knowledge of crew chief Christophe 'Beefy' Bourgignon married with de Puniet's 'ride it like you stole it' style made for an explosive series of performances.

Data specialist Brian Harden was in his second season with the team, and together they made a formidable trio.

Only twice in the opening seven races was de Puniet outside the top six, and in successive races at Silverstone, Assen and Catalunya, he made the front row. At Catalunya, HRC made the latest-spec RC212C chassis available. Fourth in that race saw a factory-spec electronics package delivered for the German round at Sachsenring.

But it was there that de Puniet's purple patch came to an abrupt and painful end. He crashed heavily in the race and his left leg was run over by Kallio's Ducati, and both tibia and fibula were broken. His powers of recovery bordered on the superhuman – back in action at Brno some 26 days later.

His strength and conditioning dulled by the lay-off, de Puniet could not replicate his early-season brilliance. That form, though, had captured the attention of Suzuki's factory team, and talks began with de Puniet's manager, Eric Mahe.

Wary that he couldn't compete with the bigger salaries being tabled by Suzuki, Cecchinello began an extensive scouting mission that led him to negotiate with Melandri and Capirossi, while Toni Elias and Alex de Angelis were also options.

At the Japanese GP, it seemed certain that de Puniet would remain at LCR, but Cecchinello had made Elias his prime target, and a deal was concluded soon afterwards.

Cecchinello funded his team using a tried-and-tested format. Playboy was undeniably the crown jewel, as title sponsor at several races. When Playboy took a back seat (as in Qatar and Malaysia, where censorship bans the magazine), Cecchinello operated a rotation system, selling rights to Givi, Elletronica Discount, Rev'it and Elf.

Roger Lee Hayden substituted at Laguna Seca, finishing 11th.

## HONDA RCV212V

*Major Sponsors and Technical Suppliers:* Playboy · Eurobet · Givi · TS Vision · Elettronica Discount · Dinamica · Elf · VIAR

*Engine:* 800cc, 76-degree V4, 360-degree crank (tbc), PVRS.  *Power:* More than 210ps

*Ancillaries:* HRC Electronics and ride-by-wire throttle and fuel injection system, Denso sparking plugs · *Lubrication:* Elf · *Fuel:* 21 litres; Elf

*Dimensions:* 2,050mm length, 1,440mm wheelbase, 1,130mm height, 645mm width.

*Transmission:* Gear primary drive, multi-plate dry slipper clutch, six-speed constant-mesh cassette-style gearbox, RK chain

*Suspension:* Front, Öhlins TTx20 42mm forks · Rear, Öhlins TTx36 shock with linkage

*Wheels:* Front, 16.5in Marchesini · Rear, 16.5in Marchesini · *Tyres:* Bridgestone

*Brakes:* Front, Nissin carbon-carbon 314mm · Rear, HRC steel 218mm

## PAGINAS AMARILLAS DUCATI

### TEAM STAFF

Jorge MARTINEZ: Team Manager
Facundo GARCIA: General Manager
Sylvia PELUFO: Administration Manager
Gino BORSOI: Sporting Manager
Maria-Jose BOTELLA: Media and Logistics Manager
Ricardo PEDROS: Media Officer

### HECTOR BARBERA PIT CREW

Luca GASBARRO: Track Engineer
Andrea ORLANDI: Technical Manager
*Mechanics*
Miguel Angel GALLEGO · Juan-Manuel ALCANIZ
Ignacio CABEZA · Salvador MORALEDA
Maurizio CASARIL: Spare Parts
Tommaso PAGANO: Electronics Engineer

#### HECTOR BARBERA
Born: 2 November, 1986 – Dos Aguas, Spain
GP Starts: 140 (18 MotoGP 75 250cc, 47 125cc)
GP Wins: (4 250cc, 6 125cc)

JORGE MARTINEZ

*Photos: Gold & Goose*

THE emergence of the Aspar Ducati squad for 2010 – Spanish team, Spanish sponsor and Spanish rider – did little to alter perception that MotoGP had become too reliant on Spain for investment and riding talent. Reservations were inconsequential, as any new team was welcomed with open arms to bolster a shrinking grid.

The outfit was created and overseen by one of the paddock's longest serving incumbents, Jorge 'Aspar' Martinez. The triple 80cc and once 125cc world champion had set up his own team in 1992, five years before he retired at the end of 1997.

That laid the foundations for Martinez to build the biggest single outfit in the grand prix paddock, playing a leading role in the smaller classes; expansion into the MotoGP arena was the fruition of long-held ambitions. The lease of a Ducati GP10 Desmosedici was in addition to top-level two-rider 125cc and Moto2 teams.

Martinez's previous attempts to graduate to MotoGP had been frustrated. He'd spoken at length with Suzuki without being able to persuade the Japanese factory to extend its commitment. Talks with Yamaha had also been doomed. He had been linked with Kawasaki as well.

His persistence finally paid off and he secured the lease of one Ducati with sponsorship from Paginas Amarillas (Yellow Pages). Martinez had once again proved to be an astute businessman, as his Valencia-based teams had always carried flagship brands from Spain.

Facundo Garcia acted as general manager, and former 125cc rider Gino Borsoi served as sporting director, his remit covering all three teams.

Martinez had been desperate to retain Bautista, who had won the team's first world title (125) in 2006, but he was enticed by a direct factory link with Suzuki, so Martinez swooped on former team rider

Hector Barbera. The Valencia rider enjoyed a respectable rookie campaign, his only non-finish coming at Laguna Seca, caused by a broken chain.

Barbera worked under Luca Gasbarro, data engineer Tommaso Pagano and technical director Andrea Orlandi. Gasbarro had been involved in countless Ducati racing projects, the most recent as crew chief to Gibernau at the ill-fated Grupo Francisco Hernando Ducati squad of 2009.

Barbera ended the season with eight top-ten finishes, and a best of eighth at Le Mans and Valencia.

With a distinguished GP career over three decades, it was patently obvious that Martinez saw his MotoGP effort as a long-term commitment. At Indianapolis, he announced that he would continue with Barbera and Ducati in 2011, and made it clear that he was planning a two-rider effort for the new 1000cc four-stroke class in 2012.

## DUCATI Desmosedici GP10

*Major Sponsors and Technical Suppliers:* Paginas Amarillas · SIID · Playstation · Pull and Bear · NH Hotels · Air Nostrum · Circuit de Valencia · Sol-Mar Rentacar Grupo Molca · Giannelli · Beta · Coca-Cola · Nicolau Jamonos · Avant-Pro · Goo Motor · Kyocera · Ferroli · Vincente Gandia · Aspadis · NOOX · Motomoclos

*Engine:* 800cc, 90-degree V4, 360-degree crank, DOHC, 4 valves per cylinder, Desmodromic valve gear, variable-length inlet tracts
    *Power:* Around 225bhp, revs up to 18,500rpm

*Ancillaries:* Magneti Marelli electronics, NGK sparking plugs, full electronic ride by wire · *Fuel:* 21 litres

*Transmission:* Gear primary drive, multi-plate dry slipper clutch, six-speed constant-mesh cassette-style gearbox, RK chain

*Suspension:* Front, Öhlins TTxTR25 48mm forks · Rear; Öhlins TTxTR 44 shock with linkage

*Wheels:* Front, 16.5in Marchesini · Rear, 16.5in Marchesini · *Tyres:* Bridgestone

*Brakes:* Front, Brembo carbon-carbon 320mm · Rear, steel 200mm

## INTERWETTEN HONDA

### TEAM STAFF

Daniel M. EPP: Team Owner and Manager

Meike KOCH: Marketing and Sponsorship Manager

Judith PIEPER-KÖHLER: Communications Manager

Jana CIZKOVA: Administration and Logistics

Zuzana VONGREJOVA: Accounting

### HIROSHI AOYAMA PIT CREW

Tom JOJIC: Crew Chief and Technical Director

*Mechanics*

Emanuel BUCHNER · Craig Stuart BURTON

Antonio Haba PEREZ

Petr CIZEK: Fuel and Tyres

Francesco FAVA: Telemetry and Data

**HIROSHI AOYAMA**
Born: 25 October, 1981 – Chiba, Japan
GP Starts: 116 (12 MotoGP, 104 250cc)
GP Wins: 9 250cc
World Championships: 1 250cc

**KOUSUKE AKIYOSHI**
Born: 12 January, 1975 – Kurume, Japan
GP Starts: 6 MotoGP

THE ongoing global financial crisis made trying to arrest the rapid decline in MotoGP grid numbers something of a thankless task. Scot Honda and Hayate folded at the end of 2009, following the demise of Sete Gibernau's Grupo Francisco Hernando Ducati outfit earlier in the year. Hope springs eternal, though, and the Interwetten Honda squad became one of two new additions to the 2010 grid.

Several teams had unveiled ambitious plans to be part of the series without ever turning a wheel in anger. The Italian-based FB Corse project – a three-cylinder concept engine designed for, but discarded by BMW several years ago – was meant to contest the championship from the first European round. Australian Garry McCoy was hired to develop the FB01, but he quit in early June, after just one serious test in Valencia in March failed to convince

IRTA and Dorna officials that the bike was anywhere near ready.

And then there was the Spanish Inmotec project, which had planned to wild-card in Catalunya with Ivan Silva, and contest other selected races. The new V4 never saw GP action; the closest it got was when the bike was put on public display in the hospitality area at Aragon.

Interwetten was the one team that did make it. Based in Zurich, it was run by highly respected owner Daniel Epp with sponsorship from Interwetten, a sport betting company founded in Vienna in 1990.

Epp was no stranger to grand prix management, having run successful 125 and 250 teams previously, most notably under the Emmi Caffe Latte banner. In 2005, he managed Thomas Luthi to the 125cc world championship, and in realising long-standing

MotoGP ambitions, he didn't desert his smaller-class roots.

The Interwetten challenge came on three fronts in 2010, with a single-rider effort in all three classes. German Marcel Schrotter rode in the 125cc class; Thomas Luthi was a consistent front-runner in the all-new and ultra-competitive Moto2 class; while its flagship venture in MotoGP was headed by Hiroshi Aoyama, last ever 250 champion.

Epp assembled a team boasting a wealth of experience. Crew chief Tom Jojic had previously worked with Kenny Roberts Junior at Team Roberts, while mechanic Craig Burton had been with Nicky Hayden when the American won the 2006 title. And Francesco Fava was a former data engineer with Fausto Gresini's squad.

Aoyama made an encouraging start to his rookie

## HONDA RCV212V

© 

*Major Sponsors and Technical Suppliers:* Interwetten.com · Polo Motorrad · HRC · Bridgestone · Motorex · Konzept-Medienhaus · Hertz Germany
Sony Germany · Elf · NGK · Nissin · RK-Excel · Arai · Arlen Ness · Albion Group · Draft FCB · Desjoyaux · Sitag

*Engine:* 800cc, 76-degree V4, 360-degree crank (tbc), PVRS. *Power:* More than 210ps

*Ancillaries:* HRC Electronics and ride-by-wire throttle and fuel injection system, NGK sparking plugs · *Lubrication:* Elf · *Fuel:* 21 litres

*Dimensions:* 2,050mm length, 1,440mm wheelbase, 1,130mm height, 645mm width.

*Transmission:* Gear primary drive, multi-plate dry slipper clutch, six-speed constant-mesh cassette-style gearbox, RK chain

*Suspension:* Front, Öhlins TTx20 42mm forks · Rear, Öhlins TTx36 shock with linkage

*Wheels:* Front, 16.5in Marchesini · Rear, 16.5in Marchesini · *Tyres:* Bridgestone

Brakes: Front, Nissin carbon-carbon 314mm · Rear, HRC steel 218mm

Photos: Gold & Goose

## ALEX DE ANGELIS
Born: 2 February, 1984 – Rimini, Italy
GP Starts: 180 (38 MotoGP, 12 Moto2, 65 250cc, 65 125cc)
GP Wins: 1 250cc 1, Moto2

campaign with a debut tenth at Qatar, which he re-peated at Mugello.

A promising year, though, was cut short in ago-nising fashion at Silverstone. Barely travelling at 40mph as he flicked left into the Vale chicane, he was viciously high-sided. The punishment scarcely fitted the crime, as the low-speed tumble fractured his T12 vertabra and put him out of action for a third of the season.

A portly Kousuke Akiyoshi – HRC test rider – filled the breach in Assen and Catalunya, and scored in both races. Then Alex de Angelis was plucked from his Moto2 misery for another shot at the big time. Having been axed by the Gresini Honda squad at the end of 2009, he struggled for redemption and scored a best of 12th in three races.

As the season passed the halfway stage, there were already familiar murmurings emanating from inside the paddock that the team was on the brink of collapse. Interwetten would stay, but would con-tribute a substantially reduced fee; Epp failed to fill the financial void, despite frantic 11th-hour efforts.

Salvation appeared to arrive at the Twin Ring Mo-tegi in early October, yet just seven days later, in Sepang, the outlook was bleak. The team's demise was all but confirmed at Phillip Island and made of-ficial by the end of the season.

*Above:* Aoyama – a season interrupted.

*Left:* Team principal Daniel Epp.

Photos: Gold & Goose

Photo: Courtesy of Yamaha

## Championship Team Points

| | | |
|---|---|---|
| 1 | Fiat Yamaha Team | 617 |
| 2 | Repsol Honda Team | 451 |
| 3 | Ducati Marlboro Team | 388 |
| 4 | Monster Yamaha Tech 3 | 279 |
| 5 | San Carlo Honda Gresini | 228 |
| 6 | Rizla Suzuki MotoGP | 129 |
| 7 | LCR Honda MotoGP | 121 |
| 8 | Pramac Racing Team | 109 |
| 9 | Paginas Amarillas Aspar | 90 |
| 10 | Interwetten Honda MotoGP | 68 |

# 2010 TEAMS AND RIDERS

By PETER McLAREN

MIKE DI MEGLIO

VLADIMIR IVANOV

TATSUYA YAMAGUCHI

MATTIA PASINI

TONI ELIAS

## MOTO2: A NEW WORLD ORDER

A NEW vision of grand prix motorcycle racing made its debut under the lights at Qatar in the form of Moto2, a controversial cut-price replacement for the 250cc class. It smashed down the rigid hierarchy that had existed in the factory-dependent two-stroke category, and fans and riders alike soon came to love the new championship, which featured 40-rider grids and action packed racing.

As required by the rules, all riders used identical 600cc four-stroke Honda-built engines, mounted inside prototype chassis designs. Dunlop was the exclusive tyre supplier.

The majority of the new Moto2 teams came from within the grand prix paddock, and it wasn't just former 250 and 125cc teams that were interested. Gresini, Aspar, Interwetten and Tech 3 entered riders in both MotoGP and Moto2 in 2010, with Tech 3 even building its own chassis.

Riders stepping down from MotoGP to 250cc may have been unheard of in recent times, but Moto2 attracted no less than eight riders with previous premier-class experience. They were Toni Elias (79 MotoGP starts), Anthony West (43), Alex de Angelis (35), Roberto Rolfo (17), Niccolo Canepa (14), Gabor Talmacsi (12), Yuki Takahashi (7) and Fonsi Nieto (1). Both Elias and de Angelis had finished on the podium in MotoGP, but only eventual Moto2 champion Elias had been a premier-class race winner.

Of the 40-riders on the full-time entry list, Spain boasted ten competitors, Italy eight and France three, with two each from Switzerland, Czech Republic, Japan and Germany. Australia, Great Britain, USA, Thailand, Qatar, Russia, Ukraine, Venezuela, Hungary, San Marino and Columbia were each represented by a single rider.

Eighteen riders had won a grand prix prior to Moto2, with Julian Simon, Mike di Meglio, Gabor Talmacsi and Thomas Luthi also previous grand prix world champions, in 125cc.

By the end of the first Moto2 season, nine different riders had won a race, on six different types of bike, with 17 riders claiming at least one podium. For comparison, there were four different race winners in MotoGP and 125cc in 2010, while the final season of 250cc racing had produced five different winners and 11 different podium finishers.

While Moto2 machines were evenly matched on paper, the fight for race victories was not always as close you might think. Seven of the 17 races (Jerez, Silverstone, Indianapolis, Motegi, Sepang, Estoril and Valencia) were won by less than a second – compared with two for MotoGP and four for 125cc – but there were also runaway wins of over four seconds at Losail, Assen, Catalunya and Aragon (where Andrea Iannone took the biggest victory of the year at 6.2 seconds).

Racing at the front generally got closer as the season went on, the leading manufacturers ironing out their weak points so that they were competitive on every type of circuit.

Qualifying was incredibly tight: at Le Mans, 27 riders qualified within one second of pole position.

Fifteen different chassis manufacturers began the inaugural Moto2 season, 14 of which scored points. Eight different manufacturers appeared on the podium.

Mike Trimby, general secretary of the teams' association, IRTA, praised the new class: "In Moto2, any team that works well gets a chance of making the podium or getting a pole once in a while. That means they've got something to sell to sponsors, whereas in 250s they had nothing to sell, unless they were a big team that could afford factory bikes."

## Moriwaki

One of the most recognisable names on the Moto2 chassis list, Moriwaki had last raced in grands prix as a wild-card during the 990cc MotoGP era, again using a Honda-powered prototype, and it was among the first to prepare a chassis for the new 600cc class.

Both Moriwaki and Team Gresini have close ties with Honda, so it was no surprise when they joined forces for Moto2. Then Gresini persuaded its former MotoGP star, Elias, to sign up for the project as a potential route back to MotoGP. The resulting Gresini-Moriwaki-Elias combination was an instant pre-season favourite.

A veteran of ten years in grand prix racing, and winner of ten races across 125cc, 250cc and MotoGP machinery, Elias had by far the most glittering CV of any Moto2 rider. But disaster struck when he was injured during the final pre-season test at Jerez, the 27-year-old requiring surgery after suffering hand and ankle fractures when he tangled with a slower rider.

Elias overcame those injuries to put the Moriwaki on pole for the first ever Moto2 race, and he claimed the manufacturer's first victory, and podium, next time out in Jerez. Six further wins followed before Elias wrapped up the title three rounds early in Malaysia.

Elias, who will return to MotoGP in 2011 with LCR Honda, won more races than any other Moto2 rider (seven), but also was the only Moriwaki rider to win. Interwetten's Thomas Luthi was the only other Moriwaki rider to stand on the podium, and that lack of depth cost Moriwaki in terms of the constructors' title.

Luthi had spent seven seasons in 125/250cc racing prior to Moto2, but his career had largely been on the decline since his title triumph in 2005.

Overlooked for the Interwetten MotoGP project after

FONSI NIETO

LUKAS PESEK

YANNICK GUERRA

HECTOR FAUBEL

JULIAN SIMON

MICHELE PIRRO

XAVIER SIMEON

a podium-less 2009, the 23-year-old came out fighting in the new Moto2 era, finishing third in only his second race to be an early title contender.

Later the Swiss rider came within 0.057 second of victory at Silverstone, despite riding with a freshly dislocated collarbone, which subsequently required surgery.

Second in the championship as late as round ten, Luthi's form tailed away slightly in the second half of the season, but he still finished the year with five rostrums and a competitive fourth in the standings. Interwetten will switch to Suter in 2011.

Luthi rode in a single-rider team, while Elias had been paired with 27-year-old grand prix rookie Vladimir Ivanov. The Ukrainian had experience of national Supersport racing in Russia, Germany and Italy, but wasn't able to make an impression in his first season at world level.

When Ivanov was injured, Gresini gave 34-year-old Japanese Tatsuya Yamaguchi (one previous 250cc start) the chance to ride at Misano, where he finished 26th, then put World Supersport rider Michele Pirro on the bike at Aragon.

The 24-year-old Italian – a former 125cc rider and future WSS race winner – performed admirably by qualifying eighth and finishing 14th, despite still recovering from recent injuries of his own. Pirro and Yuki Takahashi will form Gresini's 2011 line-up.

Holiday Gym G22 and Matteoni CP Racing also ran the Moriwaki chassis.

Holiday Gym G22 was headed by former 250cc title contender Fonsi Nieto, the only rider in Moto2 to have won a World Superbike race (in addition to five 250cc victories). The 31-year-old had a quiet start to the season, but showed flashes of his form – including a fourth place in Germany – before a nasty foot fracture

and ensuing medical drama at Indianapolis sapped his momentum.

Nieto was partnered by fellow Spaniard Yannick Guerra, who had a long association with the team's title sponsor, with a third machine occasionally run by the team for Belgian Xavier Simeon.

Both Simeon and Guerra were grand prix rookies, who came from the World Superbike support paddock. Simeon had taken eight wins and two titles (one in 600cc, the other in 1000cc) in FIM Superstock racing, while Guerra hadn't been ranked higher than 27th during three years in Superstock 600 and one season in Supersport.

Neither rode the full Moto2 season, but Simeon proved the most effective, scoring points on three occasions.

Matteoni CP Racing ran a variety of riders, including Lukas Pesek, Santiago Hernandez (brother of Yonny), Wayne Maxwell (disqualified on his GP debut at home in Australia) and Ferruccio Lamborghini (of the famous car family, who switched to Matteoni after one start for Forward Racing). None raced the full year, and only Pesek, with six years of grand prix experience, scored points.

A notable Moriwaki wild-card entry was by American Honda, which ran Roger Lee Hayden, younger brother of Nicky, at the Indianapolis round in a team managed by 1993 500cc world champion Kevin Schwantz.

Hayden, who raced full time for Pedercini Kawasaki in WSB in 2010, but also made a stand-in MotoGP appearance for LCR Honda at Laguna Seca, qualified 17th and finished the race in 11th.

Moriwaki also gave family member Shogo Moriwaki his first experience of grand prix racing at the Japanese round, but the 27-year-old didn't start the race due to a recent eye injury.

## Suter

The most represented chassis on the Moto2 grid, Suter began the season with Forward Racing, Kiefer Racing, Italtrans S.T.R., Racing Team Germany, Marc VDS Racing Team and Technomag-CIP. Then Mapfre Aspar joined its ranks from round three onwards (see RSV).

Technomag's Shoya Tomizawa gave Suter instant Moto2 success with a brilliant out-of-the-blue victory from ninth on the grid in the first ever race at Qatar. Tomizawa hadn't been higher than tenth during his first full season of grand prix racing in the 250cc class in 2009, but the exciting 19-year-old was able to fully express his talent in the new class. He backed up his debut victory with pole and a podium at round two in Jerez, and although no further podiums followed, he remained in the championship top six until his tragic death in Misano.

Despite the disruption of a chassis change, reigning 125cc world champion Julian Simon had taken over from Tomizawa as the leading Suter rider by round seven. The experienced 23-year-old, riding in his seventh grand prix season, took eight podiums on his way to second in the championship, but wasn't quite able to win.

Simon's team-mate and fellow 125cc world champion, Mike di Meglio, found adapting to a four-stroke much more taxing, scoring points on just five occasions, with a best race finish of sixth. Simon is staying with Aspar in 2011, when he will be a firm title favourite, while di Meglio is moving to Tech 3.

The Suter may not have taken the most victories – that went to Moriwaki, thanks to Elias – but it did take the constructors' title and could boast more race wins with different riders than any other chassis.

After Tomizawa's round-one victory, Forward's Jules

Photos: Gold & Goose

SCOTT REDDING

STEFAN BRADL

JULES CLUZEL

ROBERTO ROLFO

YUKI TAKAHASHI

Cluzel won at Silverstone, Italtran's Roberto Rolfo at Sepang, and Viessmann Kiefer Racing's Stefan Bradl at Estoril.

For frantic Frenchman Cluzel, it was his first win in five seasons of grand prix racing, while 30-year-old Italian Rolfo – returning to grand prix after four years in World Superbike – hadn't won since 2004. Bradl was riding in his third full year, having been a previous double 125cc race winner.

Cluzel and Rolfo both took one additional podium, but 20-year-old Bradl's only rostrum appearance of the year was on the top step. He eclipsed fellow Kiefer riders Michael Ranseder, Patrik Vostarek and Vladimir Leonov (none of whom raced the full season), while Cluzel and Rolfo comfortably outshone their respective team-mates, Claudio Corti and Robertino Pietri.

Like Aspar, Marc VDS may not have won, but the team – headed by former Kawasaki MotoGP team manager Michael Bartholemy – proved to be a front running force from mid-season onwards with British star Scott Redding.

Guided by Nicky Hayden's former MotoGP title winning crew chief, Pete Benson, 17-year-old Redding claimed his first Moto2 podium at round ten in Indianapolis and later a second place at Phillip Island. He finished eighth in the championship.

Team-mate Hector Faubel was drafted in at the last moment to replace Vincent Lonbois, after the 19-year-old Belgian had been left at the tail of the field in preseason testing. Faubel, runner-up in the 2007 125cc world championship, wasn't able to crack the top ten in Moto2. Former MotoGP rider Mika Kallio will take Faubel's seat in 2011.

Swiss Dominique Aegerter had been teamed with Tomizawa at Technomag-CIP and, although unable to repeat the late Japanese rider's heroics, the 19-year-old did a solid job under what must have been difficult circumstances, scoring points in 12 races, no easy task with such big grids.

For the last two rounds, Technomag put reigning double World Supersport champion Kenan Sofuoglu

on Tomizawa's former bike. The Turkish star, winner of more WSS races than any other rider (17), wanted a future in Moto2 and proved he more than deserved one by rocketing to a seven-second race lead on his debut.

Despite that huge advantage, the 26-year-old would be denied a fairytale win when his tyres began to deteriorate, and he crossed the finish line in fifth. But his potential was clear, and by the time he crashed out of the lead group at the following Valencia finale, he already had a 2011 Technomag contract in his pocket.

Racing Team Germany was represented by German Arne Tode until Indianapolis, after which it ran Japanese Kazuki Watanabe for four rounds, before finishing the season with Carmelo Morales.

## Speed Up

The Speed Up was a modified version of the FTR chassis, and on its day it proved staggeringly effective in the hands of Italian Andrea Iannone.

Fresh from five years in the 125cc class, where he had taken five wins and a best of seventh in the championship, Iannone didn't even finish in the points in his first two Moto2 starts. Then came a fourth at Le Mans, followed by a pole-to-victory ride at Mugello, which he repeated at Assen and Aragon.

The 20-year-old had the speed to win several more races, including Catalunya (where he was penalised for passing under a yellow flag), Estoril (where he fell after charging from 35th to within sight of the lead) and Valencia (where he was hit from behind by Elias while leading on the last lap).

The Valencia incident also cost him a chance of second in the championship, and he finished the year just two points behind Simon, after eight podiums. Elias and Iannone were the only riders to win more than one race.

Team-mate to Iannone was former 125cc champion Gabor Talmacsi. Despite his 2009 MotoGP four-stroke experience, the 29-year-old Hungarian couldn't

replicate Iannone's form, although he did manage one podium and pole for sixth in the standings.

## MotoBI

The MotoBI was built by Japanese specialist TSR in collaboration with former MotoGP team JiR.

JiR split from star rider Mattia Pasini after just six races, by which time lesser-known team-mate Simone Corsi (still a five-time 125cc race winner) had proven to be a much sounder investment, with back-to-back podiums at rounds three and four. Corsi remained consistent throughout the year, but it would be Alex de Angelis who took the MotoBI to its first victory.

De Angelis began the season on a Force GP210, but the Scot team had withdrawn by the time he returned from some substitute rides in MotoGP. Initially, JiR had replaced Pasini with Japanese rookie Yusuke Teshima, with little success, but de Angelis was typically fast from his debut at Misano.

De Angelis had been running fifth at the time of his involvement in Tomizawa's accident, but overcame the trauma to claim his first front-row start next time out at Aragon. The upward trend continued with a second place two races later in Sepang, before victory at Phillip Island.

The win was only his second in a grand prix career spanning almost 11 years.

## FTR

The British-built FTR chassis began the year with Alex Debon (Aeroport de Castello) as its only full-time rider, but then Czech Karel Abraham switched to the FTR from round three. Debon started the year in style with second to Tomizawa at Qatar, but the Spaniard wasn't seen on the podium again after a series of nasty accidents and injuries.

Abraham's five previous seasons of grand prix racing had been without a podium, but he helped justify his 2011 MotoGP ride with a debut rostrum at Japan

Photos: Gold & Goose

GABOR TALMACSI

VLADIMIR LEONOV

ALEX DEBON

DOMINIQUE AEGERTER

ANDREA IANNONE

KAREL ABRAHAM

CLAUDIO CORTI

ALEX DE ANGELIS

KENAN SOFUOGLU

SIMONE CORSI

RAFFAELE DE ROSA

and then a last-gasp victory at the Valencia finale.

FTR also supplied a chassis for 26-year-old Jason Di Salvo to make a wild-card appearance in front of his home fans at Indianapolis. Di Salvo had split from the Triumph WSS team earlier in the year, but impressed by riding from 26th to 9th at Indy.

Another FTR wild-card was Spanish-based Scotsman Kev Coghlan, who made two starts and one finish for the Joey Darcey team.

## Tech3

Herve Poncharal called upon his Tech 3 team to use all of its considerable experience, gained by winning the 2000 250cc world championship and spending nine years in MotoGP, to design its own chassis for Moto2. It was a big challenge, but the French-based team pulled out the stops and was rewarded when it became the fourth different manufacturer to win a Moto2 race, courtesy of Yuki Takahashi's victory at Catalunya.

The 26-year-old Takahashi carried Tech 3's hopes for much of the season, with Raffaele de Rosa, the 2009 250cc rookie of the year, battling to understand the four-stroke. De Rosa claimed points on just four occasions and finished inside the top ten once – a sixth place at Phillip Island.

Takahashi took a further podium at Brno, but Tech 3 was frustrated by the many crashes suffered by both riders as it sought valuable race data to further develop the bike.

Tech 3 has signed a fresh line-up of Mike di Meglio and Bradley Smith for 2011.

## Pons Kalex

Former world champion and MotoGP team owner Sito Pons joined forced with Kalex Engineering for Moto2. The team's full-time line-up saw Sito's son, Axel, partnered by fellow Spaniard Sergio Gadea. The latter had six seasons of 125cc racing, including three wins, un-

67

ANTHONY WEST

NICOLO CANEPA

VALENTIN DEBISE

JOAN OLIVE

RATTHAPARK WILAIROT

KENNY NOYES

DAMIAN CUDLIN

ALEX BALDOLINI

AXEL PONS

SERGIO GADEA

YONNY HERNANDEZ

der his belt and quickly adapted to the much heavier four-stroke.

Points in the first four races culminated in a debut Moto2 podium with second position at Mugello, by which time Gadea was fourth in the championship, but his form deteriorated thereafter.

The 19-year-old Pons, starting only his second full season of world championship competition, hadn't claimed a point by the time he was injured at Assen (round six), but he did get on the score sheet later in the season. While Pons Jr sat out two races to recover, Sito made two shrewd substitute signings in the form of Carmelo Morales and Damian Cudlin.

Morales, 32, was a double Spanish Formula Extreme champion. He qualified an excellent sixth on his grand prix debut at Catalunya and was on target for a top-ten finish, before a shocking accident on the run to the flag.

Australian Cudlin, 28, was drafted in for the Sachsenring, and underlined both his and the Pons Kalex's potential by racing from 22nd on the grid to seventh. Pons has secured the services of 2010 MotoGP rider Aleix Espargaro to ride alongside Axel in 2011.

## Bimota

The famous Bimota name was represented throughout the inaugural Moto2 season by Thai rider Ratthapark Wilairot, a midfield runner for the previous three seasons in 250cc.

The Bimota was another of the bikes that seemed to suit certain tracks much more than others, with the highlight of the season coming at round six, Assen, where Wilairot qualified second and finished fourth.

Just two more points scoring rides followed as the Bimota dropped back relative to its rivals. The 22-year-old Wilairot was the only Bimota rider to score.

As well as Wilairot, the Stop And Go Racing team began the season with grand prix rookie Bernat Martinez, but he was dropped after seven rounds in favour of fellow Spaniard Ricard Cardus. He, in turn, was replaced for two events by Javier Fores.

Another Bimota appeared late in the season in the form of M Racing, which joined the series at San Marino, having picked up former MotoGP rider Niccolo Canepa from the disbanded Team Scot. But Canepa remained at the tail of the field and lost the seat to Japanese Hiromichi Kunikawa from Motegi onwards.

## BQR-Moto2

Developed in the Spanish championship during 2009, the BQR was run by Blusens-STX throughout the 2010 season, with chassis numbers occasionally boosted by wild-card entries.

Columbian Supermoto star Yonny Hernandez, who had raced in Spanish Supersport in 2009, carried BQR's hopes, entertaining the fans with his sideways style on his way to points in nine of the 17 rounds.

Qatari team-mate Mashel Al Naimi didn't score; the top 15 also eluded BQR wild-cards Dani Rivas and Anthony Delhalle.

## I.C.P.

One of the great underdog stories of the Moto2 season came at Estoril, where Alex Baldolini, the only rider on the little known I.C.P. chassis, took advantage of the lack of dry track time heading into the race to claim a fine second position. It was his first ever podium in his ninth grand prix season.

Caretta Technology team manager Giorgio Bertelli summed up his emotions: "The bike is totally our creation, with all the difficulties you can imagine in order to develop a competitive project. This result is an incomparable thrill."

## Promoharris

Headed by Hollywood star Antonio Banderas, the Jack & Jones by A. Banderas outfit raced a Promoharris chassis, the name reflecting its joint creation by the Spanish Promoracing team and British-based manufacturer Harris Performance. Like BQR, the Promoharris had been race developed in the 2009 Spanish championship.

There were two distinct highlights for Promoharris in 2010, and both came from grand prix rookie Kenny Noyes. The former Spanish Formula Extreme frontrunner led in only his second grand prix, at Jerez, then took pole for round three at Le Mans – the first pole for an American in the intermediate class since John Kocinski in 1990.

But the Promoharris couldn't keep up over a full

race distance, or with the pace of gains made by some of the other chassis designs as the year went on. Three points scoring rides, and a best of seventh, left Noyes 24th in the championship.

Despite being one of the most experienced riders on the grid, with nine seasons of 125cc grand prix racing behind him, team-mate Joan Olive failed to score. The Spaniard tried an FTR at Misano, but returned to the Promoharris for the following round and finished the year with a best result of 21st. The team has retained Noyes for 2011, when it will switch to Suter machinery.

## MZ-RE Honda

MZ used Moto2 to revive its racing heritage in 2010, when former 250cc and World Supersport race winner Anthony West overcame a shoestring budget to claim a best finish of seventh, from five points scoring rides.

West was the only MZ rider, but, after signing a partnership with Pro Ride, the team will expand to two entries in 2011.

## Force GP210

This was the chassis of the ill-fated RSM Team Scot entry of Alex de Angelis and Niccolo Canepa. On paper, it was a strong rider line-up, being the only outfit with two former MotoGP riders, and de Angelis began promisingly by qualifying fourth for round one in Qatar. Accidents and injuries followed for the San Marinese, who had scored just 11 points by the time he accepted the offer of a temporary return to MotoGP, in place of the injured Hiroshi Aoyama, at round eight. While de Angelis was away, Team Scot briefly switched the yet-to-score Canepa to a Suter chassis for Brno, where he finished 28th, then withdrew from the championship due to financial problems.

## RSV

Initially, RSV was selected by one of the pre-season team favourites, Aspar, after Aprilia's late decision to abandon its Moto2 chassis project.

Reigning 125cc world champion Julian Simon qualified the RSV a promising second on the grid for the first two rounds, but could only claim an eighth in the races. Team-mate Mike di Meglio didn't score a point, and Aspar wasted no time in switching to the then title leading Suter design from round three onwards, stating, "The RSV is a competitive bike, but the Mapfre Aspar Team has two world champions and they can't be spending time on development during the season."

RSV's only other team, the single-rider entry of Karel Abraham, also switched at the same time (to an FTR). During its brief campaign, the RSV scored a total of ten points.

## ADV

ADV was the only chassis manufacturer to race the full season and not score a point in Moto2. It was represented only by the WTR San Marino Team, which ran a single-bike entry for Valetin Debise. The Frenchman, 21st in 250cc in 2009, took the ADV to a best race result of 16th.

# SHOYA TOMIZAWA

THE Moto2 class started in 2010. Shoya Tomizawa earned his first victory in the Qatar GP, which was the first race and which carved his name in the history of the new category.

Tomizawa was a competitor who raised great hopes that he would be the standard-bearer for Japanese riding from then on.

From the time that he was chasing for the national championships, Shoya had great boldness and he very easily went beyond the normal limits. Because of this, he had many spills – but he was a competitor who, when he fell, immediately got back into the race.

Last year he competed in the 250cc class and he fell many times, but this year he did not make as many mistakes, and people felt that he had made great progress.

Points where Shoya excelled were his skilful starts and fast first laps. These are innate qualities that a rider possesses, and not really things that can be acquired through practice. There are many attributes necessary to become a world champion and Shoya had already mastered two of these.

Even among great champions there are many who had a lot of spills when they were young. Jorge Lorenzo, for whom Shoya had great respect, was one of them. I thought that, if he went on to develop as he was doing, Shoya would certainly become a world champion.

There are a number of things that had to be learnt for this. There was a period, back when the works teams took the field in the national championships, when the bike manufacturers fostered riders who would make them well-known to the public, and they ushered them on to the GP circuit. However, nowadays there are no works teams that participate in the national championships and the route out into the world has become more difficult. Shoya found his place on the world stage in such rigorous times, and his reputation continued to grow.

A splendid thing about Shoya was that from when he started racing, he never once grumbled that the engine was slow. Perhaps he put up with it because there was no point in saying anything. Then when he came to the Moto 2 class, where he competed with the same engine and on the same tyres, he said very happily, "Can't be passed on the straight". Great champions, the champions among riders who are held in affection by everybody, are not jealous of other people, and I feel that there are many competitors who do their very best with things they have. Shoya was such a competitor.

Since Shoya died, I have learnt from his parents and many other people about a Shoya I did not know. He was a rare competitor who was mild-natured, cheerful and lively, and who never made those around him feel uncomfortable. I met Shoya for the first time was when he was a high school student. I thoroughly enjoyed the time that I spent with Shoya when he came to Grand Prix after a year and a half. I dreamed of the day that Shoya would become a world champion.

These two months, while going around the Grand Prix in the absence of Shoya, I have felt strongly that I ought to offer, with photographs and in writing, a memorial that 'there was such a splendid rider'. Just think, the fist of Shoya's right hand was still grasping the accelerator when he died. The data shows that he was speeding through turn eleven of the Misano circuit with the accelerator fully open.

I shall never forget the touch of that small hand. I want lots of people to know that Shoya, who died while pursuing his aim, was a splendid competitor. I think that may be the only thing that can now be offered to Shoya.

SATOSHI ENDO
Tochu Sports Newspaper, Japan

MARC MARQUEZ

POL ESPARGARO

NICOLAS TEROL

JOHANN ZARCO

SANDRO CORTESE

MARCEL SCHROTTER

JONAS FOLGER

BRADLEY SMITH

ESTEVE RABAT

RANDY KRUMMENACHER

## FIM 125cc WORLD CHAMPIONSHIP

# 2010 TEAMS AND RIDERS

By PETER McLAREN

THE 125cc world championship was the only GP title decided at the final round. Five manufacturers scored points during the 17-round season, but in reality the championship was dominated once again by the best teams from the Piaggio owned Derbi and Aprilia brands, using close variations of the same machine. Other less-effective Aprilia/Derbi entries, of varying technical specification, filled all but three of the re-maining places on the permanent entry list.

Variety, if little else, was provided by a single Honda effort, plus a newcomer in the form of famous scooter brand Lambretta, which ran a two-rider team. In fact, this was a new label for the former Loncin (and earlier still Malaguti) squad, with its own engine developed over the years from a Honda base. Also missing from the class was former title contender KTM, the Austrian firm having turned its back on GP racing.

Grid numbers suffered slightly due to interest in the Moto2 class, but 125cc still produced a 26-rider permanent entry list, boosted by wild-cards. Of the full-time riders, eight were from Spain, four from France, three each from Italy and Germany, two from Great Britain, and one each from Switzerland, Norway, the Netherlands, Malaysia, Japan and Czech Republic.

Officially, only Tuenti Derbi and Lambretta Reparto Corse were factory entries, with all other riders being eligible for the Michel Metraux Cup awarded to the top privateer. There were nine rookies, the best of whom proved to be Alberto Moncayo.

### Derbi/Aprilia

Three teams – Ajo (Derbi), Tuenti (Derbi) and Aspar (Aprilia) – proved the class of the field, each producing one title challenger in the form of Marc Marquez, Nico Terol and Pol Espargaro respectively. Between them,

these three Spaniards won all but one race, and each led the world championship during the season.

Fearless 17-year-old Marquez had taken a pair of poles and podiums during two action packed years with the KTM factory, before moving to the Finnish Ajo team for 2010. Ajo had won the 2008 title with Mike di Meglio.

Rider, bike and team gelled instantly, and Marquez overcame a dislocated collarbone at round two to win five successive races, from Mugello to Sachsenring, handing him the championship lead.

The victory run ended after another (opposite shoulder) dislocation at Brno, then a penalty at Indianapolis, but Marquez kept his points advantage until he was punted off at Turn One of the inaugural Aragon event (round 12 of 17).

The 19-year-old Espargaro – in his fourth season – won his third race at Aragon, but it was runner-up Terol who returned to the top of the tables for the three fly-away races.

Terol, at 22 the most experienced of the title fighting trio, moved to Aspar for 2010 to replace 2009 champion Julian Simon. He began the season perfectly with victory in Qatar, but didn't win again until returning from a one-race absence caused by back injuries at Catalunya. That one, at Brno, was the year's biggest, by 20.351 seconds. He won again at Indianapolis, and went to Japan six points clear of Espargaro and 11 ahead of Marquez. He was never again off the rostrum.

Marquez dominated the Motegi-Sepang-Phillip Island sequence and retained command of the title from round 15 in Malaysia onwards, thanks in large part to a dramatic penultimate-round victory at Estoril. He finished a memorable year with ten wins, a record 12 poles and 12 podiums.

EFREN VAZQUEZ · LUIS SALOM · DANNY WEBB

JAKUB KORNFEIL · STURLA FAGERHAUG · SIMONE GROTZKYJ · LORENZO SAVADORI · JASPER IWEMA

TOMOYOSHI KOYAMA · ADRIAN MARTIN · ALBERTO MONCAYO

Pol Espargaro, younger brother of MotoGP's Aleix, saw his title hopes end at Estoril after an all-or-nothing wet-tyre gamble went against him. Espargaro briefly led the championship after round five.

Outside the big three, the supporting act was provided by their respective team-mates, Sandro Cortese (Ajo), Bradley Smith (Aspar) and Efren Vasquez (Tuenti). Between them, the six riders claimed all but three of the 51 podium places on offer in the season and filled six of the top seven championship positions.

Remaining with Aspar, 2009's title runner-up Smith was naturally seen as a 2010 championship favourite, but he struggled with engine performance for much of the year. Three poles during the second half of the season indicated that the 19-year-old's power problems were abating, and he closed his 125cc career in style by winning the Valencia season finale.

That win was the first by a non-Spanish rider since the 2009 Catalan Grand Prix, and Smith's six podiums took him to fourth in the world championship during his fifth and final season of two-stroke racing.

Espargaro's team-mate, Vasquez, began his third season in 125 with a debut podium at round one. A rostrum return at San Marino helped the 23-year-old to a career-best fifth in the championship, 11 places higher than his 2009 ranking.

Only two riders broke the podium domination: Esteve Rabat and Tomoyoshi Koyama.

Rabat was in his fifth 125 season and his second with Blusens Aprilia. It would also prove his most successful, the 21-year-old scoring two rostrums and sixth overall. Rabat has raced for three different manufacturers in 125cc, but that's nothing compared with Koyama, who has recorded starts for Yamaha, Honda, Malaguti, KTM, Loncin and Aprilia. The 27-year-old Japanese 'veteran' rode for Racing Team Germany

(Aprilia), appropriately claiming a rostrum at the Sachsenring on his way to eighth in the championship.

Separating Rabat and Koyama in the final standings was Marquez's 20-year-old Ajo team-mate, Cortese, who took two rostrums – one less than in 2009 – in his sixth year of grand prix action.

Ajo and Tuenti were the only Derbi branded entries, but there were plenty more Aprilias. Stipa-Molenaar enjoyed top-six finishes with both Randy Krummenacher (20) and Luis Salom (18); as did Andalucia Cajasol, courtesy of Danny Webb (19) and rookie Alberto Moncayo (18). The 16-year-old German Jonas Folger couldn't repeat his 2009 podium, but did take two fourth places for Ongetta; while WTR San Marino's Johann Zarco (19) claimed double-digit points once during his second season in the class. Koyama's team-mate, Jakub Kornfeil, took his best finish of fifth on home asphalt at Brno.

Aeroport de Castello-Ajo claimed regular points with Spanish rookie Adrian Martin (17), as did CBC Corse's Jasper Iwema (20).

AirAsia and the Sepang circuit joined forces to give Malaysian Zulfahmi Khairuddin his first season in grand prix, which yielded four points finishes, while the highlight for Norwegian team-mate and fellow 18-year-old Sturla Fagerhaug was a top ten in Germany.

## Honda

Honda's only full-season entry of 2010 came from the Interwetten team, which ran Marcel Schrotter. The young German had turned heads during three wild-card rides, also on a Honda, in 2009, which included a fifth place at Valencia, but his first full season proved far tougher. The only Honda rider to score points, Schrotter was unable to better 12th place and finished the

season 18th in the standings. His bike was prepared by veteran two-stroke tuner Sepp Schloegl.

## Lambretta

Lambretta's first grand prix road racing campaign in almost 60 years saw plenty of rider changes.

The season began with rookies Marco Ravaioli (Italy) and Luis Salom (Spain), with the latter scoring the team's first and last 2010 point with 15th place at round two, before moving to Stipa-Molenaar Aprilia.

Dutchman Michael van der Mark took Salom's place and remained with the team until after the summer break at Brno, when Isaac Vinales got the ride. Fellow Spaniard Joan Perello briefly replaced Vinales, before Danny Kent, runner-up in the 2010 Red Bull Rookies Cup, joined Ravaioli from Motegi onwards. The 16-year-old Briton had made just one previous grand prix start, on an Aztec Honda at his home Silverstone round, but his performances exceeded his experience from the outset at Lambretta.

Kent's highlights included third in wet opening practice in Australia, then tenth on the grid after qualifying was cancelled at Estoril – the best starting position for the Lambretta – but he couldn't quite earn a world championship point.

## KTM

Despite not officially entering the championship, KTM finished above Lambretta in the manufacturers' standings, thanks to six points scored by wild-card Daniel Kartheininger. The German claimed a tenth-place finish, from 26th on the grid, on a drying track in front of his home fans at Sachsenring. It was his only grand prix appearance of the season.

Photos: Gold & Goose

# SPORTMAX SportSmart

# ROAD REVOLUTION
## THE NEW REFERENCE IN PERFORMANCE AND MILEAGE

## SPORTMAX SportSmart

/ NTEC RACE TYRE TECHNOLOGY FOR FASTER TRACK DAY LAPS

/ MULTI-TREAD TECHNOLOGY FRONT & REAR MAXIMIZES PURE GRIP BETWEEN 35 AND 55 DEGREES LEAN ANGLE

/ NEW ADVANCED SILICA AND RESIN FOR GREATER CONFIDENCE ON THE WET

/ BEST IN CLASS MILEAGE*

NTec | MT MULTI TREAD COMPOUND TECHNOLOGY

*IN AN INDEPENDENT TEST PERFORMED BY DEKRA IN JANUARY 2010 ON A SUZUKI GSX-R 1000 (2009) ON 120/70ZR17 AND 190/50ZR17 TYRES THE DUNLOP SPORTSMART ACHIEVED **20%** BETTER MILEAGE COMPARED TO MICHELIN POWER PURE, **30%** BETTER MILEAGE THAN PIRELLI DIABLO ROSSO AND **40%** BETTER MILEAGE THAN BRIDGESTONE BATTLAX BT-016

EXCLUSIVE TYRE OF *Moto2*

DUNLOP®

moto2

MotoGP
WORLD CHAMPIONSHIP

WWW.DUNLOPMOTORCYCLE.EU

MOTOGP · MOTO2 · 125cc
# GRANDS PRIX 2010

Photo: Gold & Goose

## By MICHAEL SCOTT

FIM WORLD CHAMPIONSHIP · ROUND 1

# QATAR GRAND PRIX

LOSAIL CIRCUIT

*Left:* Rossi profited from Stoner's fall. He would not win again for another 14 races.

*Main photo:* Rossi wins, Lorenzo follows.
*Photos: Gold & Goose*

BACK in the 1980s and early 1990s, the last time there were so many different potential race winning bikes and riders, the contest required the most extensive testing. Factory teams would go to Brazilian, Australian and South African tracks for days and days. Rationalisation came at the other end of the 1990s with group testing organised by IRTA, to which teams would still add their own tests. In 2009 came a radical cut-back in response to the financial crisis – the trip to Australia cancelled, and mid-season tests reduced to just two; for 2010, pre-season tests were cut again. Starting on 3rd February, there were just three two-day tests – two visits to Sepang (with extra time for the rookies), followed by one to Qatar. In the interests of logistics, Dorna's showpiece televised Jerez test was cancelled: bikes and equipment stayed put at Sepang, and likewise at Qatar, ready for the opening round.

This restriction would have sundry effects, in both the short and the long term. Stoner, for example, would complain later in the season that the lack of track variety had hampered understanding of Ducati's new and differently configured motor; while the crop of impressive rookies still complained of being short of time to adapt, in spite of extra days. It highlighted growing tension in the Repsol Honda garage, as Pedrosa battled with a bike that wobbled visibly on the straight on its new-to-him Öhlins suspension, and Dovizioso generally got the better of him. And it meant that

Lorenzo, who had missed the middle test, was a full third behind the rest of them.

Jorge had fallen victim to the risks that beset high-spirited youngsters on motorcycles, no matter how professional: he'd been play-racing with pal Carlos Checa on minibikes at Barcelona on 10th February and had suffered a silly crash. The tumble had hooked his right thumb out of joint and broken a bone in his hand. Even with a titanium plate, he was unable to join the second Sepang test and only made the third at Qatar after a last-minute decision. The right hand carries the heaviest load in every sense, the most important of any limb to a racer. "I feel like a footballer who cannot use his right foot," he had said at the tests, and he was still stitched and below full strength for the race.

Tests had clarified one thing: that the Losail circuit is susceptible to a heavy dew as midnight approaches. Spies, Edwards, Hayden and Stoner had all crashed in short order during tests for just such a reason. The riders wanted the time of the race changed, from 11pm to 10pm, which would make little difference to the European TV schedules, and surely not much to the scattering of 7,302 fans who turned up to watch. This was declined – local information was that this had been atypical. Happily, it proved correct.

The tests had also stressed the difference between a large crop of rookies: Spies had been close to the pace at both tracks; the ex-250 riders, with the apparent exception of Si-

*Above, from left:* Mr and Mrs – Stoner celebrates pole, but it would all go wrong in the race; Capirossi celebrated his 300th GP start; Aoyama shows his leathers with the gambling logos hastily taped over.

*Right:* Spies eventually broke away from de Puniet, Pedrosa dropped away behind.

*Photos: Gold & Goose*

*Left:* Spanish civil war – but Lorenzo was moving forward and Pedrosa backwards.

*Below:* Melandri about to endure "the worst race of my life."

*Below centre:* Moto2 class favourite Elias was walking on crutches after his big testing crash.

Photos: Gold & Goose

moncelli, were picking up speed reasonably well. The Italian seemed all at sea and had complicated matters with a heavy crash at Sepang. Barbera, by contrast, topped the speed sheets for the meeting on his new all-yellow Aspar Ducati.

Rossi had led pretty much every test session until the last under lights at Qatar, when Stoner set a flier to claim final bragging rights. So it looked much like business as usual as the pair dominated, with Stoner very much on top and Rossi's Yamaha short on top speed. Stoner's crash – the first of the year, the second in successive races and the first of a series that would wreck his title battle before it had started – upset the preconceptions of victory that everyone had shared before the race.

It was one of several reminders to come that preconceptions don't always work in motorbike racing.

There were celebrations at Suzuki, where Capirossi set a remarkable record – it was his 300th grand prix start, and he swapped his usual racing number 65 for a concessionary '300' for the race – normally, three-digit numbers are not permitted. Sadly, perennially hoped-for improvements in Suzuki performance were not evident, and his race led to a disappointing ninth.

All eyes were on the main class, of course, but the sound and fury (there was plenty of both) of the new Moto2 class swept aside any sentimental regrets about the lost 250s, and all were agog for the spectacle of 41 racing bikes peeling into the first corner.

Moto2 did not disappoint, in all sorts of ways. The sheer numbers and close qualifying times (13 within the first second) were reminiscent of the glory days of the old semi-privateer 250 class; an unexpected winner didn't disprove that the cream rises to the top, merely that the cream is not always obvious.

Remarkably, in a class that was once a national stronghold, there were only three Italians in the 125s, and none of any real account. Instead it had turned very Spanish, with Spaniards filling the front row and the first four places, and sixth as well.

There were the usual funny stories about this strange race in a strange place. Grid girls are less evident out of respect for local Arab sensitivities, and the Playboy backing was again missing from the LCR bike. But the new Interwetten Honda team of Aoyama had to hastily tape over the name on fairing and team gear. It is a gambling organisation, but they had forgotten that gambling is against the law in Qatar.

We have commented before on the hubris of running the race at night. The Pramac team provided some unintentional irony. The company and the team had espoused a bizarre 'green' *leitmotif*, painting the bikes that colour and reinforcing these credentials during the year with a variety of incongruous ecology-minded enterprises – like Philippe Starck designed wind-turbines on their trucks, which provided enough power, on a windy weekend, to service the team's lap-tops. All this with a straight face, while at Qatar a bank of Pramac diesel generators roared through the night, pounding out enough electricity to illuminate the track until after dawn with (as they had boasted at the launch) enough candlepower to light a road from Doha to Moscow, long after the racing had finished.

## MOTOGP RACE – 22 laps

Qualifying continued what had begun at the last tests: Stoner in dominant form. His pole was by a significant margin of almost four-tenths; as significant was his top-speed margin in the session over second-placed Rossi – almost 10km/h, at 329.1. Third-placed Lorenzo and de Puniet in fourth reflected similar speeds to Rossi. Dovi had outqualified a moaning Pedrosa, but both were behind sixth-placed Capirossi.

Stoner was a little slow to start, and it was Pedrosa away first, with Rossi ahead halfway around the first lap, Hayden third. Pedrosa was back in front as they finished lap two, but Stoner had already dealt with Hayden and Rossi in a single lap, and had surged into the lead by the time they swept into the right-hander at the end of the long straight.

He set his best lap next time around, and by the end of the fifth he was already better than two seconds clear of new second-place man Rossi, who had just repassed Pedrosa. Four corners later, he was down in a shower of sparks, after the front wheel had tucked under. It wasn't a fast crash, but the handlebar had broken, and he was left to walk away, the picture of dejection. His explanation was that he'd run into the corner slower than usual, and with less braking load, the tyre had slipped away. "I've had my crash for the season," he added: words that would haunt him. His easy run up front looked ominous all the same, but that too would not carry on to the following races.

Now Rossi led, but not by any comfortable margin. Pedrosa succumbed to Hayden, and on the next lap also to Dovizioso. His pace was dropping, his problems with weaving plain to see, even on the straight.

Dovizioso had no such difficulty. On lap eight, he got ahead of Hayden and started to lean on Rossi. At this point, Lorenzo was fourth, a second adrift and not yet showing any signs of anything better. Three laps later, Spies inherited fifth from Pedrosa, who got back in front for half a lap, only to run wide at turn one and lose the position for good.

Rossi had his hands full, and Dovizioso's Honda clearly had the advantage on speed – more than 10km/h. That was enough to put him ahead over the line on lap 16, although Rossi took it straight back. It was time for Rossi to take charge.

On lap 18, he pulled a second over Hayden, back ahead of the Honda again. At the same time, Lorenzo was coming and would be on Hayden's tail the next lap. As so often in his latter 250 days, his pace was improving as the end drew nigh. He went up the inside of Hayden on the fourth corner of lap 21, and did the same rather more forcefully to Dovizioso at the 12th.

Rossi's lead was still just two seconds at the start of the final lap and half that by the end. Then, on the slow-down lap, the Yamaha sputtered to a stop, out of gas. But it had been enough for the first win of the year – his 104th, and last for a long spell. He knew that it had been hard, that his bike had lacked top speed and that the year ahead would be difficult. "These are 25 very valuable points," he said.

Third was still hotly disputed, less than a second off Lorenzo's back wheel. Hayden thought he had timed it right,

following the Honda on to the last lap, then moving firmly ahead, but his defence of the last corner spoiled his exit. Dovizioso, by contrast, hooked up perfectly, and crews hanging over the pit wall were treated to the extraordinary sight of a Honda not only out-accelerating a Ducati, but also faster on top end as well. Dovi reclaimed the rostrum by 0.011 second, leaving the renascent 2006 world champion bereft.

Spies's debut fifth was impressively less than four seconds off the lead: he had overtaken only Pedrosa, but had stuck with Lorenzo well mid-race and hadn't put a foot wrong, at a track he already knew from World Superbikes.

He'd pulled clear of de Puniet, who had followed him past Pedrosa and was a lonely sixth, but happy to be second Honda. Gloomy Dani was another seven seconds away, clear of an entertaining battle for eighth. That was won by Edwards from fellow veteran Capirossi, the 300-race-old man; the pair had been joined impressively by the end by rookie Aoyama, best of the 250 gang.

The other three were replaying their past battles in a last-lap barging match. Simoncelli was the survivor with Barbera just behind, but Bautista – who had been between the pair – crashed out on the last lap.

Melandri qualified last and finished "the worst race of my life" last, mystifying for all concerned. Both Pramac riders crashed out, first Kallio and then youngster Espargaro.

## MOTO2 RACE – 20 laps

Drama began before the season for one favourite – MotoGP race winner Toni Elias had clashed with a slow 125 rider during controversial combined 125/Moto2 tests at Jerez less than two weeks before, and had broken both his left hand and his right ankle. Plated and screwed, walking on crutches, the brave little Spaniard qualified on pole nonetheless, ahead of ex-125 champion Simon, rival Bradl and ex-MotoGP firebrand de Angelis. The first 13 had qualified within a second in a fine mélange of different chassis, backgrounds and levels of experience.

It was one of the old hands who started the fireworks on lap one: de Angelis got into turn two too hot, narrowly missed Elias, only to high-side in front of Bradl, who ran into him. Both went down and out; Simon also toured into the pits with a failed clutch. Three of the four front-row starters had gone.

Cluzel took over, with Debon demoting Elias to third. But Tomizawa – like Cluzel, one of the better privateers of the 250 class – was on the move, taking fourth from compatriot Takahashi on lap three, and grabbing three more to push through to the lead with a double pass on Cluzel and Debon.

The new class had certainly stirred the pot, but few would have predicted what followed: the Japanese rider edged steadily clear, by tenths each lap. By half-distance, his lead was just over 1.4 seconds, and he would treble it by the end.

Tomizawa left behind a dwindling pack. Takahashi had been up to third on lap seven before joining Tech 3 teammate de Rosa on the crash list. Now Debon, Cluzel and Elias were glued together, with Rolfo closing after half-distance to swell the numbers in a battle that went almost to the end.

Cluzel drafted past Elias to head the group on lap 16; three laps later, Debon outbraked him at the end of the front straight. Cluzel passed him back later that lap, but on the last one Debon reversed the order finally for the second podium spot.

For Elias, pain and weakness had finally taken their toll, and he was a couple of seconds adrift. But he still had to fight for fourth with Rolfo.

There were strong battles down the field: Pasini got back ahead of a charging Luthi for sixth, Corsi close behind, but Talmacsi dropped off the back. Luthi had been 19th on lap one and set the new lap record on his run through. Gadea won a big battle for tenth.

Pons, Leonov and MZ's Anthony West also joined the crash list; Yonny Hernandez retired.

There were still 32 finishers, and a track full of noise and action plus an unexpected winner bode well for the excitement level, if not the dignity and world championship status, of the fledgling class.

*Above:* From out of the blue, Shoya Tomizawa took a runaway inaugural Moto2 win.

*Above right:* De Angelis and Bradl collide on the first lap of the first Moto2 race.

*Right:* The leading 125 pack, with Marquez heading Vazquez, Espargaro, Rabat, Cortese and the rest.

*Below:* Moto2 is go! Elias leads a brawl that would augur well for the new class.

*Photo:* Gold & Goose

## 125cc RACE – 18 laps

The last two-stroke class gave a fine display: an epic seven-strong battle for victory, with all of them not only making it to the finish, but also crossing the line with second to seventh covered by 1.3 seconds. A superb tactical ride by Nico Terol had seen him break free to win by almost 2.5 seconds.

First to fourth were all Spanish, as had been the make-up of the front row – a trend that would remain pronounced as the year wore on.

Marquez had been on pole; Vazquez led away, with Smith at the back of a gang of seven, knocked back to eighth on lap three when Cortese came through. It was the start of a disappointing afternoon for the Briton in a Spanish team, his bike clearly lacking speed down the long straight.

They all stayed together, crossing the line for lap 12 covered by seven-tenths of a second. The battle was fierce, every tiny opening exploited, with the occasional nudge. Terol had slipped to the back of the group now, waiting and watching.

Marquez had taken over from Vazquez on lap seven, and again on laps 12 and 14, only to be forced back each time. All the while, however, Terol was making his way forward, and on lap 15 he took the lead, setting fastest lap and leaving the rest to fight it out as he pulled away, once again setting fastest lap for a far greater win than anyone might have expected.

The next three were covered by less than half a second: Vazquez, Marquez and Espargaro. Close behind, Cortese, Krummenacher and Rabat crossed the line also almost side by side.

Smith had dropped to tenth, but fought back past Koyama and Masbou in the closing laps. Countryman Webb was a long way back, after finally prevailing over Zarco for 11th.

In all, there were three retirements, but amazingly not a single crash.

*Above:* Nico Terol waited his chance, then stamped his authority on the 125 class.

*Photo:* Gold & Goose

# COMMERCIALBANK GRAND PRIX OF QATAR

9-11 APRIL 2010 · FIM WORLD CHAMPIONSHIP ROUND 1

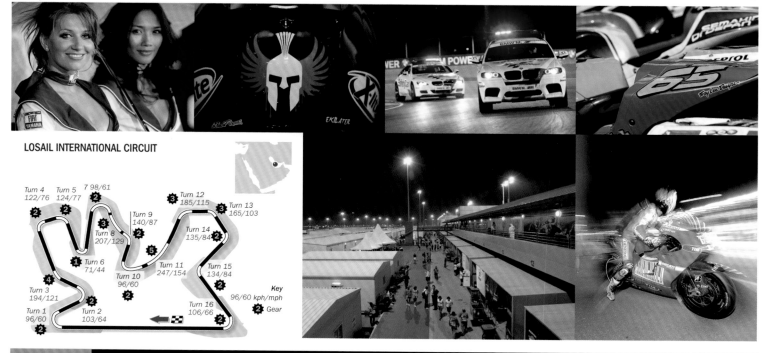

**LOSAIL INTERNATIONAL CIRCUIT**

Turn 4 122/76 · Turn 5 124/77 · 7 98/61 · Turn 12 185/115 · Turn 13 165/103
Turn 9 140/87 · Turn 8 207/129 · Turn 14 135/84
Turn 6 71/44 · Turn 11 247/154 · Turn 15 134/84
Turn 3 194/121 · Turn 10 96/60
Turn 1 96/60 · Turn 2 103/64 · Turn 16 106/66

Key 96/60 kph/mph · Gear

## MotoGP

**RACE DISTANCE: 22 laps, 73.545 miles/118.36 km · RACE WEATHER: Dry (air 24°, humidity 30%, track 26°)**

| Pos. | Rider | Nat. | No. | Entrant | Machine | Tyres | Laps | Time & speed |
|---|---|---|---|---|---|---|---|---|
| 1 | **Valentino Rossi** | ITA | 46 | Fiat Yamaha Team | Yamaha | B | 22 | 42m 50.099s 103.017mph/ 165.789km/h |
| 2 | **Jorge Lorenzo** | SPA | 99 | Fiat Yamaha Team | Yamaha | B | 22 | 42m 51.121s |
| 3 | **Andrea Dovizioso** | ITA | 4 | Repsol Honda Team | Honda | B | 22 | 42m 51.964s |
| 4 | **Nicky Hayden** | USA | 69 | Ducati Marlboro Team | Ducati | B | 22 | 42m 51.975s |
| 5 | **Ben Spies** | USA | 11 | Monster Yamaha Tech 3 | Yamaha | B | 22 | 42m 54.002s |
| 6 | **Randy de Puniet** | FRA | 14 | LCR Honda MotoGP | Honda | B | 22 | 42m 59.421s |
| 7 | **Dani Pedrosa** | SPA | 26 | Repsol Honda Team | Honda | B | 22 | 43m 06.607s |
| 8 | **Colin Edwards** | USA | 5 | Monster Yamaha Tech 3 | Yamaha | B | 22 | 43m 09.966s |
| 9 | **Loris Capirossi** | ITA | 65 | Rizla Suzuki MotoGP | Suzuki | B | 22 | 43m 10.992s |
| 10 | **Hiroshi Aoyama** | JPN | 7 | Interwetten Honda MotoGP | Honda | B | 22 | 43m 11.199s |
| 11 | **Marco Simoncelli** | ITA | 58 | San Carlo Honda Gresini | Honda | B | 22 | 43m 21.737s |
| 12 | **Hector Barbera** | SPA | 40 | Paginas Amarillas Aspar | Ducati | B | 22 | 43m 22.672s |
| 13 | **Marco Melandri** | ITA | 33 | San Carlo Honda Gresini | Honda | B | 22 | 43m 30.879s |
| | Alvaro Bautista | SPA | 19 | Rizla Suzuki MotoGP | Suzuki | B | 21 | DNF |
| | Aleix Espargaro | SPA | 41 | Pramac Racing Team | Ducati | B | 7 | DNF |
| | Casey Stoner | AUS | 27 | Ducati Marlboro Team | Ducati | B | 5 | DNF |
| | Mika Kallio | FIN | 36 | Pramac Racing Team | Ducati | B | 2 | DNF |

**Fastest lap:** Casey Stoner, on lap 5, 1m 55.537s, 104.163mph/167.634km/h.

**Lap record:** Casey Stoner, AUS (Ducati), 1m 55.153s, 104.510mph/168.193km/h (2008).

**Event best maximum speed:** Casey Stoner, 204.5mph/329.1km/h (qualifying practice).

### Qualifying

Weather: Dry
Air Temp: 26° Humidity: 26°
Track Temp: 27°

| | | |
|---|---|---|
| 1 | Stoner | 1m 55.007s |
| 2 | Rossi | 1m 55.362s |
| 3 | Lorenzo | 1m 55.520s |
| 4 | de Puniet | 1m 55.831s |
| 5 | Capirossi | 1m 55.899s |
| 6 | Dovizioso | 1m 55.963s |
| 7 | Pedrosa | 1m 55.990s |
| 8 | Edwards | 1m 56.005s |
| 9 | Hayden | 1m 56.163s |
| 10 | Aoyama | 1m 56.227s |
| 11 | Spies | 1m 56.271s |
| 12 | Kallio | 1m 56.283s |
| 13 | Bautista | 1m 56.450s |
| 14 | Espargaro | 1m 56.652s |
| 15 | Simoncelli | 1m 56.957s |
| 16 | Barbera | 1m 57.130s |
| 17 | Melandri | 1m 57.325s |

### Fastest race laps

| | | |
|---|---|---|
| 1 | Stoner | 1m 55.537s |
| 2 | Lorenzo | 1m 56.042s |
| 3 | Rossi | 1m 56.043s |
| 4 | Spies | 1m 56.087s |
| 5 | Dovizioso | 1m 56.157s |
| 6 | Hayden | 1m 56.162s |
| 7 | de Puniet | 1m 56.221s |
| 8 | Pedrosa | 1m 56.398s |
| 9 | Aoyama | 1m 56.677s |
| 10 | Edwards | 1m 56.756s |
| 11 | Capirossi | 1m 56.794s |
| 12 | Bautista | 1m 57.104s |
| 13 | Simoncelli | 1m 57.119s |
| 14 | Barbera | 1m 57.229s |
| 15 | Espargaro | 1m 57.272s |
| 16 | Melandri | 1m 57.359s |
| 17 | Kallio | 1m 57.931s |

### Championship Points

| | | |
|---|---|---|
| 1 | Rossi | 25 |
| 2 | Lorenzo | 20 |
| 3 | Dovizioso | 16 |
| 4 | Hayden | 13 |
| 5 | Spies | 11 |
| 6 | de Puniet | 10 |
| 7 | Pedrosa | 9 |
| 8 | Edwards | 8 |
| 9 | Capirossi | 7 |
| 10 | Aoyama | 6 |
| 11 | Simoncelli | 5 |
| 12 | Barbera | 4 |
| 13 | Melandri | 3 |

### Team Points

| | | |
|---|---|---|
| 1 | Fiat Yamaha Team | 45 |
| 2 | Repsol Honda Team | 25 |
| 3 | Monster Yamaha Tech 3 | 19 |
| 4 | Ducati Marlboro Team | 13 |
| 5 | LCR Honda MotoGP | 10 |
| 6 | San Carlo Honda Gresini | 8 |
| 7 | Rizla Suzuki MotoGP | 7 |
| 8 | Interwetten Honda MotoGP | 6 |
| 9 | Paginas Amarillas Aspar | 4 |

### Constructor Points

| | | |
|---|---|---|
| 1 | Yamaha | 25 |
| 2 | Honda | 16 |
| 3 | Ducati | 13 |
| 4 | Suzuki | 7 |

### Grid order / Lap chart

| Grid order | 1 | 2 | 3 | 4 | 5 | 6 | 7 | 8 | 9 | 10 | 11 | 12 | 13 | 14 | 15 | 16 | 17 | 18 | 19 | 20 | 21 | 22 | Pos |
|---|---|---|---|---|---|---|---|---|---|---|---|---|---|---|---|---|---|---|---|---|---|---|---|
| 27 STONER | 46 | 26 | 27 | 27 | 27 | 46 | 46 | 46 | 46 | 46 | 46 | 46 | 46 | 46 | 4 | 46 | 46 | 46 | 46 | 46 | 46 | 46 | 1 |
| 46 ROSSI | 26 | 27 | 26 | 26 | 46 | 69 | 69 | 4 | 4 | 4 | 4 | 4 | 4 | 4 | 46 | 4 | 69 | 4 | 4 | 99 | 99 | 99 | 2 |
| 99 LORENZO | 69 | 46 | 46 | 46 | 26 | 4 | 4 | 69 | 69 | 69 | 69 | 69 | 69 | 69 | 69 | 69 | 4 | 69 | 69 | 4 | 4 | 4 | 3 |
| 14 de PUNIET | 27 | 69 | 69 | 69 | 69 | 26 | 99 | 99 | 99 | 99 | 99 | 99 | 99 | 99 | 99 | 99 | 99 | 99 | 99 | 69 | 69 | 69 | 4 |
| 65 CAPIROSSI | 99 | 99 | 4 | 4 | 4 | 99 | 26 | 26 | 26 | 26 | 11 | 11 | 11 | 11 | 11 | 11 | 11 | 11 | 11 | 11 | 11 | 11 | 5 |
| 4 DOVIZIOSO | 4 | 4 | 99 | 99 | 99 | 11 | 11 | 11 | 11 | 11 | 14 | 14 | 14 | 14 | 14 | 14 | 14 | 14 | 14 | 14 | 14 | 14 | 6 |
| 26 PEDROSA | 11 | 11 | 11 | 11 | 11 | 14 | 14 | 14 | 14 | 14 | 26 | 26 | 26 | 26 | 26 | 26 | 26 | 26 | 26 | 26 | 26 | 26 | 7 |
| 5 EDWARDS | 65 | 65 | 14 | 14 | 14 | 65 | 65 | 65 | 65 | 5 | 5 | 5 | 5 | 5 | 5 | 5 | 5 | 5 | 5 | 5 | | | 8 |
| 69 HAYDEN | 14 | 14 | 65 | 65 | 65 | 5 | 5 | 5 | 5 | 65 | 65 | 65 | 65 | 65 | 65 | 65 | 65 | 65 | 65 | 65 | | | 9 |
| 7 AOYAMA | 58 | 58 | 5 | 5 | 5 | 58 | 58 | 58 | 58 | 7 | 7 | 7 | 7 | 7 | 7 | 7 | 7 | 7 | 7 | 7 | | | 10 |
| 11 SPIES | 5 | 5 | 58 | 58 | 58 | 41 | 41 | 7 | 7 | 58 | 58 | 58 | 58 | 58 | 58 | 58 | 58 | 58 | 58 | 58 | | | 11 |
| 36 KALLIO | 41 | 41 | 41 | 41 | 41 | 7 | 7 | 33 | 33 | 33 | 33 | 33 | 33 | 33 | 33 | 19 | 19 | 19 | 19 | 40 | | | 12 |
| 19 BAUTISTA | 7 | 33 | 33 | 33 | 33 | 33 | 33 | 19 | 19 | 19 | 19 | 19 | 19 | 19 | 19 | 40 | 40 | 40 | 40 | 33 | | | 13 |
| 41 ESPARGARO | 33 | 7 | 7 | 7 | 7 | 19 | 19 | 40 | 40 | 40 | 40 | 40 | 40 | 40 | 40 | 33 | 33 | 33 | 33 | | | | |
| 58 SIMONCELLI | 40 | 36 | 19 | 19 | 19 | 40 | 40 | | | | | | | | | | | | | | | | |
| 40 BARBERA | 19 | 40 | 40 | 40 | 40 | | | | | | | | | | | | | | | | | | |
| 33 MELANDRI | 36 | 19 | | | | | | | | | | | | | | | | | | | | | |

## Moto2

**RACE DISTANCE: 20 laps, 66.860 miles/107.600 km · RACE WEATHER: Dry (air 24°, humidity 25%, track 26°)**

| Pos. | Rider | Nat. | No. | Entrant | Machine | Laps | Time & Speed |
|---|---|---|---|---|---|---|---|
| 1 | **Shoya Tomizawa** | JPN | 48 | Technomag-CIP | Suter | 20 | 41m 11.768s |
| | | | | | | | (mph/km/h) |
| | | | | | | | 97.377/156.713 |
| 2 | **Alex Debon** | SPA | 6 | Aeroport de Castello - Ajo | FTR | 20 | 41m 16.424s |
| 3 | **Jules Cluzel** | FRA | 16 | Forward Racing | Suter | 20 | 41m 16.557s |
| 4 | **Toni Elias** | SPA | 24 | Gresini Racing Moto2 | Moriwaki | 20 | 41m 18.746s |
| 5 | **Roberto Rolfo** | ITA | 44 | Italtrans S.T.R. | Suter | 20 | 41m 18.946s |
| 6 | **Mattia Pasini** | ITA | 75 | JIR Moto2 | MotoBI | 20 | 41m 23.572s |
| 7 | **Thomas Luthi** | SWI | 12 | Interwetten Moriwaki Moto2 | Moriwaki | 20 | 41m 23.629s |
| 8 | **Simone Corsi** | ITA | 3 | JIR Moto2 | MotoBI | 20 | 41m 24.114s |
| 9 | **Gabor Talmacsi** | HUN | 2 | Fimmco Speed Up | Speed Up | 20 | 41m 25.589s |
| 10 | **Sergio Gadea** | SPA | 40 | Tenerife 40 Pons | Pons Kalex | 20 | 41m 31.957s |
| 11 | **Dominique Aegerter** | SWI | 77 | Technomag-CIP | Suter | 20 | 41m 33.057s |
| 12 | **Alex Baldolini** | ITA | 25 | Caretta Technology Race Dept. | I.C.P. | 20 | 41m 33.128s |
| 13 | **Fonsi Nieto** | SPA | 10 | Holiday Gym G22 | Moriwaki | 20 | 41m 33.603s |
| 14 | **Karel Abraham** | CZE | 17 | Cardion AB Motoracing | RSV | 20 | 41m 33.741s |
| 15 | **Lukas Pesek** | CZE | 52 | Matteoni CP Racing | Moriwaki | 20 | 41m 38.033s |
| 16 | Mike di Meglio | FRA | 63 | Mapfre Aspar Team | RSV | 20 | 41m 38.033s |
| 17 | Ratthapark Wilairot | THA | 14 | Thai Honda PTT Singha SAG | Bimota | 20 | 41m 38.367s |
| 18 | Kenny Noyes | USA | 9 | Jack & Jones by A.Banderas | Promoharris | 20 | 41m 45.601s |
| 19 | Andrea Iannone | ITA | 29 | Fimmco Speed Up | Speed Up | 20 | 41m 45.663s |
| 20 | Claudio Corti | ITA | 71 | Forward Racing | Suter | 20 | 41m 52.760s |
| 21 | Arne Tode | GER | 41 | Racing Team Germany | Suter | 20 | 41m 54.887s |
| 22 | Hector Faubel | SPA | 55 | Marc VDS Racing Team | Suter | 20 | 41m 55.017s |
| 23 | Scott Redding | GBR | 45 | Marc VDS Racing Team | Suter | 20 | 41m 57.165s |
| 24 | Valentin Debise | FRA | 53 | WTR San Marino Team | ADV | 20 | 41m 58.240s |
| 25 | Anthony Delhalle | FRA | 96 | Qatar Endurance Racing Team | BQR-Moto2 | 20 | 42m 02.925s |
| 26 | Vladimir Ivanov | UKR | 61 | Gresini Racing Moto2 | Moriwaki | 20 | 42m 06.020s |
| 27 | Niccolo Canepa | ITA | 59 | RSM Team Scot | Force GP210 | 20 | 42m 06.399s |
| 28 | Robertino Pietri | VEN | 39 | Italtrans S.T.R. | Suter | 20 | 42m 27.744s |
| 29 | Bernat Martinez | SPA | 76 | Maquinza-SAG Team | Bimota | 20 | 42m 27.990s |
| 30 | Yannick Guerra | SPA | 88 | Holiday Gym G22 | Moriwaki | 20 | 42m 32.419s |
| 31 | Mashel Al Naimi | QAT | 95 | Blusens-STX | BQR-Moto2 | 20 | 42m 32.487s |
| 32 | Joan Olive | SPA | 5 | Jack & Jones by A.Banderas | Promoharris | 20 | 42m 53.758s |
| | Anthony West | AUS | 8 | MZ Racing Team | MZ-RE Honda | 8 | DNF |
| | Yuki Takahashi | JPN | 72 | Tech 3 Racing | Tech 3 | 7 | DNF |
| | Vladimir Leonov | RUS | 21 | Vector Kiefer Racing | Suter | 7 | DNF |
| | Yonny Hernandez | COL | 68 | Blusens-STX | BQR-Moto2 | 3 | DNF |
| | Axel Pons | SPA | 80 | Tenerife 40 Pons | Pons Kalex | 3 | DNF |
| | Raffaele de Rosa | ITA | 35 | Tech 3 Racing | Tech 3 | 2 | DNF |
| | Alex de Angelis | RSM | 15 | RSM Team Scot | Force GP210 | 0 | DNF |
| | Julian Simon | SPA | 60 | Mapfre Aspar Team | RSV | 0 | DNF |
| | Stefan Bradl | GER | 65 | Viessmann Kiefer Racing | Suter | 0 | DNF |

**Qualifying: Dry**
Air: 25° Humidity: 22% Ground: 26°

| | | |
|---|---|---|
| 1 | Elias | 2m 01.904s |
| 2 | Simon | 2m 02.032s |
| 3 | Bradl | 2m 02.038s |
| 4 | de Angelis | 2m 02.101s |
| 5 | Takahashi | 2m 02.295s |
| 6 | Cluzel | 2m 02.366s |
| 7 | de Rosa | 2m 02.560s |
| 8 | Debon | 2m 02.759s |
| 9 | Tomizawa | 2m 02.771s |
| 10 | Baldolini | 2m 02.866s |
| 11 | Gadea | 2m 02.881s |
| 12 | Rolfo | 2m 02.883s |
| 13 | di Meglio | 2m 02.896s |
| 14 | Talmacsi | 2m 02.916s |
| 15 | Canepa | 2m 03.002s |
| 16 | Luthi | 2m 03.041s |
| 17 | Redding | 2m 03.129s |
| 18 | Pasini | 2m 03.155s |
| 19 | Wilairot | 2m 03.192s |
| 20 | Aegerter | 2m 03.232s |
| 21 | Iannone | 2m 03.258s |
| 22 | Tode | 2m 03.341s |
| 23 | Abraham | 2m 03.346s |
| 24 | Nieto | 2m 03.390s |
| 25 | Pesek | 2m 03.531s |
| 26 | Corsi | 2m 03.588s |
| 27 | Hernandez | 2m 03.635s |
| 28 | Corti | 2m 03.725s |
| 29 | Debise | 2m 03.752s |
| 30 | Noyes | 2m 03.792s |
| 31 | Pons | 2m 04.301s |
| 32 | Faubel | 2m 04.417s |
| 33 | Ivanov | 2m 04.470s |
| 34 | Olive | 2m 04.476s |
| 35 | Leonov | 2m 04.579s |
| 36 | Pietri | 2m 04.629s |
| 37 | Al Naimi | 2m 04.871s |
| 38 | Delhalle | 2m 04.912s |
| 39 | West | 2m 05.362s |
| 40 | Guerra | 2m 05.460s |
| 41 | Martinez | 2m 06.310s |

**Fastest race laps**

| | | |
|---|---|---|
| 1 | Luthi | 2m 02.537s |
| 2 | Tomizawa | 2m 02.728s |
| 3 | Takahashi | 2m 02.738s |
| 4 | Elias | 2m 02.758s |
| 5 | Rolfo | 2m 02.784s |
| 6 | Cluzel | 2m 02.878s |
| 7 | Debon | 2m 03.045s |
| 8 | Corsi | 2m 03.049s |
| 9 | Talmacsi | 2m 03.155s |
| 10 | Pasini | 2m 03.192s |
| 11 | Wilairot | 2m 03.219s |
| 12 | Baldolini | 2m 03.371s |
| 13 | Hernandez | 2m 03.399s |
| 14 | Noyes | 2m 03.440s |
| 15 | Gadea | 2m 03.453s |
| 16 | Iannone | 2m 03.561s |
| 17 | Pesek | 2m 03.575s |
| 18 | Abraham | 2m 03.605s |
| 19 | de Rosa | 2m 03.640s |
| 20 | Aegerter | 2m 03.641s |
| 21 | di Meglio | 2m 03.747s |
| 22 | Tode | 2m 03.752s |
| 23 | West | 2m 03.772s |
| 24 | Nieto | 2m 03.811s |
| 25 | Redding | 2m 03.874s |
| 26 | Delhalle | 2m 03.911s |
| 27 | Corti | 2m 04.157s |
| 28 | Faubel | 2m 04.258s |
| 29 | Debise | 2m 04.333s |
| 30 | Ivanov | 2m 04.419s |
| 31 | Canepa | 2m 04.450s |
| 32 | Al Naimi | 2m 04.602s |
| 33 | Pons | 2m 04.614s |
| 34 | Leonov | 2m 04.922s |
| 35 | Olive | 2m 05.051s |
| 36 | Pietri | 2m 05.934s |
| 37 | Martinez | 2m 06.112s |
| 38 | Guerra | 2m 06.214s |

**Championship Points**

| | | |
|---|---|---|
| 1 | Tomizawa | 25 |
| 2 | Debon | 20 |
| 3 | Cluzel | 16 |
| 4 | Elias | 13 |
| 5 | Rolfo | 11 |
| 6 | Pasini | 10 |
| 7 | Luthi | 9 |
| 8 | Corsi | 8 |
| 9 | Talmacsi | 7 |
| 10 | Gadea | 6 |
| 11 | Aegerter | 5 |
| 12 | Baldolini | 4 |
| 13 | Nieto | 3 |
| 14 | Abraham | 2 |
| 15 | Pesek | 1 |

**Constructors**

| | | |
|---|---|---|
| 1 | Suter | 25 |
| 2 | FTR | 20 |
| 3 | Moriwaki | 13 |
| 4 | MotoBI | 10 |
| 5 | Speed Up | 7 |
| 6 | Pons Kalex | 6 |
| 7 | I.C.P. | 4 |
| 8 | RSV | 2 |

**Fastest lap:** Thomas Luthi, on lap 4, 2m 02.537s, 98.213mph/158.058km/h (record).
**Lap record:** New category.
**Event best maximum speed:** Mattia Pasini, 172.4mph/277.5km/h (race).

---

## 125cc

**RACE DISTANCE: 18 laps, 60.174 miles/96.84 km · RACE WEATHER: Dry (air 25°, humidity 18%, track 27°)**

| Pos. | Rider | Nat. | No. | Entrant | Machine | Laps | Time & Speed |
|---|---|---|---|---|---|---|---|
| 1 | **Nicolas Terol** | SPA | 40 | Bancaja Aspar Team | Aprilia | 18 | 38m 25.644s |
| | | | | | | | (mph/km/h) |
| | | | | | | | 93.954/151.204 |
| 2 | **Efren Vazquez** | SPA | 7 | Tuenti Racing | Derbi | 18 | 38m 28.039s |
| 3 | **Marc Marquez** | SPA | 93 | Red Bull Ajo Motorsport | Derbi | 18 | 38m 28.064s |
| 4 | **Pol Espargaro** | SPA | 44 | Tuenti Racing | Derbi | 18 | 38m 28.484s |
| 5 | **Sandro Cortese** | GER | 11 | Avant Mitsubishi Ajo | Derbi | 18 | 38m 29.170s |
| 6 | **Randy Krummenacher** | SWI | 35 | Stipa-Molenaar Racing GP | Aprilia | 18 | 38m 29.213s |
| 7 | **Esteve Rabat** | SPA | 12 | Blusens-STX | Aprilia | 18 | 38m 29.336s |
| 8 | **Bradley Smith** | GBR | 38 | Bancaja Aspar Team | Aprilia | 18 | 38m 39.363s |
| 9 | **Tomoyoshi Koyama** | JPN | 71 | Racing Team Germany | Aprilia | 18 | 38m 39.981s |
| 10 | **Alexis Masbou** | FRA | 5 | Ongetta Team | Aprilia | 18 | 38m 41.561s |
| 11 | **Danny Webb** | GBR | 99 | Andalucia Cajasol | Aprilia | 18 | 38m 54.388s |
| 12 | **Johann Zarco** | FRA | 14 | WTR San Marino Team | Aprilia | 18 | 39m 01.311s |
| 13 | **Alberto Moncayo** | SPA | 23 | Andalucia Cajasol | Aprilia | 18 | 39m 02.475s |
| 14 | **Jasper Iwema** | NED | 53 | CBC Corse | Aprilia | 18 | 39m 02.498s |
| 15 | **Jonas Folger** | GER | 94 | Ongetta Team | Aprilia | 18 | 39m 04.543s |
| 16 | Marcel Schrotter | GER | 78 | Interwetten Honda 125 | Honda | 18 | 39m 04.635s |
| 17 | Louis Rossi | FRA | 69 | CBC Corse | Aprilia | 18 | 39m 07.700s |
| 18 | Sturla Fagerhaug | NOR | 50 | AirAsia-Sepang Int. Circuit | Aprilia | 18 | 39m 16.995s |
| 19 | Jakub Kornfeil | CZE | 84 | Racing Team Germany | Aprilia | 18 | 39m 22.140s |
| 20 | Adrian Martin | SPA | 26 | Aeroport de Castello - Ajo | Aprilia | 18 | 39m 22.394s |
| 21 | Zulfahmi Khairuddin | MAL | 63 | AirAsia-Sepang Int. Circuit | Aprilia | 18 | 39m 47.642s |
| 22 | Luca Marconi | ITA | 87 | Ongetta Team | Aprilia | 18 | 39m 57.718s |
| 23 | Quentin Jacquet | FRA | 80 | Stipa-Molenaar Racing GP | Aprilia | 18 | 40m 18.486s |
| | Marco Ravaioli | ITA | 72 | Lambretta Reparto Corse | Lambretta | 4 | DNF |
| | Luis Salom | SPA | 39 | Lambretta Reparto Corse | Lambretta | 2 | DNF |
| | Lorenzo Savadori | ITA | 32 | Matteoni CP Racing | Aprilia | 0 | DNF |

**Qualifying: Dry**
Air: 26° Humidity: 31% Ground: 27°

| | | |
|---|---|---|
| 1 | Marquez | 2m 06.651s |
| 2 | Espargaro | 2m 07.110s |
| 3 | Terol | 2m 07.136s |
| 4 | Vazquez | 2m 07.143s |
| 5 | Krummenacher | 2m 07.770s |
| 6 | Koyama | 2m 07.943s |
| 7 | Cortese | 2m 08.211s |
| 8 | Masbou | 2m 08.735s |
| 9 | Smith | 2m 08.835s |
| 10 | Rabat | 2m 08.850s |
| 11 | Zarco | 2m 09.382s |
| 12 | Iwema | 2m 09.388s |
| 13 | Webb | 2m 09.647s |
| 14 | Moncayo | 2m 09.649s |
| 15 | Schrotter | 2m 09.739s |
| 16 | Fagerhaug | 2m 10.010s |
| 17 | Khairuddin | 2m 10.253s |
| 18 | Folger | 2m 10.405s |
| 19 | Rossi | 2m 10.680s |
| 20 | Martin | 2m 10.859s |
| 21 | Kornfeil | 2m 10.864s |
| 22 | Savadori | 2m 11.034s |
| 23 | Salom | 2m 11.038s |
| 24 | Marconi | 2m 11.307s |
| 25 | Jacquet | 2m 13.874s |
| 26 | Ravaioli | 2m 14.311s |

**Fastest race laps**

| | | |
|---|---|---|
| 1 | Terol | 2m 06.674s |
| 2 | Espargaro | 2m 07.142s |
| 3 | Marquez | 2m 07.168s |
| 4 | Vazquez | 2m 07.196s |
| 5 | Cortese | 2m 07.227s |
| 6 | Krummenacher | 2m 07.315s |
| 7 | Rabat | 2m 07.421s |
| 8 | Koyama | 2m 07.742s |
| 9 | Smith | 2m 07.784s |
| 10 | Masbou | 2m 07.875s |
| 11 | Zarco | 2m 08.302s |
| 12 | Webb | 2m 08.391s |
| 13 | Iwema | 2m 08.850s |
| 14 | Schrotter | 2m 09.015s |
| 15 | Moncayo | 2m 09.129s |
| 16 | Folger | 2m 09.150s |
| 17 | Rossi | 2m 09.242s |
| 18 | Fagerhaug | 2m 09.469s |
| 19 | Kornfeil | 2m 10.179s |
| 20 | Martin | 2m 10.373s |
| 21 | Khairuddin | 2m 10.382s |
| 22 | Marconi | 2m 11.796s |
| 23 | Jacquet | 2m 12.662s |
| 24 | Salom | 2m 13.153s |
| 25 | Ravaioli | 2m 13.477s |

**Championship Points**

| | | |
|---|---|---|
| 1 | Terol | 25 |
| 2 | Vazquez | 20 |
| 3 | Marquez | 16 |
| 4 | Espargaro | 13 |
| 5 | Cortese | 11 |
| 6 | Krummenacher | 10 |
| 7 | Rabat | 9 |
| 8 | Smith | 8 |
| 9 | Koyama | 7 |
| 10 | Masbou | 6 |
| 11 | Webb | 5 |
| 12 | Zarco | 4 |
| 13 | Moncayo | 3 |
| 14 | Iwema | 2 |
| 15 | Folger | 1 |

**Constructors**

| | | |
|---|---|---|
| 1 | Aprilia | 25 |
| 2 | Derbi | 20 |

**Fastest lap:** Nicolas Terol, on lap 17, 2m 06.674s, 95.023mph/152.924km/h.
**Lap record:** Scott Redding, GBR (Aprilia), 2m 05.695s, 95.745mph/154.087km/h (2008).
**Event best maximum speed:** Sandro Cortese, 145.2mph/233.7km/h (race).

# SPANISH GRAND PRIX

JEREZ CIRCUIT

The clash that saved Pedrosa's
reputation as he fought back at the
final hairpin.
Photo: Gold & Goose

Above: Nicky Hayden had the beating of team-mate Stoner.

Top right: Pedrosa showed he had some fight in him.

Above right: Barbera was getting to grips with his Duke.

Right: Mary Spies, manager and number-one fan to Ben.

Photos: Gold & Goose

A SMALL volcano in Iceland gave off a steady plume of fine ash, the wind blew the wrong way, and on 15th April, eight days before first practice at Motegi, air travel over northern Europe was abruptly grounded. As the paralysis continued for day after day, the outlook for the second round grew increasingly bleak. By the weekend, Dorna had decided, and the Japanese GP became the first major international sporting event to be cancelled – actually postponed, a date was found in October.

There had been little choice. Although the bikes and pit gear had already arrived at Motegi direct from Qatar, team personnel and riders were mostly in Europe and stuck there – a back-up plan to lay on overland transport to Istanbul and charter aircraft to Japan was never very serious. Teams were informed on Saturday and the news announced on Monday. That gave Dorna another problem: how to get the bikes back to Europe for the Spanish GP at Jerez just one week later.

As restrictions were gradually eased, this proved narrowly achievable, with three charter aircraft following different routes: bikes, riders and spanner-men duly re-united for only the second race of what seemed a very desultory start to the year: World Superbike would have its fifth round on the following weekend, likewise F1.

In the interim, there was an intimation of mortality for Valentino: a crash while motocross training on the Thursday after Qatar had injured his right shoulder. It was not actually dislocated, he explained later, "but it tried to come out", and the resultant muscle and ligament damage, plus a small fracture, meant he was in pain and weak. The postponement of the Motegi round had been a blessing, giving him another week to recover.

In fact, the injury would linger far longer, and he would later explain, to a chorus of insider laughs, "With Dr Costa, sometimes it takes a little time to understand exactly." That was at Mugello: two days after that, a much more serious

injury would stop dead a championship bid that was already on the back foot.

A season alive with rumours kicked off early at the Andalucian circuit, where the usual big crowd (122,000 on race day) enjoyed the still rather watery spring sunshine. The trigger was the presence at the track of Colin Stoner, father and manager of Casey, and nowadays seldom seen trackside. From that day forth, "STONER TO HONDA?" headlines became a weekly event, soon followed by "ROSSI TO DUCATI?" in the same vein.

Other rumours were triggered almost in frustration, as another GP commission meeting passed without the MSMA coming up with any firm proposals for future MotoGP regulations. These were stuck in a very formative stage, with a three-tier proposal: the 800s to continue, for those factories that want it; 1000cc prototypes with 81mm maximum bore; and 1000cc "Claiming Rule Team" bikes, possibly production based. With time becoming short, the MSMA's only contribution was to seek a way to prevent rival factories from sneaking in via the CRT route without paying their dues. With this continuing stalemate, it is little wonder that word leaked from various sources that maybe the 1000cc bikes should be introduced in 2011 instead of 2012 – and as if in answer to this call, Moto2 chassis constructor Eskil Suter revealed that he was well advanced in constructing a BMW S100RR-powered CRT test mule, due out on track during the summer. "I believe with the extra torque and rideability, it could be competitive with the 800s," he said.

Other news from the commission was more welcome: a reduction in the penalty for going beyond the allocation of six engines. Riders would still start from the pit lane, but only ten rather than 20 seconds after the pack had passed.

In the pits, preparations for the second race reflected contrasting fortunes of the first. At Ducati, Hayden spoke of how better communication with his team had played a major part

in giving him a bike that was easier to ride fast. Then he had one of those Ducati front-end washouts in practice, coming down hard and lucky not to be hurt. Stoner had one too. As ever, the Italian stallion was proving slightly fickle.

Honda had filled the intervening time making chassis, although later Pedrosa scorned a report that there had been no fewer than six variations available to him. Certainly there was at least one, along with a new swing-arm, mainly stiffer to address his instability problems. It was not a complete fix, but it was a step in the right direction. A big one, as we would see on both Saturday and Sunday.

In the F1 paddock, there was a minor storm about the bar codes on the Marlboro Ferraris. This made them, said a panel of concerned doctors, reminiscent of cigarette packets; as a result, this was subliminal advertising. Ducati was not singled out, but carried the same bar code – and, like Ferrari, tried to pass it off as part of the team's own livery, rather than that of Marlboro. All the same, in both cases the bar codes were gone from the next race on.

Moto2 hit Europe with a bang: record close qualifying promised very close racing, and it was delivered – to the extent of a multiple crash at the hairpin on lap two that was Keystone Kops-hilarious, but might easily have been tragic. It had been triggered when Qatar winner Tomizawa crashed at the front of a tight group: as his bike hit the deck, the end cover had been ripped off the crankshaft and a deadly oil slick had been laid across the track. A hasty amendment to the technical regulations stipulated protective covers for this vulnerable part from the next race on.

Off-track, the creeping Hispanicisation of GP racing had already been remarked, with the cancelled Hungarian GP replaced at the last minute by yet another race in Spain, at a new circuit near Aragon. The Spanish influence was not only restricted to off track. This was the first of two races where all three classes were won by Spaniards. That it happened on home soil made it all the sweeter.

## MOTOGP RACE – 27 laps

Stoner started strong again, dominating free practice, but he found progress difficult thereafter as Lorenzo led on Saturday morning. Lorenzo was on top also in qualifying – until a blazing lap by Pedrosa gave him pole by almost a quarter of a second. Lorenzo and Stoner were alongside; Rossi led row two from Hayden and de Puniet.

Pedrosa leapt off the line as usual to lead Rossi, Hayden, Lorenzo and Stoner into the first corners. By the end of lap two, Stoner was fourth, but Pedrosa and Rossi were already a second clear of the two Ducatis. Dovizioso had passed fast-starting Spies and was behind Lorenzo, but also losing ground, with the midfield pack close up behind him.

Spies was in trouble. He'd qualified eighth at the first of a string of maiden tracks and was sixth first time across the line. "But when the pace started picking up, I ran into problems. I was doing everything as in practice, but the bike just wasn't responding the same way." He had no grip from the front, and survived "seven or eight" big moments in the first three laps, dropping back to 12th by lap five and pitting three laps later. Rather than change tyres and go for a point or two, he chose to save the engine instead. Bridgestone could find no fault with the tyre.

With a processional race up front, most of the action was in the midfield, where Melandri soon took over, Simoncelli harrying and sometimes passing him, Edwards and de Puniet close behind.

On lap five, Lorenzo started to gain speed, passing Stoner and closing on Hayden, only to be stuck behind him until lap ten, when the American ran wide at Dry Sack.

Pedrosa had complained about his unstable bike all weekend; the expectation was that Rossi would soon take over. But after ten laps, the Spaniard was surprised to be a second clear, the gap to Lorenzo and Hayden another 2.7 seconds, Stoner losing touch behind.

*Above:* Kallio was seventh, his best in a year that went downhill.

*Left:* Colin Stoner's presence sparked rumours that Casey would be moving to Honda. They were true.
*Photos:* Gold & Goose

*Above:* Interwetten girls were badged and free.

*Top:* Winner Lorenzo had to be rescued from the pool.

*Top right:* Noyes leads Corsi, Simon and Gadea after the Moto2 restart.

*Above right:* Tomizawa falls and lays down an oil slick in the path of the leading pack.

*Photos: Gold & Goose*

Observers were comparing the race unfavourably with the preceding Moto2 event. But after another six laps, it became clear that Lorenzo was beginning to pose a serious challenge. By lap 19, he was closing a three-second gap to Rossi by four- or five-tenths a lap. He caught him under braking for Dry Sack on lap 22.

With five laps to go, Pedrosa was sailing along with a margin of over two seconds. It seemed safe, but next time around, the gap was down to 1.5 seconds, then 1.1 seconds on lap 24. On the next lap, the flying Yamaha was on the Honda and ready to attack.

Dani held him off at Dry Sack. Lorenzo tried again around the outside at the last hairpin, but Pedrosa released the brakes, ran a little wide, and the pair collided. Lorenzo stayed on track, but once again was behind the Honda.

One lap to go. Lorenzo's next attack, again at Dry Sack, was perfectly timed, forcing Pedrosa wide. A magnificent victory was secured, and the loser's reputation also redeemed. Nobody could recall seeing Dani fight back like this. Later it emerged that he had finished the race with a full litre of fuel left in his tank. HRC admitted an electronic fault with the control programme had reduced consumption too much. The aim was to finish the race with 300 to 400cc remaining: anything more represented unused potential horsepower.

Rossi had been closing all the while, watching the battle and ready to profit from any mistakes. He was not quite close enough to pounce on the last corner.

Almost ten seconds behind, Stoner had closed again on Hayden, once he'd cleared a big bug splatter from his visor. He started the last lap eight-tenths behind and pushed even closer, only to run wide himself in the final hairpin, to finish a second adrift. He was baffled to be fifth, and increasingly worried by the front-end slides he'd been fighting throughout the race.

Dovizioso was alone behind, then came the growing gang.

Kallio had got ahead of the battling San Carlo team-mates now and again, and then for good with three laps left. Melandri stuck with him; Simoncelli succumbed first to de Puniet and on the last lap also to an impressive Bautista, who had caught and passed Edwards with four laps to go. The American was struggling for grip, almost losing 12th to Barbera at the end.

Hiro Aoyama was a distant 14th; another three laps down, Espargaro had fallen in the early stages, and then stopped twice in the pits, but he still earned a point for his efforts.

Lorenzo's brilliant win gave him the points lead from Rossi, while Pedrosa won kudos for the most unaccustomed vigour of his defence of his lead, albeit unsuccessful.

It had been, said Lorenzo, "the most wonderful race of my life", and it might also have been his last: his celebration was a running, flying jump into an artificial lake on the infield. Once in the water, however, he found that leathers, boots, gloves and a helmet were a severe hindrance to swimming ashore again, every kick pulling him under. "The water was coming up to my mouth," he said. Luckily, a track worker leapt in and helped him to dry land.

## MOTO2 RACE – 17 laps (restarted)

The first European Moto2 race promised much: qualifying times set a new record, with half the grid within one second of pole time, the coveted position occupied by Qatar winner Tomizawa, in spite of a heavy crash in the session. Simon and the still-limping Elias were next, then came Takahashi; Luthi led the second row from Bradl, Talmacsi, Gadea and rookie Noyes.

It was all a bit too close at the first attempt, and it went wrong on lap two, when an overenthusiastic attack on early leader Corsi at Dry Sack hairpin ended with Tomizawa slithering to earth. His bike spilled oil in a slick starting almost at the apex; Elias, close behind, was first to fall, followed by another five riders, including Noyes.

The red flags came out and everyone picked themselves up, with no injuries. Elias was particularly lucky: he'd been clobbered by a sliding bike soon after falling, and then had tripped over as he sprinted away through the gravel, all without exacerbating his existing hand injury. All the bikes were also ready to be patched up again for a prompt restart, the race being cut from 26 laps to 17.

What followed was reminiscent of the best of the good old days of the semi-privateer 250 class in the 1980s and early 1990s – a pack of more than ten back and forth up front, changing places at almost every corner in a battle that mixed skill and finesse with courage and desperation.

Elias and Tomizawa disputed the early lead. Then on lap five, Noyes took over, exploiting local track knowledge from his Spanish championship days to hold the pack at bay, but using up his front tyre in the process.

After ten laps, the lead pack was seven-strong and covered by 1.29 seconds. Elias and Tomizawa were prominent up front, Luthi moving through. It was the Swiss rider who took over from Noyes, only to run wide at the hairpin, taking Elias with him. Tomizawa assumed the lead, staying up front for another two laps. That was over the line – at other points on the circuit, riders were changing places over and over.

As the final laps approached, the Japanese rider tried to

repeat his breakaway of Qatar, but Luthi and Elias went with him. Luthi led on to the last lap, where the pushing and shoving was even more intense than on the first. By the end, experienced MotoGP reject Elias was in control, with Luthi third and Takahashi a close fourth.

A heartbeat behind, Corsi led Gadea, who had come through impressively from tenth on the first lap. Noyes was still close, ahead of Simon.

Elias promised more in the future, "when I am in a normal condition." Tomizawa was more concerned about apologising for spilling oil than celebrating his second place.

Alex de Angelis did not start, a heavy high-sider crash in morning warm-up having left him barely conscious and under observation in the Clinica Mobile.

## 125cc RACE – 23 laps

Qualifying was a Spanish fiesta, pole disputed between Marquez and Espargaro; Marquez took it by a tenth. Vazquez and Rabat completed row one; Terol led the second with Britons Smith and Webb at the far end.

The armada continued in the race, but Marquez was out before completing the first lap. His exhaust came adrift running through the final pair of fast rights and slipped under his back wheel, and he fell heavily, dislocating his shoulder.

Terol led the first lap; Espargaro took over the second, Vazquez and Rabat right behind. Rabat would lose touch after one-third distance, but by then Cortese had forged his way through from tenth on the first lap and was in the battle.

Then on lap 15, his rear suspension sagged visibly, the link broken, and he started to drop back rapidly.

Vazquez was also heading for trouble, sliding off on lap 19. Now there were two.

It looked like an even match until, with two laps to go, Espargaro kicked once more and drew steadily clear; Terol was almost two seconds behind when he crossed the line.

Rabat was 15 seconds adrift in third, but still two seconds ahead of a disgruntled Smith, down on speed, who had been chasing in vain all race long.

Koyama escaped from the next gang for fifth, ahead of rookie Moncaya and Zarco, with an over-powered Krummenacher eighth and Masbou closing at the finish. Iwema had been with them, but a mistake on the last lap dropped him almost 30 seconds behind. He retained tenth, two seconds ahead of the luckless Cortese, who was barely a second clear of the next gang, headed by Schrotter from fellow rookies Martin and Kornfeil. Webb had crashed out of this group with two laps left.

*Above:* The front-runners of Moto2, with Elias heading Tomizawa, Luthi and the rest.

*Left:* Third place was a career second podium for 125 rider Esteve Rabat.

*Below:* Team-mates Espargaro and Vazquez battle for inches. Terol and Cortese watch with interest.

*Photos:* Gold & Goose

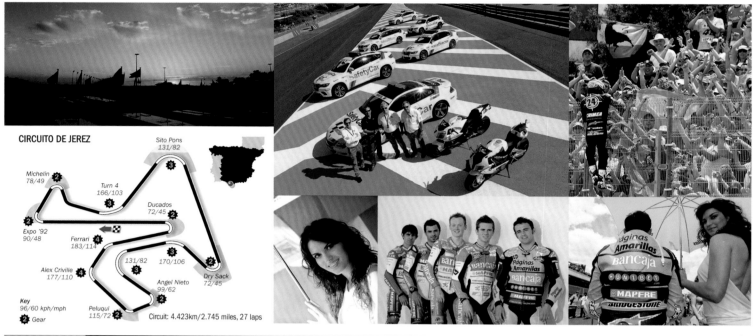

**CIRCUITO DE JEREZ**

Sito Pons 131/82
Michelin 78/49
Turn 4 166/103
Ducados 72/45
Expo '92 90/48
Ferrari 183/114
131/82
170/106
Alex Criville 177/110
Dry Sack 72/45
Angel Nieto 99/62
Key 96/60 kph/mph
Gear
Peluqui 115/72
Circuit: 4.423km/2.745 miles, 27 laps

## MotoGP · RACE DISTANCE: 27 laps, 74.205 miles/119.421 km · RACE WEATHER: Dry (air 27°, humidity 30%, track 44°)

| Pos. | Rider | Nat. | No. | Entrant | Machine | Tyres | Laps | Time & speed |
|---|---|---|---|---|---|---|---|---|
| 1 | **Jorge Lorenzo** | SPA | 99 | Fiat Yamaha Team | Yamaha | B | 27 | 45m 17.538s 98.301mph/ 158.200km/h |
| 2 | **Dani Pedrosa** | SPA | 26 | Repsol Honda Team | Honda | B | 27 | 45m 18.081s |
| 3 | **Valentino Rossi** | ITA | 46 | Fiat Yamaha Team | Yamaha | B | 27 | 45m 18.428s |
| 4 | **Nicky Hayden** | USA | 69 | Ducati Marlboro Team | Ducati | B | 27 | 45m 26.553s |
| 5 | **Casey Stoner** | AUS | 27 | Ducati Marlboro Team | Ducati | B | 27 | 45m 27.572s |
| 6 | **Andrea Dovizioso** | ITA | 4 | Repsol Honda Team | Honda | B | 27 | 45m 40.682s |
| 7 | **Mika Kallio** | FIN | 36 | Pramac Racing Team | Ducati | B | 27 | 45m 52.027s |
| 8 | **Marco Melandri** | ITA | 33 | San Carlo Honda Gresini | Honda | B | 22 | 45m 52.225s |
| 9 | **Randy de Puniet** | FRA | 14 | LCR Honda MotoGP | Honda | B | 27 | 45m 53.968s |
| 10 | **Alvaro Bautista** | SPA | 19 | Rizla Suzuki MotoGP | Suzuki | B | 21 | 45m 54.329s |
| 11 | **Marco Simoncelli** | ITA | 58 | San Carlo Honda Gresini | Honda | B | 27 | 45m 54.693s |
| 12 | **Colin Edwards** | USA | 5 | Monster Yamaha Tech 3 | Yamaha | B | 27 | 45m 55.798s |
| 13 | **Hector Barbera** | SPA | 40 | Paginas Amarillas Aspar | Ducati | B | 27 | 45m 55.909s |
| 14 | **Hiroshi Aoyama** | JPN | 7 | Interwetten Honda MotoGP | Honda | B | 27 | 46m 19.590s |
| 15 | **Aleix Espargaro** | SPA | 41 | Pramac Racing Team | Ducati | B | 24 | 46m 41.784s |
| | Ben Spies | USA | 11 | Monster Yamaha Tech 3 | Yamaha | B | 7 | DNF |
| | Loris Capirossi | ITA | 65 | Rizla Suzuki MotoGP | Suzuki | B | 2 | DNF |

**Fastest lap:** Dani Pedrosa, on lap 2, 1m 39.731s, 99.206mph/159.657km/h (record).
**Previous lap record:** Valentino Rossi, ITA (Yamaha), 1m 39.818s, 99.120mph/159.518km/h (2009).
**Event best maximum speed:** Marco Melandri, 174.6mph/281.0km/h (qualifying practice).

### Qualifying
Weather: Dry
Air Temp: 26° Humidity: 32°
Track Temp: 49°

| 1 | Pedrosa | 1m 39.202s |
|---|---|---|
| 2 | Lorenzo | 1m 39.487s |
| 3 | Stoner | 1m 39.511s |
| 4 | Rossi | 1m 39.558s |
| 5 | Hayden | 1m 39.560s |
| 6 | de Puniet | 1m 39.591s |
| 7 | Edwards | 1m 39.970s |
| 8 | Spies | 1m 39.989s |
| 9 | Dovizioso | 1m 40.021s |
| 10 | Melandri | 1m 40.027s |
| 11 | Capirossi | 1m 40.206s |
| 12 | Aoyama | 1m 40.322s |
| 13 | Bautista | 1m 40.416s |
| 14 | Barbera | 1m 40.482s |
| 15 | Espargaro | 1m 40.555s |
| 16 | Simoncelli | 1m 40.586s |
| 17 | Kallio | 1m 40.803s |

### Fastest race laps

| 1 | Pedrosa | 1m 39.731s |
|---|---|---|
| 2 | Rossi | 1m 39.733s |
| 3 | Stoner | 1m 39.988s |
| 4 | Lorenzo | 1m 40.007s |
| 5 | Hayden | 1m 40.102s |
| 6 | Dovizioso | 1m 40.405s |
| 7 | Capirossi | 1m 40.739s |
| 8 | Melandri | 1m 40.748s |
| 9 | Simoncelli | 1m 40.758s |
| 10 | Edwards | 1m 40.974s |
| 11 | de Puniet | 1m 40.992s |
| 12 | Espargaro | 1m 41.024s |
| 13 | Kallio | 1m 41.044s |
| 14 | Spies | 1m 41.102s |
| 15 | Barbera | 1m 41.266s |
| 16 | Bautista | 1m 41.274s |
| 17 | Aoyama | 1m 41.379s |

### Championship Points

| 1 | Lorenzo | 45 |
|---|---|---|
| 2 | Rossi | 41 |
| 3 | Pedrosa | 29 |
| 4 | Dovizioso | 26 |
| 5 | Hayden | 26 |
| 6 | de Puniet | 17 |
| 7 | Edwards | 12 |
| 8 | Stoner | 11 |
| 9 | Spies | 11 |
| 10 | Melandri | 11 |
| 11 | Simoncelli | 10 |
| 12 | Kallio | 9 |
| 13 | Aoyama | 8 |
| 14 | Capirossi | 7 |
| 15 | Barbera | 7 |
| 16 | Bautista | 6 |
| 17 | Espargaro | 1 |

### Team Points

| 1 | Fiat Yamaha Team | 86 |
|---|---|---|
| 2 | Repsol Honda Team | 55 |
| 3 | Ducati Marlboro Team | 37 |
| 4 | Monster Yamaha Tech 3 | 23 |
| 5 | San Carlo Honda Gresini | 21 |
| 6 | LCR Honda MotoGP | 17 |
| 7 | Rizla Suzuki MotoGP | 13 |
| 8 | Pramac Racing Team | 10 |
| 9 | Interwetten Honda MotoGP | 8 |
| 10 | Paginas Amarillas Aspar | 7 |

### Constructor Points

| 1 | Yamaha | 50 |
|---|---|---|
| 2 | Honda | 36 |
| 3 | Ducati | 26 |
| 4 | Suzuki | 13 |

### Grid order

| Grid order | 1 | 2 | 3 | 4 | 5 | 6 | 7 | 8 | 9 | 10 | 11 | 12 | 13 | 14 | 15 | 16 | 17 | 18 | 19 | 20 | 21 | 22 | 23 | 24 | 25 | 26 | 27 | |
|---|---|---|---|---|---|---|---|---|---|---|---|---|---|---|---|---|---|---|---|---|---|---|---|---|---|---|---|---|
| 26 PEDROSA | 26 | 26 | 26 | 26 | 26 | 26 | 26 | 26 | 26 | 26 | 26 | 26 | 26 | 26 | 26 | 26 | 26 | 26 | 26 | 26 | 26 | 26 | 26 | 26 | 26 | 26 | 99 | 1 |
| 99 LORENZO | 46 | 46 | 46 | 46 | 46 | 46 | 46 | 46 | 46 | 46 | 46 | 46 | 46 | 46 | 46 | 46 | 46 | 46 | 46 | 46 | 99 | 99 | 99 | 99 | 99 | 26 | | 2 |
| 27 STONER | 69 | 69 | 69 | 69 | 69 | 69 | 69 | 69 | 69 | 99 | 99 | 99 | 99 | 99 | 99 | 99 | 99 | 99 | 99 | 99 | 46 | 46 | 46 | 46 | 46 | 46 | | 3 |
| 46 ROSSI | 99 | 27 | 27 | 27 | 99 | 99 | 99 | 99 | 99 | 69 | 69 | 69 | 69 | 69 | 69 | 69 | 69 | 69 | 69 | 69 | 69 | 69 | 69 | 69 | 69 | 69 | | 4 |
| 69 HAYDEN | 27 | 99 | 99 | 99 | 27 | 27 | 27 | 27 | 27 | 27 | 27 | 27 | 27 | 27 | 27 | 27 | 27 | 27 | 27 | 27 | 27 | 27 | 27 | 27 | 27 | 27 | | 5 |
| 14 de PUNIET | 11 | 4 | 4 | 4 | 4 | 4 | 4 | 4 | 4 | 4 | 4 | 4 | 4 | 4 | 4 | 4 | 4 | 4 | 4 | 4 | 4 | 4 | 4 | 4 | 4 | 4 | | 6 |
| 5 EDWARDS | 4 | 11 | 33 | 33 | 33 | 33 | 33 | 33 | 33 | 33 | 58 | 33 | 33 | 33 | 33 | 33 | 33 | 33 | 36 | 33 | 33 | 33 | 36 | 36 | 36 | 36 | | 7 |
| 11 SPIES | 33 | 33 | 58 | 58 | 58 | 58 | 58 | 58 | 58 | 58 | 58 | 33 | 58 | 58 | 58 | 36 | 36 | 36 | 36 | 33 | 58 | 58 | 36 | 33 | 33 | 33 | | 8 |
| 4 DOVIZIOSO | 65 | 65 | 11 | 11 | 11 | 5 | 5 | 5 | 14 | 14 | 14 | 14 | 14 | 14 | 36 | 14 | 14 | 14 | 58 | 36 | 36 | 14 | 14 | 14 | 14 | 14 | | 9 |
| 33 MELANDRI | 5 | 58 | 5 | 5 | 5 | 14 | 14 | 14 | 36 | 36 | 36 | 36 | 36 | 36 | 14 | 58 | 58 | 58 | 14 | 14 | 14 | 58 | 58 | 58 | 58 | 19 | | 10 |
| 65 CAPIROSSI | 58 | 5 | 14 | 14 | 14 | 36 | 36 | 36 | 5 | 5 | 5 | 5 | 5 | 5 | 5 | 5 | 5 | 5 | 5 | 5 | 5 | 5 | 19 | 19 | 19 | 58 | | 11 |
| 7 AOYAMA | 14 | 14 | 36 | 36 | 36 | 11 | 11 | 19 | 19 | 19 | 19 | 19 | 19 | 19 | 19 | 19 | 19 | 19 | 19 | 19 | 19 | 19 | 5 | 5 | 5 | 5 | | 12 |
| 19 BAUTISTA | 36 | 36 | 40 | 40 | 40 | 40 | 40 | 40 | 40 | 40 | 40 | 40 | 40 | 40 | 40 | 40 | 40 | 40 | 40 | 40 | 40 | 40 | 40 | 40 | 40 | | | 13 |
| 40 BARBERA | 40 | 40 | 41 | 19 | 19 | 19 | 40 | 7 | 7 | 7 | 7 | 7 | 7 | 7 | 7 | 7 | 7 | 7 | 7 | 7 | 7 | 7 | 7 | 7 | 7 | | | 14 |
| 41 ESPARGARO | 19 | 41 | 19 | 7 | 7 | 7 | 7 | 41 | 41 | 41 | 41 | 41 | 41 | 41 | 41 | 41 | 41 | 41 | 41 | 41 | 41 | 41 | | | | | | 15 |
| 58 SIMONCELLI | 41 | 19 | 7 | 41 | 41 | 41 | 41 | | | | | | | | | | | | | | | | | | | | | |
| 36 KALLIO | 7 | 7 | | | | | | | | | | | | | | | | | | | | | | | | | | |

41 Lapped rider

## Moto2 RACE DISTANCE: 17 laps, 46.722 miles/75.191 km · RACE WEATHER: Dry (air 26°, humidity 31%, track 41°)

| Pos. | Rider | Nat. | No. | Entrant | Machine | Laps | Time & Speed |
|---|---|---|---|---|---|---|---|
| 1 | **Toni Elias** | SPA | 24 | Gresini Racing Moto2 | Moriwaki | 17 | 29m 58.726s (mph/km/h) 93.509/150.488 |
| 2 | **Shoya Tomizawa** | JPN | 48 | Technomag-CIP | Suter | 17 | 29m 58.916s |
| 3 | **Thomas Luthi** | SWI | 12 | Interwetten Moriwaki Moto2 | Moriwaki | 17 | 29m 58.987s |
| 4 | **Yuki Takahashi** | JPN | 72 | Tech 3 Racing | Tech 3 | 17 | 29m 59.284s |
| 5 | **Simone Corsi** | ITA | 3 | JIR Moto2 | MotoBI | 17 | 30m 00.175s |
| 6 | **Sergio Gadea** | SPA | 40 | Tenerife 40 Pons | Pons Kalex | 17 | 30m 00.222s |
| 7 | **Kenny Noyes** | USA | 9 | Jack & Jones by A.Banderas | Promoharris | 17 | 30m 00.941s |
| 8 | **Julian Simon** | SPA | 60 | Mapfre Aspar Team | RSV | 17 | 30m 01.302s |
| 9 | **Gabor Talmacsi** | HUN | 2 | Fimmco Speed Up | Speed Up | 17 | 30m 02.551s |
| 10 | **Yonny Hernandez** | COL | 68 | Blusens-STX | BQR-Moto2 | 17 | 30m 05.417s |
| 11 | **Jules Cluzel** | FRA | 16 | Forward Racing | Suter | 17 | 30m 06.849s |
| 12 | **Roberto Rolfo** | ITA | 44 | Italtrans S.T.R. | Suter | 17 | 30m 10.691s |
| 13 | **Dominique Aegerter** | SWI | 77 | Technomag-CIP | Suter | 17 | 30m 10.916s |
| 14 | **Stefan Bradl** | GER | 65 | Viessmann Kiefer Racing | Suter | 17 | 30m 11.021s |
| 15 | **Anthony West** | AUS | 8 | MZ Racing Team | MZ-RE Honda | 17 | 30m 11.271s |
| 16 | Scott Redding | GBR | 45 | Marc VDS Racing Team | Suter | 17 | 30m 11.404s |
| 17 | Ratthapark Wilairot | THA | 14 | Thai Honda PTT Singha SAG | Bimota | 17 | 30m 12.274s |
| 18 | Claudio Corti | ITA | 71 | Forward Racing | Suter | 17 | 30m 14.368s |
| 19 | Axel Pons | SPA | 80 | Tenerife 40 Pons | Pons Kalex | 17 | 30m 15.466s |
| 20 | Raffaele de Rosa | ITA | 35 | Tech 3 Racing | Tech 3 | 17 | 30m 18.094s |
| 21 | Fonsi Nieto | SPA | 10 | Holiday Gym G22 | Moriwaki | 17 | 30m 19.682s |
| 22 | Mike di Meglio | FRA | 63 | Mapfre Aspar Team | RSV | 17 | 30m 19.855s |
| 23 | Vladimir Ivanov | UKR | 61 | Gresini Racing Moto2 | Moriwaki | 17 | 30m 29.950s |
| 24 | Robertino Pietri | VEN | 39 | Italtrans S.T.R. | Suter | 17 | 30m 30.001s |
| 25 | Alex Debon | SPA | 6 | Aeroport de Castello - Ajo | FTR | 17 | 30m 32.009s |
| 26 | Lukas Pesek | CZE | 52 | Matteoni CP Racing | Moriwaki | 17 | 30m 32.816s |
| 27 | Bernat Martinez | SPA | 76 | Maquinza-SAG Team | Bimota | 17 | 30m 37.431s |
| 28 | Karel Abraham | CZE | 17 | Cardion AB Motoracing | RSV | 17 | 30m 38.110s |
| 29 | Arne Tode | GER | 41 | Racing Team Germany | Suter | 17 | 30m 42.565s |
| 30 | Amadeo Llados | SPA | 92 | Llados Racing Team | AJR | 17 | 30m 45.622s |
| 31 | Valentin Debise | FRA | 53 | WTR San Marino Team | ADV | 17 | 30m 45.806s |
| 32 | Alex Baldolini | ITA | 25 | Caretta Technology Race Dept. | I.C.P. | 17 | 30m 45.942s |
| 33 | Yannick Guerra | SPA | 88 | Holiday Gym G22 | Moriwaki | 17 | 30m 46.503s |
| 34 | Mashel Al Naimi | QAT | 95 | Blusens-STX | BQR-Moto2 | 17 | 30m 55.321s |
| | Ivan Moreno | SPA | 91 | Andalucia Cajasol | Moriwaki | 8 | DNF |
| | Niccolo Canepa | ITA | 59 | RSM Team Scot | Force GP210 | 8 | DNF |
| | Mattia Pasini | ITA | 75 | JIR Moto2 | MotoBI | 6 | DNF |
| | Hector Faubel | SPA | 55 | Marc VDS Racing Team | Suter | 2 | DNF |
| | Andrea Iannone | ITA | 29 | Fimmco Speed Up | Speed Up | 0 | DNF |
| | Joan Olive | SPA | 5 | Jack & Jones by A.Banderas | Promoharris | 0 | DNF |

**Fastest lap:** Toni Elias, on lap 14, 1m 44.710s, 94.489mph/152.065km/h (record).
**Previous lap record:** New category.
**Event best maximum speed:** Alex Debon, 155.0mph/249.5km/h (warm-up).

**Qualifying:** Dry
Air: 29° Humidity: 33% Ground: 50°

| | | |
|---|---|---|
| 1 | Tomizawa | 1m 44.372s |
| 2 | Simon | 1m 44.374s |
| 3 | Elias | 1m 44.424s |
| 4 | Takahashi | 1m 44.463s |
| 5 | Luthi | 1m 44.573s |
| 6 | Bradl | 1m 44.631s |
| 7 | Talmacsi | 1m 44.661s |
| 8 | Gadea | 1m 44.694s |
| 9 | Noyes | 1m 44.712s |
| 10 | Corsi | 1m 44.722s |
| 11 | West | 1m 44.741s |
| 12 | Hernandez | 1m 44.779s |
| 13 | Debon | 1m 44.783s |
| 14 | Cluzel | 1m 44.810s |
| 15 | de Rosa | 1m 44.943s |
| 16 | Corti | 1m 44.957s |
| 17 | Rolfo | 1m 45.063s |
| 18 | Nieto | 1m 45.149s |
| 19 | Baldolini | 1m 45.179s |
| 20 | Olive | 1m 45.183s |
| 21 | Aegerter | 1m 45.375s |
| 22 | Pons | 1m 45.404s |
| 23 | Tode | 1m 45.412s |
| 24 | Faubel | 1m 45.443s |
| 25 | Abraham | 1m 45.448s |
| 26 | de Angelis | 1m 45.515s |
| 27 | Redding | 1m 45.591s |
| 28 | di Meglio | 1m 45.653s |
| 29 | Iannone | 1m 45.704s |
| 30 | Wilairot | 1m 45.705s |
| 31 | Pietri | 1m 45.770s |
| 32 | Martinez | 1m 45.962s |
| 33 | Pesek | 1m 46.059s |
| 34 | Canepa | 1m 46.084s |
| 35 | Ivanov | 1m 46.366s |
| 36 | Pasini | 1m 46.529s |
| 37 | Llados | 1m 46.550s |
| 38 | Debise | 1m 46.772s |
| 39 | Moreno | 1m 46.806s |
| 40 | Guerra | 1m 47.068s |
| 41 | Al Naimi | 1m 47.793s |
| 42 | Leonov | No Time |

**Fastest race laps**

| | | |
|---|---|---|
| 1 | Elias | 1m 44.710s |
| 2 | Gadea | 1m 44.830s |
| 3 | Takahashi | 1m 44.944s |
| 4 | Luthi | 1m 44.966s |
| 5 | Noyes | 1m 44.992s |
| 6 | Talmacsi | 1m 45.006s |
| 7 | Debon | 1m 45.022s |
| 8 | Corsi | 1m 45.066s |
| 9 | Tomizawa | 1m 45.076s |
| 10 | Cluzel | 1m 45.182s |
| 11 | West | 1m 45.244s |
| 12 | Redding | 1m 45.253s |
| 13 | Simon | 1m 45.259s |
| 14 | Hernandez | 1m 45.338s |
| 15 | Rolfo | 1m 45.381s |
| 16 | Aegerter | 1m 45.420s |
| 17 | Wilairot | 1m 45.481s |
| 18 | Bradl | 1m 45.547s |
| 19 | Corti | 1m 45.569s |
| 20 | Pons | 1m 45.624s |
| 21 | Nieto | 1m 45.650s |
| 22 | di Meglio | 1m 45.807s |
| 23 | de Rosa | 1m 45.845s |
| 24 | Abraham | 1m 45.881s |
| 25 | Baldolini | 1m 46.128s |
| 26 | Moreno | 1m 46.375s |
| 27 | Pietri | 1m 46.405s |
| 28 | Ivanov | 1m 46.416s |
| 29 | Pesek | 1m 46.591s |
| 30 | Martinez | 1m 46.670s |
| 31 | Faubel | 1m 46.687s |
| 32 | Tode | 1m 46.821s |
| 33 | Canepa | 1m 46.940s |
| 34 | Llados | 1m 46.948s |
| 35 | Pasini | 1m 46.963s |
| 36 | Al Naimi | 1m 47.048s |
| 37 | Debise | 1m 47.147s |
| 38 | Guerra | 1m 47.409s |

**Championship Points**

| | | |
|---|---|---|
| 1 | Tomizawa | 45 |
| 2 | Elias | 38 |
| 3 | Luthi | 25 |
| 4 | Cluzel | 21 |
| 5 | Debon | 20 |
| 6 | Corsi | 19 |
| 7 | Gadea | 16 |
| 8 | Rolfo | 15 |
| 9 | Talmacsi | 14 |
| 10 | Takahashi | 13 |
| 11 | Pasini | 10 |
| 12 | Noyes | 9 |
| 13 | Simon | 8 |
| 14 | Aegerter | 8 |
| 15 | Hernandez | 6 |
| 16 | Baldolini | 4 |
| 17 | Nieto | 3 |
| 18 | Bradl | 2 |
| 19 | Abraham | 2 |
| 20 | West | 1 |
| 21 | Pesek | 1 |

**Constructors**

| | | |
|---|---|---|
| 1 | Suter | 45 |
| 2 | Moriwaki | 38 |
| 3 | MotoBI | 21 |
| 4 | FTR | 20 |
| 5 | Pons Kalex | 16 |
| 6 | Speed Up | 14 |
| 7 | Tech 3 | 13 |
| 8 | RSV | 10 |
| 9 | Promoharris | 9 |
| 10 | BQR-Moto2 | 6 |
| 11 | I.C.P. | 4 |
| 12 | MZ-RE Honda | 1 |

## 125cc RACE DISTANCE: 23 laps, 63.211 miles/101.729 km · RACE WEATHER: Dry (air 27°, humidity 39%, track 40°)

| Pos. | Rider | Nat. | No. | Entrant | Machine | Laps | Time & Speed |
|---|---|---|---|---|---|---|---|
| 1 | **Pol Espargaro** | SPA | 44 | Tuenti Racing | Derbi | 23 | 41m 36.146s (mph/km/h) 91.164/146.715 |
| 2 | **Nicolas Terol** | SPA | 40 | Bancaja Aspar Team | Aprilia | 23 | 41m 38.032s |
| 3 | **Esteve Rabat** | SPA | 12 | Blusens-STX | Aprilia | 23 | 41m 51.326s |
| 4 | **Bradley Smith** | GBR | 38 | Bancaja Aspar Team | Aprilia | 23 | 41m 53.256s |
| 5 | **Tomoyoshi Koyama** | JPN | 71 | Racing Team Germany | Aprilia | 23 | 42m 01.215s |
| 6 | **Alberto Moncayo** | SPA | 23 | Andalucia Cajasol | Aprilia | 23 | 42m 03.006s |
| 7 | **Johann Zarco** | FRA | 14 | WTR San Marino Team | Aprilia | 23 | 42m 03.248s |
| 8 | **Randy Krummenacher** | SWI | 35 | Stipa-Molenaar Racing GP | Aprilia | 23 | 42m 04.611s |
| 9 | **Alexis Masbou** | FRA | 5 | Ongetta Team | Aprilia | 23 | 42m 05.109s |
| 10 | **Jasper Iwema** | NED | 53 | CBC Corse | Aprilia | 23 | 42m 34.976s |
| 11 | **Sandro Cortese** | GER | 11 | Avant Mitsubishi Ajo | Derbi | 23 | 42m 39.181s |
| 12 | **Marcel Schrotter** | GER | 78 | Interwetten Honda 125 | Honda | 23 | 42m 40.868s |
| 13 | **Adrian Martin** | SPA | 26 | Aeroport de Castello - Ajo | Aprilia | 23 | 42m 40.987s |
| 14 | **Jakub Kornfeil** | CZE | 84 | Racing Team Germany | Aprilia | 23 | 42m 41.394s |
| 15 | **Luis Salom** | SPA | 39 | Lambretta Reparto Corse | Lambretta | 23 | 42m 45.446s |
| 16 | Isaac Vinales | SPA | 57 | Catalunya Racing Team | Aprilia | 23 | 42m 45.686s |
| 17 | Luca Marconi | ITA | 87 | Ongetta Team | Aprilia | 23 | 43m 11.072s |
| 18 | Joan Perello | SPA | 58 | SAG Castrol | Honda | 23 | 43m 18.841s |
| 19 | Johnny Rosell | SPA | 59 | SAG Castrol | Honda | 23 | 43m 27.630s |
| 20 | Zulfahmi Khairuddin | MAL | 63 | AirAsia-Sepang Int. Circuit | Aprilia | 23 | 43m 27.671s |
| 21 | Quentin Jacquet | FRA | 80 | Stipa-Molenaar Racing GP | Aprilia | 22 | 41m 36.547s |
| 22 | Marco Ravaioli | ITA | 72 | Lambretta Reparto Corse | Lambretta | 22 | 41m 39.765s |
| | Jonas Folger | GER | 94 | Ongetta Team | Aprilia | 22 | DNF |
| | Danny Webb | GBR | 99 | Andalucia Cajasol | Aprilia | 21 | DNF |
| | Efren Vazquez | SPA | 7 | Tuenti Racing | Derbi | 18 | DNF |
| | Michael van der Mark | NED | 60 | Team Sachsenring | Aprilia | 15 | DNF |
| | Louis Rossi | FRA | 69 | CBC Corse | Aprilia | 14 | DNF |
| | Riccardo Moretti | ITA | 51 | Fontana Racing | Aprilia | 5 | DNF |
| | Sturla Fagerhaug | NOR | 50 | AirAsia-Sepang Int. Circuit | Aprilia | 1 | DNF |
| | Lorenzo Savadori | ITA | 32 | Matteoni CP Racing | Aprilia | 0 | DNF |
| | Marc Marquez | SPA | 93 | Red Bull Ajo Motorsport | Derbi | 0 | DNF |

**Fastest lap:** Sandro Cortese, on lap 3, 1m 47.493s, 92.042mph/148.128km/h.
**Lap record:** Julian Simon, SPA (Aprilia), 1m 47.057s, 92.417mph/148.731km/h (2009).
**Event best maximum speed:** Marc Marquez, 135.0mph/217.2km/h (free practice 1).

**Qualifying:** Dry
Air: 25° Humidity: 34% Ground: 45°

| | | |
|---|---|---|
| 1 | Marquez | 1m 46.829s |
| 2 | Espargaro | 1m 46.933s |
| 3 | Vazquez | 1m 47.275s |
| 4 | Rabat | 1m 47.379s |
| 5 | Terol | 1m 47.443s |
| 6 | Cortese | 1m 47.645s |
| 7 | Smith | 1m 47.753s |
| 8 | Webb | 1m 48.164s |
| 9 | Moncayo | 1m 48.700s |
| 10 | Krummenacher | 1m 48.727s |
| 11 | Koyama | 1m 48.880s |
| 12 | Zarco | 1m 48.982s |
| 13 | Iwema | 1m 49.030s |
| 14 | Vinales | 1m 49.604s |
| 15 | Martin | 1m 49.752s |
| 16 | Rossi | 1m 49.817s |
| 17 | Masbou | 1m 49.826s |
| 18 | Schrotter | 1m 49.911s |
| 19 | Folger | 1m 49.925s |
| 20 | Kornfeil | 1m 49.947s |
| 21 | Marconi | 1m 50.077s |
| 22 | Savadori | 1m 50.474s |
| 23 | Fagerhaug | 1m 50.614s |
| 24 | Perello | 1m 50.724s |
| 25 | Salom | 1m 50.755s |
| 26 | Rosell | 1m 50.771s |
| 27 | Moretti | 1m 51.184s |
| 28 | Jacquet | 1m 51.797s |
| 29 | van der Mark | 1m 51.945s |
| 30 | Ravaioli | 1m 52.798s |
| 31 | Khairuddin | 1m 53.546s |

**Fastest race laps**

| | | |
|---|---|---|
| 1 | Cortese | 1m 47.493s |
| 2 | Vazquez | 1m 47.645s |
| 3 | Espargaro | 1m 47.658s |
| 4 | Terol | 1m 47.730s |
| 5 | Rabat | 1m 47.748s |
| 6 | Smith | 1m 48.120s |
| 7 | Krummenacher | 1m 48.124s |
| 8 | Moncayo | 1m 48.389s |
| 9 | Koyama | 1m 48.426s |
| 10 | Iwema | 1m 48.605s |
| 11 | Zarco | 1m 48.779s |
| 12 | Webb | 1m 48.786s |
| 13 | Masbou | 1m 48.790s |
| 14 | Folger | 1m 48.916s |
| 15 | Moretti | 1m 49.635s |
| 16 | Schrotter | 1m 49.860s |
| 17 | Kornfeil | 1m 50.336s |
| 18 | Martin | 1m 50.366s |
| 19 | Marconi | 1m 50.378s |
| 20 | Rossi | 1m 50.411s |
| 21 | Vinales | 1m 50.496s |
| 22 | Salom | 1m 50.632s |
| 23 | Perello | 1m 51.157s |
| 24 | van der Mark | 1m 51.886s |
| 25 | Jacquet | 1m 51.982s |
| 26 | Ravaioli | 1m 52.085s |
| 27 | Khairuddin | 1m 52.169s |
| 28 | Rosell | 1m 52.419s |
| 29 | Fagerhaug | 2m 02.596s |

**Championship Points**

| | | |
|---|---|---|
| 1 | Terol | 45 |
| 2 | Espargaro | 38 |
| 3 | Rabat | 25 |
| 4 | Smith | 21 |
| 5 | Vazquez | 20 |
| 6 | Koyama | 18 |
| 7 | Krummenacher | 18 |
| 8 | Marquez | 16 |
| 9 | Cortese | 16 |
| 10 | Moncayo | 13 |
| 11 | Zarco | 13 |
| 12 | Masbou | 13 |
| 13 | Iwema | 8 |
| 14 | Webb | 5 |
| 15 | Schrotter | 4 |
| 16 | Martin | 3 |
| 17 | Kornfeil | 2 |
| 18 | Salom | 1 |
| 19 | Folger | 1 |

**Constructors**

| | | |
|---|---|---|
| 1 | Derbi | 45 |
| 2 | Aprilia | 45 |
| 3 | Honda | 4 |
| 4 | Lambretta | 1 |

FIM WORLD CHAMPIONSHIP · ROUND 3

# FRENCH GRAND PRIX

LE MANS CIRCUIT

Main photo: Yamahas in control, and Lorenzo in control of Rossi.

Inset: Lorenzo's second win in a row put his team-mate under increasing pressure.
Photos: Gold & Goose

T HE championship battle that had looked so promising at the start of the year sustained a blow in France, when Casey Stoner did it again. The race had just begun and, confident that he had the pace to challenge for a win, he was closing on the other three aliens ahead. Then he was down, the red bike skittering away as the treacherous front end folded underneath the Australian. Three races, two disastrous no-scores: even he knew he was being left badly behind. "I've made the championship very difficult for myself," he said. "If not impossible."

Le Mans had accorded a warmer welcome than usual, at least with regard to the weather, with bright sunshine enjoyed by a good crowd of 82,270. Warmer and drier, and smoother to boot. Resurfacing had addressed the many complaints about bumps and low grip. But not sufficiently warmer to prevent, for a second race, an uncomfortable number of crashes in Free Practice Two. The significance of this second session is such: riders who have got up to speed the previous afternoon are faced with lower morning temperatures for the first time. The combination can lead to a bit too much confidence in cold tyres, proving that while the Bridgestones continue to earn praise from the riders for their consistency, they certainly need careful warming up. A continuation of this phenomenon over the coming races would count Rossi among its victims, and would see an experimental return to a Friday-morning first session later in the year.

The morning crashes came even though Bridgestone had acceded to rider requests and brought asymmetric mixed-compound tyres, the first of 11 races in 2010. Victims this time were Spies, Bautista and Kallio, and all were injured. The American flipped at the chicane and bashed his left ankle hard; Kallio landed on his shoulder, hurting it badly enough to cause problems for several weeks to come. Bautista knocked himself out of the race.

Some thought he should never have been in it. A week before, he'd become the latest victim of an off-track mo-

tocross training crash, breaking his left collar-bone. It was hastily plated, and now he was back on the bike and clearly struggling even before he went looping high in the air to land heavily on the same shoulder.

In the wake of Rossi and Lorenzo, and many previous examples, this raised questions about whether such high-intensity training is wise, in a cotton-wool age. Motocross is a valuable tool for keeping motorcycling reflexes sharp, especially throttle control, and also a thorough fitness regime. And with the opportunities to ride their MotoGP bikes severely restricted, the off-roaders have become even more useful. But in this season alone, Lorenzo, Rossi and now Bautista had compromised their racing with injuries sustained playbiking, and there have been plenty of examples before. One such was Nicky Hayden, who smashed his heel in a stadium supercross outing in 2008 while riding for Repsol Honda, causing him to miss two races. Honda turned a blind eye. "You can cycle and swim, run and work out at the gym like a he-man, but it's not like being on a bike. It's not something you do just for fun and jokes. Honda understood it is valuable, in spite of the risk."

Rossi had expected to be free from shoulder problems after another fortnight's recovery, but the pain was lingering. He was unable to lift his right arm above his shoulder; on the bike, he explained that hard braking (and there is plenty of that at Le Mans) was the difficulty.

All were fresh from the first of only two post-race tests: a day at Jerez, where Dani had topped the time sheets, ahead of Rossi and Lorenzo – the first two also had crashed, Rossi at low speed. Dani had made a little more chassis progress with the latest version he had raced; Dovizioso had also tried it. No one else had much in the way of new stuff to test, but it was a chance to go galloping without having to worry about engine life; Lorenzo used the time to practice 25 starts, to avoid repeating his low-key get-go from the day before.

The Honda chassis question was not only exercising Pedrosa's team: Melandri had hoped for much by switching back to his old Gresini Honda team, but he was struggling to do better than his rookie team-mate, Simoncelli, who in turn had yet to pick up the pace. Always ready to try something different (it was he who had persuaded Gresini to switch early to Bridgestone from Michelin), Melandri and his team gained permission from Honda not only to go back to the Showa suspension recently rejected by the factory team, but also to make chassis modifications, revising stiffness in key areas. It was the start of the awaited improvement.

Moto2 continued to grab attention, with Le Mans first-timer Noyes taking a surprise pole, the first American to do so in the secondary class since John Kocinski in his 250 title year of 1990. The Aspar team, dismayed by poor results so far, as well as the amount of development required by their RSV chassis, switched to class-favourite Suter gear for riders Simon and di Meglio. And a new rule allowed riders to wait until after the first free practice before deciding on their seventh and final front Dunlop, having already been allocated three each of the two compounds available.

Most of the chatter concerned the intensifying rumours: Stoner to Honda, Rossi to Ducati, the possible early introduction (as with Moto2) of one-litre privateer-level MotoGP bikes to swell the grid in 2011, the chance of running heats to accommodate more Moto2 bikes, and the imminent demise of 125 two-strokes in favour of a low-cost four-stroke alternative. Most of them were true.

## MOTOGP RACE – 28 laps

No one could remember when all practice sessions at Le Mans had been dry, and Rossi celebrated by taking pole from Lorenzo. Pedrosa was alongside, the two Ducatis next.

With the sun baking down and the track temperature a torrid 51 degrees, the slender grid of 16 (minus Bautista) filed through the first left-right combination and under the

*Above:* Playboy girl was de Puniet's grid companion.

*Top:* Early in the race, Melandri leads Dovizioso, de Puniet, Spies and Co.

Photos: Gold & Goose

Dunlop Bridge with none of the usual scrapes and tumbles, Rossi in front.

For once, Pedrosa was second, but Lorenzo managed to force past the Honda before the end of the lap. Hayden was fourth, soon to be passed by Stoner; Melandri was ahead of Dovizioso.

Stoner was closing rapidly on the three leaders when he found himself fighting a long, but losing battle with a front-end slide on the way into the first looping right-hander on only the third lap. All efforts to save it with his knee, then his elbow, were in vain, and the front eventually tucked terminally. He was distraught. All through practice, he'd been trying to provoke front-end slides, to address the problem, but it had stuck like glue. "It feels like I'm being teased," he said, adding that he had been the only rider with the pace to match Lorenzo.

On the same lap, Dovizioso also passed Hayden, but then was unable to catch his team-mate, a second's gap stretching towards two as the race approached half-distance.

Rossi was leading, but Lorenzo was with him every step of the way; Pedrosa was in close attendance. Rossi's braking distances were stretching; he was slowing them up.

Lorenzo's first attack came on lap seven. He went flying past through the daunting first corner. Rossi went straight back under him braking for the following left-right combination; Lorenzo went around the outside on the second part, but Rossi emerged in front. "Just for fun," he said. He knew the end was inevitable.

Now Jorge showed growing maturity. "A couple of years ago, maybe I would have done a crazy thing, but now I feel able to stay quiet and to ride better."

On lap 12, he swept past into the same corner combination and immediately started to pull clear. After five laps, the gap was better than three seconds and stretching. Lorenzo also set fastest lap, short of Rossi's 2008 record, on lap 15. It was a massive win.

By now, Pedrosa was dropping back, and Rossi, running out of strength, had settled for second. This gave his team serious misgivings about the forthcoming Mugello race, with its fast direction changes.

By lap 17, Dovizioso had caught Pedrosa and was looking in vain for a way past. At the same time, Hayden was also closing again.

Dovizioso waited until the last lap to make his attack, at the same place where Lorenzo had passed Rossi. Dani chased hard, at the same time trying to defend himself from Hayden, who now was almost on his back wheel. It all went wrong in the final corner, however: Pedrosa defended the entry, only to run wide in the middle of the corner, giving Nicky an open invitation for a third successive fourth place. It was revenge also for Dovizioso, who had lost third to Pedrosa in 2009.

Melandri had his best race in ages, sticking with Hayden until after half-distance. After that, he decided to "pull the oars in" and go for his best finish of the year.

Then came de Puniet, gradually losing touch and ending up eight seconds adrift.

The next group almost caught him, after a to-and-fro struggle that made up for a lack of action up front. Simoncelli had dominated for most of the race, but with two laps to go Barbera took to the front, then also Espargaro. Aoyama had played a leading role until a big wobble on lap 23 lost him almost a second.

Edwards was feeling bleak after failing to stay with the rookies. Unable to get comfortable, he couldn't find the confidence to push.

Kallio was stiff and sore, in spite of pain killing injections. "Every lap, I was a second slower than I should be," he said, but soldiering on did net him three points.

Capirossi and Spies fell almost together on lap seven at an unusual place, the fast left-hander after the Dunlop Bridge. Neither could explain it. "I saw Capirossi lose the front, and as soon as I tipped it in, I lost the front too, and I was down," said Spies.

## MOTO2 RACE – 26 laps

The closest qualifying in GP history put 27 riders within a second of pole, which was set by new boy Noyes, clearly awestruck to find himself sitting next to Rossi and Lorenzo in the Press briefing after qualifying. Takahashi, Debon and Cluzel were his front-row companions; Elias was down in seventh after falling at the start of qualifying.

The race wasn't as close, as crashes and misadventures cut the field down by a quarter in the first ten laps, and eliminated several fancied runners, including Noyes.

A crash in the first left-right corners was fortunately near the back of the huge pack, eliminating Aegerter and Abraham as popular veteran Debon headed a four-bike runaway from Elias, Noyes and Cluzel.

The first to go was Debon, called into the pits for a ride-through for jumping the start.

On lap five, Noyes also checked out, losing the front over a change of surface on the final left-hander.

This left just Elias and Cluzel up front, and on lap six the Frenchman, infused with home-race heroism, put in a daring pass and started to move away rapidly from the former MotoGP rider, setting fastest lap in the process. He led over the line, but as he tipped it into Turn One, the front gave way under him and he went tumbling into the gravel at high speed; as he lay there, he was almost hit by another sliding rider.

Takahashi had already fallen while trying to catch the leaders, with 21 laps to go; team-mate de Rosa and Luthi were also out. It went on this way, mainly over the first ten laps, with a total of 13 crashes. The unluckiest victim was de Angelis, who had been running into Turn Two when he was T-boned by the riderless bike of Simeon, who had fallen at the previous corner.

This all left Elias with a strong lead, and although second-placed Simon was less than two seconds behind all the way to the flag, the victory was clear.

Third was hotly disputed by Corsi and Iannone, the latter losing touch by a couple of seconds only in the closing laps.

Fifth was also in contention as a group closed up towards the finish. Talmacsi managed to hold them off. Nieto had been hounding him most of the way, but at the finish an impressive Gadea had moved through from 16th on lap four to sixth, with Wilairot following to consign Nieto to eighth.

Another big gang disputed ninth, Bradl eventually coming through past Rolfo, with Redding, Hernandez, Pesek and Baldolini close behind.

Tomizawa was among the crashers, falling early after battling through to 12th from a bad start; Pons, Pasini and Faubel were also on the list. In spite of his injuries, Elias extended his early overall lead again.

## 125cc RACE – 24 laps

Terol's first pole put him at the head of compatriots Espargaro and Marquez, the pair split by Cortese. Smith led the second row, at a track where his puzzling lack of top speed was of less consequence.

Terol made a blazing start and was almost a second clear at the end of lap one. "I wanted to make sure the leading group was as small as possible," he explained. Indeed, only one rider was able to catch him. Espargaro had closed up by lap three, leaving the rest trailing.

Terol did most of the leading, but Espargaro looked as though he was biding his time, and so it proved. The first time he got ahead was on lap 16, but Terol fought back to lead the next two laps. At the start of the 19th, Espargaro took over again with a daring swoop through Turn One and was never headed, winning by almost a second. He was the 13th consecutive Spanish 125 winner.

Smith held third for most of the race, a group forming up behind. By the end, it was four strong and the pressure was severe, Marquez setting a new record on the penultimate lap as he slotted into fourth.

Smith led the first third of the final lap, riding on the limit. Then a slip at Museum Corner pitched him out of the seat momentarily. It was enough to let Marquez past. Smith fought back and seemed to have stuffed it under the tough little Spaniard in the final corners. But Marquez wouldn't give way and the pair collided, sending Smith off towards the outside and letting Vazquez past him as well. Cortese was on Smith's back wheel.

Rabat had dropped back in seventh, with Koyama right with him. Webb was half a minute behind in ninth place.

*Top:* Elias took a second win in a row, and a championship lead he would never lose.

*Above:* Espargaro and Terol locked in combat – it was two in a row also for Pol, and his last for a long spell.

*Left:* Bradley Smith receives a last-minute grid download, his leathers already scuffed.

*Photos: Gold & Goose*

**LE MANS – BUGATTI**

Garage Vert
78/49

Chemin aux
Boeufs
67/42

La
Chappelle
191/119

Le Musée
244/152

"S" du Garage Bleu
130/81

Chicane
Dunlop
83/52

Courbe Dunlop
266/166

Raccordement 78/49

Key
96/60 kph/mph

Gear

Circuit: 4.180km / 2.597 miles, 28 laps

## MotoGP

**RACE DISTANCE: 28 laps, 74.812 miles/117.180 km · RACE WEATHER: Dry (air 32°, humidity 21%, track 51°)**

| Pos. | Rider | Nat. | No. | Entrant | Machine | Tyres | Laps | Time & speed |
|------|-------|------|-----|---------|---------|-------|------|--------------|
| 1 | **Jorge Lorenzo** | SPA | 99 | Fiat Yamaha Team | Yamaha | B | 28 | 44m 29.114s 98.206mph/ 158.047km/h |
| 2 | **Valentino Rossi** | ITA | 46 | Fiat Yamaha Team | Yamaha | B | 28 | 44m 34.786s |
| 3 | **Andrea Dovizioso** | ITA | 4 | Repsol Honda Team | Honda | B | 28 | 44m 36.986s |
| 4 | **Nicky Hayden** | USA | 69 | Ducati Marlboro Team | Ducati | B | 28 | 44m 38.460s |
| 5 | **Dani Pedrosa** | SPA | 26 | Repsol Honda Team | Honda | B | 28 | 44m 41.727s |
| 6 | **Marco Melandri** | ITA | 33 | San Carlo Honda Gresini | Honda | B | 28 | 44m 51.032s |
| 7 | **Randy de Puniet** | FRA | 14 | LCR Honda MotoGP | Honda | B | 28 | 44m 58.402s |
| 8 | **Hector Barbera** | SPA | 40 | Paginas Amarillas Aspar | Ducati | B | 28 | 45m 02.242s |
| 9 | **Aleix Espargaro** | SPA | 41 | Pramac Racing Team | Ducati | B | 28 | 45m 02.607s |
| 10 | **Marco Simoncelli** | ITA | 58 | San Carlo Honda Gresini | Honda | B | 28 | 45m 02.919s |
| 11 | **Hiroshi Aoyama** | JPN | 7 | Interwetten Honda MotoGP | Honda | B | 28 | 45m 03.460s |
| 12 | **Colin Edwards** | USA | 5 | Monster Yamaha Tech 3 | Yamaha | B | 28 | 45m 06.237s |
| 13 | **Mika Kallio** | FIN | 36 | Pramac Racing Team | Ducati | B | 28 | 45m 24.175s |
| | Loris Capirossi | ITA | 65 | Rizla Suzuki MotoGP | Suzuki | B | 6 | DNF |
| | Ben Spies | USA | 11 | Monster Yamaha Tech 3 | Yamaha | B | 6 | DNF |
| | Casey Stoner | AUS | 27 | Ducati Marlboro Team | Ducati | B | 2 | DNF |

**Fastest lap:** Jorge Lorenzo, on lap 15, 1m 34.545s, 99.017mph/159.352km/h.

**Lap record:** Valentino Rossi, ITA (Yamaha), 1m 34.215s, 99.363mph/159.910km/h (2008).

**Event best maximum speed:** Valentino Rossi, 180.6mph/290.6km/h (qualifying practice).

### Qualifying

Weather: Dry
Air Temp: 28° Humidity: 27°
Track Temp: 46°

| | | |
|---|---|---|
| 1 | Rossi | 1m 33.408s |
| 2 | Lorenzo | 1m 33.462s |
| 3 | Pedrosa | 1m 33.573s |
| 4 | Stoner | 1m 33.824s |
| 5 | Hayden | 1m 33.845s |
| 6 | de Puniet | 1m 34.074s |
| 7 | Dovizioso | 1m 34.204s |
| 8 | Edwards | 1m 34.304s |
| 9 | Capirossi | 1m 34.306s |
| 10 | Espargaro | 1m 34.514s |
| 11 | Melandri | 1m 34.523s |
| 12 | Spies | 1m 34.920s |
| 13 | Simoncelli | 1m 34.942s |
| 14 | Aoyama | 1m 34.979s |
| 15 | Barbera | 1m 35.323s |
| 16 | Kallio | 1m 35.810s |

### Fastest race laps

| | | |
|---|---|---|
| 1 | Lorenzo | 1m 34.545s |
| 2 | Rossi | 1m 34.586s |
| 3 | Pedrosa | 1m 34.632s |
| 4 | Dovizioso | 1m 34.756s |
| 5 | Hayden | 1m 35.006s |
| 6 | Melandri | 1m 35.127s |
| 7 | de Puniet | 1m 35.300s |
| 8 | Spies | 1m 35.403s |
| 9 | Capirossi | 1m 35.413s |
| 10 | Edwards | 1m 35.527s |
| 11 | Aoyama | 1m 35.540s |
| 12 | Stoner | 1m 35.577s |
| 13 | Barbera | 1m 35.611s |
| 14 | Espargaro | 1m 35.667s |
| 15 | Simoncelli | 1m 35.738s |
| 16 | Kallio | 1m 36.417s |

### Championship Points

| | | |
|---|---|---|
| 1 | Lorenzo | 70 |
| 2 | Rossi | 61 |
| 3 | Dovizioso | 42 |
| 4 | Pedrosa | 40 |
| 5 | Hayden | 39 |
| 6 | de Puniet | 26 |
| 7 | Melandri | 21 |
| 8 | Edwards | 16 |
| 9 | Simoncelli | 16 |
| 10 | Barbera | 15 |
| 11 | Aoyama | 13 |
| 12 | Kallio | 12 |
| 13 | Stoner | 11 |
| 14 | Spies | 11 |
| 15 | Espargaro | 8 |
| 16 | Capirossi | 7 |
| 17 | Bautista | 6 |

### Team Points

| | | |
|---|---|---|
| 1 | Fiat Yamaha Team | 131 |
| 2 | Repsol Honda Team | 82 |
| 3 | Ducati Marlboro Team | 50 |
| 4 | San Carlo Honda Gresini | 37 |
| 5 | Monster Yamaha Tech 3 | 27 |
| 6 | LCR Honda MotoGP | 26 |
| 7 | Pramac Racing Team | 20 |
| 8 | Paginas Amarillas Aspar | 15 |
| 9 | Rizla Suzuki MotoGP | 13 |
| 10 | Interwetten Honda MotoGP | 13 |

### Constructor Points

| | | |
|---|---|---|
| 1 | Yamaha | 75 |
| 2 | Honda | 52 |
| 3 | Ducati | 39 |
| 4 | Suzuki | 13 |

| Grid order | 1 | 2 | 3 | 4 | 5 | 6 | 7 | 8 | 9 | 10 | 11 | 12 | 13 | 14 | 15 | 16 | 17 | 18 | 19 | 20 | 21 | 22 | 23 | 24 | 25 | 26 | 27 | 28 | |
|------------|---|---|---|---|---|---|---|---|---|----|----|----|----|----|----|----|----|----|----|----|----|----|----|----|----|----|----|----|---|
| 46 ROSSI | 46 | 46 | 46 | 46 | 46 | 46 | 46 | 46 | 46 | 46 | 46 | 99 | 99 | 99 | 99 | 99 | 99 | 99 | 99 | 99 | 99 | 99 | 99 | 99 | 99 | 99 | 99 | 99 | 1 |
| 99 LORENZO | 99 | 99 | 99 | 99 | 99 | 99 | 99 | 99 | 99 | 99 | 99 | 46 | 46 | 46 | 46 | 46 | 46 | 46 | 46 | 46 | 46 | 46 | 46 | 46 | 46 | 46 | 46 | 46 | 2 |
| 26 PEDROSA | 26 | 26 | 26 | 26 | 26 | 26 | 26 | 26 | 26 | 26 | 26 | 26 | 26 | 26 | 26 | 26 | 26 | 26 | 26 | 26 | 26 | 26 | 26 | 26 | 26 | 26 | 26 | 4 | 3 |
| 27 STONER | 69 | 27 | 4 | 4 | 4 | 4 | 4 | 4 | 4 | 4 | 4 | 4 | 4 | 4 | 4 | 4 | 4 | 4 | 4 | 4 | 4 | 4 | 4 | 4 | 4 | 4 | 4 | 69 | 4 |
| 69 HAYDEN | 27 | 69 | 69 | 69 | 69 | 69 | 69 | 69 | 69 | 69 | 69 | 69 | 69 | 69 | 69 | 69 | 69 | 69 | 69 | 69 | 69 | 69 | 69 | 69 | 69 | 69 | 26 | 5 |
| 14 de PUNIET | 33 | 4 | 33 | 33 | 33 | 33 | 33 | 33 | 33 | 33 | 33 | 33 | 33 | 33 | 33 | 33 | 33 | 33 | 33 | 33 | 33 | 33 | 33 | 33 | 33 | 33 | 33 | 6 |
| 4 DOVIZIOSO | 4 | 33 | 14 | 14 | 14 | 14 | 14 | 14 | 14 | 14 | 14 | 14 | 14 | 14 | 14 | 14 | 14 | 14 | 14 | 14 | 14 | 14 | 14 | 14 | 14 | 14 | 14 | 7 |
| 5 EDWARDS | 14 | 14 | 5 | 5 | 5 | 65 | 58 | 58 | 58 | 58 | 58 | 58 | 58 | 58 | 58 | 58 | 58 | 58 | 58 | 58 | 58 | 58 | 58 | 58 | 40 | 40 | 8 |
| 65 CAPIROSSI | 5 | 5 | 65 | 65 | 65 | 58 | 5 | 5 | 5 | 5 | 5 | 5 | 5 | 5 | 5 | 5 | 5 | 5 | 5 | 5 | 40 | 40 | 40 | 58 | 41 | 9 |
| 41 ESPARGARO | 58 | 65 | 58 | 58 | 58 | 5 | 40 | 40 | 40 | 40 | 40 | 7 | 7 | 7 | 7 | 7 | 7 | 41 | 41 | 40 | 40 | 40 | 5 | 5 | 5 | 41 | 58 | 10 |
| 33 MELANDRI | 65 | 58 | 11 | 11 | 11 | 11 | 41 | 7 | 7 | 7 | 41 | 41 | 41 | 41 | 41 | 41 | 41 | 7 | 40 | 7 | 7 | 41 | 41 | 41 | 41 | 7 | 7 | 11 |
| 11 SPIES | 41 | 41 | 40 | 40 | 40 | 40 | 7 | 41 | 41 | 41 | 41 | 40 | 40 | 40 | 40 | 40 | 40 | 40 | 7 | 41 | 41 | 7 | 7 | 7 | 7 | 5 | 5 | 12 |
| 58 SIMONCELLI | 11 | 11 | 41 | 41 | 41 | 41 | 36 | 36 | 36 | 36 | 36 | 36 | 36 | 36 | 36 | 36 | 36 | 36 | 36 | 36 | 36 | 36 | 36 | 36 | 36 | 36 | 36 | 13 |
| 7 AOYAMA | 40 | 40 | 7 | 7 | 7 | 7 | | | | | | | | | | | | | | | | | | | | | | |
| 40 BARBERA | 7 | 36 | 36 | 36 | 36 | 36 | | | | | | | | | | | | | | | | | | | | | | |
| 36 KALLIO | 36 | 7 | | | | | | | | | | | | | | | | | | | | | | | | | | |

## Moto2 — RACE DISTANCE: 26 laps, 67.611 miles/108.810 km · RACE WEATHER: Dry (air 31°, humidity 21%, track 46°)

| Pos. | Rider | Nat. | No. | Entrant | Machine | Laps | Time & Speed |
|---|---|---|---|---|---|---|---|
| 1 | **Toni Elias** | SPA | 24 | Gresini Racing Moto2 | Moriwaki | 26 | 43m 29.277s (mph/km/h) 93.283/150.124 |
| 2 | **Julian Simon** | SPA | 60 | Mapfre Aspar Team | Suter | 26 | 43m 30.613s |
| 3 | **Simone Corsi** | ITA | 3 | JIR Moto2 | MotoBI | 26 | 43m 32.108s |
| 4 | **Andrea Iannone** | ITA | 29 | Fimmco Speed Up | Speed Up | 26 | 43m 34.157s |
| 5 | **Gabor Talmacsi** | HUN | 2 | Fimmco Speed Up | Speed Up | 26 | 43m 42.570s |
| 6 | **Sergio Gadea** | SPA | 40 | Tenerife 40 Pons | Pons Kalex | 26 | 43m 42.692s |
| 7 | **Ratthapark Wilairot** | THA | 14 | Thai Honda PTT Singha SAG | Bimota | 26 | 43m 43.571s |
| 8 | **Fonsi Nieto** | SPA | 10 | Holiday Gym G22 | Moriwaki | 26 | 43m 43.831s |
| 9 | **Stefan Bradl** | GER | 65 | Viessmann Kiefer Racing | Suter | 26 | 43m 52.780s |
| 10 | **Roberto Rolfo** | ITA | 44 | Italtrans S.T.R. | Suter | 26 | 43m 52.964s |
| 11 | **Scott Redding** | GBR | 45 | Marc VDS Racing Team | Suter | 26 | 43m 53.236s |
| 12 | **Yonny Hernandez** | COL | 68 | Blusens-STX | BQR-Moto2 | 26 | 43m 54.232s |
| 13 | **Lukas Pesek** | CZE | 52 | Matteoni CP Racing | Moriwaki | 26 | 43m 54.345s |
| 14 | **Alex Baldolini** | ITA | 25 | Caretta Technology Race Dept. | I.C.P. | 26 | 43m 55.300s |
| 15 | **Claudio Corti** | ITA | 71 | Forward Racing | Suter | 26 | 43m 58.042s |
| 16 | Alex Debon | SPA | 6 | Aeroport de Castello - Ajo | FTR | 26 | 44m 01.517s |
| 17 | Niccolo Canepa | ITA | 59 | RSM Team Scot | Force GP210 | 26 | 44m 02.884s |
| 18 | Arne Tode | GER | 41 | Racing Team Germany | Suter | 26 | 44m 04.066s |
| 19 | Thomas Luthi | SWI | 12 | Interwetten Moriwaki Moto2 | Moriwaki | 26 | 44m 12.457s |
| 20 | Mike di Meglio | FRA | 63 | Mapfre Aspar Team | Suter | 26 | 44m 12.799s |
| 21 | Vladimir Ivanov | UKR | 61 | Gresini Racing Moto2 | Moriwaki | 26 | 44m 17.038s |
| 22 | Valentin Debise | FRA | 53 | WTR San Marino Team | ADV | 26 | 44m 20.848s |
| 23 | Robertino Pietri | VEN | 39 | Italtrans S.T.R. | Suter | 26 | 44m 28.969s |
| 24 | Joan Olive | SPA | 5 | Jack & Jones by A.Banderas | Promoharris | 26 | 44m 29.216s |
| 25 | Yannick Guerra | SPA | 88 | Holiday Gym G22 | Moriwaki | 26 | 44m 36.654s |
| 26 | Anthony West | AUS | 8 | MZ Racing Team | MZ-RE Honda | 26 | 44m 45.448s |
| 27 | Vladimir Leonov | RUS | 21 | Vector Kiefer Racing | Suter | 26 | 44m 45.805s |
| 28 | Mashel Al Naimi | QAT | 95 | Blusens-STX | BQR-Moto2 | 26 | 44m 50.254s |
| 29 | Bernat Martinez | SPA | 76 | Maquinza-SAG Team | Bimota | 26 | 44m 52.259s |
| 30 | Dominique Aegerter | SWI | 77 | Technomag-CIP | Suter | 24 | 43m 36.055s |
| | Hector Faubel | SPA | 55 | Marc VDS Racing Team | Suter | 16 | DNF |
| | Mattia Pasini | ITA | 75 | JIR Moto2 | MotoBI | 7 | DNF |
| | Shoya Tomizawa | JPN | 48 | Technomag-CIP | Suter | 7 | DNF |
| | Jules Cluzel | FRA | 16 | Forward Racing | Suter | 6 | DNF |
| | Xavier Simeon | BEL | 19 | Holiday Gym G22 | Moriwaki | 6 | DNF |
| | Alex de Angelis | RSM | 15 | RSM Team Scot | Force GP210 | 6 | DNF |
| | Raffaele de Rosa | ITA | 35 | Tech 3 Racing | Tech 3 | 5 | DNF |
| | Axel Pons | SPA | 80 | Tenerife 40 Pons | Pons Kalex | 5 | DNF |
| | Kenny Noyes | USA | 9 | Jack & Jones by A.Banderas | Promoharris | 4 | DNF |
| | Yuki Takahashi | JPN | 72 | Tech 3 Racing | Tech 3 | 4 | DNF |
| | Karel Abraham | CZE | 17 | Cardion AB Motoracing | FTR | 1 | DNF |

**Fastest lap:** Jules Cluzel, on lap 3, 1m 39.169s, 94.400mph/151.922km/h (record).
**Previous lap record:** New category.
**Event best maximum speed:** Andrea Iannone, 162.6mph/261.7km/h (race).

**Qualifying:** Dry
Air: 29° Humidity 26% Ground: 45°

| | | |
|---|---|---|
| 1 | Noyes | 1m 39.234s |
| 2 | Takahashi | 1m 39.265s |
| 3 | Debon | 1m 39.320s |
| 4 | Cluzel | 1m 39.334s |
| 5 | Nieto | 1m 39.402s |
| 6 | Gadea | 1m 39.501s |
| 7 | Elias | 1m 39.517s |
| 8 | Corsi | 1m 39.598s |
| 9 | Simon | 1m 39.622s |
| 10 | Rolfo | 1m 39.695s |
| 11 | Simeon | 1m 39.761s |
| 12 | Wilairot | 1m 39.783s |
| 13 | Corti | 1m 39.787s |
| 14 | Iannone | 1m 39.787s |
| 15 | Tomizawa | 1m 39.795s |
| 16 | de Angelis | 1m 39.878s |
| 17 | Luthi | 1m 39.900s |
| 18 | Canepa | 1m 39.920s |
| 19 | Talmacsi | 1m 39.973s |
| 20 | de Rosa | 1m 40.064s |
| 21 | Redding | 1m 40.087s |
| 22 | Pesek | 1m 40.093s |
| 23 | Pons | 1m 40.163s |
| 24 | Hernandez | 1m 40.184s |
| 25 | Abraham | 1m 40.185s |
| 26 | Tode | 1m 40.200s |
| 27 | Faubel | 1m 40.203s |
| 28 | Baldolini | 1m 40.262s |
| 29 | di Meglio | 1m 40.315s |
| 30 | Aegerter | 1m 40.461s |
| 31 | Pasini | 1m 40.585s |
| 32 | West | 1m 40.632s |
| 33 | Pietri | 1m 40.666s |
| 34 | Ivanov | 1m 40.746s |
| 35 | Bradl | 1m 40.753s |
| 36 | Martinez | 1m 41.509s |
| 37 | Olive | 1m 41.532s |
| 38 | Debise | 1m 41.649s |
| 39 | Al Naimi | 1m 41.789s |
| 40 | Guerra | 1m 41.972s |
| 41 | Leonov | 1m 42.118s |

**Fastest race laps**

| | | |
|---|---|---|
| 1 | Cluzel | 1m 39.169s |
| 2 | Simon | 1m 39.504s |
| 3 | Takahashi | 1m 39.521s |
| 4 | Talmacsi | 1m 39.655s |
| 5 | Iannone | 1m 39.664s |
| 6 | Elias | 1m 39.670s |
| 7 | Corsi | 1m 39.675s |
| 8 | Wilairot | 1m 39.722s |
| 9 | Simeon | 1m 39.805s |
| 10 | de Angelis | 1m 39.813s |
| 11 | Noyes | 1m 39.816s |
| 12 | Debon | 1m 39.871s |
| 13 | Tomizawa | 1m 39.949s |
| 14 | Gadea | 1m 39.950s |
| 15 | de Rosa | 1m 39.984s |
| 16 | Luthi | 1m 40.114s |
| 17 | Nieto | 1m 40.142s |
| 18 | Bradl | 1m 40.174s |
| 19 | Redding | 1m 40.238s |
| 20 | Rolfo | 1m 40.259s |
| 21 | Pesek | 1m 40.387s |
| 22 | Canepa | 1m 40.428s |
| 23 | Hernandez | 1m 40.445s |
| 24 | Corti | 1m 40.446s |
| 25 | Baldolini | 1m 40.470s |
| 26 | Aegerter | 1m 40.476s |
| 27 | Pasini | 1m 40.571s |
| 28 | Tode | 1m 40.735s |
| 29 | di Meglio | 1m 40.754s |
| 30 | Faubel | 1m 40.765s |
| 31 | Debise | 1m 41.036s |
| 32 | Ivanov | 1m 41.050s |
| 33 | Pons | 1m 41.270s |
| 34 | Pietri | 1m 41.438s |
| 35 | Al Naimi | 1m 41.478s |
| 36 | West | 1m 41.529s |
| 37 | Martinez | 1m 41.636s |
| 38 | Guerra | 1m 41.658s |
| 39 | Olive | 1m 41.691s |
| 40 | Leonov | 1m 42.330s |

**Championship Points**

| | | |
|---|---|---|
| 1 | Elias | 63 |
| 2 | Tomizawa | 45 |
| 3 | Corsi | 35 |
| 4 | Simon | 28 |
| 5 | Gadea | 26 |
| 6 | Luthi | 25 |
| 7 | Talmacsi | 25 |
| 8 | Cluzel | 21 |
| 9 | Rolfo | 21 |
| 10 | Debon | 20 |
| 11 | Iannone | 13 |
| 12 | Takahashi | 13 |
| 13 | Nieto | 11 |
| 14 | Pasini | 10 |
| 15 | Hernandez | 10 |
| 16 | Wilairot | 9 |
| 17 | Noyes | 9 |
| 18 | Bradl | 9 |
| 19 | Aegerter | 8 |
| 20 | Baldolini | 6 |
| 21 | Redding | 5 |
| 22 | Pesek | 4 |
| 23 | Abraham | 2 |
| 24 | Corti | 1 |
| 25 | West | 1 |

**Constructors**

| | | |
|---|---|---|
| 1 | Suter | 65 |
| 2 | Moriwaki | 63 |
| 3 | MotoBI | 37 |
| 4 | Speed Up | 27 |
| 5 | Pons Kalex | 26 |
| 6 | FTR | 20 |
| 7 | Tech 3 | 13 |
| 8 | RSV | 10 |
| 9 | BQR-Moto2 | 10 |
| 10 | Bimota | 9 |
| 11 | Promoharris | 9 |
| 12 | I.C.P. | 6 |
| 13 | MZ-RE Honda | 1 |

## 125cc — RACE DISTANCE: 24 laps, 62.411 miles/100.440 km · RACE WEATHER: Dry (air 23°, humidity 37%, track 39°)

| Pos. | Rider | Nat. | No. | Entrant | Machine | Laps | Time & Speed |
|---|---|---|---|---|---|---|---|
| 1 | **Pol Espargaro** | SPA | 44 | Tuenti Racing | Derbi | 24 | 41m 52.280s (mph/km/h) 89.431/143.926 |
| 2 | **Nicolas Terol** | SPA | 40 | Bancaja Aspar Team | Aprilia | 24 | 41m 53.237s |
| 3 | **Marc Marquez** | SPA | 93 | Red Bull Ajo Motorsport | Derbi | 24 | 41m 56.708s |
| 4 | **Efren Vazquez** | SPA | 7 | Tuenti Racing | Derbi | 24 | 41m 57.016s |
| 5 | **Bradley Smith** | GBR | 38 | Bancaja Aspar Team | Aprilia | 24 | 41m 57.423s |
| 6 | **Sandro Cortese** | GER | 11 | Avant Mitsubishi Ajo | Derbi | 24 | 41m 58.127s |
| 7 | **Esteve Rabat** | SPA | 12 | Blusens-STX | Aprilia | 24 | 42m 03.327s |
| 8 | **Tomoyoshi Koyama** | JPN | 71 | Racing Team Germany | Aprilia | 24 | 42m 03.445s |
| 9 | **Danny Webb** | GBR | 99 | Andalucia Cajasol | Aprilia | 24 | 42m 30.088s |
| 10 | **Luis Salom** | SPA | 39 | Stipa-Molenaar Racing GP | Aprilia | 24 | 42m 31.865s |
| 11 | **Johann Zarco** | FRA | 14 | WTR San Marino Team | Aprilia | 24 | 42m 32.799s |
| 12 | **Jasper Iwema** | NED | 53 | CBC Corse | Aprilia | 24 | 42m 33.097s |
| 13 | **Jonas Folger** | GER | 94 | Ongetta Team | Aprilia | 24 | 42m 34.429s |
| 14 | **Randy Krummenacher** | SWI | 35 | Stipa-Molenaar Racing GP | Aprilia | 24 | 42m 37.021s |
| 15 | **Adrian Martin** | SPA | 26 | Aeroport de Castello - Ajo | Aprilia | 24 | 42m 38.600s |
| 16 | Alexis Masbou | FRA | 5 | Ongetta Team | Aprilia | 24 | 42m 38.783s |
| 17 | Alberto Moncayo | SPA | 23 | Andalucia Cajasol | Aprilia | 24 | 42m 39.259s |
| 18 | Marcel Schrotter | GER | 78 | Interwetten Honda 125 | Honda | 24 | 42m 51.906s |
| 19 | Jakub Kornfeil | CZE | 84 | Racing Team Germany | Aprilia | 24 | 42m 52.050s |
| 20 | Sturla Fagerhaug | NOR | 50 | AirAsia-Sepang Int. Circuit | Aprilia | 24 | 42m 56.685s |
| 21 | Louis Rossi | FRA | 69 | CBC Corse | Aprilia | 24 | 42m 58.011s |
| 22 | Michael van der Mark | NED | 60 | Lambretta Reparto Corse | Lambretta | 24 | 43m 21.208s |
| 23 | Kevin Szalai | FRA | 82 | Equipe de France Vitesse Espo | Honda | 24 | 43m 39.423s |
| 24 | Gregory di Carlo | FRA | 81 | Equipe de France Vitesse Espo | Honda | 23 | 41m 53.349s |
| 25 | Zulfahmi Khairuddin | MAL | 63 | AirAsia-Sepang Int. Circuit | Aprilia | 23 | 42m 19.286s |
| 26 | Morgan Berchet | FRA | 83 | Xtreme Racing Team | Honda | 23 | 42m 53.487s |
| | Marco Ravaioli | ITA | 72 | Lambretta Reparto Corse | Lambretta | 18 | DNF |
| | Riccardo Moretti | ITA | 51 | Fontana Racing | Aprilia | 16 | DNF |
| | Lorenzo Savadori | ITA | 32 | Matteoni CP Racing | Aprilia | 6 | DNF |

**Fastest lap:** Marc Marquez, on lap 23, 1m 43.787s, 90.199mph/145.162km/h (record).
**Previous lap record:** Pol Espargaro, SPA (Derbi), 1m 43.918s, 90.086mph/144.979km/h (2008).
**Event best maximum speed:** Sandro Cortese, 136.1mph/219.1km/h (race).

**Qualifying:** Dry
Air: 28° Humidity 29% Ground: 44°

| | | |
|---|---|---|
| 1 | Terol | 1m 43.719s |
| 2 | Espargaro | 1m 43.864s |
| 3 | Cortese | 1m 44.118s |
| 4 | Marquez | 1m 44.141s |
| 5 | Smith | 1m 44.172s |
| 6 | Koyama | 1m 44.358s |
| 7 | Krummenacher | 1m 44.580s |
| 8 | Webb | 1m 44.807s |
| 9 | Zarco | 1m 44.909s |
| 10 | Rabat | 1m 44.920s |
| 11 | Salom | 1m 45.021s |
| 12 | Vazquez | 1m 45.306s |
| 13 | Folger | 1m 45.618s |
| 14 | Moretti | 1m 45.657s |
| 15 | Iwema | 1m 45.754s |
| 16 | Martin | 1m 45.851s |
| 17 | Moncayo | 1m 45.955s |
| 18 | Masbou | 1m 46.035s |
| 19 | Savadori | 1m 46.372s |
| 20 | Schrotter | 1m 46.772s |
| 21 | Fagerhaug | 1m 46.777s |
| 22 | Rossi | 1m 46.782s |
| 23 | Kornfeil | 1m 46.867s |
| 24 | Khairuddin | 1m 47.643s |
| 25 | van der Mark | 1m 48.271s |
| 26 | Berchet | 1m 48.812s |
| 27 | di Carlo | 1m 48.868s |
| 28 | Szalai | 1m 48.924s |
| 29 | Ravaioli | 1m 49.023s |

**Fastest race laps**

| | | |
|---|---|---|
| 1 | Marquez | 1m 43.787s |
| 2 | Smith | 1m 43.912s |
| 3 | Vazquez | 1m 43.915s |
| 4 | Espargaro | 1m 43.945s |
| 5 | Terol | 1m 43.968s |
| 6 | Cortese | 1m 43.989s |
| 7 | Rabat | 1m 44.187s |
| 8 | Koyama | 1m 44.359s |
| 9 | Krummenacher | 1m 44.471s |
| 10 | Iwema | 1m 44.699s |
| 11 | Folger | 1m 45.311s |
| 12 | Webb | 1m 45.336s |
| 13 | Zarco | 1m 45.418s |
| 14 | Martin | 1m 45.467s |
| 15 | Salom | 1m 45.518s |
| 16 | Moretti | 1m 45.625s |
| 17 | Moncayo | 1m 45.690s |
| 18 | Masbou | 1m 45.730s |
| 19 | Fagerhaug | 1m 46.104s |
| 20 | Rossi | 1m 46.178s |
| 21 | Schrotter | 1m 46.298s |
| 22 | Kornfeil | 1m 46.341s |
| 23 | Savadori | 1m 46.948s |
| 24 | van der Mark | 1m 47.528s |
| 25 | Ravaioli | 1m 47.599s |
| 26 | Szalai | 1m 47.778s |
| 27 | Khairuddin | 1m 47.972s |
| 28 | di Carlo | 1m 48.277s |
| 29 | Berchet | 1m 49.766s |

**Championship Points**

| | | |
|---|---|---|
| 1 | Terol | 65 |
| 2 | Espargaro | 63 |
| 3 | Rabat | 34 |
| 4 | Vazquez | 33 |
| 5 | Marquez | 32 |
| 6 | Smith | 32 |
| 7 | Cortese | 26 |
| 8 | Koyama | 26 |
| 9 | Krummenacher | 20 |
| 10 | Zarco | 18 |
| 11 | Moncayo | 13 |
| 12 | Masbou | 13 |
| 13 | Webb | 12 |
| 14 | Iwema | 12 |
| 15 | Salom | 7 |
| 16 | Schrotter | 4 |
| 17 | Folger | 4 |
| 18 | Martin | 4 |
| 19 | Kornfeil | 2 |

**Constructors**

| | | |
|---|---|---|
| 1 | Derbi | 70 |
| 2 | Aprilia | 65 |
| 3 | Honda | 4 |
| 4 | Lambretta | 1 |

*Main photo:* A moment that resounded through the racing world. Rossi flies through the gravel, the angle of his right leg showing that it is already broken.

*Inset:* Writhing in agony, Rossi clutches at his injured limb.
*Photos:* Gold & Goose

FIM WORLD CHAMPIONSHIP · ROUND 4

# ITALIAN GRAND PRIX

## MUGELLO CIRCUIT

MISANO is Rossi's backyard track, but Mugello, with hillsides of fans, swooping ess-bends and long undulating straights is his racing home. He arrived at the scenic track, having won there on seven previous occasions, with a question-mark hanging over the strength of his shoulder, a Mohican crop – "a hairstyle for battle" – and a great big grin. And he promptly took an advantage of almost half a second in first practice.

He left in a yellow helicopter at lunchtime the next day, waving feebly at the camera in a morphine daze, Dr Costa trotting alongside the stretcher, shading his eyes from the bright sun that continued all weekend.

In between had been an event that was nothing more nor less than a normal racing accident, and at the same time a cataclysmic shock that resounded through Italy and around the world beyond. Television news bulletins that night carried shots of the number 46 bike flipping at a fast ess-bend, the final Biondetti chicane, then of the rider writhing on the ground clutching his misshapen right leg in agony. And then the helicopter.

The explanation was simple. Midway through the Saturday morning session, Rossi was out for a third run, already fastest and on his first flying lap. Halfway around he became mixed up with rookie Barbera. Unwilling to act as a tow truck, he slowed up by a full nine seconds over the third of four sections – usually covered in some 35 seconds – to let the yellow Ducati get well clear. Then, approaching the end of the lap, he started to nail it, coming fast out of the long Correntaio right-hander, then pitching the bike hard left while maintaining high momentum, the key to Mugello and a speciality of his.

He had made one crucial mistake: failing to take into account how much the slow run had allowed the left side of the tyre to cool. Crew chief Burgess explained: "According to the data, in that corner he was a little lower than usual, and he opened the throttle no more than usual, but a little faster." The rear spun up quicker than the electronics could manage, triggering the 171km/h high-side.

Another Saturday morning crash, but the riders still forbore to criticise the Bridgestones. It was, said Pedrosa,

"part of the character of the tyre; you have to warm them up carefully." Part of the rider's job, something he has to learn. Lorenzo said, "Every crash I have had in MotoGP was because of cold tyres." Many of those, of course, had been on Michelins.

Tyre temperature sensors, banned on cost-cutting grounds, would not have made any difference: not accurate enough – although the enforced absence of these low-cost items does prevent possible development that might make them so.

But these issues, involving all riders, remained peripheral. The shock was that, very suddenly, grand prix racing discovered what life was like without Valentino.

Completely different. A Charlie Chaplin film, but without Charlie Chaplin.

This was always going to happen one day, but people preferred not to think about it. Rossi has single-handedly carried the sport for so long that his departure was too uncomfortable to contemplate. Now it had been thrust upon us, and the effect was immediate, with reports of traffic tail-backs to the motorway as fans left in droves, not even caring enough to stay to watch the afternoon qualifying session. These reports may have been exaggerated, since 76,000 fans turned up on Sunday, 5,000 fewer than the previous year, but the effect would be felt in falling TV figures over the next few races. With some predicting that he would be out perhaps for the rest of the year, it was a bleak prospect. Happily, he came back much sooner than that.

The other effect was on the racing. This was the first of a series of races with processions up front. It was in terms of sheer sport that Rossi was missed the most.

This overshadowed other events on a busy weekend, apart from providing welcome relief from the endless rumours of which rider would be with which team in 2011.

Stoner's weekend started with yet another front-end crash early in the first free practice, but he was at pains to point out the cause was not the usual front-end queasiness, but because a big shimmy had knocked off the front brake discs more than he had anticipated, and he ran off because he had arrived at the corner too fast. Inconvenient, because on

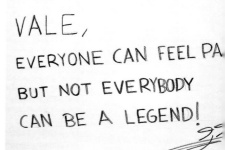

that bike he was testing the previous-generation Öhlins forks, and that bike was damaged in the crash. His problems in the early races had pushed him back to the piggy-back reservoir forks he'd used in 2009, rather than the through-rod units employed by the other top riders. This was the start of the trials, and he would stick with the older units for this and the upcoming races.

Capirossi's 192nd premier-class start put him equal second with Checa; the record-holder is Alex Barros, with an astonishing 245.

But the veteran had a worrying problem at Mugello, when a piston failed in one of his engines in practice, a hint of possible problems at the far end of the season: Suzuki was the only team to fall short in 2009 during the trial run on restricted engines.

The FIM celebrated World Environment Day with an all-riders photocall on the grid; Pramac went further, commissioning famous designer Philippe Starck to pen a special paint job, while drawing more attention to the Starck-designed wind turbines that they claim provide enough power to drive the team's laptops for the weekend. And never mind the bank of Pramac generators rumbling away to power the rest of the paddock, just a few feet away. A sense of irony was sorely missed.

Alpinestars launched its own version of the rider airbag, already pioneered by Dainese. This two-bag system protects shoulders and collarbones, but test rider Mika Kallio wasn't wearing it when he crashed at Le Mans, where he injured … his shoulder.

Moto2 rider Anthony West was given a new engine for his MZ, after it turned out that overheating at Le Mans – the result of a holed radiator – had spoiled the new one he had received there. Meanwhile, the nature of the class was made clear by another remarkable statistic: all of the top 12 in the race were former GP winners.

## MOTOGP RACE – 23 laps

In Rossi's absence, qualifying honours were disputed between Pedrosa and Lorenzo, going to the former by less than two-tenths for his second pole of the year. Stoner completed the front row, but was worried. "Usually our race pace is good, but our one-lap qualifying run not so good. This weekend, it's the opposite," he said. Hayden was barely a tenth slower, heading the second row from compatriot Edwards, who had reverted to his 2009 settings and announced, somewhat rashly, "I'm back!"

Dani got his usual flying start, but it was a couple of laps before he managed to pull any sort of a gap. Lorenzo was close until Dovizioso powered past down the long straight, and the interval started to open rapidly, from less than a second to almost three by lap five, when Pedrosa set a new lap record.

Would there be a Honda one-two? No. Lorenzo was just awaiting his chance. It came under braking for the first corner on lap six, and while Dovizioso stayed close until two-thirds distance, he was never near enough to attack and had lost touch by the finish.

All the while, Pedrosa was pulling clear: by 7.9 seconds on lap 15. And though Lorenzo did manage to close slightly after that, the Honda was still comfortably clear at the end. He was delighted.

*Above:* Pedrosa leads Lorenzo, Stoner and Spies into the first corner, after the dash from the lights.

*Left:* Lorenzo had a message for his absent rival.

*Centre left, top:* Rossi's absence was the keynote of the weekend for the local fans.

*Centre left, bottom:* Dr Costa briefs the Press on the hero's injuries.

*Far left:* Moments from disaster. Rossi checks for a clear track after running slow to avoid helping other riders with a tow.

*Photos: Gold & Goose*

Thus the top three, and definitely robbed of tension and excitement by the absence of Rossi, but there was plenty more adventure lower down the field.

Hayden had been left on the line, but he was in sixth by the end of lap one. Spies was fourth, with Stoner between them. Both former champions were past the Superbike champion within two laps, along with Melandri, who was surprising everybody, including himself, after a flying start from the fifth row.

Melandri went past Hayden as well when the American fell on the downhill entry to the Correntaio corner, where the Ducati fans pack the grandstand with red. It was a typical 2010-style Ducati front-end lose. "I'd had a couple of close calls, then it went quite early in the corner. I didn't even have my knee down, and it went way too quick for me to save it," he said. In another two laps, Kallio suffered an almost identical crash two corners earlier.

At the start of the eighth lap, the Honda surged past Stoner's Ducati under braking for the first corner. At the same time, de Puniet, riding inspired, had got ahead of Spies and was closing on the pair ahead.

The three stayed together, Spies playing a close spectator's role as Melandri and Stoner swapped back and forth, and de Puniet lurched backwards and forwards using some highly adventurous lines. The Frenchman led the trio on laps 16 and 17, succumbed to Melandri, but then pushed through once more with three laps to go.

They started the last lap de Puniet, Melandri and Stoner, but the last-named had been biding his time and trying to stay out of trouble, worried that de Puniet might bring them all down. Into the first corner, both he and Melandri passed the Frenchman, and they were still in that order when they crossed the line, Spies a second adrift.

Capirossi had been next after the start, losing time from the first lap onwards as Espargaro and Edwards queued up behind the Suzuki. On the eighth lap, Edwards swapped with Espargaro, and next time around both were past the Italian, with Aoyama following them on lap ten.

Edwards was soon slowing again, finding the effort of heaving the bike from side to side on the track's three fast ess-bends exhausting. On lap 13, he was behind even Capirossi and losing ground rapidly, his race done, his puzzlement at his condition complete.

This left Espargaro to pull clear convincingly, abandoning his companions to the trouble coming from behind, in the shape of an avenging Simoncelli. He had run into the gravel on lap one and only narrowly avoided crashing, rejoining five seconds behind the still injured and tentative Bautista.

Simoncelli's pace soon took him past the Suzuki and Barbera. Shortly after half-distance, he took Barbera with him as he passed the fading Edwards and started to slash away at a five-second gap to Capirossi, who would soon pass Aoyama. The pursuing pair caught them up with three laps to go, and Simoncelli set about them at once, passing Aoyama on one lap and Capirossi the next, and getting more than half a second clear over the line.

This had brought all of them up to Espargaro, but the Spaniard had enough in hand to stay narrowly safe in eighth. Capirossi was tenth, with Aoyama just over a second behind, while Barbera was three-tenths further back.

Edwards was another half-minute down, and Bautista ten seconds adrift of him.

## MOTO2 RACE – 21 laps

Fourteen riders qualified within the same second, and it would have been more but for Iannone's impressive pole-time gap of 0.26 second, over Elias, de Angelis and Cluzel. Tomizawa headed row two from Gadea, Talmacsi and Pons.

The volatility was reliable, however, with Debon 15th and Le Mans pole-sitter Noyes 33rd.

Iannone continued to make nonsense of the close-racing ethic of the new class, rocketing away into an early lead that just kept stretching and stretching. Any rivals hoping that his soft tyre choice would slow him down at the other end of the race were sorely disappointed; he was able to cruise to the finish still with almost three seconds in hand.

He was pursued at first by team-mate Talmacsi, but after three laps he was almost three seconds ahead, while some fast riders were piling up behind the Hungarian. One was Cluzel, who took second on lap four (Iannone now 3.5 seconds away), only to go flying off into the gravel before he was a quarter of the way around the next lap.

This left Elias second, Iannone's advantage now more than five seconds; Debon was next, then Talmacsi, Luthi, Tomizawa, Faubel and Gadea.

After ten laps, the pursuing pack had broken free and had become six strong – Faubel had been left behind and Debon had also dropped off the back, while Corsi had joined after flying through from 17th on lap one.

The next to be left trailing was Talmacsi; the remaining five battled all the way to the flag, finishing Gadea, Corsi, Luthi,

*Left:* The battle for fourth: de Puniet leads Melandri, Stoner and Spies.

*Right:* A Moto2 train. Gadea leads from Corsi, Luthi, Elias, Tomizawa and Talmacsi

*Below:* A typical Mugello 125 finish: Marques snatches a first win from Terol, Espargaro and Smith.

*Photos:* Gold & Goose

Elias and Tomizawa. Talmacsi was a lone seventh; a second behind, Takahashi headed the next big gang, with Simon and Debon completing the top ten. De Angelis was a close 11th, with Faubel and Baldolini slightly off the back by the end.

Close behind, Bradl headed the next trio going for the last points, from Nieto and Aegerter, the last-named out of luck.

Another seven riders joined Cluzel on the crash list: Pesek, replacement Delhalle, Pasini, de Rosa, di Meglio, Wilairot and Pietri; all were unhurt.

Elias extended his points lead further, but Iannone and especially Luthi were beginning to look dangerous, both finishing ahead of him.

## 125cc RACE – 20 laps

The Spanish domination was broken in qualifying when German Cortese claimed his second pole, with Espargaro second followed by Smith and Terol. Espargaro was on his way to pole when he crashed heavily at the end of the session, but luckily he was unhurt.

It was Spain again in the race, Marquez taking his first victory in a typical ultra-close battle. It would be the first of a string of them for the 17-year-old.

Terol led away from Espargaro and Vazquez, Cortese in hot pursuit. He took second as they ran into the first corner for the second time, only to slide off two corners later. Distraught, he remounted, but crashed out for good a few laps later.

Terol was trying to escape, only Espargaro going with him. They were almost three seconds ahead after five laps, but by now Marquez was ahead of Smith, the pair of them closing. By lap eight, there were four up front.

Smith and Marquez did most of the leading over the line, Espargaro looming menacingly and Terol waiting for the inevitable Mugello drafting battle at the end.

Smith led lap 18, only to be consigned to fourth as they ran into the first corner.

Now it was Marquez again; he managed to stay there for the next two laps and all the way down the long straight for the last time, with Terol second, then Espargaro and Smith, all in a bunch. The spread of 0.161 second was the third closest top four of all time in the class. The other occasions were also at Mugello, in 2007 and 2008.

There was an equivalent battle for fifth, won by Vazquez from Krummenacher and Rabat. A long way back, Koyama headed Zarco, Webb and Folger.

## AUTODROMO INTERNAZIONALE DEL MUGELLO

Arrabbiata 2 156/97
Scarperia 109/68
Palagio 106/66
Correntaio 106/66
Biondetti 1 165/103
Biondetti 2 167/104
Bucine 114/71
Savelli 117/73
San Donato 99/62
Arrabbiata 1 163/101
Materassi 119/74
Cassanova 114/71
Luco 113/70
Borgo San Lorenzo 121/75
Poggio Seco 119/74

Key 96/60 kph/mph
Gear

Circuit 5.245km / 3.259 miles, 23 laps

## MotoGP
RACE DISTANCE: 23 laps, 74.959 miles/120.635 km · RACE WEATHER: Dry (air 32°, humidity 27%, track 54°)

| Pos. | Rider | Nat. | No. | Entrant | Machine | Tyres | Laps | Time & speed |
|---|---|---|---|---|---|---|---|---|
| 1 | **Dani Pedrosa** | SPA | 26 | Repsol Honda Team | Honda | B | 23 | 42m 28.066s 105.905mph/ 170.437km/h |
| 2 | **Jorge Lorenzo** | SPA | 99 | Fiat Yamaha Team | Yamaha | B | 23 | 42m 32.080s |
| 3 | **Andrea Dovizioso** | ITA | 4 | Repsol Honda Team | Honda | B | 23 | 42m 34.262s |
| 4 | **Casey Stoner** | AUS | 27 | Ducati Marlboro Team | Ducati | B | 23 | 42m 53.769s |
| 5 | **Marco Melandri** | ITA | 33 | San Carlo Honda Gresini | Honda | B | 23 | 42m 53.801s |
| 6 | **Randy de Puniet** | FRA | 14 | LCR Honda MotoGP | Honda | B | 23 | 42m 54.031s |
| 7 | **Ben Spies** | USA | 11 | Monster Yamaha Tech 3 | Yamaha | B | 23 | 42m 56.872s |
| 8 | **Aleix Espargaro** | SPA | 41 | Pramac Racing Team | Ducati | B | 23 | 43m 08.238s |
| 9 | **Marco Simoncelli** | ITA | 58 | San Carlo Honda Gresini | Honda | B | 23 | 43m 09.460s |
| 10 | **Loris Capirossi** | ITA | 65 | Rizla Suzuki MotoGP | Suzuki | B | 23 | 43m 10.173s |
| 11 | **Hiroshi Aoyama** | JPN | 7 | Interwetten Honda MotoGP | Honda | B | 23 | 43m 11.161s |
| 12 | **Hector Barbera** | SPA | 40 | Paginas Amarillas Aspar | Ducati | B | 23 | 43m 11.429s |
| 13 | **Colin Edwards** | USA | 5 | Monster Yamaha Tech 3 | Yamaha | B | 23 | 43m 42.459s |
| 14 | **Alvaro Bautista** | SPA | 19 | Rizla Suzuki MotoGP | Suzuki | B | 23 | 43m 52.455s |
| | Mika Kallio | FIN | 36 | Pramac Racing Team | Ducati | B | 8 | DNF |
| | Nicky Hayden | USA | 69 | Ducati Marlboro Team | Ducati | B | 5 | DNF |

**Fastest lap:** Dani Pedrosa, on lap 5, 1m 49.531s, 107.118mph/172.389km/h (record).
**Previous lap record:** Casey Stoner, AUS (Ducati), 1m 50.003s, 106.658mph/171.649km/h (2008).
**Event best maximum speed:** Hector Barbera, 214.8mph/345.7km/h (warm up).

### Qualifying
Weather: Dry
Air Temp: 30° Humidity: 29°
Track Temp: 51°

| | | |
|---|---|---|
| 1 | Pedrosa | 1m 48.819s |
| 2 | Lorenzo | 1m 48.996s |
| 3 | Stoner | 1m 49.432s |
| 4 | Hayden | 1m 49.546s |
| 5 | Edwards | 1m 49.683s |
| 6 | de Puniet | 1m 49.737s |
| 7 | Spies | 1m 49.861s |
| 8 | Dovizioso | 1m 50.065s |
| 9 | Espargaro | 1m 50.168s |
| 10 | Aoyama | 1m 50.224s |
| 11 | Simoncelli | 1m 50.434s |
| 12 | Capirossi | 1m 50.475s |
| 13 | Barbera | 1m 50.561s |
| 14 | Melandri | 1m 50.664s |
| 15 | Kallio | 1m 50.970s |
| 16 | Bautista | 1m 53.243s |

### Fastest race laps

| | | |
|---|---|---|
| 1 | Pedrosa | 1m 49.531s |
| 2 | Dovizioso | 1m 50.293s |
| 3 | Lorenzo | 1m 50.418s |
| 4 | Melandri | 1m 50.620s |
| 5 | de Puniet | 1m 50.971s |
| 6 | Stoner | 1m 50.996s |
| 7 | Hayden | 1m 51.042s |
| 8 | Spies | 1m 51.092s |
| 9 | Edwards | 1m 51.497s |
| 10 | Capirossi | 1m 51.557s |
| 11 | Aoyama | 1m 51.557s |
| 12 | Simoncelli | 1m 51.569s |
| 13 | Espargaro | 1m 51.588s |
| 14 | Barbera | 1m 51.666s |
| 15 | Kallio | 1m 51.880s |
| 16 | Bautista | 1m 53.171s |

### Championship Points

| | | |
|---|---|---|
| 1 | Lorenzo | 90 |
| 2 | Pedrosa | 65 |
| 3 | Rossi | 61 |
| 4 | Dovizioso | 58 |
| 5 | Hayden | 39 |
| 6 | de Puniet | 36 |
| 7 | Melandri | 32 |
| 8 | Stoner | 24 |
| 9 | Simoncelli | 23 |
| 10 | Spies | 20 |
| 11 | Barbera | 19 |
| 12 | Edwards | 19 |
| 13 | Aoyama | 18 |
| 14 | Espargaro | 16 |
| 15 | Capirossi | 13 |
| 16 | Kallio | 12 |
| 17 | Bautista | 8 |

### Team Points

| | | |
|---|---|---|
| 1 | Fiat Yamaha Team | 151 |
| 2 | Repsol Honda Team | 123 |
| 3 | Ducati Marlboro Team | 63 |
| 4 | San Carlo Honda Gresini | 55 |
| 5 | Monster Yamaha Tech 3 | 39 |
| 6 | LCR Honda MotoGP | 36 |
| 7 | Pramac Racing Team | 28 |
| 8 | Rizla Suzuki MotoGP | 21 |
| 9 | Paginas Amarillas Aspar | 19 |
| 10 | Interwetten Honda MotoGP | 18 |

### Constructor Points

| | | |
|---|---|---|
| 1 | Yamaha | 95 |
| 2 | Honda | 77 |
| 3 | Ducati | 52 |
| 4 | Suzuki | 19 |

| Grid order | 1 | 2 | 3 | 4 | 5 | 6 | 7 | 8 | 9 | 10 | 11 | 12 | 13 | 14 | 15 | 16 | 17 | 18 | 19 | 20 | 21 | 22 | 23 | |
|---|---|---|---|---|---|---|---|---|---|---|---|---|---|---|---|---|---|---|---|---|---|---|---|---|
| 26 PEDROSA | 26 | 26 | 26 | 26 | 26 | 26 | 26 | 26 | 26 | 26 | 26 | 26 | 26 | 26 | 26 | 26 | 26 | 26 | 26 | 26 | 26 | 26 | 26 | 1 |
| 99 LORENZO | 99 | 99 | 4 | 4 | 4 | 99 | 99 | 99 | 99 | 99 | 99 | 99 | 99 | 99 | 99 | 99 | 99 | 99 | 99 | 99 | 99 | 99 | 99 | 2 |
| 27 STONER | 4 | 4 | 99 | 99 | 99 | 4 | 4 | 4 | 4 | 4 | 4 | 4 | 4 | 4 | 4 | 4 | 4 | 4 | 4 | 4 | 4 | 4 | 4 | 3 |
| 69 HAYDEN | 11 | 11 | 27 | 27 | 27 | 27 | 27 | 33 | 33 | 27 | 27 | 27 | 33 | 33 | 33 | 14 | 14 | 33 | 33 | 33 | 14 | 33 | 27 | 4 |
| 5 EDWARDS | 27 | 27 | 69 | 69 | 33 | 33 | 33 | 27 | 27 | 33 | 33 | 33 | 14 | 14 | 14 | 33 | 33 | 14 | 14 | 14 | 33 | 14 | 33 | 5 |
| 14 de PUNIET | 69 | 69 | 33 | 33 | 69 | 11 | 14 | 14 | 14 | 14 | 14 | 14 | 27 | 27 | 27 | 27 | 27 | 27 | 27 | 27 | 27 | 14 | | 6 |
| 11 SPIES | 33 | 33 | 11 | 11 | 11 | 14 | 11 | 11 | 11 | 11 | 11 | 11 | 11 | 11 | 11 | 11 | 11 | 11 | 11 | 11 | 11 | 11 | | 7 |
| 4 DOVIZIOSO | 14 | 14 | 14 | 14 | 14 | 65 | 65 | 65 | 5 | 5 | 5 | 5 | 41 | 41 | 41 | 41 | 41 | 41 | 41 | 41 | 41 | 41 | | 8 |
| 41 ESPARGARO | 41 | 41 | 65 | 65 | 65 | 41 | 41 | 5 | 41 | 41 | 41 | 41 | 7 | 7 | 7 | 7 | 65 | 65 | 65 | 65 | 58 | 58 | | 9 |
| 7 AOYAMA | 65 | 65 | 41 | 41 | 41 | 5 | 5 | 41 | 65 | 7 | 7 | 7 | 65 | 65 | 65 | 65 | 7 | 7 | 7 | 58 | 65 | 65 | | 10 |
| 58 SIMONCELLI | 5 | 5 | 5 | 5 | 5 | 7 | 7 | 7 | 7 | 65 | 65 | 65 | 5 | 58 | 58 | 58 | 58 | 58 | 58 | 7 | 7 | 7 | | 11 |
| 65 CAPIROSSI | 36 | 36 | 7 | 7 | 7 | 36 | 36 | 36 | 58 | 58 | 58 | 58 | 40 | 40 | 40 | 40 | 40 | 40 | 40 | 40 | 40 | 40 | | 12 |
| 40 BARBERA | 7 | 7 | 36 | 36 | 36 | 58 | 58 | 58 | 40 | 40 | 40 | 40 | 40 | 5 | 5 | 5 | 5 | 5 | 5 | 5 | 5 | 5 | | 13 |
| 33 MELANDRI | 40 | 19 | 19 | 58 | 58 | 40 | 40 | 40 | 19 | 19 | 19 | 19 | 19 | 19 | 19 | 19 | 19 | 19 | 19 | 19 | 19 | 19 | | 14 |
| 36 KALLIO | 19 | 40 | 58 | 40 | 40 | 19 | 19 | 19 | | | | | | | | | | | | | | | | |
| 19 BAUTISTA | 58 | 58 | 40 | 19 | 19 | | | | | | | | | | | | | | | | | | | |

## Moto2

**RACE DISTANCE:** 21 laps, 68.441 miles/110.145 km · **RACE WEATHER:** Dry (air 30°, humidity 32%, track 50°)

| Pos. | Rider | Nat. | No. | Entrant | Machine | Laps | Time & Speed |
|---|---|---|---|---|---|---|---|
| 1 | **Andrea Iannone** | ITA | 29 | Fimmco Speed Up | Speed Up | 21 | 41m 05.374s (mph/km/h) 99.939/160.836 |
| 2 | **Sergio Gadea** | SPA | 40 | Tenerife 40 Pons | Pons Kalex | 21 | 41m 08.138s |
| 3 | **Simone Corsi** | ITA | 3 | JIR Moto2 | MotoBI | 21 | 41m 08.173s |
| 4 | **Thomas Luthi** | SWI | 12 | Interwetten Moriwaki Moto2 | Moriwaki | 21 | 41m 08.188s |
| 5 | **Toni Elias** | SPA | 24 | Gresini Racing Moto2 | Moriwaki | 21 | 41m 08.778s |
| 6 | **Shoya Tomizawa** | JPN | 48 | Technomag-CIP | Suter | 21 | 41m 09.200s |
| 7 | **Gabor Talmacsi** | HUN | 2 | Fimmco Speed Up | Speed Up | 21 | 41m 12.583s |
| 8 | **Yuki Takahashi** | JPN | 72 | Tech 3 Racing | Tech 3 | 21 | 41m 13.751s |
| 9 | **Julian Simon** | SPA | 60 | Mapfre Aspar Team | Suter | 21 | 41m 13.958s |
| 10 | **Alex Debon** | SPA | 6 | Aeroport de Castello - Ajo | FTR | 21 | 41m 14.305s |
| 11 | **Alex de Angelis** | RSM | 15 | RSM Team Scot | Force GP210 | 21 | 41m 14.523s |
| 12 | **Hector Faubel** | SPA | 55 | Marc VDS Racing Team | Suter | 21 | 41m 15.365s |
| 13 | **Alex Baldolini** | ITA | 25 | Caretta Technology Race Dept. | I.C.P. | 21 | 41m 17.593s |
| 14 | **Stefan Bradl** | GER | 65 | Viessmann Kiefer Racing | Suter | 21 | 41m 24.484s |
| 15 | **Fonsi Nieto** | SPA | 10 | Holiday Gym G22 | Moriwaki | 21 | 41m 25.054s |
| 16 | Dominique Aegerter | SWI | 77 | Technomag-CIP | Suter | 21 | 41m 25.368s |
| 17 | Karel Abraham | CZE | 17 | Cardion AB Motoracing | FTR | 21 | 41m 30.343s |
| 18 | Roberto Rolfo | ITA | 44 | Italtrans S.T.R. | Suter | 21 | 41m 31.143s |
| 19 | Xavier Simeon | BEL | 19 | Holiday Gym G22 | Moriwaki | 21 | 41m 36.468s |
| 20 | Yonny Hernandez | COL | 68 | Blusens-STX | BQR-Moto2 | 21 | 41m 36.545s |
| 21 | Scott Redding | GBR | 45 | Marc VDS Racing Team | Suter | 21 | 41m 43.144s |
| 22 | Claudio Corti | ITA | 71 | Forward Racing | Suter | 21 | 41m 44.557s |
| 23 | Valentin Debise | FRA | 53 | WTR San Marino Team | ADV | 21 | 41m 44.779s |
| 24 | Arne Tode | GER | 41 | Racing Team Germany | Suter | 21 | 41m 45.987s |
| 25 | Vladimir Leonov | RUS | 21 | Vector Kiefer Racing | Suter | 21 | 41m 48.732s |
| 26 | Kenny Noyes | USA | 9 | Jack & Jones by A.Banderas | Promoharris | 21 | 41m 49.371s |
| 27 | Anthony West | AUS | 8 | MZ Racing Team | MZ-RE Honda | 21 | 41m 59.122s |
| 28 | Niccolo Canepa | ITA | 59 | RSM Team Scot | Force GP210 | 21 | 41m 59.761s |
| 29 | Bernat Martinez | SPA | 76 | Maquinza-SAG Team | Bimota | 21 | 42m 02.409s |
| 30 | Yannick Guerra | SPA | 88 | Holiday Gym G22 | Moriwaki | 21 | 42m 03.986s |
| | Robertino Pietri | VEN | 39 | Italtrans S.T.R. | Suter | 18 | DNF |
| | Ratthapark Wilairot | THA | 14 | Thai Honda PTT Singha SAG | Bimota | 16 | DNF |
| | Mike di Meglio | FRA | 63 | Mapfre Aspar Team | Suter | 15 | DNF |
| | Vladimir Ivanov | UKR | 61 | Gresini Racing Moto2 | Moriwaki | 15 | DNF |
| | Raffaele de Rosa | ITA | 35 | Tech 3 Racing | Tech 3 | 11 | DNF |
| | Mattia Pasini | ITA | 75 | JIR Moto2 | MotoBI | 7 | DNF |
| | Jules Cluzel | FRA | 16 | Forward Racing | Suter | 4 | DNF |
| | Axel Pons | SPA | 80 | Tenerife 40 Pons | Pons Kalex | 4 | DNF |
| | Anthony Delhalle | FRA | 96 | Blusens-STX | BQR-Moto2 | 3 | DNF |
| | Lukas Pesek | CZE | 52 | Matteoni CP Racing | Moriwaki | 2 | DNF |

**Fastest lap:** Andrea Iannone, on lap 2, 1m 55.647s, 101.453mph/163.272km/h (record).
**Previous lap record:** New category.
**Event best maximum speed:** Alex Debon, 180.3mph/290.1km/h (race)

**Qualifying:** Dry
Air: 27° Humidity: 31% Ground: 45°

| | | |
|---|---|---|
| 1 | Iannone | 1m 55.598s |
| 2 | Elias | 1m 55.858s |
| 3 | de Angelis | 1m 56.222s |
| 4 | Cluzel | 1m 56.272s |
| 5 | Tomizawa | 1m 56.284s |
| 6 | Gadea | 1m 56.296s |
| 7 | Talmacsi | 1m 56.305s |
| 8 | Pons | 1m 56.331s |
| 9 | Luthi | 1m 56.339s |
| 10 | Simon | 1m 56.343s |
| 11 | Baldolini | 1m 56.388s |
| 12 | Faubel | 1m 56.443s |
| 13 | Simeon | 1m 56.466s |
| 14 | de Rosa | 1m 56.543s |
| 15 | Debon | 1m 56.647s |
| 16 | Rolfo | 1m 56.649s |
| 17 | Pesek | 1m 56.652s |
| 18 | Tode | 1m 56.665s |
| 19 | Takahashi | 1m 56.716s |
| 20 | Abraham | 1m 56.718s |
| 21 | di Meglio | 1m 56.746s |
| 22 | Corti | 1m 56.799s |
| 23 | Bradl | 1m 56.851s |
| 24 | Wilairot | 1m 56.888s |
| 25 | Pasini | 1m 56.897s |
| 26 | Corsi | 1m 56.898s |
| 27 | Hernandez | 1m 56.911s |
| 28 | Redding | 1m 57.049s |
| 29 | Aegerter | 1m 57.380s |
| 30 | Ivanov | 1m 57.392s |
| 31 | Canepa | 1m 57.400s |
| 32 | Pietri | 1m 57.455s |
| 33 | Noyes | 1m 57.467s |
| 34 | Olive | 1m 57.589s |
| 35 | Nieto | 1m 57.690s |
| 36 | Martinez | 1m 57.733s |
| 37 | Debise | 1m 57.940s |
| 38 | Leonov | 1m 58.247s |
| 39 | West | 1m 58.430s |
| 40 | Guerra | 1m 58.467s |
| 41 | Delhalle | 1m 58.701s |

**Fastest race laps**

| | | |
|---|---|---|
| 1 | Iannone | 1m 55.647s |
| 2 | Tomizawa | 1m 56.213s |
| 3 | Faubel | 1m 56.227s |
| 4 | Gadea | 1m 56.248s |
| 5 | Luthi | 1m 56.263s |
| 6 | Debon | 1m 56.335s |
| 7 | Corsi | 1m 56.376s |
| 8 | Talmacsi | 1m 56.534s |
| 9 | Simon | 1m 56.548s |
| 10 | Elias | 1m 56.594s |
| 11 | Cluzel | 1m 56.640s |
| 12 | de Angelis | 1m 56.657s |
| 13 | Bradl | 1m 56.735s |
| 14 | di Meglio | 1m 56.780s |
| 15 | Wilairot | 1m 56.827s |
| 16 | Pesek | 1m 56.837s |
| 17 | Nieto | 1m 56.842s |
| 18 | Takahashi | 1m 56.874s |
| 19 | Baldolini | 1m 56.973s |
| 20 | Simeon | 1m 57.058s |
| 21 | Ivanov | 1m 57.102s |
| 22 | Pons | 1m 57.258s |
| 23 | de Rosa | 1m 57.330s |
| 24 | Redding | 1m 57.335s |
| 25 | Aegerter | 1m 57.338s |
| 26 | Hernandez | 1m 57.411s |
| 27 | Abraham | 1m 57.473s |
| 28 | Rolfo | 1m 57.503s |
| 29 | Pietri | 1m 57.526s |
| 30 | Debise | 1m 57.622s |
| 31 | Pasini | 1m 57.625s |
| 32 | Corti | 1m 57.833s |
| 33 | Leonov | 1m 57.897s |
| 34 | Noyes | 1m 57.898s |
| 35 | Martinez | 1m 58.051s |
| 36 | Canepa | 1m 58.104s |
| 37 | Tode | 1m 58.106s |
| 38 | West | 1m 58.248s |
| 39 | Delhalle | 1m 58.283s |
| 40 | Guerra | 1m 58.311s |

**Championship Points**

| | | |
|---|---|---|
| 1 | Elias | 74 |
| 2 | Tomizawa | 55 |
| 3 | Corsi | 51 |
| 4 | Gadea | 46 |
| 5 | Iannone | 38 |
| 6 | Luthi | 38 |
| 7 | Simon | 35 |
| 8 | Talmacsi | 34 |
| 9 | Debon | 26 |
| 10 | Cluzel | 21 |
| 11 | Takahashi | 21 |
| 12 | Rolfo | 21 |
| 13 | Nieto | 12 |
| 14 | Bradl | 11 |
| 15 | Pasini | 10 |
| 16 | Hernandez | 10 |
| 17 | Wilairot | 9 |
| 18 | Noyes | 9 |
| 19 | Baldolini | 9 |
| 20 | Aegerter | 8 |
| 21 | de Angelis | 5 |
| 22 | Redding | 5 |
| 23 | Faubel | 4 |
| 24 | Pesek | 4 |
| 25 | Abraham | 2 |
| 26 | Corti | 1 |
| 27 | West | 1 |

**Constructors**

| | | |
|---|---|---|
| 1 | Moriwaki | 76 |
| 2 | Suter | 75 |
| 3 | MotoBI | 53 |
| 4 | Speed Up | 52 |
| 5 | Pons Kalex | 46 |
| 6 | FTR | 26 |
| 7 | Tech 3 | 21 |
| 8 | RSV | 10 |
| 9 | BQR-Moto2 | 10 |
| 10 | Bimota | 9 |
| 11 | Promoharris | 9 |
| 12 | I.C.P. | 9 |
| 13 | Force GP210 | 5 |
| 14 | MZ-RE Honda | 1 |

## 125cc

**RACE DISTANCE:** 20 laps, 65.182 miles/104.900 km · **RACE WEATHER:** Dry (air 25°, humidity 43%, track 43°)

| Pos. | Rider | Nat. | No. | Entrant | Machine | Laps | Time & Speed |
|---|---|---|---|---|---|---|---|
| 1 | **Marc Marquez** | SPA | 93 | Red Bull Ajo Motorsport | Derbi | 20 | 39m 53.153s (mph/km/h) 98.052/157.800 |
| 2 | **Nicolas Terol** | SPA | 40 | Bancaja Aspar Team | Aprilia | 20 | 39m 53.192s |
| 3 | **Pol Espargaro** | SPA | 44 | Tuenti Racing | Derbi | 20 | 39m 53.269s |
| 4 | **Bradley Smith** | GBR | 38 | Bancaja Aspar Team | Aprilia | 20 | 39m 53.314s |
| 5 | **Efren Vazquez** | SPA | 7 | Tuenti Racing | Derbi | 20 | 40m 03.434s |
| 6 | **Randy Krummenacher** | SWI | 35 | Stipa-Molenaar Racing GP | Aprilia | 20 | 40m 03.517s |
| 7 | **Esteve Rabat** | SPA | 12 | Blusens-STX | Aprilia | 20 | 40m 03.715s |
| 8 | **Tomoyoshi Koyama** | JPN | 71 | Racing Team Germany | Aprilia | 20 | 40m 29.494s |
| 9 | **Johann Zarco** | FRA | 14 | WTR San Marino Team | Aprilia | 20 | 40m 29.564s |
| 10 | **Danny Webb** | GBR | 99 | Andalucia Cajasol | Aprilia | 20 | 40m 29.883s |
| 11 | **Jonas Folger** | GER | 94 | Ongetta Team | Aprilia | 20 | 40m 29.928s |
| 12 | **Alexis Masbou** | FRA | 5 | Ongetta Team | Aprilia | 20 | 40m 39.024s |
| 13 | **Marcel Schrotter** | GER | 78 | Interwetten Honda 125 | Honda | 20 | 40m 39.032s |
| 14 | **Jasper Iwema** | NED | 53 | CBC Corse | Aprilia | 20 | 40m 39.048s |
| 15 | **Simone Grotzkyj** | ITA | 15 | Fontana Racing | Aprilia | 20 | 40m 39.213s |
| 16 | Riccardo Moretti | ITA | 51 | Junior GP FMI | Aprilia | 20 | 40m 43.458s |
| 17 | Jakub Kornfeil | CZE | 84 | Racing Team Germany | Aprilia | 20 | 40m 43.942s |
| 18 | Alessandro Tonucci | ITA | 95 | Junior GP Racing Team FMI | Aprilia | 20 | 40m 46.298s |
| 19 | Mattia Tarozzi | ITA | 98 | Faenza Racing | Aprilia | 20 | 41m 12.600s |
| 20 | Armando Pontone | ITA | 97 | Junior GP Racing Team FMI | Aprilia | 20 | 41m 12.694s |
| 21 | Zulfahmi Khairuddin | MAL | 63 | AirAsia-Sepang Int. Circuit | Aprilia | 20 | 41m 12.698s |
| 22 | Michael van der Mark | NED | 60 | Lambretta Reparto Corse | Lambretta | 20 | 41m 14.917s |
| | Alberto Moncayo | SPA | 23 | Andalucia Cajasol | Aprilia | 16 | DNF |
| | Luigi Morciano | ITA | 92 | Junior GP Racing Team FMI | Aprilia | 16 | DNF |
| | Louis Rossi | FRA | 69 | CBC Corse | Aprilia | 14 | DNF |
| | Sturla Fagerhaug | NOR | 50 | AirAsia-Sepang Int. Circuit | Aprilia | 12 | DNF |
| | Sandro Cortese | GER | 11 | Avant Mitsubishi Ajo | Derbi | 7 | DNF |
| | Lorenzo Savadori | ITA | 32 | Matteoni CP Racing | Aprilia | 4 | DNF |
| | Tommaso Gabrielli | ITA | 96 | Racing Team Gabrielli | Aprilia | 3 | DNF |
| | Marco Ravaioli | ITA | 72 | Lambretta Reparto Corse | Lambretta | 3 | DNF |
| | Luca Marconi | ITA | 87 | Ongetta Team | Aprilia | 1 | DNF |

**Fastest lap:** Bradley Smith, on lap 8, 1m 58.009s, 99.422mph/160.004km/h (record).
**Previous lap record:** Mike di Meglio, FRA (Derbi), 1m 58.570s, 98.531mph/159.247km/h (2008).
**Event best maximum speed:** Pol Espargaro, 151.4mph/243.6km/h (race).

**Qualifying:** Dry
Air: 29° Humidity: 30% Ground: 47°

| | | |
|---|---|---|
| 1 | Cortese | 1m 58.315s |
| 2 | Espargaro | 1m 58.336s |
| 3 | Smith | 1m 58.572s |
| 4 | Terol | 1m 58.586s |
| 5 | Krummenacher | 1m 58.682s |
| 6 | Marquez | 1m 58.705s |
| 7 | Rabat | 1m 59.177s |
| 8 | Vazquez | 1m 59.341s |
| 9 | Zarco | 1m 59.617s |
| 10 | Koyama | 1m 59.692s |
| 11 | Iwema | 1m 59.809s |
| 12 | Salom | 2m 00.052s |
| 13 | Webb | 2m 00.131s |
| 14 | Moncayo | 2m 00.559s |
| 15 | Tonucci | 2m 00.774s |
| 16 | Morciano | 2m 00.890s |
| 17 | Masbou | 2m 01.300s |
| 18 | Schrotter | 2m 01.312s |
| 19 | Fagerhaug | 2m 01.351s |
| 20 | Grotzkyj | 2m 01.589s |
| 21 | Kornfeil | 2m 01.683s |
| 22 | Moretti | 2m 01.797s |
| 23 | Folger | 2m 01.868s |
| 24 | Gabrielli | 2m 01.898s |
| 25 | Savadori | 2m 02.243s |
| 26 | Tarozzi | 2m 02.417s |
| 27 | Khairuddin | 2m 02.586s |
| 28 | Pontone | 2m 02.763s |
| 29 | van der Mark | 2m 03.114s |
| 30 | Marconi | 2m 03.245s |
| 31 | Rossi | 2m 03.864s |
| 32 | Ravaioli | 2m 06.126s |
| Outside 107% | | |
| DNQ | Martin | 2m 21.695s |

**Fastest race laps**

| | | |
|---|---|---|
| 1 | Smith | 1m 58.009s |
| 2 | Marquez | 1m 58.101s |
| 3 | Espargaro | 1m 58.235s |
| 4 | Terol | 1m 58.425s |
| 5 | Cortese | 1m 58.635s |
| 6 | Vazquez | 1m 58.807s |
| 7 | Rabat | 1m 59.033s |
| 8 | Krummenacher | 1m 59.084s |
| 9 | Koyama | 1m 59.914s |
| 10 | Zarco | 1m 59.955s |
| 11 | Schrotter | 2m 00.098s |
| 12 | Rossi | 2m 00.314s |
| 13 | Masbou | 2m 00.389s |
| 14 | Webb | 2m 00.389s |
| 15 | Folger | 2m 00.463s |
| 16 | Kornfeil | 2m 00.580s |
| 17 | Iwema | 2m 00.589s |
| 18 | Grotzkyj | 2m 00.630s |
| 19 | Moncayo | 2m 00.673s |
| 20 | Tonucci | 2m 00.690s |
| 21 | Morciano | 2m 00.809s |
| 22 | Moretti | 2m 00.822s |
| 23 | Fagerhaug | 2m 01.216s |
| 24 | Gabrielli | 2m 01.966s |
| 25 | Pontone | 2m 02.283s |
| 26 | Khairuddin | 2m 02.306s |
| 27 | Tarozzi | 2m 02.323s |
| 28 | van der Mark | 2m 02.357s |
| 29 | Savadori | 2m 3.134s |
| 30 | Ravaioli | 2m 05.483s |
| 31 | Marconi | 2m 13.096s |

**Championship Points**

| | | |
|---|---|---|
| 1 | Terol | 85 |
| 2 | Espargaro | 79 |
| 3 | Marquez | 57 |
| 4 | Smith | 45 |
| 5 | Vazquez | 44 |
| 6 | Rabat | 43 |
| 7 | Koyama | 34 |
| 8 | Krummenacher | 30 |
| 9 | Cortese | 26 |
| 10 | Zarco | 25 |
| 11 | Webb | 18 |
| 12 | Masbou | 17 |
| 13 | Iwema | 14 |
| 14 | Moncayo | 13 |
| 15 | Folger | 9 |
| 16 | Salom | 7 |
| 17 | Schrotter | 7 |
| 18 | Martin | 4 |
| 19 | Kornfeil | 2 |
| 20 | Grotzkyj | 1 |

**Constructors**

| | | |
|---|---|---|
| 1 | Derbi | 95 |
| 2 | Aprilia | 85 |
| 3 | Honda | 7 |
| 4 | Lambretta | 1 |

Lap one, and Lorenzo had
already started to get clear
of Dovizioso, de Puniet and
Pedrosa.
Photo: Gold & Goose

*Above:* The battle for second: Dovizioso leads de Puniet, Hayden and Spies.

*Top right:* Two Silverstone winners: Lorenzo and Mamola.

*Above right:* Steve Parrish unveils a painting of Barry Sheene with the BRDC's Nick Whale and track boss Richard Phillips.

*Centre, left to right:* Ill-fated Aoyama at the Day of Champions; Rossi's Yamaha was present and correct, but riderless; F1's Mark Webber is an enthusiastic follower of MotoGP; Randy Mamola gave F1 commentator and former driver Martin Brundle a two-wheel experience.

*Right:* Run over by his own bike, Pedrosa was fortunate to escape serious injury.

Photos: Gold & Goose

TRADITION, tradition – and there was plenty of it, mostly updated, for the return of the British GP to Silverstone after an absence of 23 years. The wide-open Northamptonshire airfield circuit had been the first home of the race in 1976, having taken over from the Isle of Man TT, and many in the paddock had strong memories of an atmospheric, difficult and spectacularly fast track.

Much had changed, especially with the introduction of several safety-orientated chicanes and ess-bends, and some very tight infield turns, since the time when Barry Sheene and Kenny Roberts had staged that memorable battle in 1979: Roberts won by 0.03 second, Sheene coming out of near-flat-out Woodcote on the grass.

Then much had changed again, and was still changing, with the circuit under new management, and also the double beneficiary of Donington Park's slide from ambition into temporary closure. Silverstone had secured the bike GP already, because Donington's new regime had bigger plans – and then Silverstone regained the all-important car GP when it ran out of money.

That race was scheduled for three weeks time, and the F1 visitors included popular bike fan Mark Webber and designer Adrian Newey among many others, all eager to see the new GP track in action at the first major event since it had been significantly redesigned and reprofiled.

The redesign had been aimed at regaining some of the old character of the wide-open circuit: the run back from Abbey had been significantly altered, even regaining a semblance of the old wide and spectacular Woodcote. Now, however, it was approached from a third-gear loop, whereas before packs of bikes would be piling in from a full top-gear blast.

Only a handful of riders had any Silverstone experience, among them Stoner and Spies, but only a few of the first corners were as before, so it meant little. All the riders liked the track, bumps aside. Lorenzo was a fan: "It's beautiful; very difficult, and the lap takes a long time. It's long and wide, and difficult to understand." Stoner thought it "fantastic", but added that in some places it was smoother on the kerb than on the track. Double winner on the old track Randy Mamola had a riposte: "This was a common sort of racetrack for us – Assen was almost eight kilometres, and Spa-Francorchamps. These guys should get used to it and enjoy it, and ride those bumps."

Silverstone has wide-open spaces, and nowadays these include vast paved run-off areas, tailored for F1. Those on the exit of Stowe could be used to widen the exit, and a line across the kerbs and the green verge on to the run-off was especially popular with 125 riders anxious to maintain momentum. By Saturday morning, it had been banned: riders drifting wide, even inadvertently, would have that lap disallowed in qualifying, while there was a discretionary ride-through penalty in the race. The biggest loser was Takahashi, who was placed 12th fastest in Moto2 until his lap was disallowed. He ended up 38th.

The unique combination of fast bumpy corners and intermittent high winds contributed to a number of crashes,

while cool mornings were the most likely times for these to occur. On Saturday morning, Dovizioso, Barbera, Spies and Simoncelli all fell without serious injury – Barbera's bike continued to run on its side for a minute or more, apparently without damage to the engine. In qualifying, Pedrosa had a really lucky escape. Near the end of a fast lap, a quirk of trajectory as he was flicked over the high-side meant his bike stayed wheels-down and ran right over him, passing up between his legs, the footpeg ripping his leathers. His Honda head-butted the barrier and Dani was stretchered away, but emerged unhurt. Then, in race-morning warm-up, there was another cold-tyre incident. Two-fifty champion Aoyama was victim of a particularly nasty high-side at Vale, sustaining fractures to his vertebrae that would keep him out for many weeks.

The absence of Rossi, by now at home, but still on his back, was palpable; the evidence was another runaway winner. Lorenzo had emerged as confident standard-bearer, but was, at least in public, radiating his usual calm and refusing to become over-excited about his points lead. "I'm in no rush," he said. Stoner offered an amusing aside on the difference of racing without Rossi present. "The fans are more polite," he said. "That's the only difference. They all love him so much that when he's there, they hate all the other riders."

It was probable that there were fewer of them through his absence; race day attendance of 70,123 was almost 20,000 fewer than at Donington in 2009.

At this point, everyone expected him to be away until Brno at the earliest; Yamaha had one more race before he had to be replaced (giving Rossi, upon his return, a potentially useful bank of unused mileage on his allocation of engines). Speculation suggested that Spies might be given a run on his bikes; more plausibly that former factory rider Edwards would be put in as a safe pair of hands.

Meantime, potential future Ducati team-mate Hayden was looking forward to the prospect. "He improves bikes, teams, packages. Specially if he brings that guy [Jerry Burgess] who calls the shots with him. I think Rossi would win on the Ducati."

Surprising news put Kevin Schwantz in charge of a one-race wild-card entry from American Honda for Indianapolis, with Roger Lee Hayden in the saddle. A career-long Suzuki man, the 1993 world champion, had been courting a top spot in the factory team for some time, but had finally abandoned hope. "I've asked and I've asked Suzuki and the Japanese. I made up my mind a year ago that if something else came to me and it happened to be with a different brand, I wasn't going to stand around and wait any more," he told America's *Cycle News*.

The annual charity Day of Champions transferred with the race from Donington, and enjoyed the best weather the day before a cloudy and blustery weekend, netting £10,000 more than 2009 at the auction, with a total of £185,607.

## MOTOGP RACE – 20 laps

Lorenzo's first pole since Estoril in 2009 was under double threat at the end of the session: by Pedrosa, until he fell off under his own bike, and also de Puniet, until he also crashed on his best lap. Even so, he ended up an impressive second, and Pedrosa third. Dani fell again in morning warm-up and was by now a little beaten up.

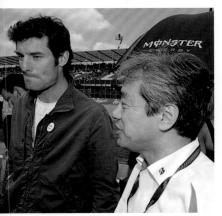

Stoner was a surprising sixth on the grid, behind Dovizioso and Hayden, with a problem that was troubling others: putting and keeping enough heat in the tyres. Stoner said that his were actually cooling down. All but three riders – Pedrosa, Hayden and de Puniet – would choose the softer option for the race.

The lead changed hands four times on the first lap, and then never again. Lorenzo was first away, Pedrosa passed him at the end of the Hangar Straight, Jorge passed him straight back at the next corner. Then Dani made one more lunge and got ahead, only to run out wide with a big slide. As he tried to push on, the front kept tucking and he was obliged to back off to wait "until the harder tyre came in later. I don't know why, but it went the other way."

Lorenzo got his head down and reeled off a handful of fastest laps, the fourth setting the new record. By now, he was already 1.6 seconds ahead, and the gap kept on stretching, to almost eight seconds at half-distance. "I expected Dani to stay with me for three or four laps, but he went to the rear, so I just concentrated on my own race."

Pedrosa finished lap one fourth, and kept on losing time and places from then to the finish.

Dovizioso had taken over second, only to be displaced by de Puniet. The contrast in styles was obvious as the pair disputed the position over the next 16 laps: the wilder de Puniet was ahead more often than not, and once again impressing with his determination to ride a lesser bike on the giddy limit.

Hayden had a reasonable start, but at first found Pedrosa hard to pass. He got ahead on lap three when the Honda ran wide again and started to work on a gap that was around two seconds. By the end of lap seven, he was with the pair up front, but stuck behind them.

Pedrosa delayed the pursuit, but on lap nine Spies and his close companion, Simoncelli, both got past the factory bike and started to close a gap of 1.2 seconds, catching up just after half-distance. Now the group disputing second numbered five.

And Stoner? He'd been in trouble from the very moment he had engaged the clutch. "The bike jumped, shuddered and shook. It felt like the clutch exploded. I got it engaged, but then I got pushed around in Turn One." Apart from a couple of false neutrals, he had no more trouble, but he had finished lap one 12th and had plenty of work to do.

He had the pace for second and, he opined, "maybe even a battle for the win". On lap five, he took eighth from Edwards, the American having another disappointing run, and complaining of heavy steering and consequent arm-pump.

It took Stoner five more laps to catch Pedrosa, and another four to get by, with the Spaniard's late braking and the Honda's strong acceleration. His next target, an increasingly confident Simoncelli, was easier, and he blew by a couple of corners later. Now there were six laps to go and a gap of two seconds to the group ahead.

This was led by Dovizioso, from Hayden and Spies, with de Puniet starting to fade. Stoner was ahead of the Frenchman on lap 18.

From there to the end, he was locked on to the back of the quartet, with Spies pushing conspicuously hard just in front of him.

On the last lap, Spies passed Hayden, but was passed right back. The Ducati rider was targeting Dovizioso, but almost fell when he attacked, giving Spies a second chance. The Superbike champion's first rostrum was well earned.

Second to fourth was covered by three-quarters of a second, with de Puniet still just about in touch. Pedrosa closed on Simoncelli again at the end, but not by enough to make a difference; Edwards trailed in behind. Espargaro had been in narrow control of the group disputing last place for the latter half of the race, with Barbera next, and Bautista finally getting the better of Kallio.

## MOTO2 RACE – 18 laps

Volatile in its formative stages, Moto2 gave a second surprise pole to follow that at Le Mans, with rookie Claudio Corti slotting in fully four-tenths faster than team-mate Cluzel. Bradl and Simon completed the front row, displacing earlier leader and spectacular ex-Supermotard stylist Yonny Hernandez.

Unusually, the first race of the day, a feast of close racing, had a strong British interest: youngest-ever GP winner Scott

Redding was in the thick of a lead pack that crossed the line within half a second. There was also one genuine unsung hero. Luthi had dislocated his collarbone in a motocross spill the week before. Heavily strapped and telling no one, he all but won.

Corti led the first lap after Cluzel ran wide into the first corner. Nieto had a flying start from the third row and was riding forcefully with the two leaders, taking over up front on laps two and three.

Bradl had been slow away from the front row, 14th after lap one; on the second, he missed his braking for the tight Vale chicane and took Corsi out with him as he crashed.

Nieto was displaced again by Corti, then Simon led laps five to eight as his fellow Spaniard dropped out of touch.

Now Cluzel joined them, leading for the first time on lap nine. But the next group of seven was closing up, Luthi prominent among it. He had qualified ninth, but had lost eight places on the hectic first lap and had been cutting through ever since.

Redding had finished lap one 15th, but also had charged through; he took over the lead of the chase pack from Debon on lap nine, now 2.4 seconds from the leaders. He'd cut it down to 1.6 when Luthi caught and passed him, and the pair escaped to make a lead pack of five by lap 13.

The fighting was intense, and the first casualty was Corti, who slithered off on lap 17, remounting to finish last.

Luthi was clearly the strongest of the surviving quartet and took the lead on lap 16. He was still leading as they started the last lap, but not at the end of it. "I couldn't see where they were, so I decided to push as hard as I could, and I pushed too hard and almost crashed," he explained.

His little slip let Cluzel through for a first GP victory; Simon was third, his second rostrum of the year; Redding a close, but disappointed fourth. Debon led the next group from Tomizawa, di Meglio and Simeon. Their numbers had been depleted on the last lap, when a suspected spillage on the track saw Hernandez, Baldolini, Abraham and Faubel crash out.

Elias was promoted to tenth by this after a bad race, test-track modifications having proved counter-productive on arrival to leave him unable to escape the midfield barging match. His points lead over Tomizawa shrank by four.

Delhalle and Talmacsi also crashed out, while the luckless Pasini toured into the pits to retire.

*Above:* The Moto2 podium, with heroic Luthi, first-time winner Cluzel and Simon.

*Top left:* I got third! Spies informs winner Lorenzo that he will join him on the rostrum.

*Top right:* Espargaro and Marquez fought almost all the way to the flag.
*Photos: Gold & Goose*

## 125cc RACE – 17 laps

Smith did his best against the Spanish armada, his bike speed problems at last behind him, and looked as though he might top qualifying. Marquez, however, was at the start of a remarkable run and took his second pole in succession at the end. Espargaro and Terol completed the front row.

Marquez led away for the last race of the day, pursued by Espargaro, with Smith third, although he had been displaced by lap three by team-mate Terol. Vazquez was with them, and their scrap gave the leading pair a chance to escape.

By half-distance, they were four seconds clear, their battle intensifying to the thrilling final lap. They swapped back and forth with a series of increasingly forceful moves. Then Espargaro tried too hard to get back around the outside and only saved the crash by picking up, running across the gravel, then recovering on the paved run-off. This gave Marquez a second win in succession by better than 2.5 seconds.

Ten seconds down, the next trio were equally hard at it. Vazquez was at the rear when he crashed out on the final lap. Terol also almost crashed, leaving Smith to take a popular rostrum finish in front of his home crowd, his first of the year.

Koyama was a lonely fifth. A long way behind, Cortese had come through from another poor start to take over the lead of the next group from Krummenacher. Zarco and Rabat were still close behind.

Espargaro took the title lead, but Marquez was closing on him and Terol.

*Above:* Bradley Smith made the podium in his home race.

*Above left:* Brit Scott Redding had the best Moto2 race of the season to date.

*Left:* Cluzel leads Luthi, Simon and Redding in a close Moto2 battle for the lead.

*Photos:* Gold & Goose

OFFICIAL TIMEKEEPER

**SILVERSTONE GRAND PRIX CIRCUIT**

Club
Vale
Luffield
Woodcote
Abbey
Brooklands
Stowe
Farm
Wellington Straight
Hangar straight
Village
The Loop
Copse
Becketts
Aintree
Chapel
Maggotts

Circuit: 3.667m/5.901km, 20 laps

## MotoGP
**RACE DISTANCE:** 20 laps, 73.347 miles/118.040 km · **RACE WEATHER:** Dry (air 17°, humidity 27%, track 29°)

| Pos. | Rider | Nat. | No. | Entrant | Machine | Tyres | Laps | Time & speed |
|---|---|---|---|---|---|---|---|---|
| 1 | **Jorge Lorenzo** | SPA | 99 | Fiat Yamaha Team | Yamaha | B | 20 | 41m 34.083s |
| | | | | | | | | 105.869mph/ |
| | | | | | | | | 170.380km/h |
| 2 | **Andrea Dovizioso** | ITA | 4 | Repsol Honda Team | Honda | B | 20 | 41m 40.826s |
| 3 | **Ben Spies** | USA | 11 | Monster Yamaha Tech 3 | Yamaha | B | 20 | 41m 41.180s |
| 4 | **Nicky Hayden** | USA | 69 | Ducati Marlboro Team | Ducati | B | 20 | 41m 41.397s |
| 5 | **Casey Stoner** | AUS | 27 | Ducati Marlboro Team | Ducati | B | 20 | 41m 41.577s |
| 6 | **Randy de Puniet** | FRA | 14 | LCR Honda MotoGP | Honda | B | 20 | 41m 43.138s |
| 7 | **Marco Simoncelli** | ITA | 58 | San Carlo Honda Gresini | Honda | B | 20 | 41m 48.508s |
| 8 | **Dani Pedrosa** | SPA | 26 | Repsol Honda Team | Honda | B | 20 | 41m 49.396s |
| 9 | **Colin Edwards** | USA | 5 | Monster Yamaha Tech 3 | Yamaha | B | 20 | 42m 02.037s |
| 10 | **Aleix Espargaro** | SPA | 41 | Pramac Racing Team | Ducati | B | 20 | 42m 16.477s |
| 11 | **Hector Barbera** | SPA | 40 | Paginas Amarillas Aspar | Ducati | B | 20 | 42m 17.448s |
| 12 | **Alvaro Bautista** | SPA | 19 | Rizla Suzuki MotoGP | Suzuki | B | 20 | 42m 17.491s |
| 13 | **Mika Kallio** | FIN | 36 | Pramac Racing Team | Ducati | B | 20 | 42m 17.663s |
| | Loris Capirossi | ITA | 65 | Rizla Suzuki MotoGP | Suzuki | B | 13 | DNF |
| | Marco Melandri | ITA | 33 | San Carlo Honda Gresini | Honda | B | 0 | DNF |

**Fastest lap:** Jorge Lorenzo, on lap 4, 2m 03.526s, 106.879mph/172.005km/h (record).
**Previous lap record:** New circuit.
**Event best maximum speed:** Dani Pedrosa, 201.3mph/323.9km/h (qualifying practice).

**Qualifying**
Weather: Dry
Air Temp: 16° Humidity: 37°
Track Temp: 27°

| | | |
|---|---|---|
| 1 | Lorenzo | 2m 03.308s |
| 2 | de Puniet | 2m 03.434s |
| 3 | Pedrosa | 2m 03.586s |
| 4 | Dovizioso | 2m 03.995s |
| 5 | Hayden | 2m 04.332s |
| 6 | Stoner | 2m 04.394s |
| 7 | Spies | 2m 04.477s |
| 8 | Melandri | 2m 04.555s |
| 9 | Simoncelli | 2m 04.868s |
| 10 | Edwards | 2m 05.035s |
| 11 | Barbera | 2m 05.354s |
| 12 | Aoyama | 2m 05.712s |
| 13 | Espargaro | 2m 05.748s |
| 14 | Capirossi | 2m 05.821s |
| 15 | Bautista | 2m 06.607s |
| 16 | Kallio | 2m 06.980s |

**Fastest race laps**

| | | |
|---|---|---|
| 1 | Lorenzo | 2m 03.526s |
| 2 | Stoner | 2m 03.886s |
| 3 | Dovizioso | 2m 04.117s |
| 4 | de Puniet | 2m 04.135s |
| 5 | Pedrosa | 2m 04.191s |
| 6 | Spies | 2m 04.194s |
| 7 | Hayden | 2m 04.223s |
| 8 | Simoncelli | 2m 04.521s |
| 9 | Edwards | 2m 04.666s |
| 10 | Espargaro | 2m 05.510s |
| 11 | Bautista | 2m 05.762s |
| 12 | Barbera | 2m 05.798s |
| 13 | Kallio | 2m 05.839s |
| 14 | Capirossi | 2m 06.028s |

**Championship Points**

| | | |
|---|---|---|
| 1 | Lorenzo | 115 |
| 2 | Dovizioso | 78 |
| 3 | Pedrosa | 73 |
| 4 | Rossi | 61 |
| 5 | Hayden | 52 |
| 6 | de Puniet | 46 |
| 7 | Spies | 36 |
| 8 | Stoner | 35 |
| 9 | Melandri | 32 |
| 10 | Simoncelli | 32 |
| 11 | Edwards | 26 |
| 12 | Barbera | 24 |
| 13 | Espargaro | 22 |
| 14 | Aoyama | 18 |
| 15 | Kallio | 15 |
| 16 | Capirossi | 13 |
| 17 | Bautista | 12 |

**Team Points**

| | | |
|---|---|---|
| 1 | Fiat Yamaha Team | 176 |
| 2 | Repsol Honda Team | 151 |
| 3 | Ducati Marlboro Team | 87 |
| 4 | San Carlo Honda Gresini | 64 |
| 5 | Monster Yamaha Tech 3 | 62 |
| 6 | LCR Honda MotoGP | 46 |
| 7 | Pramac Racing Team | 37 |
| 8 | Rizla Suzuki MotoGP | 25 |
| 9 | Paginas Amarillas Aspar | 24 |
| 10 | Interwetten Honda MotoGP | 18 |

**Constructor Points**

| | | |
|---|---|---|
| 1 | Yamaha | 120 |
| 2 | Honda | 97 |
| 3 | Ducati | 65 |
| 4 | Suzuki | 23 |

| Grid order | 1 | 2 | 3 | 4 | 5 | 6 | 7 | 8 | 9 | 10 | 11 | 12 | 13 | 14 | 15 | 16 | 17 | 18 | 19 | 20 | |
|---|---|---|---|---|---|---|---|---|---|---|---|---|---|---|---|---|---|---|---|---|---|
| 99 LORENZO | 99 | 99 | 99 | 99 | 99 | 99 | 99 | 99 | 99 | 99 | 99 | 99 | 99 | 99 | 99 | 99 | 99 | 99 | 99 | 99 | 1 |
| 14 de PUNIET | 4 | 14 | 14 | 14 | 14 | 14 | 4 | 4 | 14 | 14 | 4 | 4 | 4 | 4 | 4 | 4 | 4 | 4 | 4 | 4 | 2 |
| 26 PEDROSA | 14 | 4 | 4 | 4 | 4 | 4 | 14 | 14 | 4 | 4 | 14 | 14 | 14 | 14 | 14 | 14 | 69 | 69 | 69 | 11 | 3 |
| 4 DOVIZIOSO | 26 | 26 | 69 | 69 | 69 | 69 | 69 | 69 | 69 | 69 | 69 | 69 | 69 | 69 | 69 | 69 | 11 | 11 | 11 | 69 | 4 |
| 69 HAYDEN | 69 | 69 | 26 | 26 | 26 | 26 | 26 | 26 | 11 | 11 | 11 | 11 | 11 | 11 | 11 | 11 | 14 | 27 | 27 | 27 | 5 |
| 27 STONER | 11 | 58 | 58 | 58 | 58 | 11 | 11 | 11 | 58 | 58 | 58 | 58 | 58 | 27 | 27 | 27 | 27 | 14 | 14 | 14 | 6 |
| 11 SPIES | 58 | 11 | 11 | 11 | 11 | 58 | 58 | 58 | 26 | 26 | 26 | 26 | 26 | 58 | 58 | 58 | 58 | 58 | 58 | 58 | 7 |
| 33 MELANDRI | 5 | 5 | 5 | 5 | 27 | 27 | 27 | 27 | 27 | 27 | 27 | 27 | 27 | 26 | 26 | 26 | 26 | 26 | 26 | 26 | 8 |
| 58 SIMONCELLI | 65 | 65 | 65 | 27 | 5 | 5 | 5 | 5 | 5 | 5 | 5 | 5 | 5 | 5 | 5 | 5 | 5 | 5 | 5 | 5 | 9 |
| 5 EDWARDS | 40 | 40 | 27 | 40 | 40 | 40 | 40 | 41 | 41 | 41 | 41 | 41 | 41 | 41 | 41 | 41 | 41 | 41 | 41 | 41 | 10 |
| 40 BARBERA | 36 | 27 | 40 | 65 | 65 | 65 | 65 | 65 | 19 | 19 | 19 | 19 | 19 | 19 | 36 | 40 | 40 | 40 | 40 | 40 | 11 |
| 41 ESPARGARO | 27 | 41 | 41 | 41 | 41 | 41 | 41 | 19 | 65 | 65 | 65 | 40 | 40 | 40 | 40 | 40 | 36 | 19 | 19 | 19 | 12 |
| 65 CAPIROSSI | 41 | 36 | 36 | 36 | 19 | 19 | 19 | 40 | 40 | 40 | 40 | 65 | 65 | 36 | 36 | 19 | 19 | 36 | 36 | 36 | 13 |
| 19 BAUTISTA | 19 | 19 | 19 | 19 | 36 | 36 | 36 | 36 | 36 | 36 | 36 | 36 | 36 | | | | | | | | |
| 36 KALLIO | | | | | | | | | | | | | | | | | | | | | |

## Moto2 RACE DISTANCE: 18 laps, 66.012 miles/106.236 km · RACE WEATHER: Dry (air 16°, humidity 26%, track 20°)

| Pos. | Rider | Nat. | No. | Entrant | Machine | Laps | Time & Speed |
|---|---|---|---|---|---|---|---|
| 1 | **Jules Cluzel** | FRA | 16 | Forward Racing | Suter | 18 | 39m 19.472s (mph/km/h) 100.719/162.091 |
| 2 | **Thomas Luthi** | SWI | 12 | Interwetten Moriwaki Moto2 | Moriwaki | 18 | 39m 19.529s |
| 3 | **Julian Simon** | SPA | 60 | Mapfre Aspar Team | Suter | 18 | 39m 19.794s |
| 4 | **Scott Redding** | GBR | 45 | Marc VDS Racing Team | Suter | 18 | 39m 19.992s |
| 5 | **Alex Debon** | SPA | 6 | Aeroport de Castello - Ajo | FTR | 18 | 39m 24.743s |
| 6 | **Shoya Tomizawa** | JPN | 48 | Technomag-CIP | Suter | 18 | 39m 24.849s |
| 7 | **Mike di Meglio** | FRA | 63 | Mapfre Aspar Team | Suter | 18 | 39m 24.956s |
| 8 | **Xavier Simeon** | BEL | 19 | Holiday Gym G22 | Moriwaki | 18 | 39m 25.181s |
| 9 | **Dominique Aegerter** | SWI | 77 | Technomag-CIP | Suter | 18 | 39m 29.712s |
| 10 | **Toni Elias** | SPA | 24 | Gresini Racing Moto2 | Moriwaki | 18 | 39m 29.883s |
| 11 | **Fonsi Nieto** | SPA | 10 | Holiday Gym G22 | Moriwaki | 18 | 39m 30.173s |
| 12 | **Andrea Iannone** | ITA | 29 | Fimmco Speed Up | Speed Up | 18 | 39m 30.213s |
| 13 | **Ratthapark Wilairot** | THA | 14 | Thai Honda PTT Singha SAG | Bimota | 18 | 39m 30.431s |
| 14 | **Arne Tode** | GER | 41 | Racing Team Germany | Suter | 18 | 39m 35.534s |
| 15 | **Sergio Gadea** | SPA | 40 | Tenerife 40 Pons | Pons Kalex | 18 | 39m 35.633s |
| 16 | Niccolo Canepa | ITA | 59 | RSM Team Scot | Force GP210 | 18 | 39m 43.590s |
| 17 | Anthony West | AUS | 8 | MZ Racing Team | MZ-RE Honda | 18 | 39m 49.035s |
| 18 | Yuki Takahashi | JPN | 72 | Tech 3 Racing | Tech 3 | 18 | 39m 49.424s |
| 19 | Vladimir Ivanov | UKR | 61 | Gresini Racing Moto2 | Moriwaki | 18 | 39m 49.690s |
| 20 | Lukas Pesek | CZE | 52 | Matteoni CP Racing | Moriwaki | 18 | 39m 50.761s |
| 21 | Kenny Noyes | USA | 9 | Jack & Jones by A.Banderas | Promoharris | 18 | 39m 50.895s |
| 22 | Kev Coghlan | GBR | 54 | Monlau Joey Darcey | FTR | 18 | 39m 51.187s |
| 23 | Axel Pons | SPA | 80 | Tenerife 40 Pons | Pons Kalex | 18 | 39m 51.291s |
| 24 | Roberto Rolfo | ITA | 44 | Italtrans S.T.R. | Suter | 18 | 39m 54.919s |
| 25 | Bernat Martinez | SPA | 76 | Maquinza-SAG Team | Bimota | 18 | 39m 55.323s |
| 26 | Valentin Debise | FRA | 53 | WTR San Marino Team | ADV | 18 | 40m 02.396s |
| 27 | Robertino Pietri | VEN | 39 | Italtrans S.T.R. | Suter | 18 | 40m 11.038s |
| 28 | Raffaele de Rosa | ITA | 35 | Tech 3 Racing | Tech 3 | 18 | 40m 16.001s |
| 29 | Vladimir Leonov | RUS | 21 | Vector Kiefer Racing | Suter | 18 | 40m 17.833s |
| 30 | Claudio Corti | ITA | 71 | Forward Racing | Suter | 18 | 40m 38.143s |
| | Joan Olive | SPA | 5 | Jack & Jones by A.Banderas | Promoharris | 18 | Finish in pitlane |
| | Yonny Hernandez | COL | 68 | Blusens-STX | BQR-Moto2 | 17 | DNF |
| | Alex Baldolini | ITA | 25 | Caretta Technology Race Dept. | I.C.P. | 17 | DNF |
| | Karel Abraham | CZE | 17 | Cardion AB Motoracing | FTR | 17 | DNF |
| | Hector Faubel | SPA | 55 | Marc VDS Racing Team | Suter | 17 | DNF |
| | Mattia Pasini | ITA | 75 | JIR Moto2 | MotoBI | 16 | DNF |
| | Gabor Talmacsi | HUN | 2 | Fimmco Speed Up | Speed Up | 15 | DNF |
| | Anthony Delhalle | FRA | 96 | Blusens-STX | BQR-Moto2 | 13 | DNF |
| | Simone Corsi | ITA | 3 | JIR Moto2 | MotoBI | 1 | DNF |
| | Stefan Bradl | GER | 65 | Viessmann Kiefer Racing | Suter | 1 | DNF |

**Fastest lap:** Thomas Luthi, on lap 12, 2m 09.886s, 101.646mph/163.583km/h (record).
**Previous lap record:** New category.
**Event best maximum speed:** Andrea Iannone, 172.4mph/277.5km/h (race).

**Qualifying:** Dry
Air: 14° Humidity: 37% Ground: 23°

| | | |
|---|---|---|
| 1 | Corti | 2m 09.624s |
| 2 | Cluzel | 2m 10.037s |
| 3 | Bradl | 2m 10.413s |
| 4 | Simon | 2m 10.419s |
| 5 | Hernandez | 2m 10.475s |
| 6 | Simeon | 2m 10.492s |
| 7 | Baldolini | 2m 10.578s |
| 8 | Tode | 2m 10.634s |
| 9 | Luthi | 2m 10.654s |
| 10 | Nieto | 2m 10.668s |
| 11 | Tomizawa | 2m 10.688s |
| 12 | Redding | 2m 10.768s |
| 13 | Aegerter | 2m 10.773s |
| 14 | Abraham | 2m 10.802s |
| 15 | Corsi | 2m 10.821s |
| 16 | Iannone | 2m 10.846s |
| 17 | Debon | 2m 10.864s |
| 18 | Elias | 2m 11.050s |
| 19 | Talmacsi | 2m 11.177s |
| 20 | Pons | 2m 11.190s |
| 21 | Pasini | 2m 11.212s |
| 22 | Gadea | 2m 11.221s |
| 23 | Noyes | 2m 11.410s |
| 24 | Wilairot | 2m 11.421s |
| 25 | Pesek | 2m 11.457s |
| 26 | Canepa | 2m 11.461s |
| 27 | Rolfo | 2m 11.537s |
| 28 | Martinez | 2m 11.613s |
| 29 | Pietri | 2m 11.684s |
| 30 | Coghlan | 2m 11.694s |
| 31 | di Meglio | 2m 11.815s |
| 32 | Faubel | 2m 11.948s |
| 33 | West | 2m 12.052s |
| 34 | Ivanov | 2m 12.167s |
| 35 | Olive | 2m 12.340s |
| 36 | de Rosa | 2m 12.360s |
| 37 | Delhalle | 2m 12.502s |
| 38 | Takahashi | 2m 12.568s |
| 39 | Debise | 2m 13.106s |
| 40 | Leonov | 2m 13.240s |

**Fastest race laps**

| | | |
|---|---|---|
| 1 | Luthi | 2m 09.886s |
| 2 | Redding | 2m 10.015s |
| 3 | Wilairot | 2m 10.283s |
| 4 | Cluzel | 2m 10.322s |
| 5 | Corti | 2m 10.342s |
| 6 | Hernandez | 2m 10.354s |
| 7 | Debon | 2m 10.489s |
| 8 | Simon | 2m 10.492s |
| 9 | Tomizawa | 2m 10.493s |
| 10 | Elias | 2m 10.513s |
| 11 | Baldolini | 2m 10.595s |
| 12 | Aegerter | 2m 10.599s |
| 13 | Simeon | 2m 10.624s |
| 14 | Nieto | 2m 10.649s |
| 15 | Iannone | 2m 10.663s |
| 16 | di Meglio | 2m 10.665s |
| 17 | Canepa | 2m 10.673s |
| 18 | Abraham | 2m 10.832s |
| 19 | Coghlan | 2m 10.849s |
| 20 | Pasini | 2m 10.941s |
| 21 | Talmacsi | 2m 10.952s |
| 22 | Gadea | 2m 11.014s |
| 23 | Tode | 2m 11.069s |
| 24 | Faubel | 2m 11.197s |
| 25 | West | 2m 11.327s |
| 26 | Pesek | 2m 11.340s |
| 27 | Noyes | 2m 11.349s |
| 28 | Pons | 2m 11.434s |
| 29 | Ivanov | 2m 11.457s |
| 30 | Delhalle | 2m 11.458s |
| 31 | Rolfo | 2m 11.519s |
| 32 | Takahashi | 2m 11.521s |
| 33 | Martinez | 2m 11.723s |
| 34 | Leonov | 2m 12.190s |
| 35 | Debise | 2m 12.201s |
| 36 | Pietri | 2m 12.391s |
| 37 | de Rosa | 2m 12.395s |
| 38 | Olive | 2m 12.748s |
| 39 | Corsi | 2m 17.092s |
| 40 | Bradl | 2m 17.551s |

**Championship Points**

| | | |
|---|---|---|
| 1 | Elias | 80 |
| 2 | Tomizawa | 65 |
| 3 | Luthi | 58 |
| 4 | Simon | 51 |
| 5 | Corsi | 51 |
| 6 | Gadea | 47 |
| 7 | Cluzel | 46 |
| 8 | Iannone | 42 |
| 9 | Debon | 37 |
| 10 | Talmacsi | 34 |
| 11 | Takahashi | 21 |
| 12 | Rolfo | 21 |
| 13 | Redding | 18 |
| 14 | Nieto | 17 |
| 15 | Aegerter | 15 |
| 16 | Wilairot | 12 |
| 17 | Bradl | 11 |
| 18 | Pasini | 10 |
| 19 | Hernandez | 10 |
| 20 | di Meglio | 9 |
| 21 | Noyes | 9 |
| 22 | Baldolini | 9 |
| 23 | Simeon | 8 |
| 24 | de Angelis | 5 |
| 25 | Faubel | 4 |
| 26 | Pesek | 4 |
| 27 | Tode | 2 |
| 28 | Abraham | 2 |
| 29 | Corti | 1 |
| 30 | West | 1 |

**Constructors**

| | | |
|---|---|---|
| 1 | Suter | 100 |
| 2 | Moriwaki | 96 |
| 3 | Speed Up | 56 |
| 4 | MotoBI | 53 |
| 5 | Pons Kalex | 47 |
| 6 | FTR | 37 |
| 7 | Tech 3 | 21 |
| 8 | Bimota | 12 |
| 9 | RSV | 10 |
| 10 | BQR-Moto2 | 10 |
| 11 | Promoharris | 9 |
| 12 | I.C.P. | 9 |
| 13 | Force GP210 | 5 |
| 14 | MZ-RE Honda | 1 |

## 125cc RACE DISTANCE: 17 laps, 62.345 miles/100.334 km · RACE WEATHER: Dry (air 20°, humidity 25%, track 38°)

| Pos. | Rider | Nat. | No. | Entrant | Machine | Laps | Time & Speed |
|---|---|---|---|---|---|---|---|
| 1 | **Marc Marquez** | SPA | 93 | Red Bull Ajo Motorsport | Derbi | 17 | 38m 12.837s (mph/km/h) 97.888/157.535 |
| 2 | **Pol Espargaro** | SPA | 44 | Tuenti Racing | Derbi | 17 | 38m 15.413s |
| 3 | **Bradley Smith** | GBR | 38 | Bancaja Aspar Team | Aprilia | 17 | 38m 26.283s |
| 4 | **Nicolas Terol** | SPA | 40 | Bancaja Aspar Team | Aprilia | 17 | 38m 29.954s |
| 5 | **Tomoyoshi Koyama** | JPN | 71 | Racing Team Germany | Aprilia | 17 | 38m 48.478s |
| 6 | **Sandro Cortese** | GER | 11 | Avant Mitsubishi Ajo | Derbi | 17 | 38m 52.021s |
| 7 | **Randy Krummenacher** | SWI | 35 | Stipa-Molenaar Racing GP | Aprilia | 17 | 38m 52.095s |
| 8 | **Johann Zarco** | FRA | 14 | WTR San Marino Team | Aprilia | 17 | 38m 52.786s |
| 9 | **Esteve Rabat** | SPA | 12 | Blusens-STX | Aprilia | 17 | 38m 53.347s |
| 10 | **Danny Webb** | GBR | 99 | Andalucia Cajasol | Aprilia | 17 | 39m 03.124s |
| 11 | **Efren Vazquez** | SPA | 7 | Tuenti Racing | Derbi | 17 | 39m 16.340s |
| 12 | **Alberto Moncayo** | SPA | 23 | Andalucia Cajasol | Aprilia | 17 | 39m 16.902s |
| 13 | **Jasper Iwema** | NED | 53 | CBC Corse | Aprilia | 17 | 39m 19.985s |
| 14 | **Simone Grotzkyj** | ITA | 15 | Fontana Racing | Aprilia | 17 | 39m 20.428s |
| 15 | **Jonas Folger** | GER | 94 | Ongetta Team | Aprilia | 17 | 39m 20.438s |
| 16 | Adrian Martin | SPA | 26 | Aeroport de Castello - Ajo | Aprilia | 17 | 39m 20.882s |
| 17 | Marcel Schrotter | GER | 78 | Interwetten Honda 125 | Honda | 17 | 39m 25.309s |
| 18 | Sturla Fagerhaug | NOR | 50 | AirAsia-Sepang Int. Circuit | Aprilia | 17 | 39m 29.770s |
| 19 | Louis Rossi | FRA | 69 | CBC Corse | Aprilia | 17 | 39m 50.976s |
| 20 | Jakub Kornfeil | CZE | 84 | Racing Team Germany | Aprilia | 17 | 39m 54.061s |
| 21 | Lorenzo Savadori | ITA | 32 | Matteoni CP Racing | Aprilia | 17 | 39m 54.253s |
| 22 | Michael van der Mark | NED | 60 | Lambretta Reparto Corse | Lambretta | 17 | 39m 55.150s |
| 23 | Luca Marconi | ITA | 87 | Ongetta Team | Aprilia | 17 | 39m 55.479s |
| 24 | Deane Brown | GBR | 75 | Colin Appleyard/Macadam Racing | Honda | 16 | 38m 17.501s |
| | Taylor Mackenzie | GBR | 73 | KRP | Honda | 16 | DNF |
| | Zulfahmi Khairuddin | MAL | 63 | AirAsia-Sepang Int. Circuit | Aprilia | 11 | DNF |
| | Danny Kent | GBR | 52 | Aztec Grand Prix | Honda | 11 | DNF |
| | James Lodge | GBR | 74 | RS Earnshaws Motorcycles | Honda | 8 | DNF |
| | Alexis Masbou | FRA | 5 | Ongetta Team | Aprilia | 5 | DNF |
| | Luis Salom | SPA | 39 | Stipa-Molenaar Racing GP | Aprilia | 4 | DNF |
| | Marco Ravaioli | ITA | 72 | Lambretta Reparto Corse | Lambretta | 4 | DNF |

**Fastest lap:** Pol Espargaro, on lap 14, 2m 13.781s, 98.686mph/158.820km/h (record).
**Previous lap record:** New circuit.
**Event best maximum speed:** Efren Vazquez, 144.7mph/232.9km/h (race).

**Qualifying:** Dry
Air: 16° Humidity: 37% Ground: 25°

| | | |
|---|---|---|
| 1 | Marquez | 2m 14.667s |
| 2 | Smith | 2m 14.966s |
| 3 | Espargaro | 2m 15.112s |
| 4 | Terol | 2m 15.571s |
| 5 | Zarco | 2m 16.208s |
| 6 | Rabat | 2m 16.425s |
| 7 | Koyama | 2m 16.660s |
| 8 | Webb | 2m 16.689s |
| 9 | Vazquez | 2m 16.714s |
| 10 | Krummenacher | 2m 16.918s |
| 11 | Cortese | 2m 17.192s |
| 12 | Moncayo | 2m 17.248s |
| 13 | Salom | 2m 17.406s |
| 14 | Iwema | 2m 17.669s |
| 15 | Grotzkyj | 2m 17.873s |
| 16 | Fagerhaug | 2m 18.212s |
| 17 | Martin | 2m 18.832s |
| 18 | Masbou | 2m 18.948s |
| 19 | Rossi | 2m 19.090s |
| 20 | Schrotter | 2m 19.299s |
| 21 | Kornfeil | 2m 19.320s |
| 22 | Khairuddin | 2m 20.480s |
| 23 | Savadori | 2m 20.583s |
| 24 | Folger | 2m 20.936s |
| 25 | van der Mark | 2m 20.989s |
| 26 | Brown | 2m 21.967s |
| 27 | Mackenzie | 2m 21.988s |
| 28 | Marconi | 2m 22.073s |
| 29 | Kent | 2m 22.279s |
| 30 | Ravaioli | 2m 22.773s |
| 31 | Lodge | 2m 22.885s |
| Outside 107% | | |
| DNQ | Reid | 2m 26.896s |

**Fastest race laps**

| | | |
|---|---|---|
| 1 | Espargaro | 2m 13.781s |
| 2 | Marquez | 2m 14.020s |
| 3 | Terol | 2m 14.617s |
| 4 | Smith | 2m 14.689s |
| 5 | Vazquez | 2m 14.852s |
| 6 | Koyama | 2m 15.738s |
| 7 | Salom | 2m 16.193s |
| 8 | Cortese | 2m 16.198s |
| 9 | Krummenacher | 2m 16.214s |
| 10 | Zarco | 2m 16.316s |
| 11 | Rabat | 2m 16.465s |
| 12 | Webb | 2m 16.674s |
| 13 | Grotzkyj | 2m 17.035s |
| 14 | Masbou | 2m 17.592s |
| 15 | Folger | 2m 17.674s |
| 16 | Iwema | 2m 17.708s |
| 17 | Moncayo | 2m 17.774s |
| 18 | Schrotter | 2m 17.828s |
| 19 | Martin | 2m 17.854s |
| 20 | Fagerhaug | 2m 17.909s |
| 21 | Kornfeil | 2m 17.984s |
| 22 | Khairuddin | 2m 18.947s |
| 23 | Savadori | 2m 18.992s |
| 24 | Rossi | 2m 19.344s |
| 25 | Mackenzie | 2m 19.703s |
| 26 | Marconi | 2m 19.752s |
| 27 | van der Mark | 2m 19.869s |
| 28 | Brown | 2m 20.911s |
| 29 | Kent | 2m 21.212s |
| 30 | Ravaioli | 2m 21.657s |
| 31 | Lodge | 2m 21.776s |

**Championship Points**

| | | |
|---|---|---|
| 1 | Espargaro | 99 |
| 2 | Terol | 98 |
| 3 | Marquez | 82 |
| 4 | Smith | 61 |
| 5 | Rabat | 50 |
| 6 | Vazquez | 49 |
| 7 | Koyama | 45 |
| 8 | Krummenacher | 39 |
| 9 | Cortese | 36 |
| 10 | Zarco | 33 |
| 11 | Webb | 24 |
| 12 | Moncayo | 17 |
| 13 | Masbou | 17 |
| 14 | Iwema | 17 |
| 15 | Folger | 10 |
| 16 | Salom | 7 |
| 17 | Schrotter | 7 |
| 18 | Martin | 4 |
| 19 | Grotzkyj | 3 |
| 20 | Kornfeil | 2 |

**Constructors**

| | | |
|---|---|---|
| 1 | Derbi | 120 |
| 2 | Aprilia | 101 |
| 3 | Honda | 7 |
| 4 | Lambretta | 1 |

FIM WORLD CHAMPIONSHIP · ROUND 6

# DUTCH TT

ASSEN CIRCUIT

On his way to another convincing win, Lorenzo stretches Pedrosa and Stoner, while Dovizioso fades behind.
*Photos:* Gold & Goose

N 2009, Rossi had claimed his hundredth victory at the classic Dutch circuit, scene of so many racing milestones during its 103 years of existence. The absence of the star attraction seemed to have little effect on the numbers, with 97,146 there on race day. The effect on the racing, as we had seen before, was another walk-away win.

Just because he wasn't there didn't mean Valentino wasn't the centre of attention. The rumours had cranked up into overdrive with reports of a huge 15-million-euro offer from Marlboro Ducati.

So it was a relief to get back to the nuts and bolts of racing at this one-third point of the 18-race season. Nuts and bolts as in engines, two of which chose the Dutch track to expire. One belonged to Jorge Lorenzo, the unit he had used for the first two races, and for most free and some qualifying practices ever since. A few puffs of smoke and a tour to the pits, and it was not seen again. The other was Hayden's, with a similar story, believed to be a piston or ring failure. It was also quite well used: he'd raced it at the previous three rounds. But at some 1,600km, as Ducati revealed, it was not quite enough. With 18 races and an average of around 600km per race, that meant a rough total of 10,800km for the year, coming out at around 1,800km for each unit. And that if you wanted to run the last race right up to the end of your last engine's life.

Engines were at the heart of a plea from Moto2 leader Elias: the modest 125-odd horsepower of the mildly tuned stock engines was too little to challenge the riders or provide opportunities for the better ones. As a result, experienced and less-experienced riders inevitably stayed close together, with high-risk consequences. Elias also suggested a three-bike grid formation, to stagger the numbers arriving at the bottleneck of a tight first corner. "Moto2 is the most dangerous class right now," he told MOTOCOURSE.

And there were other nut-and-bolt issues, revealed in an extraordinary practice accident suffered by runner-up Tomizawa. Running on to and then off the kerb on a corner exit, his rear wheel snagged and flicked the bike sideways. That broke the steering damper mount, and amazed TV viewers watched as the bike flapped its front wheel violently from lock to lock and he ran straight on at the next corner. He regained control on the paved run-off, but by then it was too late and he had to abandon ship before hitting the barrier. Faubel had suffered a similar failure on a Suter machine.

Another Moto2 prang (there are always plenty) caused controversy: Wilairot was running slowly, outside the white line, towards the pit entry at the same time as veteran tearaway Debon was drifting wide from the exit of Ramshoek corner. They collided: the Spaniard broke his collarbone, and Wilairot was fined 3,000 euros – a harsh penalty for being in the wrong place at the wrong time.

Back in MotoGP, Melandri also suffered severe consequences after a strange crash. He'd run on to the paved run-off, and then across a strip of grass to regain the track. His back wheel caught, however, and he was flicked and high-sided to land heavily, dislocating his shoulder. That put him out for the weekend and conceivably longer. Once again, though, Melandri would turn out to be tougher than that.

Another injury to the thin field threw the question of substitute riders into focus. Yamaha was veering towards the safe hands of factory tester Wataru Yoshikawa to take over Valentino's bike on the following weekend at Catalunya for what would turn out to be just one race. Interwetten Honda had also looked to Japan to fill Aoyama's vacant seat at short notice: the bike was ridden by Kousuke Akiyoshi, a former Suzuki factory rider and tester.

Stoner had complained after Silverstone of having suffered arm-pump for the first time, blaming an undersuit that was too tight. That corrected, it struck again: "After three laps, I knew I had a problem." This is a vexing complaint, and Lorenzo, Hayden and Elias among others had all had surgery to correct this compartment syndrome problem in

*Above:* Pedrosa made progress, but he was still forced to battle his squirming Honda.

*Top left:* Giacomo Agostini had a run on his title winning 1975 Yamaha, and then tried Rossi's M1.

*Above left:* Kousuke Akiyoshi took over the Interwetten Honda in place of the injured Aoyama.

*Left:* Melandri's hopes of career recovery were put on hold by a shoulder injury.

*Photos:* Gold & Goose

the previous 18 months. Stoner, hoping for the best, kept his practice laps to a minimum, running 68 over three sessions compared with almost 90 for Lorenzo.

The first part of the short new track remained unchanged and highly technical (i.e., slow), increasing the stress Stoner had hoped to avoid, but a change at the end of the revised Veenslang was generally welcomed: a slower corner with hard braking was replaced by a fast fifth-gear kink. This removed one overtaking point, but restored some of the feel of the classic track.

There was a GP commission meeting with some significant, though hardly unexpected news: of the execution of the last of the racing two-strokes, the current 125s to be replaced by four-stroke 250 singles from 2012. Discussions centred on an 81mm-bore purpose-built unit, handily one quarter of a 1000cc four, and it was rumoured that Honda already had just such a unit under development.

The other interesting item concerned an experimental return to four practice sessions instead of three. This was at the request of the riders; for MotoGP, the actual track time would remain the same: four 45-minute sessions instead of three hour-long sessions. "We're just wasting time sitting around talking on Friday mornings anyway," said Stoner. The experiment would take place at the Aragon round.

Since, in 2009, the same riders had complained that 45 minutes was not long enough for a session, and they had been extended to an hour as a result, the response to the change back would be interesting. But many would miss the relaxed atmosphere of Friday mornings. With engines out of

bounds, nowadays mechanics have much less to do, and there had been a chance to circulate and chew the fat, more like racing in an earlier age.

## MOTOGP RACE – 26 laps

Lorenzo was on top of every practice and smooth as you like, joined on the front row by de Puniet, gaining confidence and aggression race by race. Stoner was alongside, while Spies headed row two, fresh from his first GP rostrum and enjoying a return to a track that he knew after a spell of strange ones. Pedrosa was seventh and somewhat at sea, having made a raft of changes front to rear for the race, which successfully eliminated the braking and cornering instability.

It looked as though it would be another runaway like Silverstone. The race began, and the lone Fiat Yamaha was off. Spies made a flying start into second and stayed there, all elbows, for the first three laps, pursuers piling up behind him. By now, Lorenzo was almost 1.5 seconds clear and appeared set for a lonely afternoon.

The revitalised Pedrosa was pushing hard to find a way past the Superbike champion, Stoner doing the same to him, with Dovizioso right behind and de Puniet dogging him.

On lap three, Pedrosa did get past, with a fine move at the far double-rights, Mandeveen and Duikersloot, slipping inside halfway through. At the start of the next lap, Stoner also took the American at the first corner, and then Dovizioso pushed inside into the Strubben. Second to fifth in less than a full lap.

Now the chase was on, and Pedrosa was making the running. He set a new record, only two-hundredths slower than pole time, on the fourth lap; by the fifth, he had caught the leader and had started pushing him hard. At the same time, Stoner also closed up, and by the seventh lap had tagged on behind.

It was a fierce enough battle, but rather austere – tense, but no actual overtaking. And Lorenzo had it under control. He had chosen the harder tyre option; the other two were on the softer choice. Nuances of different performance levels would play into his hands later. "I knew I had to wait a little and let the tyres go down before I could take an advantage," he explained.

After the tenth lap, he made a little gap, up to more than a second on the 13th. But there was no respite: it wasn't until the 19th that it had stretched to more than two seconds, Stoner by now a similar distance behind in third. Arm-pump was the problem once again, hindering his throttle and brake operation. It was, however, his first rostrum of the year. "The bike is capable of a lot better than I am at the moment," he said.

Dovizioso gradually lost touch, and Spies behind him. Then, after half-distance, the American closed again and started to attack. On lap 16, he outbraked the Italian at the chicane. At the same time, de Puniet had also closed back up and was putting the pressure on Dovizioso, the pair passing and repassing.

They changed places four times on the last lap alone, and while Dovizioso managed to be in front when it mattered, this combat quite foiled his own hopes of attacking Spies, who was two seconds ahead over the line.

Hayden had been slow at the start and knocked about on the first lap. Then he lost a lot of time passing Edwards and afterwards Simoncelli, which took five laps. Now he was close to de Puniet, but his pace wasn't; gradually he

*Above:* Wilairot leads the Moto2 gang into the first corner, from Iannone (29), Elias (24) and Tomizawa (48), with Luthi (12) prominent in the pack.

*Right:* Winner Lorenzo with team manager and former rider Wilco Zeelenberg paid tribute to the football World Cup.

*Top right:* Iannone took a second runaway Moto2 win.

*Above far right:* Marquez and Terol fight for the 125 victory. The battle would last all season.

*Far right, top:* Alex Debon broke his collarbone for the first of three times this year.

*Far right:* Vito Ippolito, FIM President.

*Photos: Gold & Goose*

pair had collided in qualifying. This moved Tomizawa up and promoted Luthi to the front row; Elias led row two.

Wilairot, smarting from his heavy punishment, led into the first corners, but Iannone was ahead by the time they reached the new Ruskenhoek kink; by the end of the lap so was Nieto, fast away and set to delay the pursuit.

By the end of lap two, Iannone had doubled his lead to almost two seconds, while both Wilairot and Elias were back ahead of Nieto. From there on, the Italian was on his own, better than five seconds clear at half-distance and more than nine on lap 18. He was able to ease his pace and still win by a comfortable four-and-a-half seconds.

The race wasn't as close as previous rounds, the slow corners at the start of the lap playing a part in splitting up the groups. All the same, although Elias and Wilairot stayed together, the Spaniard was back ahead from lap three. Nieto would lose places slowly over the next three laps, dropping to ninth before crashing out on lap seven; he remounted to retire in the pits.

The pair never got close to Iannone and at half-distance were two seconds clear of Luthi, with Tomizawa and Simon closing up on the Swiss rider.

With four laps to go, there were five disputing second, and the freshly injured Luthi was one of the strongest. Elias held on to second; Luthi forced past Wilairot for third with two laps to go. Tomizawa and Simon were a couple of seconds adrift.

Cluzel had dropped back at the finish into the hands of the next group, narrowly fending off di Meglio and Abraham.

The group had been bigger, but had split by the finish, with Takahashi, Redding, Corsi and Talmacsi disputing tenth place, all over the line within less than two seconds.

There were only two fallers apart from Nieto: Tode and, at the end, Simeon. Meanwhile, luckless Mattia Pasini was still struggling to get to grips with the four-stroke and make his mark: he qualified 15th and raced to a lonely 14th.

Elias extended his points lead over Tomizawa, but both Luthi and Iannone were closing in.

## 125cc RACE – 22 laps

The march of Marquez continued with his fourth pole in six races by better than half a second. Smith was alongside, then Terol and Espargaro.

Pol bogged on the line and was swamped; Marquez got away perfectly and led from start to finish.

He wasn't alone: Terol was on him, and for the next sixteen-and-a-half laps they circulated in very close company, Terol setting the lap record on the 12th.

Their lonely duel was resolved on lap 17 by a heedless backmarker. Dutch wild-card Jerry van de Bunt was disputing last place with countrymen Dubbink and Bijsterbosch. The others gave way, but de Bunt let Marquez through, then slammed the door closed just as Terol was coming through on the inside. De Bunt crashed, while Terol lost a crucial one-and-a-half seconds.

Smith was knocked from second to fourth at the end of the first lap, and delayed thereafter by a determined Vazquez, who responded to every passing move by passing right back. Espargaro, eighth on lap one, caught and passed them both at the chicane.

Vazquez would crash out at the fast Ramshoek on lap four; Espargaro made a strong attempt to catch the leaders, closing to within 1.7 seconds. But that was the most he could do, and from there on he had a lonely race to third, enlivened in the final stages when Smith closed again to within just over a second.

Cortese came through to a lone and distant fifth; Krummenacher won a fierce last-laps battle for sixth with Webb, after catching up all race long. Team-mate Salom was eighth, narrowly ahead of Grotzky and Folger.

Terol regained the points lead from Espargaro, but Marquez was coming up strongly with a third successive win.

---

dropped away, eventually finishing ten seconds behind, although comfortably three seconds ahead of Edwards. Both were somewhat dismayed, Edwards increasingly so, and he soon began railing publicly against the satellite Yamaha's lack of horsepower.

Simoncelli had been caught by Espargaro, and they went back and forth, the Italian finally prevailing for ninth. There was an equally fierce tussle for 11th, won by Kallio from Barbera. The Suzukis had another awful afternoon, Capirossi losing out to Barbera and dropping back to a lonely 13th; Bautista was one place and seven seconds behind. Only Akiyoshi was further back, one lap down.

There were no crashes or retirements, and with only 15 starters, points for everybody.

Most of all for Lorenzo. His points lead over Pedrosa was now 47 – almost a two-race margin. As comforting for the Spaniard was that he was 79 points and more than three races clear of the still-absent Rossi. One third of the way through the season, it was a very comfortable position.

## MOTO2 RACE – 24 laps

Jam-packed as ever, Moto2 yielded two remarkable performances. The first was another runaway by Iannone, who joined Elias to become the second to win two races. The second was a fine aggressive ride by Luthi, not merely bearing the pain from dislocating his collarbone before Silverstone, but having aggravated it considerably: a slide in practice had fractured the injured joint. Luthi gritted his teeth, raced to third and flew straight home to Switzerland to have a plate in his shoulder replaced, to be ready to race the following weekend in Catalunya.

Iannone had claimed a clear pole, the first 15 riders being within the same second. Wilairot was alongside, while Debon had been third fastest, but he was out of the race after the

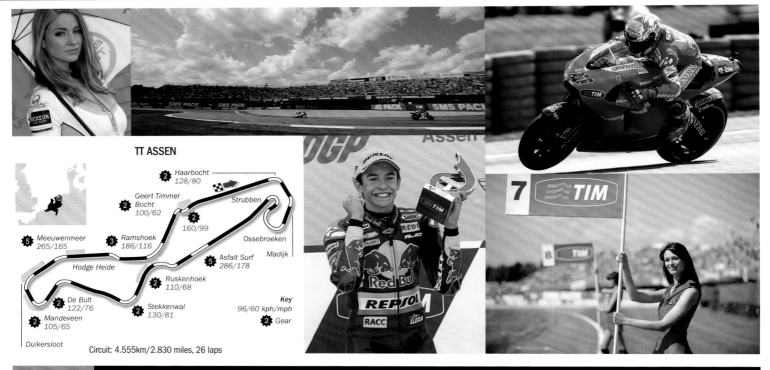

## TT ASSEN

- Haarbocht 128/80
- Geert Timmer Bocht 100/62
- Strubben 160/99
- Meeuwenmeer 265/165
- Ramshoek 186/116
- Ossebroeken
- Hodge Heide
- Asfalt Surf 286/178
- Madijk
- Ruskenhoek 110/68
- De Bult 122/76
- Stekkenwal 130/81
- Mandeveen 105/65
- Duikersloot

**Key** 96/60 kph/mph · Gear

Circuit: 4.555km/2.830 miles, 26 laps

7 ≋ TIM

---

## MotoGP

**RACE DISTANCE: 26 laps, 73.379 miles/118.092 km · RACE WEATHER: Dry (air 23°, humidity 23%, track 48°)**

| Pos. | Rider | Nat. | No. | Entrant | Machine | Tyres | Laps | Time & speed |
|------|-------|------|-----|---------|---------|-------|------|--------------|
| 1 | Jorge Lorenzo | SPA | 99 | Fiat Yamaha Team | Yamaha | B | 26 | 41m 18.629s 106.576mph/ 171.518km/h |
| 2 | Dani Pedrosa | SPA | 26 | Repsol Honda Team | Honda | B | 26 | 41m 21.564s |
| 3 | Casey Stoner | AUS | 27 | Ducati Marlboro Team | Ducati | B | 26 | 41m 25.651s |
| 4 | Ben Spies | USA | 11 | Monster Yamaha Tech 3 | Yamaha | B | 26 | 41m 31.894s |
| 5 | Andrea Dovizioso | ITA | 4 | Repsol Honda Team | Honda | B | 26 | 41m 33.952s |
| 6 | Randy de Puniet | FRA | 14 | LCR Honda MotoGP | Honda | B | 26 | 41m 34.401s |
| 7 | Nicky Hayden | USA | 69 | Ducati Marlboro Team | Ducati | B | 26 | 41m 44.496s |
| 8 | Colin Edwards | USA | 5 | Monster Yamaha Tech 3 | Yamaha | B | 26 | 41m 47.620s |
| 9 | Marco Simoncelli | ITA | 58 | San Carlo Honda Gresini | Honda | B | 26 | 41m 54.287s |
| 10 | Aleix Espargaro | SPA | 41 | Pramac Racing Team | Ducati | B | 26 | 41m 54.466s |
| 11 | Mika Kallio | FIN | 36 | Pramac Racing Team | Ducati | B | 26 | 42m 15.398s |
| 12 | Hector Barbera | SPA | 40 | Paginas Amarillas Aspar | Ducati | B | 26 | 42m 15.519s |
| 13 | Loris Capirossi | ITA | 65 | Rizla Suzuki MotoGP | Suzuki | B | 26 | 42m 19.244s |
| 14 | Alvaro Bautista | SPA | 19 | Rizla Suzuki MotoGP | Suzuki | B | 26 | 42m 26.703s |
| 15 | Kousuke Akiyoshi | JPN | 64 | Interwetten Honda MotoGP | Honda | B | 25 | 41m 42.019s |

Fastest lap: Dani Pedrosa, on lap 4, 1m 34.525s, 107.486mph/172.982km/h (record).

Previous lap record: New circuit.

Event best maximum speed: Marco Melandri, 194.1mph/312.3km/h (free practice 2).

### Qualifying

**Weather:** Dry
**Air Temp:** 23° **Humidity:** 34°
**Track Temp:** 42°

| | | |
|---|---|---|
| 1 | Lorenzo | 1m 34.515s |
| 2 | de Puniet | 1m 34.797s |
| 3 | Stoner | 1m 34.803s |
| 4 | Spies | 1m 34.929s |
| 5 | Hayden | 1m 34.999s |
| 6 | Dovizioso | 1m 35.015s |
| 7 | Pedrosa | 1m 35.162s |
| 8 | Simoncelli | 1m 35.283s |
| 9 | Edwards | 1m 35.393s |
| 10 | Espargaro | 1m 35.593s |
| 11 | Capirossi | 1m 35.664s |
| 12 | Bautista | 1m 36.344s |
| 13 | Kallio | 1m 36.502s |
| 14 | Barbera | 1m 36.569s |
| 15 | Akiyoshi | 1m 38.198s |

### Fastest race laps

| | | |
|---|---|---|
| 1 | Pedrosa | 1m 34.525s |
| 2 | Lorenzo | 1m 34.626s |
| 3 | Stoner | 1m 34.761s |
| 4 | Dovizioso | 1m 35.063s |
| 5 | Spies | 1m 35.068s |
| 6 | de Puniet | 1m 35.266s |
| 7 | Hayden | 1m 35.312s |
| 8 | Simoncelli | 1m 35.643s |
| 9 | Espargaro | 1m 35.644s |
| 10 | Edwards | 1m 35.647s |
| 11 | Capirossi | 1m 36.219s |
| 12 | Barbera | 1m 36.281s |
| 13 | Kallio | 1m 36.450s |
| 14 | Bautista | 1m 37.143s |
| 15 | Akiyoshi | 1m 38.056s |

### Championship Points

| | | |
|---|---|---|
| 1 | Lorenzo | 140 |
| 2 | Pedrosa | 93 |
| 3 | Dovizioso | 89 |
| 4 | Rossi | 61 |
| 5 | Hayden | 61 |
| 6 | de Puniet | 56 |
| 7 | Stoner | 51 |
| 8 | Spies | 49 |
| 9 | Simoncelli | 39 |
| 10 | Edwards | 34 |
| 11 | Melandri | 32 |
| 12 | Espargaro | 28 |
| 13 | Barbera | 28 |
| 14 | Kallio | 20 |
| 15 | Aoyama | 18 |
| 16 | Capirossi | 16 |
| 17 | Bautista | 14 |
| 18 | Akiyoshi | 1 |

### Team Points

| | | |
|---|---|---|
| 1 | Fiat Yamaha Team | 201 |
| 2 | Repsol Honda Team | 182 |
| 3 | Ducati Marlboro Team | 112 |
| 4 | Monster Yamaha Tech 3 | 83 |
| 5 | San Carlo Honda Gresini | 71 |
| 6 | LCR Honda MotoGP | 56 |
| 7 | Pramac Racing Team | 48 |
| 8 | Rizla Suzuki MotoGP | 30 |
| 9 | Paginas Amarillas Aspar | 28 |
| 10 | Interwetten Honda MotoGP | 19 |

### Constructor Points

| | | |
|---|---|---|
| 1 | Yamaha | 145 |
| 2 | Honda | 117 |
| 3 | Ducati | 81 |
| 4 | Suzuki | 26 |

| Grid order | 1 | 2 | 3 | 4 | 5 | 6 | 7 | 8 | 9 | 10 | 11 | 12 | 13 | 14 | 15 | 16 | 17 | 18 | 19 | 20 | 21 | 22 | 23 | 24 | 25 | 26 | |
|---|---|---|---|---|---|---|---|---|---|---|---|---|---|---|---|---|---|---|---|---|---|---|---|---|---|---|---|
| 99 LORENZO | 99 | 99 | 99 | 99 | 99 | 99 | 99 | 99 | 99 | 99 | 99 | 99 | 99 | 99 | 99 | 99 | 99 | 99 | 99 | 99 | 99 | 99 | 99 | 99 | 99 | 99 | 1 |
| 14 de PUNIET | 11 | 11 | 26 | 26 | 26 | 26 | 26 | 26 | 26 | 26 | 26 | 26 | 26 | 26 | 26 | 26 | 26 | 26 | 26 | 26 | 26 | 26 | 26 | 26 | 26 | 26 | 2 |
| 27 STONER | 26 | 26 | 11 | 27 | 27 | 27 | 27 | 27 | 27 | 27 | 27 | 27 | 27 | 27 | 27 | 27 | 27 | 27 | 27 | 27 | 27 | 27 | 27 | 27 | 27 | 27 | 3 |
| 11 SPIES | 27 | 27 | 27 | 4 | 4 | 4 | 4 | 4 | 4 | 4 | 4 | 4 | 4 | 4 | 4 | 11 | 11 | 11 | 11 | 11 | 11 | 11 | 11 | 11 | 11 | 11 | 4 |
| 69 HAYDEN | 4 | 4 | 4 | 11 | 11 | 11 | 11 | 11 | 11 | 11 | 11 | 11 | 11 | 11 | 11 | 4 | 4 | 14 | 14 | 14 | 14 | 14 | 14 | 4 | 4 | | 5 |
| 4 DOVIZIOSO | 14 | 14 | 14 | 14 | 14 | 14 | 14 | 14 | 14 | 14 | 14 | 14 | 14 | 14 | 14 | 14 | 4 | 4 | 4 | 4 | 4 | 4 | 14 | 14 | | | 6 |
| 26 PEDROSA | 58 | 58 | 58 | 58 | 69 | 69 | 69 | 69 | 69 | 69 | 69 | 69 | 69 | 69 | 69 | 69 | 69 | 69 | 69 | 69 | 69 | 69 | 69 | 69 | | | 7 |
| 58 SIMONCELLI | 5 | 5 | 69 | 69 | 58 | 5 | 5 | 5 | 5 | 5 | 5 | 5 | 5 | 5 | 5 | 5 | 5 | 5 | 5 | 5 | 5 | 5 | 5 | 5 | | | 8 |
| 5 EDWARDS | 69 | 69 | 5 | 5 | 5 | 58 | 58 | 58 | 58 | 58 | 58 | 58 | 58 | 41 | 41 | 41 | 41 | 41 | 41 | 58 | 58 | 58 | 58 | 58 | | | 9 |
| 41 ESPARGARO | 36 | 36 | 41 | 41 | 41 | 41 | 41 | 41 | 41 | 41 | 41 | 41 | 41 | 58 | 58 | 58 | 58 | 58 | 58 | 41 | 41 | 41 | 41 | 41 | | | 10 |
| 65 CAPIROSSI | 41 | 41 | 36 | 36 | 36 | 40 | 40 | 36 | 36 | 36 | 36 | 36 | 40 | 40 | 40 | 65 | 65 | 65 | 65 | 65 | 36 | 36 | 36 | 36 | | | 11 |
| 19 BAUTISTA | 65 | 40 | 40 | 40 | 36 | 36 | 36 | 40 | 40 | 40 | 40 | 40 | 36 | 36 | 65 | 40 | 40 | 40 | 40 | 36 | 65 | 40 | 40 | 40 | | | 12 |
| 36 KALLIO | 40 | 65 | 65 | 65 | 65 | 65 | 65 | 65 | 65 | 65 | 65 | 65 | 65 | 36 | 36 | 36 | 36 | 40 | 40 | 65 | 65 | 65 | 65 | 65 | | | 13 |
| 40 BARBERA | 19 | 19 | 19 | 19 | 19 | 19 | 19 | 19 | 19 | 19 | 19 | 19 | 19 | 19 | 19 | 19 | 19 | 19 | 19 | 19 | 19 | 19 | 19 | 19 | | | 14 |
| 64 AKIYOSHI | 64 | 64 | 64 | 64 | 64 | 64 | 64 | 64 | 64 | 64 | 64 | 64 | 64 | 64 | 64 | 64 | 64 | 64 | 64 | 64 | 64 | 64 | 64 | 64 | | | 15 |

64 Lapped rider

## Moto2

**RACE DISTANCE: 24 laps, 67.734 miles/109.008 km · RACE WEATHER: Dry (air 20°, humidity 44%, track 33°)**

| Pos. | Rider | Nat. | No. | Entrant | Machine | Laps | Time & Speed |
|---|---|---|---|---|---|---|---|
| 1 | **Andrea Iannone** | ITA | 29 | Fimmco Speed Up | Speed Up | 24 | 40m 00.383s (mph/km/h) 101.585/163.485 |
| 2 | **Toni Elias** | SPA | 24 | Gresini Racing Moto2 | Moriwaki | 24 | 40m 04.875s |
| 3 | **Thomas Luthi** | SWI | 12 | Interwetten Moriwaki Moto2 | Moriwaki | 24 | 40m 05.773s |
| 4 | **Ratthapark Wilairot** | THA | 14 | Thai Honda PTT Singha SAG | Bimota | 24 | 40m 05.856s |
| 5 | **Shoya Tomizawa** | JPN | 48 | Technomag-CIP | Suter | 24 | 40m 07.788s |
| 6 | **Julian Simon** | SPA | 60 | Mapfre Aspar Team | Suter | 24 | 40m 08.049s |
| 7 | **Jules Cluzel** | FRA | 16 | Forward Racing | Suter | 24 | 40m 16.406s |
| 8 | **Mike di Meglio** | FRA | 63 | Mapfre Aspar Team | Suter | 24 | 40m 16.505s |
| 9 | **Karel Abraham** | CZE | 17 | Cardion AB Motoracing | FTR | 24 | 40m 17.342s |
| 10 | **Yuki Takahashi** | JPN | 72 | Tech 3 Racing | Tech 3 | 24 | 40m 19.984s |
| 11 | **Scott Redding** | GBR | 45 | Marc VDS Racing Team | Suter | 24 | 40m 20.570s |
| 12 | **Simone Corsi** | ITA | 3 | JIR Moto2 | MotoBI | 24 | 40m 20.806s |
| 13 | **Gabor Talmacsi** | HUN | 2 | Fimmco Speed Up | Speed Up | 24 | 40m 21.741s |
| 14 | **Mattia Pasini** | ITA | 75 | JIR Moto2 | MotoBI | 24 | 40m 27.037s |
| 15 | **Yonny Hernandez** | COL | 68 | Blusens-STX | BQR-Moto2 | 24 | 40m 34.407s |
| 16 | Alex Baldolini | ITA | 25 | Caretta Technology Race Dept. | I.C.P. | 24 | 40m 34.428s |
| 17 | Claudio Corti | ITA | 71 | Forward Racing | Suter | 24 | 40m 34.760s |
| 18 | Dominique Aegerter | SWI | 77 | Technomag-CIP | Suter | 24 | 40m 34.864s |
| 19 | Stefan Bradl | GER | 65 | Viessmann Kiefer Racing | Suter | 24 | 40m 37.666s |
| 20 | Alex de Angelis | RSM | 15 | RSM Team Scot | Force GP210 | 24 | 40m 42.908s |
| 21 | Vladimir Ivanov | UKR | 61 | Gresini Racing Moto2 | Moriwaki | 24 | 40m 43.778s |
| 22 | Kenny Noyes | USA | 9 | Jack & Jones by A.Banderas | Promoharris | 24 | 40m 47.167s |
| 23 | Sergio Gadea | SPA | 40 | Tenerife 40 Pons | Pons Kalex | 24 | 40m 47.179s |
| 24 | Niccolo Canepa | ITA | 59 | RSM Team Scot | Force GP210 | 24 | 40m 59.707s |
| 25 | Hector Faubel | SPA | 55 | Marc VDS Racing Team | Suter | 24 | 41m 00.551s |
| 26 | Robertino Pietri | VEN | 39 | Italtrans S.T.R. | Suter | 24 | 41m 02.251s |
| 27 | Raffaele de Rosa | ITA | 35 | Tech 3 Racing | Tech 3 | 24 | 41m 02.834s |
| 28 | Bernat Martinez | SPA | 76 | Maquinza-SAG Team | Bimota | 24 | 41m 07.700s |
| 29 | Vladimir Leonov | RUS | 21 | Vector Kiefer Racing | Suter | 24 | 41m 10.490s |
| 30 | Valentin Debise | FRA | 53 | WTR San Marino Team | ADV | 24 | 41m 38.002s |
| 31 | Mashel Al Naimi | QAT | 95 | Blusens-STX | BQR-Moto2 | 24 | 41m 41.418s |
| 32 | Joan Olive | SPA | 5 | Jack & Jones by A.Banderas | Promoharris | 24 | 41m 41.928s |
| | Xavier Simeon | BEL | 19 | Holiday Gym G22 | Moriwaki | 23 | DNF |
| | Lukas Pesek | CZE | 52 | Matteoni CP Racing | Moriwaki | 16 | DNF |
| | Arne Tode | GER | 41 | Racing Team Germany | Suter | 15 | DNF |
| | Roberto Rolfo | ITA | 44 | Italtrans S.T.R. | Suter | 14 | DNF |
| | Anthony West | AUS | 8 | MZ Racing Team | MZ-RE Honda | 10 | DNF |
| | Fonsi Nieto | SPA | 10 | Holiday Gym G22 | Moriwaki | 7 | DNF |

**Fastest lap:** Andrea Iannone, on lap 5, 1m 38.917s, 102.714mph/165.302km/h (record).
**Previous lap record:** New category.
**Event best maximum speed:** Sergio Gadea, 163.9mph/263.7km/h (free practice 2).

**Qualifying:** Dry
Air: 23° Humidity: 34% Ground: 41°

| | | |
|---|---|---|
| 1 | Iannone | 1m 39.092s |
| 2 | Wilairot | 1m 39.307s |
| 3 | Debon | 1m 39.584s |
| 4 | Tomizawa | 1m 39.664s |
| 5 | Luthi | 1m 39.671s |
| 6 | Elias | 1m 39.711s |
| 7 | Simon | 1m 39.755s |
| 8 | Nieto | 1m 39.777s |
| 9 | Corti | 1m 39.798s |
| 10 | Cluzel | 1m 39.829s |
| 11 | Pesek | 1m 39.856s |
| 12 | Abraham | 1m 39.990s |
| 13 | Takahashi | 1m 40.025s |
| 14 | Rolfo | 1m 40.043s |
| 15 | Pasini | 1m 40.085s |
| 16 | Bradl | 1m 40.225s |
| 17 | di Meglio | 1m 40.232s |
| 18 | West | 1m 40.246s |
| 19 | Corsi | 1m 40.262s |
| 20 | Redding | 1m 40.313s |
| 21 | Tode | 1m 40.413s |
| 22 | Hernandez | 1m 40.427s |
| 23 | Talmacsi | 1m 40.475s |
| 24 | Debise | 1m 40.578s |
| 25 | Gadea | 1m 40.659s |
| 26 | de Angelis | 1m 40.660s |
| 27 | de Rosa | 1m 40.676s |
| 28 | Baldolini | 1m 40.708s |
| 29 | Ivanov | 1m 40.716s |
| 30 | Simeon | 1m 40.762s |
| 31 | Canepa | 1m 40.888s |
| 32 | Pons | 1m 40.968s |
| 33 | Aegerter | 1m 41.006s |
| 34 | Noyes | 1m 41.218s |
| 35 | Faubel | 1m 41.316s |
| 36 | Pietri | 1m 41.368s |
| 37 | Olive | 1m 41.953s |
| 38 | Leonov | 1m 41.967s |
| 39 | Martinez | 1m 42.643s |
| 40 | Al Naimi | 1m 43.072s |

**Fastest race laps**

| | | |
|---|---|---|
| 1 | Iannone | 1m 38.917s |
| 2 | Elias | 1m 39.263s |
| 3 | Wilairot | 1m 39.288s |
| 4 | Luthi | 1m 39.414s |
| 5 | Redding | 1m 39.438s |
| 6 | Simon | 1m 39.621s |
| 7 | Tomizawa | 1m 39.651s |
| 8 | Cluzel | 1m 39.673s |
| 9 | Abraham | 1m 39.805s |
| 10 | Takahashi | 1m 39.958s |
| 11 | Talmacsi | 1m 39.964s |
| 12 | Pasini | 1m 39.978s |
| 13 | Corsi | 1m 39.981s |
| 14 | Bradl | 1m 39.994s |
| 15 | di Meglio | 1m 40.020s |
| 16 | Hernandez | 1m 40.089s |
| 17 | Rolfo | 1m 40.142s |
| 18 | Nieto | 1m 40.199s |
| 19 | Corti | 1m 40.259s |
| 20 | Baldolini | 1m 40.310s |
| 21 | de Angelis | 1m 40.333s |
| 22 | Gadea | 1m 40.553s |
| 23 | Aegerter | 1m 40.577s |
| 24 | Simeon | 1m 40.686s |
| 25 | Noyes | 1m 40.699s |
| 26 | Ivanov | 1m 40.741s |
| 27 | Tode | 1m 40.803s |
| 28 | Pesek | 1m 40.803s |
| 29 | de Rosa | 1m 41.119s |
| 30 | Pietri | 1m 41.155s |
| 31 | Faubel | 1m 41.222s |
| 32 | Canepa | 1m 41.389s |
| 33 | Debise | 1m 41.505s |
| 34 | Martinez | 1m 41.711s |
| 35 | Leonov | 1m 41.750s |
| 36 | West | 1m 42.086s |
| 37 | Olive | 1m 42.521s |
| 38 | Al Naimi | 1m 42.572s |

**Championship Points**

| | | |
|---|---|---|
| 1 | Elias | 100 |
| 2 | Tomizawa | 76 |
| 3 | Luthi | 74 |
| 4 | Iannone | 67 |
| 5 | Simon | 61 |
| 6 | Cluzel | 55 |
| 7 | Corsi | 55 |
| 8 | Gadea | 47 |
| 9 | Debon | 37 |
| 10 | Talmacsi | 37 |
| 11 | Takahashi | 27 |
| 12 | Wilairot | 25 |
| 13 | Redding | 23 |
| 14 | Rolfo | 21 |
| 15 | di Meglio | 17 |
| 16 | Nieto | 17 |
| 17 | Aegerter | 15 |
| 18 | Pasini | 12 |
| 19 | Bradl | 11 |
| 20 | Hernandez | 11 |
| 21 | Noyes | 9 |
| 22 | Abraham | 9 |
| 23 | Baldolini | 9 |
| 24 | Simeon | 8 |
| 25 | de Angelis | 5 |
| 26 | Faubel | 4 |
| 27 | Pesek | 4 |
| 28 | Tode | 2 |
| 29 | Corti | 1 |
| 30 | West | 1 |

**Constructors**

| | | |
|---|---|---|
| 1 | Moriwaki | 116 |
| 2 | Suter | 111 |
| 3 | Speed Up | 81 |
| 4 | MotoBI | 57 |
| 5 | Pons Kalex | 47 |
| 6 | FTR | 44 |
| 7 | Tech 3 | 27 |
| 8 | Bimota | 25 |
| 9 | BQR-Moto2 | 11 |
| 10 | RSV | 10 |
| 11 | Promoharris | 9 |
| 12 | I.C.P. | 9 |
| 13 | Force GP210 | 5 |
| 14 | MZ-RE Honda | 1 |

## 125cc

**RACE DISTANCE: 22 laps, 62.090 miles/99.924 km · RACE WEATHER: Dry (air 19°, humidity 50%, track 22°)**

| Pos. | Rider | Nat. | No. | Entrant | Machine | Laps | Time & Speed |
|---|---|---|---|---|---|---|---|
| 1 | **Marc Marquez** | SPA | 93 | Red Bull Ajo Motorsport | Derbi | 22 | 37m 48.923s (mph/km/h) 98.515/158.545 |
| 2 | **Nicolas Terol** | SPA | 40 | Bancaja Aspar Team | Aprilia | 22 | 37m 51.255s |
| 3 | **Pol Espargaro** | SPA | 44 | Tuenti Racing | Derbi | 22 | 37m 57.057s |
| 4 | **Bradley Smith** | GBR | 38 | Bancaja Aspar Team | Aprilia | 22 | 37m 58.559s |
| 5 | **Sandro Cortese** | GER | 11 | Avant Mitsubishi Ajo | Derbi | 22 | 38m 25.884s |
| 6 | **Randy Krummenacher** | SWI | 35 | Stipa-Molenaar Racing GP | Aprilia | 22 | 38m 28.014s |
| 7 | **Danny Webb** | GBR | 99 | Andalucia Cajasol | Aprilia | 22 | 38m 28.320s |
| 8 | **Luis Salom** | SPA | 39 | Stipa-Molenaar Racing GP | Aprilia | 22 | 38m 33.933s |
| 9 | **Simone Grotzkyj** | ITA | 15 | Fontana Racing | Aprilia | 22 | 38m 34.595s |
| 10 | **Jonas Folger** | GER | 94 | Ongetta Team | Aprilia | 22 | 38m 36.954s |
| 11 | **Alberto Moncayo** | SPA | 23 | Andalucia Cajasol | Aprilia | 22 | 38m 37.380s |
| 12 | **Johann Zarco** | FRA | 14 | WTR San Marino Team | Aprilia | 22 | 38m 37.756s |
| 13 | **Jasper Iwema** | NED | 53 | CBC Corse | Aprilia | 22 | 38m 43.131s |
| 14 | **Tomoyoshi Koyama** | JPN | 71 | Racing Team Germany | Aprilia | 22 | 38m 47.978s |
| 15 | **Jakub Kornfeil** | CZE | 84 | Racing Team Germany | Aprilia | 22 | 38m 50.427s |
| 16 | Adrian Martin | SPA | 26 | Aeroport de Castello - Ajo | Aprilia | 22 | 39m 04.992s |
| 17 | Sturla Fagerhaug | NOR | 50 | AirAsia-Sepang Int. Circuit | Aprilia | 22 | 39m 05.098s |
| 18 | Marcel Schrotter | GER | 78 | Interwetten Honda 125 | Honda | 22 | 39m 06.952s |
| 19 | Louis Rossi | FRA | 69 | CBC Corse | Aprilia | 22 | 39m 10.661s |
| 20 | Toni Finsterbusch | GER | 68 | Freudenberg Racing Team | KTM | 22 | 39m 25.186s |
| 21 | Michael van der Mark | NED | 60 | Lambretta Reparto Corse | Lambretta | 22 | 39m 25.368s |
| 22 | Zulfahmi Khairuddin | MAL | 63 | AirAsia-Sepang Int. Circuit | Aprilia | 22 | 39m 29.604s |
| 23 | Pepijn Bijsterbosch | NED | 66 | Racing Team Bijsterbosch | Honda | 21 | 38m 24.288s |
| 24 | Ernst Dubbink | NED | 64 | RV Racing | Honda | 21 | 39m 32.479s |
| | Alexis Masbou | FRA | 5 | Ongetta Team | Aprilia | 20 | DNF |
| | Jerry van de Bunt | NED | 67 | Jerrys Racing | Honda | 16 | DNF |
| | Roy Pouw | NED | 65 | Team Holland Mototechnic | Aprilia | 14 | DNF |
| | Marco Ravaioli | ITA | 72 | Lambretta Reparto Corse | Lambretta | 11 | DNF |
| | Luca Marconi | ITA | 87 | Ongetta Team | Aprilia | 6 | DNF |
| | Esteve Rabat | SPA | 12 | Blusens-STX | Aprilia | 4 | DNF |
| | Efren Vazquez | SPA | 7 | Tuenti Racing | Derbi | 3 | DNF |
| | Lorenzo Savadori | ITA | 32 | Matteoni CP Racing | Aprilia | 0 | DNF |

**Fastest lap:** Nicolas Terol, on lap 12, 1m 42.428s, 99.193mph/159.636km/h (record).
**Previous lap record:** New circuit.
**Event best maximum speed:** Nicolas Terol, 136.8mph/220.1km/h (qualifying practice).

**Qualifying:** Dry
Air: 22° Humidity: 40% Ground: 35°

| | | |
|---|---|---|
| 1 | Marquez | 1m 42.191s |
| 2 | Smith | 1m 42.775s |
| 3 | Terol | 1m 42.865s |
| 4 | Espargaro | 1m 43.299s |
| 5 | Cortese | 1m 43.480s |
| 6 | Iwema | 1m 43.670s |
| 7 | Vazquez | 1m 43.752s |
| 8 | Rabat | 1m 43.934s |
| 9 | Moncayo | 1m 44.106s |
| 10 | Grotzkyj | 1m 44.224s |
| 11 | Webb | 1m 44.225s |
| 12 | Krummenacher | 1m 44.282s |
| 13 | Masbou | 1m 44.427s |
| 14 | Koyama | 1m 44.671s |
| 15 | Salom | 1m 44.671s |
| 16 | Kornfeil | 1m 45.193s |
| 17 | Zarco | 1m 45.204s |
| 18 | Schrotter | 1m 45.321s |
| 19 | Fagerhaug | 1m 45.365s |
| 20 | Martin | 1m 45.731s |
| 21 | Rossi | 1m 46.201s |
| 22 | Finsterbusch | 1m 46.257s |
| 23 | Marconi | 1m 46.725s |
| 24 | van der Mark | 1m 46.882s |
| 25 | Khairuddin | 1m 46.941s |
| 26 | Savadori | 1m 46.960s |
| 27 | Ravaioli | 1m 47.760s |
| 28 | Dubbink | 1m 48.385s |
| 29 | van de Bunt | 1m 48.711s |
| 30 | Bijsterbosch | 1m 49.044s |
| Outside 107% | | |
| *(but inside during free practice)* | | |
| | Pouw | 1m 49.871s |
| | Folger | 1m 51.839s |

**Fastest race laps**

| | | |
|---|---|---|
| 1 | Terol | 1m 42.428s |
| 2 | Marquez | 1m 42.446s |
| 3 | Espargaro | 1m 42.642s |
| 4 | Smith | 1m 42.833s |
| 5 | Rabat | 1m 43.402s |
| 6 | Vazquez | 1m 43.700s |
| 7 | Cortese | 1m 43.813s |
| 8 | Webb | 1m 43.972s |
| 9 | Krummenacher | 1m 44.050s |
| 10 | Salom | 1m 44.143s |
| 11 | Grotzkyj | 1m 44.195s |
| 12 | Zarco | 1m 44.342s |
| 13 | Folger | 1m 44.436s |
| 14 | Moncayo | 1m 44.582s |
| 15 | Iwema | 1m 44.617s |
| 16 | Kornfeil | 1m 44.739s |
| 17 | Koyama | 1m 44.785s |
| 18 | Masbou | 1m 45.032s |
| 19 | Martin | 1m 45.145s |
| 20 | Fagerhaug | 1m 45.228s |
| 21 | Schrotter | 1m 45.631s |
| 22 | Rossi | 1m 45.888s |
| 23 | Marconi | 1m 46.118s |
| 24 | Finsterbusch | 1m 46.379s |
| 25 | Khairuddin | 1m 46.527s |
| 26 | van der Mark | 1m 46.582s |
| 27 | Ravaioli | 1m 48.061s |
| 28 | Pouw | 1m 48.082s |
| 29 | van de Bunt | 1m 48.100s |
| 30 | Bijsterbosch | 1m 48.235s |
| 31 | Dubbink | 1m 48.579s |

**Championship Points**

| | | |
|---|---|---|
| 1 | Terol | 118 |
| 2 | Espargaro | 115 |
| 3 | Marquez | 107 |
| 4 | Smith | 74 |
| 5 | Rabat | 50 |
| 6 | Vazquez | 49 |
| 7 | Krummenacher | 49 |
| 8 | Cortese | 47 |
| 9 | Koyama | 47 |
| 10 | Zarco | 37 |
| 11 | Webb | 33 |
| 12 | Moncayo | 22 |
| 13 | Iwema | 20 |
| 14 | Masbou | 17 |
| 15 | Folger | 16 |
| 16 | Salom | 15 |
| 17 | Grotzkyj | 10 |
| 18 | Schrotter | 7 |
| 19 | Martin | 4 |
| 20 | Kornfeil | 3 |

**Constructors**

| | | |
|---|---|---|
| 1 | Derbi | 145 |
| 2 | Aprilia | 121 |
| 3 | Honda | 7 |
| 4 | Lambretta | 1 |

# CATALUNYA GRAND PRIX

*Inset above left:* Dani contemplates what might have been.

*Inset above:* Lorenzo stayed on dry land to celebrate his second home win of the year.

*Main photo:* You take the high road, and I'll take the low road. Pedrosa led into the first corner, but didn't make the turn.
Photos: Gold & Goose

*Right:* Some like it hot, especially the Suzukis. Bautista and Capirossi sandwich Simoncelli, with Hayden and Spies behind in the team's best race of the season to date,

*Below:* A second rostrum in succession marked improving results for Casey Stoner.

*Below right:* Burgess had Yoshikawa in place of Rossi: "We don't expect to learn very much."

*Bottom left:* De Angelis celebrates his next-race return to MotoGP with Interwetten team boss Daniel Epp.

*Bottom right:* Edwards made some fruity remarks about the competitiveness of his Tech3 Yamaha.

*Photos:* Gold & Goose

FOR a third successive weekend, the Rossi-less paddock gathered – to race and to talk about him in his absence. Thus Lorenzo's third win in a row (all from pole), achieved with the calm maturity that was becoming increasingly familiar, was not to be a revenge for 2009, when Rossi had bamboozled him on the last corner. Both Honda riders suffered sundry front-end vagueness that spoiled an otherwise strong rivalry; Stoner was afflicted with something rather similar. In the end, Lorenzo's second home win in the big class was rather clinical.

The fatigue was accentuated by blazing heat, while there was another of those heart-stopping accidents in Moto2. This time, only two bikes were involved: Spanish-resident American Kenny Noyes and former national championship rival Carmelo Morales, a 31-year-old track veteran substituting for the injured Axel Pons. Noyes had worked through all race long, gaining places after being run off the track in another epic nine-bike first-corner crash. He had snatched seventh from Morales, Rossi-style, on the last corner. Desperately, Morales tried to get back, but clipped Noyes's rear wheel, which flung him and his bike in a high arc through the air in front of the grandstands, in a real bullfighting moment. Struck by the looping bike as he landed, he lay in an ominously crumpled heap as Noyes's team owner, actor Anthony Banderas, threw up his hands in unfeigned horror in the pit. Amazingly, Morales escaped with only bangs and bruises: motorcycle racing can be unexpectedly kind as well as cruel.

The Stoner-to-Honda move was all but openly acknowledged, and was confirmed officially in the week after the race by carefully timed and worded announcements from Ducati and Honda. Some unkind tongues suggested that this new prospect had dulled Stoner's urge, after the year had started so badly. Others were occupied with a new rumour: Red Bull to step in to sponsor a Honda super-team for 2011, with three riders – Stoner, Pedrosa and Dovizioso.

Rossi to Ducati was now also generally accepted and expected, but in the absence of confirmation had to remain a rumour: anything can go wrong with these things until the ink is actually dry on the contracts. One clue was the presence of engineering director Filippo Preziosi. "He's not here just to check the fork springs," commented Rossi's potential new team-mate, Hayden. Later in the year, Preziosi would insist to *MOTOCOURSE* that while he had spoken to Rossi several times during this and previous years, even now it was still "as enemies. We cannot have any in-depth discussion until the end of the season."

The other Rossi story concerned his return from injury. His own cheery statements spoke of excellent progress in recovery, with Brno his target for return – but there were whispers that he might be back even sooner, at the very next race. They would turn out to be true. In the meantime, three races now missed, it was time for Yamaha to field a replacement.

There was plenty of speculation about who would get the ride: Edwards was considered a good candidate, Spies was ready to have a go, Superbike rider Crutchlow was another name in the frame, possibly to take the place of one or the other at Tech 3. And Garry McCoy, having walked out on his testing role with the apparently foundering FB Corse MotoGP project, was in the paddock to suggest that he might be given a go. In the end, Yamaha went for the safe hands of factory tester Wataru Yoshikawa, among whose instructions was surely one to keep the revs down and preserve the

engines. As Rossi's crew chief, Burgess, opined, "We don't expect to learn very much. He hasn't raced for ten years." Instead he and Interwetten replacement Kousuke Akiyoshi, a former Suzuki tester, engaged in a private contest at the rear.

De Puniet's efforts and prowess had been recognised by HRC, with a stiffer chassis/swing-arm combination; Stoner was apparently free from the arm-pump problems that had plagued his previous two races, after some minor adjustment to hand control positions. He was in a feisty enough mood as well to complain about people, especially Espargaro, following him in practice; and others, notably Capirossi, lingering on line while going slowly. "It's getting like the 125 class," he said. Similarly, Spies complained of his qualifying lap being spoiled by the Spanish rookie, but, as Espargaro told *MOTO-COURSE*, "I try to do my job and to be fast, but sometimes you need some help. This is how you learn … Casey is in the top three always, and when I see him, I try to copy him."

Spies had team-mate Edwards to complain on his behalf about another matter, in an outspoken interview with Britain's *Motorcycle News*, about a lack of development for their sub-factory machines. "It's the same bike as last year, just with a slower engine. I look like a f***ing moron, and if Ben had a bike that was worth a sh*t, he'd be on the podium every weekend."

The small field and austere MotoGP race once again meant that the all-action Moto2 event threatened to steal the show, although not quite as expected, with Iannone taking another runaway by such a margin that his rivals were becoming suspicious, as well as somewhat spaced out behind him. One of those racing mess-ups intervened, however, to spoil his race.

Like the results, the cast showed some instability: luckless Mattia Pasini was dropped amid some acrimony by his JiR team, his place being taken by Japanese rookie Yusuki Teshima; while Team Scot, only surviving after a personal top-up contribution from its chief sponsor, prepared to lose de Angelis, who would return to MotoGP in the following week to race the Interwetten machine. At MZ, Ralf Waldmann had left the pit crew, and rider West was threatening the same, with his bike overweight and the team's resources

pitifully slender. The first top-ten finish of the year cheered things up somewhat.

Tales of heroism abounded this season; Luthi was back from surgery and took a third successive rostrum with his freshly plated collarbone. Two others were absent with injuries: Axel Pons and Stefan Bradl, both having been hurt in motocross crashes.

## MOTOGP RACE – 25 laps

Lorenzo dominated free practice and qualifying; his third successive pole was by four-tenths. Stoner was alongside, also strong throughout. The surprising face on the front row belonged to de Puniet, in the ascendancy, although still not confident of sustaining that pace.

He'd knocked Dani down to the second row by eight-hundredths; Spies had a good final run to get ahead of Dovizioso. And leading row three? None other than Capirossi with team-mate Bautista at the far end of it, the Suzukis enjoying hot conditions in a brief respite from their problems.

The sun was blazing down on a crowd of 81,250, with a track temperature of 49 degrees further complicating the choice of dual-compound tyres at a track where grip is always an issue. Of the fast men, only de Puniet chose the extra-hard.

No surprises when Pedrosa rocketed away to lead the sprint to the first 90-degree corner. A big surprise when he missed his braking point and had to take to the escape road on the inside of the gravel trap to get the bike turned. "A big wobble" had knocked his brake pads off and he had to pump the lever. Lorenzo led everyone past, and Dani slotted back in around tenth.

Stoner and Dovizioso were with the leader, de Puniet hanging on behind, but soon losing a little ground, forced to wait to see if his tyre choice would pay dividends. Lorenzo's serenity would be disturbed at the start of lap four. Dovi had pushed past Stoner two laps before into the first tight right at the bottom of the hill, and now he moved inside Lorenzo at the end of the main straight.

But it did not last. Next time around, the Honda was a little

*Above:* Capirossi enjoyed Suzuki's brief revival.

*Right:* De Puniet is congratulated by his crew after a fine fourth place.

*Far right:* Debon (airborne) hit di Meglio (red bike) and triggered Moto2 mayhem on the first corner.

*Top right:* Takahashi and Luthi battle it out after inheriting the lead from Iannone.

*Above centre right:* Karel Abraham (17), here leading Elias and Corsi, had his best result so far.

*Above far right:* Morales lies prone after his sickening crash with Noyes.

*Right:* Terol is heading for a hard landing on the last lap of the 125 race. Smith is out of the picture, Pol Espargaro passes for third.

Photos: Gold & Goose

wide as they started the climb up to the back straight, and Lorenzo was through. He was never headed again, although Dovizioso kept the pressure on until lap 15. He was just four-tenths adrift when his efforts finally failed and he slipped off at the end of the back straight, rejoining at the back.

Lorenzo was some 5.6 seconds clear, and he stretched the gap to almost seven seconds before finally slacking off for another dominant win that gave him a two-race championship advantage.

Pedrosa had stormed back into the picture after his first-corner blunder: ahead of off-form Hayden in ninth at the end of lap one, and four places higher next time around, having despatched Melandri, Spies, Bautista and Simoncelli with great authority. His next victim was de Puniet at the start of lap six.

The pair of them got past Stoner at the same time: the Ducati rider had exactly the same braking problem as Pedrosa, also recovering on the paved run-off to tuck in behind de Puniet. It took the best part of four laps before he could find his way past the fast Frenchman with his wild riding style, and now the satellite Honda would drop off the pace as Stoner set about Pedrosa.

That battle for what had become second went to the flag, but Stoner was never close enough to make a convincing attack. "I was waiting for a mistake, but Dani never made any," he said.

De Puniet had his own problems, with Simoncelli now starting to close – until the Italian crashed out in the effort.

The now safely distant pursuit was led by Bautista, a couple of seconds clear of a three-bike maul. Spies had been in front, but a slip on lap eight let both Capirossi and Melandri past, and it stayed that way for almost ten laps, with Capirossi actually getting away ahead to within a second of his younger team-mate.

At the start of lap 18, track first-timer Spies showed improving late pace once again, moving past Melandri and starting to hunt down the veteran ahead. He attacked at the start of lap 23; Capirossi fought back, but Spies was ahead again through the third corner. He closed rapidly on Bautista as the older rider dropped away disheartened, and probably would have been ahead one lap later. Bautista's fifth rewarded a fine ride, and with his team-mate seventh it was by far the team's best result of a dire season.

Battered Hayden had been with the gang at the back, but rallied slightly to catch and pass Melandri with three laps to go. Barbera had lost touch behind, likewise a disgruntled Edwards, whose season kept getting worse in spite of "riding as well as I ever have".

The rest trailed in – Kallio, then Akiyoshi, who had pulled well clear of countryman and near anagram Yoshikawa, with Dovizioso between them. Espargaro had joined Simoncelli on the crash list.

## MOTO2 RACE - 23 laps

A strict race-control safety briefing had little effect on the massed Moto2 grid, the race starting and finishing with massive crashes. There was plenty of intervening drama as well, as runaway leader Iannone ended up being given a ride-through penalty.

The Italian on the puzzlingly fast green bike – wearing a factory Aprilia fairing – had claimed pole by better than a quarter of a second from Takahashi, Luthi and Elias.

Luthi led the massive pack funnelling into Turn One from Takahashi, Simon and Iannone; not far behind, all hell broke loose as Debon, already injured at Assen, came from 13th on the grid down the inside on to the grass. He ran back at the apex straight into di Meglio and Tomizawa, triggering mayhem. Among the pile of bikes clattering into the gravel

were Pietri and Rolfo, while Faubel and Aegerter remounted, only to retire. Cluzel, Gadea, Baldolini and Tomizawa got going again, with nine bikes down and several more put off the track.

Luthi still led as they started lap two, now with Elias on him and a short gap to Takahashi, Iannone and Simon. Then came Iannone's Turn-One disaster as, head down, he swept past Takahashi under braking. He hadn't seen the flags, being busy targeting Elias as well, so he finished lap two in second place and took the lead as they finished the next lap.

As he embarked on yet another astonishing runaway, race officials examined the evidence, and his team started to try to signal him to drop behind Takahashi again. Thoroughly bemused by this, he kept racing until race direction decided he had run out of time, and he was called in for a ride-through penalty on lap 16. His lead had been two seconds; he rejoined in 17th, but was back up to 13th at the end.

Takahashi, meanwhile, had broken free from the tussle for the lead, and went on to win his and the Tech 3 team's first Moto2 race by five seconds. An aluminium plate hastily welded to the steering head area of the chassis to make it more rigid seemed to have done the trick.

The battle for second raged between Luthi and Simon, being narrowly won by the older rider. Only a couple of seconds behind, Karel Abraham had the race of his life. He caught and passed an off-form Elias, and managed to stay half a second clear at the flag. The points leader had his hands full anyway with an aggressive Corsi.

Ten seconds behind, Noyes had been storming through after finishing lap one 28th, put off track in the turn-one mêlée. His last victim was Morales, whose attempt to regain seventh ended in catastrophe only narrowly averted.

Nieto came through to lead the next gang over the line, with Anthony West's shoestring MZ an excellent ninth, heading de Angelis, Talmacsi and the spectacular Hernandez.

Tomizawa and Redding retired; Wilairot and Canepa were among a handful of other crashes, Canepa's bike burning out spectacularly in what was a heavy blow for his Scot team.

## 125cc RACE – 22 laps

It was more marvel of Marquez as the home boy marched on to a third pole/win weekend in succession, and his fourth win in a row. With the mature accuracy of a much more experienced rider, his was a classic start-to-finish victory, pulling steadily away. One might have called it majestic, if the epithet didn't seem wrong for one so young. After all, at 17, he was too young to be given champagne on the rostrum. But not to gain the championship lead.

Actually he led only from the second corner, but played no part in a three-way scrap for second that lasted until a few corners from the end.

That was between team-mates Smith and Terol, and local hero Espargaro. All took turns up front, with Terol getting most of it, but they were seldom more than a few inches apart, lap after lap, in a fine demonstration of two-stroke combat.

It was Smith heading the trio over the line for the last four laps, but on the final lap Terol had got in front again. Smith lined him up for a daring overtake into the corner after the back straight; Terol's attempt at resistance instead sent him tumbling. The crash looked innocuous enough, but left him with a fractured vertebra and out for the next race.

Espargaro was inches behind in third, with the consolation of a new lap record.

Fully 40 seconds behind, Cortese also made a last-corner pass to secure fourth by a whisker from Vazquez; they had battled all race long.

Another four seconds away, a quartet crossed the line almost side by side for seventh. It went to the experienced Koyama from Krummenacher, Zarco and Folger, all covered by 0.09 second.

MotoGP · TISSOT SWISS WATCHES SINCE 1853 · OFFICIAL TIMEKEEPER

**CIRCUIT DE CATALUNYA**

Renault 145/90 — 3
Repsol 116/72 — 3
Seat 79/49 — 2
Campsa 140/87 — 3
Abolafio 158/98 — 2
Europcar 146/91 — 3
Total 104/88 — 2
Banc Sabadell 101/63 — 2
TV3 110/69 — 3
320/199
La Caixa 83/52 — 2
Tourisme de Catalunya 145/90 — 4

Key
96/60 kph/mph
2 Gear

Circuit: 4.727km/2.892 miles, 25 laps

## MotoGP
**RACE DISTANCE:** 25 laps, 73.431 miles/118.175 km · **RACE WEATHER:** Dry (air 34°, humidity 17%, track 49°)

| Pos. | Rider | Nat. | No. | Entrant | Machine | Tyres | Laps | Time & speed |
|---|---|---|---|---|---|---|---|---|
| 1 | Jorge Lorenzo | SPA | 99 | Fiat Yamaha Team | Yamaha | B | 25 | 43m 22.805s 101.563mph/163.450km/h |
| 2 | Dani Pedrosa | SPA | 26 | Repsol Honda Team | Honda | B | 25 | 43m 27.559s |
| 3 | Casey Stoner | AUS | 27 | Ducati Marlboro Team | Ducati | B | 25 | 43m 27.761s |
| 4 | Randy de Puniet | FRA | 14 | LCR Honda MotoGP | Honda | B | 25 | 43m 40.862s |
| 5 | Alvaro Bautista | SPA | 19 | Rizla Suzuki MotoGP | Suzuki | B | 25 | 43m 44.166s |
| 6 | Ben Spies | USA | 11 | Monster Yamaha Tech 3 | Yamaha | B | 25 | 43m 44.308s |
| 7 | Loris Capirossi | ITA | 65 | Rizla Suzuki MotoGP | Suzuki | B | 25 | 43m 46.986s |
| 8 | Nicky Hayden | USA | 69 | Ducati Marlboro Team | Ducati | B | 25 | 43m 50.746s |
| 9 | Marco Melandri | ITA | 33 | San Carlo Honda Gresini | Honda | B | 25 | 43m 50.851s |
| 10 | Hector Barbera | SPA | 40 | Paginas Amarillas Aspar | Ducati | B | 25 | 43m 55.244s |
| 11 | Colin Edwards | USA | 5 | Monster Yamaha Tech 3 | Yamaha | B | 25 | 44m 01.211s |
| 12 | Mika Kallio | FIN | 36 | Pramac Racing Team | Ducati | B | 25 | 44m 21.062s |
| 13 | Kousuke Akiyoshi | JPN | 64 | Interwetten Honda MotoGP | Honda | B | 25 | 44m 32.153s |
| 14 | Andrea Dovizioso | ITA | 4 | Repsol Honda Team | Honda | B | 25 | 44m 55.207s |
| 15 | Wataru Yoshikawa | JPN | 8 | Fiat Yamaha Team | Yamaha | B | 25 | 44m 58.042s |
|  | Marco Simoncelli | ITA | 58 | San Carlo Honda Gresini | Honda | B | 13 | DNF |
|  | Aleix Espargaro | SPA | 41 | Pramac Racing Team | Ducati | B | 5 | DNF |

**Fastest lap:** Andrea Dovizioso, on lap 3, 1m 43.154s, 102.506mph/164.968km/h.
**Lap record:** Dani Pedrosa, SPA (Honda), 1m 42.358s, 103.304mph/166.251km/h (2008).
**Event best maximum speed:** Dani Pedrosa, 205.7mph/331.0km/h (free practice 2).

### Qualifying
Weather: Dry
Air Temp: 35° Humidity: 19°
Track Temp: 53°

| | | |
|---|---|---|
| 1 | Lorenzo | 1m 42.046s |
| 2 | Stoner | 1m 42.410s |
| 3 | de Puniet | 1m 42.512s |
| 4 | Pedrosa | 1m 42.592s |
| 5 | Spies | 1m 42.710s |
| 6 | Dovizioso | 1m 42.866s |
| 7 | Capirossi | 1m 42.903s |
| 8 | Simoncelli | 1m 42.994s |
| 9 | Bautista | 1m 43.025s |
| 10 | Edwards | 1m 43.059s |
| 11 | Hayden | 1m 43.068s |
| 12 | Espargaro | 1m 43.380s |
| 13 | Barbera | 1m 43.417s |
| 14 | Melandri | 1m 43.621s |
| 15 | Kallio | 1m 43.685s |
| 16 | Akiyoshi | 1m 45.577s |
| 17 | Yoshikawa | 1m 45.759s |

### Fastest race laps
| | | |
|---|---|---|
| 1 | Dovizioso | 1m 43.154s |
| 2 | Stoner | 1m 43.276s |
| 3 | Lorenzo | 1m 43.310s |
| 4 | Pedrosa | 1m 43.317s |
| 5 | Simoncelli | 1m 43.837s |
| 6 | de Puniet | 1m 43.887s |
| 7 | Bautista | 1m 43.929s |
| 8 | Edwards | 1m 44.141s |
| 9 | Spies | 1m 44.156s |
| 10 | Capirossi | 1m 44.190s |
| 11 | Melandri | 1m 44.232s |
| 12 | Espargaro | 1m 44.326s |
| 13 | Hayden | 1m 44.390s |
| 14 | Barbera | 1m 44.433s |
| 15 | Kallio | 1m 44.952s |
| 16 | Akiyoshi | 1m 45.695s |
| 17 | Yoshikawa | 1m 47.258s |

### Championship Points
| | | |
|---|---|---|
| 1 | Lorenzo | 165 |
| 2 | Pedrosa | 113 |
| 3 | Dovizioso | 91 |
| 4 | Hayden | 69 |
| 5 | de Puniet | 69 |
| 6 | Stoner | 67 |
| 7 | Rossi | 61 |
| 8 | Spies | 59 |
| 9 | Melandri | 39 |
| 10 | Simoncelli | 39 |
| 11 | Edwards | 39 |
| 12 | Barbera | 34 |
| 13 | Espargaro | 28 |
| 14 | Bautista | 25 |
| 15 | Capirossi | 25 |
| 16 | Kallio | 24 |
| 17 | Aoyama | 18 |
| 18 | Akiyoshi | 4 |
| 19 | Yoshikawa | 1 |

### Team Points
| | | |
|---|---|---|
| 1 | Fiat Yamaha Team | 227 |
| 2 | Repsol Honda Team | 204 |
| 3 | Ducati Marlboro Team | 136 |
| 4 | Monster Yamaha Tech 3 | 98 |
| 5 | San Carlo Honda Gresini | 78 |
| 6 | LCR Honda MotoGP | 69 |
| 7 | Pramac Racing Team | 52 |
| 8 | Rizla Suzuki MotoGP | 50 |
| 9 | Paginas Amarillas Aspar | 34 |
| 10 | Interwetten Honda MotoGP | 22 |

### Constructor Points
| | | |
|---|---|---|
| 1 | Yamaha | 170 |
| 2 | Honda | 137 |
| 3 | Ducati | 97 |
| 4 | Suzuki | 37 |

### Grid order / lap chart

| Grid order | 1 | 2 | 3 | 4 | 5 | 6 | 7 | 8 | 9 | 10 | 11 | 12 | 13 | 14 | 15 | 16 | 17 | 18 | 19 | 20 | 21 | 22 | 23 | 24 | 25 | Pos |
|---|---|---|---|---|---|---|---|---|---|---|---|---|---|---|---|---|---|---|---|---|---|---|---|---|---|---|
| 99 LORENZO | 99 | 99 | 99 | 4 | 99 | 99 | 99 | 99 | 99 | 99 | 99 | 99 | 99 | 99 | 99 | 99 | 99 | 99 | 99 | 99 | 99 | 99 | 99 | 99 | 99 | 1 |
| 27 STONER | 27 | 4 | 4 | 99 | 4 | 4 | 4 | 4 | 4 | 4 | 4 | 4 | 4 | 26 | 26 | 26 | 26 | 26 | 26 | 26 | 26 | 26 | 26 | 26 | 26 | 2 |
| 14 de PUNIET | 4 | 27 | 27 | 27 | 27 | 26 | 26 | 26 | 26 | 26 | 26 | 26 | 26 | 27 | 27 | 27 | 27 | 27 | 27 | 27 | 27 | 27 | 27 | 27 | 27 | 3 |
| 26 PEDROSA | 14 | 14 | 14 | 14 | 14 | 14 | 14 | 14 | 27 | 27 | 27 | 27 | 27 | 14 | 14 | 14 | 14 | 14 | 14 | 14 | 14 | 14 | 14 | 14 | 14 | 4 |
| 11 SPIES | 58 | 26 | 26 | 26 | 26 | 27 | 27 | 27 | 14 | 14 | 14 | 14 | 14 | 14 | 19 | 19 | 19 | 19 | 19 | 19 | 19 | 19 | 19 | 19 | 19 | 5 |
| 4 DOVIZIOSO | 19 | 58 | 58 | 58 | 58 | 58 | 58 | 58 | 58 | 58 | 58 | 58 | 58 | 19 | 65 | 65 | 65 | 65 | 65 | 65 | 65 | 11 | 11 | 11 | 11 | 6 |
| 65 CAPIROSSI | 65 | 19 | 19 | 19 | 19 | 19 | 19 | 19 | 19 | 19 | 19 | 19 | 19 | 65 | 33 | 33 | 33 | 11 | 11 | 11 | 11 | 11 | 65 | 65 | 65 | 7 |
| 58 SIMONCELLI | 11 | 11 | 11 | 33 | 11 | 11 | 11 | 65 | 33 | 33 | 33 | 65 | 65 | 33 | 11 | 11 | 33 | 33 | 33 | 33 | 33 | 69 | 69 | 69 | 69 | 8 |
| 19 BAUTISTA | 26 | 33 | 33 | 11 | 33 | 33 | 65 | 33 | 65 | 65 | 65 | 33 | 33 | 11 | 5 | 69 | 69 | 69 | 69 | 69 | 69 | 33 | 33 | 33 | 33 | 9 |
| 5 EDWARDS | 69 | 65 | 65 | 65 | 65 | 65 | 33 | 11 | 11 | 11 | 11 | 11 | 11 | 5 | 69 | 5 | 40 | 40 | 40 | 40 | 40 | 40 | 40 | 40 | 40 | 10 |
| 69 HAYDEN | 33 | 41 | 41 | 41 | 41 | 69 | 69 | 69 | 5 | 5 | 5 | 5 | 5 | 69 | 40 | 40 | 5 | 5 | 5 | 5 | 5 | 5 | 5 | 5 | 5 | 11 |
| 41 ESPARGARO | 41 | 69 | 69 | 69 | 69 | 40 | 5 | 5 | 69 | 69 | 69 | 69 | 69 | 40 | 36 | 36 | 36 | 36 | 36 | 36 | 36 | 36 | 36 | 36 | 36 | 12 |
| 40 BARBERA | 40 | 40 | 40 | 40 | 40 | 5 | 40 | 40 | 40 | 40 | 40 | 40 | 40 | 36 | 64 | 64 | 64 | 64 | 64 | 64 | 64 | 64 | 64 | 64 | 64 | 13 |
| 33 MELANDRI | 36 | 5 | 5 | 5 | 5 | 36 | 36 | 36 | 36 | 36 | 36 | 36 | 36 | 64 | 8 | 8 | 8 | 8 | 8 | 8 | 4 | 4 | 4 | 4 | 4 | 14 |
| 36 KALLIO | 5 | 36 | 36 | 36 | 36 | 64 | 64 | 64 | 64 | 64 | 64 | 64 | 64 | 8 | 4 | 4 | 4 | 4 | 4 | 4 | 8 | 8 | 8 | 8 | 8 | 15 |
| 64 AKIYOSHI | 64 | 64 | 64 | 64 | 64 | 8 | 8 | 8 | 8 | 8 | 8 | 8 | 8 | | | | | | | | | | | | | |
| 8 YOSHIKAWA | 8 | 8 | 8 | 8 | 8 | | | | | | | | | | | | | | | | | | | | | |

## Moto2

RACE DISTANCE: 23 laps, 67.556 miles/108.721 km · RACE WEATHER: Dry (air 32°, humidity 16%, track 49°)

| Pos. | Rider | Nat. | No. | Entrant | Machine | Laps | Time & Speed |
|---|---|---|---|---|---|---|---|
| 1 | **Yuki Takahashi** | JPN | 72 | Tech 3 Racing | Tech 3 | 23 | 41m 42.451s (mph/km/h) 97.185/156.404 |
| 2 | **Thomas Luthi** | SWI | 12 | Interwetten Moriwaki Moto2 | Moriwaki | 23 | 41m 47.488s |
| 3 | **Julian Simon** | SPA | 60 | Mapfre Aspar Team | Suter | 23 | 41m 47.651s |
| 4 | **Karel Abraham** | CZE | 17 | Cardion AB Motoracing | FTR | 23 | 41m 49.157s |
| 5 | **Toni Elias** | SPA | 24 | Gresini Racing Moto2 | Moriwaki | 23 | 41m 49.820s |
| 6 | **Simone Corsi** | ITA | 3 | JIR Moto2 | MotoBI | 23 | 41m 49.865s |
| 7 | **Kenny Noyes** | USA | 9 | Jack & Jones by A.Banderas | Promoharris | 23 | 41m 59.461s |
| 8 | **Fonsi Nieto** | SPA | 10 | Holiday Gym G22 | Moriwaki | 23 | 42m 03.006s |
| 9 | **Anthony West** | AUS | 8 | MZ Racing Team | MZ-RE Honda | 23 | 42m 03.452s |
| 10 | **Alex de Angelis** | RSM | 15 | RSM Team Scot | Force GP210 | 23 | 42m 03.820s |
| 11 | **Gabor Talmacsi** | HUN | 2 | Fimmco Speed Up | Speed Up | 23 | 42m 04.664s |
| 12 | **Yonny Hernandez** | COL | 68 | Blusens-STX | BQR-Moto2 | 23 | 42m 05.475s |
| 13 | **Andrea Iannone** | ITA | 29 | Fimmco Speed Up | Speed Up | 23 | 42m 07.748s |
| 14 | **Jules Cluzel** | FRA | 16 | Forward Racing | Suter | 23 | 42m 09.125s |
| 15 | **Yusuke Teshima** | JPN | 11 | JIR Moto2 | MotoBI | 23 | 42m 09.247s |
| 16 | Raffaele de Rosa | ITA | 35 | Tech 3 Racing | Tech 3 | 23 | 42m 09.892s |
| 17 | Arne Tode | GER | 41 | Racing Team Germany | Suter | 23 | 42m 10.125s |
| 18 | Vladimir Ivanov | UKR | 61 | Gresini Racing Moto2 | Moriwaki | 23 | 42m 17.644s |
| 19 | Jordi Torres | SPA | 18 | MR Griful | Promoharris | 23 | 42m 19.875s |
| 20 | Valentin Debise | FRA | 53 | WTR San Marino Team | ADV | 23 | 42m 23.955s |
| 21 | Joan Olive | SPA | 5 | Jack & Jones by A.Banderas | Promoharris | 23 | 42m 24.161s |
| 22 | Claudio Corti | ITA | 71 | Forward Racing | Suter | 23 | 42m 24.417s |
| 23 | Ricard Cardus | SPA | 4 | Viessmann Kiefer Racing | Suter | 23 | 42m 31.675s |
| 24 | Xavier Simeon | BEL | 19 | Holiday Gym G22 | Moriwaki | 23 | 42m 45.921s |
| 25 | Sergio Gadea | SPA | 40 | Tenerife 40 Pons | Pons Kalex | 23 | 42m 55.265s |
| 26 | Mashel Al Naimi | QAT | 95 | Blusens-STX | BQR-Moto2 | 23 | 43m 05.247s |
| | Carmelo Morales | SPA | 31 | Tenerife 40 Pons | Pons Kalex | 22 | DNF |
| | Bernat Martinez | SPA | 76 | Maquinza-SAG Team | Bimota | 20 | DNF |
| | Alex Baldolini | ITA | 25 | Caretta Technology Race Dept. | I.C.P. | 19 | DNF |
| | Scott Redding | GBR | 45 | Marc VDS Racing Team | Suter | 12 | DNF |
| | Ratthapark Wilairot | THA | 14 | Thai Honda PTT Singha SAG | Bimota | 9 | DNF |
| | Dani Rivas | SPA | 7 | MR Griful | Promoharris | 4 | DNF |
| | Shoya Tomizawa | JPN | 48 | Technomag-CIP | Suter | 4 | DNF |
| | Niccolo Canepa | ITA | 59 | RSM Team Scot | Force GP210 | 3 | DNF |
| | Lukas Pesek | CZE | 52 | Matteoni CP Racing | Moriwaki | 3 | DNF |
| | Vladimir Leonov | RUS | 21 | Vector Kiefer Racing | Suter | 1 | DNF |
| | Dominique Aegerter | SWI | 77 | Technomag-CIP | Suter | 1 | DNF |
| | Hector Faubel | SPA | 55 | Marc VDS Racing Team | Suter | 1 | DNF |
| | Robertino Pietri | VEN | 39 | Italtrans S.T.R. | Suter | 0 | DNF |
| | Roberto Rolfo | ITA | 44 | Italtrans S.T.R. | Suter | 0 | DNF |
| | Alex Debon | SPA | 6 | Aeroport de Castello - Ajo | FTR | 0 | DNF |
| | Mike di Meglio | FRA | 63 | Mapfre Aspar Team | Suter | 0 | DNF |

**Fastest lap:** Andrea Iannone, on lap 4, 1m 47.543s, 98.323mph/158.236km/h (record).
**Previous lap record:** New category.
**Event best maximum speed:** Andrea Iannone, 174.6mph/281.0km/h (warm up).

**Qualifying:** Dry
Air: 34° Humidity: 18% Ground: 52°

| | | |
|---|---|---|
| 1 | Iannone | 1m 47.493s |
| 2 | Takahashi | 1m 47.760s |
| 3 | Luthi | 1m 47.973s |
| 4 | Elias | 1m 48.089s |
| 5 | Cluzel | 1m 48.133s |
| 6 | Morales | 1m 48.164s |
| 7 | Tomizawa | 1m 48.192s |
| 8 | Wilairot | 1m 48.224s |
| 9 | Noyes | 1m 48.291s |
| 10 | Rolfo | 1m 48.366s |
| 11 | Simon | 1m 48.373s |
| 12 | Abraham | 1m 48.438s |
| 13 | Corsi | 1m 48.447s |
| 14 | Redding | 1m 48.480s |
| 15 | Faubel | 1m 48.491s |
| 16 | Aegerter | 1m 48.495s |
| 17 | Nieto | 1m 48.563s |
| 18 | Gadea | 1m 48.571s |
| 19 | Tode | 1m 48.587s |
| 20 | Debon | 1m 48.613s |
| 21 | di Meglio | 1m 48.620s |
| 22 | de Rosa | 1m 48.621s |
| 23 | Hernandez | 1m 48.640s |
| 24 | Pesek | 1m 48.677s |
| 25 | Torres | 1m 48.745s |
| 26 | Baldolini | 1m 48.803s |
| 27 | Cardus | 1m 48.807s |
| 28 | Rivas | 1m 48.888s |
| 29 | West | 1m 48.928s |
| 30 | de Angelis | 1m 48.942s |
| 31 | Ivanov | 1m 49.036s |
| 32 | Talmacsi | 1m 49.047s |
| 33 | Canepa | 1m 49.131s |
| 34 | Simeon | 1m 49.169s |
| 35 | Martinez | 1m 49.188s |
| 36 | Teshima | 1m 49.209s |
| 37 | Corti | 1m 49.272s |
| 38 | Olive | 1m 49.314s |
| 39 | Debise | 1m 49.439s |
| 40 | Al Naimi | 1m 49.723s |
| 41 | Leonov | 1m 50.150s |
| 42 | Pietri | 1m 50.183s |

**Fastest race laps**

| | | |
|---|---|---|
| 1 | Iannone | 1m 47.543s |
| 2 | Abraham | 1m 47.826s |
| 3 | Takahashi | 1m 47.949s |
| 4 | Simon | 1m 47.982s |
| 5 | Corsi | 1m 48.043s |
| 6 | Luthi | 1m 48.061s |
| 7 | Hernandez | 1m 48.082s |
| 8 | Talmacsi | 1m 48.163s |
| 9 | Tomizawa | 1m 48.173s |
| 10 | Wilairot | 1m 48.258s |
| 11 | Pesek | 1m 48.326s |
| 12 | Morales | 1m 48.330s |
| 13 | Redding | 1m 48.461s |
| 14 | Noyes | 1m 48.528s |
| 15 | Elias | 1m 48.574s |
| 16 | Cluzel | 1m 48.592s |
| 17 | de Rosa | 1m 48.606s |
| 18 | West | 1m 48.697s |
| 19 | Nieto | 1m 48.716s |
| 20 | Gadea | 1m 48.799s |
| 21 | Tode | 1m 48.811s |
| 22 | de Angelis | 1m 48.841s |
| 23 | Simeon | 1m 48.886s |
| 24 | Torres | 1m 48.894s |
| 25 | Ivanov | 1m 49.008s |
| 26 | Baldolini | 1m 49.020s |
| 27 | Rivas | 1m 49.166s |
| 28 | Canepa | 1m 49.178s |
| 29 | Teshima | 1m 49.241s |
| 30 | Cardus | 1m 49.360s |
| 31 | Debise | 1m 49.375s |
| 32 | Corti | 1m 49.409s |
| 33 | Martinez | 1m 49.621s |
| 34 | Olive | 1m 49.629s |
| 35 | Al Naimi | 1m 49.723s |
| 36 | Leonov | 1m 59.408s |

**Championship Points**

| | | |
|---|---|---|
| 1 | Elias | 111 |
| 2 | Luthi | 94 |
| 3 | Simon | 77 |
| 4 | Tomizawa | 76 |
| 5 | Iannone | 70 |
| 6 | Corsi | 65 |
| 7 | Cluzel | 57 |
| 8 | Takahashi | 52 |
| 9 | Gadea | 47 |
| 10 | Talmacsi | 42 |
| 11 | Debon | 37 |
| 12 | Wilairot | 25 |
| 13 | Nieto | 25 |
| 14 | Redding | 23 |
| 15 | Abraham | 22 |
| 16 | Rolfo | 21 |
| 17 | Noyes | 18 |
| 18 | di Meglio | 17 |
| 19 | Aegerter | 15 |
| 20 | Hernandez | 15 |
| 21 | Pasini | 12 |
| 22 | Bradl | 11 |
| 23 | de Angelis | 11 |
| 24 | Baldolini | 9 |
| 25 | Simeon | 8 |
| 26 | West | 8 |
| 27 | Faubel | 4 |
| 28 | Pesek | 4 |
| 29 | Tode | 2 |
| 30 | Teshima | 1 |
| 31 | Corti | 1 |

**Constructors**

| | | |
|---|---|---|
| 1 | Moriwaki | 136 |
| 2 | Suter | 127 |
| 3 | Speed Up | 86 |
| 4 | MotoBI | 67 |
| 5 | FTR | 57 |
| 6 | Tech 3 | 52 |
| 7 | Pons Kalex | 47 |
| 8 | Bimota | 25 |
| 9 | Promoharris | 18 |
| 10 | BQR-Moto2 | 15 |
| 11 | Force GP210 | 11 |
| 12 | RSV | 10 |
| 13 | I.C.P. | 9 |
| 14 | MZ-RE Honda | 8 |

## 125cc

RACE DISTANCE: 22 laps, 64.619 miles/103.994 km · RACE WEATHER: Dry (air 31°, humidity 21%, track 44°)

| Pos. | Rider | Nat. | No. | Entrant | Machine | Laps | Time & Speed |
|---|---|---|---|---|---|---|---|
| 1 | **Marc Marquez** | SPA | 93 | Red Bull Ajo Motorsport | Derbi | 22 | 40m 46.315s (mph/km/h) 95.093/153.037 |
| 2 | **Bradley Smith** | GBR | 38 | Bancaja Aspar Team | Aprilia | 22 | 40m 50.953s |
| 3 | **Pol Espargaro** | SPA | 44 | Tuenti Racing | Derbi | 22 | 40m 51.311s |
| 4 | **Sandro Cortese** | GER | 11 | Avant Mitsubishi Ajo | Derbi | 22 | 41m 31.681s |
| 5 | **Efren Vazquez** | SPA | 7 | Tuenti Racing | Derbi | 22 | 41m 31.748s |
| 6 | **Tomoyoshi Koyama** | JPN | 71 | Racing Team Germany | Aprilia | 22 | 41m 36.000s |
| 7 | **Randy Krummenacher** | SWI | 35 | Stipa-Molenaar Racing GP | Aprilia | 22 | 41m 36.050s |
| 8 | **Johann Zarco** | FRA | 14 | WTR San Marino Team | Aprilia | 22 | 41m 36.058s |
| 9 | **Jonas Folger** | GER | 94 | Ongetta Team | Aprilia | 22 | 41m 36.090s |
| 10 | **Danny Webb** | GBR | 99 | Andalucia Cajasol | Aprilia | 22 | 41m 39.430s |
| 11 | **Adrian Martin** | SPA | 26 | Aeroport de Castello - Ajo | Aprilia | 22 | 41m 44.984s |
| 12 | **Simone Grotzkyj** | ITA | 15 | Fontana Racing | Aprilia | 22 | 41m 45.115s |
| 13 | **Alberto Moncayo** | SPA | 23 | Andalucia Cajasol | Aprilia | 22 | 41m 48.365s |
| 14 | **Marcel Schrotter** | GER | 78 | Interwetten Honda 125 | Honda | 22 | 42m 01.812s |
| 15 | **Zulfahmi Khairuddin** | MAL | 63 | AirAsia-Sepang Int. Circuit | Aprilia | 22 | 42m 02.344s |
| 16 | Jakub Kornfeil | CZE | 84 | Racing Team Germany | Aprilia | 22 | 42m 12.756s |
| 17 | Louis Rossi | FRA | 69 | CBC Corse | Aprilia | 22 | 42m 19.928s |
| 18 | Luca Marconi | ITA | 87 | Ongetta Team | Aprilia | 22 | 42m 22.501s |
| 19 | Joan Perello | SPA | 58 | SAG Castrol | Honda | 22 | 42m 22.538s |
| 20 | Michael van der Mark | NED | 60 | Lambretta Reparto Corse | Lambretta | 22 | 42m 22.655s |
| 21 | Johnny Rosell | SPA | 59 | SAG Castrol | Honda | 22 | 42m 30.119s |
| 22 | Marco Ravaioli | ITA | 72 | Lambretta Reparto Corse | Lambretta | 22 | 42m 41.646s |
| 23 | Peter Sebestyen | HUN | 56 | Right Guard Racing | Aprilia | 21 | 42m 09.743s |
| | Nicolas Terol | SPA | 40 | Bancaja Aspar Team | Aprilia | 21 | DNF |
| | Luis Salom | SPA | 39 | Stipa-Molenaar Racing GP | Aprilia | 14 | DNF |
| | Eduard Lopez | SPA | 17 | Catalunya Racing Team | Aprilia | 11 | DNF |
| | Isaac Vinales | SPA | 55 | Catalunya Racing Team | Aprilia | 10 | DNF |
| | Sturla Fagerhaug | NOR | 50 | AirAsia-Sepang Int. Circuit | Aprilia | 7 | DNF |
| | Alexis Masbou | FRA | 5 | Ongetta Team | Aprilia | 5 | DNF |
| | Esteve Rabat | SPA | 12 | Blusens-STX | Aprilia | 0 | DNF |
| | Jasper Iwema | NED | 53 | CBC Corse | Aprilia | 0 | DNF |
| | Lorenzo Savadori | ITA | 32 | Matteoni CP Racing | Aprilia | 0 | DNS |

**Fastest lap:** Pol Espargaro, on lap 9, 1m 50.590s, 95.614mph/153.876km/h.
**Lap record:** Randy Krummenacher, SWI (KTM), 1m 50.732s, 95.492mph/153.679km/h (2007).
**Event best maximum speed:** Efren Vazquez, 147.9mph/238.0km/h (free practice 2).

**Qualifying:** Dry
Air: 34° Humidity: 19% Ground: 52°

| | | |
|---|---|---|
| 1 | Marquez | 1m 50.543s |
| 2 | Espargaro | 1m 50.809s |
| 3 | Smith | 1m 51.019s |
| 4 | Terol | 1m 51.066s |
| 5 | Cortese | 1m 51.546s |
| 6 | Koyama | 1m 51.824s |
| 7 | Rabat | 1m 51.890s |
| 8 | Vazquez | 1m 51.951s |
| 9 | Masbou | 1m 52.316s |
| 10 | Zarco | 1m 52.478s |
| 11 | Grotzkyj | 1m 52.538s |
| 12 | Folger | 1m 52.580s |
| 13 | Moncayo | 1m 52.758s |
| 14 | Krummenacher | 1m 52.765s |
| 15 | Salom | 1m 52.801s |
| 16 | Webb | 1m 52.861s |
| 17 | Fagerhaug | 1m 52.884s |
| 18 | Khairuddin | 1m 53.179s |
| 19 | Martin | 1m 53.486s |
| 20 | Iwema | 1m 53.525s |
| 21 | Vinales | 1m 53.609s |
| 22 | Rosell | 1m 53.824s |
| 23 | Schrotter | 1m 54.055s |
| 24 | Rossi | 1m 54.510s |
| 25 | Marconi | 1m 54.695s |
| 26 | Perello | 1m 54.735s |
| 27 | van der Mark | 1m 55.157s |
| 28 | Kornfeil | 1m 55.777s |
| 29 | Savadori | 1m 56.211s |
| 30 | Ravaioli | 1m 56.544s |
| 31 | Lopez | 1m 57.198s |
| 32 | Sebestyen | 1m 57.404s |

**Fastest race laps**

| | | |
|---|---|---|
| 1 | Espargaro | 1m 50.590s |
| 2 | Marquez | 1m 50.628s |
| 3 | Terol | 1m 50.636s |
| 4 | Smith | 1m 50.684s |
| 5 | Cortese | 1m 51.638s |
| 6 | Salom | 1m 52.048s |
| 7 | Vazquez | 1m 52.163s |
| 8 | Krummenacher | 1m 52.270s |
| 9 | Folger | 1m 52.293s |
| 10 | Zarco | 1m 52.351s |
| 11 | Grotzkyj | 1m 52.444s |
| 12 | Koyama | 1m 52.505s |
| 13 | Masbou | 1m 52.674s |
| 14 | Webb | 1m 52.716s |
| 15 | Martin | 1m 52.765s |
| 16 | Moncayo | 1m 52.882s |
| 17 | Fagerhaug | 1m 53.541s |
| 18 | Khairuddin | 1m 53.626s |
| 19 | Schrotter | 1m 53.814s |
| 20 | Kornfeil | 1m 53.901s |
| 21 | Rosell | 1m 54.171s |
| 22 | Marconi | 1m 54.402s |
| 23 | Perello | 1m 54.416s |
| 24 | Rossi | 1m 54.431s |
| 25 | Vinales | 1m 54.481s |
| 26 | van der Mark | 1m 54.742s |
| 27 | Ravaioli | 1m 55.161s |
| 28 | Lopez | 1m 55.509s |
| 29 | Sebestyen | 1m 58.457s |

**Championship Points**

| | | |
|---|---|---|
| 1 | Marquez | 132 |
| 2 | Espargaro | 131 |
| 3 | Terol | 118 |
| 4 | Smith | 94 |
| 5 | Vazquez | 60 |
| 6 | Cortese | 60 |
| 7 | Krummenacher | 58 |
| 8 | Koyama | 57 |
| 9 | Rabat | 50 |
| 10 | Zarco | 45 |
| 11 | Webb | 39 |
| 12 | Moncayo | 25 |
| 13 | Folger | 23 |
| 14 | Iwema | 20 |
| 15 | Masbou | 17 |
| 16 | Salom | 15 |
| 17 | Grotzkyj | 14 |
| 18 | Martin | 9 |
| 19 | Schrotter | 9 |
| 20 | Kornfeil | 3 |
| 21 | Khairuddin | 1 |

**Constructors**

| | | |
|---|---|---|
| 1 | Derbi | 170 |
| 2 | Aprilia | 141 |
| 3 | Honda | 9 |
| 4 | Lambretta | 1 |

# GERMAN GRAND PRIX

## SACHSENRING

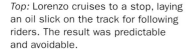

Top: Lorenzo cruises to a stop, laying an oil slick on the track for following riders. The result was predictable and avoidable.

Above: Red bike gives you wings! Ducati's little aerofoils.

Above right: He's back! Rossi's garage was even more than usually besieged by photographers anxious to capture the defining moment...

Right: ...and this is it. With leathers and boots reinforced, Rossi used a crutch to get to and from the bike.

Above far right: Catastrophe in three parts. Espargaro is sent looping, and Bautista (just visible) can't avoid the wreckage; the Frenchman's bike flames up in a fiery aftermath; de Puniet is stretchered away with a broken leg.

Photos: Gold & Goose

THE ovation at the opening Press briefing on Thursday evening said it all. The main man was back. Two races earlier than predicted, walking with a crutch, but ready to race. Rossi was in cheerful mood: the worst time had been the first 15 days, lying on his back immobilised. Since then, in spite of dull hours spent in a hyperbaric chamber, recovery had gone quickly. He'd come back for this race and the next because they were both on left-hand tracks, putting less strain on his right leg; he was here to play himself back in. "I need to get back on my M1, get the right feeling, make it step by step, and in the last five races try to win."

It would take at least that long: the recuperation had also set back recovery of his troublesome shoulder, while in the weeks to come the inability to run would mean a long haul back to the sort of fitness needed to race Lorenzo and Co. For now, racing in general was much relieved at the return of its megastar, and he was clearly as happy to be back.

He'd tested an R1 Superbike at Misano eight days before, then more seriously on Monday, on Bridgestone tyres this time, lapping faster than Toseland had on Pirellis the day before, according to reports. The last hurdle was the German track doctor: easily surmounted when Rossi showed him 90 per cent of knee movement and 95 per cent in his ankle, and proved that he could walk. Good enough to race, then, in specially enlarged and reinforced leathers and boots, and making setting changes to make the bike more agile, taking less physical effort to turn.

With the season approaching halfway, engine wear was starting to become an issue, especially, but not only for Suzuki. The issue was highlighted in spectacular fashion by Lorenzo, who demonstrated that two-stroke racers might benefit from some re-education. In short, his Fiat Yamaha motor came apart on the front straight, but it wasn't until a convenient break in the barrier beyond the pit lane and by the first corner that the points leader coasted to a stop and swung the bike off the track.

The engine had been used for the first time, sparingly, at Qatar, and had raced in France and England, having covered some 1,500km – planned useful life is 1,800km, so it was nearing the limit. The blow-up was comprehensive and abrupt. Piston or gudgeon-pin failure had led to a broken

conrod flailing around and smashing the crankcase, and the loss of an awful lot of oil. At first, career two-stroke rider Lorenzo was not sure what had happened, and he escaped censure for his rather slow reactions. "Only when I got to the corner, I felt oil on my boot," he said.

Spies and de Puniet paid the price, the first to arrive, falling the instant they hit the oil in the braking zone. De Puniet slammed into Spies's bike painfully; his weekend would get worse. The riders accepted this likelihood, if reluctantly. "I'll discuss it at the safety commission. If it happens more, we'll have to do something about it," said Stoner; while Pedrosa added, "Today, I was lucky not to be the first one there. It's a tricky point, and not easy to find a solution."

There was something new at Ducati – the return of fairing-flank winglets, an aerodynamic device of questionable value that has been seen, briefly, on factory Suzukis in the 1970s and more recently on factory Yamahas. Questionable value, that is, in terms of downforce, although this was the official raison d'être given by team manager Vito Guareschi. But the stature of Ducati's aerodynamicist, Alan Jenkins, and the factory's reliance on wind-tunnel testing suggested more than just a frippery: possibly the winglets, or more importantly their end-plates, had a role to play in controlling air-flow along the sides of the fairing, and encouraging greater flow through the radiator exit ducts to improve cooling. Either way, the riders felt little difference, although Stoner imagined "some positives on faster corners. Though this is a slower track. Maybe we'll notice more somewhere faster." The wings would come and go over the coming races.

Dorna had introduced an innovation that would take root: an on-board camera with a gyroscope that kept the lens – and the viewer's head – aligned with the horizon while the bike leaned to and fro in the foreground. Along with the advent of HD cameras and the continued use of close-up camera angles, like those scrutinising a rider's right hand on throttle and brake, this was another step forward in standard-setting coverage.

Lorenzo continued to build on his statistics, arriving in Germany as one of seven riders to finish on the podium in the first seven races. The others were famous names indeed: John Surtees, Mike Hailwood, Giacomo Agostini, Wayne

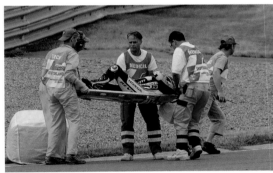

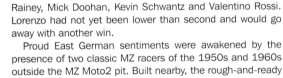

Rainey, Mick Doohan, Kevin Schwantz and Valentino Rossi. Lorenzo had not yet been lower than second and would go away with another win.

Proud East German sentiments were awakened by the presence of two classic MZ racers of the 1950s and 1960s outside the MZ Moto2 pit. Built nearby, the rough-and-ready machines had developed the rotary-valve/expansion-chamber techniques that had created the high-performance two-stroke. And had formed the foundation of Suzuki's success, after rider Ernst Degner had fled Communism with all MZ's secrets. Factory owner and team chief Martin Wimmer had a new aluminium space-frame chassis, which saved a massive 6kg compared with the steel version, but reverted to the familiarity of the old type when it looked as though the weekend might turn wet. Sadly, it didn't happen.

Moto2 struggler Talmacsi received a kick in the teeth when Hungarian petro-chemical giant MOL withdrew his sponsorship. Badly outclassed by team-mate Iannone, the former 125 champion had fallen short of the target number of points in the sponsorship contract. The news, arriving on Saturday, still came as a shock.

On the positive side, after testing at the new Aragon circuit, Simon, Tomizawa and Cluzel had all received revised Suter chassis, closing the gap on the FTR and Moriwaki riders.

## MOTOGP RACE – 21 laps

Pedrosa was leading when qualifying was stopped after Lorenzo's blow-up. But Jorge returned to the pits for his spare bike, as an army of marshals scrubbed the track, and took a fourth successive pole, while Stoner also slipped ahead of the Honda, barely two-hundredths from pole and blaming traffic for not being one place higher.

Dovizioso headed row two from the amazing Rossi, who said after two sessions, "I had to suffer a bit." Barbera impressed in sixth; de Puniet led row three, any chance of another front row ruined after hitting the oil.

The race would also be interrupted, after just nine laps. Pedrosa had got away first, but by the end of lap one, Lorenzo was in front, and he, Pedrosa and Stoner soon began pulling clear. Rossi had closed on Dovi, while Hayden had

charged to sixth from 15th on the grid. Valuable, since race positions determined the restart grid.

Slow away, de Puniet was scrapping his way through a tight pack, now ninth and pressing Barbera. Then on the looping Omega curve, he fell in the middle of the track. Melandri and Capirossi got past, but Espargaro hit his fallen bike, while Kallio ran over the rider; then Bautista ploughed into the shambles as well.

De Puniet was hurt: the Pramac Ducati had snapped both lower bones in his left leg. The red flags came out as he was stretchered away, and a 21-lap restart was scheduled 40 minutes after the first.

Edwards had crashed out two laps earlier; Bautista and Espargaro were ready to ride, the former even lining up on his spare, but they had not returned to the pits within five minutes with their bikes, and were out per regulations. Just 13 starters, down to 12 when Kallio fell at Turn One.

Up front, it went much as before. Dani jumped straight into the lead; Lorenzo took over on the second lap, and by the fifth lap, Stoner was ahead of Dovisioso once more in a close third.

Pedrosa was pushing hard. His first pass came at the start of lap nine, but he ran wide and Lorenzo was immediately ahead again. Next time around, Pedrosa's turn-one move started earlier and was more assured, and he took a lead he would retain to the end.

By lap 14, Lorenzo had given up hope. He was more than a second adrift, and the gap would stretch to the end. But he was also under no threat from behind, for Stoner was now almost three seconds adrift and under attack by old rival Rossi.

The returnee had finished the first lap sixth, behind Hayden, but was past by the second, and on lap six he pounced successfully on Dovizioso at the bottom of the 'waterfall' hill into the second-last corner.

He soon whittled down the two seconds to Stoner and by lap 12 was leaning on his old rival. Their battle was the highlight of an otherwise tedious race.

Rossi's first attack came on lap 15; two laps later, Stoner was ahead. They changed places twice more and started the last lap with Rossi ahead. He stayed tight into the penultimate corner, the last real passing place. Stoner, however,

*Above:* Capirossi commiserates with returnee de Angelis after beating him into last place by just over a tenth.

*Top:* "Not with a broken leg you don't." Stoner had to put a hard move on Rossi to keep him off the rostrum.

*Photos: Gold & Goose*

determined not to be beaten by a rider with a broken leg, had other plans.

Rossi's tight entry slowed his exit and speed up the hill; Stoner had taken a late line to come out faster – and in the way as Rossi came across to the final apex. "We touched a little," said the Australian – Rossi denied it later, but added mischievously, "But we didn't touch in America in 2008 either." (A famous epic battle where loser Stoner had accused him of rough tactics.) A fighting fourth, three-tenths off the rostrum, marked an amazing comeback.

Behind them, Dovisioso had fallen into the clutches of Simoncelli and Hayden, and for the second half of the race the three were locked together, Dovi mostly in front until Hayden took over from lap 13 to 18. But it was only by a bike length or two, and with three laps to go, he had a slide going on to the fast straight downhill swoop and dropped to the back of the close trio.

Spies had finished lap one in tenth and took time to escape from the brawl, finally getting ahead of first Barbera and, on lap nine, Melandri. By now, he was more than five seconds behind the three in front, but he had closed the gap to 1.3 seconds by lap 19 before backing off.

Barbera was a second behind him, Melandri dropping another second away at the back, the shoulder he had dislocated at Assen still troubling him. Another ten seconds away, a listless Capirossi narrowly fended off de Angelis, whose MotoGP return on the Interwetten Honda had proven harder than expected.

## MOTO2 RACE – 29 laps

Iannone raised eyebrows once again by taking a third pole in a row, by an astonishing 0.673 second. From second to 25th were covered by a single second. Tode was second, Elias and Simon alongside, Talmacsi heading the second from Corsi, Bradl and Tomizawa. Luthi was 21st, two places down on West's overweight MZ; Cluzel and Gadea were 31st and 32nd respectively.

By some miracle, the expected first-corner crash only took out five riders from near the back – de Rosa, Olive, Pesek, Faubel and Cardus.

Talmacsi led, team-mate Iannone taking over on lap two for his by now expected breakaway. By lap ten, he was almost two seconds clear, while Talmacsi was still five seconds ahead of the pursuit.

It wouldn't last, because by now Elias, out of the top ten on lap one, had taken third from Corsi. The Spaniard was in no mood for compromise. Now fully adjusted to a late setting change, he was circulating almost as fast as Iannone's lap-three record, while the leader's pace was slackening.

With Corsi dogging his tracks, Elias scythed the gap to the Hungarian. By lap 17, the pair was on him, and two laps later both were ahead.

Corsi crashed out next time around, but now Elias was within two seconds of Iannone and closing rapidly. It took Elias just over one more lap to dive under the Italian into the first tight corner, and this time Iannone had no real response, try as he might. He was more than three seconds behind at the finish.

"I made a bad start and lost a lot of time with other riders, but when I took my rhythm I made many overtakes and I could catch the leaders," explained Elias. "It was hard, but when I was in front I was able to go away."

Now Talmacsi had been caught by the next group, down to just four, with Abraham behind Rolfo, then Nieto and substitute Damien Cudlin, on the Pons bike in a first GP outing for the 27-year-old jobbing Australian rider.

By the finish, Rolfo was narrowly ahead of Nieto and Abraham, with the heartbroken Talmacsi sixth and impressive Cudlin inches behind. Aegerter was a couple of seconds further back, with the returned Bradl on his heels. Both had passed Yonny Hernandez on the last lap.

The crash list, as usual, was impressive. Championship contenders Simon and Luthi both crashed out, the former while battling up front, the latter well out of touch at the back. Other fallers included race winner Takahashi, fast-at-home Arne Tode, Debon yet again, Gadea and di Meglio.

Elias stretched his points lead impressively, showing real quality and consistency in circumstances that had other riders up one weekend and down the next.

*Above:* Marquez (93) and Espargaro (44) took off for a lonely battle, once the track had dried. Krummenacher (35) ended up 11th.

*Above left:* Nieto leads Rolfo in the battle for the Moto2 rostrum. The order was reversed at the flag.

*Left:* Elias celebrates a second Moto2 win and an enhanced championship points lead.

*Below:* Substituting Australian Damian Cudlin took a fine Moto2 seventh on the Tenerife Pons.

*Bottom:* Anthony West stayed mired in midfield at his MZ's home track.

*Below right:* Koyama beams after finishing second in the 125cc race.

Photos: Gold & Goose

## 125cc RACE – 27 laps

The absence of Terol made a bit more room up front, while Marquez secured his fourth pole in a row by better than half a second. Espargaro was next, with Smith and Cortese alongside; Krummenacher headed row two.

There'd been rain for morning warm-up, and there were still a few damp patches on a drying track for the first race of the day. Just the conditions for a couple of German heroes to fit wet tyres and attempt a runaway.

Folger took off for a big early lead – two seconds on the first lap – followed by countryman Schrotter. Folger had almost a three-second lead after four laps, and Schrotter was almost four ahead of the pursuit, led by Smith. But now the situation began to change rapidly as the track dried.

Three laps later, Marquez and Espargaro had broken three seconds clear in the lead, jousting almost all race long, neither able to escape.

The issue was settled dramatically with three laps left. Espargaro was ahead when he ran wide coming out of the second-last corner, touched the grass and was thrown violently. Marquez, right behind, narrowly escaped being hit by flying bike and/or body, and was left to cruise to a fifth win in a row by 17.5 seconds.

The battle for second was distant, but fierce, Koyama prevailing at the finish. Cortese had been 12th on lap one, but caught the gang with seven laps to go and regained third from Rabat on the final corner.

Smith lost touch at the end for fifth; sixth-placed Zarco was almost half a minute behind. Krummenacher crashed out of a strong place in this group with three laps to go, remounting for 11th.

Webb headed the next group for seventh, from Vazquez and Fagerhaug. Wild-card Daniel Kartheininger was tenth; Schrotter was 14th, Folger 16th, with only 18 finishing.

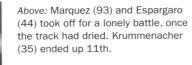

OFFICIAL TIMEKEEPER

## SACHSENRING GP CIRCUIT

Castrol Omega 86/54
Karthallen 180/112
Turn 9 147/91
Sternquell 128/80
Coca Cola Kurve 76/47
Turn 6 114/71
Turn 10 211/132
Queckenburg Kurve 104/65
Sachsen Kurve 123/77
Turn 11 146/90
Turn 12 208/130

Key
96/60 kph/mph
Gear
Circuit 3.671km/ 2.281 miles, 30 Laps

## MotoGP

**RACE (PART 2) DISTANCE: 21 laps, 47.902 miles/77.091 km · RACE WEATHER: Dry (air 21°, humidity 44%, track 31°)**

| Pos. | Rider | Nat. | No. | Entrant | Machine | Tyres | Laps | Time & speed |
|---|---|---|---|---|---|---|---|---|
| 1 | **Dani Pedrosa** | SPA | 26 | Repsol Honda Team | Honda | B | 21 | 28m 50.476s / 99.653mph/ 160.376km/h |
| 2 | **Jorge Lorenzo** | SPA | 99 | Fiat Yamaha Team | Yamaha | B | 21 | 28m 53.831s |
| 3 | **Casey Stoner** | AUS | 27 | Ducati Marlboro Team | Ducati | B | 21 | 28m 55.733s |
| 4 | **Valentino Rossi** | ITA | 46 | Fiat Yamaha Team | Yamaha | B | 21 | 28m 56.099s |
| 5 | **Andrea Dovizioso** | ITA | 4 | Repsol Honda Team | Honda | B | 21 | 29m 07.634s |
| 6 | **Marco Simoncelli** | ITA | 58 | San Carlo Honda Gresini | Honda | B | 21 | 29m 08.233s |
| 7 | **Nicky Hayden** | USA | 69 | Ducati Marlboro Team | Ducati | B | 21 | 29m 08.411s |
| 8 | **Ben Spies** | USA | 11 | Monster Yamaha Tech 3 | Yamaha | B | 21 | 29m 11.433s |
| 9 | **Hector Barbera** | SPA | 40 | Paginas Amarillas Aspar | Ducati | B | 21 | 29m 12.476s |
| 10 | **Marco Melandri** | ITA | 33 | San Carlo Honda Gresini | Honda | B | 21 | 29m 25.693s |
| 11 | **Loris Capirossi** | ITA | 65 | Rizla Suzuki MotoGP | Suzuki | B | 21 | 29m 35.518s |
| 12 | **Alex de Angelis** | RSM | 15 | Interwetten Honda MotoGP | Honda | B | 21 | 29m 35.680s |
| | Mika Kallio | FIN | 36 | Pramac Racing Team | Ducati | B | 0 | DNF |
| | Randy de Puniet | FRA | 14 | LCR Honda MotoGP | Honda | B | 0 | DNS 2nd race |
| | Alvaro Bautista | SPA | 19 | Rizla Suzuki MotoGP | Suzuki | B | 0 | DNS 2nd race |
| | Colin Edwards | USA | 5 | Monster Yamaha Tech 3 | Yamaha | B | 0 | DNS 2nd race |
| | Aleix Espargaro | SPA | 41 | Pramac Racing Team | Ducati | B | 0 | DNS 2nd race |

**Fastest lap:** Dani Pedrosa, on lap 12, 1m 21.882s, 100.288mph/161.398km/h (record).
**Previous lap record:** Dani Pedrosa, SPA (Honda), 1m 22.126s, 99.990mph/160.918km/h (2009).
**Event best maximum speed:** Dani Pedrosa, 176.7mph/284.4km/h (race part 2).

### Qualifying
Weather: Dry
Air Temp: 24° Humidity: 59°
Track Temp: 31°

| | | |
|---|---|---|
| 1 | Lorenzo | 1m 21.817s |
| 2 | Stoner | 1m 21.841s |
| 3 | Pedrosa | 1m 21.948s |
| 4 | Dovizioso | 1m 22.263s |
| 5 | Rossi | 1m 22.395s |
| 6 | Barbera | 1m 22.454s |
| 7 | de Puniet | 1m 22.610s |
| 8 | Simoncelli | 1m 22.624s |
| 9 | Espargaro | 1m 22.910s |
| 10 | Melandri | 1m 22.917s |
| 11 | Kallio | 1m 22.961s |
| 12 | Edwards | 1m 23.026s |
| 13 | Spies | 1m 23.028s |
| 14 | Capirossi | 1m 23.040s |
| 15 | Hayden | 1m 23.090s |
| 16 | Bautista | 1m 23.193s |
| 17 | de Angelis | 1m 23.515s |

### Fastest race laps
| | | |
|---|---|---|
| 1 | Pedrosa | 1m 21.882s |
| 2 | Rossi | 1m 22.035s |
| 3 | Lorenzo | 1m 22.099s |
| 4 | Stoner | 1m 22.135s |
| 5 | Dovizioso | 1m 22.592s |
| 6 | Hayden | 1m 22.604s |
| 7 | Simoncelli | 1m 22.644s |
| 8 | Spies | 1m 22.652s |
| 9 | Barbera | 1m 22.983s |
| 10 | Melandri | 1m 23.091s |
| 11 | de Angelis | 1m 23.865s |
| 12 | Capirossi | 1m 23.965s |

### Championship Points
| | | |
|---|---|---|
| 1 | Lorenzo | 185 |
| 2 | Pedrosa | 138 |
| 3 | Dovizioso | 102 |
| 4 | Stoner | 83 |
| 5 | Hayden | 78 |
| 6 | Rossi | 74 |
| 7 | de Puniet | 69 |
| 8 | Spies | 67 |
| 9 | Simoncelli | 49 |
| 10 | Melandri | 45 |
| 11 | Barbera | 41 |
| 12 | Edwards | 39 |
| 13 | Capirossi | 30 |
| 14 | Espargaro | 28 |
| 15 | Bautista | 25 |
| 16 | Kallio | 24 |
| 17 | Aoyama | 18 |
| 18 | de Angelis | 4 |
| 19 | Akiyoshi | 4 |
| 20 | Yoshikawa | 1 |

### Team Points
| | | |
|---|---|---|
| 1 | Fiat Yamaha Team | 260 |
| 2 | Repsol Honda Team | 240 |
| 3 | Ducati Marlboro Team | 161 |
| 4 | Monster Yamaha Tech 3 | 106 |
| 5 | San Carlo Honda Gresini | 94 |
| 6 | LCR Honda MotoGP | 69 |
| 7 | Rizla Suzuki MotoGP | 55 |
| 8 | Pramac Racing Team | 52 |
| 9 | Paginas Amarillas Aspar | 41 |
| 10 | Interwetten Honda MotoGP | 26 |

### Constructor Points
| | | |
|---|---|---|
| 1 | Yamaha | 25 |
| 2 | Honda | 16 |
| 3 | Ducati | 13 |
| 4 | Suzuki | 7 |

| Grid order | 1 | 2 | 3 | 4 | 5 | 6 | 7 | 8 | 9 | 10 | 11 | 12 | 13 | 14 | 15 | 16 | 17 | 18 | 19 | 20 | 21 | |
|---|---|---|---|---|---|---|---|---|---|---|---|---|---|---|---|---|---|---|---|---|---|---|
| 99 LORENZO | 26 | 99 | 99 | 99 | 99 | 99 | 99 | 99 | 99 | 26 | 26 | 26 | 26 | 26 | 26 | 26 | 26 | 26 | 26 | 26 | 26 | 1 |
| 26 PEDROSA | 99 | 26 | 26 | 26 | 26 | 26 | 26 | 26 | 26 | 99 | 99 | 99 | 99 | 99 | 99 | 99 | 99 | 99 | 99 | 99 | 99 | 2 |
| 27 STONER | 4 | 4 | 4 | 4 | 27 | 27 | 27 | 27 | 27 | 27 | 27 | 27 | 27 | 27 | 46 | 46 | 27 | 46 | 27 | 46 | 27 | 3 |
| 4 DOVIZIOSO | 27 | 27 | 27 | 27 | 4 | 46 | 46 | 46 | 46 | 46 | 46 | 46 | 46 | 46 | 27 | 27 | 46 | 27 | 46 | 27 | 46 | 4 |
| 46 ROSSI | 69 | 46 | 46 | 46 | 46 | 4 | 4 | 4 | 4 | 4 | 58 | 4 | 69 | 69 | 69 | 69 | 69 | 4 | 4 | 4 | 4 | 5 |
| 69 HAYDEN | 46 | 69 | 58 | 58 | 58 | 58 | 58 | 58 | 58 | 58 | 4 | 69 | 4 | 58 | 58 | 58 | 58 | 58 | 58 | 58 | 58 | 6 |
| 58 SIMONCELLI | 58 | 58 | 69 | 69 | 69 | 69 | 69 | 69 | 69 | 69 | 69 | 58 | 58 | 4 | 4 | 4 | 4 | 69 | 69 | 69 | 7 |
| 40 BARBERA | 33 | 33 | 33 | 40 | 40 | 40 | 40 | 33 | 11 | 11 | 11 | 11 | 11 | 11 | 11 | 11 | 11 | 11 | 11 | 11 | 8 |
| 33 MELANDRI | 40 | 40 | 40 | 33 | 33 | 33 | 33 | 11 | 33 | 33 | 33 | 40 | 40 | 40 | 40 | 40 | 40 | 40 | 40 | 40 | 9 |
| 65 CAPIROSSI | 11 | 11 | 11 | 11 | 11 | 11 | 11 | 40 | 40 | 40 | 40 | 33 | 33 | 33 | 33 | 33 | 33 | 33 | 33 | 33 | 10 |
| 36 KALLIO | 65 | 65 | 65 | 65 | 65 | 65 | 65 | 65 | 65 | 65 | 65 | 65 | 65 | 65 | 65 | 65 | 65 | 65 | 65 | 65 | 11 |
| 11 SPIES | 15 | 15 | 15 | 15 | 15 | 15 | 15 | 15 | 15 | 15 | 15 | 15 | 15 | 15 | 15 | 15 | 15 | 15 | 15 | 15 | 12 |
| 15 de ANGELIS | | | | | | | | | | | | | | | | | | | | | | |

## Moto2

**RACE DISTANCE: 29 laps, 66.151 miles/106.459 km · RACE WEATHER: Dry (air 19°, humidity 56%, track 27°)**

| Pos. | Rider | Nat. | No. | Entrant | Machine | Laps | Time & Speed |
|---|---|---|---|---|---|---|---|
| 1 | **Toni Elias** | SPA | 24 | Gresini Racing Moto2 | Moriwaki | 29 | 41m 57.745s (mph/km/h) 94.585/152.220 |
| 2 | **Andrea Iannone** | ITA | 29 | Fimmco Speed Up | Speed Up | 29 | 42m 01.042s |
| 3 | **Roberto Rolfo** | ITA | 44 | Italtrans S.T.R. | Suter | 29 | 42m 04.319s |
| 4 | **Fonsi Nieto** | SPA | 10 | Holiday Gym G22 | Moriwaki | 29 | 42m 04.526s |
| 5 | **Karel Abraham** | CZE | 17 | Cardion AB Motoracing | FTR | 29 | 42m 05.141s |
| 6 | **Gabor Talmacsi** | HUN | 2 | Fimmco Speed Up | Speed Up | 29 | 42m 07.300s |
| 7 | **Damian Cudlin** | AUS | 50 | Tenerife 40 Pons | Pons Kalex | 29 | 42m 07.442s |
| 8 | **Dominique Aegerter** | SWI | 77 | Technomag-CIP | Suter | 29 | 42m 09.118s |
| 9 | **Stefan Bradl** | GER | 65 | Viessmann Kiefer Racing | Suter | 29 | 42m 10.897s |
| 10 | **Yonny Hernandez** | COL | 68 | Blusens-STX | BQR-Moto2 | 29 | 42m 11.471s |
| 11 | **Alex Baldolini** | ITA | 25 | Caretta Technology Race Dept. | I.C.P. | 29 | 42m 13.547s |
| 12 | **Jules Cluzel** | FRA | 16 | Forward Racing | Suter | 29 | 42m 15.411s |
| 13 | **Anthony West** | AUS | 8 | MZ Racing Team | MZ-RE Honda | 29 | 42m 23.672s |
| 14 | **Vladimir Ivanov** | UKR | 61 | Gresini Racing Moto2 | Moriwaki | 29 | 42m 24.221s |
| 15 | **Xavier Simeon** | BEL | 19 | Holiday Gym G22 | Moriwaki | 29 | 42m 24.371s |
| 16 | Valentin Debise | FRA | 53 | WTR San Marino Team | ADV | 29 | 42m 25.210s |
| 17 | Ratthapark Wilairot | THA | 14 | Thai Honda PTT Singha SAG | Bimota | 29 | 42m 26.752s |
| 18 | Shoya Tomizawa | JPN | 48 | Technomag-CIP | Suter | 29 | 42m 40.706s |
| 19 | Yusuke Teshima | JPN | 11 | JIR Moto2 | MotoBI | 29 | 42m 40.886s |
| 20 | Niccolo Canepa | ITA | 59 | RSM Team Scot | Force GP210 | 29 | 42m 41.022s |
| 21 | Kenny Noyes | USA | 9 | Jack & Jones by A.Banderas | Promoharris | 29 | 42m 41.325s |
| 22 | Claudio Corti | ITA | 71 | Forward Racing | Suter | 29 | 42m 41.916s |
| 23 | Sascha Hommel | GER | 32 | MGM Racing Performance MC | Kalex | 29 | 42m 50.127s |
| 24 | Vladimir Leonov | RUS | 21 | Vector Kiefer Racing | Suter | 29 | 43m 01.979s |
| 25 | Hector Faubel | SPA | 55 | Marc VDS Racing Team | Suter | 29 | 43m 16.956s |
| 26 | Yannick Guerra | SPA | 88 | Holiday Gym G22 | Moriwaki | 29 | 43m 20.823s |
| 27 | Arne Tode | GER | 41 | Racing Team Germany | Suter | 29 | 43m 25.896s |
| | Mike di Meglio | FRA | 63 | Mapfre Aspar Team | Suter | 28 | DNF |
| | Raffaele de Rosa | ITA | 35 | Tech 3 Racing | Tech 3 | 25 | DNF |
| | Robertino Pietri | VEN | 39 | Italtrans S.T.R. | Suter | 24 | DNF |
| | Simone Corsi | ITA | 3 | JIR Moto2 | MotoBI | 19 | DNF |
| | Mashel Al Naimi | QAT | 95 | Blusens-STX | BQR-Moto2 | 17 | DNF |
| | Scott Redding | GBR | 45 | Marc VDS Racing Team | Suter | 10 | DNF |
| | Alex Debon | SPA | 6 | Aeroport de Castello - Ajo | FTR | 10 | DNF |
| | Thomas Luthi | SWI | 12 | Interwetten Moriwaki Moto2 | Moriwaki | 9 | DNF |
| | Sergio Gadea | SPA | 40 | Tenerife 40 Pons | Pons Kalex | 7 | DNF |
| | Julian Simon | SPA | 60 | Mapfre Aspar Team | Suter | 3 | DNF |
| | Yuki Takahashi | JPN | 72 | Tech 3 Racing | Tech 3 | 1 | DNF |
| | Ricard Cardus | SPA | 4 | Maquinza-SAG Team | Bimota | 0 | DNF |
| | Joan Olive | SPA | 5 | Jack & Jones by A.Banderas | Promoharris | 0 | DNF |
| | Lukas Pesek | CZE | 52 | Matteoni CP Racing | Moriwaki | 0 | DNF |

**Fastest lap:** Andrea Iannone, on lap 3, 1m 25.629s, 95.899mph/154.335km/h (record).
**Previous lap record:** New category.
**Event best maximum speed:** Stefan Bradl, 153.3mph/246.7km/h (race).

**Qualifying:** Dry
Air: 25° Humidity: 42% Ground: 33°

| | | |
|---|---|---|
| 1 | Iannone | 1m 24.982s |
| 2 | Tode | 1m 25.655s |
| 3 | Elias | 1m 25.664s |
| 4 | Simon | 1m 25.758s |
| 5 | Talmacsi | 1m 25.772s |
| 6 | Corsi | 1m 25.830s |
| 7 | Bradl | 1m 25.918s |
| 8 | Tomizawa | 1m 25.967s |
| 9 | Aegerter | 1m 26.028s |
| 10 | Debon | 1m 26.104s |
| 11 | Abraham | 1m 26.110s |
| 12 | Rolfo | 1m 26.114s |
| 13 | Takahashi | 1m 26.120s |
| 14 | Hernandez | 1m 26.156s |
| 15 | Redding | 1m 26.246s |
| 16 | Baldolini | 1m 26.274s |
| 17 | Nieto | 1m 26.319s |
| 18 | Wilairot | 1m 26.320s |
| 19 | West | 1m 26.320s |
| 20 | di Meglio | 1m 26.462s |
| 21 | Luthi | 1m 26.492s |
| 22 | Cudlin | 1m 26.522s |
| 23 | Corti | 1m 26.533s |
| 24 | de Rosa | 1m 26.600s |
| 25 | Simeon | 1m 26.600s |
| 26 | Cardus | 1m 26.670s |
| 27 | Faubel | 1m 26.736s |
| 28 | Ivanov | 1m 26.755s |
| 29 | Hommel | 1m 26.761s |
| 30 | Teshima | 1m 26.824s |
| 31 | Cluzel | 1m 26.831s |
| 32 | Gadea | 1m 26.981s |
| 33 | Pesek | 1m 27.051s |
| 34 | Olive | 1m 27.080s |
| 35 | Noyes | 1m 27.144s |
| 36 | Debise | 1m 27.171s |
| 37 | Leonov | 1m 27.180s |
| 38 | Pietri | 1m 27.682s |
| 39 | Canepa | 1m 27.801s |
| 40 | Al Naimi | 1m 28.146s |
| 41 | Guerra | 1m 28.790s |

**Fastest race laps**

| | | |
|---|---|---|
| 1 | Iannone | 1m 25.629s |
| 2 | Talmacsi | 1m 25.881s |
| 3 | Elias | 1m 25.934s |
| 4 | Nieto | 1m 25.998s |
| 5 | Simon | 1m 26.178s |
| 6 | Cudlin | 1m 26.224s |
| 7 | Abraham | 1m 26.229s |
| 8 | Corsi | 1m 26.251s |
| 9 | Rolfo | 1m 26.315s |
| 10 | di Meglio | 1m 26.352s |
| 11 | Aegerter | 1m 26.438s |
| 12 | Baldolini | 1m 26.448s |
| 13 | Hernandez | 1m 26.488s |
| 14 | de Rosa | 1m 26.540s |
| 15 | Debon | 1m 26.541s |
| 16 | Redding | 1m 26.600s |
| 17 | Bradl | 1m 26.654s |
| 18 | Cluzel | 1m 26.663s |
| 19 | West | 1m 26.665s |
| 20 | Tomizawa | 1m 26.735s |
| 21 | Wilairot | 1m 26.771s |
| 22 | Simeon | 1m 26.781s |
| 23 | Ivanov | 1m 26.824s |
| 24 | Debise | 1m 26.949s |
| 25 | Luthi | 1m 27.137s |
| 26 | Faubel | 1m 27.175s |
| 27 | Tode | 1m 27.259s |
| 28 | Noyes | 1m 27.263s |
| 29 | Canepa | 1m 27.306s |
| 30 | Corti | 1m 27.444s |
| 31 | Teshima | 1m 27.515s |
| 32 | Al Naimi | 1m 27.634s |
| 33 | Hommel | 1m 27.708s |
| 34 | Leonov | 1m 27.804s |
| 35 | Pietri | 1m 27.869s |
| 36 | Guerra | 1m 28.150s |
| 37 | Gadea | 1m 28.805s |
| 38 | Takahashi | 1m 32.854s |

**Championship Points**

| | | |
|---|---|---|
| 1 | Elias | 136 |
| 2 | Luthi | 94 |
| 3 | Iannone | 90 |
| 4 | Simon | 77 |
| 5 | Tomizawa | 76 |
| 6 | Corsi | 65 |
| 7 | Cluzel | 61 |
| 8 | Takahashi | 52 |
| 9 | Talmacsi | 52 |
| 10 | Gadea | 47 |
| 11 | Nieto | 38 |
| 12 | Debon | 37 |
| 13 | Rolfo | 37 |
| 14 | Abraham | 33 |
| 15 | Wilairot | 25 |
| 16 | Redding | 23 |
| 17 | Aegerter | 23 |
| 18 | Hernandez | 21 |
| 19 | Noyes | 18 |
| 20 | Bradl | 18 |
| 21 | di Meglio | 17 |
| 22 | Baldolini | 14 |
| 23 | Pasini | 12 |
| 24 | West | 11 |
| 25 | de Angelis | 11 |
| 26 | Cudlin | 9 |
| 27 | Simeon | 9 |
| 28 | Faubel | 4 |
| 29 | Pesek | 4 |
| 30 | Ivanov | 2 |
| 31 | Tode | 2 |
| 32 | Teshima | 1 |
| 33 | Corti | 1 |

**Constructors**

| | | |
|---|---|---|
| 1 | Moriwaki | 161 |
| 2 | Suter | 143 |
| 3 | Speed Up | 106 |
| 4 | FTR | 68 |
| 5 | MotoBI | 67 |
| 6 | Pons Kalex | 56 |
| 7 | Tech 3 | 52 |
| 8 | Bimota | 25 |
| 9 | BQR-Moto2 | 21 |
| 10 | Promoharris | 18 |
| 11 | I.C.P. | 14 |
| 12 | MZ-RE Honda | 11 |
| 13 | Force GP210 | 11 |
| 14 | RSV | 10 |

## 125cc

**RACE DISTANCE: 27 laps, 61.588 miles/99.117 km · RACE WEATHER: Wet (air 17°, humidity 72%, track 22°)**

| Pos. | Rider | Nat. | No. | Entrant | Machine | Laps | Time & Speed |
|---|---|---|---|---|---|---|---|
| 1 | **Marc Marquez** | SPA | 93 | Red Bull Ajo Motorsport | Derbi | 27 | 41m 28.274s (mph/km/h) 89.105/143.401 |
| 2 | **Tomoyoshi Koyama** | JPN | 71 | Racing Team Germany | Aprilia | 27 | 41m 45.852s |
| 3 | **Sandro Cortese** | GER | 11 | Avant Mitsubishi Ajo | Derbi | 27 | 41m 46.537s |
| 4 | **Esteve Rabat** | SPA | 12 | Blusens-STX | Aprilia | 27 | 41m 47.372s |
| 5 | **Bradley Smith** | GBR | 38 | Bancaja Aspar Team | Aprilia | 27 | 41m 47.987s |
| 6 | **Johann Zarco** | FRA | 14 | WTR San Marino Team | Aprilia | 27 | 42m 13.250s |
| 7 | **Danny Webb** | GBR | 99 | Andalucia Cajasol | Aprilia | 27 | 42m 21.517s |
| 8 | **Efren Vazquez** | SPA | 7 | Tuenti Racing | Derbi | 27 | 42m 21.576s |
| 9 | **Sturla Fagerhaug** | NOR | 50 | AirAsia-Sepang Int. Circuit | Aprilia | 27 | 42m 21.863s |
| 10 | **Daniel Kartheininger** | GER | 61 | Freudenberg Racing Team | KTM | 27 | 42m 33.352s |
| 11 | **Randy Krummenacher** | SWI | 35 | Stipa-Molenaar Racing GP | Aprilia | 27 | 42m 41.758s |
| 12 | **Lorenzo Savadori** | ITA | 32 | Matteoni CP Racing | Aprilia | 27 | 42m 41.993s |
| 13 | **Alexis Masbou** | FRA | 5 | Ongetta Team | Aprilia | 27 | 42m 49.953s |
| 14 | **Marcel Schrotter** | GER | 78 | Interwetten Honda 125 | Honda | 26 | 42m 09.972s |
| 15 | **Zulfahmi Khairuddin** | MAL | 63 | AirAsia-Sepang Int. Circuit | Aprilia | 26 | 42m 12.796s |
| 16 | Jonas Folger | GER | 94 | Ongetta Team | Aprilia | 26 | 42m 20.190s |
| 17 | Jakub Kornfeil | CZE | 84 | Racing Team Germany | Aprilia | 26 | 42m 35.741s |
| 18 | Kevin Hanus | GER | 86 | Thomas Sabo Team Hanusch | Honda | 23 | 41m 40.444s |
| | Pol Espargaro | SPA | 44 | Tuenti Racing | Derbi | 24 | DNF |
| | Michael van der Mark | NED | 60 | Lambretta Reparto Corse | Lambretta | 23 | DNF |
| | Jasper Iwema | NED | 53 | CBC Corse | Aprilia | 16 | DNF |
| | Simone Grotzkyj | ITA | 15 | Fontana Racing | Aprilia | 15 | DNF |
| | Toni Finsterbusch | GER | 68 | Freudenberg Racing Team | KTM | 15 | DNF |
| | Adrian Martin | SPA | 26 | Aeroport de Castello - Ajo | Aprilia | 14 | DNF |
| | Luca Marconi | ITA | 87 | Ongetta Team | Aprilia | 10 | DNF |
| | Louis Rossi | FRA | 69 | CBC Corse | Aprilia | 8 | DNF |
| | Marvin Fritz | GER | 62 | LHF Project Racing | Honda | 7 | DNF |
| | Eric Hubsch | GER | 85 | Team Sachsenring | Aprilia | 6 | DNF |
| | Marco Ravaioli | ITA | 72 | Lambretta Reparto Corse | Lambretta | 4 | DNF |
| | Alberto Moncayo | SPA | 23 | Andalucia Cajasol | Aprilia | 2 | DNF |
| | Luis Salom | SPA | 39 | Stipa-Molenaar Racing GP | Aprilia | 0 | DNF |

**Fastest lap:** Marc Marquez, on lap 15, 1m 28.702s, 92.577mph/148.988km/h.
**Lap record:** Gabor Talmacsi, HUN (Aprilia), 1m 26.909s, 94.487mph/152.062km/h (2007).
**Event best maximum speed:** Marc Marquez, 130.9mph/210.6km/h (qualifying practice).

**Qualifying:** Dry
Air: 23° Humidity: 62% Ground: 33°

| | | |
|---|---|---|
| 1 | Marquez | 1m 26.053s |
| 2 | Espargaro | 1m 26.596s |
| 3 | Smith | 1m 27.378s |
| 4 | Cortese | 1m 27.387s |
| 5 | Krummenacher | 1m 27.480s |
| 6 | Vazquez | 1m 27.647s |
| 7 | Koyama | 1m 27.824s |
| 8 | Zarco | 1m 28.069s |
| 9 | Rabat | 1m 28.075s |
| 10 | Webb | 1m 28.324s |
| 11 | Folger | 1m 28.499s |
| 12 | Iwema | 1m 28.720s |
| 13 | Moncayo | 1m 28.826s |
| 14 | Masbou | 1m 28.854s |
| 15 | Schrotter | 1m 28.975s |
| 16 | Kornfeil | 1m 29.054s |
| 17 | Grotzkyj | 1m 29.091s |
| 18 | Finsterbusch | 1m 29.225s |
| 19 | Martin | 1m 29.397s |
| 20 | Khairuddin | 1m 29.506s |
| 21 | Salom | 1m 29.577s |
| 22 | Fagerhaug | 1m 29.819s |
| 23 | van der Mark | 1m 29.868s |
| 24 | Rossi | 1m 30.123s |
| 25 | Savadori | 1m 30.138s |
| 26 | Kartheininger | 1m 30.476s |
| 27 | Marconi | 1m 30.634s |
| 28 | Hubsch | 1m 30.656s |
| 29 | Fritz | 1m 31.502s |
| 30 | Hanus | 1m 31.519s |
| 31 | Ravaioli | 1m 31.703s |

**Fastest race laps**

| | | |
|---|---|---|
| 1 | Marquez | 1m 28.702s |
| 2 | Espargaro | 1m 28.877s |
| 3 | Cortese | 1m 29.131s |
| 4 | Koyama | 1m 29.174s |
| 5 | Rabat | 1m 29.331s |
| 6 | Smith | 1m 29.496s |
| 7 | Krummenacher | 1m 29.662s |
| 8 | Webb | 1m 29.932s |
| 9 | Zarco | 1m 30.207s |
| 10 | Fagerhaug | 1m 30.270s |
| 11 | Vazquez | 1m 30.302s |
| 12 | Kartheininger | 1m 30.646s |
| 13 | Savadori | 1m 31.127s |
| 14 | Iwema | 1m 31.693s |
| 15 | Masbou | 1m 31.710s |
| 16 | Martin | 1m 31.839s |
| 17 | Finsterbusch | 1m 31.941s |
| 18 | Grotzkyj | 1m 32.731s |
| 19 | Hanus | 1m 34.545s |
| 20 | Khairuddin | 1m 35.450s |
| 21 | Fritz | 1m 35.525s |
| 22 | Folger | 1m 35.762s |
| 23 | Schrotter | 1m 36.244s |
| 24 | van der Mark | 1m 36.362s |
| 25 | Kornfeil | 1m 36.758s |
| 26 | Hubsch | 1m 38.128s |
| 27 | Rossi | 1m 39.225s |
| 28 | Marconi | 1m 40.035s |
| 29 | Ravaioli | 1m 40.284s |
| 30 | Moncayo | 1m 44.263s |

**Championship Points**

| | | |
|---|---|---|
| 1 | Marquez | 157 |
| 2 | Espargaro | 131 |
| 3 | Terol | 118 |
| 4 | Smith | 105 |
| 5 | Koyama | 77 |
| 6 | Cortese | 76 |
| 7 | Vazquez | 68 |
| 8 | Rabat | 63 |
| 9 | Krummenacher | 63 |
| 10 | Zarco | 55 |
| 11 | Webb | 48 |
| 12 | Moncayo | 25 |
| 13 | Folger | 23 |
| 14 | Masbou | 20 |
| 15 | Iwema | 20 |
| 16 | Salom | 15 |
| 17 | Grotzkyj | 14 |
| 18 | Schrotter | 11 |
| 19 | Martin | 9 |
| 20 | Fagerhaug | 7 |
| 21 | Kartheininger | 6 |
| 22 | Savadori | 4 |
| 23 | Kornfeil | 3 |
| 24 | Khairuddin | 2 |

**Constructors**

| | | |
|---|---|---|
| 1 | Derbi | 195 |
| 2 | Aprilia | 161 |
| 3 | Honda | 11 |
| 4 | KTM | 6 |
| 5 | Lambretta | 1 |

# UNITED STATES GRAND PRIX

## LAGUNA SECA CIRCUIT

*Main photo:* Jorge Lorenzo was uncatchable on his way to the moon.

*Inset above:* Lorenzo looked vexed. Valentino highly tickled when they played the Italian anthem instead of the Spanish refrain.

*Photos:* Gold & Goose

*Above:* Stoner's distant second was his best finish yet.

*Centre, from top:* Show time for Rossi: 500 Tweeters on the fairing, life influences (including inter alia Jerry Burgess) on his helmet; California girl goes green; King Kenny is enthroned.

*Top far right:* Wild-card Roger Lee Hayden found life tough on de Puniet's Honda.

*Above centre right:* Brother Nicky Hayden spent some coin on a designer hairdo.

*Above far right:* For once, Vale's yellow bunting was outnumbered, by star-spangled banners.

*Photos: Gold & Goose*

IN the sixth consecutive return to Laguna Seca, actually the 12th race held at the short and intense track in the scrubby hills set back from the Monterey harbour, modern MotoGP seemed finally to have adjusted to life at the American circuit.

Certainly, things are done differently there: from the makeshift pits and 'container' offices to the officious parking attendants, conveying a continent of righteous authority just in the inflexions to the word "Sir". But with the track surface settled and the Corkscrew becoming increasingly familiar, this was the first year when there was no chorus of complaints about the venue. Although there were plenty about the tyres Bridgestone had brought along.

In return, California responded with trademark warm weather and a good crowd of 51,546. It was reported that more than 20,000 of these had bought tickets only after Valentino had confirmed his attendance: his response in turn was a rostrum place, from where he threw his single crutch into the crowd below, all the more to upstage Jorge Lorenzo, whose sixth win of the year had been in copybook style, but far less exciting than Vale's fighting ride.

A moment of confusion had already primed the pump, after track officials had selected the wrong national anthem. Instead of the more sombre strain of the Spanish refrain, the PA blared out the jaunty opening notes of the Italian anthem, a sprightly tune written by Verdi. It surely wasn't a calculated slap in the face to Jorge, but both he and Rossi recognised the mistake long before officials hastily started again; and Rossi made the most of it.

Yamaha always makes the most of the Californian race, and the company's annual party was based on the signing of an agreement to continue the association with the circuit until 2014, when the current MotoGP contract expires. Later in the weekend, three of the company's greatest past champions – Kenny Roberts, Eddie Lawson and Wayne Rainey – were feted by the crowd, sitting on their title-winning bikes.

Roberts and Lawson also rode demonstration laps on the simple and now archaic-looking 500 two-strokes.

Local resident Rainey, still associated with the company's racing effort, held everyone's attention as he expounded on the situation between Lorenzo and Rossi within the factory team. Yamaha had been quite right, he said, to give full support to Jorge in spite of Rossi's opposition. "You have two strong riders. There's really one that's going to lead the team, and the situation has changed this year for Rossi because of injuries," the triple champion said. "I had many very fast, challenging team-mates, and no matter what, it's the rider's job to get the team working with him. Rossi's been fighting to that end. Lorenzo's also been fighting for that.

"Riders are always trying to get, or at least have the illusion, that your team-mate thinks the team is built around you. But with the injuries to Rossi, Yamaha's had to go with Lorenzo. They still have to win the championship, and it's by no means over."

Two riders had potential rostrum finishes snatched away. One was Pedrosa, who was leading like a runaway rabbit when he crashed out for his first non-finish of the year. The other was Ben Spies, whose pace had him on target for a top finish at a track he knew intimately, but whose fates had other ideas. With ten laps to go, he was shadowing Rossi as the Italian moved forward toward the top three. Then suddenly he was slower and dropping back. His problem was both mundane and costly: his visor was popping open as he hammered over the bumps, head down on the bike, and he had to keep taking a hand off the bars to close it. All the more frustrating as it had happened during practice: "A two-cent piece of tape could have fixed it," said frustrated team boss Poncharal.

Stoner's patience with the control Bridgestone tyres was wearing thin, at a track where even the soft-option asymmetric tyres had to be carefully coaxed up to operating temperatures. "No matter how soft it is, it's difficult to get it

working." At the same time, the softer/harder-choice tyres were so close that sometimes "the softer compound is better for withstanding temperatures. Now with every soft tyre at every track, we can do the race, no problem. No matter how hot the race is, we can run with the soft tyre. For me, this is ridiculous, because as soon as we have low temperatures, it becomes dangerous." he said. His crusade would bear fruit at the far end of the year, when Bridgestone agreed to provide tyres that did not overlap to the same degree. Motorcycle racing chief Hiroshi Yamada credited the riders' safety commission for persuading the company to change: "Originally, the target was to give the riders a choice of tyre for the race, but there were issues with warm-up performance and now they want something different," he told *MOTOCOURSE* later in the season.

Rossi waspishly brushed aside questions about his forthcoming move to Ducati: the announcement would come at Brno; the rumour mill was now grinding around his crew, as news broke that Burgess would return to Honda to head Stoner's crew. Both the Australian and HRC vice-president Shuhei Nakamoto admitted they'd chatted informally. "He would be welcome back at HRC any time," said Nakamoto. But it was no more than a rumour, reflecting increasing interest in a question that would not be settled until much later in the year.

Satellite Honda riders had sundry upgrades for the race, with both Gresini teams now also getting the factory electronics package already given to de Puniet in Germany. Nakamoto explained that there was no change to overall horsepower, but improved traction and wheelie control. "At the same time, the engineers have to learn how to use it," he added. There was similar generosity at Yamaha, where Spies and Edwards both enjoyed a power-up electronics package that left Edwards back-pedalling on his earlier remarks, at least in public, with "a big thanks to Yamaha for giving me their support as always". The new spec made the lap time

easier and more comfortable, he opined. At the same time, news leaked that he was in serious talks with Ducati to head the factory Superbike team in 2011. Later this would require more back-pedalling, when the factory unexpectedly pulled out of the series.

As usual, various new liveries etc were essayed for this show-boating event, some more successful than others – Lorenzo's post-race moon walk through the Corkscrew gravel trap was slightly mystifying; while the combination of the yellow stripes on Rossi's leathers with the off-white effect of Fiat Yamaha's 500 portraits of Twitter fans on the fairing made him rather resemble a Pramac Ducati rider, at least from afar or on TV. Ben Spies went especially Texan; Rossi's helmet bore portraits of friends and life influences, echoing the theme of his bike.

Others just got on with it as best they could – like Roger Lee Hayden, who was moonlighting from his SBK Kawasaki job as substitute for de Puniet on the LCR Honda. Not short of local knowledge, he had been tenth in 2007 as a Kawasaki wild-card, but found a modern 800cc MotoGP bike a hard mistress, the greatest difficulty being mastering the carbon brakes.

## MOTOGP RACE – 32 laps

Lorenzo was unstoppable in practice, in spite of strong efforts by Stoner. Alongside, first time on the front row, was Dovizioso's Honda, with "a good pace, but still not enough".

Pedrosa was only 0.038 second slower, heading a second row covered by just 0.071 second. Spies was alongside, his front-row hopes thwarted when Kallio crashed in front of him on his best lap. Rossi was next, an unimaginable 0.009 second slower around the short lap. He was suffering slightly with the up-and-down track's physical demands, but more in his shoulders than his legs, "the left shoulder because it has to compensate for the right one".

*Inset top left:* Lorenzo's Land just went orbital: the winner's moon-walk celebration.

*Inset left:* Petty visor problems spoiled Spies's hopes at home.

*Inset bottom left:* Rossi's crucial pass on Dovizioso.

*Inset below:* Dorna Sport's CEO Carmelo Ezpeleta.

*Main photo:* Pedrosa leads Stoner and winner Lorenzo around the daunting Turn One: Laguna atmosphere is unique.

*Photos: Gold & Goose*

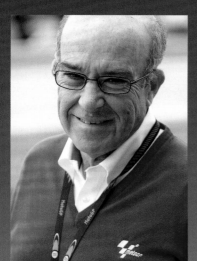

Old hands Hayden and Edwards headed row three from fast first-timer Simoncelli.

The first lap was hectic, Pedrosa for once not the first away. It was Jorge off the line, but Pedrosa got him back with a bold around-the-outside run through Turn One, and Stoner followed, Spies also soon afterwards, although Lorenzo got back ahead of the American down the hill.

Over the next five laps, the front three escaped, Stoner setting a new record on the fourth. But he was battling a familiar problem – a front end that lacked bite, and on lap six, after a third and worst-yet slide, he ran wide and Lorenzo was ahead.

At this point, the gap to the leader was eight-tenths, and more than a second two laps later. But now the Yamaha closed up again. "Dani was braking so hard and pushing so fast, I knew if I kept pushing maybe he would make a mistake, and he did." It was lap 12, and Lorenzo was less than a second behind the Honda when the leader lost the front at the downhill Rainey Curve, and he was gone in a cloud of dust. "Sometimes it's like this," he said gloomily.

Stoner was already 1.5 seconds down, and after half-distance his attack was spent; he switched attention to staying on track to get to the end. The gap was more than four seconds in the closing stages, and second was his best finish so far.

A tense battle, but with only the one overtaking move. The battle for third more than made up for it for the fans lining the hillsides.

After a hectic lap three, Dovizioso headed a close gang, from Rossi and Hayden, Spies knocked back three places, Simoncelli, Melandri and Edwards close behind. The last three would soon drop away in their own battle; the four up front stayed close for the first ten laps. Then Rossi started to lose ground on his younger countryman. Dovi was some two

seconds ahead at the mid-point. Was the taxing track taking its toll on Rossi's injuries?

Over the last ten laps, however, it all came to life again. First Spies passed Hayden on lap 20 and was looking for a way past Rossi as well, until his visor problems. At the same time, Rossi was speeding up: "I tried to ride to my maximum and make no mistakes, and I caught Andrea again." At the end of lap 27, he outbraked the Honda smoothly into the last tight corner, fought off Dovi's counterattack into turn one and kept holding him back to the flag. "I have pain everywhere; after Sachsenring, this track was much harder than I expected. This is like a victory for us," he grinned happily.

By the finish, a flawed final attack by Dovi at the last corner put him almost within reach of Hayden's late charge. Fifth still made him the best American, and they finished in line. Spies was four seconds behind, and Edwards another 20 seconds away. He'd had a long and strong battle with the Gresini team-mates, but had emerged clear victor after Simoncelli crashed out on lap 19 and Melandri dropped away towards the end.

A fierce fight for ninth gave it to Kallio from Capirossi by one-thousandth. Espargaro, supported in the pit by brother Pol, had passed both of them and was pulling away when he crashed on lap 29.

One lap down, Roger Lee Hayden battled with de Angelis almost all race long, finishing a creditable six-tenths ahead.

Bautista had crashed out right at the beginning; Barbera struggled at the back for four laps until his chain broke, a problem some blamed on the Ducati's sometimes very harsh clutch off the start line.

Jorge's sixth assured win and Pedrosa's zero stretched the former's lead to 72 points – almost three full race wins. His difficulty over the summer break would be to avoid becoming too complacent.

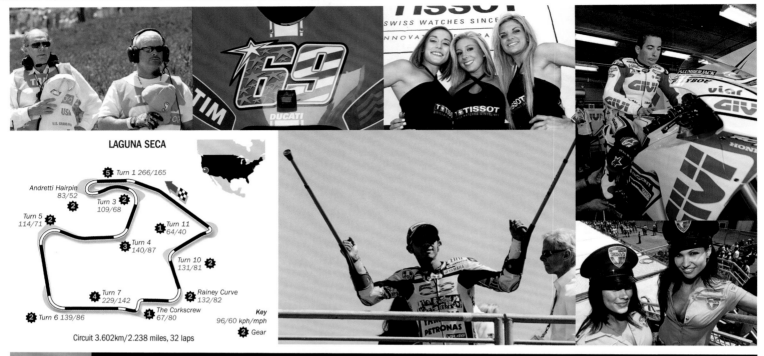

## LAGUNA SECA

Turn 1 266/165
Andretti Hairpin 83/52
Turn 3 109/68
Turn 5 114/71
Turn 11 64/40
Turn 4 140/87
Turn 10 131/81
Turn 7 229/142
Rainey Curve 132/82
The Corkscrew 67/80
Turn 6 139/86

Key
96/60 kph/mph
Gear

Circuit 3.602km/2.238 miles, 32 laps

## MotoGP

RACE DISTANCE: 32 laps, 71.781 miles/115.52 km · RACE WEATHER: Dry (air 23°, humidity 44%, track 40°)

| Pos. | Rider | Nat. | No. | Entrant | Machine | Tyres | Laps | Time & speed |
|---|---|---|---|---|---|---|---|---|
| 1 | **Jorge Lorenzo** | SPA | 99 | Fiat Yamaha Team | Yamaha | B | 32 | 43m 54.873s 98.073mph/ 157.833km/h |
| 2 | **Casey Stoner** | AUS | 27 | Ducati Marlboro Team | Ducati | B | 32 | 43m 58.390s |
| 3 | **Valentino Rossi** | ITA | 46 | Fiat Yamaha Team | Yamaha | B | 32 | 44m 08.293s |
| 4 | **Andrea Dovizioso** | ITA | 4 | Repsol Honda Team | Honda | B | 32 | 44m 09.061s |
| 5 | **Nicky Hayden** | USA | 69 | Ducati Marlboro Team | Ducati | B | 32 | 44m 09.474s |
| 6 | **Ben Spies** | USA | 11 | Monster Yamaha Tech 3 | Yamaha | B | 32 | 44m 13.910s |
| 7 | **Colin Edwards** | USA | 5 | Monster Yamaha Tech 3 | Yamaha | B | 32 | 44m 35.594s |
| 8 | **Marco Melandri** | ITA | 33 | San Carlo Honda Gresini | Honda | B | 32 | 44m 42.092s |
| 9 | **Mika Kallio** | FIN | 36 | Pramac Racing Team | Ducati | B | 32 | 44m 47.686s |
| 10 | **Loris Capirossi** | ITA | 65 | Rizla Suzuki MotoGP | Suzuki | B | 32 | 44m 47.687s |
| 11 | **Roger Lee Hayden** | USA | 95 | LCR Honda MotoGP | Honda | B | 32 | 45m 08.962s |
| 12 | **Alex de Angelis** | RSM | 15 | Interwetten Honda MotoGP | Honda | B | 32 | 45m 09.539s |
| | Aleix Espargaro | SPA | 41 | Pramac Racing Team | Ducati | B | 28 | DNF |
| | Marco Simoncelli | ITA | 58 | San Carlo Honda Gresini | Honda | B | 18 | DNF |
| | Dani Pedrosa | SPA | 26 | Repsol Honda Team | Honda | B | 11 | DNF |
| | Hector Barbera | SPA | 40 | Paginas Amarillas Aspar | Ducati | B | 3 | DNF |
| | Alvaro Bautista | SPA | 19 | Rizla Suzuki MotoGP | Suzuki | B | 2 | DNF |

**Fastest lap:** Casey Stoner, on lap 4, 1m 21.376s, 99.235mph/159.703km/h (record).
**Previous lap record:** Casey Stoner, AUS (Ducati), 1m 21.488s, 99.098mph/159.483km/h (2008).
**Event best maximum speed:** Casey Stoner, 165.9mph/267.0km/h (free practice 2).

### Qualifying
Weather: Dry
Air Temp: 25° Humidity: 39°
Track Temp: 47°

| |  |  |
|---|---|---|
| 1 | Lorenzo | 1m 20.978s |
| 2 | Stoner | 1m 21.169s |
| 3 | Dovizioso | 1m 21.617s |
| 4 | Pedrosa | 1m 21.655s |
| 5 | Spies | 1m 21.679s |
| 6 | Rossi | 1m 21.688s |
| 7 | N. Hayden | 1m 21.920s |
| 8 | Edwards | 1m 22.217s |
| 9 | Simoncelli | 1m 22.300s |
| 10 | Barbera | 1m 22.366s |
| 11 | Melandri | 1m 22.407s |
| 12 | Capirossi | 1m 22.647s |
| 13 | Espargaro | 1m 22.712s |
| 14 | Bautista | 1m 22.770s |
| 15 | Kallio | 1m 23.127s |
| 16 | de Angelis | 1m 23.226s |
| 17 | R. Hayden | 1m 23.764s |

### Fastest race laps

| |  |  |
|---|---|---|
| 1 | Stoner | 1m 21.376s |
| 2 | Lorenzo | 1m 21.487s |
| 3 | Pedrosa | 1m 21.602s |
| 4 | Dovizioso | 1m 22.039s |
| 5 | Spies | 1m 22.055s |
| 6 | N. Hayden | 1m 22.112s |
| 7 | Rossi | 1m 22.116s |
| 8 | Melandri | 1m 22.706s |
| 9 | Simoncelli | 1m 22.736s |
| 10 | Edwards | 1m 22.772s |
| 11 | Espargaro | 1m 23.029s |
| 12 | Capirossi | 1m 23.125s |
| 13 | Kallio | 1m 23.318s |
| 14 | de Angelis | 1m 23.455s |
| 15 | R. Hayden | 1m 23.673s |
| 16 | Bautista | 1m 24.198s |
| 17 | Barbera | 1m 24.472s |

### Championship Points

| |  |  |
|---|---|---|
| 1 | Lorenzo | 210 |
| 2 | Pedrosa | 138 |
| 3 | Dovizioso | 115 |
| 4 | Stoner | 103 |
| 5 | Rossi | 90 |
| 6 | N. Hayden | 89 |
| 7 | Spies | 77 |
| 8 | de Puniet | 69 |
| 9 | Melandri | 53 |
| 10 | Simoncelli | 49 |
| 11 | Edwards | 48 |
| 12 | Barbera | 41 |
| 13 | Capirossi | 36 |
| 14 | Kallio | 31 |
| 15 | Espargaro | 28 |
| 16 | Bautista | 25 |
| 17 | Aoyama | 18 |
| 18 | de Angelis | 8 |
| 19 | R. Hayden | 5 |
| 20 | Akiyoshi | 4 |
| 21 | Yoshikawa | 1 |

### Team Points

| | Team | Points |
|---|---|---|
| 1 | Fiat Yamaha Team | 301 |
| 2 | Repsol Honda Team | 253 |
| 3 | Ducati Marlboro Team | 192 |
| 4 | Monster Yamaha Tech 3 | 125 |
| 5 | San Carlo Honda Gresini | 102 |
| 6 | LCR Honda MotoGP | 74 |
| 7 | Rizla Suzuki MotoGP | 61 |
| 8 | Pramac Racing Team | 59 |
| 9 | Paginas Amarillas Aspar | 41 |
| 10 | Interwetten Honda MotoGP | 30 |

### Constructor Points

| | Constructor | Points |
|---|---|---|
| 1 | Yamaha | 215 |
| 2 | Honda | 175 |
| 3 | Ducati | 133 |
| 4 | Suzuki | 48 |

| Grid order | 1 | 2 | 3 | 4 | 5 | 6 | 7 | 8 | 9 | 10 | 11 | 12 | 13 | 14 | 15 | 16 | 17 | 18 | 19 | 20 | 21 | 22 | 23 | 24 | 25 | 26 | 27 | 28 | 29 | 30 | 31 | 32 | |
|---|---|---|---|---|---|---|---|---|---|---|---|---|---|---|---|---|---|---|---|---|---|---|---|---|---|---|---|---|---|---|---|---|---|
| 99 LORENZO | 26 | 26 | 26 | 26 | 26 | 26 | 26 | 26 | 26 | 26 | 26 | 99 | 99 | 99 | 99 | 99 | 99 | 99 | 99 | 99 | 99 | 99 | 99 | 99 | 99 | 99 | 99 | 99 | 99 | 99 | 99 | 99 | 1 |
| 27 STONER | 27 | 27 | 27 | 27 | 27 | 99 | 99 | 99 | 99 | 99 | 99 | 27 | 27 | 27 | 27 | 27 | 27 | 27 | 27 | 27 | 27 | 27 | 27 | 27 | 27 | 27 | 27 | 27 | 27 | 27 | 27 | 27 | 2 |
| 4 DOVISIOSO | 99 | 99 | 99 | 99 | 99 | 27 | 27 | 27 | 27 | 27 | 27 | 4 | 4 | 4 | 4 | 4 | 4 | 4 | 4 | 4 | 4 | 4 | 4 | 4 | 4 | 46 | 46 | 46 | 46 | 46 | 46 | 46 | 3 |
| 26 PEDROSA | 11 | 11 | 4 | 4 | 4 | 4 | 4 | 4 | 4 | 4 | 4 | 46 | 46 | 46 | 46 | 46 | 46 | 46 | 46 | 46 | 46 | 46 | 46 | 46 | 46 | 4 | 4 | 4 | 4 | 4 | 4 | 4 | 4 |
| 11 SPIES | 4 | 4 | 46 | 46 | 46 | 46 | 46 | 46 | 46 | 46 | 46 | 69 | 69 | 69 | 69 | 69 | 69 | 69 | 69 | 69 | 11 | 11 | 11 | 11 | 69 | 69 | 69 | 69 | 69 | 69 | 69 | 69 | 5 |
| 46 ROSSI | 46 | 46 | 69 | 69 | 69 | 69 | 69 | 69 | 69 | 69 | 69 | 11 | 11 | 11 | 11 | 11 | 11 | 11 | 11 | 11 | 69 | 69 | 69 | 69 | 11 | 11 | 11 | 11 | 11 | 11 | 11 | 11 | 6 |
| 69 HAYDEN | 69 | 69 | 11 | 11 | 11 | 11 | 11 | 11 | 11 | 11 | 11 | 58 | 58 | 58 | 5 | 5 | 5 | 5 | 5 | 5 | 5 | 5 | 5 | 5 | 5 | 5 | 5 | 5 | 5 | 5 | 5 | 5 | 7 |
| 5 EDWARDS | 58 | 58 | 58 | 33 | 33 | 33 | 33 | 33 | 33 | 58 | 58 | 5 | 5 | 5 | 58 | 33 | 33 | 33 | 33 | 33 | 33 | 33 | 33 | 33 | 33 | 33 | 33 | 33 | 33 | 33 | 33 | 33 | 8 |
| 58 SIMONCELLI | 5 | 33 | 33 | 58 | 58 | 58 | 58 | 58 | 58 | 5 | 5 | 33 | 33 | 33 | 33 | 58 | 58 | 58 | 65 | 65 | 65 | 65 | 65 | 65 | 65 | 65 | 41 | 41 | 65 | 65 | 65 | 36 | 9 |
| 40 BARBERA | 33 | 5 | 5 | 5 | 5 | 5 | 5 | 5 | 5 | 33 | 33 | 65 | 65 | 65 | 65 | 65 | 65 | 65 | 41 | 41 | 41 | 41 | 41 | 41 | 41 | 41 | 65 | 65 | 36 | 36 | 36 | 65 | 10 |
| 33 MELANDRI | 36 | 36 | 65 | 65 | 65 | 65 | 65 | 65 | 65 | 65 | 65 | 36 | 36 | 36 | 36 | 36 | 41 | 41 | 36 | 36 | 36 | 36 | 36 | 36 | 36 | 36 | 36 | 36 | 15 | 15 | 95 | 95 | 11 |
| 65 CAPIROSSI | 65 | 65 | 36 | 36 | 36 | 36 | 36 | 36 | 36 | 36 | 36 | 41 | 41 | 41 | 41 | 41 | 36 | 36 | 15 | 15 | 15 | 15 | 15 | 15 | 15 | 15 | 15 | 15 | 95 | 95 | 15 | 15 | 12 |
| 41 ESPARGARO | 41 | 41 | 15 | 15 | 41 | 41 | 41 | 41 | 41 | 41 | 41 | 15 | 15 | 15 | 15 | 15 | 15 | 15 | 95 | 95 | 95 | 95 | 95 | 95 | 95 | 95 | 95 | 95 | | | | | |
| 19 BAUTISTA | 15 | 19 | 95 | 95 | 15 | 15 | 15 | 15 | 15 | 15 | 15 | 95 | 95 | 95 | 95 | 95 | 95 | 95 | | | | | | | | | | | | | | | |
| 36 KALLIO | 19 | 15 | 41 | 41 | 95 | 95 | 95 | 95 | 95 | 95 | 95 | | | | | | | | | | | | | | | | | | | | | | |
| 15 de ANGELIS | 40 | 95 | 40 | | | | | | | | | | | | | | | | | | | | | | | | | | | | | | |
| 95 HAYDEN, R | 95 | 40 | | | | | | | | | | | | | | | | | | | | | | | | | | | | | | | |

FIM WORLD CHAMPIONSHIP · ROUND 10

# CZECH REPUBLIC GRAND

BRNO CIRCUIT

*Insets above:* Rossi and Burgess in urgent discussion – about moving to Ducati?

*Inset top left:* Stoner, still searching.

*Main photo:* Lorenzo leads Pedrosa, Spies, Dovizioso and Stoner into the first corner on lap four. The gaps would grow.
*Photos:* Gold & Goose

*Photos:* Gold & Goose

*Above:* Spies came close to his first pole, but he would have to wait one more race.

*Opposite, from top:* Cal Crutchlow was in town, finalising his 2011 move to Tech 3 Yamaha; Aoyama was back at work, but not yet in action; Elias kept smiling as he watched the first Moto2 session – he was banned; grim faces at launch of new MotoGP team, with team owner Karel Abraham Senior, Ducati's Cicognani, and Dorna's Ezpeleta.

RECONVENED after the two free weekends (three for the smaller classes) of the summer break, racing was ready for some major announcements at Brno. Some were life changing, like the confirmation of the end of two-stroke GP racing; none was unexpected. The most eagerly awaited was the least surprising: some four hours after the race, Ducati Motor Holding president Gabriele Del Torchio confirmed that the red brigade had agreed a two-year contract with Italy's national hero. Valentino Rossi and Ducati were an item.

The occasion was marked by a piece of pure Rossiness, something only he could have got away with. It took the form of a love letter, written by hand and complete with crossings-out, to the love of his life for the previous seven years: "she – my M1 Yamaha".

When translated from the Italian, the letter thanked Yamaha chief Masao Furusawa and a couple of other Japanese staff, plus Jerry Burgess and his pit crew. Then Valentino waxed lyrical.

"Many things have changed since that far-off time in 2004, but especially 'she', my M1, has changed. At that time, she was a poor middle-grid-position MotoGP bike, derided by most of the riders and the MotoGP workers. Now, after having helped her to grow and improve, you can see her smiling in her garage, courted and admired, treated as top of the class.

"Unfortunately, even the most beautiful love stories finish, but they leave a lot of wonderful memories, like when my M1

and I kissed for the first time on the grass at Welkom, when she looked straight in my eyes and told me, 'I love you.'"

It is easy to forget the role played by Yamaha in transforming that shy gooseberry of 2003 into MotoGP's favourite dancing partner: the greatest contribution was the cross-plane-crank engine devised by Furusawa, but one should not underestimate the role played by the sensitivity and understanding of Rossi and his pragmatic crew chief, Jerry Burgess, in refining that package. It was still not clear whether Burgess and crew would be following Vale into the all-Italian Castello Ducati, but Del Torchio expressed confidence that the rider could work the same magic with the Desmosedici, operating hand in hand with design guru Filippo Preziosi.

The black cap for two-strokes came from Saturday's GP Commission meeting, when it was formally announced that a new Moto3 breed of 250 four-strokes, sharing the 81mm maximum bore of the 2012 MotoGP 1000cc bikes, would take over in 2012. At the same time, specs for 2012 1000cc MotoGP bikes were confirmed with that bore size. Claiming Rule Teams, able to use production-based components, would be allowed 12 instead of six engines, and 24 rather than 21 litres of fuel. The selection of these CRTs would be "by unanimous decision of the GP Commission", which allayed any factory fears that this could be a low-cost back-door entry for new factories.

The other business of the commission was to find a way to bend the engine-life rules to give Suzuki a second chance,

a notion originally suggested by Ducati. An extra clause was added to the rule: "For 2010 the manufacturer members of MSMA who did not win at least two dry races in 2008 and 2009 seasons can use nine engines instead of six". New manufacturers in 2012 would be given the same concession for their first year.

The Suzuki sanction was necessary politically and practically. There were already rumours that the smallest and least-competitive factory team might pull out at the end of the season, although these were denied on the spot; there would be more speculation later in the year of radical cutbacks to come. Dorna especially was anxious to encourage this long-standing GP supporter to stay, and so was everyone else. The practical aspect was obvious. While several riders, including Lorenzo, Spies, Stoner and Hayden, had already broken out their fourth of six engines at the halfway point of the year, Bautista was on his fifth, and three of his used engines had been removed from allocation. He definitely wasn't going to get through the year, while team-mate Capirossi was close behind.

Of the others, Stoner was beginning to run thin – four engines commissioned and two scrapped. The factory Hondas were exemplary, both riders still only on their third engines, with all three still available for use; most of the satellite riders were similarly well off.

There were a number of crashes, including – late in qualifying – one each by the Fiat Yamaha rivals, fortunately without injury. Doubly fortunate was practice faller Randy de Puniet, who had just slashed Rossi's record to get back on a racing bike to 26 (rather than 41) days after his own tib-and-fib fractures, duly screwed and plated directly after the German GP. He'd passed the final test, with the track doctor ("He touched my leg and saw I could walk."). He could race, but was unable to walk for several days afterwards and remained weak for the races to come.

Ben Spies shrugged off the burden of a US $1.9-million judgment against him, in favour of former manager Doug Gonda, qualifying on the front row for the first time. He almost had pole: at the Press conference, his first such, he watched the fastest in each class being presented with their special Tissots. "If I'd realised I would have a free watch, I might have got in his way on the fast lap," he joked.

His route to the factory team was now pre-ordained if not official; his Tech 3 replacement, Cal Crutchlow, was on hand and soon would be signing up, Britain's latest bright hope, in the tracks of the unlucky and unsuccessful James Toseland.

Aoyama was back, but not to race: he would join tests the following day to see how his recovering back injury held up. A new MotoGP Ducati team was announced for 2011: 250/Moto2 rider Karel Abraham, financed by his multi-millionaire father's firm, AB Cardion. This led Stoner to comment critically on a system whereby money rather than obvious talent prevailed, though to be fair, Abraham had shown some good rides in Moto2. Not here at home, however: he crashed heavily in practice and was out of the race.

If the crowd of more than 148,000 were to be underwhelmed by a processional front group in MotoGP, as always there were plenty of things happening in Moto2, where rivals had been outraged at the leniency shown to Toni Elias. His Gresini team had inadvertently violated the no-test rule with a home gallop at Misano during the break. He was disqualified from the first free practice and fined 3,000 euros, a price any team would willingly pay for a valuable extra day of testing.

Another Suter was added to the grid when the financially struggling RSM Team Scot swapped from its exclusive Force GP210 chassis, built in Italy by Rapid Inside. The team cited development difficulties, but there were rumours of a financial dispute, while it had already lost one chassis when Canepa's bike burned out at Catalunya – second rider de Angelis was still on Aoyama's MotoGP bike. Things would get worse for the team.

*Above:* Melandri battles for Honda honours with de Puniet; the Ducatis of Barbera and Espargaro trail.

*Top centre:* A fourth win of the season for Elias also gave Team Gresini its 100th podium.

*Top far right:* Terol came back from his Catalunya crash to win.

*Above centre right:* Dunlop were kept busy supplying the whole of the 40-plus Moto2 field.

*Above far right:* Takahashi, here heading Debon and Talmacsi mid-race, went on to take second in Moto2.

*Right:* Rabat leads Krummenacher early in the 125cc race.

*Below right:* Marquez dislocated his other shoulder, but bravely raced to a potentially valuable nine points.
*Photos:* Gold & Goose

## MOTOGP RACE – 22 laps

Spies led qualifying with minutes to go; Rossi and Lorenzo both fell trying to beat him, the latter at such speed that his bike landed on top of the tyre wall. Pedrosa stayed on, ousting the upstart by three-tenths. Lorenzo remained third. Rossi was fifth, behind a frustrated Stoner, ahead of Dovizioso; a somewhat revived Edwards led the third row from Hayden and Barbera. The second American was in trouble: an awkward fall in practice had chipped the wrist end of his left radius, both painful and potentially problematic. "It ain't gonna be gravy out there," he said.

Nor was it, though the race pace was surprisingly slow – 19 seconds slower than 2009, with Lorenzo's fastest lap almost a full second down on his record from that year. Heavy rain on the preceding two nights had washed the track, and the same Bridgestones didn't seem to perform as the year before.

Pedrosa led into the first corner as usual, but excessive caution on cold tyres lost him two places by the end of the first lap, with Lorenzo leading and Spies tucked in behind. Dani was back in front of Spies next time around, and for the first eight laps it looked as though he might be able to make a race of it.

But Lorenzo pushed again, and at the end of lap nine, the gap was 0.9 second, and starting to stretch by one- or two-tenths every lap. By the 13th, Lorenzo was two seconds clear, and he kept on for a fine seventh win, by better than five seconds.

Pedrosa was equally alone. Spies stayed close for a while, but was a second down at the end of lap five, and that gap also kept on stretching as he ran into front-grip difficulties.

Dovizioso might have played a major part. He'd passed Stoner for fourth on lap three and was pushing hard to close on Spies when he fell on the exit of Turn Nine. He and his bike ended up in the middle of the track; Rossi, close behind, ran between them as Dovi frantically sought an escape route. He remounted, only to retire.

Now Stoner's pace started to improve even as Spies's slowed. On lap eight, the Ducati was on the Yamaha's back wheel, and ahead next time around. But Pedrosa was four

seconds away and still going quicker than Stoner. That gap kept stretching as the race wore on, just as the gap to Spies behind did the same.

By lap four, the next group was already three seconds adrift. At this point, it was Hayden in front, having got ahead of fast-starting Edwards on lap three. Rossi took another lap to follow Hayden through, and now it seemed that he might still have a chance to push on and catch the leaders, as he had threatened to do the day before.

Not so. He was badly off the leaders' pace. He passed Hayden on lap six, but he didn't get away from the two Americans for several more laps, and all the while the gap to Stoner was widening – 3.5 seconds on lap six, more than four behind Spies at the finish. Dismal compared with expectations; the next day, he traced the setting mishap that had robbed him of faith in the front wheel.

Behind him, Hayden gradually slipped out of touch; Edwards lost ground even quicker.

Simoncelli had started well and hung on to the back of this trio until the sixth. He was all alone for the middle part of the race.

Behind, Kallio had got ahead of Melandri and de Puniet, only to slip off on lap eight. By now, Espargaro, Barbera and de Angelis had closed up, with Bautista also tagging on. This group was the most exciting, although de Angelis was soon losing ground at the back, while Espargaro also dropped off after two dozen laps.

The rest stayed hard at it, with de Puniet taking over from Melandri on lap 11. They were four seconds behind Simoncelli, but the rookie was slowing, and they all caught up on lap 19, Melandri ahead once more. He and Barbera were straight past Simoncelli and then de Puniet also. They finished in that order – but Simoncelli was lucky. Bautista had also passed him on the last climb up the hill, only to slither into the gravel on the second-last corner. The brave Spaniard had been a doubtful starter, after a back-bruising crash the day before.

Espargaro and de Angelis trailed in; Capirossi had crashed out from near the back on the second lap, at least saving some engine miles.

he had recovered to tenth and was gaining all the time. By lap five, he was fourth, Elias now behind him after running wide the lap before and losing four places. On the sixth, he scythed past Rolfo, Cluzel and Debon to take the lead.

It looked like another remarkable run-away might be on the cards, and he had a second in hand three laps later. But Elias had also moved back through and now was second; he was fully aware also that he dare not let the Italian get away. "I was too quiet early on, but when I saw Andrea going away, I knew it was time to push."

By lap 12, he had closed up again, and on the 13th lap he took a lead that he would never relinquish, gradually moving ahead.

Veteran Rolfo had closed up with him, and might even have given him some trouble. But no sooner had he got past Iannone than suddenly he slowed and pulled to the side of the track, oil pouring from his blown Honda motor.

Iannone still was not safe, however. Takahashi had been to and fro among the chase pack, but he was getting faster as the race wore on. On lap 15, he passed Cluzel, then quickly closed a two-second gap to the slowing Iannone, whose tyres were shot.

He was ahead on the penultimate lap and held the Italian at bay to the line.

Cluzel came under attack in the closing laps, caught by a rapid trio led by Simon from Talmacsi and Debon. The Frenchman held them off by inches.

Corsi was ninth; Bradl regained tenth from Tomizawa on the final lap; Luthi was a distant eleventh.

Elias's fourth win was Team Gresini's 100th rostrum, and it stretched his points lead to 55.

## 125cc RACE – 19 laps

A change of exhaust pipe – identical spec, different performance – boosted Smith to his first pole of the year by almost half a second as the speed missing all season was mysteriously restored. Terol was back from injury, and straight into second, with Espargaro alongside. Marquez completed the front row in spite of a heavy crash on Friday that had dislocated his left shoulder – his right had popped out at Jerez. He missed Saturday morning, but returned for qualifying in the afternoon.

The day started wet, and the first race was delayed by seven minutes as another heavy shower swept through. All but one rider started on wet tyres, the exception being Dutchman Iwema, who pulled in after the sighting lap to start from the pit lane. By lap ten, he was over a minute adrift, but the drying track played into his hands and he cut through to a career-best eighth.

A sideshow – Terol was the main event. He took the lead from Vazquez on lap two and simply charged away. By half-distance, he was 20 seconds clear, and he maintained that for a triumphal return, his second win of the season.

The battle for second was distant, but absorbing. Espargaro had passed Vazquez on lap eight, the pair staying close. All the while, Rabat had been picking his way through, displacing Folger from the front of the pursuit pack on lap eight and rapidly pulling away to close on his compatriots with four laps to go, splitting them next time around.

Vazquez got back ahead on the penultimate lap, only to slip off on the second-last corner. The disturbance bought Espargaro enough space to stay narrowly ahead.

Folger led the next group of five from best-yet Czech rookie Kornfeil and Smith, Marquez a second adrift after a brave ride.

Iwema was only two seconds down; then came Koyama and Salom. Fastest lap went to Zarco after he'd pitted for slicks, but he finished 19th and out of the points.

Webb crashed out on the first lap, joined on the crash list by Masbou and Fagerhaug, who remounted.

Terol's victory placed him firmly back into the championship equation.

## MOTO2 RACE – 20 laps

Volatile as ever, the second class saw five different leaders over the 20 laps, and the usual wildly changing fortunes in the close-packed pursuit.

Elias bounced back from his practice ban to head the second free session, but Tomizawa took his second pole, crediting a break in the traffic, two-tenths ahead of Iannone, then Elias and Rolfo, up front for the first time. Takahashi led the second row, times more spread than usual on this long track, and only the first seven within a second of the leader.

Tomizawa led away, but after some bad slides, handling problems dropped him back in the midfield maelstrom after four laps. Corsi was next to lead, Cluzel in hot pursuit, but next time around, Debon had lunged past both of them for one lap of glory.

All-action racing.

Iannone was swamped off the start, but by the end of it

OFFICIAL TIMEKEEPER

### AUTODROM BRNO

Turn 5 111/69
Turn 9 100/62
Kevin Schwantz 109/68
Turn 4 110/69
Stadion 92/57
Turn 8 100/62
Turn 3 92/57
Turn 12 117/73
Frantisëk Štasny 127/79
Horizont 93/58
Turn 14 190/118
Turn 12 117/73

**Key**
96/60 kph/mph
Gear

Circuit 5.403km/3.357 miles, 22 laps

## MotoGP

RACE DISTANCE: 22 laps, 73.860 miles/118.866 km · RACE WEATHER: Dry (air 26°, humidity 43%, track 40°)

| Pos. | Rider | Nat. | No. | Entrant | Machine | Tyres | Laps | Time & speed |
|------|-------|------|-----|---------|---------|-------|------|--------------|
| 1 | **Jorge Lorenzo** | SPA | 99 | Fiat Yamaha Team | Yamaha | B | 22 | 43m 22.638s 102.163mph/ 164.416km/h |
| 2 | **Dani Pedrosa** | SPA | 26 | Repsol Honda Team | Honda | B | 22 | 43m 28.132s |
| 3 | **Casey Stoner** | AUS | 27 | Ducati Marlboro Team | Ducati | B | 22 | 43m 34.064s |
| 4 | **Ben Spies** | USA | 11 | Monster Yamaha Tech 3 | Yamaha | B | 22 | 43m 36.361s |
| 5 | **Valentino Rossi** | ITA | 46 | Fiat Yamaha Team | Yamaha | B | 22 | 43m 40.568s |
| 6 | **Nicky Hayden** | USA | 69 | Ducati Marlboro Team | Ducati | B | 22 | 43m 49.453s |
| 7 | **Colin Edwards** | USA | 5 | Monster Yamaha Tech 3 | Yamaha | B | 22 | 43m 56.034s |
| 8 | **Marco Melandri** | ITA | 33 | San Carlo Honda Gresini | Honda | B | 22 | 44m 02.044s |
| 9 | **Hector Barbera** | SPA | 40 | Paginas Amarillas Aspar | Ducati | B | 22 | 44m 02.277s |
| 10 | **Randy de Puniet** | FRA | 14 | LCR Honda MotoGP | Honda | B | 22 | 44m 03.531s |
| 11 | **Marco Simoncelli** | ITA | 58 | San Carlo Honda Gresini | Honda | B | 22 | 44m 04.670s |
| 12 | **Aleix Espargaro** | SPA | 41 | Pramac Racing Team | Ducati | B | 22 | 44m 09.729s |
| 13 | **Alex de Angelis** | RSM | 15 | Interwetten Honda MotoGP | Honda | B | 22 | 44m 14.006s |
| | Alvaro Bautista | SPA | 19 | Rizla Suzuki MotoGP | Suzuki | B | 21 | DNF |
| | Mika Kallio | FIN | 36 | Pramac Racing Team | Ducati | B | 7 | DNF |
| | Andrea Dovizioso | ITA | 4 | Repsol Honda Team | Honda | B | 6 | DNF |
| | Loris Capirossi | ITA | 65 | Rizla Suzuki MotoGP | Suzuki | B | 2 | DNF |

**Fastest lap:** Jorge Lorenzo, on lap 11, 1m 57.524s, 102.839mph/165.504km/h.
**Lap record:** Jorge Lorenzo, SPA (Yamaha), 1m 56.670s, 103.593mph/166.716km/h (2009).
**Event best maximum speed:** Dani Pedrosa, 188.5mph/303.4km/h (qualifying practice).

### Qualifying
Weather: Dry
Air Temp: 25° Humidity: 61°
Track Temp: 38°

| | | |
|---|---|---|
| 1 | Pedrosa | 1m 56.508s |
| 2 | Spies | 1m 56.846s |
| 3 | Lorenzo | 1m 56.865s |
| 4 | Stoner | 1m 56.868s |
| 5 | Rossi | 1m 57.059s |
| 6 | Dovizioso | 1m 57.117s |
| 7 | Edwards | 1m 57.222s |
| 8 | Hayden | 1m 57.635s |
| 9 | Barbera | 1m 57.960s |
| 10 | Capirossi | 1m 57.981s |
| 11 | de Puniet | 1m 58.089s |
| 12 | Simoncelli | 1m 58.169s |
| 13 | Kallio | 1m 58.182s |
| 14 | Melandri | 1m 58.430s |
| 15 | de Angelis | 1m 58.522s |
| 16 | Espargaro | 1m 58.700s |

### Fastest race laps

| | | |
|---|---|---|
| 1 | Lorenzo | 1m 57.524s |
| 2 | Pedrosa | 1m 57.712s |
| 3 | Spies | 1m 58.001s |
| 4 | Dovizioso | 1m 58.045s |
| 5 | Stoner | 1m 58.121s |
| 6 | Rossi | 1m 58.240s |
| 7 | Hayden | 1m 58.433s |
| 8 | Edwards | 1m 58.469s |
| 9 | Simoncelli | 1m 58.630s |
| 10 | Bautista | 1m 59.197s |
| 11 | Barbera | 1m 59.251s |
| 12 | Melandri | 1m 59.328s |
| 13 | de Puniet | 1m 59.416s |
| 14 | de Angelis | 1m 59.487s |
| 15 | Kallio | 1m 59.524s |
| 16 | Espargaro | 1m 59.611s |
| 17 | Capirossi | 2m 08.360s |

### Championship Points

| | | |
|---|---|---|
| 1 | Lorenzo | 235 |
| 2 | Pedrosa | 158 |
| 3 | Stoner | 119 |
| 4 | Dovizioso | 115 |
| 5 | Rossi | 101 |
| 6 | N. Hayden | 99 |
| 7 | Spies | 90 |
| 8 | de Puniet | 75 |
| 9 | Melandri | 61 |
| 10 | Edwards | 57 |
| 11 | Simoncelli | 54 |
| 12 | Barbera | 48 |
| 13 | Capirossi | 36 |
| 14 | Espargaro | 32 |
| 15 | Kallio | 31 |
| 16 | Bautista | 25 |
| 17 | Aoyama | 18 |
| 18 | de Angelis | 11 |
| 19 | R. Hayden | 5 |
| 20 | Akiyoshi | 4 |
| 21 | Yoshikawa | 1 |

| Grid order | 1 | 2 | 3 | 4 | 5 | 6 | 7 | 8 | 9 | 10 | 11 | 12 | 13 | 14 | 15 | 16 | 17 | 18 | 19 | 20 | 21 | 22 | |
|------------|---|---|---|---|---|---|---|---|---|----|----|----|----|----|----|----|----|----|----|----|----|----|---|
| 26 PEDROSA | 99 | 99 | 99 | 99 | 99 | 99 | 99 | 99 | 99 | 99 | 99 | 99 | 99 | 99 | 99 | 99 | 99 | 99 | 99 | 99 | 99 | 99 | 1 |
| 11 SPIES | 11 | 26 | 26 | 26 | 26 | 26 | 26 | 26 | 26 | 26 | 26 | 26 | 26 | 26 | 26 | 26 | 26 | 26 | 26 | 26 | 26 | 26 | 2 |
| 99 LORENZO | 26 | 11 | 11 | 11 | 11 | 11 | 11 | 11 | 27 | 27 | 27 | 27 | 27 | 27 | 27 | 27 | 27 | 27 | 27 | 27 | 27 | 27 | 3 |
| 27 STONER | 27 | 27 | 4 | 27 | 27 | 27 | 27 | 27 | 11 | 11 | 11 | 11 | 11 | 11 | 11 | 11 | 11 | 11 | 11 | 11 | 11 | 11 | 4 |
| 46 ROSSI | 4 | 4 | 27 | 69 | 69 | 46 | 46 | 46 | 46 | 46 | 46 | 46 | 46 | 46 | 46 | 46 | 46 | 46 | 46 | 46 | 46 | 46 | 5 |
| 4 DOVIZIOSO | 5 | 5 | 69 | 46 | 46 | 69 | 69 | 69 | 69 | 69 | 69 | 69 | 69 | 69 | 69 | 69 | 69 | 69 | 69 | 69 | 69 | 69 | 6 |
| 5 EDWARDS | 69 | 69 | 5 | 5 | 5 | 5 | 5 | 5 | 5 | 5 | 5 | 5 | 5 | 5 | 5 | 5 | 5 | 5 | 5 | 5 | 5 | 5 | 7 |
| 69 HAYDEN | 46 | 46 | 46 | 58 | 58 | 58 | 58 | 58 | 58 | 58 | 58 | 58 | 58 | 58 | 58 | 58 | 58 | 58 | 58 | 33 | 33 | 33 | 8 |
| 40 BARBERA | 58 | 58 | 58 | 36 | 36 | 36 | 36 | 33 | 33 | 33 | 14 | 14 | 14 | 14 | 14 | 14 | 33 | 33 | 40 | 40 | 40 | | 9 |
| 65 CAPIROSSI | 36 | 36 | 33 | 33 | 33 | 33 | 33 | 14 | 14 | 14 | 33 | 33 | 33 | 33 | 40 | 40 | 33 | 14 | 40 | 58 | 14 | 14 | 10 |
| 14 de PUNIET | 33 | 36 | 36 | 14 | 14 | 14 | 14 | 41 | 14 | 40 | 40 | 40 | 40 | 33 | 33 | 40 | 40 | 14 | 14 | 58 | 58 | | 11 |
| 58 SIMONCELLI | 14 | 14 | 14 | 41 | 41 | 41 | 41 | 40 | 40 | 41 | 41 | 19 | 19 | 19 | 19 | 19 | 19 | 19 | 19 | 19 | 41 | | 12 |
| 36 KALLIO | 15 | 41 | 41 | 15 | 40 | 40 | 40 | 15 | 15 | 15 | 19 | 41 | 41 | 41 | 41 | 41 | 41 | 41 | 41 | 41 | 15 | | 13 |
| 33 MELANDRI | 41 | 15 | 15 | 40 | 15 | 15 | 15 | 19 | 19 | 19 | 15 | 15 | 15 | 15 | 15 | 15 | 15 | 15 | | | | | |
| 15 de ANGELIS | 65 | 40 | 40 | 19 | 19 | 19 | 19 | | | | | | | | | | | | | | | | |
| 41 ESPARGARO | 40 | 19 | 19 | 4 | 4 | 4 | | | | | | | | | | | | | | | | | |
| 19 BAUTISTA | 19 | | | | | | | | | | | | | | | | | | | | | | |

### Team Points

| | | |
|---|---|---|
| 1 | Fiat Yamaha Team | 337 |
| 2 | Repsol Honda Team | 273 |
| 3 | Ducati Marlboro Team | 218 |
| 4 | Monster Yamaha Tech 3 | 147 |
| 5 | San Carlo Honda Gresini | 115 |
| 6 | LCR Honda MotoGP | 80 |
| 7 | Pramac Racing Team | 63 |
| 8 | Rizla Suzuki MotoGP | 61 |
| 9 | Paginas Amarillas Aspar | 48 |
| 10 | Interwetten Honda MotoGP | 33 |

### Constructor Points

| | | |
|---|---|---|
| 1 | Yamaha | 240 |
| 2 | Honda | 195 |
| 3 | Ducati | 149 |
| 4 | Suzuki | 48 |

## Moto2

**RACE DISTANCE: 20 laps, 67.145 miles/108.060 km · RACE WEATHER: Dry (air 25°, humidity 57%, track 36°)**

| Pos. | Rider | Nat. | No. | Entrant | Machine | Laps | Time & Speed |
|---|---|---|---|---|---|---|---|
| 1 | **Toni Elias** | SPA | 24 | Gresini Racing Moto2 | Moriwaki | 20 | 41m 51.715s (mph/km/h) 96.238/154.880 |
| 2 | **Yuki Takahashi** | JPN | 72 | Tech 3 Racing | Tech 3 | 20 | 41m 54.027s |
| 3 | **Andrea Iannone** | ITA | 29 | Fimmco Speed Up | Speed Up | 20 | 41m 54.674s |
| 4 | **Jules Cluzel** | FRA | 16 | Forward Racing | Suter | 20 | 41m 58.620s |
| 5 | **Julian Simon** | SPA | 60 | Mapfre Aspar Team | Suter | 20 | 41m 58.689s |
| 6 | **Gabor Talmacsi** | HUN | 2 | Fimmco Speed Up | Speed Up | 20 | 41m 58.739s |
| 7 | **Alex Debon** | SPA | 6 | Aeroport de Castello - Ajo | FTR | 20 | 41m 59.523s |
| 8 | **Simone Corsi** | ITA | 3 | JIR Moto2 | MotoBI | 20 | 42m 03.406s |
| 9 | **Stefan Bradl** | GER | 65 | Viessmann Kiefer Racing | Suter | 20 | 42m 07.673s |
| 10 | **Shoya Tomizawa** | JPN | 48 | Technomag-CIP | Suter | 20 | 42m 07.689s |
| 11 | **Thomas Luthi** | SWI | 12 | Interwetten Moriwaki Moto2 | Moriwaki | 20 | 42m 08.201s |
| 12 | **Hector Faubel** | SPA | 55 | Marc VDS Racing Team | Suter | 20 | 42m 08.205s |
| 13 | **Fonsi Nieto** | SPA | 10 | Holiday Gym G22 | Moriwaki | 20 | 42m 11.141s |
| 14 | **Sergio Gadea** | SPA | 40 | Tenerife 40 Pons | Pons Kalex | 20 | 42m 11.845s |
| 15 | **Raffaele de Rosa** | ITA | 35 | Tech 3 Racing | Tech 3 | 20 | 42m 11.942s |
| 16 | Dominique Aegerter | SWI | 77 | Technomag-CIP | Suter | 20 | 42m 11.948s |
| 17 | Alex Baldolini | ITA | 25 | Caretta Technology Race Dept. | I.C.P. | 20 | 42m 17.453s |
| 18 | Anthony West | AUS | 8 | MZ Racing Team | MZ-RE Honda | 20 | 42m 19.241s |
| 19 | Xavier Simeon | BEL | 19 | Holiday Gym G22 | Moriwaki | 20 | 42m 19.426s |
| 20 | Mike di Meglio | FRA | 63 | Mapfre Aspar Team | Suter | 20 | 42m 20.610s |
| 21 | Ratthapark Wilairot | THA | 14 | Thai Honda PTT Singha SAG | Bimota | 20 | 42m 27.978s |
| 22 | Scott Redding | GBR | 45 | Marc VDS Racing Team | Suter | 20 | 42m 35.996s |
| 23 | Yonny Hernandez | COL | 68 | Blusens-STX | BQR-Moto2 | 20 | 42m 38.161s |
| 24 | Ricard Cardus | SPA | 4 | Maquinza-SAG Team | Bimota | 20 | 42m 39.335s |
| 25 | Axel Pons | SPA | 80 | Tenerife 40 Pons | Pons Kalex | 20 | 42m 39.513s |
| 26 | Claudio Corti | ITA | 71 | Forward Racing | Suter | 20 | 42m 39.681s |
| 27 | Vladimir Ivanov | UKR | 61 | Gresini Racing Moto2 | Moriwaki | 20 | 42m 40.214s |
| 28 | Niccolo Canepa | ITA | 59 | RSM Team Scot | Force GP210 | 20 | 42m 43.708s |
| 29 | Robertino Pietri | VEN | 39 | Italtrans S.T.R. | Suter | 20 | 42m 43.958s |
| 30 | Mashel Al Naimi | QAT | 95 | Blusens-STX | BQR-Moto2 | 20 | 42m 44.866s |
| 31 | Joan Olive | SPA | 5 | Jack & Jones by A.Banderas | Promoharris | 20 | 42m 45.193s |
| 32 | Valentin Debise | FRA | 53 | WTR San Marino Team | ADV | 20 | 42m 51.795s |
| 33 | Yannick Guerra | SPA | 88 | Holiday Gym G22 | Moriwaki | 20 | 42m 59.957s |
| | Roberto Rolfo | ITA | 44 | Italtrans S.T.R. | Suter | 14 | DNF |
| | Yusuke Teshima | JPN | 11 | JIR Moto2 | MotoBI | 12 | DNF |
| | Lukas Pesek | CZE | 52 | Matteoni CP Racing | Moriwaki | 9 | DNF |
| | Patrik Vostarek | CZE | 81 | Vector Kiefer Racing | Suter | 2 | DNF |
| | Kenny Noyes | USA | 9 | Jack & Jones by A.Banderas | Promoharris | 1 | DNF |
| | Arne Tode | GER | 41 | Racing Team Germany | Suter | 0 | DNF |
| | Karel Abraham | CZE | 17 | Cardion AB Motoracing | FTR | 0 | DNS |

**Fastest lap:** Toni Elias, on lap 16, 2m 04.315s, 97.222mph/156.463km/h (record).
**Previous lap record:** New category.
**Event best maximum speed:** Andrea Iannone, 161.7mph/260.2km/h (race).

**Qualifying:** Dry
Air: 25° Humidity: 46% Ground: 42°

| | | |
|---|---|---|
| 1 | Tomizawa | 2m 03.452s |
| 2 | Iannone | 2m 03.684s |
| 3 | Elias | 2m 03.741s |
| 4 | Rolfo | 2m 03.794s |
| 5 | Takahashi | 2m 04.145s |
| 6 | Aegerter | 2m 04.251s |
| 7 | Corsi | 2m 04.383s |
| 8 | Tode | 2m 04.484s |
| 9 | Simon | 2m 04.519s |
| 10 | Redding | 2m 04.528s |
| 11 | Cluzel | 2m 04.597s |
| 12 | Nieto | 2m 04.602s |
| 13 | Luthi | 2m 04.605s |
| 14 | Baldolini | 2m 04.735s |
| 15 | Debon | 2m 04.775s |
| 16 | Talmacsi | 2m 04.899s |
| 17 | de Rosa | 2m 04.929s |
| 18 | di Meglio | 2m 04.976s |
| 19 | Faubel | 2m 04.989s |
| 20 | Bradl | 2m 05.029s |
| 21 | Pons | 2m 05.268s |
| 22 | Gadea | 2m 05.387s |
| 23 | Corti | 2m 05.402s |
| 24 | Wilairot | 2m 05.426s |
| 25 | Pesek | 2m 05.486s |
| 26 | Ivanov | 2m 05.517s |
| 27 | Vostarek | 2m 05.558s |
| 28 | Debise | 2m 05.650s |
| 29 | Teshima | 2m 05.658s |
| 30 | Canepa | 2m 05.760s |
| 31 | Noyes | 2m 05.802s |
| 32 | West | 2m 05.805s |
| 33 | Hernandez | 2m 05.871s |
| 34 | Abraham | 2m 05.877s |
| 35 | Simeon | 2m 05.906s |
| 36 | Cardus | 2m 06.047s |
| 37 | Al Naimi | 2m 06.130s |
| 38 | Pietri | 2m 06.458s |
| 39 | Olive | 2m 06.707s |
| 40 | Guerra | 2m 07.711s |

**Fastest race laps**

| | | |
|---|---|---|
| 1 | Elias | 2m 04.315s |
| 2 | Takahashi | 2m 04.618s |
| 3 | Iannone | 2m 04.676s |
| 4 | Rolfo | 2m 04.739s |
| 5 | Cluzel | 2m 04.868s |
| 6 | Debon | 2m 04.890s |
| 7 | Simon | 2m 04.947s |
| 8 | Talmacsi | 2m 05.126s |
| 9 | Luthi | 2m 05.145s |
| 10 | Corsi | 2m 05.237s |
| 11 | Bradl | 2m 05.433s |
| 12 | Tomizawa | 2m 05.473s |
| 13 | Faubel | 2m 05.483s |
| 14 | West | 2m 05.485s |
| 15 | de Rosa | 2m 05.534s |
| 16 | Nieto | 2m 05.542s |
| 17 | di Meglio | 2m 05.599s |
| 18 | Pesek | 2m 05.606s |
| 19 | Redding | 2m 05.647s |
| 20 | Gadea | 2m 05.663s |
| 21 | Baldolini | 2m 05.779s |
| 22 | Simeon | 2m 05.881s |
| 23 | Aegerter | 2m 05.887s |
| 24 | Wilairot | 2m 05.939s |
| 25 | Pons | 2m 06.282s |
| 26 | Pietri | 2m 06.284s |
| 27 | Corti | 2m 06.583s |
| 28 | Canepa | 2m 06.627s |
| 29 | Al Naimi | 2m 06.637s |
| 30 | Cardus | 2m 06.650s |
| 31 | Hernandez | 2m 06.665s |
| 32 | Ivanov | 2m 06.746s |
| 33 | Teshima | 2m 06.758s |
| 34 | Olive | 2m 06.809s |
| 35 | Debise | 2m 07.279s |
| 36 | Guerra | 2m 07.853s |
| 37 | Vostarek | 2m 08.190s |
| 38 | Noyes | 2m 16.906s |

**Championship Points**

| | | |
|---|---|---|
| 1 | Elias | 161 |
| 2 | Iannone | 106 |
| 3 | Luthi | 99 |
| 4 | Simon | 88 |
| 5 | Tomizawa | 82 |
| 6 | Cluzel | 74 |
| 7 | Corsi | 73 |
| 8 | Takahashi | 72 |
| 9 | Talmacsi | 62 |
| 10 | Gadea | 49 |
| 11 | Debon | 46 |
| 12 | Nieto | 41 |
| 13 | Rolfo | 37 |
| 14 | Abraham | 33 |
| 15 | Wilairot | 25 |
| 16 | Bradl | 25 |
| 17 | Redding | 23 |
| 18 | Aegerter | 23 |
| 19 | Hernandez | 21 |
| 20 | Noyes | 18 |
| 21 | di Meglio | 17 |
| 22 | Baldolini | 14 |
| 23 | Pasini | 12 |
| 24 | West | 11 |
| 25 | de Angelis | 11 |
| 26 | Cudlin | 9 |
| 27 | Simeon | 9 |
| 28 | Faubel | 8 |
| 29 | Pesek | 4 |
| 30 | Ivanov | 2 |
| 31 | Tode | 2 |
| 32 | de Rosa | 1 |
| 33 | Teshima | 1 |
| 34 | Corti | 1 |

**Constructors**

| | | |
|---|---|---|
| 1 | Moriwaki | 186 |
| 2 | Suter | 156 |
| 3 | Speed Up | 122 |
| 4 | FTR | 77 |
| 5 | MotoBI | 75 |
| 6 | Tech 3 | 72 |
| 7 | Pons Kalex | 58 |
| 8 | Bimota | 25 |
| 9 | BQR-Moto2 | 21 |
| 10 | Promoharris | 18 |
| 11 | I.C.P. | 14 |
| 12 | MZ-RE Honda | 11 |
| 13 | Force GP210 | 11 |
| 14 | RSV | 10 |

## 125cc

**RACE DISTANCE: 19 laps, 63.788 miles/102.657 km · RACE WEATHER: Wet (air 22°, humidity 88%, track 24°)**

| Pos. | Rider | Nat. | No. | Entrant | Machine | Laps | Time & Speed |
|---|---|---|---|---|---|---|---|
| 1 | **Nicolas Terol** | SPA | 40 | Bancaja Aspar Team | Aprilia | 19 | 43m 49.303s (mph/km/h) 87.337/140.556 |
| 2 | **Pol Espargaro** | SPA | 44 | Tuenti Racing | Derbi | 19 | 44m 09.654s |
| 3 | **Esteve Rabat** | SPA | 12 | Blusens-STX | Aprilia | 19 | 44m 09.858s |
| 4 | **Jonas Folger** | GER | 94 | Ongetta Team | Aprilia | 19 | 44m 18.832s |
| 5 | **Jakub Kornfeil** | CZE | 84 | Racing Team Germany | Aprilia | 19 | 44m 19.217s |
| 6 | **Bradley Smith** | GBR | 38 | Bancaja Aspar Team | Aprilia | 19 | 44m 19.289s |
| 7 | **Marc Marquez** | SPA | 93 | Red Bull Ajo Motorsport | Derbi | 19 | 44m 20.708s |
| 8 | **Jasper Iwema** | NED | 53 | CBC Corse | Aprilia | 19 | 44m 22.276s |
| 9 | **Tomoyoshi Koyama** | JPN | 71 | Racing Team Germany | Aprilia | 19 | 44m 31.145s |
| 10 | **Luis Salom** | SPA | 39 | Stipa-Molenaar Racing GP | Aprilia | 19 | 44m 35.431s |
| 11 | **Adrian Martin** | SPA | 26 | Aeroport de Castello - Ajo | Aprilia | 19 | 44m 36.062s |
| 12 | **Alberto Moncayo** | SPA | 23 | Andalucia Cajasol | Aprilia | 19 | 44m 36.933s |
| 13 | **Marcel Schrotter** | GER | 78 | Interwetten Honda 125 | Honda | 19 | 44m 39.960s |
| 14 | **Louis Rossi** | FRA | 69 | CBC Corse | Aprilia | 19 | 44m 40.031s |
| 15 | **Zulfahmi Khairuddin** | MAL | 63 | AirAsia-Sepang Int. Circuit | Aprilia | 19 | 44m 44.793s |
| 16 | Sandro Cortese | GER | 11 | Avant Mitsubishi Ajo | Derbi | 19 | 44m 50.205s |
| 17 | Randy Krummenacher | SWI | 35 | Stipa-Molenaar Racing GP | Aprilia | 19 | 44m 51.677s |
| 18 | Alessandro Tonucci | ITA | 95 | Junior GP Racing Team FMI | Aprilia | 19 | 45m 20.039s |
| 19 | Johann Zarco | FRA | 14 | WTR San Marino Team | Aprilia | 19 | 45m 39.919s |
| 20 | Sturla Fagerhaug | NOR | 50 | AirAsia-Sepang Int. Circuit | Aprilia | 19 | 45m 43.114s |
| 21 | Marco Ravaioli | ITA | 72 | Lambretta Reparto Corse | Lambretta | 19 | 45m 43.722s |
| 22 | Isaac Vinales | SPA | 55 | Lambretta Reparto Corse | Lambretta | 19 | 45m 44.013s |
| 23 | Luca Marconi | ITA | 87 | Ongetta Team | Aprilia | 19 | 45m 52.555s |
| | Efren Vazquez | SPA | 7 | Tuenti Racing | Derbi | 17 | DNF |
| | Simone Grotzkyj | ITA | 15 | Fontana Racing | Aprilia | 13 | DNF |
| | Ladislav Chmelik | CZE | 48 | Moto FGR | Honda | 11 | DNF |
| | Lorenzo Savadori | ITA | 32 | Matteoni CP Racing | Aprilia | 10 | DNF |
| | Luigi Morciano | ITA | 92 | Junior GP Racing Team FMI | Aprilia | 8 | DNF |
| | Alexis Masbou | FRA | 5 | Ongetta Team | Aprilia | 1 | DNF |
| | Danny Webb | GBR | 99 | Andalucia Cajasol | Aprilia | 0 | DNF |

**Fastest lap:** Johann Zarco, on lap 17, 2m 12.642s, 91.118mph/146.641km/h.
**Lap record:** Lucio Cecchinello, ITA (Aprilia), 2m 07.836s, 94.544mph/152.154km/h (2003).
**Event best maximum speed:** Esteve Rabat, 138.9mph/223.5km/h (qualifying practice).

**Qualifying:** Dry
Air: 25° Humidity: 62% Ground: 37°

| | | |
|---|---|---|
| 1 | Smith | 2m 07.146s |
| 2 | Terol | 2m 07.630s |
| 3 | Espargaro | 2m 08.073s |
| 4 | Marquez | 2m 08.186s |
| 5 | Cortese | 2m 08.339s |
| 6 | Vazquez | 2m 08.674s |
| 7 | Krummenacher | 2m 08.974s |
| 8 | Koyama | 2m 09.166s |
| 9 | Zarco | 2m 09.349s |
| 10 | Salom | 2m 09.496s |
| 11 | Webb | 2m 09.639s |
| 12 | Rabat | 2m 09.793s |
| 13 | Folger | 2m 10.188s |
| 14 | Kornfeil | 2m 10.313s |
| 15 | Moncayo | 2m 10.424s |
| 16 | Masbou | 2m 10.435s |
| 17 | Iwema | 2m 10.443s |
| 18 | Schrotter | 2m 10.610s |
| 19 | Grotzkyj | 2m 10.674s |
| 20 | Fagerhaug | 2m 10.774s |
| 21 | Rossi | 2m 11.017s |
| 22 | Martin | 2m 11.022s |
| 23 | Khairuddin | 2m 11.131s |
| 24 | Savadori | 2m 11.553s |
| 25 | Vinales | 2m 11.562s |
| 26 | Morciano | 2m 11.817s |
| 27 | Tonucci | 2m 12.281s |
| 28 | Ravaioli | 2m 12.772s |
| 29 | Marconi | 2m 12.929s |
| **Outside 107%** | | |
| *(but inside during free practice)* | | |
| | Chmelik | 2m 17.738s |
| **Outside 107%** | | |
| DNQ | Touskova | 2m 18.162s |

**Fastest race laps**

| | | |
|---|---|---|
| 1 | Zarco | 2m 12.642s |
| 2 | Iwema | 2m 13.010s |
| 3 | Terol | 2m 15.622s |
| 4 | Smith | 2m 17.851s |
| 5 | Rabat | 2m 17.878s |
| 6 | Kornfeil | 2m 18.203s |
| 7 | Espargaro | 2m 18.413s |
| 8 | Vazquez | 2m 18.548s |
| 9 | Folger | 2m 18.769s |
| 10 | Marquez | 2m 18.974s |
| 11 | Koyama | 2m 19.139s |
| 12 | Salom | 2m 19.386s |
| 13 | Rossi | 2m 19.467s |
| 14 | Khairuddin | 2m 19.568s |
| 15 | Moncayo | 2m 19.569s |
| 16 | Martin | 2m 19.606s |
| 17 | Schrotter | 2m 19.700s |
| 18 | Cortese | 2m 20.010s |
| 19 | Krummenacher | 2m 20.527s |
| 20 | Fagerhaug | 2m 20.598s |
| 21 | Grotzkyj | 2m 20.923s |
| 22 | Tonucci | 2m 20.985s |
| 23 | Ravaioli | 2m 22.041s |
| 24 | Savadori | 2m 22.329s |
| 25 | Vinales | 2m 22.329s |
| 26 | Marconi | 2m 23.618s |
| 27 | Morciano | 2m 24.279s |
| 28 | Chmelik | 2m 25.291s |
| 29 | Masbou | 2m 33.022s |

**Championship Points**

| | | |
|---|---|---|
| 1 | Marquez | 166 |
| 2 | Espargaro | 151 |
| 3 | Terol | 143 |
| 4 | Smith | 115 |
| 5 | Koyama | 84 |
| 6 | Rabat | 79 |
| 7 | Cortese | 76 |
| 8 | Vazquez | 68 |
| 9 | Krummenacher | 63 |
| 10 | Zarco | 55 |
| 11 | Webb | 48 |
| 12 | Folger | 36 |
| 13 | Moncayo | 29 |
| 14 | Iwema | 28 |
| 15 | Salom | 21 |
| 16 | Masbou | 20 |
| 17 | Kornfeil | 14 |
| 18 | Grotzkyj | 14 |
| 19 | Martin | 14 |
| 20 | Schrotter | 14 |
| 21 | Fagerhaug | 7 |
| 22 | Kartheininger | 6 |
| 23 | Savadori | 4 |
| 24 | Khairuddin | 3 |
| 25 | Rossi | 2 |

**Constructors**

| | | |
|---|---|---|
| 1 | Derbi | 215 |
| 2 | Aprilia | 186 |
| 3 | Honda | 14 |
| 4 | KTM | 6 |
| 5 | Lambretta | 1 |

*Main photo:* The city dwarfs the grandstands, grandstands dwarf the crowd, and Spies leads on lap one.

*Inset right:* Pedrosa clearly shows the effort of his win.

*Inset below:* Spies on pole for the first time, in special livery for his second home race.

*Inset bottom:* Jay Leno played the celebrity flagman.
*Photos:* Gold & Goose

# INDIANAPOLIS GRAND PRIX

INDIANAPOLIS CIRCUIT

*Above:* Ducati's big chief Del Torchio and project director Alessandro Cicognani watch and wait.

*Top:* Spies leads Pedrosa, but he just wasn't fast enough.

*Top right:* Riders in the MD250H series pose for a photo. Their race was marred by tragedy with the death of Peter Lenz (red shirt, third young rider from right, second row).

*Above centre right:* Nicky Hayden revisited his dirt-track days.

*Above right:* New forks, same old problem – Stoner suffered a third race crash.

Photos: Gold & Goose

THE second trip to America was a repeat, in many ways, of the first. Different winner in Dani Pedrosa, but repeat rostrum by Lorenzo, repeat of the heat, and a repeat of having to adapt to a track that fell a long way short of the usual standards.

Fittingly for the overpowering venue – the grandstands simply dwarfed a good crowd of almost 63,000 – it was also extraordinary. Here's one fact: Rossi crashed three times. He'd had trouble on Saturday night remembering when he'd ever had two crashes, then he did it again in race-morning warm-up. The team had enough of the special-paint 500-photo fairings, but Valentino ran out of the special leathers designed to go with them.

He was far from the only one to crash, at a track that race faller Stoner described with typical forthrightness as "a pile". Spies and Hayden also fell victim to the bumps in practice, the latter receiving an ugly surface wound to his left arm as a result of holding his injured wrist out of the way as he slid. One problem is the mix of three surfaces: one on the main straight, a second running on to the infield section and a third not quite halfway around, where the track was realigned for the first hurricane-struck Indy round in 2008. Another is bumps under braking, like the one that tipped Rossi down in 2009. They are bad enough to dictate strange lines that are smoother, and thus faster, than the ideal line; and tricky enough to catch out even the best.

Stoner's criticism was more explicit, and with good reason. His race crash was the Desmosedici signature front-end lose: he'd switched to the latest 2011 Öhlins front forks and said they'd improved matters, but that turned out to be wishful thinking. In practice, however, it had definitely been the track at fault. Sliding his knee on the inside kerb in the usual way, he had hit a slightly sunken drain cover. This dislodged his knee slider and delivered a painful blow in the process. His protests, and those of his team, to the organisers were of little avail, for exactly the same thing happened to Nicky Hayden (other knee) soon after the start of the race. As he'd been one of two Americans on the front row and was on target to take a hat trick of rostrums at the circuit just a drive

away from his Kentucky home, this was a cruel fate. He soldiered on, lacking a crucial element of control, and dropped back to still stalwart sixth.

The other American on the front row, at the best end, was Spies. His first pole, coming on the heels of his first front row, "ticks all the boxes," he said. Far from having track knowledge on his side, he had less experience than most – Indy was never used for AMA racing, and he had missed 2009 riding a Superbike.

His expected move to the now officially vacant Rossi slot in the factory team was confirmed before the race, as was Hayden's continuation at Ducati, alongside the defecting Italian.

All of these, and Lorenzo as well, might have felt a little chill, however, at the strength of Pedrosa's package: although complaints about balance and handling lingered on, as they will, there was no doubt that the bike could not only come out of the corners well, but also had the horsepower to sustain that surge in a demoralising fashion. It didn't show much in the top-speed figures (Melandri's off-works Gresini bike was fastest, at 319.7km/h, Stoner's Duke at 319.0), but it was emphatic when Pedrosa simply powered past early leader Spies in the race.

Lorenzo likewise couldn't hold the speedy Honda, even though his was the fastest Yamaha, 5km/h down. Third was his worst result of the season, but his progress still looked serene: he had equalled Doohan's record of rostrums at the first 11 rounds, and wore a special Iron Man helmet design.

No such fancy stuff on the annual Indy Mile, attended by all and enlivened by a memory-lane run by Nicky Hayden.

Other GP regulars were even closer to home: one Spanish journalist and a Dorna TV operative were turned back on entry to the US for visa problems (others entering on the same tourist visas passed without trouble), while Scott Redding was detained for some three hours before he was allowed in.

The weather was blazing for those who did get there: the track at 56 degrees and ambient at 35. This underlined a growing concern about the Bridgestone control tyres: in spite of the punishing heat, the softer option was by and large the choice for the race. Only four riders went with the harder

rear: Edwards, who stopped for a tyre change, then retired; Stoner, who crashed out early; Dovizioso, who dropped gradually out of contention; and Pedrosa. He ran away to win. All the same, as Stoner would point out with increasing vehemence in the races to come, it's simply all wrong that the so-called softer tyre should be able to do race distance in these conditions: "And we haven't had any cold races yet, either. What will happen then?" In fact, the heat also made the track slick, but Bridgestone would respond at the far end of the season, promising a wider divergence between the two supplied tyre compounds. It also pointed out that breadth of performance capability was a major design target, and therefore some overlap was inevitable.

Edwards's retirement perhaps had less to do with tyres than to a traumatic incident that had cast a shadow over the weekend.

A round of the USGPRU's learner-class MD250H series was a curtain-raiser, and was the subject of keen interest, since the 40bhp 250 single-cylinder Moriwaki-Honda machines are a precursor to Moto3, replacing the 125 class in 2012. The series is open to riders as young as 12, and 13-year-old Peter Lenz was leading on points after four wins, and had some high-level support, including spending time at Indy with Edwards in the pit.

Lenz fell on the warm-up lap, was struck by a following rider and fatally injured – the youngest to die at Indianapolis in 101 years of racing.

## MOTOGP RACE – 28 laps

Qualifying was close, the first six within six-tenths: Spies exulting in his first pole and Hayden in his first front row on a Ducati. Lorenzo was between them; Pedrosa was behind in the middle of the second row, flanked by Dovizioso in fourth and Stoner seventh. Rossi was seventh, heading row three.

It was Spies away from the start, pursued by Dovizioso, Hayden and Pedrosa, with the Yamahas of Lorenzo and Rossi right behind by the time they came back across the yard of bricks for the first time.

*Above:* Hayden's hopes were dashed when his knee-slider caught a kerb and came loose.

*Top:* Lorenzo had a ready smile for the fans.

*Left:* A plaintive Rossi seeks answers from Burgess during practice.

Photos: Gold & Goose

Pedrosa found his way past Hayden on the second lap, but the American would soon suffer the blow that cost him all his chances – his left knee slider was ripped off halfway around lap three, and the third time down the long straight he was clutching at the pad, trying to reattach it to the Velcro base. He was unsuccessful, however, since the Velcro itself had become unstitched from his leathers. He started to lose places at once.

Stoner had finished the first lap in ninth, behind both Gresini riders. While Simoncelli made a slip next time around and dropped behind both of them, Melandri – who, at 28, had just become the youngest rider to make 200 GP starts – was resisting fiercely when he slipped off, the first crash of the race.

Pedrosa was gaining pace, setting the first of a series of fastest laps on the third and directly past his team-mate, gaining a second's gap almost at once. Less than a second behind Spies, he was closing inexorably, and the American hero's run at the front would finish at the end of lap seven, when the Spaniard powered past over the stripe. "I just wasn't fast enough," he said.

Spies hung on as best he could, but he was right, and by half-distance, Pedrosa was 3.7 seconds clear in a trademark run-away performance, as convincing as you like. Surprisingly, perhaps, it marked the first time he had ever won three races in one season.

Lorenzo was straight past Hayden on lap three, and over the next two Rossi and Stoner also got ahead. Stoner was gaining confidence and pushing Rossi hard. Then on lap eight, his old nightmare recurred: the front folded under him and he was down. A broken handlebar ended his race.

Dovizioso's hard tyre choice worked the opposite way to his team-mate's and gradually he dropped away from Spies towards Lorenzo. By lap ten, he was coming under attack, only for Lorenzo to run wide; next time around, Dovizioso suffered a big slide, losing the advantage again. The issue was settled at the start of lap 12, when he moved inside into the first corner and claimed the rostrum for good.

There was one more change in the top four when Rossi, clearly not at his best, upped his pace to close on Dovizioso, passing him quite easily on lap 21. The Honda was slowing, but Lorenzo was still only 1.7 seconds ahead. Next time around, however, it was more than two, and Rossi's attack was soon spent as he settled for a safe fourth.

Dovizioso's fifth was likewise secure, and Hayden seemed to have sixth under control, with Simoncelli five seconds behind at half-distance, the rookie's hands full in fending off

Bautista and Kallio in a good long battle, Espargaro close behind. They were still at it on lap 19, when Kallio hit a bump under braking and crashed out.

Simoncelli put on a spurt in the closing laps to close to within 1.5 seconds of Hayden, hounded all the way by Bautista, with Espargaro losing touch at the end.

Another six seconds behind, Barbera held on to tenth. He had been caught gradually by Capirossi in the closing stages, and the veteran had got ahead at the start of the final lap, only to be forced off track when the rookie pushed back ahead.

Aoyama was back, riding carefully in a corset after being out of action for ten weeks, but he was only a couple of seconds behind; de Puniet was a distant 13th and last after a feat of endurance: his injured leg had flared up after Brno, leaving him immobilised for several days.

Edwards had dropped back steadily to last on his hard tyre, pitting on lap 12 to change to the softer option, only to retire five laps later, his mind too full of the morning's tragedy to concentrate.

*Above:* Moto2 winner Elias leads Simon and Redding.

*Top left:* Another top ten for the improving Simoncelli, heading Bautista, Kallio and Espargaro.

*Top:* Sick and tired, and victorious: an exhausted Elias on the podium.

*Centre:* A podium also for Simon...

*Left:* ...and for Scott Redding, the youngest rider in Moto2.

*Right:* Terol inherited a massive lead in the 125cc race.

*Photos: Gold & Goose*

## MOTO2 RACE – 17 laps (shortened)

The new class claimed a new record: not one, but two mass pile-ups in the second corner. This brought out the red flag, for a hasty restart.

The front two in the title race had problems already: Elias was suffering from high 39-degree fever and fatigue; Iannone had injured a wrist and ankle in a heavy qualifying crash after only three laps. He was 26th on the grid. Simon took pole from front-row first-timers Faubel, Redding and Corsi; Elias was on row two.

Simon led the field away from second-row qualifier Ant West on the MZ; Elias was fourth. But two second-corner pile-ups left a tangle of bikes that workers were unable to clear in time, and the race was stopped forthwith.

It was hard to find culprits for the crash in the endemic overcrowding. The worst victim was Tomizawa, unable to make the restart; while Corsi was too late to get to the grid and obliged to start from the pit lane. Two others – de Rosa and wild-card Roger Lee Hayden – at first were held back, having not got back to the pits in time in the first place, but a hasty revision (with Hayden's team boss, Kevin Schwantz, leading a lively debate) saw the rule waived.

With the race distance cut from 23 to 17 laps, they started again, Elias taking the gap left in the front row by Corsi's absence to seize the lead going into the first corner.

Redding slipped past West to follow him, Simon in fourth, but soon up to third.

On lap five, Simon took over the lead, but was unable to escape. Redding, youngest rider in the class, hung on valiantly, regaining what he lost on the straight under brakes and in the corners.

Then Elias swept past Simon into the lead at the start of lap 12 with a daring round-the-outside line into the fast turn one. Simon went with him as he pushed the pace, and though he was less than half a second adrift over the line, he was never close enough to attack. "I kept the only energy I had to push for the last five laps," said an exhausted Elias.

Iannone had finished lap one 13th, and Corsi 22nd, and they were cutting through in tandem; by half-distance, they lay fourth and fifth. They didn't get any higher, but were closing steadily on Redding, alone in third. The Briton had enough in hand, however, to earn his first class rostrum, keeping the Italians almost two seconds behind at the end.

Another couple of seconds away, Gadea narrowly won a long battle with Luthi and Talmacsi; Wilairot had been with them until he crashed out.

Impressive US wild-card Jason di Salvo narrowly prevailed in the next battle for ninth, inches ahead of West and Aegerter. West had gained tenth only on the line.

Hayden was 17th, 1.4 seconds out of the points after battling with no rear brake.

The first multiple pile-up aside, the number to fall victim to the bumpy and slippery surface gave MotoGP riders something to worry about as the heat kept building. Here's the list: Debon, Ivanov, Faubel (a fiery spectacular), Bradl, Tashima, Cardus, Takahashi, Rolfo, de Rosa, Cluzel and Wilairot.

## 125cc RACE – 23 laps

Marquez, Terol, Smith and Cortese held the front row; Espargaro and Vazquez led the second, the first two half a second clear of the rest. They controlled the race, Marquez pulling away impressively and Terol in a lone pursuit – until it all went wrong for the teenager when he slipped off. He remounted, however, and charged back to fifth, gaining three places on the last lap, only to be dropped to tenth by a controversial penalty: he had taken an inadvertent short cut and was docked 20 seconds.

Thus it was a second runaway win in a row for Terol, and his third of the year, demonstrating the strength of his return from injury and spicing up the title contest in the process, as he closed to within four points.

Marquez crashed out just after one-third-distance; Terol was more than two seconds adrift when unexpectedly he was promoted to the lead.

Smith had come through to the front of a battle for second, but on unlucky lap 13 he also fell victim to the bumpy, slippery surface, slumping in despair as he came to rest, his last championship hopes gone.

That left Tuenti team-mates Espargaro and Vazquez under pressure from Cortese, who had come through forcefully from tenth on the first lap after yet another poor start. He was in front by the finish and the trio was spaced out.

Marquez crossed the line ahead of a battling gang: Rabat, Webb and Krummenacher. He'd been 1.7 seconds behind when he ran off on the penultimate lap, but the error meant he'd close up enough to pass them on the last. His penalty promoted Moncaya and Folger to eighth and ninth.

## INDIANAPOLIS MOTOR SPEEDWAY

Turn 6 110/68
Turn 5
Turn 7
Turn 10 95/59
Hulman Boulevard
Turn 8
Turn 13 125/78
Turn 12
Turn 3
Turn 9 85/53
Turn 2 90/56
Turn 4
Turn 11
Turn 14
Turn 15 105/65
Turn 1 150/93
Turn 16

**Key**
96/60 kph/mph
Gear
Circuit 4.218km/2.621 miles, 28 laps

## MotoGP

**RACE DISTANCE: 28 laps, 73.352 miles/118.048 km · RACE WEATHER: Dry (air 35°, humidity 26%, track 56°)**

| Pos. | Rider | Nat. | No. | Entrant | Machine | Tyres | Laps | Time & speed |
|---|---|---|---|---|---|---|---|---|
| 1 | Dani Pedrosa | SPA | 26 | Repsol Honda Team | Honda | B | 28 | 47m 31.615s 92.602mph/ 149.028km/h |
| 2 | Ben Spies | USA | 11 | Monster Yamaha Tech 3 | Yamaha | B | 28 | 47m 35.190s |
| 3 | Jorge Lorenzo | SPA | 99 | Fiat Yamaha Team | Yamaha | B | 28 | 47m 38.427s |
| 4 | Valentino Rossi | ITA | 46 | Fiat Yamaha Team | Yamaha | B | 28 | 47m 44.248s |
| 5 | Andrea Dovizioso | ITA | 4 | Repsol Honda Team | Honda | B | 28 | 47m 53.500s |
| 6 | Nicky Hayden | USA | 69 | Ducati Marlboro Team | Ducati | B | 28 | 48m 06.753s |
| 7 | Marco Simoncelli | ITA | 58 | San Carlo Honda Gresini | Honda | B | 28 | 48m 08.355s |
| 8 | Alvaro Bautista | SPA | 19 | Rizla Suzuki MotoGP | Suzuki | B | 28 | 48m 08.440s |
| 9 | Aleix Espargaro | SPA | 41 | Pramac Racing Team | Ducati | B | 28 | 48m 16.520s |
| 10 | Hector Barbera | SPA | 40 | Paginas Amarillas Aspar | Ducati | B | 28 | 48m 22.983s |
| 11 | Loris Capirossi | ITA | 65 | Rizla Suzuki MotoGP | Suzuki | B | 28 | 48m 27.001s |
| 12 | Hiroshi Aoyama | JPN | 7 | Interwetten Honda MotoGP | Honda | B | 28 | 48m 29.518s |
| 13 | Randy de Puniet | FRA | 14 | LCR Honda MotoGP | Honda | B | 28 | 48m 35.754s |
| | Mika Kallio | FIN | 36 | Pramac Racing Team | Ducati | B | 18 | DNF |
| | Colin Edwards | USA | 5 | Monster Yamaha Tech 3 | Yamaha | B | 16 | DNF |
| | Casey Stoner | AUS | 27 | Ducati Marlboro Team | Ducati | B | 7 | DNF |
| | Marco Melandri | ITA | 33 | San Carlo Honda Gresini | Honda | B | 2 | DNF |

**Fastest lap:** Dani Pedrosa, on lap 11, 1m 40.896s, 93.472mph/150.428km/h.
**Lap record:** Jorge Lorenzo, SPA (Yamaha), 1m 40.152s, 103.593mph/151.545km/h (2009).
**Event best maximum speed:** Marco Melandri, 198.7mph/319.7km/h (free practice 1).

**Qualifying**
Weather: Dry
Air Temp: 33° Humidity: 15°
Track Temp: 54°

| | | |
|---|---|---|
| 1 | Spies | 1m 40.105s |
| 2 | Lorenzo | 1m 40.325s |
| 3 | Hayden | 1m 40.336s |
| 4 | Dovizioso | 1m 40.559s |
| 5 | Pedrosa | 1m 40.637s |
| 6 | Stoner | 1m 40.664s |
| 7 | Rossi | 1m 41.005s |
| 8 | Simoncelli | 1m 41.092s |
| 9 | Edwards | 1m 41.232s |
| 10 | Capirossi | 1m 41.512s |
| 11 | Bautista | 1m 41.534s |
| 12 | Melandri | 1m 41.623s |
| 13 | Aoyama | 1m 41.631s |
| 14 | Espargaro | 1m 41.649s |
| 15 | Kallio | 1m 41.856s |
| 16 | Barbera | 1m 41.896s |
| 17 | de Puniet | 1m 41.923s |

**Fastest race laps**

| | | |
|---|---|---|
| 1 | Pedrosa | 1m 40.896s |
| 2 | Spies | 1m 41.417s |
| 3 | Stoner | 1m 41.417s |
| 4 | Rossi | 1m 41.436s |
| 5 | Lorenzo | 1m 41.490s |
| 6 | Dovizioso | 1m 41.569s |
| 7 | Melandri | 1m 42.010s |
| 8 | Hayden | 1m 42.182s |
| 9 | Bautista | 1m 42.288s |
| 10 | Kallio | 1m 42.299s |
| 11 | Espargaro | 1m 42.416s |
| 12 | Edwards | 1m 42.435s |
| 13 | Simoncelli | 1m 42.450s |
| 14 | Barbera | 1m 42.708s |
| 15 | Capirossi | 1m 42.757s |
| 16 | de Puniet | 1m 42.866s |
| 17 | Aoyama | 1m 42.917s |

**Championship Points**

| | | |
|---|---|---|
| 1 | Lorenzo | 251 |
| 2 | Pedrosa | 183 |
| 3 | Dovizioso | 126 |
| 4 | Stoner | 119 |
| 5 | Rossi | 114 |
| 6 | Spies | 110 |
| 7 | N. Hayden | 109 |
| 8 | de Puniet | 78 |
| 9 | Simoncelli | 63 |
| 10 | Melandri | 61 |
| 11 | Edwards | 57 |
| 12 | Barbera | 54 |
| 13 | Capirossi | 41 |
| 14 | Espargaro | 39 |
| 15 | Bautista | 33 |
| 16 | Kallio | 31 |
| 17 | Aoyama | 22 |
| 18 | de Angelis | 11 |
| 19 | R. Hayden | 5 |
| 20 | Akiyoshi | 4 |
| 21 | Yoshikawa | 1 |

| Grid order | 1 | 2 | 3 | 4 | 5 | 6 | 7 | 8 | 9 | 10 | 11 | 12 | 13 | 14 | 15 | 16 | 17 | 18 | 19 | 20 | 21 | 22 | 23 | 24 | 25 | 26 | 27 | 28 | |
|---|---|---|---|---|---|---|---|---|---|---|---|---|---|---|---|---|---|---|---|---|---|---|---|---|---|---|---|---|---|
| 11 SPIES | 11 | 11 | 11 | 11 | 11 | 11 | 26 | 26 | 26 | 26 | 26 | 26 | 26 | 26 | 26 | 26 | 26 | 26 | 26 | 26 | 26 | 26 | 26 | 26 | 26 | 26 | 26 | 26 | 1 |
| 99 LORENZO | 4 | 4 | 4 | 26 | 26 | 26 | 11 | 11 | 11 | 11 | 11 | 11 | 11 | 11 | 11 | 11 | 11 | 11 | 11 | 11 | 11 | 11 | 11 | 11 | 11 | 11 | 11 | 11 | 2 |
| 69 HAYDEN | 69 | 26 | 26 | 4 | 4 | 4 | 4 | 4 | 4 | 4 | 4 | 99 | 99 | 99 | 99 | 99 | 99 | 99 | 99 | 99 | 99 | 99 | 99 | 99 | 99 | 99 | 99 | 99 | 3 |
| 4 DOVIZIOSO | 26 | 69 | 99 | 99 | 99 | 99 | 99 | 99 | 99 | 99 | 99 | 4 | 4 | 4 | 4 | 4 | 4 | 4 | 46 | 46 | 46 | 46 | 46 | 46 | 46 | 46 | 46 | 46 | 4 |
| 26 PEDROSA | 99 | 99 | 69 | 46 | 46 | 46 | 46 | 46 | 46 | 46 | 46 | 46 | 46 | 46 | 46 | 46 | 46 | 46 | 4 | 4 | 4 | 4 | 4 | 4 | 4 | 4 | 4 | 4 | 5 |
| 27 STONER | 46 | 46 | 46 | 69 | 69 | 27 | 27 | 69 | 69 | 69 | 69 | 69 | 69 | 69 | 69 | 69 | 69 | 69 | 69 | 69 | 69 | 69 | 69 | 69 | 69 | 69 | 69 | 69 | 6 |
| 46 ROSSI | 58 | 33 | 27 | 27 | 27 | 69 | 69 | 58 | 58 | 58 | 58 | 58 | 58 | 58 | 58 | 58 | 58 | 58 | 58 | 58 | 58 | 58 | 58 | 58 | 58 | 58 | 58 | 58 | 7 |
| 58 SIMONCELLI | 33 | 27 | 58 | 58 | 58 | 58 | 58 | 19 | 19 | 19 | 19 | 19 | 19 | 19 | 19 | 19 | 19 | 19 | 19 | 19 | 19 | 19 | 19 | 19 | 19 | 19 | 19 | 19 | 8 |
| 5 EDWARDS | 27 | 58 | 5 | 36 | 36 | 36 | 36 | 36 | 36 | 36 | 36 | 36 | 36 | 36 | 36 | 36 | 36 | 36 | 41 | 41 | 41 | 41 | 41 | 41 | 41 | 41 | 41 | 41 | 9 |
| 65 CAPIROSSI | 5 | 5 | 36 | 5 | 19 | 19 | 19 | 41 | 41 | 41 | 41 | 41 | 41 | 41 | 41 | 41 | 41 | 41 | 40 | 40 | 40 | 40 | 40 | 40 | 40 | 40 | 65 | 40 | 10 |
| 19 BAUTISTA | 65 | 36 | 19 | 19 | 41 | 41 | 41 | 40 | 40 | 40 | 40 | 40 | 40 | 40 | 40 | 40 | 40 | 40 | 65 | 65 | 65 | 65 | 65 | 65 | 65 | 65 | 40 | 65 | 11 |
| 33 MELANDRI | 36 | 65 | 65 | 65 | 5 | 5 | 5 | 65 | 65 | 65 | 65 | 65 | 65 | 65 | 65 | 65 | 65 | 65 | 7 | 7 | 7 | 7 | 7 | 7 | 7 | 7 | 7 | 7 | 12 |
| 7 AOYAMA | 19 | 19 | 41 | 41 | 65 | 40 | 40 | 14 | 14 | 14 | 14 | 14 | 14 | 14 | 14 | 14 | 14 | 14 | 14 | 14 | 14 | 14 | 14 | 14 | 14 | 14 | 14 | 14 | 13 |
| 41 ESPARGARO | 41 | 41 | 40 | 40 | 40 | 65 | 65 | 7 | 7 | 7 | 7 | 7 | 7 | 7 | 7 | 7 | 7 | 7 | | | | | | | | | | | |
| 36 KALLIO | 40 | 40 | 7 | 7 | 7 | 7 | 7 | 5 | 5 | 5 | 5 | 5 | 5 | 5 | 5 | 5 | | | | | | | | | | | | | |
| 40 BARBERA | 7 | 7 | 14 | 14 | 14 | 14 | 14 | | | | | | | | | | | | | | | | | | | | | | |
| 14 de PUNIET | 14 | 14 | | | | | | | | | | | | | | | | | | | | | | | | | | | |

5 Lapped rider

**Team Points**

| | | |
|---|---|---|
| 1 | Fiat Yamaha Team | 366 |
| 2 | Repsol Honda Team | 309 |
| 3 | Ducati Marlboro Team | 228 |
| 4 | Monster Yamaha Tech 3 | 167 |
| 5 | San Carlo Honda Gresini | 124 |
| 6 | LCR Honda MotoGP | 83 |
| 7 | Rizla Suzuki MotoGP | 74 |
| 8 | Pramac Racing Team | 70 |
| 9 | Paginas Amarillas Aspar | 54 |
| 10 | Interwetten Honda MotoGP | 37 |

**Constructor Points**

| | | |
|---|---|---|
| 1 | Yamaha | 260 |
| 2 | Honda | 220 |
| 3 | Ducati | 159 |
| 4 | Suzuki | 56 |

## Moto2

**RACE DISTANCE: 17 laps, 44.535 miles/71.672 km · RACE WEATHER: Dry (air 34°, humidity 26%, track 52°)**

| Pos. | Rider | Nat. | No. | Entrant | Machine | Laps | Time & Speed |
|---|---|---|---|---|---|---|---|
| 1 | **Toni Elias** | SPA | 24 | Gresini Racing Moto2 | Moriwaki | 17 | 30m 27.480s |
| | | | | | | | (mph/km/h) |
| | | | | | | | 97.730/141.188 |
| 2 | **Julian Simon** | SPA | 60 | Mapfre Aspar Team | Suter | 17 | 30m 27.885s |
| 3 | **Scott Redding** | GBR | 45 | Marc VDS Racing Team | Suter | 17 | 30m 31.707s |
| 4 | **Andrea Iannone** | ITA | 29 | Fimmco Speed Up | Speed Up | 17 | 30m 33.458s |
| 5 | **Simone Corsi** | ITA | 3 | JIR Moto2 | MotoBI | 17 | 30m 34.538s |
| 6 | **Sergio Gadea** | SPA | 40 | Tenerife 40 Pons | Pons Kalex | 17 | 30m 36.912s |
| 7 | **Thomas Luthi** | SWI | 12 | Interwetten Moriwaki Moto2 | Moriwaki | 17 | 30m 37.295s |
| 8 | **Gabor Talmacsi** | HUN | 2 | Fimmco Speed Up | Speed Up | 17 | 30m 37.621s |
| 9 | **Jason Di Salvo** | USA | 42 | GP Tech | FTR | 17 | 30m 45.044s |
| 10 | **Anthony West** | AUS | 8 | MZ Racing Team | MZ-RE Honda | 17 | 30m 45.072s |
| 11 | **Dominique Aegerter** | SWI | 77 | Technomag-CIP | Suter | 17 | 30m 45.098s |
| 12 | **Mike di Meglio** | FRA | 63 | Mapfre Aspar Team | Suter | 17 | 30m 48.007s |
| 13 | **Claudio Corti** | ITA | 71 | Forward Racing | Suter | 17 | 30m 53.488s |
| 14 | **Axel Pons** | SPA | 80 | Tenerife 40 Pons | Pons Kalex | 17 | 30m 55.833s |
| 15 | **Yonny Hernandez** | COL | 68 | Blusens-STX | BQR-Moto2 | 17 | 30m 57.960s |
| 16 | Alex Baldolini | ITA | 25 | Caretta Technology Race Dept. | I.C.P. | 17 | 30m 58.018s |
| 17 | Roger Lee Hayden | USA | 34 | American Honda | Moriwaki | 17 | 30m 59.340s |
| 18 | Valentin Debise | FRA | 53 | WTR San Marino Team | ADV | 17 | 30m 59.735s |
| 19 | Kenny Noyes | USA | 9 | Jack & Jones by A.Banderas | Promoharris | 17 | 30m 59.980s |
| 20 | Lukas Pesek | CZE | 52 | Matteoni CP Racing | Moriwaki | 17 | 31m 00.009s |
| 21 | Robertino Pietri | VEN | 39 | Italtrans S.T.R. | Suter | 17 | 31m 12.049s |
| 22 | Joan Olive | SPA | 5 | Jack & Jones by A.Banderas | Promoharris | 17 | 31m 12.436s |
| 23 | Arne Tode | GER | 41 | Racing Team Germany | Suter | 17 | 31m 20.473s |
| 24 | Yannick Guerra | SPA | 88 | Holiday Gym G22 | Moriwaki | 17 | 31m 24.961s |
| 25 | Roberto Rolfo | ITA | 44 | Italtrans S.T.R. | Suter | 17 | 31m 43.884s |
| 26 | Yuki Takahashi | JPN | 72 | Tech 3 Racing | Tech 3 | 14 | 31m 00.519s |
| | Mashel Al Naimi | QAT | 95 | Blusens-STX | BQR-Moto2 | 12 | DNF |
| | Jules Cluzel | FRA | 16 | Forward Racing | Suter | 11 | DNF |
| | Ratthapark Wilairot | THA | 14 | Thai Honda PTT Singha SAG | Bimota | 11 | DNF |
| | Raffaele de Rosa | ITA | 35 | Tech 3 Racing | Tech 3 | 6 | DNF |
| | Stefan Bradl | GER | 65 | Viessmann Kiefer Racing | Suter | 5 | DNF |
| | Ricard Cardus | SPA | 4 | Maquinza-SAG Team | Bimota | 2 | DNF |
| | Yusuke Teshima | JPN | 11 | JIR Moto2 | MotoBI | 2 | DNF |
| | Hector Faubel | SPA | 55 | Marc VDS Racing Team | Suter | 1 | DNF |
| | Alex Debon | SPA | 6 | Aeroport de Castello - Ajo | FTR | 1 | DNF |
| | Vladimir Ivanov | UKR | 61 | Gresini Racing Moto2 | Moriwaki | 1 | DNF |
| | Shoya Tomizawa | JPN | 48 | Technomag-CIP | Suter | 0 | DNS |
| | Michael Ranseder | AUT | 56 | Vector Kiefer Racing | Suter | 0 | DNS |

**Fastest lap:** Julian Simon, on lap 2, 1m 46.580s, 88.486mph/142.405km/h (record).
**Previous lap record:** New category.
**Event best maximum speed:** Sergio Gadea, 171.3mph/275.7km/h (free practice 1).

**Qualifying: Dry**
Air: 36° Humidity: 14% Ground: 57°

| | | |
|---|---|---|
| 1 | Simon | 1m 46.139s |
| 2 | Faubel | 1m 46.287s |
| 3 | Redding | 1m 46.334s |
| 4 | Corsi | 1m 46.358s |
| 5 | West | 1m 46.365s |
| 6 | Elias | 1m 46.368s |
| 7 | Wilairot | 1m 46.454s |
| 8 | Gadea | 1m 46.561s |
| 9 | Bradl | 1m 46.709s |
| 10 | de Rosa | 1m 46.739s |
| 11 | Ranseder | 1m 46.821s |
| 12 | Nieto | 1m 46.900s |
| 13 | Takahashi | 1m 46.935s |
| 14 | Corti | 1m 46.942s |
| 15 | Pesek | 1m 46.959s |
| 16 | Talmacsi | 1m 46.962s |
| 17 | Luthi | 1m 47.004s |
| 18 | Cluzel | 1m 47.031s |
| 19 | Rolfo | 1m 47.052s |
| 20 | Baldolini | 1m 47.062s |
| 21 | Aegerter | 1m 47.075s |
| 22 | di Meglio | 1m 47.084s |
| 23 | Hernandez | 1m 47.098s |
| 24 | Tomizawa | 1m 47.171s |
| 25 | Ivanov | 1m 47.224s |
| 26 | Iannone | 1m 47.261s |
| 27 | Di Salvo | 1m 47.302s |
| 28 | Pons | 1m 47.313s |
| 29 | Hayden | 1m 47.390s |
| 30 | Noyes | 1m 47.514s |
| 31 | Debise | 1m 47.551s |
| 32 | Tode | 1m 47.581s |
| 33 | Pietri | 1m 47.751s |
| 34 | Debon | 1m 47.796s |
| 35 | Cardus | 1m 47.937s |
| 36 | Olive | 1m 48.188s |
| 37 | Teshima | 1m 48.275s |
| 38 | Al Naimi | 1m 48.421s |
| 39 | Guerra | 1m 48.905s |

**Fastest race laps**

| | | |
|---|---|---|
| 1 | Simon | 1m 46.580s |
| 2 | Elias | 1m 46.770s |
| 3 | Iannone | 1m 46.862s |
| 4 | Corsi | 1m 46.907s |
| 5 | Redding | 1m 46.920s |
| 6 | Gadea | 1m 47.128s |
| 7 | Talmacsi | 1m 47.172s |
| 8 | Cluzel | 1m 47.206s |
| 9 | Luthi | 1m 47.242s |
| 10 | Di Salvo | 1m 47.328s |
| 11 | Wilairot | 1m 47.369s |
| 12 | Baldolini | 1m 47.402s |
| 13 | de Rosa | 1m 47.421s |
| 14 | di Meglio | 1m 47.526s |
| 15 | Corti | 1m 47.614s |
| 16 | Pons | 1m 47.634s |
| 17 | West | 1m 47.635s |
| 18 | Aegerter | 1m 47.637s |
| 19 | Debise | 1m 47.878s |
| 20 | Hernandez | 1m 47.956s |
| 21 | Rolfo | 1m 48.001s |
| 22 | Noyes | 1m 48.024s |
| 23 | Hayden | 1m 48.051s |
| 24 | Takahashi | 1m 48.191s |
| 25 | Pesek | 1m 48.284s |
| 26 | Pietri | 1m 48.561s |
| 27 | Al Naimi | 1m 49.053s |
| 28 | Olive | 1m 49.156s |
| 29 | Tode | 1m 49.457s |
| 30 | Guerra | 1m 49.756s |
| 31 | Teshima | 1m 49.802s |
| 32 | Cardus | 1m 49.896s |
| 33 | Bradl | 1m 50.003s |
| 34 | Faubel | 1m 53.275s |
| 35 | Debon | 1m 58.102s |
| 36 | Ivanov | 1m 58.152s |

**Championship Points**

| | | |
|---|---|---|
| 1 | Elias | 186 |
| 2 | Iannone | 119 |
| 3 | Luthi | 108 |
| 4 | Simon | 108 |
| 5 | Corsi | 84 |
| 6 | Tomizawa | 82 |
| 7 | Cluzel | 74 |
| 8 | Takahashi | 72 |
| 9 | Talmacsi | 70 |
| 10 | Gadea | 59 |
| 11 | Debon | 46 |
| 12 | Nieto | 41 |
| 13 | Redding | 39 |
| 14 | Rolfo | 37 |
| 15 | Abraham | 33 |
| 16 | Aegerter | 28 |
| 17 | Wilairot | 25 |
| 18 | Bradl | 25 |
| 19 | Hernandez | 22 |
| 20 | di Meglio | 21 |
| 21 | Noyes | 18 |
| 22 | West | 17 |
| 23 | Baldolini | 14 |
| 24 | Pasini | 12 |
| 25 | de Angelis | 11 |
| 26 | Cudlin | 9 |
| 27 | Simeon | 9 |
| 28 | Faubel | 8 |
| 29 | Di Salvo | 7 |
| 30 | Corti | 4 |
| 31 | Pesek | 4 |
| 32 | Pons | 2 |
| 33 | Ivanov | 2 |
| 34 | Tode | 2 |
| 35 | de Rosa | 1 |
| 36 | Teshima | 1 |

**Constructors**

| | | |
|---|---|---|
| 1 | Moriwaki | 211 |
| 2 | Suter | 176 |
| 3 | Speed Up | 135 |
| 4 | MotoBI | 86 |
| 5 | FTR | 84 |
| 6 | Tech 3 | 72 |
| 7 | Pons Kalex | 68 |
| 8 | Bimota | 25 |
| 9 | BQR-Moto2 | 22 |
| 10 | Promoharris | 18 |
| 11 | MZ-RE Honda | 17 |
| 12 | I.C.P. | 14 |
| 13 | Force GP210 | 11 |
| 14 | RSV | 10 |

---

## 125cc

**RACE DISTANCE: 23 laps, 60.253 miles/96.968 km · RACE WEATHER: Dry (air 33°, humidity 35%, track 50°)**

| Pos. | Rider | Nat. | No. | Entrant | Machine | Laps | Time & Speed |
|---|---|---|---|---|---|---|---|
| 1 | **Nicolas Terol** | SPA | 40 | Bancaja Aspar Team | Aprilia | 23 | 42m 19.223s |
| | | | | | | | (mph/km/h) |
| | | | | | | | 85.424/137.477 |
| 2 | **Sandro Cortese** | GER | 11 | Avant Mitsubishi Ajo | Derbi | 23 | 42m 24.218s |
| 3 | **Pol Espargaro** | SPA | 44 | Tuenti Racing | Derbi | 23 | 42m 30.079s |
| 4 | **Efren Vazquez** | SPA | 7 | Tuenti Racing | Derbi | 23 | 42m 34.625s |
| 5 | **Esteve Rabat** | SPA | 12 | Blusens-STX | Aprilia | 23 | 42m 39.135s |
| 6 | **Danny Webb** | GBR | 99 | Andalucia Cajasol | Aprilia | 23 | 42m 39.316s |
| 7 | **Randy Krummenacher** | SWI | 35 | Stipa-Molenaar Racing GP | Aprilia | 23 | 42m 39.925s |
| 8 | **Alberto Moncayo** | SPA | 23 | Andalucia Cajasol | Aprilia | 23 | 42m 46.020s |
| 9 | **Jonas Folger** | GER | 94 | Ongetta Team | Aprilia | 23 | 42m 46.889s |
| 10 | **Marc Marquez** | SPA | 93 | Red Bull Ajo Motorsport | Derbi | 23 | 42m 59.063s |
| 11 | **Jasper Iwema** | NED | 53 | CBC Corse | Aprilia | 23 | 43m 05.376s |
| 12 | **Luis Salom** | SPA | 39 | Stipa-Molenaar Racing GP | Aprilia | 23 | 43m 11.779s |
| 13 | **Johann Zarco** | FRA | 14 | WTR San Marino Team | Aprilia | 23 | 43m 13.577s |
| 14 | **Jakub Kornfeil** | CZE | 84 | Racing Team Germany | Aprilia | 23 | 43m 13.625s |
| 15 | **Lorenzo Savadori** | ITA | 32 | Matteoni CP Racing | Aprilia | 23 | 43m 26.431s |
| 16 | Marco Ravaioli | ITA | 72 | Lambretta Reparto Corse | Lambretta | 23 | 43m 43.340s |
| 17 | Simone Grotzkyj | ITA | 15 | Fontana Racing | Aprilia | 23 | 43m 45.113s |
| 18 | Luca Marconi | ITA | 87 | Ongetta Team | Aprilia | 23 | 44m 12.841s |
| | Tomoyoshi Koyama | JPN | 71 | Racing Team Germany | Aprilia | 14 | DNF |
| | Bradley Smith | GBR | 38 | Bancaja Aspar Team | Aprilia | 12 | DNF |
| | Adrian Martin | SPA | 26 | Aeroport de Castello - Ajo | Aprilia | 12 | DNF |
| | Zulfahmi Khairuddin | MAL | 63 | AirAsia-Sepang Int. Circuit | Aprilia | 11 | DNF |
| | Marcel Schrotter | GER | 78 | Interwetten Honda 125 | Honda | 8 | DNF |
| | Isaac Vinales | SPA | 55 | Lambretta Reparto Corse | Lambretta | 3 | DNF |
| | Louis Rossi | FRA | 69 | CBC Corse | Aprilia | 1 | DNF |

**Fastest lap:** Marc Marquez, on lap 7, 1m 48.672s, 86.783mph/139.664km/h (record).
**Previous lap record:** Bradley Smith, GBR (Aprilia), 1m 49.039s, 86.491mph/139.194km/h (2009).
**Event best maximum speed:** Efren Vasquez, 142.9mph/230.0km/h (free practice 1).

**Qualifying: Dry**
Air: 32° Humidity: 15% Ground: 47°

| | | |
|---|---|---|
| 1 | Marquez | 1m 48.124s |
| 2 | Terol | 1m 48.603s |
| 3 | Smith | 1m 49.026s |
| 4 | Cortese | 1m 49.110s |
| 5 | Espargaro | 1m 49.664s |
| 6 | Vazquez | 1m 49.769s |
| 7 | Salom | 1m 49.938s |
| 8 | Zarco | 1m 50.010s |
| 9 | Koyama | 1m 50.027s |
| 10 | Rabat | 1m 50.078s |
| 11 | Webb | 1m 50.095s |
| 12 | Folger | 1m 50.150s |
| 13 | Krummenacher | 1m 50.283s |
| 14 | Grotzkyj | 1m 50.384s |
| 15 | Moncayo | 1m 50.510s |
| 16 | Masbou | 1m 50.690s |
| 17 | Schrotter | 1m 50.992s |
| 18 | Kornfeil | 1m 51.031s |
| 19 | Iwema | 1m 51.181s |
| 20 | Martin | 1m 51.323s |
| 21 | Savadori | 1m 51.430s |
| 22 | Vinales | 1m 52.157s |
| 23 | Khairuddin | 1m 52.529s |
| 24 | Rossi | 1m 52.572s |
| 25 | Ravaioli | 1m 53.031s |
| 26 | Marconi | 1m 53.517s |

**Outside 107%**
*(but inside during free practice)*

| | | |
|---|---|---|
| | Turner | No Time |

**Fastest race laps**

| | | |
|---|---|---|
| 1 | Marquez | 1m 48.672s |
| 2 | Terol | 1m 48.912s |
| 3 | Cortese | 1m 49.438s |
| 4 | Smith | 1m 49.542s |
| 5 | Vazquez | 1m 49.726s |
| 6 | Espargaro | 1m 49.801s |
| 7 | Salom | 1m 49.895s |
| 8 | Koyama | 1m 49.992s |
| 9 | Rabat | 1m 50.055s |
| 10 | Webb | 1m 50.091s |
| 11 | Moncayo | 1m 50.220s |
| 12 | Krummenacher | 1m 50.414s |
| 13 | Folger | 1m 50.459s |
| 14 | Zarco | 1m 51.074s |
| 15 | Iwema | 1m 51.127s |
| 16 | Schrotter | 1m 51.267s |
| 17 | Grotzkyj | 1m 51.657s |
| 18 | Martin | 1m 51.677s |
| 19 | Kornfeil | 1m 51.892s |
| 20 | Savadori | 1m 52.181s |
| 21 | Vinales | 1m 52.391s |
| 22 | Khairuddin | 1m 52.545s |
| 23 | Ravaioli | 1m 52.846s |
| 24 | Marconi | 1m 53.201s |

**Championship Points**

| | | |
|---|---|---|
| 1 | Marquez | 172 |
| 2 | Terol | 168 |
| 3 | Espargaro | 167 |
| 4 | Smith | 115 |
| 5 | Cortese | 96 |
| 6 | Rabat | 90 |
| 7 | Koyama | 84 |
| 8 | Vazquez | 81 |
| 9 | Krummenacher | 72 |
| 10 | Webb | 58 |
| 11 | Zarco | 58 |
| 12 | Folger | 43 |
| 13 | Moncayo | 37 |
| 14 | Iwema | 33 |
| 15 | Salom | 25 |
| 16 | Masbou | 20 |
| 17 | Kornfeil | 16 |
| 18 | Grotzkyj | 14 |
| 19 | Martin | 14 |
| 20 | Schrotter | 14 |
| 21 | Fagerhaug | 7 |
| 22 | Kartheininger | 6 |
| 23 | Savadori | 5 |
| 24 | Khairuddin | 3 |
| 25 | Rossi | 2 |

**Constructors**

| | | |
|---|---|---|
| 1 | Derbi | 235 |
| 2 | Aprilia | 211 |
| 3 | Honda | 14 |
| 4 | KTM | 6 |
| 5 | Lambretta | 1 |

# SAN MARINO GRAND PRIX

FIM WORLD CHAMPIONSHIP · ROUND 12

MISANO CIRCUIT

Never mind the yellow flags,
Pedrosa was untouchable
at Misano. Lorenzo is just a
speck in the distance.
*Photos: Gold & Goose*

*Above:* Stricken, Tomizawa receives urgent attention on the track.

*Top centre right:* A shaken Scott Redding: lucky to escape serious injury.

*Above centre right:* Eskil Suter (centre) showed his 2012 MotoGP CRT prototype, with BMW power.

Photos: Gold & Goose

RACING and mortality are constant companions. Happily, it is only seldom that they collide. This is a tribute to safety improvements – in equipment and technology, circuit design and medical standards.

Against some injuries, however, there is no defence. There had been a shocking reminder at Indy of what happens when a fallen rider is struck by following motorcycles. So soon afterwards came grand prix racing's first fatal crash in seven years. Runaway Qatar Moto2 winner Shoya Tomizawa, lying fourth on lap 12 of 26, lost the front on the fastest corner of the track. By a quirk of physics, instead of sliding outwards, the bike touched the Astroturf, spun and bounced itself and the rider directly into the path of the pair following right behind. Alex de Angelis was the first to hit, Scott Redding next. He was already hard on the brakes, back wheel in the air, and he was thrown looping to land on his back almost halfway to the next corner.

Hit by two bikes, Tomizawa suffered grievous injuries. He was hastily removed (so hastily that one of the stretcher-bearers tripped in the gravel, and he was almost dropped) to be revived by a ventilator in the ambulance and transported to the medical centre, where his heart was beating weakly and irregularly. Transferred by road to the nearby Riccione hospital, he was certified dead soon afterwards.

By then, the MotoGP race had already started, after a silence of one minute had been observed on the grid in honour of Indy victim Peter Lenz.

The timing was important, for Italian legal reasons: in the same way, Ayrton Senna was artificially revived, then allowed to die in hospital, when he crashed at Imola in 1994, a gruesome charade that at least allows events to continue at the track. The truth remained the same: although everything possible was done to save the popular and friendly Japanese rider, his injuries were too terrible.

Yet there was a storm of criticism for the way the incident had been handled.

The first concerned the fact that the race had not been red-flagged, as such a serious incident seemed to require.

Race director Paul Butler's excuse was valid in itself: the track had been cleared of victims, debris and personnel in record time, and there was no reason why the race should not continue.

The second followed on: why was the track cleared so quickly? De Angelis had walked away. In Tomizawa's case, immediate removal to a fully equipped ambulance alongside the crash was justifiable. Not so the brusque removal of Redding. A spinal injury was highly possible after such an impact: surely he should have been examined more than perfunctorily where he lay.

As it turned out, the shocked British teenager escaped with nothing worse than a bad gash on his back; Butler's response to criticism was that the medical staff on the ground had to be left to make the decision on the spot. Correct enough, but not enough to still the continuing rumble of criticism, and a feeling that medical protocol might benefit from more rigorous standardisation, and that good taste would have been better served with a red flag.

The crash also focused attention again on trackside furniture. Some thought the artificial turf had caused the unusual movement of the bike, although this was hard to substantiate. The material, at least when dry, has more grip than grass, according to Hayden, to the extent that "sometimes you see the 125s using it as part of their line", but not an excessive amount. Of more concern to him and team-mate Stoner was the combination of Astroturf with paved run-off areas beyond, because of the way they give riders the chance to make a mistake and then recover from it. "A track should punish a rider for making a mistake," opined the Australian. This element encouraged recklessness, he suggested, urging a return to grass and then gravel. Track safety was designed with cars in mind, he said, but bike riders are at much greater risk of injury – the standards should be set for them.

Stoner had an outspoken weekend in general, as his drought of wins stretched to 13. Having tried the 2011-spec forks at Indy and suffered yet another copybook front-end crash, he had run out of options and wasn't going to get

anything more from the factory, which now was concentrating on 2011's bike for Rossi. "The bike works well. But it doesn't work great, and we just can't get any more out of it. My only chance is if some of the other riders have some sort of disaster," he said. He would soon prove himself to be a rotten prophet.

Blazing sunshine on the holiday coast augured well for the event, and the weather stayed benign, with the usual emphasis of Rossi-ness for the local hero, and swathes of yellow in the stands as usual.

The tragedy overshadowed what had otherwise been a balmy and relaxed weekend. In Rossi's back yard, the yellow was everywhere, along with plenty of hooting and good cheer. A good crowd of 50,918 turned out for the second GP on Italian soil. Oddly, Valentino's may not have been the most famous name on the grid: Ferruccio Lamborghini, grandson of the eponymous founder of the supercar firm, was racing as a wild-card in the Moto2 class. The 19-year-old national racer qualified an impressive 20th out of 39, and finished 23rd.

A good crowd of paddock insiders had turned out also two days before, to see the first of the 2012-generation production-based MotoGP machines. As the year before, with his Moto2 bike, it was former rider Eskil Suter hosting the display. The bike was very much like the Suter that is the most numerous chassis in the new class, small and in its present form below the 145kg minimum weight. The compact dimensions were possible because the BMW S1000RR engine he had used was of very similar size to the Moto2 Honda 600. It is much more powerful: 195 bhp in standard form, with Suter targeting 210 in a programme of development in 2011, backed by the well-financed Marc VDS Moto2 team, but not in any way, Suter insisted, by BMW itself.

Off-track, the annual 'Dedikato' charity event, run by the Gresini team in memory of the last GP fatality, Daijiro Kato, turned a mite sour with an on-stage spat between two Italian riders facing different circumstances. One was Melandri, who had been confirmed as being bound for Superbikes with

Sterilgarda Yamaha; the other was Capirossi, on the verge of agreement to move to Pramac Ducati for 2011, and about to start his 200th GP (second only to Alex Barros, on 245). Delegates included Rossi and Schwantz, and the surprised crowd heard Melandri attack the older rider for staying in MotoGP "only to be a number", denying space to younger riders. "You had better wear your mask when you sign the contract, because it will be like a highway robbery," he said. Capirossi's riposte was, "You are only jealous because you are 15 years younger than me [actually only nine], and you can only find a ride in World Superbikes."

Melandri's move was a series swap with Cal Crutchlow, whose two-year deal with the Tech 3 Yamaha squad was officially confirmed during the weekend (as was another year with Aspar Ducati for Barbera). The other Yamaha signing remained in abeyance, although Lorenzo's manager, Marcos Hirsch, was present, and the rider said, "I am sure something will happen soon."

## MOTOGP RACE – 28 laps

With the track running directly into two tight corners, it is important to qualify ahead of any potential collisions: national pride was also at stake in a titanic end-of-session struggle between Lorenzo and Pedrosa, the older rider winning pole. Stoner was third, suffering another front-end fall directly after his fast lap; Rossi headed row two from Spies and de Puniet, saying that the track's three hard braking areas were punishing his shoulder. "I lose 0.1 of a second at each one," he said.

Hayden was 14th with no real explanation, but serious concerns. In three previous visits, he hadn't got past the first corners unscathed: knocked off in 2007 and 2009, and pulling out with injuries in 2008. Now he was right in the firing line once more.

Again, he left without seeing the third corner, and this time he was the unwilling aggressor, forced to lift on the change of direction and running right into an unexpectedly slow Ca-

*Above:* Ferruccio Lamborghini – Moto2 new boy with a famous name.

*Top:* Hayden and Capirossi clash on turn two. The American has never got to the third corner here; his Italian victim suffered a tricky finger injury.

*Above centre:* Departing Gresini rider Melandri had his Yamaha Superbike contract confirmed.

*Above left:* Ducati's Stoner and crew chief Cristian Gabarrini were still looking puzzled.

*Photos: Gold & Goose*

pirossi. Both were out, the Italian missing the next race while a badly broken finger was elaborately mended.

They missed out on a processional race. As usual, Pedrosa was fast off the line and led into the first corner. He carried on pulling away from there, never remotely threatened and able to let a lead of five seconds at half-distance drop back to two at the flag. It was in no way exciting, but still a fine fourth win of the year, adding a frisson to the championship as he closed a little on Lorenzo, and underlining Honda's steadily building strength.

Lorenzo's afternoon was no more eventful. He passed Stoner before the first lap was done and carried on in a similar way to his countryman, just that little bit slower. Stoner stuck with him for a couple of laps, but by the eighth, the gap was up to one second and would continue to grow.

Rossi finished the first lap fourth and at first was losing time on Stoner, even as Dovizioso was closing on him, to become a close companion as Valentino's pace improved. By lap nine, the pair had caught the fading Stoner. Rossi's first pass on the Ducati was reversed at the next corner, but two laps later, on the 11th, he attacked again on the second-last corner, a right-hander, and managed to hold the place through the following left to head the Ducati over the line.

Next time around, Dovizioso was also past the Australian, relatively easily, and he chased Rossi from there to the end. At around the 20th lap, Dovi pushed harder and even looked as though he might get ahead. Rossi would have none of it, however, and by the end he was three seconds clear.

Stoner had plodded on as best he could and was another 12 seconds away by the end. He blamed the familiar problems: "Everything seemed okay until race day, but every time we try to get the front to stick better, we have problems with too little weight on the rear. We can't get the balance right."

Edwards had been sixth from the start and likewise was losing ground on Stoner. A long way behind, Spies had been bumped back to tenth in the first corners. He stayed there for four laps, then embarked on the most entertaining ride of the afternoon. Picking off Melandri and de Puniet in three corners, he took five laps to close a 1.7-second gap to his team-mate and one more to get ahead. He was more than five seconds away by the end.

Now Melandri was mixed up with de Puniet and Barbera, both of whom were ahead by lap eight, with Espargaro following on. The quartet stayed close and became a quintet as Bautista tagged on behind.

Soon after half-distance, they started shuffling. Melandri

got back in front while Bautista was picking his way through. Then de Puniet was pushed off by a strong attack from Barbera, dropping out of touch.

Bautista was still coming, and both he and Barbera passed Melandri on lap 22. The Suzuki kept on pulling away to secure eighth by better than 2.5 seconds; Barbera was next, then Melandri. Espargaro was out of touch at the end, with Aoyama closing right up at the finish and de Puniet three seconds adrift.

Marco Simoncelli was 14th, still half a minute behind after running right off the track and almost crashing on lap five; he had been lying sixth, ahead of Edwards. Kallio retired with 11 laps remaining.

## MOTO2 RACE – 26 laps

The turbulent entry list saw de Angelis take the place of Japan's Yusuki Teshima in the JiR team, Teshima himself having been a replacement for Pasini, who was back as a wild-card. Nieto was out after breaking his ankle and suffering medical complications at Indianapolis, replaced by Xavier Simeon; Mikki Ranseder was in for a second race, as permanent replacement for too-slow Vladimir Leonov in the Viessman-Kiefer team; and Tatsuya Yamaguchi had taken Vladimir Ivanov's place at Gresini.

Elias took his second pole of the year, with Redding alongside for a second successive front row. Simon and Cluzel completed row one; the patched-up Iannone (two fractures in his wrist) led the second.

A massive crash on the first tight corners was rather surprisingly avoided, and all 39 starters took off for a typical demonstration of Moto2 mayhem – ultra-close and spiced with danger.

Cluzel led away, displaced on lap two by Iannone, who galloped off, set for one of his trademark runaway wins. But it was not to be: he had jumped a few inches forward over the line at the start, and although he stopped again, it was still enough for a ride-through penalty. He came in at the end of lap three, leaving Tomizawa in the lead for three laps while Elias followed along, waiting his chance. It came on lap seven, and he took a lead he would hold to the end.

Corsi pushed through to second, and on lap 11 Simon was also ahead of Tomizawa, who was under increasing pressure from de Angelis, through impressively from 11th on the first lap, and Redding, with Cluzel now a little way behind.

The Japanese rider would not finish the next lap, meeting

*Left:* A sombre MotoGP podium, with flags at half-mast and no champagne. The riders have just heard the news about Tomizawa.

*Far left:* Dovi chases Rossi hard for the last podium position; Stoner loses ground behind.

*Below:* Moto2 winner Elias leads Corsi and the ill-fated Tomizawa early in the race.

*Photos:* Gold & Goose

his terrible fate on the exit from the near flat-out corner at the end of the back straight. De Angelis and Redding went out with him, the former amazingly walking away from what had, to the unscathed Cluzel, been a shockingly violent incident.

This took the thrill out of the race and spaced out the contenders. Now Elias was able to move steadily away, while Corsi ceded second to Simon on lap 15 and would continue to lose ground.

Simon closed on the slowing Elias over the last laps, but he was still almost two seconds behind at the flag.

By then, Luthi had come through from 14th on lap one, taking third from Corsi with three laps to go. Bradl had tagged on behind, but was still following Corsi at the end for fifth, ahead of the numbed Cluzel and Talmacsi, all three crossing the line within less than three-quarters of a second. Impressive replacement Simeon had been battling with Talmacsi, but ran off on the last lap, finishing 19th; Takahashi had also been with this group, but crashed out on lap 21.

Aegerter, Corti and then a distant Rolfo completed the top ten. Pasini crashed out, as did di Meglio and Gadea.

## 125cc RACE – 23 laps

After two bad races, title leader Marquez recaptured his demoralising form. A surprised Smith had just pipped him for pole, but the Englishman lost touch as a pack of four took off in the early laps, led first by Espargaro and on lap three by Marquez for the first time. Terol and Vazquez were the other two, the last-named intent on trying to help team-mate Espargaro's points score.

Terol took over up front on lap six for a six-lap spell and Vazquez faded, to come under pressure from Cortese, who had moved ahead of Smith. But then, as Marquez took over up front once more, the pair closed on the leaders again.

At two-thirds distance, Terol grabbed the lead back and raised the pace. Only Marquez was able to match him, and then with five laps left he pushed once more. It looked almost as though Terol had let him past, but if so, it was a bad mistake, because the teenager put the hammer down and pulled steadily away to win by better than two seconds, exploiting the better grip from his tyres in the closing lap, "the opposite from usual".

The battle for third was compelling as Smith caught up over the last eight laps. At the end, it was narrowly won by Vazquez, who abandoned his team-mate to defend his own position. Smith was a close fourth, then Cortese and Espargaro, half a second back.

A long way behind, Rabat held Koyama narrowly at bay almost all race. The top ten was rounded out by another three-man battle, Krummenacher through at the end, past Webb and Folger. Salom, Savadori and wild-card Bonati crashed out.

*Top left:* Stefan Bradl came through for fifth.

*Above left:* Elias and Luthi are given news of the fatal crash directly after the race.

*Left:* Second-place Simon gave Iannone a lift home. The Italian had led, been given a ride-through penalty, ridden through back into the points – and then broken down.

*Right:* Winner Marquez leads Espargaro, Terol, Vazquez and Cortese in the 125 race.

*Photo:* Gold & Goose

OFFICIAL TIMEKEEPER

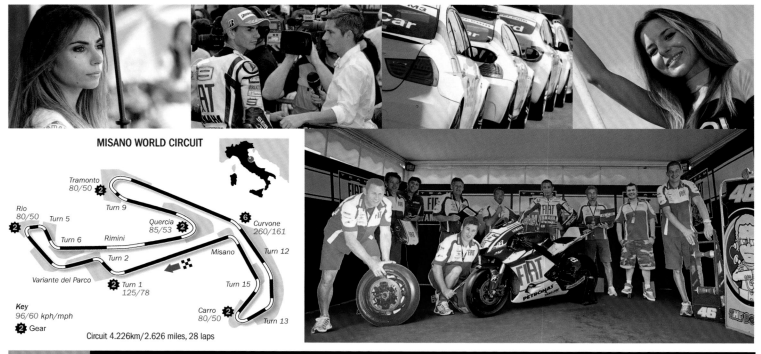

**MISANO WORLD CIRCUIT**

Tramonto 80/50
Rio 80/50
Turn 5
Turn 9
Quercia 85/53
Curvone 260/161
Turn 6
Rimini
Turn 2
Misano
Turn 12
Variante del Parco
Turn 1 125/78
Turn 15
Carro 80/50
Turn 13

**Key**
96/60 kph/mph
Gear

Circuit 4.226km/2.626 miles, 28 laps

## MotoGP

RACE DISTANCE: 28 laps, 73.526 miles/118.328 km · RACE WEATHER: Dry (air 27°, humidity 43%, track 39°)

| Pos. | Rider | Nat. | No. | Entrant | Machine | Tyres | Laps | Time & speed |
|---|---|---|---|---|---|---|---|---|
| 1 | **Dani Pedrosa** | SPA | 26 | Repsol Honda Team | Honda | B | 28 | 44m 22.059s 99.431mph/ 160.019km/h |
| 2 | **Jorge Lorenzo** | SPA | 99 | Fiat Yamaha Team | Yamaha | B | 28 | 44m 23.959s |
| 3 | **Valentino Rossi** | ITA | 46 | Fiat Yamaha Team | Yamaha | B | 28 | 44m 25.242s |
| 4 | **Andrea Dovizioso** | ITA | 4 | Repsol Honda Team | Honda | B | 28 | 44m 28.513s |
| 5 | **Casey Stoner** | AUS | 27 | Ducati Marlboro Team | Ducati | B | 28 | 44m 40.538s |
| 6 | **Ben Spies** | USA | 11 | Monster Yamaha Tech 3 | Yamaha | B | 28 | 44m 50.444s |
| 7 | **Colin Edwards** | USA | 5 | Monster Yamaha Tech 3 | Yamaha | B | 28 | 44m 56.993s |
| 8 | **Alvaro Bautista** | SPA | 19 | Rizla Suzuki MotoGP | Suzuki | B | 28 | 45m 00.216s |
| 9 | **Hector Barbera** | SPA | 40 | Paginas Amarillas Aspar | Ducati | B | 28 | 45m 03.002s |
| 10 | **Marco Melandri** | ITA | 33 | San Carlo Honda Gresini | Honda | B | 28 | 45m 04.436s |
| 11 | **Aleix Espargaro** | SPA | 41 | Pramac Racing Team | Ducati | B | 28 | 45m 07.965s |
| 12 | **Hiroshi Aoyama** | JPN | 7 | Interwetten Honda MotoGP | Honda | B | 28 | 45m 08.453s |
| 13 | **Randy de Puniet** | FRA | 14 | LCR Honda MotoGP | Honda | B | 28 | 45m 12.540s |
| 14 | **Marco Simoncelli** | ITA | 58 | San Carlo Honda Gresini | Honda | B | 28 | 45m 45.202s |
| | Mika Kallio | FIN | 36 | Pramac Racing Team | Ducati | B | 17 | DNF |
| | Nicky Hayden | USA | 69 | Ducati Marlboro Team | Ducati | B | 3 | DNF |
| | Loris Capirossi | ITA | 65 | Rizla Suzuki MotoGP | Suzuki | B | 0 | DNF |

**Fastest lap:** Dani Pedrosa, on lap 7, 1m 34.340s, 100.204mph/161.263km/h (record).

**Previous lap record:** Valentino Rossi, ITA (Yamaha), 1m 34.746s, 99.775mph/160.572km/h (2009).

**Event best maximum speed:** Dani Pedrosa, 174.2mph/280.4km/h (free practice 2).

### Qualifying
Weather: Dry
Air Temp: 26° Humidity: 33°
Track Temp: 42°

| | | |
|---|---|---|
| 1 | Pedrosa | 1m 33.948s |
| 2 | Lorenzo | 1m 34.256s |
| 3 | Stoner | 1m 34.397s |
| 4 | Rossi | 1m 34.470s |
| 5 | Spies | 1m 34.472s |
| 6 | de Puniet | 1m 34.751s |
| 7 | Edwards | 1m 34.782s |
| 8 | Dovizioso | 1m 34.826s |
| 9 | Simoncelli | 1m 34.934s |
| 10 | Melandri | 1m 35.018s |
| 11 | Capirossi | 1m 35.096s |
| 12 | Barbera | 1m 35.259s |
| 13 | Aoyama | 1m 35.286s |
| 14 | Hayden | 1m 35.303s |
| 15 | Espargaro | 1m 35.438s |
| 16 | Bautista | 1m 35.629s |
| 17 | Kallio | 1m 35.724s |

### Fastest race laps

| | | |
|---|---|---|
| 1 | Pedrosa | 1m 34.340s |
| 2 | Rossi | 1m 34.461s |
| 3 | Dovizioso | 1m 34.562s |
| 4 | Lorenzo | 1m 34.613s |
| 5 | Stoner | 1m 34.835s |
| 6 | Bautista | 1m 35.240s |
| 7 | Spies | 1m 35.537s |
| 8 | Edwards | 1m 35.546s |
| 9 | Simoncelli | 1m 35.553s |
| 10 | Barbera | 1m 35.644s |
| 11 | Espargaro | 1m 35.694s |
| 12 | Melandri | 1m 35.727s |
| 13 | Aoyama | 1m 35.834s |
| 14 | de Puniet | 1m 35.905s |
| 15 | Kallio | 1m 36.240s |
| 16 | Hayden | 1m 52.418s |

### Championship Points

| | | |
|---|---|---|
| 1 | Lorenzo | 271 |
| 2 | Pedrosa | 208 |
| 3 | Dovizioso | 139 |
| 4 | Rossi | 130 |
| 5 | Stoner | 130 |
| 6 | Spies | 120 |
| 7 | N. Hayden | 109 |
| 8 | de Puniet | 81 |
| 9 | Melandri | 67 |
| 10 | Edwards | 66 |
| 11 | Simoncelli | 65 |
| 12 | Barbera | 61 |
| 13 | Espargaro | 44 |
| 14 | Bautista | 41 |
| 15 | Capirossi | 41 |
| 16 | Kallio | 31 |
| 17 | Aoyama | 26 |
| 18 | de Angelis | 11 |
| 19 | R. Hayden | 5 |
| 20 | Akiyoshi | 4 |
| 21 | Yoshikawa | 1 |

### Team Points

| | | |
|---|---|---|
| 1 | Fiat Yamaha Team | 402 |
| 2 | Repsol Honda Team | 347 |
| 3 | Ducati Marlboro Team | 239 |
| 4 | Monster Yamaha Tech 3 | 186 |
| 5 | San Carlo Honda Gresini | 132 |
| 6 | LCR Honda MotoGP | 86 |
| 7 | Rizla Suzuki MotoGP | 82 |
| 8 | Pramac Racing Team | 75 |
| 9 | Paginas Amarillas Aspar | 61 |
| 10 | Interwetten Honda MotoGP | 41 |

### Constructor Points

| | | |
|---|---|---|
| 1 | Yamaha | 280 |
| 2 | Honda | 245 |
| 3 | Ducati | 170 |
| 4 | Suzuki | 64 |

| Grid order | 1 | 2 | 3 | 4 | 5 | 6 | 7 | 8 | 9 | 10 | 11 | 12 | 13 | 14 | 15 | 16 | 17 | 18 | 19 | 20 | 21 | 22 | 23 | 24 | 25 | 26 | 27 | 28 | |
|---|---|---|---|---|---|---|---|---|---|---|---|---|---|---|---|---|---|---|---|---|---|---|---|---|---|---|---|---|---|
| 26 PEDROSA | 26 | 26 | 26 | 26 | 26 | 26 | 26 | 26 | 26 | 26 | 26 | 26 | 26 | 26 | 26 | 26 | 26 | 26 | 26 | 26 | 26 | 26 | 26 | 26 | 26 | 26 | 26 | 26 | 1 |
| 99 LORENZO | 99 | 99 | 99 | 99 | 99 | 99 | 99 | 99 | 99 | 99 | 99 | 99 | 99 | 99 | 99 | 99 | 99 | 99 | 99 | 99 | 99 | 99 | 99 | 99 | 99 | 99 | 99 | 99 | 2 |
| 27 STONER | 27 | 27 | 27 | 27 | 27 | 27 | 27 | 27 | 27 | 27 | 46 | 46 | 46 | 46 | 46 | 46 | 46 | 46 | 46 | 46 | 46 | 46 | 46 | 46 | 46 | 46 | 46 | 46 | 3 |
| 46 ROSSI | 46 | 46 | 46 | 46 | 46 | 46 | 46 | 46 | 46 | 46 | 27 | 4 | 4 | 4 | 4 | 4 | 4 | 4 | 4 | 4 | 4 | 4 | 4 | 4 | 4 | 4 | 4 | 4 | 4 |
| 11 SPIES | 4 | 4 | 4 | 4 | 4 | 4 | 4 | 4 | 4 | 4 | 4 | 27 | 27 | 27 | 27 | 27 | 27 | 27 | 27 | 27 | 27 | 27 | 27 | 27 | 27 | 27 | 27 | 27 | 5 |
| 14 de PUNIET | 5 | 58 | 58 | 58 | 5 | 5 | 5 | 5 | 5 | 5 | 5 | 11 | 11 | 11 | 11 | 11 | 11 | 11 | 11 | 11 | 11 | 11 | 11 | 11 | 11 | 11 | 11 | 11 | 6 |
| 5 EDWARDS | 58 | 5 | 5 | 5 | 14 | 11 | 11 | 11 | 11 | 11 | 11 | 5 | 5 | 5 | 5 | 5 | 5 | 5 | 5 | 5 | 5 | 5 | 5 | 5 | 5 | 5 | 5 | 7 | 7 |
| 4 DOVIZIOSO | 14 | 14 | 14 | 14 | 33 | 33 | 33 | 14 | 14 | 14 | 14 | 14 | 14 | 14 | 14 | 33 | 33 | 33 | 19 | 19 | 19 | 19 | 19 | 19 | 19 | 19 | 19 | 19 | 8 |
| 58 SIMONCELLI | 33 | 33 | 33 | 33 | 11 | 14 | 14 | 40 | 40 | 40 | 40 | 40 | 40 | 33 | 33 | 14 | 19 | 40 | 40 | 40 | 40 | 40 | 40 | 33 | 33 | 33 | 40 | 9 | |
| 33 MELANDRI | 11 | 11 | 11 | 11 | 40 | 40 | 40 | 33 | 33 | 33 | 33 | 33 | 33 | 40 | 40 | 40 | 40 | 19 | 33 | 33 | 33 | 33 | 33 | 40 | 40 | 40 | 33 | 10 | |
| 65 CAPIROSSI | 40 | 40 | 40 | 40 | 41 | 41 | 41 | 41 | 41 | 41 | 41 | 41 | 41 | 41 | 41 | 19 | 41 | 41 | 14 | 14 | 14 | 14 | 14 | 14 | 41 | 41 | 41 | 11 | |
| 40 BARBERA | 7 | 41 | 41 | 41 | 7 | 7 | 7 | 7 | 7 | 19 | 19 | 19 | 19 | 19 | 19 | 41 | 14 | 14 | 41 | 41 | 41 | 41 | 41 | 7 | 7 | 7 | 7 | 12 | |
| 7 AOYAMA | 41 | 7 | 7 | 7 | 36 | 19 | 19 | 19 | 19 | 7 | 7 | 7 | 7 | 7 | 7 | 7 | 7 | 7 | 7 | 7 | 7 | 7 | 7 | 14 | 14 | 14 | 14 | 13 | |
| 69 HAYDEN | 19 | 19 | 19 | 36 | 19 | 36 | 36 | 36 | 36 | 36 | 36 | 36 | 36 | 36 | 36 | 36 | 36 | 58 | 58 | 58 | 58 | 58 | 58 | 58 | 58 | 58 | 58 | 14 | |
| 41 ESPARGARO | 36 | 36 | 36 | 19 | 58 | 58 | 58 | 58 | 58 | 58 | 58 | 58 | 58 | 58 | 58 | 58 | | | | | | | | | | | | | |
| 19 BAUTISTA | 69 | 69 | 69 | | | | | | | | | | | | | | | | | | | | | | | | | | |
| 36 KALLIO | | | | | | | | | | | | | | | | | | | | | | | | | | | | | |

## Moto2

RACE DISTANCE: 26 laps, 68.274 miles/109.876 km · RACE WEATHER: Dry (air 26°, humidity 37%, track 37°)

| Pos. | Rider | Nat. | No. | Entrant | Machine | Laps | Time & Speed |
|---|---|---|---|---|---|---|---|
| 1 | **Toni Elias** | SPA | 24 | Gresini Racing Moto2 | Moriwaki | 26 | 43m 33.996s (mph/km/h) 94.027/151.321 |
| 2 | **Julian Simon** | SPA | 60 | Mapfre Aspar Team | Suter | 26 | 43m 35.965s |
| 3 | **Thomas Luthi** | SWI | 12 | Interwetten Moriwaki Moto2 | Moriwaki | 26 | 43m 45.913s |
| 4 | **Simone Corsi** | ITA | 3 | JIR Moto2 | MotoBI | 26 | 43m 49.405s |
| 5 | **Stefan Bradl** | GER | 65 | Viessmann Kiefer Racing | Suter | 26 | 43m 50.215s |
| 6 | **Jules Cluzel** | FRA | 16 | Forward Racing | Suter | 26 | 43m 50.672s |
| 7 | **Gabor Talmacsi** | HUN | 2 | Fimmco Speed Up | Speed Up | 26 | 43m 50.848s |
| 8 | **Dominique Aegerter** | SWI | 77 | Technomag-CIP | Suter | 26 | 43m 52.326s |
| 9 | **Claudio Corti** | ITA | 71 | Forward Racing | Suter | 26 | 43m 54.646s |
| 10 | **Roberto Rolfo** | ITA | 44 | Italtrans S.T.R. | Suter | 26 | 44m 03.674s |
| 11 | **Yonny Hernandez** | COL | 68 | Blusens-STX | BQR-Moto2 | 26 | 44m 06.716s |
| 12 | **Ratthapark Wilairot** | THA | 14 | Thai Honda PTT Singha SAG | Bimota | 26 | 44m 09.094s |
| 13 | **Raffaele de Rosa** | ITA | 35 | Tech 3 Racing | Tech 3 | 26 | 44m 09.424s |
| 14 | **Michael Ranseder** | AUT | 56 | Vector Kiefer Racing | Suter | 26 | 44m 09.929s |
| 15 | **Lukas Pesek** | CZE | 52 | Matteoni CP Racing | Moriwaki | 26 | 44m 11.008s |
| 16 | Hector Faubel | SPA | 55 | Marc VDS Racing Team | Suter | 26 | 44m 14.946s |
| 17 | Anthony West | AUS | 8 | MZ Racing Team | MZ-RE Honda | 26 | 44m 15.748s |
| 18 | Axel Pons | SPA | 80 | Tenerife 40 Pons | Pons Kalex | 26 | 44m 15.874s |
| 19 | Xavier Simeon | BEL | 19 | Holiday Gym G22 | Moriwaki | 26 | 44m 21.562s |
| 20 | Ricard Cardus | SPA | 4 | Maquinza-SAG Team | Bimota | 26 | 44m 31.022s |
| 21 | Joan Olive | SPA | 5 | Jack & Jones by A.Banderas | FTR | 26 | 44m 31.115s |
| 22 | Valentin Debise | FRA | 53 | WTR San Marino Team | ADV | 26 | 44m 34.829s |
| 23 | Ferruccio Lamborghini | ITA | 70 | Forward Racing | Suter | 26 | 44m 36.312s |
| 24 | Kenny Noyes | USA | 9 | Jack & Jones by A.Banderas | Promoharris | 26 | 44m 39.791s |
| 25 | Tatsuya Yamaguchi | JPN | 99 | Gresini Racing Moto2 | Moriwaki | 26 | 44m 43.973s |
| 26 | Yannick Guerra | SPA | 88 | Holiday Gym G22 | Moriwaki | 26 | 44m 50.516s |
| 27 | Mashel Al Naimi | QAT | 95 | Blusens-STX | BQR-Moto2 | 26 | 44m 50.559s |
| 28 | Niccolo Canepa | ITA | 59 | M Racing | Bimota | 26 | 44m 51.475s |
| 29 | Robertino Pietri | VEN | 39 | Italtrans S.T.R. | Suter | 26 | 45m 15.035s |
| | Andrea Iannone | ITA | 29 | Fimmco Speed Up | Speed Up | 23 | DNF |
| | Alex Baldolini | ITA | 25 | Caretta Technology Race Dept. | I.C.P. | 23 | DNF |
| | Yuki Takahashi | JPN | 72 | Tech 3 Racing | Tech 3 | 21 | DNF |
| | Sergio Gadea | SPA | 40 | Tenerife 40 Pons | Pons Kalex | 14 | DNF |
| | Shoya Tomizawa | JPN | 48 | Technomag-CIP | Suter | 11 | DNF |
| | Alex de Angelis | RSM | 15 | JIR Moto2 | MotoBI | 11 | DNF |
| | Scott Redding | GBR | 45 | Marc VDS Racing Team | Suter | 11 | DNF |
| | Mattia Pasini | ITA | 75 | Italtrans S.T.R. | Suter | 10 | DNF |
| | Mike di Meglio | FRA | 63 | Mapfre Aspar Team | Suter | 7 | DNF |

**Fastest lap:** Alex de Angelis, on lap 8, 1m 39.430s, 95.075mph/153.008km/h (record).
**Previous lap record:** New category.
**Event best maximum speed:** Alex de Angelis, 149.9mph/241.3km/h (warm up).

**Qualifying:** Dry
Air: 26° Humidity: 31% Ground: 42°

| | | |
|---|---|---|
| 1 | Elias | 1m 38.991s |
| 2 | Redding | 1m 39.035s |
| 3 | Simon | 1m 39.280s |
| 4 | Cluzel | 1m 39.413s |
| 5 | Iannone | 1m 39.426s |
| 6 | Corsi | 1m 39.664s |
| 7 | de Angelis | 1m 39.686s |
| 8 | Tomizawa | 1m 39.778s |
| 9 | Pasini | 1m 39.856s |
| 10 | Talmacsi | 1m 39.857s |
| 11 | Faubel | 1m 40.045s |
| 12 | Aegerter | 1m 40.047s |
| 13 | Takahashi | 1m 40.075s |
| 14 | Corti | 1m 40.101s |
| 15 | Luthi | 1m 40.101s |
| 16 | Simeon | 1m 40.153s |
| 17 | Bradl | 1m 40.164s |
| 18 | Gadea | 1m 40.184s |
| 19 | di Meglio | 1m 40.201s |
| 20 | Lamborghini | 1m 40.290s |
| 21 | Baldolini | 1m 40.523s |
| 22 | Ranseder | 1m 40.531s |
| 23 | Hernandez | 1m 40.579s |
| 24 | Rolfo | 1m 40.677s |
| 25 | Abraham | 1m 40.732s |
| 26 | Pons | 1m 40.751s |
| 27 | Pietri | 1m 40.880s |
| 28 | de Rosa | 1m 40.930s |
| 29 | Yamaguchi | 1m 41.074s |
| 30 | Pesek | 1m 41.147s |
| 31 | Debise | 1m 41.178s |
| 32 | Wilairot | 1m 41.269s |
| 33 | Canepa | 1m 41.522s |
| 34 | West | 1m 41.526s |
| 35 | Noyes | 1m 41.794s |
| 36 | Olive | 1m 41.853s |
| 37 | Cardus | 1m 42.061s |
| 38 | Al Naimi | 1m 42.657s |
| 39 | Guerra | 1m 42.827s |

**Fastest race laps**

| | | |
|---|---|---|
| 1 | de Angelis | 1m 39.430s |
| 2 | Redding | 1m 39.618s |
| 3 | Simon | 1m 39.703s |
| 4 | Tomizawa | 1m 39.730s |
| 5 | Elias | 1m 39.764s |
| 6 | Bradl | 1m 39.872s |
| 7 | Corsi | 1m 39.877s |
| 8 | Cluzel | 1m 39.911s |
| 9 | Iannone | 1m 40.108s |
| 10 | Takahashi | 1m 40.130s |
| 11 | Luthi | 1m 40.131s |
| 12 | Corti | 1m 40.140s |
| 13 | Pasini | 1m 40.195s |
| 14 | Talmacsi | 1m 40.196s |
| 15 | di Meglio | 1m 40.253s |
| 16 | Simeon | 1m 40.285s |
| 17 | Aegerter | 1m 40.328s |
| 18 | Ranseder | 1m 40.369s |
| 19 | Wilairot | 1m 40.560s |
| 20 | Gadea | 1m 40.571s |
| 21 | Rolfo | 1m 40.710s |
| 22 | Hernandez | 1m 40.743s |
| 23 | Pesek | 1m 40.833s |
| 24 | Faubel | 1m 40.867s |
| 25 | West | 1m 40.907s |
| 26 | Baldolini | 1m 41.004s |
| 27 | de Rosa | 1m 41.044s |
| 28 | Pons | 1m 41.050s |
| 29 | Cardus | 1m 41.467s |
| 30 | Lamborghini | 1m 41.542s |
| 31 | Olive | 1m 41.769s |
| 32 | Debise | 1m 41.801s |
| 33 | Pietri | 1m 41.893s |
| 34 | Al Naimi | 1m 41.987s |
| 35 | Noyes | 1m 42.013s |
| 36 | Yamaguchi | 1m 42.018s |
| 37 | Guerra | 1m 42.261s |
| 38 | Canepa | 1m 42.519s |

**Championship Points**

| | | |
|---|---|---|
| 1 | Elias | 211 |
| 2 | Simon | 128 |
| 3 | Luthi | 124 |
| 4 | Iannone | 119 |
| 5 | Corsi | 97 |
| 6 | Cluzel | 84 |
| 7 | Tomizawa | 82 |
| 8 | Talmacsi | 79 |
| 9 | Takahashi | 72 |
| 10 | Gadea | 59 |
| 11 | Debon | 46 |
| 12 | Rolfo | 43 |
| 13 | Nieto | 41 |
| 14 | Redding | 39 |
| 15 | Bradl | 36 |
| 16 | Aegerter | 36 |
| 17 | Abraham | 33 |
| 18 | Wilairot | 29 |
| 19 | Hernandez | 27 |
| 20 | di Meglio | 21 |
| 21 | Noyes | 18 |
| 22 | West | 17 |
| 23 | Baldolini | 14 |
| 24 | Pasini | 12 |
| 25 | Corti | 11 |
| 26 | de Angelis | 11 |
| 27 | Cudlin | 9 |
| 28 | Simeon | 9 |
| 29 | Faubel | 8 |
| 30 | Di Salvo | 7 |
| 31 | Pesek | 5 |
| 32 | de Rosa | 4 |
| 33 | Ranseder | 2 |
| 34 | Pons | 2 |
| 35 | Ivanov | 2 |
| 36 | Tode | 2 |
| 37 | Teshima | 1 |

**Constructors**

| | | |
|---|---|---|
| 1 | Moriwaki | 236 |
| 2 | Suter | 196 |
| 3 | Speed Up | 144 |
| 4 | MotoBI | 99 |
| 5 | FTR | 84 |
| 6 | Tech 3 | 75 |
| 7 | Pons Kalex | 68 |
| 8 | Bimota | 29 |
| 9 | BQR-Moto2 | 27 |
| 10 | Promoharris | 18 |
| 11 | MZ-RE Honda | 17 |
| 12 | I.C.P. | 14 |
| 13 | Force GP210 | 11 |
| 14 | RSV | 10 |

## 125cc

RACE DISTANCE: 23 laps, 60.396 miles/97.198 km · RACE WEATHER: Dry (air 25°, humidity 35%, track 34°)

| Pos. | Rider | Nat. | No. | Entrant | Machine | Laps | Time & Speed |
|---|---|---|---|---|---|---|---|
| 1 | **Marc Marquez** | SPA | 93 | Red Bull Ajo Motorsport | Derbi | 23 | 39m 56.117s (mph/km/h) 90.741/146.033 |
| 2 | **Nicolas Terol** | SPA | 40 | Bancaja Aspar Team | Aprilia | 23 | 39m 58.302s |
| 3 | **Efren Vazquez** | SPA | 7 | Tuenti Racing | Derbi | 23 | 40m 01.745s |
| 4 | **Bradley Smith** | GBR | 38 | Bancaja Aspar Team | Aprilia | 23 | 40m 02.029s |
| 5 | **Sandro Cortese** | GER | 11 | Avant Mitsubishi Ajo | Derbi | 23 | 40m 02.495s |
| 6 | **Pol Espargaro** | SPA | 44 | Tuenti Racing | Derbi | 23 | 40m 03.208s |
| 7 | **Esteve Rabat** | SPA | 12 | Blusens-STX | Aprilia | 23 | 40m 19.952s |
| 8 | **Tomoyoshi Koyama** | JPN | 71 | Racing Team Germany | Aprilia | 23 | 40m 20.008s |
| 9 | **Randy Krummenacher** | SWI | 35 | Stipa-Molenaar Racing GP | Aprilia | 23 | 40m 26.031s |
| 10 | **Danny Webb** | GBR | 99 | Andalucia Cajasol | Aprilia | 23 | 40m 26.086s |
| 11 | **Jonas Folger** | GER | 94 | Ongetta Team | Aprilia | 23 | 40m 26.290s |
| 12 | **Johann Zarco** | FRA | 14 | WTR San Marino Team | Aprilia | 23 | 40m 34.528s |
| 13 | **Alberto Moncayo** | SPA | 23 | Andalucia Cajasol | Aprilia | 23 | 40m 34.806s |
| 14 | **Simone Grotzkyj** | ITA | 15 | Fontana Racing | Aprilia | 23 | 40m 42.611s |
| 15 | **Adrian Martin** | SPA | 26 | Aeroport de Castello - Ajo | Aprilia | 23 | 40m 42.686s |
| 16 | Jakub Kornfeil | CZE | 84 | Racing Team Germany | Aprilia | 23 | 40m 56.386s |
| 17 | Marcel Schrotter | GER | 78 | Interwetten Honda 125 | Honda | 23 | 40m 57.825s |
| 18 | Armando Pontone | ITA | 97 | Junior GP FMI | Aprilia | 23 | 41m 03.494s |
| 19 | Louis Rossi | FRA | 69 | CBC Corse | Aprilia | 23 | 41m 03.531s |
| 20 | Alessandro Tonucci | ITA | 95 | Junior GP Racing Team FMI | Aprilia | 23 | 41m 03.604s |
| 21 | Jasper Iwema | NED | 53 | CBC Corse | Aprilia | 23 | 41m 04.022s |
| 22 | Tommaso Gabrielli | ITA | 96 | Racing Team Gabrielli | Aprilia | 23 | 41m 25.785s |
| 23 | Marco Ravaioli | ITA | 72 | Lambretta Reparto Corse | Lambretta | 23 | 41m 26.735s |
| 24 | Francesco Mauriello | ITA | 76 | Team Semprucci | Aprilia | 23 | 41m 26.758s |
| 25 | Joan Perello | SPA | 36 | Lambretta Reparto Corse | Lambretta | 22 | 40m 09.448s |
| | Luca Marconi | ITA | 87 | Ongetta Team | Aprilia | 16 | DNF |
| | Sturla Fagerhaug | NOR | 50 | AirAsia-Sepang Int. Circuit | Aprilia | 14 | DNF |
| | Lorenzo Savadori | ITA | 32 | Matteoni CP Racing | Aprilia | 12 | DNF |
| | Giovanni Bonati | ITA | 79 | Junior GP FMI | Aprilia | 12 | DNF |
| | Alexis Masbou | FRA | 5 | Ongetta Team | Aprilia | 8 | DNF |
| | Luis Salom | SPA | 39 | Stipa-Molenaar Racing GP | Aprilia | 7 | DNF |
| | Zulfahmi Khairuddin | MAL | 63 | AirAsia-Sepang Int. Circuit | Aprilia | 1 | DNF |

**Fastest lap:** Marc Marquez, on lap 19, 1m 43.195s, 91.606mph/147.425km/h (record).
**Previous lap record:** Pol Espargaro, SPA (Derbi), 1m 43.613s, 91.236mph/146.830km/h (2009).
**Event best maximum speed:** Efren Vasquez, 126.9mph/204.3km/h (free practice 2).

**Qualifying:** Dry
Air: 25° Humidity: 35% Ground: 42°

| | | |
|---|---|---|
| 1 | Smith | 1m 43.329s |
| 2 | Marquez | 1m 43.487s |
| 3 | Terol | 1m 43.644s |
| 4 | Espargaro | 1m 43.809s |
| 5 | Koyama | 1m 44.272s |
| 6 | Cortese | 1m 44.341s |
| 7 | Vazquez | 1m 44.479s |
| 8 | Rabat | 1m 44.561s |
| 9 | Webb | 1m 44.816s |
| 10 | Zarco | 1m 44.929s |
| 11 | Folger | 1m 44.975s |
| 12 | Salom | 1m 45.020s |
| 13 | Krummenacher | 1m 45.103s |
| 14 | Moncayo | 1m 45.166s |
| 15 | Grotzkyj | 1m 45.217s |
| 16 | Martin | 1m 45.661s |
| 17 | Iwema | 1m 46.048s |
| 18 | Schrotter | 1m 46.309s |
| 19 | Kornfeil | 1m 46.366s |
| 20 | Khairuddin | 1m 46.368s |
| 21 | Rossi | 1m 46.557s |
| 22 | Pontone | 1m 46.916s |
| 23 | Savadori | 1m 46.932s |
| 24 | Marconi | 1m 46.940s |
| 25 | Tonucci | 1m 47.235s |
| 26 | Mauriello | 1m 47.455s |
| 27 | Gabrielli | 1m 47.732s |
| 28 | Perello | 1m 47.809s |
| 29 | Ravaioli | 1m 47.973s |
| 30 | Masbou | 1m 48.111s |
| 31 | Fagerhaug | 1m 48.324s |
| 32 | Bonati | 1m 48.346s |

**Fastest race laps**

| | | |
|---|---|---|
| 1 | Marquez | 1m 43.195s |
| 2 | Terol | 1m 43.544s |
| 3 | Cortese | 1m 43.546s |
| 4 | Smith | 1m 43.550s |
| 5 | Espargaro | 1m 43.566s |
| 6 | Vazquez | 1m 43.580s |
| 7 | Koyama | 1m 44.504s |
| 8 | Rabat | 1m 44.514s |
| 9 | Krummenacher | 1m 44.565s |
| 10 | Webb | 1m 44.744s |
| 11 | Folger | 1m 44.770s |
| 12 | Moncayo | 1m 44.809s |
| 13 | Zarco | 1m 45.051s |
| 14 | Salom | 1m 45.108s |
| 15 | Martin | 1m 45.153s |
| 16 | Grotzkyj | 1m 45.186s |
| 17 | Kornfeil | 1m 45.589s |
| 18 | Tonucci | 1m 45.700s |
| 19 | Schrotter | 1m 45.815s |
| 20 | Pontone | 1m 45.879s |
| 21 | Savadori | 1m 45.887s |
| 22 | Rossi | 1m 45.931s |
| 23 | Iwema | 1m 45.933s |
| 24 | Mauriello | 1m 46.417s |
| 25 | Gabrielli | 1m 46.492s |
| 26 | Ravaioli | 1m 46.620s |
| 27 | Marconi | 1m 47.074s |
| 28 | Bonati | 1m 47.454s |
| 29 | Fagerhaug | 1m 47.515s |
| 30 | Masbou | 1m 47.544s |
| 31 | Perello | 1m 47.917s |
| 32 | Khairuddin | 1m 57.718s |

**Championship Points**

| | | |
|---|---|---|
| 1 | Marquez | 197 |
| 2 | Terol | 188 |
| 3 | Espargaro | 177 |
| 4 | Smith | 128 |
| 5 | Cortese | 107 |
| 6 | Rabat | 99 |
| 7 | Vazquez | 97 |
| 8 | Koyama | 92 |
| 9 | Krummenacher | 79 |
| 10 | Webb | 64 |
| 11 | Zarco | 62 |
| 12 | Folger | 48 |
| 13 | Moncayo | 40 |
| 14 | Iwema | 33 |
| 15 | Salom | 25 |
| 16 | Masbou | 20 |
| 17 | Kornfeil | 16 |
| 18 | Grotzkyj | 16 |
| 19 | Martin | 15 |
| 20 | Schrotter | 14 |
| 21 | Fagerhaug | 7 |
| 22 | Kartheininger | 6 |
| 23 | Savadori | 5 |
| 24 | Khairuddin | 3 |
| 25 | Rossi | 2 |

**Constructors**

| | | |
|---|---|---|
| 1 | Derbi | 260 |
| 2 | Aprilia | 231 |
| 3 | Honda | 14 |
| 4 | KTM | 6 |
| 5 | Lambretta | 1 |

Winner Stoner wasted no time in getting clear of Lorenzo, Pedrosa and Hayden (hidden). Spies is next, then Simoncelli, Dovizioso and Barbera, and only then Rossi.
*Photos: Gold & Goose*

FIM WORLD CHAMPIONSHIP · ROUND 13

# ARAGÓN GRAND PRIX

ARAGÓN CIRCUIT

Above: King Juan Carlos (behind the bike) joined all involved in a heartfelt tribute to Tomizawa.

Above right: Inmotec – at the track, but on display only.

Right: Bautista was eighth for a third race in a row.

Far right, top: Simoncelli leads Rossi in the early stages.

Far right, bottom: De Puniet bails out.

Photos: Gold & Goose

WITH the second successive cancellation of the proposed Hungarian GP came an unprecedented fourth round in Spain. By some irony of fate, the round at the new Aragon Motorland circuit broke a run of 12 GPs in a row where there had been Spanish winners in all three classes, thanks to Stoner and Iannone. Not that it made much difference, because by the end of Sunday's racing, it had become mathematically impossible for anyone but a Spanish rider to win the major class, and extremely unlikely in either of the others. With five races left to run, it only remained to be seen which Spaniards would actually take the honours.

The track itself won immediate plaudits: a fantastic facility built with public funds at a cost of 50.5-million euros. The nearby small town of Alcaniz had a traditional street-race circuit; on this flimsy basis, a consortium of provincial, regional and municipal authorities had founded a thoroughly modern type of racetrack-plus, incorporating "technology, sport, leisure and culture". Opened just over a year previously, it all looked very raw, and a massive Friday-night traffic jam didn't bode well – but it was caused only because a new bypass was being opened, so the circuit access roads were ready literally just in time.

Apart from a long lap of 5.078km, including a straight claimed to be 1.7km long, but closer to just 1km, and incorporating several other shorter track options, the facility boasts a kart track and off-road facilities for supermotard, and both auto- and moto-cross. There is also the Norman Foster designed Technology Centre, attached to the University of Zaragoza up on the hillside, with leisure and shopping facilities yet to come. The surroundings are rural in the extreme: hilly, dry and thinly populated, and with a stony scenic beauty that reflects what some called "the real Spain". The downside was a serious shortage of accommodation, with a

number of paddock folk facing a drive to and from the circuit of an hour or much more.

The riders were in almost universal approval: the Herman Tilke designed layout had a variety of fast and slow corners, and included a tight, but wide first-gear hairpin, as well as plenty of elevation changes and even a sort of simulation of Laguna's Corkscrew. It was, said Rossi, "a typical Tilke track, more like Sepang than Istanbul." Stoner, however, was one who fell short of total admiration: it was essentially a car circuit, with few overtaking opportunities other than the last turn, he said. "I don't hate the track, but it's not fun. At Mugello, Phillip Island and Brno, there are corners where you can really hang it out. Here, almost all the corners you brake all the way in on the edge of the tyre."

He was one of only three MotoGP riders not to have tested at the circuit on a road bike, and in Hayden's case, a Moto2 bike, when his Ducati broke down. The other two were Edwards and Spies. A GP bike was so different, thought Casey, that you could learn nothing much more than the direction of the corners, "and that only takes a couple of laps anyway." Events were to prove both assertions correct, as a rebalancing exercise on his Ducati – a longer front end and a shorter swing-arm combined with a more forward seating position – turned his fortunes around decisively.

Most riders welcomed the experimental return to four practice sessions, although inevitably there were complaints that 45 minutes (less for the smaller classes) was not long enough to make and assess meaningful adjustments. This was the original complaint that had triggered the change to three sessions; all the same, general approval meant that it was decided to return to four sessions for the last two rounds, in Portugal and Valencia. Another experiment switched practice order to match race-day order, so that MotoGP practised after Moto2 rather than before. This was meant to see if strange race-day effects noticed in MotoGP were the result of 40-odd bikes rubbering up the track directly beforehand. Results were inconclusive and the notion abandoned.

Pedrosa, one who said he preferred three longer practice sessions, was confirmed for two more years with HRC; the Repsol sponsorship was not yet signed and rumours of a three-rider factory team once again soon followed. It was also confirmed that Edwards would round out his career with one more year with the Tech 3 squad rather than returning to World Superbikes, to mentor new boy Crutchlow.

More shifts in Moto2: Pesek dropped from a reportedly financially troubled Matteoni CP team in favour of second Columbian rider Santiago Herrero, from the same family as Yonny Hernandez; Pasini back replacing Ranseder (busy with German Supersport championship commitments – he lost) at Vector Kiefer; Canepa back for a second race with the new Bimota-equipped M-team; and Michele Pirro taking the second Gresini seat.

The tragedy at Misano was still very fresh in the mind, and a minute's silence was held in Tomizawa's memory after morning warm-up, attended by King Juan Carlos, as well as most of the paddock. There was also a well-attended riders' safety briefing, where race direction assured the riders that

existing protocol of a red flag for an unconscious rider would be rigidly adhered to in future.

The Inmotec was at Aragon, half fulfilling a promise that it would appear during 2010. The plan was for wild-card entries, but the bike was just a static display thanks to budget cuts, according to project founder and veteran Spanish race entrant Oscar Gorria, although testing continued. The 80-degree V4 motor was on display alongside a complete bike, revealing that it is a semi-frameless design in Ducati style, with the swing-arm pivoting on the engine casings and a small front sub-frame carrying the steering head.

The weekend ended with a bombshell from Rossi, who had struggled to sixth and gave a briefing to Press between the team trucks. Barely audible above fans chanting his name and clearly favouring his right shoulder, he announced that he was considering quitting the season early to have corrective surgery, giving him plenty of time to recover before 2011. He would decide after the next two races, he said.

## MOTOGP RACE – 23 laps

For the first time since the opening round at Qatar, Stoner was able to sustain his habitual fast early practice pace to claim pole, by three-tenths from Lorenzo and Pedrosa. Hayden led row two, with Rossi fourth, troubled by his shoulder under braking, and his Yamaha's relatively sluggish acceleration and top speed, almost 10km/h down: a power-up engine was promised for the next race. Capirossi was absent, recuperating from intricate surgery to his right hand's little finger.

Stoner terrified his team with a tumble during morning warm-up after touching a white line. The mistake would not be repeated: he made a perfect start from pole to lead into the first corner, from Lorenzo and Hayden, with Pedrosa fourth and Rossi right behind, and about to be mugged by Simoncelli and Dovizioso.

Then came a heart-stopping moment as Pedrosa opened the throttle on the way out of the first corner – the back of his Honda skipped and stepped out, and he fought for control,

*Above:* Two Ducatis on the podium, with Hayden's first top three on the red bike. Project leader Cicognani joined the party.

*Top:* Spies and Dovizioso battle it out. Only one will reach the end.

*Opposite, main photo:* Iannone took another Moto2 runaway to break a run of Spanish wins. Here he leads Simon (60), Cortese (3) and team-mate Talmacsi.

*Opposite, inset top:* Pole-sitter Marquez is introduced to King Juan Carlos on the grid. His race was short-lived.

*Opposite, inset right:* A jubilant Pol Espargaro celebrates his first 125cc win in nine races.

Photos: Gold & Goose

losing another place to Spies. He powered past the Yamaha first time down the straight, however, a move that he would repeat over the ensuing laps, blitzing Hayden's Ducati and next time Lorenzo's Yamaha.

Stoner had quickly reversed a lap-one pass by Lorenzo and by now had pulled out by just short of 1.5 seconds; on the next lap, Pedrosa took one-and-a-half tenths out of it. It looked like he was hunting him down, but the Australian got the message and took a few tenths back over the next three laps.

On the ninth came Pedrosa's supreme effort, setting a new lap record, and for the first time he was less than a second adrift, if only by a hundredth. He would never be that close again, and by lap 18 the gap had grown to more than two seconds for the first time, thereafter growing faster as the Honda rider started to suffer wheelspin problems.

Lorenzo had been losing ground, more than a second adrift of Pedrosa by lap five, and with Hayden already dogging his every move. They stayed inches apart as the laps wound down. Lorenzo wasn't making any mistakes, and the American didn't have anything else to throw at him. At the same time, "I really didn't want another fourth," he explained; he pushed past the Spaniard on the last lap at the last right-left before the straight. "It was a bit of a backyard move," he admitted.

Lorenzo was angry as he pitted, his first time off the rostrum all year, and Yamaha's first time in 47 races! After he

had calmed down, he explained how, while the move had been rough, "it is allowed. I didn't want to close the door because I thought he would probably try it anyway, and maybe we would both crash. Fourth is not so bad."

At half-distance, Spies had closed to within less than a second of this pair. By now, however, Dovizioso was also coming up. He'd taken five laps to get ahead of fast-starting Simoncelli and was poised about a second behind the American. Then he started to get closer, and on lap 15 he was ready to attack. The battle intensified as the end of the race approached, but Spies was giving an object lesson in being hard to pass.

When Dovi did finally succeed, on horsepower on lap 22, Ben straight away tried to outbrake him and go around the outside at the looping last corner. He only narrowly failed, eventually succeeding under braking at the first corner of the last lap. By the end of it, he was alone and Dovizioso was walking disconsolately to the barrier while marshals wheeled his fallen Honda to safety.

Rossi had taken until lap 12 to get ahead of Simoncelli, and his compatriot stuck with him, even trying to get back ahead until a slip of his own caused him to lose touch with four laps to go.

As so often, the best actual racing was in the next group. At half-distance, Barbera had been a second ahead of Bautista, and two ahead of the next trio. But now it was Melandri at the front of that group, and by lap 19 he had closed up on the pair ahead, with Espargaro on his tail. De Puniet was the other combatant, but he slipped off on lap 16 after dropping to the back of the gang.

Bautista proved the strongest in yet another boost to the morale of the troubled Suzuki team, passing Barbera with two laps to go. Melandri followed him next time, and Espargaro also on the final lap.

Edwards recovered to a distant 12th after dropping to last. "For whatever reason, I'm just not fast enough, and I haven't figured it out yet," he said. By the end, he was well clear of Aoyama and Kallio.

## MOTO2 RACE – 21 laps

Elias was making a strong bid for pole when he crashed, lucky not to be hit by following riders, not only as he slid along, but also as he ran back across the track for his bike, pushing it home the wrong way down the pit lane. He got out again, but ended up 12th, one place ahead of Scottish wild-card Kevin Coghlan. Not that there wasn't a strong element of chance: 20 riders were within a second of pole, with frequent front-runner Luthi the last of them.

It was Iannone on pole, snitching it from Redding and fellow Misano accident victim de Angelis. Simon completed the first row, Corse led the second.

Iannone once again made a nonsense of the closeness, galloping away in the early laps to stamp his domination on the race and take a third win of the year by a massive margin. He would likely have had two more similar wins, but for incurring ride-through penalties at Catalunya (overtaking under the yellow flag) and Misano (jumped start).

The other thing the Italian broke was a record run of consecutive all-class Spanish wins. The earlier 125 race had been the 15th in a row for Spanish riders.

He had started from pole and led from the first corner – a valuable position, given that once again there was one of those class trademark multiple crashes. It started on the way in, taking down the ever-luckless Pasini, Baldolini, Hernandez, Nieto and Cardus.

A pack of three chased after the disappearing green FTR. Simon headed Corsi and Talmacsi, glued together until Talmacsi found his way past Corsi on lap 14. The Hungarian stayed on Simon's tail to the very end for his first podium in the class.

Elias had dropped to 14th on the first lap, but was up to

seventh, ahead of Redding and Aegerter by the end of the fifth, behind Cluzel and de Angelis. The last named, however, would last only two more laps before sliding off; on the same lap, Elias took to the front of the tight group.

Cluzel went with him as he gradually whittled away at a gap that had grown to almost four seconds by half-distance. Then with five laps to go, Elias broke the tow and was closing on a slowing Corsi. He was quickly past and left him behind to close within a second of Talmacsi by the finish.

Cluzel was sixth, under pressure in the last laps from Aegerter; Redding had dropped more than five seconds away at the end.

Bradl snatched the lead of the next gang from Luthi on the last lap, for ninth. Corti was still right behind; Takahashi and di Meglio were less than a second adrift. Pietri, de Rosa, Al Naimi and Pons all swelled the crash list; Coghlan retired.

It ended a run of four wins for Elias, but his title lead was not much troubled.

## 125cc RACE – 19 laps

Marquez took his eighth pole by more than half a second; team-mate Cortese was alongside, then Terol and Vazquez. Espargaro crashed heavily, but got back out to qualify fifth, heading the second row.

The most significant event happened going into the first

corner. Krummenacher, from row two, got squeezed on to the inside kerb and couldn't stop in time. He slammed straight into Marquez. His race was over, and his despairing histrionics at the trackside showed how the apologetic Austrian had blown the championship wide open again.

This left Espargaro and Terol to a game of cat and mouse, each letting the other past at least once. But who would pounce on the last lap?

Terol led at the start of it, repulsing the first attack at the first right-left combination. Espargaro tried again at the next one, but wasn't close enough. Then came the long, long straight, and the younger rider timed his slipstream perfectly to pull out and pass Terol firmly enough to hold him at bay to the line by 0.050 second, his third win of the year, after a ten-race gap. "I couldn't get away, but I always thought I could win," he said. Both moved ahead of Marquez on points, Terol in front.

Smith had led the first two laps, but gradually he lost touch to cross the line a safe third. Cortese did the same behind him, only to be repassed for fourth by Vazquez and narrowly defeating Koyama.

A long way behind, Rabat had come through from a bad start, followed by Folger all the way. Webb dropped back in ninth, but kept ahead of Salom.

Krummenacher remounted, but he was black-flagged for dangerous riding. Wrong victim in the wrong country.

**OFFICIAL TIMEKEEPER**

## MOTORLAND ARAGÓN

Turn 10, Turn 9, Turn 5, Turn 8, Turn 11, Turn 7, Turn 4, Turn 6, Turn 3, Turn 2, Turn 1, Turn 12, Turn 13, Turn 14, Turn 15, Turn 18, Turn 17, Turn 16

New venue for 2010

Circuit 5.345km/3.321 miles, 23 laps

## MotoGP

RACE DISTANCE: 23 laps, 72.572 miles/116.794 km · RACE WEATHER: Dry (air 23°, humidity 32%, track 39°)

| Pos. | Rider | Nat. | No. | Entrant | Machine | Tyres | Laps | Time & speed |
|---|---|---|---|---|---|---|---|---|
| 1 | **Casey Stoner** | AUS | 27 | Ducati Marlboro Team | Ducati | B | 23 | 42m 16.530s 102.999mph/ 165.761km/h |
| 2 | **Dani Pedrosa** | SPA | 26 | Repsol Honda Team | Honda | B | 23 | 42m 21.678s |
| 3 | **Nicky Hayden** | USA | 69 | Ducati Marlboro Team | Ducati | B | 23 | 42m 26.026s |
| 4 | **Jorge Lorenzo** | SPA | 99 | Fiat Yamaha Team | Yamaha | B | 23 | 42m 26.110s |
| 5 | **Ben Spies** | USA | 11 | Monster Yamaha Tech 3 | Yamaha | B | 23 | 42m 30.301s |
| 6 | **Valentino Rossi** | ITA | 46 | Fiat Yamaha Team | Yamaha | B | 23 | 42m 43.860s |
| 7 | **Marco Simoncelli** | ITA | 58 | San Carlo Honda Gresini | Honda | B | 23 | 42m 45.041s |
| 8 | **Alvaro Bautista** | SPA | 19 | Rizla Suzuki MotoGP | Suzuki | B | 23 | 42m 51.784s |
| 9 | **Marco Melandri** | ITA | 33 | San Carlo Honda Gresini | Honda | B | 23 | 42m 51.923s |
| 10 | **Aleix Espargaro** | SPA | 41 | Pramac Racing Team | Ducati | B | 23 | 42m 51.997s |
| 11 | **Hector Barbera** | SPA | 40 | Paginas Amarillas Aspar | Ducati | B | 23 | 42m 52.052s |
| 12 | **Colin Edwards** | USA | 5 | Monster Yamaha Tech 3 | Yamaha | B | 23 | 43m 01.890s |
| 13 | **Hiroshi Aoyama** | JPN | 7 | Interwetten Honda MotoGP | Honda | B | 23 | 43m 04.849s |
| 14 | **Mika Kallio** | FIN | 36 | Pramac Racing Team | Ducati | B | 23 | 43m 14.577s |
| | Andrea Dovizioso | ITA | 4 | Repsol Honda Team | Honda | B | 22 | DNF |
| | Randy de Puniet | FRA | 14 | LCR Honda MotoGP | Honda | B | 15 | DNF |

**Fastest lap:** Dani Pedrosa, on lap 9, 1m 49.521s, 103.716mph/166.915km/h (record).

**Previous lap record:** New circuit.

**Event best maximum speed:** Dani Pedrosa, 204.7mph/329.5km/h (free practice 3).

### Qualifying

**Weather:** Dry
**Air Temp:** 19° **Humidity:** 41°
**Track Temp:** 26°

| | | |
|---|---|---|
| 1 | Stoner | 1m 48.942s |
| 2 | Lorenzo | 1m 49.251s |
| 3 | Pedrosa | 1m 49.343s |
| 4 | Hayden | 1m 49.506s |
| 5 | Spies | 1m 49.565s |
| 6 | de Puniet | 1m 49.952s |
| 7 | Rossi | 1m 50.017s |
| 8 | Dovizioso | 1m 50.046s |
| 9 | Simoncelli | 1m 50.088s |
| 10 | Barbera | 1m 50.323s |
| 11 | Edwards | 1m 50.440s |
| 12 | Bautista | 1m 50.523s |
| 13 | Espargaro | 1m 50.537s |
| 14 | Melandri | 1m 50.580s |
| 15 | Aoyama | 1m 50.836s |
| 16 | Kallio | 1m 51.490s |

### Fastest race laps

| | | |
|---|---|---|
| 1 | Pedrosa | 1m 49.521s |
| 2 | Stoner | 1m 49.555s |
| 3 | Hayden | 1m 49.935s |
| 4 | Spies | 1m 50.116s |
| 5 | Dovizioso | 1m 50.234s |
| 6 | Lorenzo | 1m 50.273s |
| 7 | Simoncelli | 1m 50.688s |
| 8 | Rossi | 1m 50.701s |
| 9 | Bautista | 1m 50.958s |
| 10 | Barbera | 1m 50.999s |
| 11 | Espargaro | 1m 51.035s |
| 12 | Melandri | 1m 51.145s |
| 13 | Edwards | 1m 51.292s |
| 14 | Aoyama | 1m 51.306s |
| 15 | de Puniet | 1m 51.327s |
| 16 | Kallio | 1m 51.818s |

### Championship Points

| | | |
|---|---|---|
| 1 | Lorenzo | 284 |
| 2 | Pedrosa | 228 |
| 3 | Stoner | 155 |
| 4 | Rossi | 140 |
| 5 | Dovizioso | 139 |
| 6 | Spies | 131 |
| 7 | N. Hayden | 125 |
| 8 | de Puniet | 81 |
| 9 | Melandri | 74 |
| 10 | Simoncelli | 74 |
| 11 | Edwards | 70 |
| 12 | Barbera | 66 |
| 13 | Espargaro | 50 |
| 14 | Bautista | 49 |
| 15 | Capirossi | 41 |
| 16 | Kallio | 33 |
| 17 | Aoyama | 29 |
| 18 | de Angelis | 11 |
| 19 | R. Hayden | 5 |
| 20 | Akiyoshi | 4 |
| 21 | Yoshikawa | 1 |

| Grid order | 1 | 2 | 3 | 4 | 5 | 6 | 7 | 8 | 9 | 10 | 11 | 12 | 13 | 14 | 15 | 16 | 17 | 18 | 19 | 20 | 21 | 22 | 23 | |
|---|---|---|---|---|---|---|---|---|---|---|---|---|---|---|---|---|---|---|---|---|---|---|---|---|
| 27 STONER | 27 | 27 | 27 | 27 | 27 | 27 | 27 | 27 | 27 | 27 | 27 | 27 | 27 | 27 | 27 | 27 | 27 | 27 | 27 | 27 | 27 | 27 | 27 | 1 |
| 99 LORENZO | 99 | 99 | 26 | 26 | 26 | 26 | 26 | 26 | 26 | 26 | 26 | 26 | 26 | 26 | 26 | 26 | 26 | 26 | 26 | 26 | 26 | 26 | 26 | 2 |
| 26 PEDROSA | 69 | 26 | 99 | 99 | 99 | 99 | 99 | 99 | 99 | 99 | 99 | 99 | 99 | 99 | 99 | 99 | 99 | 99 | 99 | 99 | 99 | 99 | 69 | 3 |
| 69 HAYDEN | 26 | 69 | 69 | 69 | 69 | 69 | 69 | 69 | 69 | 69 | 69 | 69 | 69 | 69 | 69 | 69 | 69 | 69 | 69 | 69 | 69 | 69 | 99 | 4 |
| 11 SPIES | 11 | 11 | 11 | 11 | 11 | 11 | 11 | 11 | 11 | 11 | 11 | 11 | 11 | 11 | 11 | 11 | 11 | 11 | 11 | 11 | 11 | 4 | 11 | 5 |
| 14 de PUNIET | 58 | 58 | 58 | 58 | 4 | 4 | 4 | 4 | 4 | 4 | 4 | 4 | 4 | 4 | 4 | 4 | 4 | 4 | 4 | 4 | 4 | 11 | 46 | 6 |
| 46 ROSSI | 4 | 4 | 4 | 4 | 58 | 58 | 58 | 58 | 58 | 58 | 58 | 46 | 46 | 46 | 46 | 46 | 46 | 46 | 46 | 46 | 46 | 46 | 58 | 7 |
| 4 DOVIZIOSO | 46 | 46 | 40 | 40 | 46 | 46 | 46 | 46 | 46 | 46 | 46 | 58 | 58 | 58 | 58 | 58 | 58 | 58 | 58 | 58 | 58 | 19 | | 8 |
| 58 SIMONCELLI | 40 | 40 | 46 | 46 | 40 | 40 | 40 | 40 | 40 | 40 | 40 | 40 | 40 | 40 | 40 | 40 | 40 | 40 | 40 | 40 | 19 | 33 | | 9 |
| 40 BARBERA | 14 | 14 | 14 | 14 | 14 | 14 | 19 | 19 | 19 | 19 | 19 | 19 | 19 | 19 | 19 | 19 | 19 | 19 | 19 | 19 | 33 | 41 | | 10 |
| 5 EDWARDS | 19 | 19 | 19 | 19 | 19 | 19 | 14 | 14 | 14 | 14 | 33 | 33 | 33 | 33 | 33 | 33 | 33 | 33 | 33 | 33 | 40 | 40 | | 11 |
| 19 BAUTISTA | 33 | 33 | 33 | 33 | 33 | 33 | 33 | 33 | 33 | 33 | 14 | 14 | 14 | 41 | 41 | 41 | 41 | 41 | 41 | 41 | 41 | 5 | | 12 |
| 41 ESPARGARO | 41 | 41 | 41 | 41 | 41 | 41 | 41 | 41 | 41 | 41 | 41 | 41 | 41 | 14 | 14 | 5 | 5 | 5 | 5 | 5 | 5 | 7 | | 13 |
| 33 MELANDRI | 5 | 5 | 5 | 36 | 36 | 36 | 36 | 36 | 36 | 5 | 5 | 5 | 5 | 5 | 5 | 7 | 7 | 7 | 7 | 7 | 7 | 36 | | 14 |
| 7 AOYAMA | 36 | 36 | 36 | 7 | 7 | 7 | 7 | 5 | 5 | 36 | 36 | 36 | 7 | 7 | 7 | 36 | 36 | 36 | 36 | 36 | 36 | | | |
| 36 KALLIO | 7 | 7 | 7 | 5 | 5 | 5 | 5 | 7 | 7 | 7 | 7 | 7 | 36 | 36 | 36 | | | | | | | | | |

### Team Points

| | | |
|---|---|---|
| 1 | Fiat Yamaha Team | 425 |
| 2 | Repsol Honda Team | 367 |
| 3 | Ducati Marlboro Team | 280 |
| 4 | Monster Yamaha Tech 3 | 201 |
| 5 | San Carlo Honda Gresini | 148 |
| 6 | Rizla Suzuki MotoGP | 90 |
| 7 | LCR Honda MotoGP | 86 |
| 8 | Pramac Racing Team | 83 |
| 9 | Paginas Amarillas Aspar | 66 |
| 10 | Interwetten Honda MotoGP | 44 |

### Constructor Points

| | | |
|---|---|---|
| 1 | Yamaha | 293 |
| 2 | Honda | 265 |
| 3 | Ducati | 195 |
| 4 | Suzuki | 72 |

## Moto2

RACE DISTANCE: 21 laps, 66.262 miles/106.638 km · RACE WEATHER: Dry (air 21°, humidity 33%, track 31°)

| Pos. | Rider | Nat. | No. | Entrant | Machine | Laps | Time & Speed |
|---|---|---|---|---|---|---|---|
| 1 | **Andrea Iannone** | ITA | 29 | Fimmco Speed Up | Speed Up | 21 | 40m 33.264s (mph/km/h) 98.034/157.770 |
| 2 | **Julian Simon** | SPA | 60 | Mapfre Aspar Team | Suter | 21 | 40m 39.467s |
| 3 | **Gabor Talmacsi** | HUN | 2 | Fimmco Speed Up | Speed Up | 21 | 40m 39.540s |
| 4 | **Toni Elias** | SPA | 24 | Gresini Racing Moto2 | Moriwaki | 21 | 40m 40.387s |
| 5 | **Simone Corsi** | ITA | 3 | JIR Moto2 | MotoBI | 21 | 40m 42.424s |
| 6 | **Jules Cluzel** | FRA | 16 | Forward Racing | Suter | 21 | 40m 46.145s |
| 7 | **Dominique Aegerter** | SWI | 77 | Technomag-CIP | Suter | 21 | 40m 46.251s |
| 8 | **Scott Redding** | GBR | 45 | Marc VDS Racing Team | Suter | 21 | 40m 52.145s |
| 9 | **Stefan Bradl** | GER | 65 | Viessmann Kiefer Racing | Suter | 21 | 40m 54.157s |
| 10 | **Thomas Luthi** | SWI | 12 | Interwetten Moriwaki Moto2 | Moriwaki | 21 | 40m 54.435s |
| 11 | **Claudio Corti** | ITA | 71 | Forward Racing | Suter | 21 | 40m 54.690s |
| 12 | **Yuki Takahashi** | JPN | 72 | Tech 3 Racing | Tech 3 | 21 | 40m 55.242s |
| 13 | **Mike di Meglio** | FRA | 63 | Mapfre Aspar Team | Suter | 21 | 40m 55.435s |
| 14 | **Michele Pirro** | ITA | 51 | Gresini Racing Moto2 | Moriwaki | 21 | 40m 58.011s |
| 15 | **Ratthapark Wilairot** | THA | 14 | Thai Honda PTT Singha SAG | Bimota | 21 | 41m 03.716s |
| 16 | Roman Ramos | SPA | 43 | MIR Racing | MIR Racing | 21 | 41m 04.980s |
| 17 | Hector Faubel | SPA | 55 | Marc VDS Racing Team | Suter | 21 | 41m 06.858s |
| 18 | Karel Abraham | CZE | 17 | Cardion AB Motoracing | FTR | 21 | 41m 07.065s |
| 19 | Roberto Rolfo | ITA | 44 | Italtrans S.T.R. | Suter | 21 | 41m 10.885s |
| 20 | Sergio Gadea | SPA | 40 | Tenerife 40 Pons | Pons Kalex | 21 | 41m 12.692s |
| 21 | Anthony West | AUS | 8 | MZ Racing Team | MZ-RE Honda | 21 | 41m 17.063s |
| 22 | Alex Debon | SPA | 6 | Aeroport de Castello - Ajo | FTR | 21 | 41m 18.119s |
| 23 | Santiago Hernandez | COL | 64 | Matteoni CP Racing | Moriwaki | 21 | 41m 18.428s |
| 24 | Yannick Guerra | SPA | 88 | Holiday Gym G22 | Moriwaki | 21 | 41m 33.190s |
| 25 | Kazuki Watanabe | JPN | 28 | Racing Team Germany | Suter | 21 | 41m 44.440s |
| 26 | Niccolo Canepa | ITA | 59 | Bimota - M Racing | Bimota | 21 | 41m 44.472s |
| 27 | Valentin Debise | FRA | 53 | WTR San Marino Team | ADV | 21 | 41m 44.628s |
| 28 | Joan Olive | SPA | 5 | Jack & Jones by A.Banderas | Promoharris | 21 | 41m 55.488s |
| | Axel Pons | SPA | 80 | Tenerife 40 Pons | Pons Kalex | 13 | DNF |
| | Mashel Al Naimi | QAT | 95 | Blusens-STX | BQR-Moto2 | 12 | DNF |
| | Kenny Noyes | USA | 9 | Jack & Jones by A.Banderas | Promoharris | 12 | DNF |
| | Raffaele de Rosa | ITA | 35 | Tech 3 Racing | Tech 3 | 10 | DNF |
| | Mattia Pasini | ITA | 75 | Vector Kiefer Racing | Suter | 9 | DNF |
| | Robertino Pietri | VEN | 39 | Italtrans S.T.R. | Suter | 8 | DNF |
| | Alex de Angelis | RSM | 15 | JIR Moto2 | MotoBI | 6 | DNF |
| | Kev Coghlan | GBR | 54 | Monlau Joey Darcey | FTR | 1 | DNF |
| | Fonsi Nieto | SPA | 10 | Holiday Gym G22 | Moriwaki | 0 | DNF |
| | Alex Baldolini | ITA | 25 | Caretta Technology Race Dept. | I.C.P. | 0 | DNF |
| | Ricard Cardus | SPA | 4 | Maquinza-SAG Team | Bimota | 0 | DNF |
| | Yonny Hernandez | COL | 68 | Blusens-STX | BQR-Moto2 | 0 | DNF |

**Fastest lap:** Andrea Iannone, on lap 7, 1m 55.003s, 98.773mph/158.959km/h (record).

**Previous lap record:** New category.

**Event best maximum speed:** Andrea Iannone, 173.6mph/279.4km/h (qualifying practice).

**Qualifying:** Dry

Air: 19° Humidity: 44% Ground: 28°

| | | |
|---|---|---|
| 1 | Iannone | 1m 55.148s |
| 2 | Redding | 1m 55.189s |
| 3 | de Angelis | 1m 55.194s |
| 4 | Simon | 1m 55.364s |
| 5 | Corsi | 1m 55.499s |
| 6 | Corti | 1m 55.585s |
| 7 | Talmacsi | 1m 55.627s |
| 8 | Pirro | 1m 55.752s |
| 9 | Bradl | 1m 55.752s |
| 10 | de Rosa | 1m 55.794s |
| 11 | Aegerter | 1m 55.819s |
| 12 | Elias | 1m 55.838s |
| 13 | Coghlan | 1m 55.859s |
| 14 | Cluzel | 1m 55.882s |
| 15 | di Meglio | 1m 55.941s |
| 16 | Y. Hernandez | 1m 56.036s |
| 17 | Baldolini | 1m 56.045s |
| 18 | Cardus | 1m 56.069s |
| 19 | Faubel | 1m 56.111s |
| 20 | Luthi | 1m 56.124s |
| 21 | Wilairot | 1m 56.220s |
| 22 | Abraham | 1m 56.223s |
| 23 | Rolfo | 1m 56.251s |
| 24 | Pasini | 1m 56.341s |
| 25 | Gadea | 1m 56.411s |
| 26 | Takahashi | 1m 56.440s |
| 27 | Debon | 1m 56.574s |
| 28 | West | 1m 56.584s |
| 29 | Ramos | 1m 56.596s |
| 30 | Pons | 1m 56.691s |
| 31 | S. Hernandez | 1m 57.063s |
| 32 | Nieto | 1m 57.159s |
| 33 | Debise | 1m 57.191s |
| 34 | Al Naimi | 1m 57.474s |
| 35 | Noyes | 1m 57.524s |
| 36 | Canepa | 1m 57.582s |
| 37 | Pietri | 1m 57.796s |
| 38 | Guerra | 1m 57.948s |
| 39 | Olive | 1m 58.052s |
| 40 | Watanabe | 1m 58.258s |

**Fastest race laps**

| | | |
|---|---|---|
| 1 | Iannone | 1m 55.003s |
| 2 | Elias | 1m 55.460s |
| 3 | Corsi | 1m 55.545s |
| 4 | Talmacsi | 1m 55.562s |
| 5 | Simon | 1m 55.563s |
| 6 | Takahashi | 1m 55.580s |
| 7 | de Angelis | 1m 55.713s |
| 8 | Redding | 1m 55.794s |
| 9 | Cluzel | 1m 55.813s |
| 10 | Aegerter | 1m 55.859s |
| 11 | Luthi | 1m 55.904s |
| 12 | Pirro | 1m 55.992s |
| 13 | Corti | 1m 55.993s |
| 14 | Faubel | 1m 56.029s |
| 15 | Bradl | 1m 56.030s |
| 16 | Wilairot | 1m 56.250s |
| 17 | di Meglio | 1m 56.251s |
| 18 | de Rosa | 1m 56.277s |
| 19 | Ramos | 1m 56.314s |
| 20 | Abraham | 1m 56.412s |
| 21 | Gadea | 1m 56.479s |
| 22 | S. Hernandez | 1m 56.532s |
| 23 | Rolfo | 1m 56.591s |
| 24 | West | 1m 56.676s |
| 25 | Noyes | 1m 56.679s |
| 26 | Pons | 1m 56.781s |
| 27 | Debon | 1m 56.909s |
| 28 | Pasini | 1m 57.073s |
| 29 | Guerra | 1m 57.251s |
| 30 | Watanabe | 1m 57.789s |
| 31 | Canepa | 1m 58.132s |
| 32 | Pietri | 1m 58.152s |
| 33 | Debise | 1m 58.194s |
| 34 | Al Naimi | 1m 58.691s |
| 35 | Olive | 1m 58.786s |

**Championship Points**

| | | |
|---|---|---|
| 1 | Elias | 224 |
| 2 | Simon | 148 |
| 3 | Iannone | 144 |
| 4 | Luthi | 130 |
| 5 | Corsi | 108 |
| 6 | Talmacsi | 95 |
| 7 | Cluzel | 94 |
| 8 | Tomizawa | 82 |
| 9 | Takahashi | 76 |
| 10 | Gadea | 59 |
| 11 | Redding | 47 |
| 12 | Debon | 46 |
| 13 | Aegerter | 45 |
| 14 | Rolfo | 43 |
| 15 | Bradl | 43 |
| 16 | Nieto | 41 |
| 17 | Abraham | 33 |
| 18 | Wilairot | 30 |
| 19 | Y. Hernandez | 27 |
| 20 | di Meglio | 24 |
| 21 | Noyes | 18 |
| 22 | West | 17 |
| 23 | Corti | 16 |
| 24 | Baldolini | 14 |
| 25 | Pasini | 12 |
| 26 | de Angelis | 11 |
| 27 | Cudlin | 9 |
| 28 | Simeon | 9 |
| 29 | Faubel | 8 |
| 30 | Di Salvo | 7 |
| 31 | Pesek | 5 |
| 32 | de Rosa | 4 |
| 33 | Pirro | 2 |
| 34 | Ranseder | 2 |
| 35 | Pons | 2 |
| 36 | Ivanov | 2 |
| 37 | Tode | 2 |
| 38 | Teshima | 1 |

**Constructors**

| | | |
|---|---|---|
| 1 | Moriwaki | 249 |
| 2 | Suter | 216 |
| 3 | Speed Up | 169 |
| 4 | MotoBI | 110 |
| 5 | FTR | 84 |
| 6 | Tech 3 | 79 |
| 7 | Pons Kalex | 68 |
| 8 | Bimota | 30 |
| 9 | BQR-Moto2 | 27 |
| 10 | Promoharris | 18 |
| 11 | MZ-RE Honda | 17 |
| 12 | I.C.P. | 14 |
| 13 | Force GP210 | 11 |
| 14 | RSV | 10 |

## 125cc

RACE DISTANCE: 19 laps, 59.951 miles/96.482 km · RACE WEATHER: Dry (air 18°, humidity 37%, track 27°)

| Pos. | Rider | Nat. | No. | Entrant | Machine | Laps | Time & Speed |
|---|---|---|---|---|---|---|---|
| 1 | **Pol Espargaro** | SPA | 44 | Tuenti Racing | Derbi | 19 | 38m 14.248s (mph/km/h) 94.071/151.393 |
| 2 | **Nicolas Terol** | SPA | 40 | Bancaja Aspar Team | Aprilia | 19 | 38m 14.298s |
| 3 | **Bradley Smith** | GBR | 38 | Bancaja Aspar Team | Aprilia | 19 | 38m 23.708s |
| 4 | **Efren Vazquez** | SPA | 7 | Tuenti Racing | Derbi | 19 | 38m 30.247s |
| 5 | **Sandro Cortese** | GER | 11 | Avant Mitsubishi Ajo | Derbi | 19 | 38m 32.644s |
| 6 | **Tomoyoshi Koyama** | JPN | 71 | Racing Team Germany | Aprilia | 19 | 38m 33.215s |
| 7 | **Esteve Rabat** | SPA | 12 | Blusens-STX | Aprilia | 19 | 38m 40.219s |
| 8 | **Jonas Folger** | GER | 94 | Ongetta Team | Aprilia | 19 | 38m 40.377s |
| 9 | **Danny Webb** | GBR | 99 | Andalucia Cajasol | Aprilia | 19 | 38m 53.965s |
| 10 | **Luis Salom** | SPA | 39 | Stipa-Molenaar Racing GP | Aprilia | 19 | 38m 56.967s |
| 11 | **Adrian Martin** | SPA | 26 | Aeroport de Castello - Ajo | Aprilia | 19 | 39m 02.883s |
| 12 | **Johann Zarco** | FRA | 14 | WTR San Marino Team | Aprilia | 19 | 39m 10.313s |
| 13 | **Marcel Schrotter** | GER | 78 | Interwetten Honda 125 | Honda | 19 | 39m 16.174s |
| 14 | **Jakub Kornfeil** | CZE | 84 | Racing Team Germany | Aprilia | 19 | 39m 16.268s |
| 15 | **Sturla Fagerhaug** | NOR | 50 | AirAsia-Sepang Int. Circuit | Aprilia | 19 | 39m 29.278s |
| 16 | Zulfahmi Khairuddin | MAL | 63 | AirAsia-Sepang Int. Circuit | Aprilia | 19 | 39m 32.937s |
| 17 | Alberto Moncayo | SPA | 23 | Andalucia Cajasol | Aprilia | 19 | 39m 33.100s |
| 18 | Marco Ravaioli | ITA | 72 | Lambretta Reparto Corse | Lambretta | 19 | 39m 50.433s |
| 19 | Joan Perello | SPA | 58 | SAG Castrol | Honda | 19 | 40m 08.526s |
| 20 | Robin Barbosa | SPA | 37 | Ongetta Team | Aprilia | 19 | 40m 08.812s |
| 21 | Alejandro Pardo | SPA | 27 | Matteoni CP Racing | Aprilia | 18 | 38m 53.728s |
| 22 | Josep Rodriguez | SPA | 28 | Hune Racing | Aprilia | 18 | 38m 54.720s |
| | Simone Grotzkyj | ITA | 15 | Fontana Racing | Aprilia | 15 | DNF |
| | Louis Rossi | FRA | 69 | CBC Corse | Aprilia | 13 | DNF |
| | Pedro Rodriguez | SPA | 16 | Ongetta Team | Aprilia | 11 | DNF |
| | Peter Sebestyen | HUN | 56 | Right Guard Racing | Aprilia | 10 | DNF |
| | Jasper Iwema | NED | 53 | CBC Corse | Aprilia | 8 | DNF |
| | Kevin Hanus | GER | 86 | Thomas Sabo Team Hanusch | Honda | 0 | DNF |
| | Marc Marquez | SPA | 93 | Red Bull Ajo Motorsport | Derbi | 0 | DNF |
| | Randy Krummenacher | SWI | 35 | Stipa-Molenaar Racing GP | Aprilia | 0 | DSQ |

**Fastest lap:** Pol Espargaro, on lap 5, 1m 59.509s, 95.048mph/152.965km/h (record).

**Previous lap record:** New circuit.

**Event best maximum speed:** Marc Marquez, 147.5mph/237.3km/h (free practice 3).

**Qualifying:** Dry

Air: 20° Humidity: 40% Ground: 27°

| | | |
|---|---|---|
| 1 | Marquez | 1m 59.335s |
| 2 | Cortese | 1m 59.898s |
| 3 | Terol | 1m 59.970s |
| 4 | Vazquez | 2m 00.265s |
| 5 | Espargaro | 2m 00.294s |
| 6 | Smith | 2m 00.417s |
| 7 | Krummenacher | 2m 00.842s |
| 8 | Zarco | 2m 01.281s |
| 9 | Folger | 2m 01.332s |
| 10 | Koyama | 2m 01.339s |
| 11 | Rabat | 2m 01.688s |
| 12 | Webb | 2m 01.814s |
| 13 | Salom | 2m 02.026s |
| 14 | Martin | 2m 02.568s |
| 15 | Khairuddin | 2m 02.594s |
| 16 | Moncayo | 2m 02.612s |
| 17 | Iwema | 2m 03.028s |
| 18 | Kornfeil | 2m 03.052s |
| 19 | Schrotter | 2m 03.385s |
| 20 | J. Rodriguez | 2m 03.408s |
| 21 | Grotzkyj | 2m 03.420s |
| 22 | Rossi | 2m 03.822s |
| 23 | P. Rodriguez | 2m 04.480s |
| 24 | Fagerhaug | 2m 04.607s |
| 25 | Perello | 2m 04.904s |
| 26 | Vinales | 2m 05.206s |
| 27 | Barbosa | 2m 05.302s |
| 28 | Sebestyen | 2m 05.710s |
| 29 | Ravaioli | 2m 05.820s |
| 30 | Pardo | 2m 06.193s |
| 31 | Hanus | 2m 07.150s |

**Fastest race laps**

| | | |
|---|---|---|
| 1 | Espargaro | 1m 59.509s |
| 2 | Terol | 1m 59.611s |
| 3 | Cortese | 1m 59.724s |
| 4 | Smith | 1m 59.820s |
| 5 | Koyama | 2m 00.578s |
| 6 | Rabat | 2m 00.656s |
| 7 | Vazquez | 2m 00.676s |
| 8 | Folger | 2m 00.868s |
| 9 | Salom | 2m 01.445s |
| 10 | Moncayo | 2m 01.591s |
| 11 | Zarco | 2m 01.692s |
| 12 | Webb | 2m 01.812s |
| 13 | Martin | 2m 01.876s |
| 14 | Krummenacher | 2m 02.087s |
| 15 | Grotzkyj | 2m 02.212s |
| 16 | Schrotter | 2m 02.584s |
| 17 | Iwema | 2m 02.720s |
| 18 | Kornfeil | 2m 03.054s |
| 19 | Fagerhaug | 2m 03.396s |
| 20 | Rossi | 2m 03.835s |
| 21 | Khairuddin | 2m 03.852s |
| 22 | Ravaioli | 2m 04.338s |
| 23 | Barbosa | 2m 04.689s |
| 24 | J. Rodriguez | 2m 04.842s |
| 25 | P. Rodriguez | 2m 05.417s |
| 26 | Sebestyen | 2m 05.446s |
| 27 | Perello | 2m 05.609s |
| 28 | Pardo | 2m 07.276s |

**Championship Points**

| | | |
|---|---|---|
| 1 | Terol | 208 |
| 2 | Espargaro | 202 |
| 3 | Marquez | 197 |
| 4 | Smith | 144 |
| 5 | Cortese | 118 |
| 6 | Vazquez | 110 |
| 7 | Rabat | 108 |
| 8 | Koyama | 102 |
| 9 | Krummenacher | 79 |
| 10 | Webb | 71 |
| 11 | Zarco | 66 |
| 12 | Folger | 56 |
| 13 | Moncayo | 40 |
| 14 | Iwema | 33 |
| 15 | Salom | 31 |
| 16 | Masbou | 20 |
| 17 | Martin | 20 |
| 18 | Kornfeil | 18 |
| 19 | Schrotter | 17 |
| 20 | Grotzkyj | 16 |
| 21 | Fagerhaug | 8 |
| 22 | Kartheininger | 6 |
| 23 | Savadori | 5 |
| 24 | Khairuddin | 3 |
| 25 | Rossi | 2 |

**Constructors**

| | | |
|---|---|---|
| 1 | Derbi | 285 |
| 2 | Aprilia | 251 |
| 3 | Honda | 17 |
| 4 | KTM | 6 |
| 5 | Lambretta | 1 |

*Above:* Scraping paint and ruffling feathers: Rossi's battle with team-mate Lorenzo was the highlight of the race.

*Above centre, from top:* Capirossi with Suzuki top brass on the grid; a floral display in honour of Tomizawa; 50th anniversary run for Hishiki Tetsuya on a 1960 Honda RC143.

*Photos: Gold & Goose*

THREE signal events marked out the delayed visit to Motegi. The first was Stoner's second consecutive win, which added to a remarkable record for Ducati, in the heartland of its Japanese rivals. Since 2005, the Italian bikes have won four out of six races, the first three by Capirossi (2005–07).

The second took place almost before proceedings had even begun, when Lorenzo's last remaining title rival Pedrosa crashed out on only his third lap: an awkward tumble that slammed him down while trapping his left foot under the bike. Suspected ankle fractures were later downgraded to a sprain, but the impact had broken his collarbone in two places. He was out of the race, and effectively out of the championship.

The third lit a sky-rocket under the last two laps of the race, as soon-to-be ex-team-mates Rossi and Lorenzo fought a bitter battle for the last rostrum place. Rossi took it by increasingly forceful riding, including a couple of collisions; Lorenzo went straight to Yamaha to complain about his "barely legal" tactics, given that there was a championship at stake.

Pedrosa's crash at the Honda-owned circuit was catastrophic for the rider, who flew directly back to Spain for a two-hour operation on Sunday, a titanium plate and eight screws restoring integrity to his collarbone. It was humiliating for his employer, because the crash had been caused by a mechanical failure. The throttle-closing cable (the system being only part fly-by-wire) had snagged – there was talk of an assembly fault – and just where he was trying to slow down, the bike kept on accelerating. An on-board camera had recorded the engine note just before the crash, so there was no doubt about the cause.

The Rossi-Lorenzo dispute went deeper, and it simmered for longer.

That Rossi was in a position to fight at all had come as a bit of a surprise. With its five hard braking zones, he'd expected Motegi to be the most punishing track yet for his injured shoulder. Not so, he discovered, after setting fastest time in the first free practice. Because the braking was accomplished in a straight line, it was not so difficult after all. The effect grew stronger after his first front-row qualifying position since Le Mans way back in May, although he still had doubts about his endurance.

They were overcome by the sheer thrill of the race: he and Lorenzo changed places six times in the last two laps, and touched at least twice in a battle as fierce as they had ever had before. To Valentino, it had been "great racing between two great rivals – and really funny for everybody." With Pedrosa absent, any need to comply with his promise to help his team-mate if necessary no longer applied. To Lorenzo – as with Gibernau at Jerez in 2005 and Stoner at Laguna in 2008 – his tactics had been too strong.

His complaint to the Yamaha bosses put Rossi's old strongest ally, Masao Furusawa, in the awkward position of having to give Valentino a dressing down. How seriously the rider took this was demonstrated by his cheerful comments a week later. "After the race, Yamaha asked me to race with more attention. So if I am fighting again with Lorenzo, I will try to beat him again... with more attention." He continued, "I said to Yamaha, what do you expect from me, to arrive behind? If I know this, I will stay at home."

Rossi's unexpected strength did cause a conundrum. Instead of struggling as he had at previous races, he had been able to "ride as I like". His shoulder was not recovered, but his racing spirit certainly had. Now he started to reconsider his plan to skip the last two or three races.

A rather different post-race meeting took place behind closed doors at Dorna HQ, between CEO Carmelo Ezpeleta and Suzuki factory representatives. Scheduled earlier in the weekend, it had been postponed until Sunday evening. The Japanese proposed fielding just one rider in 2011, probably to return at full strength with the 1000cc class in 2012. Ezpeleta pointed to the contract. Trouble was they interpreted it differently: Dorna thought it was a commitment

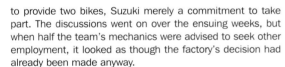

to provide two bikes, Suzuki merely a commitment to take part. The discussions went on over the ensuing weeks, but when half the team's mechanics were advised to seek other employment, it looked as though the factory's decision had already been made anyway.

The long-awaited confirmation of Lorenzo's continued employment by Yamaha came at last: a two-year contract. One class down, Scott Redding also signed on with the Marc VDS team, the greater significance being a likely move to MotoGP in 2012.

The weekend marked the closing of Moto2 entries for 2011, with a massive over-subscription, which clashed with IRTA's wish to reduce grid numbers from the current 40-odd to a more manageable figure in the mid-thirties. In all, 36 teams had applied, looking for positions for 61 riders. Pruning had been ruthless: 15 teams with 29 riders were offered confirmed places, with the rest to be decided later. This included all the significant current teams in the class. IRTA also demanded a five-year commitment and a deposit of 20,000 euros, to be refunded one fifth at a time over the next five years.

Yamaha delivered the promised power-up engine, which both factory riders described as a little better in acceleration and at the top end. For Lorenzo, however, it was his sixth and final new engine of the year, and he elected to use the older version on Sunday, a third race outing for that fifth engine. He did have all but one of his old engines still available, but most were well used, and the chance of an extra engine, and a resultant pit-lane starting penalty, loomed over him. Several other riders, including all but one of the satellite Honda riders (de Puniet), were also on their sixth engine, while Bautista was starting to exploit Suzuki's special dispensation with his seventh.

A final moving ceremony honoured Tomizawa, with his parents and brother joining team members and race management dignitaries on the rostrum on Sunday morning. Led by Toni Elias, his fellow Moto2 riders had voted him the winner of the Michel Metraux trophy, formerly for the top 250 pri-

vateer until the new class meant that there were no longer any factory bikes; the trophy was presented by IRTA founder Metraux's son.

## MOTOGP RACE – 24 laps

It was a jubilant front row, after Dovizioso cheered up Honda with his maiden pole position. Even happier was second-placed Rossi, his first front row since round four. "It feels like ten years," he said. And Stoner was relieved at the very least to be third, after chasing settings and ride height down and then halfway back up again. He had to tolerate the wheelies in exchange for better weight transfer and bite into and out of the corners. Lorenzo led row two.

Dovizioso got the jump from Stoner and Rossi, but ran wide on the exit from the first corner to let Stoner through into a lead he would hold until the end. However, it was not without the most persistent of pressure; Dovizioso was seldom more than three-tenths away for the first half of the race and only dropped to a second on the 17th lap. He finally gave up after a near high-side two laps from the end. It was an impressive ride from the now sole HRC home representative. "He really made me work for it," said Stoner.

The Australian's ride was even more impressive. He controlled the race from the front, setting one fastest lap after another, and sustained his sub-1m 48s pace right to the very end, the only rider to do so. Two wins in a row. Dovizioso praised Stoner's relentless pace. "I don't know what he had to eat today," he joked – a (possibly inadvertent) reference to the Australian's spell away from racing in 2009 with diet related fatigue problems.

It had been a two-man race, because Lorenzo had followed his first-turn overtake by slipping also past Rossi into the next braking zone. He had chosen the older engine because of concerns about fuel consumption; Rossi was using the power-up new engine. Even so, it took him six laps to get back past his team-mate, by which time the leaders were all

*Above:* Delight for Rossi and his Yamaha crew after "a funny race". The other side of the Fiat Yamaha garage was less amused.

*Top:* Pedrosa goes down and out. Mechanical failure ruined his last slender title hopes.

*Photos:* Gold & Goose

*Above:* Edwards leads Simoncelli and Capirossi, with Melandri and de Puniet behind. Fifth was the veteran's best result so far.

*Photo: Gold & Goose*

but two seconds clear. Otherwise, the rejuvenated Valentino said, he might have been in the fight for victory. He gave chase anyway, taking his own turn for fastest lap of the race on the seventh, but it was in vain, and the gap never did get much smaller.

Lorenzo was ever-present, just a few tenths behind, and as the laps wore down, he sensed that Rossi was beginning to tire and took his chance. The first pass came on lap 18, cutting underneath into turn five, into the first tunnel. But he ran wide and Rossi took it straight back. Now, shoulder pain forgotten, Valentino embarked on one of his classic rides.

Time and again, Lorenzo showed him his front wheel; Rossi would hang his right leg out wide under braking, as if threatening a kick-boxing response.

The last two laps were a minor epic. Lorenzo passed again into turn five; Rossi dived straight back under him at the apex. They collided as he regained the position. Lorenzo tried once more in the ensuing S-curve, nosing in front. They collided even harder as Rossi pushed him straight back.

Jorge's next attempt was more considered, hanging back through the first tunnel for a swooping drive out of it, to surge past into the braking zone for the next left. It looked as though he had done enough, but Rossi had one more card to play: a block-pass at the V-curve. From there to the end, he never gave Lorenzo another chance.

Afterwards, he congratulated his beaten rival. Lorenzo, on the other hand, told all and sundry that he thought Rossi's moves had been a bit strong, threatening to give it back to him should it happen again. This from a rider who was, in his 250 days, suspended for a race for barging while overtaking at this same circuit.

Hayden was up to tenth at the end of lap one, while Spies had been bumped to eighth. As they arrived at turn five on lap two, they both ran off one after the other. Hayden had problems regaining the track; Spies rejoined a mite quicker

to finish the lap second last, three seconds down on Kallio. Over the following laps, however, he gave a demonstration of considered overtaking as he picked his way steadily forward to eighth.

The fight for fifth finally went to a persistent Edwards from fast-starting Simoncelli. Bautista had closed impressively to within two seconds, from 12th on lap one. It would have been better still for Suzuki, but as the Spaniard had come up to take seventh from team-mate Capirossi, the other Suzuki's engine had expired, evidently nipping up in the process and almost throwing the rider off.

De Puniet was ninth, in spite of running off; Aoyama was a couple of seconds adrift and narrowly ahead of Melandri, who had also run off and rejoined. Hayden took until the last lap to get to the front of the privateer battle for 12th, from Barbera and Espargaro, with Kallio way behind.

## MOTO2 RACE – 23 laps

A masterful performance made Elias untouchable in the race, and almost so in the championship. He might easily have chosen to cruise to a safe finish. Instead he fought to the end, never putting a wheel wrong. His race-long attacker was his last very remote championship rival and compatriot, Simon, and he was still just three-tenths behind at the flag.

Simon was on pole, from Redding, Takahashi and Elias, and it was the Japanese rider ahead into the first corner. But Elias was in front on the way out, and he led from there all the way to the finish. He was never alone, though. Every time he looked over his shoulder, inches away was Simon's red Suter. Actually Simon did nose ahead briefly early on, but he was repulsed immediately.

The biggest gap between them across the line was 0.536 second, on lap 18. Most times it was three- or four-tenths. But for Simon, the distance might as well have been a mile,

for all the chance Elias ever gave him of reversing the situation. It was his fifth win in six races, and all the sweeter at the home race of his Moriwaki chassis – the next generation was founder's son Shogo Moriwaki, who was entered in the class and qualified 27th, but who withdrew from the race with injuries from a qualifying crash.

The leading pair had left Takashi behind, with the blossoming Redding on his heels. Before half-distance, they were being hunted down by de Angelis and Abraham, now obviously fully recovered from his Brno injuries and intent on showing that his 'rich-man's-son' entry to MotoGP in 2011 was also justified by his ability.

After 15 laps, de Angelis was in front and pulling clear, with Redding losing time at the back of the group. But there was more to come as they all closed up again.

One by one, the chasers passed Takahashi. Abraham was the strongest of them all, dropping Redding to close on de Angelis, and then attack very firmly on the last lap. The Czech rider almost fell coming out of the final underpass and the pair collided, but he was in the right place to fend off his experienced rival. Abraham's first rostrum was a big boost to his reputation.

Five seconds behind, Bradl had been alone for most of the race in seventh, but almost lost it on the last lap. Luthi had been storming through from 18th on the second lap, and had broken free from the pursuit pack to close up by a full second on the last lap alone. He had left behind Rolfo and Debon, scrapping to the line.

Corsi was 11th, Iannone 13th, neither ever in the hunt. Iannone's earlier title hopes were now a mathematical impossibility. Cluzel had been with the front pack early on, but fell back out of the points to 16th.

Teshima, now wild-carding for FCC, was the first to crash, on lap one, followed by Nieto, Kunikawa, Hernandez, Olive and Baldolini, the last-named twice.

## 125cc RACE – 20 laps

After getting knocked off at the first corner at Aragon, and out of the points lead, Marquez had much to prove at Motegi. He did so in that demoralising fashion with which his rivals were becoming increasingly familiar, starting out with his ninth pole of the season.

The Derbi led into the first corner, but then Terol nipped ahead and stayed there for the next seven laps as the pair drew clear of the pursuing Smith.

But Marquez was biding his time. "When I saw he was a little bit on the limit, I pushed, then step by step I could go away." The margin stretched steadily to almost three seconds, Marquez able to slack off and win comfortably by 2.6.

Terol's dogged pursuit had carried him well clear of Smith, who had seen off a strong challenge from fourth-placed Espargaro and Cortese, the latter tumbling out before half-distance, then remounting for an eventual 12th.

Smith was lucky to survive a crash going into the first corner, when Vazquez touched his back wheel and fell, and in turn was struck by Folger; both went down heavily. Vazquez was taken to hospital for a CAT scan, but was cleared and able to race again the next week.

The front four were spaced out, but there was a lively scrap for fifth, with Koyama mainly getting the better of Moncaya and Rabat – until he crashed out, scrambling back to finish last.

Webb was a lone seventh; Salom inched fellow Spaniard Martin for eighth; Zarco outdrafted Krummenacher and Cortese in a gang going for tenth.

The race lacked close action up front. Not so the title chase. Terol still led on 228, but Marquez was up to second, six points behind; Espargaro was third on 215. Smith (160) was only mathematically still in the hunt.

*Above:* Marquez was back to his dominant form.

*Top:* Elias held off a determined challenge from Simon all race long.

*Top left:* Future MotoGP rider Karel Abraham took a career-first podium in Moto2.

*Above left:* Winner Stoner congratulates his race-long pursuer, Dovizioso.
*Photo: Gold & Goose*

## TWIN RING MOTEGI

Victory Corner 85/53
Turn 1 98/61
90° Corner 78/49
Turn 3 96/60
V Corner 77/48
Turn 4 132/82
Turn 5 81/50
Turn 2 95/59
S Curve 120/75
130R 191/119
Hairpin 61/38

Key
96/60 kph/mph
Gear

Circuit: 4.801km/2.983 miles, 24 laps

Press Tent
Resting Place

---

## MotoGP
**RACE DISTANCE:** 24 laps, 71.597 miles/115.224 km · **RACE WEATHER:** Dry (air 23°, humidity 44%, track 34°)

| Pos. | Rider | Nat. | No. | Entrant | Machine | Tyres | Laps | Time & speed |
|---|---|---|---|---|---|---|---|---|
| 1 | **Casey Stoner** | AUS | 27 | Ducati Marlboro Team | Ducati | B | 24 | 43m 12.266s 99.429mph/ 160.016km/h |
| 2 | **Andrea Dovizioso** | ITA | 4 | Repsol Honda Team | Honda | B | 24 | 43m 16.134s |
| 3 | **Valentino Rossi** | ITA | 46 | Fiat Yamaha Team | Yamaha | B | 24 | 43m 17.973s |
| 4 | **Jorge Lorenzo** | SPA | 99 | Fiat Yamaha Team | Yamaha | B | 24 | 43m 18.487s |
| 5 | **Colin Edwards** | USA | 5 | Monster Yamaha Tech 3 | Yamaha | B | 24 | 43m 39.358s |
| 6 | **Marco Simoncelli** | ITA | 58 | San Carlo Honda Gresini | Honda | B | 24 | 43m 42.287s |
| 7 | **Alvaro Bautista** | SPA | 19 | Rizla Suzuki MotoGP | Suzuki | B | 24 | 43m 44.092s |
| 8 | **Ben Spies** | USA | 11 | Monster Yamaha Tech 3 | Yamaha | B | 24 | 43m 47.838s |
| 9 | **Randy de Puniet** | FRA | 14 | LCR Honda MotoGP | Honda | B | 24 | 43m 59.830s |
| 10 | **Hiroshi Aoyama** | JPN | 7 | Interwetten Honda MotoGP | Honda | B | 24 | 44m 01.864s |
| 11 | **Marco Melandri** | ITA | 33 | San Carlo Honda Gresini | Honda | B | 24 | 44m 02.265s |
| 12 | **Nicky Hayden** | USA | 69 | Ducati Marlboro Team | Ducati | B | 24 | 44m 02.969s |
| 13 | **Hector Barbera** | SPA | 40 | Paginas Amarillas Aspar | Ducati | B | 24 | 44m 03.688s |
| 14 | **Aleix Espargaro** | SPA | 41 | Pramac Racing Team | Ducati | B | 24 | 44m 05.109s |
| 15 | **Mika Kallio** | FIN | 36 | Pramac Racing Team | Ducati | B | 24 | 44m 26.934s |
| | Loris Capirossi | ITA | 65 | Rizla Suzuki MotoGP | Suzuki | B | 21 | DNF |

**Fastest lap:** Valentino Rossi, on lap 7, 1m 47.395s, 100.000mph/160.934km/h.

**Lap record:** Casey Stoner, AUS (Ducati), 1m 47.091s, 100.284mph/161.391km/h (2008).

**Event best maximum speed:** Casey Stoner, 182.9mph/294.4km/h (qualifying practice).

### Qualifying
Weather: Dry
Air Temp: 24° Humidity: 40°
Track Temp: 41°

| |  |  |
|---|---|---|
| 1 | Dovizioso | 1m 47.001s |
| 2 | Rossi | 1m 47.055s |
| 3 | Stoner | 1m 47.105s |
| 4 | Lorenzo | 1m 47.206s |
| 5 | Edwards | 1m 47.464s |
| 6 | Spies | 1m 47.648s |
| 7 | de Puniet | 1m 47.752s |
| 8 | Simoncelli | 1m 47.914s |
| 9 | Bautista | 1m 48.002s |
| 10 | Capirossi | 1m 48.068s |
| 11 | Hayden | 1m 48.182s |
| 12 | Melandri | 1m 48.238s |
| 13 | Espargaro | 1m 48.371s |
| 14 | Aoyama | 1m 48.396s |
| 15 | Barbera | 1m 48.535s |
| 16 | Kallio | 1m 49.480s |

### Fastest race laps
| |  |  |
|---|---|---|
| 1 | Rossi | 1m 47.395s |
| 2 | Stoner | 1m 47.410s |
| 3 | Dovizioso | 1m 47.428s |
| 4 | Lorenzo | 1m 47.561s |
| 5 | de Puniet | 1m 48.276s |
| 6 | Bautista | 1m 48.307s |
| 7 | Spies | 1m 48.394s |
| 8 | Edwards | 1m 48.424s |
| 9 | Simoncelli | 1m 48.433s |
| 10 | Capirossi | 1m 48.434s |
| 11 | Melandri | 1m 48.713s |
| 12 | Hayden | 1m 48.793s |
| 13 | Barbera | 1m 49.131s |
| 14 | Aoyama | 1m 49.133s |
| 15 | Espargaro | 1m 49.244s |
| 16 | Kallio | 1m 49.832s |

### Championship Points
| |  |  |
|---|---|---|
| 1 | Lorenzo | 297 |
| 2 | Pedrosa | 228 |
| 3 | Stoner | 180 |
| 4 | Dovizioso | 159 |
| 5 | Rossi | 156 |
| 6 | Spies | 139 |
| 7 | N. Hayden | 129 |
| 8 | de Puniet | 88 |
| 9 | Simoncelli | 84 |
| 10 | Edwards | 81 |
| 11 | Melandri | 79 |
| 12 | Barbera | 69 |
| 13 | Bautista | 58 |
| 14 | Espargaro | 52 |
| 15 | Capirossi | 41 |
| 16 | Aoyama | 35 |
| 17 | Kallio | 34 |
| 18 | de Angelis | 11 |
| 19 | R. Hayden | 5 |
| 20 | Akiyoshi | 4 |
| 21 | Yoshikawa | 1 |

| Grid order | 1 | 2 | 3 | 4 | 5 | 6 | 7 | 8 | 9 | 10 | 11 | 12 | 13 | 14 | 15 | 16 | 17 | 18 | 19 | 20 | 21 | 22 | 23 | 24 | |
|---|---|---|---|---|---|---|---|---|---|---|---|---|---|---|---|---|---|---|---|---|---|---|---|---|---|
| 4 DOVIZIOSO | 27 | 27 | 27 | 27 | 27 | 27 | 27 | 27 | 27 | 27 | 27 | 27 | 27 | 27 | 27 | 27 | 27 | 27 | 27 | 27 | 27 | 27 | 27 | 27 | 1 |
| 46 ROSSI | 4 | 4 | 4 | 4 | 4 | 4 | 4 | 4 | 4 | 4 | 4 | 4 | 4 | 4 | 4 | 4 | 4 | 4 | 4 | 4 | 4 | 4 | 4 | 4 | 2 |
| 27 STONER | 99 | 99 | 99 | 99 | 99 | 46 | 46 | 46 | 46 | 46 | 46 | 46 | 46 | 46 | 46 | 46 | 46 | 46 | 46 | 46 | 46 | 46 | 46 | 46 | 3 |
| 99 LORENZO | 46 | 46 | 46 | 46 | 46 | 99 | 99 | 99 | 99 | 99 | 99 | 99 | 99 | 99 | 99 | 99 | 99 | 99 | 99 | 99 | 99 | 99 | 99 | 99 | 4 |
| 5 EDWARDS | 5 | 5 | 58 | 58 | 58 | 58 | 58 | 58 | 58 | 58 | 58 | 58 | 58 | 58 | 58 | 58 | 58 | 58 | 5 | 5 | 5 | 5 | 5 | 5 | 5 |
| 11 SPIES | 65 | 58 | 5 | 5 | 5 | 5 | 5 | 5 | 5 | 5 | 5 | 5 | 5 | 5 | 5 | 5 | 5 | 5 | 58 | 58 | 58 | 58 | 58 | 58 | 6 |
| 14 de PUNIET | 58 | 65 | 65 | 65 | 65 | 65 | 65 | 65 | 65 | 65 | 65 | 65 | 65 | 65 | 65 | 65 | 65 | 65 | 65 | 19 | 19 | 19 | | | 7 |
| 58 SIMONCELLI | 11 | 33 | 33 | 14 | 14 | 14 | 14 | 14 | 14 | 33 | 33 | 33 | 33 | 33 | 19 | 19 | 19 | 19 | 19 | 19 | 11 | 11 | 11 | | 8 |
| 19 BAUTISTA | 33 | 14 | 14 | 33 | 33 | 33 | 33 | 33 | 33 | 19 | 19 | 19 | 19 | 19 | 33 | 33 | 33 | 33 | 33 | 33 | 11 | 14 | 14 | 14 | 9 |
| 65 CAPIROSSI | 69 | 19 | 19 | 19 | 19 | 19 | 19 | 19 | 19 | 14 | 14 | 11 | 11 | 11 | 11 | 11 | 11 | 11 | 11 | 33 | 7 | 7 | 7 | | 10 |
| 69 HAYDEN | 14 | 40 | 40 | 40 | 40 | 40 | 40 | 40 | 11 | 11 | 11 | 14 | 14 | 14 | 14 | 14 | 14 | 14 | 14 | 33 | 33 | 33 | | 11 |
| 33 MELANDRI | 19 | 41 | 41 | 41 | 41 | 41 | 7 | 11 | 40 | 40 | 40 | 40 | 7 | 7 | 7 | 7 | 7 | 7 | 7 | 40 | 40 | 69 | | 12 |
| 41 ESPARGARO | 40 | 7 | 7 | 7 | 7 | 7 | 41 | 7 | 7 | 7 | 7 | 7 | 40 | 40 | 40 | 40 | 41 | 41 | 40 | 40 | 69 | 69 | 40 | | 13 |
| 7 AOYAMA | 41 | 36 | 36 | 11 | 11 | 11 | 11 | 41 | 41 | 41 | 41 | 41 | 41 | 41 | 41 | 41 | 40 | 40 | 41 | 41 | 41 | 41 | 41 | | 14 |
| 40 BARBERA | 7 | 11 | 11 | 36 | 36 | 36 | 36 | 36 | 36 | 36 | 36 | 69 | 69 | 69 | 69 | 69 | 69 | 69 | 69 | 36 | 36 | 36 | | 15 |
| 36 KALLIO | 36 | 69 | 69 | 69 | 69 | 69 | 69 | 69 | 69 | 69 | 36 | 36 | 36 | 36 | 36 | 36 | 36 | 36 | 36 | | | | | | |

### Team Points
| | Team | Points |
|---|---|---|
| 1 | Fiat Yamaha Team | 454 |
| 2 | Repsol Honda Team | 387 |
| 3 | Ducati Marlboro Team | 309 |
| 4 | Monster Yamaha Tech 3 | 220 |
| 5 | San Carlo Honda Gresini | 163 |
| 6 | Rizla Suzuki MotoGP | 99 |
| 7 | LCR Honda MotoGP | 93 |
| 8 | Pramac Racing Team | 86 |
| 9 | Paginas Amarillas Aspar | 69 |
| 10 | Interwetten Honda MotoGP | 50 |

### Constructor Points
| | Constructor | Points |
|---|---|---|
| 1 | Yamaha | 309 |
| 2 | Honda | 285 |
| 3 | Ducati | 220 |
| 4 | Suzuki | 81 |

## Moto2

RACE DISTANCE: 23 laps, 68.614 miles/110.423 km · RACE WEATHER: Dry (air 23°, humidity 43%, track 34°)

| Pos. | Rider | Nat. | No. | Entrant | Machine | Laps | Time & Speed |
|---|---|---|---|---|---|---|---|
| 1 | **Toni Elias** | SPA | 24 | Gresini Racing Moto2 | Moriwaki | 23 | 43m 50.930s |
| | | | | | | | (mph/km/h) |
| | | | | | | | 93.886/151.095 |
| 2 | **Julian Simon** | SPA | 60 | Mapfre Aspar Team | Suter | 23 | 43m 51.245s |
| 3 | **Karel Abraham** | CZE | 17 | Cardion AB Motoracing | FTR | 23 | 44m 00.769s |
| 4 | **Alex de Angelis** | RSM | 15 | JIR Moto2 | MotoBI | 23 | 44m 01.108s |
| 5 | **Scott Redding** | GBR | 45 | Marc VDS Racing Team | Suter | 23 | 44m 02.167s |
| 6 | **Yuki Takahashi** | JPN | 72 | Tech 3 Racing | Tech 3 | 23 | 44m 03.708s |
| 7 | **Stefan Bradl** | GER | 65 | Viessmann Kiefer Racing | Suter | 23 | 44m0 8.214s |
| 8 | **Thomas Luthi** | SWI | 12 | Interwetten Moriwaki Moto2 | Moriwaki | 23 | 44m 08.822s |
| 9 | **Roberto Rolfo** | ITA | 44 | Italtrans S.T.R. | Suter | 23 | 44m 10.165s |
| 10 | **Alex Debon** | SPA | 6 | Aeroport de Castello - Ajo | FTR | 23 | 44m 10.498s |
| 11 | **Simone Corsi** | ITA | 3 | JIR Moto2 | MotoBI | 23 | 44m 13.643s |
| 12 | **Dominique Aegerter** | SWI | 77 | Technomag-CIP | Suter | 23 | 44m 14.347s |
| 13 | **Andrea Iannone** | ITA | 29 | Fimmco Speed Up | Speed Up | 23 | 44m 16.777s |
| 14 | **Claudio Corti** | ITA | 71 | Forward Racing | Suter | 23 | 44m 18.458s |
| 15 | **Raffaele de Rosa** | ITA | 35 | Tech 3 Racing | Tech 3 | 23 | 44m 19.626s |
| 16 | Jules Cluzel | FRA | 16 | Forward Racing | Suter | 23 | 44m 20.559s |
| 17 | Sergio Gadea | SPA | 40 | Tenerife 40 Pons | Pons Kalex | 23 | 44m 25.002s |
| 18 | Mike di Meglio | FRA | 63 | Mapfre Aspar Team | Suter | 23 | 44m 28.017s |
| 19 | Axel Pons | SPA | 80 | Tenerife 40 Pons | Pons Kalex | 23 | 44m 31.390s |
| 20 | Michael Ranseder | AUT | 56 | Vector Kiefer Racing | Suter | 23 | 44m 31.583s |
| 21 | Gabor Talmacsi | HUN | 2 | Fimmco Speed Up | Speed Up | 23 | 44m 31.785s |
| 22 | Kenny Noyes | USA | 9 | Jack & Jones by A.Banderas | Promoharris | 23 | 44m 33.217s |
| 23 | Anthony West | AUS | 8 | MZ Racing Team | MZ-RE Honda | 23 | 44m 35.744s |
| 24 | Ratthapark Wilairot | THA | 14 | Thai Honda PTT Singha SAG | Bimota | 23 | 44m 37.675s |
| 25 | Kazuki Watanabe | JPN | 28 | Racing Team Germany | Suter | 23 | 44m 40.679s |
| 26 | Valentin Debise | FRA | 53 | WTR San Marino Team | ADV | 23 | 44m 40.894s |
| 27 | Ricard Cardus | SPA | 4 | Maquinza-SAG Team | Bimota | 23 | 45m 05.279s |
| 28 | Mashel Al Naimi | QAT | 95 | Blusens-STX | BQR-Moto2 | 23 | 45m 06.753s |
| 29 | Yannick Guerra | SPA | 88 | Holiday Gym G22 | Moriwaki | 23 | 45m 07.119s |
| 30 | Hector Faubel | SPA | 55 | Marc VDS Racing Team | Suter | 23 | 45m 12.830s |
| 31 | Robertino Pietri | VEN | 39 | Italtrans S.T.R. | Suter | 23 | 45m 16.954s |
| 32 | Vladimir Ivanov | UKR | 61 | Gresini Racing Moto2 | Moriwaki | 23 | 45m 18.603s |
| 33 | Ferruccio Lamborghini | ITA | 70 | Matteoni Racing | Moriwaki | 23 | 45m 32.574s |
| 34 | Kouki Takahashi | JPN | 93 | Burning Blood RT | RBB | 23 | 45m 36.500s |
| | Joan Olive | SPA | 5 | Jack & Jones by A.Banderas | Promoharris | 21 | DNF |
| | Alex Baldolini | ITA | 25 | Caretta Technology Race Dept. | I.C.P. | 21 | DNF |
| | Yonny Hernandez | COL | 68 | Blusens-STX | BQR-Moto2 | 20 | DNF |
| | Hiromichi Kunikawa | JPN | 66 | Bimota - M Racing | Bimota | 11 | DNF |
| | Fonsi Nieto | SPA | 10 | Holiday Gym G22 | Moriwaki | 3 | DNF |
| | Yusuke Teshima | JPN | 11 | FCC TSR | TSR | 0 | DNF |

**Fastest lap:** Julian Simon, on lap 6, 1m 53.653s, 94.494mph/152.073km/h (record).

**Previous lap record:** New category.

**Event best maximum speed:** Andrea Iannone, 161.6mph/260.1km/h (race).

**Qualifying:** Dry

Air: 24° Humidity: 41% Ground: 37°

| | | |
|---|---|---|
| 1 | Simon | 1m 53.008s |
| 2 | Redding | 1m 53.292s |
| 3 | Y. Takahashi | 1m 53.439s |
| 4 | Elias | 1m 53.504s |
| 5 | Corti | 1m 53.507s |
| 6 | de Angelis | 1m 53.545s |
| 7 | Abraham | 1m 53.561s |
| 8 | Bradl | 1m 53.591s |
| 9 | Hernandez | 1m 53.601s |
| 10 | Iannone | 1m 53.747s |
| 11 | Rolfo | 1m 53.817s |
| 12 | Aegerter | 1m 53.830s |
| 13 | Cluzel | 1m 53.920s |
| 14 | Nieto | 1m 53.929s |
| 15 | Baldolini | 1m 53.954s |
| 16 | Luthi | 1m 53.961s |
| 17 | de Rosa | 1m 54.070s |
| 18 | Corsi | 1m 54.252s |
| 19 | di Meglio | 1m 54.363s |
| 20 | Gadea | 1m 54.390s |
| 21 | Noyes | 1m 54.417s |
| 22 | Wilairot | 1m 54.498s |
| 23 | Ranseder | 1m 54.504s |
| 24 | Faubel | 1m 54.529s |
| 25 | Teshima | 1m 54.565s |
| 26 | Debon | 1m 54.596s |
| 27 | Moriwaki | 1m 54.631s |
| 28 | Talmacsi | 1m 54.645s |
| 29 | Pons | 1m 54.837s |
| 30 | Watanabe | 1m 55.413s |
| 31 | West | 1m 55.544s |
| 32 | Debise | 1m 55.548s |
| 33 | Lamborghini | 1m 55.955s |
| 34 | Cardus | 1m 56.139s |
| 35 | Pietri | 1m 56.148s |
| 36 | Al Naimi | 1m 56.280s |
| 37 | Olive | 1m 56.445s |
| 38 | Guerra | 1m 56.474s |
| 39 | Ivanov | 1m 56.624s |
| 40 | Kunikawa | 1m 56.849s |
| 41 | K. Takahashi | 1m 57.115s |

**Fastest race laps**

| | | |
|---|---|---|
| 1 | Simon | 1m 53.653s |
| 2 | Elias | 1m 53.666s |
| 3 | de Angelis | 1m 53.737s |
| 4 | Abraham | 1m 53.866s |
| 5 | Y. Takahashi | 1m 53.997s |
| 6 | Iannone | 1m 54.013s |
| 7 | Debon | 1m 54.015s |
| 8 | Corsi | 1m 54.022s |
| 9 | Redding | 1m 54.040s |
| 10 | Luthi | 1m 54.162s |
| 11 | Bradl | 1m 54.219s |
| 12 | Rolfo | 1m 54.269s |
| 13 | de Rosa | 1m 54.325s |
| 14 | Aegerter | 1m 54.388s |
| 15 | Cluzel | 1m 54.429s |
| 16 | Hernandez | 1m 54.487s |
| 17 | Corti | 1m 54.569s |
| 18 | Talmacsi | 1m 54.802s |
| 19 | Faubel | 1m 54.802s |
| 20 | Pons | 1m 54.904s |
| 21 | Noyes | 1m 54.946s |
| 22 | Gadea | 1m 55.000s |
| 23 | Ranseder | 1m 55.005s |
| 24 | di Meglio | 1m 55.017s |
| 25 | Watanabe | 1m 55.090s |
| 26 | Baldolini | 1m 55.149s |
| 27 | Wilairot | 1m 55.150s |
| 28 | West | 1m 55.340s |
| 29 | Nieto | 1m 55.381s |
| 30 | Debise | 1m 55.547s |
| 31 | Cardus | 1m 56.008s |
| 32 | Al Naimi | 1m 56.322s |
| 33 | Kunikawa | 1m 56.499s |
| 34 | Guerra | 1m 56.602s |
| 35 | Olive | 1m 56.688s |
| 36 | Ivanov | 1m 56.742s |
| 37 | Pietri | 1m 56.900s |
| 38 | K. Takahashi | 1m 57.142s |
| 39 | Lamborghini | 1m 57.286s |

**Championship Points**

| | | |
|---|---|---|
| 1 | Elias | 249 |
| 2 | Simon | 168 |
| 3 | Iannone | 147 |
| 4 | Luthi | 138 |
| 5 | Corsi | 113 |
| 6 | Talmacsi | 95 |
| 7 | Cluzel | 94 |
| 8 | Y. Takahashi | 86 |
| 9 | Tomizawa | 82 |
| 10 | Gadea | 59 |
| 11 | Redding | 58 |
| 12 | Debon | 52 |
| 13 | Bradl | 52 |
| 14 | Rolfo | 50 |
| 15 | Abraham | 49 |
| 16 | Aegerter | 49 |
| 17 | Nieto | 41 |
| 18 | Wilairot | 30 |
| 19 | Y. Hernandez | 27 |
| 20 | de Angelis | 24 |
| 21 | di Meglio | 24 |
| 22 | Noyes | 18 |
| 23 | Corti | 18 |
| 24 | West | 17 |
| 25 | Baldolini | 14 |
| 26 | Pasini | 12 |
| 27 | Cudlin | 9 |
| 28 | Simeon | 9 |
| 29 | Faubel | 8 |
| 30 | Di Salvo | 7 |
| 31 | de Rosa | 5 |
| 32 | Pesek | 5 |
| 33 | Pirro | 2 |
| 34 | Ranseder | 2 |
| 35 | Pons | 2 |
| 36 | Ivanov | 2 |
| 37 | Tode | 2 |
| 38 | Teshima | 1 |

**Constructors**

| | | |
|---|---|---|
| 1 | Moriwaki | 274 |
| 2 | Suter | 236 |
| 3 | Speed Up | 172 |
| 4 | MotoBI | 123 |
| 5 | FTR | 100 |
| 6 | Tech 3 | 89 |
| 7 | Pons Kalex | 68 |
| 8 | Bimota | 30 |
| 9 | BQR-Moto2 | 27 |
| 10 | Promoharris | 18 |
| 11 | MZ-RE Honda | 17 |
| 12 | I.C.P. | 14 |
| 13 | Force GP210 | 11 |
| 14 | RSV | 10 |

## 125cc

RACE DISTANCE: 20 laps, 59.664 miles/96.020 km · RACE WEATHER: Dry (air 24°, humidity 40%, track 34°)

| Pos. | Rider | Nat. | No. | Entrant | Machine | Laps | Time & Speed |
|---|---|---|---|---|---|---|---|
| 1 | **Marc Marquez** | SPA | 93 | Red Bull Ajo Motorsport | Derbi | 20 | 39m 46.937s |
| | | | | | | | (mph/km/h) |
| | | | | | | | 89.986/144.818 |
| 2 | **Nicolas Terol** | SPA | 40 | Bancaja Aspar Team | Aprilia | 20 | 39m 49.549s |
| 3 | **Bradley Smith** | GBR | 38 | Bancaja Aspar Team | Aprilia | 20 | 39m 55.333s |
| 4 | **Pol Espargaro** | SPA | 44 | Tuenti Racing | Derbi | 20 | 40m 05.810s |
| 5 | **Alberto Moncayo** | SPA | 23 | Andalucia Cajasol | Aprilia | 20 | 40m 18.910s |
| 6 | **Esteve Rabat** | SPA | 12 | Blusens-STX | Aprilia | 20 | 40m 19.076s |
| 7 | **Danny Webb** | GBR | 99 | Andalucia Cajasol | Aprilia | 20 | 40m 33.653s |
| 8 | **Luis Salom** | SPA | 39 | Stipa-Molenaar Racing GP | Aprilia | 20 | 40m 36.381s |
| 9 | **Adrian Martin** | SPA | 26 | Aeroport de Castello - Ajo | Aprilia | 20 | 40m 36.804s |
| 10 | **Johann Zarco** | FRA | 14 | WTR San Marino Team | Aprilia | 20 | 40m 42.849s |
| 11 | **Randy Krummenacher** | SWI | 35 | Stipa-Molenaar Racing GP | Aprilia | 20 | 40m 43.621s |
| 12 | **Sandro Cortese** | GER | 11 | Avant Mitsubishi Ajo | Derbi | 20 | 40m 43.675s |
| 13 | **Simone Grotzkyj** | ITA | 15 | Fontana Racing | Aprilia | 20 | 40m 52.925s |
| 14 | **Marcel Schrotter** | GER | 78 | Interwetten Honda 125 | Honda | 20 | 40m 57.276s |
| 15 | **Jasper Iwema** | NED | 53 | CBC Corse | Aprilia | 20 | 40m 57.455s |
| 16 | Hikari Ookubo | JPN | 88 | 18 Garage Racing Team | Honda | 20 | 41m 08.075s |
| 17 | Takehiro Yamamoto | JPN | 43 | Team Nobby | Honda | 20 | 41m 08.090s |
| 18 | Louis Rossi | FRA | 69 | CBC Corse | Aprilia | 20 | 41m 08.340s |
| 19 | Zulfahmi Khairuddin | MAL | 63 | AirAsia-Sepang Int. Circuit | Aprilia | 20 | 41m 11.952s |
| 20 | Syunya Mori | JPN | 32 | Racing Sayama | Honda | 20 | 41m 12.123s |
| 21 | Sasuke Shinozaki | JPN | 91 | Team Tec2 | Yamaha | 20 | 41m 13.343s |
| 22 | Tomoyoshi Koyama | JPN | 71 | Racing Team Germany | Aprilia | 20 | 41m 27.671s |
| 23 | Luca Marconi | ITA | 87 | Ongetta Team | Aprilia | 19 | 39m 51.105s |
| 24 | Yuma Yahagi | JPN | 89 | Endurance | Honda | 19 | 39m 51.325s |
| | Danny Kent | GBR | 52 | Lambretta Reparto Corse | Lambretta | 11 | DNF |
| | Lorenzo Savadori | SPA | 32 | Matteoni CP Racing | Aprilia | 8 | DNF |
| | Jakub Kornfeil | CZE | 84 | Racing Team Germany | Aprilia | 3 | DNF |
| | Tommaso Gabrielli | ITA | 96 | Ongetta Team | Aprilia | 1 | DNF |
| | Sturla Fagerhaug | NOR | 50 | AirAsia-Sepang Int. Circuit | Aprilia | 0 | DNF |
| | Efren Vazquez | SPA | 7 | Tuenti Racing | Derbi | 0 | DNF |
| | Jonas Folger | GER | 94 | Ongetta Team | Aprilia | 0 | DNF |

**Fastest lap:** Sandro Cortese, on lap 4, 1m 58.666s, 90.502mph/145.649km/h.

**Lap record:** Mika Kallio, FIN (KTM), 1m 57.666s, 91.271mph/146.886km/h (2006).

**Event best maximum speed:** Marc Marquez, 140.2mph/225.7km/h (race).

**Qualifying:** Dry

Air: 23° Humidity: 41% Ground: 36°

| | | |
|---|---|---|
| 1 | Marquez | 1m 58.030s |
| 2 | Terol | 1m 58.447s |
| 3 | Smith | 1m 59.026s |
| 4 | Cortese | 1m 59.102s |
| 5 | Koyama | 1m 59.209s |
| 6 | Rabat | 1m 59.660s |
| 7 | Espargaro | 1m 59.873s |
| 8 | Grotzkyj | 1m 59.991s |
| 9 | Moncayo | 2m 00.177s |
| 10 | Vazquez | 2m 00.249s |
| 11 | Folger | 2m 00.345s |
| 12 | Krummenacher | 2m 00.595s |
| 13 | Webb | 2m 00.634s |
| 14 | Salom | 2m 01.015s |
| 15 | Martin | 2m 01.083s |
| 16 | Kent | 2m 01.109s |
| 17 | Yamamoto | 2m 01.285s |
| 18 | Zarco | 2m 01.411s |
| 19 | Ravaioli | 2m 01.660s |
| 20 | Kornfeil | 2m 01.684s |
| 21 | Schrotter | 2m 01.763s |
| 22 | Iwema | 2m 02.071s |
| 23 | Rossi | 2m 02.240s |
| 24 | Fagerhaug | 2m 02.309s |
| 25 | Shinozaki | 2m 02.521s |
| 26 | Ookubo | 2m 02.816s |
| 27 | Khairuddin | 2m 03.316s |
| 28 | Mori | 2m 03.592s |
| 29 | Savadori | 2m 04.109s |
| 30 | Yahagi | 2m 04.619s |
| 31 | Marconi | 2m0 5.921s |
| Outside 107% | | |
| DNQ | Gabrielli | 2m 14.113s |

**Fastest race laps**

| | | |
|---|---|---|
| 1 | Cortese | 1m 58.666s |
| 2 | Marquez | 1m 58.673s |
| 3 | Terol | 1m 58.705s |
| 4 | Smith | 1m 58.990s |
| 5 | Espargaro | 1m 59.141s |
| 6 | Koyama | 1m 59.784s |
| 7 | Moncayo | 1m 59.801s |
| 8 | Rabat | 1m 59.932s |
| 9 | Webb | 2m 00.135s |
| 10 | Salom | 2m 00.807s |
| 11 | Martin | 2m 00.963s |
| 12 | Zarco | 2m 01.029s |
| 13 | Krummenacher | 2m 01.073s |
| 14 | Kent | 2m 01.170s |
| 15 | Grotzkyj | 2m 01.271s |
| 16 | Iwema | 2m 01.465s |
| 17 | Schrotter | 2m 01.690s |
| 18 | Yamamoto | 2m 01.791s |
| 19 | Ookubo | 2m 01.920s |
| 20 | Rossi | 2m 02.080s |
| 21 | Mori | 2m 02.225s |
| 22 | Khairuddin | 2m 02.272s |
| 23 | Shinozaki | 2m 02.337s |
| 24 | Savadori | 2m 03.562s |
| 25 | Marconi | 2m 04.386s |
| 26 | Yahagi | 2m 04.564s |
| 27 | Kornfeil | 2m 07.292s |
| 28 | Gabrielli | 2m 33.768s |

**Championship Points**

| | | |
|---|---|---|
| 1 | Terol | 228 |
| 2 | Marquez | 222 |
| 3 | Espargaro | 215 |
| 4 | Smith | 160 |
| 5 | Cortese | 122 |
| 6 | Rabat | 118 |
| 7 | Vazquez | 110 |
| 8 | Koyama | 102 |
| 9 | Krummenacher | 84 |
| 10 | Webb | 80 |
| 11 | Zarco | 72 |
| 12 | Folger | 56 |
| 13 | Moncayo | 51 |
| 14 | Salom | 39 |
| 15 | Iwema | 34 |
| 16 | Martin | 27 |
| 17 | Masbou | 20 |
| 18 | Grotzkyj | 19 |
| 19 | Schrotter | 19 |
| 20 | Kornfeil | 18 |
| 21 | Fagerhaug | 8 |
| 22 | Kartheininger | 6 |
| 23 | Savadori | 5 |
| 24 | Khairuddin | 3 |
| 25 | Rossi | 2 |

**Constructors**

| | | |
|---|---|---|
| 1 | Derbi | 310 |
| 2 | Aprilia | 271 |
| 3 | Honda | 19 |
| 4 | KTM | 6 |
| 5 | Lambretta | 1 |

Everyone a winner, but Rossi steals the show.

*Inset above:* Elias celebrates his Moto2 championship.

*Inset above right:* Jorge Lorenzo and his crew.

*Inset left:* Lorenzo takes the chequered flag.

*Main photo:* Rossi took his first win since the opening race of the year.

*Photos:* Gold & Goose

FIM WORLD CHAMPIONSHIP · ROUND 15

# MALAYSIAN GRAND PRIX

SEPANG CIRCUIT

*Above:* Rossi had to fight all the way to keep Dovizioso behind, but Lorenzo was happy to settle for third.

*Top & above right:* Shades and degrees: Rossi looks cool as ever, while Edwards adopted a towel-head solution to the Sepang heat.

*Right:* Suzukis like hot weather. Bautista battled with Hayden and beat him.

Photos: Gold & Goose

A QUICK change of currency, cuisine, climate and clothing, and the gang was back on track just five days after Motegi for the 20th Malaysian GP, the gruelling schedule mollified slightly by the chance to spend a day or two by the swimming pool. And then go racing for a weekend when Spanish riders secured two out of three titles, and effectively annexed the third as well (the last mathematical rival to Marquez, Terol and Espargaro, Smith, was eliminated).

Back in Europe, a storm had been brewing as the Spanish media sprang to the defence of fledgling champion Lorenzo, so severely mugged by Rossi at Motegi. A cry was taken up that the superstar should be disciplined in some way for his borderline dangerous riding, but that favouritism meant he could get away with almost anything. For evidence, they pointed at the same race: video evidence showed that Rossi had jumped the start, yet nothing had been done about it.

Race director Paul Butler mounted a vigorous defence of the start-line question. Clearly Rossi's bike had jumped forward slightly, but it did not seem to go over the line, and most crucially he hadn't gained any advantage. "It can happen that a bike moves a few inches when the rider puts it into gear, and if the front wheel crosses the line then we have no choice. But if it's just a nano-second of movement and the rider gains no advantage, as Rossi clearly did not, then we don't see any need to penalise."

The charge of favouritism was harder to dismiss, although Butler thought such accusations were inevitable, "like saying the ref is favouring Manchester United when they are playing at Old Trafford". Of the past cases mentioned – barging Stoner via a corner-cutting short cut at Laguna in 2008 and

pushing Gibernau into the gravel at Jerez in 2005 – "the thing with Gibernau was on the borderline, but nobody who knows Valentino could believe he is capable of deliberately dangerous riding," he said.

Just very hard riding. Classic racing, in fact. What we all want to see. A view borne out by post-race comments from ex-racers, including Rainey and Gardner. Although not all current racers: Stoner was typically open in his criticism and free with his threats, saying, "It all looks sweet and pretty on the TV, but on the bike..." Valentino should, he thought, have shown more respect for a team-mate on the brink of the title. "He could've lost it right there with a team-mate's pass. When Jorge has got the championship wrapped up, I think Valentino may have his hands full. As for Valentino and me, it won't happen again; if it does, it'll come back tenfold."

The championship did indeed come to pass for Lorenzo at Sepang, and mindful of the need to finish, he did shrink back this time when hand-to-hand combat was on offer with Rossi. For the older rider, it was just an interlude in a classic ride – one of his best ever – from 11th on the first lap to his first victory since Qatar at the beginning of the season. It was enough for him to put aside plans to quit early for surgery and look forward to Australia. His winning was enough in itself to steal Lorenzo's glory; that it was an iconic 46th win on a Yamaha gave him another emblem to brandish on the rostrum, to steal a bit more thunder. "Forty-six is good," he said, "but 47 is better." Although he did say all the right things: that Lorenzo was "a great champion" who thoroughly deserved to win. "I look forward to some great battles next year," he added.

At Malaysia also came confirmation that the Interwetten Honda team would withdraw from MotoGP to concentrate on 125 and Moto2. With Pramac soon to announce it was planning to drop to one rider as well, the grid was shrinking before one's eyes, and Dorna was quick to act, with whatever rescue it could. At the same time, HRC was firming up plans for a possible three-man factory team, freeing up the seat being held for Dovizioso at Gresini, and thus the factory was able to steer the displaced Hiro Aoyama in that direction.

All races were cut by one lap compared to 2009, not as some thought because of fuel consumption, but in response to the heat, and the danger of fatigue. With track temperatures soaring to 56 degrees and humidity hovering towards a sweaty 40 per cent as usual, this made sense. Dovizioso shunned the 'camel-back' drinking system used by most other riders, but looked fresh after yet another strong race. There was one conspicuous victim of the conditions, however. Scott Redding was running with the leaders when suddenly he dropped back. Weak and suffering vision problems, he had to be helped off his bike when he made it back to the pits, vowing to review his training regime.

## MOTOGP RACE – 20 laps

The race was delayed by two hours to 4pm to avoid clashing with F1 from Suzuka. "At two, it is 90 per cent certain not to rain. At four, the same 90 per cent is the other way," Rossi had warned. Happily, race day's tropical downpour came later.

Lorenzo took pole, from a beaming Hayden and Dovizioso; Spies led row two, and only then came Stoner and Rossi, the former blaming circumstances and the latter elusive set-up. The Yamaha rider's crew would need to find yet another magic fix in warm-up. They duly obliged.

Lorenzo got away cleanly from pole, followed by Dovizioso, Spies and the two Ducatis. Rossi was slow off the line and swamped in the jostle through the first corners, 11th at the first timing point.

Stoner was soon past Hayden as Spies started to lose places, his early laps spoiled as he waited for his tyre to come in. Now the Ducati rider was with Lorenzo and Dovizio-

Lorenzo himself seemed dazed, on autopilot after becoming Spain's second champion so far in 2010, but only the nation's second ever in the premier class. "It was the hardest race in the championship. Now I have got the maximum a rider can get from a motorcycle. I need to be by myself for five minutes to take in what I have done." It was a tremendous achievement after a fault-free year. He had set a new record, on the rostrum for the first 12 races, and had ridden all year not only with speed and a style ever closer to the immaculate, but also with very few mistakes, while rivals were tumbling to destruction on all sides.

The latest to do so was Stoner, who crashed before even completing a lap of a race he thought might give him a third win in a row. Pedrosa's crash in Japan, triggered by mechanical failure, had given Lorenzo his first crown with three races to spare. There had been fevered talk that Dani, released from hospital with a titanium plate and eight screws on Tuesday, would be flying out to take part at Sepang. All nonsense, and even his attempt a week later in Australia would prove too soon.

The outcome of Suzuki's post-Motegi meeting was still not clear, as Dorna and the factory were wrangling over contract terms; but the factory's decision was clear enough: on the eve of the Malaysian race, half of the pit crew were told they were "free to seek other employment" for the 2011 season. Most prominent among the victims on the British crew was Capirossi's crew chief, Stuart Shenton, one of the most experienced in the paddock, whose background encompassed not only factory Honda riders, among them Freddie Spencer, but also the title won for Suzuki by Kevin Schwantz.

so as they braked for the final hairpin for the first time, fully confident that he had the pace to go for a third win in a row. But as he braked, the front tucked and he was down. He blamed tyres that were not yet warm enough, adding, "though I don't think I could have been more careful."

Hayden was third, almost a second behind Jorge and Dovi. As in their 250 days, they were glued together, and they stayed that way for the first eight laps. The spur came from behind. Rossi had finished lap one ninth, then had scythed through the middle orders to take third off charging Simoncelli by lap four. The gap to the leaders was just under two seconds, but little by little it started to come down.

He had halved it by lap eight, as Dovizioso took the lead – a clean outbraking move into the first corner. Instead of securing his escape, however, it slowed the pair and Rossi tagged on behind, with fastest lap of the race.

Lorenzo put up more than token resistance when Rossi pushed past on the entry to the first left-right set, but it was to no avail – Valentino had the bit between his teeth. He did the same thing to Dovizioso at the next such corner set one lap later, the 11th, and led a GP for the first time since before he had broken his leg at Mugello in June.

But Dovizioso wasn't finished. Four laps later, he pushed alongside, only to be directly repulsed. Then on lap 15, he pulled the Turn Five-Six move on Rossi to get ahead, only to have it done straight back to him at Nine-Ten.

By now, Lorenzo was dropping back out of harm's way, but Dovi kept on pushing, starting the last lap 0.27 second behind. Rossi did everything right to stay far enough ahead to avoid an outbraking move at the last hairpin, although he ran wide in the process. There were still barely two-tenths in it over the line.

His comeback win was a second brilliant ride in succession; Dovizioso's close second was also a big achievement: "Last year, we were 40 seconds behind the winner here, so to be just 0.2 second behind means we've moved forward a lot."

There was good racing down the field. Hayden had been a couple of seconds adrift of Simoncelli, Spies stuck behind him until lap eight. Once past, Ben was away; but Hayden

had trouble coming from behind, with a gang of four now led by the inspired Bautista, from Edwards, Aoyama and de Puniet. The Suzuki was revelling again in the heat.

Edwards crashed out on lap nine at the same time as Hayden succumbed to Bautista; next time around, Aoyama was also ahead of the Ducati, with de Puniet fading behind into the clutches of Melandri.

Soon after half-distance, Spies had caught Simoncelli and was stuck for a couple of laps. This allowed Bautista, Aoyama and Hayden to close up once more, and when Spies did escape on lap 14, there were again four riders hard at it.

Bautista soon escaped, while some trademark tough tactics by Simoncelli not only deposed Aoyama, but also gave Hayden his chance to pass them both. He stayed sixth, while Aoyama regained the advantage from Simoncelli, who was under attack by team-mate Melandri over the line.

De Puniet was another eight seconds away; then came the battling satellite Ducati pair, Barbera narrowly regaining 11th from Kallio with two laps to go.

Capirossi, going strong in spite of a painful foot injury from a crash in free practice, had another engine failure on lap five – officially "an electrical problem". Espargaro had crashed out two laps later.

Edwards had pitted for repairs and had resumed to get points for the team. Then he politely slowed on the last lap to let the battling leaders past. As a result, it turned out he had completed one too few laps to be classified.

## MOTO2 RACE – 19 laps

Simon was on pole for a second race in succession, from de Angelis, Luthi and Elias, and it was Luthi away first, Elias slotting ahead by the end of the lap. His task was simple: as long as he finished one place behind Simon, he would be champion, and team chief Gresini had suggested that a battle like the one in Japan should be avoided.

Luthi regained the lead third time around, with Redding now in a strong fourth, ahead of Iannone; Simon was behind them after finishing lap one seventh.

Iannone was pushing hardest and deposed Luthi for a

*Above:* Lap nine, and Rossi has caught the leaders, Dovizioso and Lorenzo, after fighting up from 11th.

*Above right:* The Yamaha team celebrates the MotoGP title: (l to r) team chief Lin Jarvis, Yoshiaki Hayasaki, champion Lorenzo and his team manager, Wilco Zeelenberg.

*Right:* Surprise Moto2 race winner Robie Rolfo leads de Angelis.

*Below right:* The usual suspects. Marc Marquez took another 125cc win ahead of Espargaro and Terol.

*Photos: Gold & Goose*

long spell up front, until after half-distance. Luthi crashed out trying to get back on lap seven. Elias stayed with the Italian, and since lap four had the company of Simon, who was briefly ahead at the end of lap five. His next attack ended in him running off track. He rejoined in seventh, desperate to get back at his rival, but crashed out terminally at the first corner in the attempt.

Significant events were taking place a second behind Iannone and Elias. Redding was scrapping with de Angelis, but the Briton was starting to fade. Rolfo had been there all the time, however, and by half-distance he was ahead of the Briton and closing on de Angelis, who in turn had closed up on Elias.

Both were ahead of him next time around, lap 11, and were taking the fight to leader Iannone. On the next lap, Rolfo, who had cannily saved his tyres best, picked off de Angelis and then Iannone to take a lead he would hold to the end.

He was under attack by de Angelis to the line, however, winning by 0.040 second thanks to his smooth, high corner speed and skilful defensive riding.

Iannone had fallen back into the hands of Elias, who attacked successfully on lap 16. But when the Italian came back with a forceful move through the first two corners, he let him go, crossing the line safely as champion, half a second adrift.

In the world of Spanish racing, it was a rare all-Italian-speaking rostrum (de Angelis hails from San Marino, which is within Italy).

Redding had dropped back into the next gang, only to fall further back and pull into the pits after 13 laps, a strong early ride ending in complete physical exhaustion in the heat.

That left a four-strong group hard at it, with Bradl and Abraham heading Debon and Aegerter. By the end, wise veteran Debon was leading the group from Abraham, Bradl and Aegerter, all across the line within seven-tenths.

Jules Cluzel lost touch with them for ninth; Corsi came storming through to tenth after starting from the back of the grid – a crash on his second lap in qualifying had left him without a lap time.

Now the title fight switched to second, with Simon under threat from Iannone, although Luthi was dropping away.

## 125cc RACE – 18 laps

Marquez had qualified on pole by a slightly smaller margin than usual, from Smith, Terol and Espargaro. He got the jump into the first corners, but a forceful Terol muscled him aside and by the end of the first lap had a handsome lead of better than a second. Some shuffling behind him had helped this escape, with Espargaro now second from Smith, Marquez and the recovered Vazquez, who were all over one another.

Next time around, a swoop into the hairpin put Marquez second, the gap the same. Inevitably it started to shrink, and by lap five he had not only caught Terol, but also had got ahead for the first time. And Espargaro had gone with him.

They exchanged blows for the next eight or nine laps, and then Marquez decided he'd had enough and started to pull away remorselessly at three- or four-tenths a lap. He was 2.3 seconds ahead at the end for his eighth win of the year and second in eight days, to regain the lead also on points.

In the meantime, Terol could do nothing about the determined Espargaro, and by the finish he was more than a second adrift.

The next trio had been scrapping all race long, with Smith doing most of the leading, but after a ding-dong final lap in which they all changed places at least once, it was Vazquez narrowly ahead, then Smith and Cortese.

Rabat was a distant and lonely seventh, while another trio scrapped over the last top-ten positions. Their times were identical, but a video finish gave eighth to Salom from Koyama, with Krummenacher inches behind.

# SHELL ADVANCE MALAYSIAN MOTORCYCLE GP

8-10 October 2010 · FIM WORLD CHAMPIONSHIP ROUND 15

OFFICIAL TIMEKEEPER

## SEPANG INTERNATIONAL CIRCUIT

Langkawi curve 83/52
Genting Curve 140/87
Turn 3 179/112
Turn 5 152/95
Pangkor Laut Chicane 70/44
Hairpin 72/45
Turn 7 124/77
KLIA Curve 127/79
Berjaya Tioman Corner 63/58
Sunway Lagoon Corner 87/54
Turn 12 154/96
Kenyir Lake 103/64

Key 96/60 kph/mph

Circuit 5.548km /3.447 miles  Race: 21 laps

Gear

## MotoGP

**RACE DISTANCE: 20 laps, 68.947 miles/110.960 km · RACE WEATHER: Dry (air 33°, humidity 27%, track 43°)**

| Pos. | Rider | Nat. | No. | Entrant | Machine | Tyres | Laps | Time & speed |
|---|---|---|---|---|---|---|---|---|
| 1 | **Valentino Rossi** | ITA | 46 | Fiat Yamaha Team | Yamaha | B | 20 | 41m 03.448s 100.757mph/ 162.153km/h |
| 2 | **Andrea Dovizioso** | ITA | 4 | Repsol Honda Team | Honda | B | 20 | 41m 03.672s |
| 3 | **Jorge Lorenzo** | SPA | 99 | Fiat Yamaha Team | Yamaha | B | 20 | 41m 09.483s |
| 4 | **Ben Spies** | USA | 11 | Monster Yamaha Tech 3 | Yamaha | B | 20 | 41m 17.124s |
| 5 | **Alvaro Bautista** | SPA | 19 | Rizla Suzuki MotoGP | Suzuki | B | 20 | 41m 18.850s |
| 6 | **Nicky Hayden** | USA | 69 | Ducati Marlboro Team | Ducati | B | 20 | 41m 22.274s |
| 7 | **Hiroshi Aoyama** | JPN | 7 | Interwetten Honda MotoGP | Honda | B | 20 | 41m 23.666s |
| 8 | **Marco Simoncelli** | ITA | 58 | San Carlo Honda Gresini | Honda | B | 20 | 41m 27.022s |
| 9 | **Marco Melandri** | ITA | 33 | San Carlo Honda Gresini | Honda | B | 20 | 41m 27.412s |
| 10 | **Randy de Puniet** | FRA | 14 | LCR Honda MotoGP | Honda | B | 20 | 41m 35.298s |
| 11 | **Hector Barbera** | SPA | 40 | Paginas Amarillas Aspar | Ducati | B | 20 | 41m 42.027s |
| 12 | **Mika Kallio** | FIN | 36 | Pramac Racing Team | Ducati | B | 20 | 41m 42.297s |
| | Colin Edwards | USA | 5 | Monster Yamaha Tech 3 | Yamaha | B | 6 | Not Classified |
| | Aleix Espargaro | SPA | 41 | Pramac Racing Team | Ducati | B | 6 | DNF |
| | Loris Capirossi | ITA | 65 | Rizla Suzuki MotoGP | Suzuki | B | 4 | DNF |
| | Casey Stoner | AUS | 27 | Ducati Marlboro Team | Ducati | B | 0 | DNF |

**Fastest lap:** Valentino Rossi, on lap 9, 2m 2.117s, 101.628mph/163.554km/h.

**Lap record:** Casey Stoner, AUS (Ducati), 2m 2.108s, 101.635mph/163.566km/h (2007).

**Event best maximum speed:** Hector Barbera, 194.9mph/313.6km/h (free practice 2).

### Qualifying

Weather: Dry
Air Temp: 34° Humidity: 37°
Track Temp: 52°

| Pos | Rider | Time |
|---|---|---|
| 1 | Lorenzo | 2m 1.537s |
| 2 | Hayden | 2m 1.637s |
| 3 | Dovizioso | 2m 1.829s |
| 4 | Spies | 2m 1.993s |
| 5 | Stoner | 2m 2.023s |
| 6 | Rossi | 2m 2.030s |
| 7 | Edwards | 2m 2.097s |
| 8 | Bautista | 2m 2.394s |
| 9 | Capirossi | 2m 2.522s |
| 10 | Melandri | 2m 2.624s |
| 11 | Simoncelli | 2m 2.690s |
| 12 | Espargaro | 2m 2.723s |
| 13 | de Puniet | 2m 2.775s |
| 14 | Aoyama | 2m 2.778s |
| 15 | Barbera | 2m 2.928s |
| 16 | Kallio | 2m 4.167s |

### Fastest race laps

| Pos | Rider | Time |
|---|---|---|
| 1 | Rossi | 2m 2.117s |
| 2 | Dovizioso | 2m 2.427s |
| 3 | Lorenzo | 2m 2.624s |
| 4 | Aoyama | 2m 2.683s |
| 5 | Spies | 2m 2.773s |
| 6 | Bautista | 2m 2.895s |
| 7 | Simoncelli | 2m 2.898s |
| 8 | Hayden | 2m 3.062s |
| 9 | Edwards | 2m 3.363s |
| 10 | de Puniet | 2m 3.366s |
| 11 | Melandri | 2m 3.418s |
| 12 | Barbera | 2m 3.819s |
| 13 | Kallio | 2m 4.152s |
| 14 | Espargaro | 2m 4.270s |
| 15 | Capirossi | 2m 4.425s |

### Championship Points

| Pos | Rider | Pts |
|---|---|---|
| 1 | Lorenzo | 313 |
| 2 | Pedrosa | 228 |
| 3 | Rossi | 181 |
| 4 | Stoner | 180 |
| 5 | Dovizioso | 179 |
| 6 | Spies | 152 |
| 7 | N. Hayden | 139 |
| 8 | de Puniet | 94 |
| 9 | Simoncelli | 92 |
| 10 | Melandri | 86 |
| 11 | Edwards | 81 |
| 12 | Barbera | 74 |
| 13 | Bautista | 69 |
| 14 | Espargaro | 52 |
| 15 | Aoyama | 44 |
| 16 | Capirossi | 41 |
| 17 | Kallio | 38 |
| 18 | de Angelis | 11 |
| 19 | R. Hayden | 5 |
| 20 | Akiyoshi | 4 |
| 21 | Yoshikawa | 1 |

### Team Points

| Pos | Team | Pts |
|---|---|---|
| 1 | Fiat Yamaha Team | 495 |
| 2 | Repsol Honda Team | 407 |
| 3 | Ducati Marlboro Team | 319 |
| 4 | Monster Yamaha Tech 3 | 233 |
| 5 | San Carlo Honda Gresini | 178 |
| 6 | Rizla Suzuki MotoGP | 110 |
| 7 | LCR Honda MotoGP | 99 |
| 8 | Pramac Racing Team | 90 |
| 9 | Paginas Amarillas Aspar | 74 |
| 10 | Interwetten Honda MotoGP | 59 |

### Constructor Points

| Pos | Constructor | Pts |
|---|---|---|
| 1 | Yamaha | 334 |
| 2 | Honda | 305 |
| 3 | Ducati | 230 |
| 4 | Suzuki | 92 |

### Grid order / lap chart

| Grid order | 1 | 2 | 3 | 4 | 5 | 6 | 7 | 8 | 9 | 10 | 11 | 12 | 13 | 14 | 15 | 16 | 17 | 18 | 19 | 20 | Pos |
|---|---|---|---|---|---|---|---|---|---|---|---|---|---|---|---|---|---|---|---|---|---|
| 99 LORENZO | 99 | 99 | 99 | 99 | 99 | 99 | 99 | 99 | 4 | 4 | 46 | 46 | 46 | 46 | 46 | 46 | 46 | 46 | 46 | 46 | 1 |
| 69 HAYDEN | 4 | 4 | 4 | 4 | 4 | 4 | 4 | 4 | 99 | 46 | 4 | 4 | 4 | 4 | 4 | 4 | 4 | 4 | 4 | 4 | 2 |
| 4 DOVIZIOSO | 69 | 69 | 58 | 46 | 46 | 46 | 46 | 46 | 46 | 99 | 99 | 99 | 99 | 99 | 99 | 99 | 99 | 99 | 99 | 99 | 3 |
| 11 SPIES | 11 | 58 | 46 | 58 | 58 | 58 | 58 | 58 | 58 | 58 | 58 | 58 | 58 | 11 | 11 | 11 | 11 | 11 | 11 | 11 | 4 |
| 27 STONER | 58 | 11 | 69 | 69 | 69 | 69 | 69 | 11 | 11 | 11 | 11 | 11 | 11 | 58 | 58 | 58 | 19 | 19 | 19 | 19 | 5 |
| 46 ROSSI | 5 | 46 | 11 | 11 | 11 | 11 | 11 | 69 | 19 | 19 | 19 | 19 | 19 | 19 | 19 | 7 | 58 | 7 | 69 | 69 | 6 |
| 5 EDWARDS | 65 | 5 | 33 | 5 | 33 | 19 | 19 | 19 | 69 | 7 | 7 | 7 | 7 | 7 | 7 | 19 | 7 | 58 | 7 | 7 | 7 |
| 19 BAUTISTA | 33 | 33 | 5 | 33 | 5 | 5 | 5 | 5 | 7 | 69 | 69 | 69 | 69 | 69 | 69 | 69 | 69 | 69 | 58 | 58 | 8 |
| 65 CAPIROSSI | 46 | 65 | 19 | 19 | 19 | 14 | 7 | 7 | 14 | 14 | 14 | 14 | 14 | 33 | 33 | 33 | 33 | 33 | 33 | 33 | 9 |
| 33 MELANDRI | 19 | 19 | 65 | 14 | 14 | 7 | 14 | 14 | 33 | 33 | 33 | 33 | 33 | 14 | 14 | 14 | 14 | 14 | 14 | 14 | 10 |
| 58 SIMONCELLI | 14 | 14 | 14 | 65 | 7 | 33 | 33 | 33 | 40 | 40 | 40 | 40 | 40 | 40 | 36 | 36 | 36 | 36 | 40 | 40 | 11 |
| 41 ESPARGARO | 41 | 40 | 7 | 7 | 40 | 41 | 40 | 40 | 36 | 36 | 36 | 36 | 36 | 36 | 40 | 40 | 40 | 40 | 36 | 36 | 12 |
| 14 de PUNIET | 40 | 7 | 40 | 40 | 36 | 36 | 36 | 36 | 5 | 5 | 5 | 5 | 5 | 5 | | | | | | | |
| 7 AOYAMA | 7 | 41 | 36 | 36 | 41 | 40 | | | | | | | | | | | | | | | |
| 40 BARBERA | 36 | 36 | 41 | 41 | | | | | | | | | | | | | | | | | |
| 36 KALLIO | | | | | | | | | | | | | | | | | | | | | |

5 Lapped rider

## Moto2

RACE DISTANCE: 19 laps, 65.500 miles/105.412 km · RACE WEATHER: Dry (air 33°, humidity 34%, track 44°)

| Pos. | Rider | Nat. | No. | Entrant | Machine | Laps | Time & Speed |
|---|---|---|---|---|---|---|---|
| 1 | **Roberto Rolfo** | ITA | 44 | Italtrans S.T.R. | Suter | 19 | 41m 09.412s (mph/km/h) 95.488/153.673 |
| 2 | **Alex de Angelis** | RSM | 15 | JIR Moto2 | MotoBI | 19 | 41m 09.452s |
| 3 | **Andrea Iannone** | ITA | 29 | Fimmco Speed Up | Speed Up | 19 | 41m 15.327s |
| 4 | **Toni Elias** | SPA | 24 | Gresini Racing Moto2 | Moriwaki | 19 | 41m 15.734s |
| 5 | **Alex Debon** | SPA | 6 | Aeroport de Castello - Ajo | FTR | 19 | 41m 21.324s |
| 6 | **Karel Abraham** | CZE | 17 | Cardion AB Motoracing | FTR | 19 | 41m 21.870s |
| 7 | **Stefan Bradl** | GER | 65 | Viessmann Kiefer Racing | Suter | 19 | 41m 21.931s |
| 8 | **Dominique Aegerter** | SWI | 77 | Technomag-CIP | Suter | 19 | 41m 22.001s |
| 9 | **Jules Cluzel** | FRA | 16 | Forward Racing | Suter | 19 | 41m 24.422s |
| 10 | **Simone Corsi** | ITA | 3 | JIR Moto2 | MotoBI | 19 | 41m 26.119s |
| 11 | **Hector Faubel** | SPA | 55 | Marc VDS Racing Team | Suter | 19 | 41m 29.591s |
| 12 | **Alex Baldolini** | ITA | 25 | Caretta Technology Race Dept. | I.C.P. | 19 | 41m 29.874s |
| 13 | **Yonny Hernandez** | COL | 68 | Blusens-STX | BQR-Moto2 | 19 | 41m 31.050s |
| 14 | **Michael Ranseder** | AUT | 56 | Vector Kiefer Racing | Suter | 19 | 41m 31.800s |
| 15 | **Claudio Corti** | ITA | 71 | Forward Racing | Suter | 19 | 41m 33.924s |
| 16 | Ratthapark Wilairot | THA | 14 | Thai Honda PTT Singha SAG | Bimota | 19 | 41m 35.778s |
| 17 | Axel Pons | SPA | 80 | Tenerife 40 Pons | Pons Kalex | 19 | 41m 40.142s |
| 18 | Kenny Noyes | USA | 9 | Jack & Jones by A.Banderas | Promoharris | 19 | 41m 40.492s |
| 19 | Fonsi Nieto | SPA | 10 | Holiday Gym G22 | Moriwaki | 19 | 41m 41.651s |
| 20 | Valentin Debise | FRA | 53 | WTR San Marino Team | ADV | 19 | 41m 43.216s |
| 21 | Julian Simon | SPA | 60 | Mapfre Aspar Team | Suter | 19 | 41m 48.860s |
| 22 | Mohamad Zamri Baba | MAL | 87 | Petronas SIC TWMR Malaysia | Moriwaki | 19 | 41m 55.443s |
| 23 | Joan Olive | SPA | 5 | Jack & Jones by A.Banderas | Promoharris | 19 | 41m 56.669s |
| 24 | Anthony West | AUS | 8 | MZ Racing Team | MZ-RE Honda | 19 | 41m 59.470s |
| 25 | Kazuki Watanabe | JPN | 28 | Racing Team Germany | Suter | 19 | 42m 00.242s |
| 26 | Mike di Meglio | FRA | 63 | Mapfre Aspar Team | Suter | 19 | 42m 01.383s |
| 27 | Robertino Pietri | VEN | 39 | Italtrans S.T.R. | Suter | 19 | 42m 08.567s |
| 28 | Hiromichi Kunikawa | JPN | 66 | Bimota - M Racing | Bimota | 19 | 42m 26.171s |
| 29 | Mashel Al Naimi | QAT | 95 | Blusens-STX | BQR-Moto2 | 19 | 42m 53.361s |
| | Gabor Talmacsi | HUN | 2 | Fimmco Speed Up | Speed Up | 13 | DNF |
| | Scott Redding | GBR | 45 | Marc VDS Racing Team | Suter | 13 | DNF |
| | Sergio Gadea | SPA | 40 | Tenerife 40 Pons | Pons Kalex | 13 | DNF |
| | Raffaele de Rosa | ITA | 35 | Tech 3 Racing | Tech 3 | 10 | DNF |
| | Yuki Takahashi | JPN | 72 | Tech 3 Racing | Tech 3 | 8 | DNF |
| | Thomas Luthi | SWI | 12 | Interwetten Moriwaki Moto2 | Moriwaki | 7 | DNF |
| | Vladimir Ivanov | UKR | 61 | Gresini Racing Moto2 | Moriwaki | 6 | DNF |
| | Javier Fores | SPA | 46 | Maquinza-SAG Team | Bimota | 6 | DNF |
| | Ferruccio Lamborghini | ITA | 70 | Matteoni Racing | Moriwaki | 6 | DNF |
| | Yannick Guerra | SPA | 88 | Holiday Gym G22 | Moriwaki | 1 | DNF |

**Fastest lap:** Julian Simon, on lap 7, 2m 8.691s, 96.436mph/155.199km/h (record).

**Previous lap record:** New category.

**Event best maximum speed:** Jules Cluzel, 165.2mph/265.9km/h (race).

**Qualifying:** Dry

Air: 37° Humidity: 28% Ground: 56°

| | | |
|---|---|---|
| 1 | Simon | 2m 08.562s |
| 2 | de Angelis | 2m 08.754s |
| 3 | Luthi | 2m 08.860s |
| 4 | Elias | 2m 08.863s |
| 5 | Rolfo | 2m 08.920s |
| 6 | Iannone | 2m 09.004s |
| 7 | Abraham | 2m 09.187s |
| 8 | Redding | 2m 09.335s |
| 9 | Ranseder | 2m 09.409s |
| 10 | Debon | 2m 09.429s |
| 11 | Aegerter | 2m 09.430s |
| 12 | Corti | 2m 09.489s |
| 13 | Cluzel | 2m 09.563s |
| 14 | Baldolini | 2m 09.587s |
| 15 | Talmacsi | 2m 09.714s |
| 16 | Nieto | 2m 09.746s |
| 17 | Faubel | 2m 09.794s |
| 18 | Takahashi | 2m 09.852s |
| 19 | di Meglio | 2m 09.879s |
| 20 | de Rosa | 2m 09.900s |
| 21 | Gadea | 2m 09.959s |
| 22 | Bradl | 2m 09.988s |
| 23 | Wilairot | 2m 10.059s |
| 24 | Pons | 2m 10.129s |
| 25 | Noyes | 2m 10.194s |
| 26 | West | 2m 10.444s |
| 27 | Hernandez | 2m 10.566s |
| 28 | Olive | 2m 10.885s |
| 29 | Debise | 2m 10.971s |
| 30 | Fores | 2m 11.069s |
| 31 | Zamri Baba | 2m 11.289s |
| 32 | Watanabe | 2m 11.351s |
| 33 | Ivanov | 2m 11.496s |
| 34 | Pietri | 2m 11.972s |
| 35 | Guerra | 2m 12.253s |
| 36 | Lamborghini | 2m 12.645s |
| 37 | Al Naimi | 2m 12.952s |
| 38 | Kunikawa | 2m 13.458s |
| *Outside 107%* | | |
| DNQ | Corsi | 3m 20.426s |

**Fastest race laps**

| | | |
|---|---|---|
| 1 | Simon | 2m 08.691s |
| 2 | Iannone | 2m 08.865s |
| 3 | de Angelis | 2m 09.037s |
| 4 | Elias | 2m 09.057s |
| 5 | Rolfo | 2m 09.140s |
| 6 | Luthi | 2m 09.259s |
| 7 | Redding | 2m 09.324s |
| 8 | Abraham | 2m 09.328s |
| 9 | Bradl | 2m 09.341s |
| 10 | Hernandez | 2m 09.431s |
| 11 | Aegerter | 2m 09.474s |
| 12 | Corti | 2m 09.619s |
| 13 | Debon | 2m 09.637s |
| 14 | Faubel | 2m 09.674s |
| 15 | Talmacsi | 2m 09.690s |
| 16 | Cluzel | 2m 09.713s |
| 17 | Wilairot | 2m 09.736s |
| 18 | Corsi | 2m 09.741s |
| 19 | Baldolini | 2m 09.757s |
| 20 | Ranseder | 2m 09.868s |
| 21 | Takahashi | 2m 09.905s |
| 22 | Pons | 2m 10.061s |
| 23 | Gadea | 2m 10.131s |
| 24 | Noyes | 2m 10.324s |
| 25 | di Meglio | 2m 10.416s |
| 26 | Nieto | 2m 10.585s |
| 27 | Debise | 2m 10.635s |
| 28 | de Rosa | 2m 10.746s |
| 29 | Olive | 2m 10.936s |
| 30 | West | 2m 10.962s |
| 31 | Watanabe | 2m 11.097s |
| 32 | Zamri Baba | 2m 11.175s |
| 33 | Ivanov | 2m 11.626s |
| 34 | Fores | 2m 11.741s |
| 35 | Pietri | 2m 11.748s |
| 36 | Kunikawa | 2m 12.817s |
| 37 | Lamborghini | 2m 12.857s |
| 38 | Al Naimi | 2m 12.950s |
| 39 | Guerra | 2m 23.685s |

**Championship Points**

| | | |
|---|---|---|
| 1 | Elias | 262 |
| 2 | Simon | 168 |
| 3 | Iannone | 163 |
| 4 | Luthi | 138 |
| 5 | Corsi | 119 |
| 6 | Cluzel | 101 |
| 7 | Talmacsi | 95 |
| 8 | Y. Takahashi | 86 |
| 9 | Tomizawa | 82 |
| 10 | Rolfo | 75 |
| 11 | Debon | 63 |
| 12 | Bradl | 61 |
| 13 | Gadea | 59 |
| 14 | Abraham | 59 |
| 15 | Redding | 58 |
| 16 | Aegerter | 57 |
| 17 | de Angelis | 44 |
| 18 | Nieto | 41 |
| 19 | Wilairot | 30 |
| 20 | Y. Hernandez | 30 |
| 21 | di Meglio | 24 |
| 22 | Corti | 19 |
| 23 | Noyes | 18 |
| 24 | Baldolini | 18 |
| 25 | West | 17 |
| 26 | Faubel | 13 |
| 27 | Pasini | 12 |
| 28 | Cudlin | 9 |
| 29 | Simeon | 9 |
| 30 | Di Salvo | 7 |
| 31 | de Rosa | 5 |
| 32 | Pesek | 5 |
| 33 | Ranseder | 4 |
| 34 | Pirro | 2 |
| 35 | Pons | 2 |
| 36 | Ivanov | 2 |
| 37 | Tode | 2 |
| 38 | Teshima | 1 |

**Constructors**

| | | |
|---|---|---|
| 1 | Moriwaki | 287 |
| 2 | Suter | 261 |
| 3 | Speed Up | 188 |
| 4 | MotoBI | 143 |
| 5 | FTR | 111 |
| 6 | Tech 3 | 89 |
| 7 | Pons Kalex | 68 |
| 8 | Bimota | 30 |
| 9 | BQR-Moto2 | 30 |
| 10 | Promoharris | 18 |
| 11 | I.C.P. | 18 |
| 12 | MZ-RE Honda | 17 |
| 13 | Force GP210 | 11 |
| 14 | RSV | 10 |

## 125cc

RACE DISTANCE: 18 laps, 62.053 miles/99.864 km · RACE WEATHER: Dry (air 33°, humidity 44%, track 44°)

| Pos. | Rider | Nat. | No. | Entrant | Machine | Laps | Time & Speed |
|---|---|---|---|---|---|---|---|
| 1 | **Marc Marquez** | SPA | 93 | Red Bull Ajo Motorsport | Derbi | 18 | 40m 29.035s (mph/km/h) 91.966/148.005 |
| 2 | **Pol Espargaro** | SPA | 44 | Tuenti Racing | Derbi | 18 | 40m 31.376s |
| 3 | **Nicolas Terol** | SPA | 40 | Bancaja Aspar Team | Aprilia | 18 | 40m 32.691s |
| 4 | **Efren Vazquez** | SPA | 7 | Tuenti Racing | Derbi | 18 | 40m 35.815s |
| 5 | **Bradley Smith** | GBR | 38 | Bancaja Aspar Team | Aprilia | 18 | 40m 36.168s |
| 6 | **Sandro Cortese** | GER | 11 | Avant Mitsubishi Ajo | Derbi | 18 | 40m 36.332s |
| 7 | **Esteve Rabat** | SPA | 12 | Blusens-STX | Aprilia | 18 | 40m 55.683s |
| 8 | **Luis Salom** | SPA | 39 | Stipa-Molenaar Racing GP | Aprilia | 18 | 40m 58.374s |
| 9 | **Tomoyoshi Koyama** | JPN | 71 | Racing Team Germany | Aprilia | 18 | 40m 58.374s |
| 10 | **Randy Krummenacher** | SWI | 35 | Stipa-Molenaar Racing GP | Aprilia | 18 | 40m 58.400s |
| 11 | **Johann Zarco** | FRA | 14 | WTR San Marino Team | Aprilia | 18 | 41m 05.364s |
| 12 | **Alberto Moncayo** | SPA | 23 | Andalucia Cajasol | Aprilia | 18 | 41m 06.580s |
| 13 | **Adrian Martin** | SPA | 26 | Aeroport de Castello - Ajo | Aprilia | 18 | 41m 20.297s |
| 14 | **Jakub Kornfeil** | CZE | 84 | Racing Team Germany | Aprilia | 18 | 41m 23.669s |
| 15 | **Marcel Schrotter** | GER | 78 | Interwetten Honda 125 | Honda | 18 | 41m 23.670s |
| 16 | Zulfahmi Khairuddin | MAL | 63 | AirAsia-Sepang Int. Circuit | Aprilia | 18 | 41m 27.616s |
| 17 | Louis Rossi | FRA | 69 | CBC Corse | Aprilia | 18 | 41m 44.253s |
| 18 | Marco Ravaioli | ITA | 72 | Lambretta Reparto Corse | Lambretta | 18 | 41m 44.630s |
| 19 | Tommaso Gabrielli | ITA | 96 | Ongetta Team | Aprilia | 18 | 42m 29.213s |
| | Danny Webb | GBR | 99 | Andalucia Cajasol | Aprilia | 11 | DNF |
| | Danny Kent | GBR | 52 | Lambretta Reparto Corse | Lambretta | 11 | DNF |
| | Jasper Iwema | NED | 53 | CBC Corse | Aprilia | 7 | DNF |
| | Sturla Fagerhaug | NOR | 50 | AirAsia-Sepang Int. Circuit | Aprilia | 6 | DNF |
| | Simone Grotzkyj | ITA | 15 | Fontana Racing | Aprilia | 5 | DNF |
| | Luca Marconi | ITA | 87 | Ongetta Team | Aprilia | 5 | DNF |
| | Lorenzo Savadori | SPA | 32 | Matteoni Racing | Aprilia | 3 | DNF |

**Fastest lap:** Marc Marquez, on lap 13, 2m 13.773s, 92.773mph/149.303km/h.

**Lap record:** Alvaro Bautista, SPA (Aprilia), 2m 13.118s, 93.229mph/150.038km/h (2006).

**Event best maximum speed:** Danny Webb, 139.3mph/224.2km/h (race).

**Qualifying:** Dry

Air: 35° Humidity: 37% Ground: 52°

| | | |
|---|---|---|
| 1 | Marquez | 2m 13.398s |
| 2 | Smith | 2m 13.691s |
| 3 | Terol | 2m 14.104s |
| 4 | Espargaro | 2m 14.105s |
| 5 | Vazquez | 2m 14.415s |
| 6 | Cortese | 2m 14.551s |
| 7 | Rabat | 2m 14.772s |
| 8 | Salom | 2m 15.494s |
| 9 | Koyama | 2m 15.541s |
| 10 | Krummenacher | 2m 15.967s |
| 11 | Zarco | 2m 16.150s |
| 12 | Webb | 2m 16.286s |
| 13 | Kent | 2m 16.392s |
| 14 | Moncayo | 2m 16.543s |
| 15 | Martin | 2m 16.706s |
| 16 | Grotzkyj | 2m 17.151s |
| 17 | Rossi | 2m 17.154s |
| 18 | Schrotter | 2m 17.268s |
| 19 | Kornfeil | 2m 17.441s |
| 20 | Savadori | 2m 17.802s |
| 21 | Fagerhaug | 2m 17.878s |
| 22 | Khairuddin | 2m 17.896s |
| 23 | Ravaioli | 2m 17.953s |
| 24 | Iwema | 2m 18.515s |
| 25 | Marconi | 2m 19.444s |
| 26 | Gabrielli | 2m 21.190s |

**Fastest race laps**

| | | |
|---|---|---|
| 1 | Marquez | 2m 13.773s |
| 2 | Espargaro | 2m 14.079s |
| 3 | Vazquez | 2m 14.245s |
| 4 | Terol | 2m 14.270s |
| 5 | Smith | 2m 14.407s |
| 6 | Cortese | 2m 14.461s |
| 7 | Rabat | 2m 14.801s |
| 8 | Salom | 2m 15.150s |
| 9 | Krummenacher | 2m 15.482s |
| 10 | Zarco | 2m 15.553s |
| 11 | Webb | 2m 15.623s |
| 12 | Moncayo | 2m 15.671s |
| 13 | Koyama | 2m 15.703s |
| 14 | Martin | 2m 16.660s |
| 15 | Grotzkyj | 2m 16.710s |
| 16 | Kent | 2m 16.730s |
| 17 | Fagerhaug | 2m 16.735s |
| 18 | Schrotter | 2m 16.782s |
| 19 | Kornfeil | 2m 16.883s |
| 20 | Iwema | 2m 17.065s |
| 21 | Khairuddin | 2m 17.315s |
| 22 | Ravaioli | 2m 17.444s |
| 23 | Rossi | 2m 17.463s |
| 24 | Marconi | 2m 19.080s |
| 25 | Savadori | 2m 19.150s |
| 26 | Gabrielli | 2m 19.695s |

**Championship Points**

| | | |
|---|---|---|
| 1 | Marquez | 247 |
| 2 | Terol | 244 |
| 3 | Espargaro | 235 |
| 4 | Smith | 171 |
| 5 | Cortese | 132 |
| 6 | Rabat | 127 |
| 7 | Vazquez | 123 |
| 8 | Koyama | 109 |
| 9 | Krummenacher | 90 |
| 10 | Webb | 80 |
| 11 | Zarco | 77 |
| 12 | Folger | 56 |
| 13 | Moncayo | 55 |
| 14 | Salom | 47 |
| 15 | Iwema | 34 |
| 16 | Martin | 30 |
| 17 | Kornfeil | 20 |
| 18 | Masbou | 20 |
| 19 | Schrotter | 20 |
| 20 | Grotzkyj | 19 |
| 21 | Fagerhaug | 8 |
| 22 | Kartheininger | 6 |
| 23 | Savadori | 5 |
| 24 | Khairuddin | 3 |
| 25 | Rossi | 2 |

**Constructors**

| | | |
|---|---|---|
| 1 | Derbi | 335 |
| 2 | Aprilia | 287 |
| 3 | Honda | 20 |
| 4 | KTM | 6 |
| 5 | Lambretta | 1 |

Main photo: Master of the Island. Stoner came home to a fourth successive Australian victory.

Inset: Well beaten, Lorenzo congratulates Stoner.
Photos: Gold & Goose

*Above:* Chill wind at the back of the grid. Kallio *(left)* prepares for his last MotoGP race on the Pramac Ducati; Bautista and his Suzuki are wrapped up well.

*Clockwise, from top right:* Wayne Maxwell made an impression in Moto2, in more than one way; stormy weather as the squalls swept in off the sea; stormy conversation? Past champions Mick Doohan and Wayne Gardner; Capirossi prepares for the weather. Another qualifying crash ruled him out of the race; Hayden appreciated the hardiness of the fans.

*Right:* A startled seagull clears the way for Lorenzo, Simoncelli, Hayden and Dovizioso.

*Photos:* Gold & Goose

IT was Hayden who articulated it: "These may be the most hardcore fans on the whole circuit. They beat me to the track Friday morning in the pouring rain, and I normally get here pretty early. They were already lined up. I'm not sure we got any more bigger troopers than these people."

The island overlooking the icy Bass Strait laid on a typical October weather welcome, with heavy overnight rain on Thursday that persisted on Friday, along with high winds, rendering the track too dangerous for use: a decision that was reached after there had been a serious accident on the straight in a support-class session.

Conditions eased, and some diligent work to clear standing water allowed Friday's first free session to get under way after a two-hour delay. But hypothermic temperatures, high winds and more rain remained a theme that overlaid the visit to one of GP racing's greatest circuits. Luckily, all the races were dry, and the hardiness of the 41,500-plus crowd was richly rewarded.

In short, Casey Stoner steamed from pole to flag for one of those dominant wins that are something of a trademark, celebrating his 25th birthday with his third pole of the year and winning by a yawning 8.5 seconds. Remarkably, for he is not a circuit specialist, it was his fourth home GP win in succession. And the valuable 25 points put him within reach of Pedrosa for second overall.

For the Spaniard missed the race, a brave attempt at returning terminated after increasing pain from his injury, less than two weeks after surgery. "I didn't see myself being safe for 27 laps. To risk two or three points or crash I think is not so much for me," he said on Saturday, before leaving for the airport. Dani had taken part in practice and qualifying, but the effort was far greater than the reward, with his best lap over three seconds down on Stoner's pole, to put him 15th on the 17-strong grid.

The dire weather prompted renewed calls for the Australian GP to be moved to earlier in the season. Rossi was the most vocal spokesman: this is a particularly favourite track, and the fun is so often spoiled by the early-autumn squalls. Pleas to the safety commission were likely to fall on deaf ears, however. For one thing, the island climate is capable of producing squalls at most times of the year; more significantly, the GP Corporation organises the F1 car GP at Albert Park as well and needs the events to be at opposite ends of the season.

Rossi's efforts at the previous two rounds, along with his frequent public mentions of the importance of their long "special relationship", had finally won from Yamaha the reprieve he and Ducati had been waiting for. After his victory in Malaysia, Masao Furusawa had told him that he would be released early from his contract. It could be a decision

Furusawa's successor (he would retire at year's end) might regret. This gave Ducati a crucial three-month start on the task of adapting the bike to the rider and crew, and vice versa. An indication of an open-minded approach came in reports from Italy that Ducati would have both Big Bang and Screamer engine variations at Valencia for Rossi's test. But it put the squeeze on his recovery programme, with surgery now definitely deferred until the second week of November at the earliest, and only a few weeks more than the two-months minimum recovery time before the first test of 2011.

As for now, the rider was feeling the strain of the three weeks of racing and also the cold, which made the pain worse. Scheduled for tests directly on returning home, he said, "I hope they don't tell me I have damaged it more, and I must not race more this season."

For a second race in a row, the grid was sparse: one fewer starter than at Sepang meant just 15. Not only was Pedrosa missing, but also Capirossi, who had hurt his foot badly at Sepang and now crashed again in qualifying while fighting to overcome the Suzuki's reluctance to grip in cold conditions. He limped away from the bike, but was ruled unfit to start after a badly strained left thigh muscle was added to his existing injuries.

Dorna was trying to stem the tide, with news in the paddock that Pramac might be boosted back to two riders with support from the series organisers. Toni Elias was earmarked for the position, but his bad memories of a year with the same team prompted him to turn that down. Instead he seemed set for a job swap, with Randy de Puniet bound for Pramac and Elias taking over his LCR Honda.

This would be Kallio's last ride for Pramac Ducati, after a troubled season in which the Finn had failed to build on his early promise and had been faced with off-track distractions as well. The surprise choice to take over for the last two races was Carlos Checa, who had already tested the Desmosedici, ostensibly as a reward for finishing top Duke in Superbikes, beating the factory team. Now at 38, three years after leaving GPs, he would be back for Estoril and Valencia, to add two more to his tally of 219 starts. But not, as it turned out, to his two premier-class wins.

Among all the usual flurries in Moto2 came an impressive debut from Australian Wayne Maxwell (27, and something of a circuit specialist), who substituted for the injured Lamborghini on the Matteoni Moriwaki. He qualified on row three and was second fastest (to race winner de Angelis) in morning warm-up. High hopes for the race were ruined,

however, when he tangled with Faubel on the first lap and they crashed. Perhaps understandably, Maxwell's temper took over, and he ran across to punch Faubel and push him back into the gravel. It was all captured on TV, and although he rejoined, he was soon disqualified, and fined 5,000 euros for an unfortunate moment of madness.

Poignantly, the race was fought between the two riders who had been victims at Misano of the crash that had taken Tomizawa's life, de Angelis and Redding. De Angelis referred to the late rider, and revealed that he and Redding had agreed not to spray champagne on the rostrum – only to discover that, at 17, Redding was under age and wouldn't be getting any to spray.

## MOTOGP RACE – 27 laps

The wind was cool and the clouds were building, but mercifully the sun stayed out for the main race of the day.

Stoner was on pole by a massive margin of more than six-tenths, with Lorenzo second. But then the list departed again from the usual, with Spies (a debut Superbike race winner here) on the front row for the third time. The blossoming Simoncelli led row two, from Edwards and Hayden. Rossi wasn't even seventh; that was de Puniet, with the Doctor alongside, still chasing settings again, having lost out on his qualifying lap when Hayden slipped off at Honda Hairpin just ahead of him. Dovizioso's sole factory Honda was next, after "I was fighting the wind, and the wind won."

The Italian's race would not last long. He got a good start to finish the first lap fifth, but on the third he almost crashed at Honda Hairpin as his steering damper mounting came adrift and jammed the bars as he tried to take full lock. Soon afterwards, he was in the pits and the factory team's garage doors were slammed shut after a second embarrassing mechanical or assembly failure in three races. It was also a major blow to his hopes, as the group contesting third (or possibly second) drew ahead.

Stoner, meanwhile, was in complete control, getting a good drive off the line to lead into the fast first corner and gallop off down to the seaside and back over the hill to cross the line the first time with a gap of 1.5 seconds. He added another second over the next two laps, by which time any threat from second-placed Lorenzo was remote, and kept on stretching it as the laps wore on. "I have to admit, I was feeling the pressure: before the race, I was more nervous than normally. Maybe I should be like that more often, because I

didn't make any mistakes," he said later. As for Lorenzo: "It's
really difficult to touch Casey here. When I saw him go away,
I thought that second would be okay."

If it was a case of lead and follow up front, Rossi once
again laid claim to much of the glory. He was shuffled back
to ninth in the busy first corners, but proceeded to give an
exhibition of overtaking: Melandri on lap two, Edwards next.

Spies had also been pushed back in the first two corners,
again feeling his way in with the tyres while others jostled
their way past. Now Rossi was behind him, and he in turn
was right behind Hayden, who was trying to get back in front
of Simoncelli.

They all piled up together, Spies getting to the front of
them all on lap five, then Rossi sweeping through to pass
the American into Turn One. Then Spies dropped to the back
of the gang and was stuck behind Simoncelli as Rossi and
Hayden moved away in unison. The pursuing Ducati seemed
able to match anything the Yamaha could do. But did Hayden have enough left over to pass? It would be another clos-
ing-laps battle, resolved in the familiar way.

Nicky passed Rossi at Honda Hairpin on lap 25 and held
the lead until halfway around the last lap. But Rossi never
gave up, and the last time at the same hairpin, he barged
past on the inside, giving Nicky no option but to lift and accept a depressing fourth place. "I am happy with the result,"
said Rossi, "but I expected to be faster. I was sliding a lot,
fighting with the bike ... but it was a great battle with Nicky."
Hayden was far from the first to be defeated by Rossi in this
way, but all the same he looked bleak. "Fourth place; it's
kinda hard to dress it up really."

Spies and Simoncelli remained engaged behind them, the
American ahead on lap 12, Simoncelli again seven laps later.
But when Spies made one of his well-timed swoops ahead
again on lap 23, it was for keeps, and he had opened a little
gap by the end. Fifth secured Rookie of the Year for Spies,
sixth equalled the improving Simoncelli's best of the year.

Edwards was a lonely seventh; ten seconds back, Espargaro finally passed Melandri's factory Honda.

De Puniet ran off early on and dropped to last, but came
through to take tenth, narrowly ahead of Kallio and Bautista.
A little behind, Aoyama finally got the better of Barbera.

## MOTO2 RACE – 25 laps

Ex-MotoGP riders Toni Elias and Alex de Angelis had started
the first Moto2 season as favourites. The first went on to
dominate the series; de Angelis found only problems. Crashes took their toll, then his employer, Team Scot, shut up
shop. By now, the San Marinan was in an entirely unproduc-
tive spell, substituting for Aoyama in MotoGP, returning as
a replacement rider with JiR at Misano, only to become an
innocent victim of the horror crash there.

At last, things came on track. He took his first pole, rather
cruelly deposing fellow Misano victim Redding from his first
pole, and went on to a long expected first win.

The race, which soon stretched the front field out around
the sweeping track, was between de Angelis, Redding and
second-row starter Iannone. The trio took only four laps to
put a couple of seconds on duelling Suter-mounted pair
Bradl and Simon.

Redding took to the front almost from the start, leading for
all but one lap up to half-distance. The other two were right
with him, and they skirmished over the next few laps, with
Iannone also leading for one more lap, the 15th.

But de Angelis was strongest, and when he got back
ahead next time around, he stayed there and even started to
pull away to lead at the flag by better than two seconds. He
dedicated the win, his career second, to Tomizawa, saying, "I
am sure he was watching from above."

Redding in turn eventually gained a small, but sustainable
breathing space on Iannone. The youngest rider on the grid,
he had been gaining maturity rapidly over recent races. Particularly conspicuous here was his disadvantage on the straight
and the way he hauled back lost ground everywhere else.

Di Meglio actually led into the first corner – he had qualified on the front row in his first half-decent showing of the
year. He dropped back into the battle for fourth, and then
lost touch with the pair after half-distance as Simon moved
past him and ahead of Bradl. He kept the German at bay to
the line.

There was a huge pack in pursuit. Luthi was doing most of
the leading over the line, along with Elias, Abraham, Aegerter
and Debon. The new champion looked apprehensive amid all

*Left:* Alex de Angelis bounced back to winning form after enduring a switch-back season.

*Below:* Battle for Moto2 victory – de Angelis leads Redding and Iannone.
*Photo:* Gold & Goose

the clashing of fairings and moved clear up front on the final lap, to be followed by Corsi (through again from the back, 16th on lap one), Debon, Abraham, Luthi, Nieto, Aegerter, Pons and Corti, with seventh to 15th across the line within 1.4 seconds.

Amazingly, apart from the first-lap tangle between Faubel and Maxwell, there were no crashes; non-finishers Kunikawa, Ranseder and Al Naimi all retired in the pits.

And the battle for second in the championship, between Simon and Iannone, became even closer.

## 125cc RACE – 23 laps

Marquez's third win in a row, his ninth of the year, was both majestic and familiar. He started from pole for the 11th time and dominated from the first lap to the last. His only slip came after a race in which he had found the gusting wind increasingly difficult. On the slow-down lap, while checking the results on the big screen, he ran off into the sodden grass. "I am sorry for my mechanics, because the bike is very dirty," he said.

Smith had led lap one until the teenager took over on the last corners, but it was Espargaro who had assumed the pursuit, while Terol pulled through even faster from seventh on lap one. He caught Espargaro on lap eight and steamed past. Perhaps he could even make a run on Marquez, now a distant, but not insuperable 2.7 seconds ahead. But the Derbi rider stuck with him as they pulled clear of the rest, and with seven laps to go, he scythed past through the daunting first corner and pulled away for second.

An epic three-way battle for fourth was down to two by the last lap, with Vazquez and Smith crossing the line side by side. It took a video finish to give the place to the Spaniard.

Rabat was off the back by the finish, but all three of them had dropped Koyama. The rest of the top ten were well spaced: Salom from team-mate Krummenacher, then Webb, nursing a broken bone in his right hand.

Cortese crashed out early on, Moncayo likewise on the first lap.

The championship was swinging towards Marquez, but one non-finish could still make all the difference.

*Above:* Marquez had another lonely afternoon for his ninth win.

*Left:* The 17-year-old celebrates with a can of soft-drink.
*Photo:* Gold & Goose

**OFFICIAL TIMEKEEPER**

### PHILLIP ISLAND

Southern Loop 126/78
Gardner Straight 313/195
Doohan 186/116
Turn 12 174/108
Key kph/mph Gear
Honda Corner 70/44
Turn 10 72/45
Turn 3 263/164
Turn 11 129/80
Siberia 103/64
Turn 8 239/149
Turn 7 228/142
Lukey Heights 151/94

Key 96/60 kph/mph Gear

| MotoGP | RACE DISTANCE: 27 laps, 74.624 miles/120.096 km · RACE WEATHER: Dry (air 15°, humidity 53%, track 29°) |
|---|---|

| Pos. | Rider | Nat. | No. | Entrant | Machine | Tyres | Laps | Time & speed |
|---|---|---|---|---|---|---|---|---|
| 1 | **Casey Stoner** | AUS | 27 | Ducati Marlboro Team | Ducati | B | 27 | 41m 09.128s 108.802mph/ 175.100km/h |
| 2 | **Jorge Lorenzo** | SPA | 99 | Fiat Yamaha Team | Yamaha | B | 27 | 41m 17.726s |
| 3 | **Valentino Rossi** | ITA | 46 | Fiat Yamaha Team | Yamaha | B | 27 | 41m 27.125s |
| 4 | **Nicky Hayden** | USA | 69 | Ducati Marlboro Team | Ducati | B | 27 | 41m 27.163s |
| 5 | **Ben Spies** | USA | 11 | Monster Yamaha Tech 3 | Yamaha | B | 27 | 41m 31.339s |
| 6 | **Marco Simoncelli** | ITA | 58 | San Carlo Honda Gresini | Honda | B | 27 | 41m 34.145s |
| 7 | **Colin Edwards** | USA | 5 | Monster Yamaha Tech 3 | Yamaha | B | 27 | 41m 44.296s |
| 8 | **Aleix Espargaro** | SPA | 41 | Pramac Racing Team | Ducati | B | 27 | 41m 55.322s |
| 9 | **Marco Melandri** | ITA | 33 | San Carlo Honda Gresini | Honda | B | 27 | 41m 55.422s |
| 10 | **Randy de Puniet** | FRA | 14 | LCR Honda MotoGP | Honda | B | 27 | 42m 08.763s |
| 11 | **Mika Kallio** | FIN | 36 | Pramac Racing Team | Ducati | B | 27 | 42m 08.792s |
| 12 | **Alvaro Bautista** | SPA | 19 | Rizla Suzuki MotoGP | Suzuki | B | 27 | 42m 08.860s |
| 13 | **Hiroshi Aoyama** | JPN | 7 | Interwetten Honda MotoGP | Honda | B | 27 | 42m 14.157s |
| 14 | **Hector Barbera** | SPA | 40 | Paginas Amarillas Aspar | Ducati | B | 27 | 42m 14.181s |
| | Andrea Dovizioso | ITA | 4 | Repsol Honda Team | Honda | B | 3 | DNF |
| | Loris Capirossi | ITA | 65 | Rizla Suzuki MotoGP | Suzuki | B | 0 | DNS |
| | Dani Pedrosa | SPA | 26 | Repsol Honda Team | Honda | B | 0 | DNS |

**Fastest lap:** Casey Stoner, on lap 7, 1m 30.458s, 109.995mph/177.019km/h.

**Lap record:** Nicky Hayden, USA (Honda), 1m 30.059s, 110.482mph/177.803km/h (2008).

**Event best maximum speed:** Casey Stoner, 203.3mph/327.1km/h (warm up).

### Qualifying

Weather: Dry
Air Temp: 11° Humidity: 47°
Track Temp: 22°

| | | |
|---|---|---|
| 1 | Stoner | 1m 30.107s |
| 2 | Lorenzo | 1m 30.775s |
| 3 | Spies | 1m 31.386s |
| 4 | Simoncelli | 1m 31.402s |
| 5 | Edwards | 1m 31.415s |
| 6 | Hayden | 1m 31.530s |
| 7 | de Puniet | 1m 31.554s |
| 8 | Rossi | 1m 31.627s |
| 9 | Dovizioso | 1m 32.018s |
| 10 | Melandri | 1m 32.367s |
| 11 | Espargaro | 1m 32.542s |
| 12 | Kallio | 1m 32.816s |
| 13 | Aoyama | 1m 33.190s |
| 14 | Bautista | 1m 33.224s |
| 15 | Pedrosa | 1m 33.384s |
| 16 | Barbera | 1m 33.390s |
| 17 | Capirossi | 1m 34.269s |

### Fastest race laps

| | | |
|---|---|---|
| 1 | Stoner | 1m 30.458s |
| 2 | Lorenzo | 1m 30.796s |
| 3 | Hayden | 1m 31.059s |
| 4 | Rossi | 1m 31.072s |
| 5 | Spies | 1m 31.529s |
| 6 | Simoncelli | 1m 31.547s |
| 7 | Edwards | 1m 31.665s |
| 8 | Dovizioso | 1m 31.716s |
| 9 | Espargaro | 1m 32.088s |
| 10 | de Puniet | 1m 32.217s |
| 11 | Melandri | 1m 32.314s |
| 12 | Kallio | 1m 32.342s |
| 13 | Barbera | 1m 32.841s |
| 14 | Bautista | 1m 32.869s |
| 15 | Aoyama | 1m 33.059s |

### Championship Points

| | | |
|---|---|---|
| 1 | Lorenzo | 333 |
| 2 | Pedrosa | 228 |
| 3 | Stoner | 205 |
| 4 | Rossi | 197 |
| 5 | Dovizioso | 179 |
| 6 | Spies | 163 |
| 7 | N. Hayden | 152 |
| 8 | Simoncelli | 102 |
| 9 | de Puniet | 100 |
| 10 | Melandri | 93 |
| 11 | Edwards | 90 |
| 12 | Barbera | 76 |
| 13 | Bautista | 73 |
| 14 | Espargaro | 60 |
| 15 | Aoyama | 47 |
| 16 | Kallio | 43 |
| 17 | Capirossi | 41 |
| 18 | de Angelis | 11 |
| 19 | R. Hayden | 5 |
| 20 | Akiyoshi | 4 |
| 21 | Yoshikawa | 1 |

### Team Points

| | | |
|---|---|---|
| 1 | Fiat Yamaha Team | 531 |
| 2 | Repsol Honda Team | 407 |
| 3 | Ducati Marlboro Team | 357 |
| 4 | Monster Yamaha Tech 3 | 253 |
| 5 | San Carlo Honda Gresini | 195 |
| 6 | Rizla Suzuki MotoGP | 114 |
| 7 | LCR Honda MotoGP | 105 |
| 8 | Pramac Racing Team | 103 |
| 9 | Paginas Amarillas Aspar | 76 |
| 10 | Interwetten Honda MotoGP | 62 |

### Constructor Points

| | | |
|---|---|---|
| 1 | Yamaha | 354 |
| 2 | Honda | 315 |
| 3 | Ducati | 255 |
| 4 | Suzuki | 96 |

| Grid order | 1 | 2 | 3 | 4 | 5 | 6 | 7 | 8 | 9 | 10 | 11 | 12 | 13 | 14 | 15 | 16 | 17 | 18 | 19 | 20 | 21 | 22 | 23 | 24 | 25 | 26 | 27 | |
|---|---|---|---|---|---|---|---|---|---|---|---|---|---|---|---|---|---|---|---|---|---|---|---|---|---|---|---|---|
| 27 STONER | 27 | 27 | 27 | 27 | 27 | 27 | 27 | 27 | 27 | 27 | 27 | 27 | 27 | 27 | 27 | 27 | 27 | 27 | 27 | 27 | 27 | 27 | 27 | 27 | 27 | 27 | 27 | 1 |
| 99 LORENZO | 99 | 99 | 99 | 99 | 99 | 99 | 99 | 99 | 99 | 99 | 99 | 99 | 99 | 99 | 99 | 99 | 99 | 99 | 99 | 99 | 99 | 99 | 99 | 99 | 99 | 99 | 99 | 2 |
| 11 SPIES | 69 | 58 | 58 | 69 | 11 | 11 | 11 | 46 | 46 | 46 | 46 | 46 | 46 | 46 | 46 | 46 | 46 | 46 | 46 | 46 | 46 | 46 | 46 | 69 | 69 | 46 | | 3 |
| 58 SIMONCELLI | 58 | 69 | 69 | 58 | 69 | 69 | 46 | 58 | 69 | 69 | 69 | 69 | 69 | 69 | 69 | 69 | 69 | 69 | 69 | 69 | 69 | 69 | 46 | 46 | 69 | | | 4 |
| 5 EDWARDS | 4 | 4 | 11 | 11 | 58 | 46 | 58 | 69 | 58 | 58 | 58 | 11 | 11 | 11 | 11 | 11 | 11 | 11 | 58 | 58 | 58 | 58 | 11 | 11 | 11 | 11 | 11 | 5 |
| 69 HAYDEN | 11 | 11 | 46 | 46 | 46 | 58 | 69 | 11 | 11 | 11 | 11 | 58 | 58 | 58 | 58 | 58 | 58 | 58 | 11 | 11 | 11 | 11 | 58 | 58 | 58 | 58 | | 6 |
| 14 de PUNIET | 5 | 5 | 5 | 5 | 5 | 5 | 5 | 5 | 5 | 5 | 5 | 5 | 5 | 5 | 5 | 5 | 5 | 5 | 5 | 5 | 5 | 5 | 5 | 5 | 5 | 5 | 5 | 7 |
| 46 ROSSI | 33 | 46 | 33 | 33 | 33 | 33 | 41 | 41 | 41 | 41 | 33 | 33 | 33 | 33 | 33 | 33 | 33 | 33 | 33 | 33 | 33 | 33 | 33 | 33 | 33 | 41 | | 8 |
| 4 DOVIZIOSO | 46 | 33 | 14 | 41 | 41 | 41 | 33 | 33 | 33 | 33 | 41 | 41 | 41 | 41 | 41 | 41 | 41 | 41 | 41 | 41 | 41 | 41 | 41 | 41 | 41 | 33 | | 9 |
| 33 MELANDRI | 14 | 14 | 19 | 36 | 36 | 36 | 36 | 36 | 36 | 36 | 36 | 36 | 36 | 36 | 36 | 36 | 36 | 36 | 36 | 36 | 36 | 36 | 19 | 14 | 14 | 14 | | 10 |
| 41 ESPARGARO | 19 | 19 | 36 | 19 | 19 | 19 | 19 | 19 | 19 | 19 | 19 | 19 | 19 | 19 | 19 | 19 | 19 | 19 | 19 | 19 | 19 | 19 | 36 | 19 | 19 | 36 | | 11 |
| 36 KALLIO | 36 | 36 | 41 | 7 | 7 | 7 | 7 | 40 | 40 | 40 | 7 | 7 | 7 | 7 | 7 | 7 | 14 | 14 | 14 | 14 | 14 | 14 | 14 | 36 | 36 | 19 | | 12 |
| 7 AOYAMA | 41 | 41 | 40 | 40 | 40 | 40 | 40 | 7 | 7 | 7 | 40 | 40 | 40 | 40 | 40 | 40 | 40 | 40 | 40 | 7 | 7 | 7 | 7 | 7 | 7 | 7 | | 13 |
| 19 BAUTISTA | 7 | 40 | 7 | 14 | 14 | 14 | 14 | 14 | 14 | 14 | 14 | 14 | 14 | 14 | 14 | 7 | 7 | 7 | 7 | 40 | 40 | 40 | 40 | 40 | 40 | 40 | | 14 |
| 40 BARBERA | 40 | 7 | 4 | | | | | | | | | | | | | | | | | | | | | | | | | |

## Moto2 — RACE DISTANCE: 25 laps, 69.096 miles/111.200 km · RACE WEATHER: Dry (air 15°, humidity 55%, track 27°)

| Pos. | Rider | Nat. | No. | Entrant | Machine | Laps | Time & Speed |
|------|-------|------|-----|---------|---------|------|--------------|
| 1 | **Alex de Angelis** | RSM | 15 | JIR Moto2 | MotoBI | 25 | 39m 51.102s |
| | | | | | | | (mph/km/h) |
| | | | | | | | 104.030/167.420 |
| 2 | **Scott Redding** | GBR | 45 | Marc VDS Racing Team | Suter | 25 | 39m 53.274s |
| 3 | **Andrea Iannone** | ITA | 29 | Fimmco Speed Up | Speed Up | 25 | 39m 54.076s |
| 4 | **Julian Simon** | SPA | 60 | Mapfre Aspar Team | Suter | 25 | 40m 01.446s |
| 5 | **Stefan Bradl** | GER | 65 | Viessmann Kiefer Racing | Suter | 25 | 40m 01.719s |
| 6 | **Mike di Meglio** | FRA | 63 | Mapfre Aspar Team | Suter | 25 | 40m 08.949s |
| 7 | **Toni Elias** | SPA | 24 | Gresini Racing Moto2 | Moriwaki | 25 | 40m 18.247s |
| 8 | **Simone Corsi** | ITA | 3 | JIR Moto2 | MotoBI | 25 | 40m 18.351s |
| 9 | **Alex Debon** | SPA | 6 | Aeroport de Castello - Ajo | FTR | 25 | 40m 18.500s |
| 10 | **Karel Abraham** | CZE | 17 | Cardion AB Motoracing | FTR | 25 | 40m 18.768s |
| 11 | **Thomas Luthi** | SWI | 12 | Interwetten Moriwaki Moto2 | Moriwaki | 25 | 40m 18.779s |
| 12 | **Fonsi Nieto** | SPA | 10 | Holiday Gym G22 | Moriwaki | 25 | 40m 18.953s |
| 13 | **Dominique Aegerter** | SWI | 77 | Technomag-CIP | Suter | 25 | 40m 19.435s |
| 14 | **Axel Pons** | SPA | 80 | Tenerife 40 Pons | Pons Kalex | 25 | 40m 19.540s |
| 15 | **Claudio Corti** | ITA | 71 | Forward Racing | Suter | 25 | 40m 19.599s |
| 16 | Raffaele de Rosa | ITA | 35 | Tech 3 Racing | Tech 3 | 25 | 40m 23.746s |
| 17 | Yuki Takahashi | JPN | 72 | Tech 3 Racing | Tech 3 | 25 | 40m 28.773s |
| 18 | Gabor Talmacsi | HUN | 2 | Fimmco Speed Up | Speed Up | 25 | 40m 34.035s |
| 19 | Yonny Hernandez | COL | 68 | Blusens-STX | BQR-Moto2 | 25 | 40m 37.246s |
| 20 | Alex Baldolini | ITA | 25 | Caretta Technology Race Dept. | I.C.P. | 25 | 40m 37.266s |
| 21 | Anthony West | AUS | 8 | MZ Racing Team | MZ-RE Honda | 25 | 40m 37.472s |
| 22 | Ratthapark Wilairot | THA | 14 | Thai Honda PTT Singha SAG | Bimota | 25 | 40m 42.943s |
| 23 | Jules Cluzel | FRA | 16 | Forward Racing | Suter | 25 | 40m 45.216s |
| 24 | Sergio Gadea | SPA | 40 | Tenerife 40 Pons | Pons Kalex | 25 | 40m 51.831s |
| 25 | Javier Fores | SPA | 46 | Maquinza-SAG Team | Bimota | 25 | 40m 55.242s |
| 26 | Roberto Rolfo | ITA | 44 | Italtrans S.T.R. | Suter | 25 | 40m 55.287s |
| 27 | Robertino Pietri | VEN | 39 | Italtrans S.T.R. | Suter | 25 | 41m 00.401s |
| 28 | Valentin Debise | FRA | 53 | WTR San Marino Team | ADV | 25 | 41m 00.896s |
| 29 | Vladimir Ivanov | UKR | 61 | Gresini Racing Moto2 | Moriwaki | 25 | 41m 07.162s |
| 30 | Alexander Cudlin | AUS | 49 | Qatar Moto2 Team | BQR-Moto2 | 25 | 41m 07.297s |
| 31 | Kenny Noyes | USA | 9 | Jack & Jones by A.Banderas | Promoharris | 25 | 41m 25.258s |
| 32 | Kazuki Watanabe | JPN | 28 | Racing Team Germany | Suter | 24 | 40m 01.861s |
| 33 | Yannick Guerra | SPA | 88 | Holiday Gym G22 | Moriwaki | 24 | 40m 11.052s |
| 34 | Joan Olive | SPA | 5 | Jack & Jones by A.Banderas | Promoharris | 24 | 40m 11.915s |
| | Mashel Al Naimi | QAT | 95 | Blusens-STX | BQR-Moto2 | 20 | DNF |
| | Michael Ranseder | AUT | 56 | Vector Kiefer Racing | Suter | 18 | DNF |
| | Hiromichi Kunikawa | JPN | 66 | Bimota - M Racing | Bimota | 10 | DNF |
| | Hector Faubel | SPA | 55 | Marc VDS Racing Team | Suter | 0 | DNF |
| | Wayne Maxwell | AUS | 47 | Matteoni Racing | Moriwaki | 3 | DSQ |

**Fastest lap:** Andrea Iannone, on lap 2, 1m 34.771s, 104.989mph/168.963km/h (record).
**Previous lap record:** New category.
**Event best maximum speed:** Toni Elias, 176.1mph/283.4km/h (race).

### Qualifying: Dry
Air: 13° Humidity: 57% Ground: 24°

| | | |
|---|---|---|
| 1 | de Angelis | 1m 35.148s |
| 2 | Redding | 1m 35.378s |
| 3 | Bradl | 1m 35.578s |
| 4 | di Meglio | 1m 35.696s |
| 5 | Iannone | 1m 35.870s |
| 6 | Simon | 1m 35.883s |
| 7 | Ranseder | 1m 35.935s |
| 8 | de Rosa | 1m 36.091s |
| 9 | Elias | 1m 36.105s |
| 10 | Abraham | 1m 36.133s |
| 11 | Maxwell | 1m 36.146s |
| 12 | Luthi | 1m 36.212s |
| 13 | Faubel | 1m 36.243s |
| 14 | Corsi | 1m 36.245s |
| 15 | Nieto | 1m 36.304s |
| 16 | Corti | 1m 36.319s |
| 17 | Cluzel | 1m 36.326s |
| 18 | Pons | 1m 36.348s |
| 19 | Takahashi | 1m 36.389s |
| 20 | Baldolini | 1m 36.392s |
| 21 | Debon | 1m 36.448s |
| 22 | Talmacsi | 1m 36.515s |
| 23 | West | 1m 36.719s |
| 24 | Hernandez | 1m 36.775s |
| 25 | Rolfo | 1m 36.840s |
| 26 | Aegerter | 1m 37.169s |
| 27 | Wilairot | 1m 37.229s |
| 28 | Gadea | 1m 37.335s |
| 29 | Fores | 1m 37.373s |
| 30 | Debise | 1m 37.634s |
| 31 | Ivanov | 1m 37.798s |
| 32 | Pietri | 1m 38.129s |
| 33 | Cudlin | 1m 38.422s |
| 34 | Watanabe | 1m 38.781s |
| 35 | Noyes | 1m 38.835s |
| 36 | Olive | 1m 39.318s |
| 37 | Guerra | 1m 40.095s |
| 38 | Al Naimi | 1m 40.274s |
| 39 | Kunikawa | 1m 41.716s |

### Fastest race laps

| | | |
|---|---|---|
| 1 | Iannone | 1m 34.771s |
| 2 | de Angelis | 1m 34.931s |
| 3 | Redding | 1m 34.983s |
| 4 | Bradl | 1m 35.198s |
| 5 | di Meglio | 1m 35.219s |
| 6 | Simon | 1m 35.223s |
| 7 | Pons | 1m 35.532s |
| 8 | Elias | 1m 35.545s |
| 9 | Abraham | 1m 35.613s |
| 10 | Corti | 1m 35.690s |
| 11 | Debon | 1m 35.712s |
| 12 | Ranseder | 1m 35.757s |
| 13 | Aegerter | 1m 35.766s |
| 14 | Luthi | 1m 35.795s |
| 15 | Corsi | 1m 35.860s |
| 16 | Talmacsi | 1m 35.898s |
| 17 | Nieto | 1m 35.962s |
| 18 | de Rosa | 1m 36.022s |
| 19 | Hernandez | 1m 36.145s |
| 20 | Takahashi | 1m 36.309s |
| 21 | Cluzel | 1m 36.359s |
| 22 | Baldolini | 1m 36.456s |
| 23 | Wilairot | 1m 36.530s |
| 24 | West | 1m 36.538s |
| 25 | Gadea | 1m 36.852s |
| 26 | Fores | 1m 36.912s |
| 27 | Debise | 1m 37.000s |
| 28 | Rolfo | 1m 37.103s |
| 29 | Ivanov | 1m 37.226s |
| 30 | Cudlin | 1m 37.471s |
| 31 | Maxwell | 1m 37.553s |
| 32 | Pietri | 1m 37.585s |
| 33 | Noyes | 1m 37.710s |
| 34 | Olive | 1m 38.807s |
| 35 | Watanabe | 1m 39.034s |
| 36 | Guerra | 1m 39.409s |
| 37 | Al Naimi | 1m 39.613s |
| 38 | Kunikawa | 1m 39.740s |

### Championship Points

| | | |
|---|---|---|
| 1 | Elias | 271 |
| 2 | Simon | 181 |
| 3 | Iannone | 179 |
| 4 | Luthi | 143 |
| 5 | Corsi | 127 |
| 6 | Cluzel | 101 |
| 7 | Talmacsi | 95 |
| 8 | Y. Takahashi | 86 |
| 9 | Tomizawa | 82 |
| 10 | Redding | 78 |
| 11 | Rolfo | 75 |
| 12 | Bradl | 72 |
| 13 | Debon | 70 |
| 14 | de Angelis | 69 |
| 15 | Abraham | 65 |
| 16 | Aegerter | 60 |
| 17 | Gadea | 59 |
| 18 | Nieto | 45 |
| 19 | di Meglio | 34 |
| 20 | Wilairot | 30 |
| 21 | Y. Hernandez | 30 |
| 22 | Corti | 20 |
| 23 | Noyes | 18 |
| 24 | Baldolini | 18 |
| 25 | West | 17 |
| 26 | Faubel | 13 |
| 27 | Pasini | 12 |
| 28 | Cudlin | 9 |
| 29 | Simeon | 9 |
| 30 | Di Salvo | 7 |
| 31 | de Rosa | 5 |
| 32 | Pesek | 5 |
| 33 | Pons | 4 |
| 34 | Ranseder | 4 |
| 35 | Pirro | 2 |
| 36 | Ivanov | 2 |
| 37 | Tode | 2 |
| 38 | Teshima | 1 |

### Constructors

| | | |
|---|---|---|
| 1 | Moriwaki | 296 |
| 2 | Suter | 281 |
| 3 | Speed Up | 204 |
| 4 | MotoBI | 168 |
| 5 | FTR | 118 |
| 6 | Tech 3 | 89 |
| 7 | Pons Kalex | 70 |
| 8 | Bimota | 30 |
| 9 | BQR-Moto2 | 30 |
| 10 | Promoharris | 18 |
| 11 | I.C.P. | 18 |
| 12 | MZ-RE Honda | 17 |
| 13 | Force GP210 | 11 |
| 14 | RSV | 10 |

## 125cc — RACE DISTANCE: 23 laps, 63.569 miles/102.304 km · RACE WEATHER: Dry (air 15°, humidity 55%, track 21°)

| Pos. | Rider | Nat. | No. | Entrant | Machine | Laps | Time & Speed |
|------|-------|------|-----|---------|---------|------|--------------|
| 1 | **Marc Marquez** | SPA | 93 | Red Bull Ajo Motorsport | Derbi | 23 | 38m 13.008s |
| | | | | | | | (mph/km/h) |
| | | | | | | | 99.802/160.616 |
| 2 | **Pol Espargaro** | SPA | 44 | Tuenti Racing | Derbi | 23 | 38m 19.070s |
| 3 | **Nicolas Terol** | SPA | 40 | Bancaja Aspar Team | Aprilia | 23 | 38m 24.584s |
| 4 | **Efren Vazquez** | SPA | 7 | Tuenti Racing | Derbi | 23 | 38m 32.040s |
| 5 | **Bradley Smith** | GBR | 38 | Bancaja Aspar Team | Aprilia | 23 | 38m 32.041s |
| 6 | **Esteve Rabat** | SPA | 12 | Blusens-STX | Aprilia | 23 | 38m 33.601s |
| 7 | **Tomoyoshi Koyama** | JPN | 71 | Racing Team Germany | Aprilia | 23 | 38m 44.527s |
| 8 | **Luis Salom** | SPA | 39 | Stipa-Molenaar Racing GP | Aprilia | 23 | 38m 59.606s |
| 9 | **Randy Krummenacher** | SWI | 35 | Stipa-Molenaar Racing GP | Aprilia | 23 | 39m 01.738s |
| 10 | **Danny Webb** | GBR | 99 | Andalucia Cajasol | Aprilia | 23 | 39m 11.464s |
| 11 | **Adrian Martin** | SPA | 26 | Aeroport de Castello - Ajo | Aprilia | 23 | 39m 28.865s |
| 12 | **Sturla Fagerhaug** | NOR | 50 | AirAsia-Sepang Int. Circuit | Aprilia | 23 | 39m 32.514s |
| 13 | **Marcel Schrotter** | GER | 78 | Interwetten Honda 125 | Honda | 23 | 39m 32.548s |
| 14 | **Jakub Kornfeil** | CZE | 84 | Racing Team Germany | Aprilia | 23 | 39m 32.551s |
| 15 | **Simone Grotzkyj** | ITA | 15 | Fontana Racing | Aprilia | 23 | 39m 45.130s |
| 16 | Jasper Iwema | NED | 53 | CBC Corse | Aprilia | 23 | 39m 55.374s |
| 17 | Louis Rossi | FRA | 69 | CBC Corse | Aprilia | 22 | 38m 24.002s |
| 18 | Joshua Hook | AUS | 46 | Hook Racing.com | Aprilia | 22 | 38m 34.103s |
| 19 | Luca Marconi | ITA | 87 | Ongetta Team | Aprilia | 22 | 38m 35.556s |
| 20 | Joel Taylor | AUS | 57 | BRP Racing | Aprilia | 22 | 38m 40.941s |
| 21 | Danny Kent | GBR | 52 | Lambretta Reparto Corse | Lambretta | 22 | 38m 46.555s |
| | Lorenzo Savadori | ITA | 32 | Matteoni Racing | Aprilia | 3 | DNF |
| | Sandro Cortese | GER | 11 | Avant Mitsubishi Ajo | Derbi | 2 | DNF |
| | Johann Zarco | FRA | 14 | WTR San Marino Team | Aprilia | 0 | DNF |
| | Alberto Moncayo | SPA | 23 | Andalucia Cajasol | Aprilia | 0 | DNF |

**Fastest lap:** Marc Marquez, on lap 9, 1m 38.305s, 91.606mph/162.888km/h.
**Lap record:** Alvaro Bautista, SPA (Aprilia), 1m 36.927s, 102.653mph/165.204km/h (2006).
**Event best maximum speed:** Nicolas Terol, 147.9mph/238.0km/h (race).

### Qualifying: Dry
Air: 14° Humidity: 46% Ground: 24°

| | | |
|---|---|---|
| 1 | Marquez | 1m 38.236s |
| 2 | Cortese | 1m 38.852s |
| 3 | Espargaro | 1m 38.991s |
| 4 | Terol | 1m 39.084s |
| 5 | Smith | 1m 39.363s |
| 6 | Rabat | 1m 40.124s |
| 7 | Vazquez | 1m 40.641s |
| 8 | Koyama | 1m 40.728s |
| 9 | Salom | 1m 40.787s |
| 10 | Moncayo | 1m 41.212s |
| 11 | Webb | 1m 41.458s |
| 12 | Krummenacher | 1m 41.490s |
| 13 | Grotzkyj | 1m 42.071s |
| 14 | Zarco | 1m 42.202s |
| 15 | Schrotter | 1m 42.252s |
| 16 | Savadori | 1m 42.326s |
| 17 | Martin | 1m 42.556s |
| 18 | Kornfeil | 1m 42.601s |
| 19 | Fagerhaug | 1m 42.657s |
| 20 | Marconi | 1m 43.365s |
| 21 | Iwema | 1m 43.403s |
| 22 | Hook | 1m 43.808s |
| 23 | Kent | 1m 43.990s |
| 24 | Rossi | 1m 44.271s |
| *Outside 107%* | | |
| DNQ | Taylor | 1m 45.456s |
| DNQ | Khairuddin | 1m 45.673s |
| DNQ | Day | 1m 46.347s |
| DNQ | Ravaioli | 1m 47.797s |
| DNQ | Zamora | 1m 47.961s |
| DNQ | Diles | 1m 48.757s |
| DNQ | Gabrielli | 1m 48.873s |

### Fastest race laps

| | | |
|---|---|---|
| 1 | Marquez | 1m 38.305s |
| 2 | Terol | 1m 38.321s |
| 3 | Espargaro | 1m 38.767s |
| 4 | Smith | 1m 39.423s |
| 5 | Vazquez | 1m 39.481s |
| 6 | Koyama | 1m 39.486s |
| 7 | Rabat | 1m 39.500s |
| 8 | Salom | 1m 40.156s |
| 9 | Cortese | 1m 40.725s |
| 10 | Krummenacher | 1m 40.910s |
| 11 | Webb | 1m 40.978s |
| 12 | Martin | 1m 41.101s |
| 13 | Schrotter | 1m 41.721s |
| 14 | Fagerhaug | 1m 41.961s |
| 15 | Kornfeil | 1m 42.073s |
| 16 | Grotzkyj | 1m 42.339s |
| 17 | Savadori | 1m 42.780s |
| 18 | Iwema | 1m 42.975s |
| 19 | Rossi | 1m 43.297s |
| 20 | Hook | 1m 43.602s |
| 21 | Marconi | 1m 43.981s |
| 22 | Taylor | 1m 44.262s |
| 23 | Kent | 1m 44.319s |

### Championship Points

| | | |
|---|---|---|
| 1 | Marquez | 272 |
| 2 | Terol | 260 |
| 3 | Espargaro | 255 |
| 4 | Smith | 182 |
| 5 | Rabat | 137 |
| 6 | Vazquez | 136 |
| 7 | Cortese | 132 |
| 8 | Koyama | 118 |
| 9 | Krummenacher | 97 |
| 10 | Webb | 86 |
| 11 | Zarco | 77 |
| 12 | Folger | 56 |
| 13 | Moncayo | 55 |
| 14 | Salom | 55 |
| 15 | Martin | 35 |
| 16 | Iwema | 34 |
| 17 | Schrotter | 23 |
| 18 | Kornfeil | 22 |
| 19 | Masbou | 20 |
| 20 | Grotzkyj | 20 |
| 21 | Fagerhaug | 12 |
| 22 | Kartheininger | 6 |
| 23 | Savadori | 5 |
| 24 | Khairuddin | 3 |
| 25 | Rossi | 2 |

### Constructors

| | | |
|---|---|---|
| 1 | Derbi | 360 |
| 2 | Aprilia | 303 |
| 3 | Honda | 23 |
| 4 | KTM | 6 |
| 5 | Lambretta | 1 |

# PORTUGUESE GRAND PRIX

ESTORIL CIRCUIT

F inclement weather is a sign that the gods are angry, then somebody in Estoril must have done something to make them very cross. After an almost completely dry season, and far worse than at Phillip Island, severe storms sweeping in off the nearby Atlantic were given increased fury by the mountainous ridge behind the track. Conditions were so bad that practice schedules (already revised to return to four sessions) had to be rejigged several times, and eventually the final qualifying session was cancelled as fresh torrents arrived. The starting grid would be determined by free practice times, all of which were some 12 seconds off the lap record.

By now, most riders agreed that, not having turned a single lap on slick tyres, they would prefer the race to be wet as well. Unless morning warm-up (extended by ten minutes to half an hour) were to be dry. It wasn't, but then the weather did improve, and when it came time to go racing, it had dried out. This was the worst of all worlds. With one extra sighting lap allowed for familiarisation, it meant that set-up and tyre choice became a matter of educated guesswork. Not for the first time, Lorenzo and crew chief Forcada guessed best.

This was especially vexing for the riders, at a track of great variety, incorporating plenty of elevation changes and some highly-technical slow corners, as well as a long fast entry to a long fast straight. A fun circuit: as Rossi put it, "more like a mountain road than a typical racetrack".

For the fans, 40,143 of whom had braved the conditions,

it meant a highly entertaining afternoon's racing. Bad weather is often the catalyst for good racing, and Estoril was no exception. Especially in the rain stricken 125 class, where Marquez seized victory from the jaws of defeat, after crashing on the sighting lap for the restart.

Ben Spies found the worst possible result. He was still cruising on the warm-up lap for the race on his new slicks when, to his puzzlement, down he went, in first gear. The fall repeated the injury he'd suffered at Le Mans – tendon damage to his left ankle. But this was just one of a new record number of crashes over the weekend, at least since they were first officially logged in 1996: 128 of them. That number included Lorenzo and Edwards, for each of them only the third time off the bike all year. The previous record had been set in 2007 at Donington Park, in similar conditions, at 109.

The most spectacular was a five-bike pile-up on the first lap of the 125 race, while Stoner suffered exactly the same crash as Lorenzo, almost to the inch, on the entry to the last sweeping right-hander. There were remarkably few injuries, although Moto2 charger Alex Debon did break his collarbone for the third time in the season. The first was when he had collided with Wilairot at Assen; he returned a week later to trigger the first-corner pile-up at Catalunya, incurring further fractures. On that occasion, a titanium plate had been inserted, but this plate was bent in the latest fall. Having decided to retire, and determined not to miss his final race, he was back again a week later at Valencia. Spanish journalists believed that the latest surgery would be the tenth repair to that particular bone, which has been broken a dozen times.

The big news of the weekend concerned Moto2: the final list of teams for 2011 was released late on Sunday evening, after a weekend of head scratching by IRTA, trying to cut the number to 36. "It was impossible," said Dorna's Ezpeleta. "We hope that in 2012 some teams will want to move to Moto3 or to MotoGP." The major teams of 2010 stayed in place: a couple of interesting additions were Monlau Competicion, a one-rider entry earmarked for Marquez; and Iodaracing Project. This is an Italian team devised by important past personage Giampiero Sacchi, involved in some way or another with a great deal of Italian GP milestones, including riders from Biaggi and Rossi to Simoncelli, and in senior positions with Aprilia and latterly the own-brand Gilera team. Iodaracing had another surprise at Estoril: the first showing of a bike built for a Moto3 class, for which technical regulations had not been finalised.

Sacchi hosted the launch, showing the TR001 – small, red, and not terribly exciting. It was the first motorcycle built to match the 125-replacement class, with a 250cc TM Racing off-road engine in a 125-size chassis. With a modest 40 horsepower and a simple fabricated aluminium frame, with Öhlins suspension, it had been built down to a price. The long-stroke engine had bore and stroke dimensions of 77x53.6mm, against the 81mm maximum bore mooted for Moto3. As a first attempt, it may have been short of the mark, but it certainly was a possibility for a junior one-make national series.

Capirossi was back, defying earlier medical predictions after being ruled out in Australia: although his enthusiasm had been waning through the course of a difficult season, he was anxious to do his duty, not only to Suzuki, but also to his mechanics, most of whom would be out of a job at the end of the year. One advantage of his non-starts and non-finishes was that he was still within the six-engine allocation, with the chance of finishing the year without having to take advantage of the special nine-engine 'Suzuki Sanction'. For the rider, a two-year contract at Pramac Ducati was officially confirmed during the weekend.

Other rider confirmations included Bradley Smith, to join Mike di Meglio in the cleaned-out Tech 3 Moto2 team, and Max Neukirchner to join the MZ Moto2 squad. Plenty more would follow a week later at Valencia.

## MOTOGP RACE – 28 laps

Cancellation of practice played havoc; the top six had all put in a good lap late on Friday afternoon. It was Lorenzo's seventh pole of the year, with Hayden alongside and then Rossi. Hayden had been only 13th on Saturday after a crash on his preferred bike. "I'll take the front row anyway; don't ask, don't apologise," he said.

Stoner was fourth, with Spies and Melandri alongside; Dovizioso led row three from de Puniet and Edwards. Pedrosa was 12th, on the far end of row four.

With Spies's second-row slot vacant, the rest lined up on a mainly dry track. Lorenzo led away, chased into the first corner by Dovizioso, Hayden and Rossi; the Spaniard was still narrowly ahead at the end of the first lap.

Hayden took over for one lap, but next time around both Yamahas were in front, while Dovizioso had dropped to fifth, behind Stoner. The Australian passed his team-mate, and on lap five he had a grandstand seat as Rossi dived underneath Lorenzo at the slow flip-flop chicane. Then, one corner later, his own race was over, as the front tucked under on the entry to the complex double-apex final corner. A week later, asked directly whether five race crashes in 2010 meant that he had returned to being a 'win-it-or-bin-it' rider, he told *MOTOCOURSE*, "This year, I've chosen to be. This last one in Portugal … I wasn't pushing too hard, but at the same time I'm not going out there to finish third. A long time ago, this

*Opposite page, top:* Simoncelli gave Dovizioso and Hayden a torrid time: fourth was his best of the year.

*Opposite page, centre, from left:* Moto3 in the making – the Iodaracing TR001 bike; Dovi's dashboard carried a photo of his baby daughter; Rossi and Brivio, both coming to an end with Yamaha.

*Opposite page, bottom:* Just like the beach at Brighton – this was why qualifying was cancelled.

*Below:* Aleix Espargaro crashed out on the first lap.
*Photos:* Gold & Goose

*Above:* Bradl just edges out Baldolini on the line.

*Top:* The battle at the back: veterans Checa and Capirossi at the tail of the MotoGP race. The Spaniard retired with arm-pump problems.

*Right:* Stefan Bradl, eighth different Moto2 winner of the year.

*Photos: Gold & Goose*

*Above:* Marquez's recovery from disaster was extraordinary. Here he is about to snatch the lead from Terol.

*Top:* No respect. Class rookie Sofuoglu takes the lead in Moto2, ahead of Talmacsi (2) and Hernandez. He ran away, until he wore out his tyres.

*Left:* Baldolini was thrilled with second place – his first rostrum in 143 Grand Prix starts.

*Photos:* Gold & Goose

season was gone for me. So I want to get as many wins as I can. Whether the bike's capable of it or not."

Rossi's move signalled what looked very much like a masterful breakaway, but actually it was a more desperate strategy. "We started blind, so I had to try to take some risks at the beginning," he explained. "Because the setting was … okay, but it was not enough."

All the same, he wasn't hanging around. By lap six, the gap was eight-tenths; next time around he had doubled it, and it seemed that he would carry on the same way. But by now Lorenzo was almost two seconds ahead of Hayden and gaining speed – the gap started to shrink faster and faster. "At the beginning, I saw some wet patches, and I knew I would have to be very careful. When Vale overtook me and he went, I thought he had gone. He was maybe taking more risks than me. But I was patient, I caught my pace better every lap."

By the end of the 14th, halfway to the finish, Lorenzo was on his team-mate's back wheel, and at the start of the 17th, he outbraked him easily at the end of the straight and immediately started to pull away. By lap 21, he was 2.5 seconds clear and Rossi had given up the hopeless pursuit. Lorenzo kept on pulling away to win by 8.6 seconds.

Rossi was safe. The action was all for third.

Hayden was alone for the first half, Simoncelli and Dovizioso being locked in combat a couple of seconds behind. De Puniet was with them and Pedrosa was closing, after finishing the first lap tenth, Edwards on his tail.

The first change came on the corner after the back straight on lap 12, as Dovizioso came close to high-siding and dropped behind de Puniet. Simoncelli now led from Pedrosa, all closing on a sliding Hayden. Pedrosa would drop away again as his left arm lost strength and feeling; Dovizioso would get back up with Simoncelli.

With Edwards close, it was a tight group of six, but by lap 23 Simoncelli and Dovizioso had got away with Hayden in tow; de Puniet and Edwards were a little way back, Pedrosa losing ground behind.

The last lap was fierce. Dovizioso started ahead, but again Simoncelli bullied his way past at the chicane. He led all the way until they started the final run down the long straight, but then Dovizioso pulled alongside and powered into a small, but crucial lead. Fourth was still a fine result for Simoncelli; Hayden was just six-tenths behind.

De Puniet and Edwards were still close, Pedrosa another four seconds down. Melandri was almost half a minute adrift by the end, four seconds clear of an almost race-long fight between Barbera and Bautista, won by the former by less than two-tenths. Aoyama had been with them, but had dropped away at the end. Capirossi was a distant 13th.

Checa had been ahead of the Barbera/Bautista/Aoyama group in the early stages, but soon began to suffer severe arm-pump and retired. Aleix Espargaro, his erstwhile Pramac Ducati team-mate, crashed out on the first lap.

## MOTO2 RACE – 26 laps

Five races on, the Technomag-CIP team had found a replacement for Tomizawa, and it was an intriguing choice: new World 600 Supersport champion Kenan Sofuoglu. Actually a double Supersport champion, and slightly surprised to find that no matter how much more agile the chassis, the control Honda CBR600 motor fitted to his Suter frame was a great deal less racy and mettlesome than that of his Ten Kate machine. Sofuoglu would make a blazing start, seizing a huge lead for the first half of the race and fighting hard all the way to an eventual fifth. Viewers were puzzled to see him hitting his left handlebar down the straights. Later he explained that after hasty repairs following a warm-up crash, the clip-on was loose and kept closing on the corners.

Pole went to Talmacsi after the Hungarian had fitted slicks on Friday afternoon. "The track was still damp, but it was

worth the risk," he said. Simon and Elias were alongside, with first-timer Sofuoglu fourth for a debut front row.

Others were out of luck, notably triple race winner Iannone, 35th and the last rider to set an official qualifying time; and recent front-runner Scott Redding (25th), who said, "I'll have to bust more moves than Michael Jackson if I'm going to fight my way through the field and grab a decent result."

Sofuoglu showed scant respect for his rivals as he took the lead from Hernandez and Talmacsi on lap three, and simply charged away as Hernandez crashed out in pursuit. By lap 12, he had a massive lead of better than seven seconds.

By then, Talmacsi had fallen back into a massive and volatile pack, which included Elias, again looking uneasy in the midst of the turmoil – until he crashed out on lap 15.

Conditions were still tricky and favoured the brave. Bradl and Baldolini had got to the front and started to pull clear by then, closing rapidly on Sofuoglu, who was still beating at his handlebar, his lap times erratic on the patchy track and his tyres suffering from his early attack.

They caught him on lap 19 and took off for a two-man battle that went to the flag. Baldolini did get ahead briefly, but at the flag the German was in front by 0.068 second. Iannone had been charging through astonishingly quickly; by lap 19, he had taken the lead of the chase group and was working on catching the leaders, now just one second away. The effort was too great for his tyres, however, and he crashed out.

Redding had been languishing at the back of the top 20. Then, with ten laps to go, he suddenly picked up his pace, setting fastest lap as he rapidly caught the group disputing third. He almost made it to the front, taking fourth behind de Angelis, with Sofuoglu, de Rosa, West (the MZ's best result), Talmacsi, Dominique Aegerter and Abraham making up the top ten; Faubel was inches behind.

Eight riders crashed, including Takahashi, Morales and Pons. Simon finished a troubled 12th, which still increased his narrow points advantage over Iannone, 185 to 179.

## 125cc RACE – 9 laps (restarted)

Smith felt lucky to have claimed a third pole of the year, ahead of Webb and Terol. Marquez was 11th and Espargaro 12th. But the first attempt was thrown into shambles when light showers struck soon after the start. Five riders were eliminated in just one crash at the chicane on the first lap, when Cortese fell, followed directly by Grotzky, Danny Kent, Louis Rossi and Martin. Iwema and Marconi had crashed a couple of corners earlier. The track was cleared quickly, but by the time the red flags came out after seven laps, five more riders had crashed, including Rabat and Vazquez, the only one to make the restart.

Terol was leading, from Marquez, Smith and Espargaro, making the front row for the restart. Except Marquez wasn't there. He had crashed on the sighting lap. Frantically, he scrambled back on and got going again.

With ten minutes to go, he was back in the pits having his fairing replaced and the controls straightened out; he only just made it out again, to start from the back row of the grid.

Terol and Smith led away, but Marquez got off the back like a rocket. He arrived at the first corner fourth and finished the first lap third. From then on, Smith did his best to keep him at bay and let Terol escape, but to no avail.

Terol still led as they started the last lap, but Marquez took over under braking for the first corner, quickly repulsed an attack at the end of the back straight when Terol ran wide, and led his last remaining title rival over the line by 0.150 second. Smith was a close third.

Espargaro had ended his last chances with a desperate gamble on wet tyres. Instead the track dried quite quickly, and he dropped to tenth, half a minute behind the leaders.

Folger was a distant fourth, holding off Salom, with Moncayo sixth. The rest were mainly spaced out: Vazquez, Webb, and only then Espargaro.

### CIRCUITO DO ESTORIL

Key
96/60 kph/mph
**2** Gear

Turn 8 145/90
Variante 58/36 **1**
Turn 3 74/46
Orelha 87/54 **2**
Esses 105/65 **2**
Turn 2 131/82 **2**
VIP 81/50 **4**
Recta da Meta 245/153 **5**
Turn 1 76/47 **1**
Parabolica Interior 95/59 **2**
Parabolica 210/131 **5**

Circuit 4.182km/2.598 miles  Race: 28 laps

## MotoGP

**RACE DISTANCE: 28 laps, 72.760 miles/117.096 km · RACE WEATHER: Dry (air 19°, humidity 41%, track 26°)**

| Pos. | Rider | Nat. | No. | Entrant | Machine | Tyres | Laps | Time & speed |
|---|---|---|---|---|---|---|---|---|
| 1 | **Jorge Lorenzo** | SPA | 99 | Fiat Yamaha Team | Yamaha | B | 28 | 46m 17.962s 94.291mph/ 151.746km/h |
| 2 | **Valentino Rossi** | ITA | 46 | Fiat Yamaha Team | Yamaha | B | 28 | 46m 26.591s |
| 3 | **Andrea Dovizioso** | ITA | 4 | Repsol Honda Team | Honda | B | 28 | 46m 44.437s |
| 4 | **Marco Simoncelli** | ITA | 58 | San Carlo Honda Gresini | Honda | B | 28 | 46m 44.496s |
| 5 | **Nicky Hayden** | USA | 69 | Ducati Marlboro Team | Ducati | B | 28 | 46m 45.116s |
| 6 | **Randy de Puniet** | FRA | 14 | LCR Honda MotoGP | Honda | B | 28 | 46m 46.259s |
| 7 | **Colin Edwards** | USA | 5 | Monster Yamaha Tech 3 | Yamaha | B | 28 | 46m 48.071s |
| 8 | **Dani Pedrosa** | SPA | 26 | Repsol Honda Team | Honda | B | 28 | 47m 02.909s |
| 9 | **Marco Melandri** | ITA | 33 | San Carlo Honda Gresini | Honda | B | 28 | 47m 31.611s |
| 10 | **Hector Barbera** | SPA | 40 | Paginas Amarillas Aspar | Ducati | B | 28 | 47m 35.683s |
| 11 | **Alvaro Bautista** | SPA | 19 | Rizla Suzuki MotoGP | Suzuki | B | 28 | 47m 35.870s |
| 12 | **Hiroshi Aoyama** | JPN | 7 | Interwetten Honda MotoGP | Honda | B | 28 | 47m 50.987s |
| 13 | **Loris Capirossi** | ITA | 65 | Rizla Suzuki MotoGP | Suzuki | B | 28 | 47m 57.714s |
| | Carlos Checa | SPA | 71 | Pramac Racing Team | Ducati | B | 13 | DNF |
| | Casey Stoner | AUS | 27 | Ducati Marlboro Team | Ducati | B | 4 | DNF |
| | Aleix Espargaro | SPA | 41 | Pramac Racing Team | Ducati | B | 0 | DNF |
| | Ben Spies | USA | 11 | Monster Yamaha Tech 3 | Yamaha | B | 0 | DNS |

**Fastest lap:** Jorge Lorenzo, on lap 20, 1m 37.928s, 95.528mph/153.737km/h.
**Lap record:** Dani Pedrosa, SPA (Honda), 1m 36.937s, 99.505mph/155.309km/h (2009).
**Event best maximum speed:** Jorge Lorenzo, 199.7mph/321.4km/h (race).

### Qualifying

Cancelled: Weather conditions

| | | |
|---|---|---|
| 1 | Lorenzo | 1m 48.522s |
| 2 | Hayden | 1m 48.657s |
| 3 | Rossi | 1m 48.883s |
| 4 | Stoner | 1m 49.061s |
| 5 | Spies | 1m 49.721s |
| 6 | Melandri | 1m 49.784s |
| 7 | Dovizioso | 1m 50.007s |
| 8 | de Puniet | 1m 50.043s |
| 9 | Edwards | 1m 50.313s |
| 10 | Simoncelli | 1m 50.500s |
| 11 | Espargaro | 1m 50.787s |
| 12 | Pedrosa | 1m 50.824s |
| 13 | Capirossi | 1m 51.518s |
| 14 | Bautista | 1m 52.734s |
| 15 | Barbera | 1m 53.131s |
| 16 | Aoyama | 1m 53.317s |
| 17 | Checa | 1m 53.933s |

*Grid positions decided by best time set in free practice.*

### Fastest race laps

| | | |
|---|---|---|
| 1 | Lorenzo | 1m 37.928s |
| 2 | Rossi | 1m 38.325s |
| 3 | Hayden | 1m 38.871s |
| 4 | Stoner | 1m 39.012s |
| 5 | Dovizioso | 1m 39.038s |
| 6 | Edwards | 1m 39.051s |
| 7 | Simoncelli | 1m 39.077s |
| 8 | de Puniet | 1m 39.143s |
| 9 | Pedrosa | 1m 39.173s |
| 10 | Aoyama | 1m 40.569s |
| 11 | Bautista | 1m 40.709s |
| 12 | Melandri | 1m 40.827s |
| 13 | Barbera | 1m 40.828s |
| 14 | Capirossi | 1m 41.579s |
| 15 | Checa | 1m 41.889s |

### Championship Points

| | | |
|---|---|---|
| 1 | Lorenzo | 358 |
| 2 | Pedrosa | 236 |
| 3 | Rossi | 217 |
| 4 | Stoner | 205 |
| 5 | Dovizioso | 195 |
| 6 | Spies | 163 |
| 7 | N. Hayden | 163 |
| 8 | Simoncelli | 115 |
| 9 | de Puniet | 110 |
| 10 | Melandri | 100 |
| 11 | Edwards | 99 |
| 12 | Barbera | 82 |
| 13 | Bautista | 78 |
| 14 | Espargaro | 60 |
| 15 | Aoyama | 51 |
| 16 | Capirossi | 44 |
| 17 | Kallio | 43 |
| 18 | de Angelis | 11 |
| 19 | R. Hayden | 5 |
| 20 | Akiyoshi | 4 |
| 21 | Yoshikawa | 1 |

| Grid order | 1 | 2 | 3 | 4 | 5 | 6 | 7 | 8 | 9 | 10 | 11 | 12 | 13 | 14 | 15 | 16 | 17 | 18 | 19 | 20 | 21 | 22 | 23 | 24 | 25 | 26 | 27 | 28 |
|---|---|---|---|---|---|---|---|---|---|---|---|---|---|---|---|---|---|---|---|---|---|---|---|---|---|---|---|---|
| 99 LORENZO | 99 | 69 | 99 | 46 | 46 | 46 | 46 | 46 | 46 | 46 | 46 | 46 | 46 | 46 | 46 | 46 | 99 | 99 | 99 | 99 | 99 | 99 | 99 | 99 | 99 | 99 | 99 | 99 |
| 69 HAYDEN | 69 | 99 | 46 | 99 | 99 | 99 | 99 | 99 | 99 | 99 | 99 | 99 | 99 | 99 | 99 | 99 | 46 | 46 | 46 | 46 | 46 | 46 | 46 | 46 | 46 | 46 | 46 | 2 |
| 46 ROSSI | 4 | 46 | 69 | 27 | 69 | 69 | 69 | 69 | 69 | 69 | 69 | 69 | 69 | 69 | 69 | 69 | 58 | 58 | 58 | 58 | 58 | 4 | 4 | 58 | 58 | 58 | 4 | 4 | 3 |
| 27 STONER | 46 | 27 | 27 | 69 | 4 | 58 | 58 | 58 | 58 | 58 | 58 | 58 | 58 | 58 | 58 | 58 | 69 | 4 | 4 | 4 | 4 | 58 | 58 | 4 | 4 | 4 | 58 | 58 | 4 |
| 11 SPIES | 14 | 4 | 4 | 4 | 58 | 58 | 4 | 4 | 4 | 4 | 4 | 26 | 26 | 26 | 26 | 26 | 26 | 69 | 69 | 26 | 69 | 69 | 69 | 69 | 69 | 69 | 69 | 69 | 5 |
| 33 MELANDRI | 27 | 14 | 14 | 58 | 14 | 14 | 26 | 26 | 26 | 26 | 26 | 14 | 14 | 14 | 14 | 14 | 4 | 26 | 26 | 69 | 14 | 14 | 14 | 14 | 14 | 14 | 14 | 14 | 6 |
| 4 DOVIZIOSO | 33 | 58 | 58 | 14 | 26 | 26 | 14 | 14 | 14 | 14 | 14 | 4 | 4 | 4 | 4 | 4 | 14 | 5 | 5 | 5 | 26 | 5 | 5 | 5 | 5 | 5 | 5 | 5 | 7 |
| 14 de PUNIET | 5 | 33 | 5 | 26 | 5 | 5 | 5 | 5 | 5 | 5 | 5 | 5 | 5 | 5 | 5 | 5 | 5 | 14 | 14 | 14 | 5 | 26 | 26 | 26 | 26 | 26 | 26 | 26 | 8 |
| 5 EDWARDS | 58 | 5 | 26 | 5 | 33 | 33 | 33 | 33 | 33 | 33 | 33 | 33 | 33 | 33 | 33 | 33 | 33 | 33 | 33 | 33 | 33 | 33 | 33 | 33 | 33 | 33 | 33 | 33 | 9 |
| 58 SIMONCELLI | 26 | 26 | 33 | 33 | 19 | 19 | 19 | 19 | 19 | 19 | 19 | 19 | 19 | 19 | 19 | 19 | 7 | 7 | 7 | 7 | 7 | 7 | 7 | 40 | 40 | 19 | 40 | 40 | 10 |
| 41 ESPARGARO | 19 | 19 | 19 | 19 | 71 | 7 | 7 | 7 | 7 | 7 | 7 | 7 | 7 | 7 | 7 | 7 | 19 | 40 | 19 | 40 | 19 | 40 | 40 | 19 | 19 | 40 | 19 | 19 | 11 |
| 26 PEDROSA | 65 | 7 | 71 | 71 | 7 | 71 | 71 | 40 | 40 | 40 | 40 | 40 | 40 | 40 | 40 | 40 | 40 | 19 | 40 | 19 | 40 | 19 | 19 | 40 | 7 | 7 | 7 | 7 | 12 |
| 65 CAPIROSSI | 7 | 71 | 7 | 7 | 40 | 40 | 40 | 71 | 71 | 71 | 71 | 71 | 65 | 65 | 65 | 65 | 65 | 65 | 65 | 65 | 65 | 65 | 65 | 65 | 65 | 65 | 65 | 65 | 13 |
| 19 BAUTISTA | 71 | 65 | 40 | 40 | 65 | 65 | 65 | 65 | 65 | 65 | 65 | 65 | 71 | | | | | | | | | | | | | | | | |
| 40 BARBERA | 40 | 40 | 65 | 65 | | | | | | | | | | | | | | | | | | | | | | | | | |
| 7 AOYAMA | | | | | | | | | | | | | | | | | | | | | | | | | | | | | |
| 71 CHECA | | | | | | | | | | | | | | | | | | | | | | | | | | | | | |

### Team Points

| | | |
|---|---|---|
| 1 | Fiat Yamaha Team | 576 |
| 2 | Repsol Honda Team | 431 |
| 3 | Ducati Marlboro Team | 368 |
| 4 | Monster Yamaha Tech 3 | 262 |
| 5 | San Carlo Honda Gresini | 215 |
| 6 | Rizla Suzuki MotoGP | 122 |
| 7 | LCR Honda MotoGP | 115 |
| 8 | Pramac Racing Team | 103 |
| 9 | Paginas Amarillas Aspar | 82 |
| 10 | Interwetten Honda MotoGP | 66 |

### Constructor Points

| | | |
|---|---|---|
| 1 | Yamaha | 379 |
| 2 | Honda | 331 |
| 3 | Ducati | 266 |
| 4 | Suzuki | 101 |

## Moto2

**RACE DISTANCE: 26 laps, 67.563 miles/108.732 km · RACE WEATHER: Dry (air 18°, humidity 28%, track 21°)**

| Pos. | Rider | Nat. | No. | Entrant | Machine | Laps | Time & Speed |
|---|---|---|---|---|---|---|---|
| 1 | Stefan Bradl | GER | 65 | Viessmann Kiefer Racing | Suter | 26 | 46m 59.723s |
| | | | | | | | (mph/km/h) |
| | | | | | | | 86.259/138.820 |
| 2 | Alex Baldolini | ITA | 25 | Caretta Technology Race Dept. | I.C.P. | 26 | 46m 59.791s |
| 3 | Alex de Angelis | RSM | 15 | JIR Moto2 | MotoBI | 26 | 47m 02.553s |
| 4 | Scott Redding | GBR | 45 | Marc VDS Racing Team | Suter | 26 | 47m 02.565s |
| 5 | Kenan Sofuoglu | TUR | 54 | Technomag-CIP | Suter | 26 | 47m 02.670s |
| 6 | Raffaele de Rosa | ITA | 35 | Tech 3 Racing | Tech 3 | 26 | 47m 03.034s |
| 7 | Anthony West | AUS | 8 | MZ Racing Team | MZ-RE Honda | 26 | 47m 03.108s |
| 8 | Gabor Talmacsi | HUN | 2 | Fimmco Speed Up | Speed Up | 26 | 47m 03.675s |
| 9 | Dominique Aegerter | SWI | 77 | Technomag-CIP | Suter | 26 | 47m 04.007s |
| 10 | Karel Abraham | CZE | 17 | Cardion AB Motoracing | FTR | 26 | 47m 04.034s |
| 11 | Hector Faubel | SPA | 55 | Marc VDS Racing Team | Suter | 26 | 47m 04.215s |
| 12 | Julian Simon | SPA | 60 | Mapfre Aspar Team | Suter | 26 | 47m 12.729s |
| 13 | Axel Pons | SPA | 80 | Tenerife 40 Pons | Pons Kalex | 26 | 47m 26.252s |
| 14 | Simone Corsi | ITA | 3 | JIR Moto2 | MotoBI | 26 | 47m 27.483s |
| 15 | Robertino Pietri | VEN | 39 | Italtrans S.T.R. | Suter | 26 | 47m 27.982s |
| 16 | Thomas Luthi | SWI | 12 | Interwetten Moriwaki Moto2 | Moriwaki | 26 | 47m 28.034s |
| 17 | Jules Cluzel | FRA | 16 | Forward Racing | Suter | 26 | 47m 28.056s |
| 18 | Yonny Hernandez | COL | 68 | Blusens-STX | BQR-Moto2 | 26 | 47m 37.596s |
| 19 | Claudio Corti | ITA | 71 | Forward Racing | Suter | 26 | 47m 37.815s |
| 20 | Carmelo Morales | SPA | 31 | Racing Team Germany | Suter | 26 | 47m 37.950s |
| 21 | Andrea Iannone | ITA | 29 | Fimmco Speed Up | Speed Up | 26 | 47m 46.699s |
| 22 | Sergio Gadea | SPA | 40 | Tenerife 40 Pons | Pons Kalex | 26 | 48m 01.502s |
| 23 | Xavier Simeon | BEL | 19 | Holiday Gym G22 | Moriwaki | 26 | 48m 25.595s |
| 24 | Fonsi Nieto | SPA | 10 | Holiday Gym G22 | Moriwaki | 26 | 48m 25.752s |
| 25 | Vladimir Ivanov | UKR | 61 | Gresini Racing Moto2 | Moriwaki | 26 | 48m 51.413s |
| 26 | Yuki Takahashi | JPN | 72 | Tech 3 Racing | Tech 3 | 25 | 47m 16.237s |
| 27 | Ferruccio Lamborghini | ITA | 70 | Matteoni Racing | Moriwaki | 25 | 47m 17.559s |
| 28 | Yannick Guerra | SPA | 88 | Holiday Gym G22 | Moriwaki | 25 | 48m 14.677s |
| 29 | Mashel Al Naimi | QAT | 95 | Blusens-STX | BQR-Moto2 | 25 | 48m 15.919s |
| | Ricard Cardus | SPA | 4 | Maquinza-SAG Team | Bimota | 23 | DNF |
| | Roberto Rolfo | ITA | 44 | Italtrans S.T.R. | Suter | 22 | DNF |
| | Dani Rivas | SPA | 7 | Blusens-STX | BQR-Moto2 | 19 | DNF |
| | Toni Elias | SPA | 24 | Gresini Racing Moto2 | Moriwaki | 17 | DNF |
| | Ratthapark Wilairot | THA | 14 | Thai Honda PTT Singha SAG | Bimota | 14 | DNF |
| | Valentin Debise | FRA | 53 | WTR San Marino Team | ADV | 13 | DNF |
| | Kenny Noyes | USA | 9 | Jack & Jones by A.Banderas | Promoharris | 13 | DNF |
| | Michael Ranseder | AUT | 56 | Vector Kiefer Racing | Suter | 5 | DNF |

**Fastest lap:** Scott Redding, on lap 23, 1m 45.456s, 88.708mph/142.762km/h (record).
**Previous lap record:** New category.
**Event best maximum speed:** Axel Pons, 178.1mph/286.7km/h (race).

### Qualifying

Cancelled: Weather conditions

| | | |
|---|---|---|
| 1 | Talmacsi | 1m 50.916s |
| 2 | Simon | 1m 51.304s |
| 3 | Elias | 1m 51.359s |
| 4 | Sofuoglu | 1m 51.949s |
| 5 | de Rosa | 1m 52.808s |
| 6 | de Angelis | 1m 53.233s |
| 7 | Hernandez | 1m 54.214s |
| 8 | Aegerter | 1m 54.247s |
| 9 | Takahashi | 1m 54.302s |
| 10 | Bradl | 1m 54.556s |
| 11 | Baldolini | 1m 54.568s |
| 12 | Luthi | 1m 54.594s |
| 13 | Pietri | 1m 54.665s |
| 14 | Cardus | 1m 55.040s |
| 15 | Debise | 1m 55.169s |
| 16 | Morales | 1m 55.415s |
| 17 | Corti | 1m 55.428s |
| 18 | Corsi | 1m 55.646s |
| 19 | Debon | 1m 55.765s |
| 20 | Pons | 1m 55.834s |
| 21 | West | 1m 55.863s |
| 22 | Noyes | 1m 55.940s |
| 23 | Abraham | 1m 55.988s |
| 24 | Faubel | 1m 56.082s |
| 25 | Redding | 1m 56.174s |
| 26 | Ranseder | 1m 56.281s |
| 27 | Cluzel | 1m 56.445s |
| 28 | Rivas | 1m 56.862s |
| 29 | Nieto | 1m 57.050s |
| 30 | Rolfo | 1m 57.359s |
| 31 | Lamborghini | 1m 57.391s |
| 32 | Wilairot | 1m 57.499s |
| 33 | Simeon | 1m 57.519s |
| 34 | Gadea | 1m 57.855s |
| 35 | Iannone | 1m 57.921s |
| 36 | Ivanov | 1m 58.814s |
| 37 | Guerra | 1m 59.070s |
| 38 | Al Naimi | 2m 00.622s |
| DNQ | di Meglio | 2m 00.146s |
| DNQ | Olive | 2m 00.233s |
| DNQ | Kunikawa | 2m 07.182s |

\* Grid positions decided by best time set in free practice.

### Fastest race laps

| | | |
|---|---|---|
| 1 | Redding | 1m 45.456s |
| 2 | Iannone | 1m 45.704s |
| 3 | Abraham | 1m 45.714s |
| 4 | West | 1m 46.042s |
| 5 | Faubel | 1m 46.043s |
| 6 | Pons | 1m 46.094s |
| 7 | Baldolini | 1m 46.457s |
| 8 | Aegerter | 1m 46.530s |
| 9 | Bradl | 1m 46.536s |
| 10 | Sofuoglu | 1m 46.588s |
| 11 | de Rosa | 1m 46.619s |
| 12 | Corsi | 1m 46.657s |
| 13 | de Angelis | 1m 46.679s |
| 14 | Talmacsi | 1m 46.690s |
| 15 | Morales | 1m 46.696s |
| 16 | Elias | 1m 46.734s |
| 17 | Simon | 1m 46.762s |
| 18 | Corti | 1m 46.938s |
| 19 | Pietri | 1m 47.088s |
| 20 | Noyes | 1m 47.104s |
| 21 | Luthi | 1m 47.150s |
| 22 | Cluzel | 1m 47.193s |
| 23 | Hernandez | 1m 47.216s |
| 24 | Debise | 1m 48.086s |
| 25 | Simeon | 1m 48.169s |
| 26 | Nieto | 1m 48.270s |
| 27 | Cardus | 1m 48.348s |
| 28 | Takahashi | 1m 48.406s |
| 29 | Gadea | 1m 48.447s |
| 30 | Rivas | 1m 48.472s |
| 31 | Rolfo | 1m 48.787s |
| 32 | Ivanov | 1m 49.155s |
| 33 | Lamborghini | 1m 49.410s |
| 34 | Guerra | 1m 51.025s |
| 35 | Wilairot | 1m 51.133s |
| 36 | Al Naimi | 1m 52.778s |
| 37 | Ranseder | 1m 56.170s |

### Championship Points

| | | |
|---|---|---|
| 1 | Elias | 271 |
| 2 | Simon | 185 |
| 3 | Iannone | 179 |
| 4 | Luthi | 143 |
| 5 | Corsi | 129 |
| 6 | Talmacsi | 103 |
| 7 | Cluzel | 101 |
| 8 | Bradl | 97 |
| 9 | Redding | 91 |
| 10 | Y. Takahashi | 86 |
| 11 | de Angelis | 85 |
| 12 | Tomizawa | 82 |
| 13 | Rolfo | 75 |
| 14 | Abraham | 71 |
| 15 | Debon | 70 |
| 16 | Aegerter | 67 |
| 17 | Gadea | 59 |
| 18 | Nieto | 45 |
| 19 | Baldolini | 38 |
| 20 | di Meglio | 34 |
| 21 | Wilairot | 30 |
| 22 | Y. Hernandez | 30 |
| 23 | West | 26 |
| 24 | Corti | 20 |
| 25 | Noyes | 18 |
| 26 | Faubel | 18 |
| 27 | de Rosa | 15 |
| 28 | Pasini | 12 |
| 29 | Sofuoglu | 11 |
| 30 | Cudlin | 9 |
| 31 | Simeon | 9 |
| 32 | Di Salvo | 7 |
| 33 | Pons | 7 |
| 34 | Pesek | 5 |
| 35 | Ranseder | 4 |
| 36 | Pirro | 2 |
| 37 | Ivanov | 2 |
| 38 | Tode | 2 |
| 39 | Pietri | 1 |
| 40 | Teshima | 1 |

### Constructors

| | | |
|---|---|---|
| 1 | Suter | 306 |
| 2 | Moriwaki | 296 |
| 3 | Speed Up | 212 |
| 4 | MotoBI | 184 |
| 5 | FTR | 124 |
| 6 | Tech 3 | 99 |
| 7 | Pons Kalex | 73 |
| 8 | I.C.P. | 38 |
| 9 | Bimota | 30 |
| 10 | BQR-Moto2 | 30 |
| 11 | MZ-RE Honda | 26 |
| 12 | Promoharris | 18 |
| 13 | Force GP210 | 11 |
| 14 | RSV | 10 |

---

## 125cc

**RACE (Part 2) DISTANCE: 9 laps, 23.387 miles/37.638 km · RACE WEATHER: Wet (air 18°, humidity 41%, track 25°)**

| Pos. | Rider | Nat. | No. | Entrant | Machine | Laps | Time & Speed |
|---|---|---|---|---|---|---|---|
| 1 | Marc Marquez | SPA | 93 | Red Bull Ajo Motorsport | Derbi | 9 | 16m 27.878s |
| | | | | | | | (mph/km/h) |
| | | | | | | | 85.227/137.159 |
| 2 | Nicolas Terol | SPA | 40 | Bancaja Aspar Team | Aprilia | 9 | 16m 28.028s |
| 3 | Bradley Smith | GBR | 38 | Bancaja Aspar Team | Aprilia | 9 | 16m 28.090s |
| 4 | Jonas Folger | GER | 94 | Ongetta Team | Aprilia | 9 | 16m 46.256s |
| 5 | Luis Salom | SPA | 39 | Stipa-Molenaar Racing GP | Aprilia | 9 | 16m 47.265s |
| 6 | Alberto Moncayo | SPA | 23 | Andalucia Cajasol | Aprilia | 9 | 16m 50.383s |
| 7 | Randy Krummenacher | SWI | 35 | Stipa-Molenaar Racing GP | Aprilia | 9 | 16m 54.577s |
| 8 | Efren Vazquez | SPA | 7 | Tuenti Racing | Derbi | 9 | 16m 54.581s |
| 9 | Danny Webb | GBR | 99 | Andalucia Cajasol | Aprilia | 9 | 16m 59.381s |
| 10 | Pol Espargaro | SPA | 44 | Tuenti Racing | Derbi | 9 | 17m 08.701s |
| 11 | Jakub Kornfeil | CZE | 84 | Racing Team Germany | Aprilia | 9 | 17m 14.884s |
| 12 | Simone Grotzkyj | ITA | 15 | Fontana Racing | Aprilia | 9 | 17m 16.651s |
| 13 | Alessandro Tonucci | ITA | 95 | Junior GP Racing Team FMI | Aprilia | 9 | 17m 22.296s |
| 14 | Luigi Morciano | ITA | 92 | Junior GP Racing Team FMI | Aprilia | 9 | 17m 30.112s |
| 15 | Zulfahmi Khairuddin | MAL | 63 | AirAsia-Sepang Int. Circuit | Aprilia | 9 | 17m 43.311s |
| | Robin Barbosa | FRA | 37 | H43/Hernandez Racing | Aprilia | 1 | DNF |
| | Esteve Rabat | SPA | 12 | Blusens-STX | Aprilia | 0 | DNS |
| | Tomoyoshi Koyama | JPN | 71 | Racing Team Germany | Aprilia | 0 | DNS |
| | Adrian Martin | SPA | 26 | Aeroport de Castello - Ajo | Aprilia | 0 | DNS |
| | Sturla Fagerhaug | NOR | 50 | AirAsia-Sepang Int. Circuit | Aprilia | 0 | DNS |
| | Marcel Schrotter | GER | 78 | Interwetten Honda 125 | Honda | 0 | DNS |
| | Jasper Iwema | NED | 53 | CBC Corse | Aprilia | 0 | DNS |
| | Louis Rossi | FRA | 69 | CBC Corse | Aprilia | 0 | DNS |
| | Luca Marconi | ITA | 87 | Ongetta Team | Aprilia | 0 | DNS |
| | Danny Kent | GBR | 52 | Lambretta Reparto Corse | Lambretta | 0 | DNS |
| | Lorenzo Savadori | ITA | 32 | Matteoni Racing | Aprilia | 0 | DNS |
| | Sandro Cortese | GER | 11 | Avant Mitsubishi Ajo | Derbi | 0 | DNS |
| | Johann Zarco | FRA | 14 | WTR San Marino Team | Aprilia | 0 | DNS |

**Fastest lap:** Marc Marquez, on lap 8, 1m 48.088s, 91.606mph/139.286km/h.
**Lap record:** Gabor Talmacsi, HUN (Aprilia), 1m 45.027s, 89.070mph/143.345km/h (2007).
**Event best maximum speed:** Marc Marquez, 152.4mph/245.3km/h (race part 2).

### Qualifying

Cancelled: Weather conditions

| | | |
|---|---|---|
| 1 | Smith | 2m 00.148s |
| 2 | Webb | 2m 02.646s |
| 3 | Moncayo | 2m 03.025s |
| 4 | Terol | 2m 03.823s |
| 5 | Cortese | 2m 03.957s |
| 6 | Schrotter | 2m 04.134s |
| 7 | Koyama | 2m 04.718s |
| 8 | Salom | 2m 04.949s |
| 9 | Savadori | 2m 04.982s |
| 10 | Kent | 2m 05.098s |
| 11 | Marquez | 2m 05.169s |
| 12 | Espargaro | 2m 05.292s |
| 13 | Krummenacher | 2m 05.451s |
| 14 | Vazquez | 2m 05.552s |
| 15 | Kornfeil | 2m 05.699s |
| 16 | Rabat | 2m 05.757s |
| 17 | Folger | 2m 06.031s |
| 18 | Zarco | 2m 06.553s |
| 19 | Martin | 2m 06.943s |
| 20 | Fagerhaug | 2m 07.430s |
| 21 | Rossi | 2m 07.584s |
| 22 | Marconi | 2m 07.712s |
| 23 | Morciano | 2m 07.768s |
| 24 | Tonucci | 2m 08.203s |
| 25 | Khairuddin | 2m 08.638s |
| 26 | Barbosa | 2m 09.267s |
| 27 | Iwema | 2m 09.413s |
| 28 | Grotzkyj | 2m 09.918s |
| DNQ | Gabrielli | 2m 13.986s |
| DNQ | Ravaioli | 2m 14.264s |

\* Grid positions decided by best time set in free practice.

### Fastest race laps

| | | |
|---|---|---|
| 1 | Marquez | 1m 48.088s |
| 2 | Terol | 1m 48.181s |
| 3 | Smith | 1m 48.205s |
| 4 | Folger | 1m 50.205s |
| 5 | Salom | 1m 50.549s |
| 6 | Moncayo | 1m 51.002s |
| 7 | Krummenacher | 1m 51.140s |
| 8 | Vazquez | 1m 51.511s |
| 9 | Webb | 1m 51.758s |
| 10 | Espargaro | 1m 52.270s |
| 11 | Grotzkyj | 1m 52.370s |
| 12 | Kornfeil | 1m 52.990s |
| 13 | Tonucci | 1m 53.381s |
| 14 | Morciano | 1m 54.333s |
| 15 | Khairuddin | 1m 56.410s |
| 16 | Barbosa | 2m 06.855s |

### Championship Points

| | | |
|---|---|---|
| 1 | Marquez | 297 |
| 2 | Terol | 280 |
| 3 | Espargaro | 261 |
| 4 | Smith | 198 |
| 5 | Vazquez | 144 |
| 6 | Rabat | 137 |
| 7 | Cortese | 132 |
| 8 | Koyama | 118 |
| 9 | Krummenacher | 106 |
| 10 | Webb | 93 |
| 11 | Zarco | 77 |
| 12 | Folger | 69 |
| 13 | Salom | 66 |
| 14 | Moncayo | 65 |
| 15 | Martin | 35 |
| 16 | Iwema | 34 |
| 17 | Kornfeil | 27 |
| 18 | Grotzkyj | 24 |
| 19 | Schrotter | 23 |
| 20 | Masbou | 20 |
| 21 | Fagerhaug | 12 |
| 22 | Kartheininger | 6 |
| 23 | Savadori | 5 |
| 24 | Khairuddin | 4 |
| 25 | Tonucci | 3 |
| 26 | Morciano | 2 |
| 27 | Rossi | 2 |

### Constructors

| | | |
|---|---|---|
| 1 | Derbi | 385 |
| 2 | Aprilia | 323 |
| 3 | Honda | 23 |
| 4 | KTM | 6 |
| 5 | Lambretta | 1 |

# VALENCIA GRAND PRIX

## VALENCIA CIRCUIT

*Inset above:* Lorenzo added another win to a year of achievement.

*Inset top:* Marquez completed a hat trick of Spanish champions in 2010.

*Inset right:* Vale, and thanks for the fun of it all. Rossi ended an era.

*Photos:* Gold & Goose

Bradley Smith chose Spain to break a run of 26 Spanish 125 victories. On a day of other celebrations, he was almost overlooked.
Photo: Gold & Goose

NOT only was the season ending at Valencia. Not only was it a pivotal race, followed the very next day by the start of the 2011 season, with testing on Monday for Moto2, and the following two days for the big bikes. It also marked the end of several eras.

As always, it was Rossi in the limelight, riding his M1 Yamaha for the last time after seven happy years. He wasn't able to take a valedictory victory to match his maiden-race win in Welkom in 2004, but he closed the deal in the same way he had begun it after his classic defeat of Biaggi's Honda in the Highveld sunshine – with a smacking kiss to the nose of the fairing after the race, wearing a T-shirt emblazoned with 'BYE BYE BABY'.

In his wake came a massed departure from Yamaha. Director Masao Furusawa would stay until compulsory retirement in March, but all of Rossi's mechanics, his favourite chef and others, including Davide Brivio, were also wearing the Fiat-Yamaha pyjamas for the final time.

Of no less significance was a similar exodus from Ducati, Stoner taking Gabarrini and his men with him to the new third-rider slot at Repsol Honda.

And some others, less in the public eye. IRTA threw a party for long-time Dunlop chief Jeremy Ferguson, like Furusawa at the age for compulsory retirement, after 45 years with the tyre company (starting at the 1967 Monte Carlo Rally), 25 of them in the senior role in the motorcycle GP paddock. And, with no fanfare, it was the last race for equally long-serving and oft-times near legendary two-stroke guru Sepp Schloegl. The Bavarian's tuning magic over the past 40 years had won championships for Dieter Braun in the 1970s, Toni Mang in the 1980s and Thomas Luthi in the new century; and runner-up slots in the 1980s and 1990s with Reinhold Roth, Helmut Bradl and Ralf Waldmann. His last season was with young German Marcel Schrotter, on the only Honda in the 125 class.

And there was a tense atmosphere at Suzuki, where almost half the crew were having their final race with the factory team, at least for the moment. Stuart Shenton and his guys had the satisfaction of finishing Loris Capirossi's season with six engines. In fact, nobody failed to reach the chequered flag due to running out of engines. All but two riders used the full allocation of six (Bautista eight, of Suzuki's possible nine). The exceptions were Pedrosa, who did miss three races, and Barbera, who missed none. De Puniet did use six, but only raced five, the last one being broken out only for practice at Valencia.

But had any cost savings been achieved? It was hard to get a definite answer from Yamaha at the annual technical briefing; only that while there had been a significant saving in the number of units built, there had also been a significant increase in development costs in achieving the longer service life required. Yamaha, slightly implausibly, denied any extra unit cost in special metals or coatings for longer life. Ducati and others told a different story, the Italians describing another extra expense: mile upon mile of endurance testing at Mugello, by the factory's off-track team.

Yamaha's annual update forum took a different form in 2010, with a film of the departing Rossi, talking about his bikes year by year.

In 2004, first year of the cross-plane crank, he had chosen the engine "with less power, but a lot softer feeling. The delivery was more sweet." He won. And the next year, on "the best, the most competitive, with a lot more power. It was very precise in all areas."

In 2006, chatter had been solved only in time for Michelin tyre problems to strike. And 2007 was the year "we went from 1000cc to 800, and also less fuel. I think it was a bad decision." The first year Hayden's Honda won the title, the second Stoner's Ducati ran away with it.

Then came two more straight titles. In 2008, "a big step. The power and fuel consumption were better, and electronics were very much improved. For the first time, the control could be modified corner by corner." And for 2009, "she became even more clever".

It was left to Yamaha's new champion to describe only small changes to the 2010 bike – and to sound a warning. "Our competitors have caught us. On some tracks, they are better. We need more power and more traction."

Moto3 regulations for the 125 replacement class starting in 2012 were firmed up at Valencia, with the GP Commission finalising technical requirements. The most significant were a rev limit of 14,000rpm, chain cam drive and indirect injection limited to five bar. They may use eight engines per season, with a maximum price of 12,000 euros apiece; engine manufacturers must be prepared to supply a minimum of 15 riders, and of course there will be a control ECU.

Pedrosa's doctors had cleared him of nerve damage after the numbing at Portugal; while Rossi and Spies were both due for the surgeon's knife in the near future; all were on hand not just for the race, but also tests on the following three days. Especially Rossi and Stoner, each with a brand-new bike to try.

In the case of Moto2, it was preceded by a flurry of new signings: Sofuoglu to Technomag-CIP, Takahashi to Gresini with Michele Pirro, Kallio to Marc VDS and Kevin Coghlan to Debon's new team.

Tests in that class saw Simon setting the pace from Bradl and Redding. In MotoGP, Lorenzo was fastest, but Stoner led on slightly slower times on day two, clearly revelling in his new Honda. Rossi was down in 15th.

Suzuki's switch to one rider for 2011 was confirmed the day after the Valencia GP, with the question of Dorna's response left hanging in the air.

Bridgestone's widening of the range between the two tyre options for the last three races drew mixed comments from the riders – but the previous harshest critic, Stoner, was very positive: "I couldn't really be any more happy with the changes. We were struggling all season to get temperature into the tyres. With the [cooler] conditions we've got at the moment, we have very good performance from the side of the tyre we use the least. It's a good step." Rossi proved, however, that in the end, riders will always complain about tyres. Asked his thoughts, he replied, "The soft tyre is better than last year, which was too soft. But the hard tyre is worse."

## MOTOGP RACE – 30 laps

Stoner's fourth pole of the season emphatically deposed Lorenzo with four minutes to go. Then came a surprise: a first front row and top Honda slot for rookie Simoncelli. Rossi eventually came up to fourth at the end, saying, "It's my fault. My style doesn't suit this track." Hayden and Spies completed row two; Edwards led the third from Pedrosa and Dovizioso, the last rider within a second of pole.

Stoner made a furious start, with Lorenzo, Hayden and Simoncelli following him into the first corner. But Pedrosa was rocketing through and seized second very forcefully from Lorenzo into the second corner, pushing the champion wide and behind Simoncelli.

By the end of the lap, Hayden was ahead of Pedrosa, and as they started the next, Lorenzo passed Simoncelli into the first corner, only to be passed back into the second. The next time it happened, Lorenzo shook his head in anger, but worse was to follow at the final corner. Lorenzo dived for the inside, but Simoncelli was already there, slamming the door and taking Lorenzo's front wheel. The Spaniard actually seemed to crash, but by a miracle he ended up back on board, dropping two more places behind Dovizioso and Rossi, who had finished lap one eighth.

At the start of lap three, Hayden hit the bump stops into the first corner, and was down and out. But Stoner was not relieved of pressure, with Pedrosa seven-tenths behind, and by lap six right on his tail, setting fastest lap.

*Above:* The end of lap two, and Stoner pulls the express past the signal box – from Hayden, Pedrosa, Simoncelli, Rossi, Spies, Lorenzo, Barbera (yellow) and Melandri.

*Left, top:* Race faces on for Forcada and Lorenzo.

*Left, bottom:* Capirossi reads his Suzuki GSV-R owner's manual one last time.

*Far left:* Stoner was on the giddy limit to stay ahead of the Yamahas, trying for one last Ducati win.

*Photos: Gold & Goose*

Above: The end of the affair. Rossi bids a fond farewell to his Yamaha.

Top right: Elias runs into the back of Iannone. Simon (60) is baulked, while Abraham (17) pounces to snatch victory.

Above right: Karel Abraham signed off his Moto2 season with a win, before moving on to MotoGP in 2011.

Above far right: A long-time coming. Victory at last for Bradley Smith in his last 125cc race.

Right: The 17-year-old Marquez celebrated his champonship victory with a hilarious tableau.

Photos: Gold & Goose

By now, Rossi was third after passing Simoncelli, and Lorenzo was about to follow him through, making a clean pass this time after powering past on the straight. But Pedrosa would fade again, weakened by his injuries, and on lap ten, both Yamahas overtook on consecutive corners.

Lorenzo was soon ahead of Rossi, and by half-distance both of them were right on the Ducati's back wheel. Stoner never had a moment's peace and struggled to match the pace: "I braked as hard and as late as I could to keep them behind me."

This tactic was successful until lap 23, when he ran wide out of the first corner on to the kerb and into a fearsome wobble, giving Lorenzo his chance into the second corner. Stoner stayed close for a couple of laps, but soon the gap began to grow. The new champion drew steadily clear to win by 4.5 seconds, leaving Stoner to a safe second.

Lorenzo was proud of amassing a record number of points, but also of how he had coped with being beaten up in the early laps: "I used to be known as a crazy rider, but I stayed calm and concentrated, and lap by lap I recovered."

Rossi had already dropped back by a second or so when the lead changed. Struggling with fatigue and his trouble-some injuries, he accepted a safe third. There was a time in the early stages when he had thought he might win, but "I started to feel pain in my right arm, then my left arm, then my leg. I am not fit, and if you are not at 100 per cent, you don't have the chance to win."

Fourth was another nine seconds down, but bitterly dis-puted to the finish. Pedrosa dropped back through the group, where Simoncelli and Dovizioso were going to and fro. All the while, Spies had been closing, and with four laps to go, he pounced on first one and then the other Honda, pulling clear by over a second across the line. Dovizioso was fifth, Simoncelli sixth, and Pedrosa was another six seconds away in seventh.

Behind, Barbera had led a gang of six all the way, Bautista having come through from the back of it to take ninth, from de Puniet and Espargaro, eighth to tenth places covered by half a second.

Edwards had lost touch, citing a lack of grip; Melandri had also dropped to the back of the group in his last MotoGP race, fading in the closing stages. The American passed him for 12th on the last lap. Hiro Aoyama (Interwetten Honda) and Carlos Checa (Pramac Ducati) trailed in; Loris Capirossi had retired from his last race with Rizla Suzuki.

So in the end, Pedrosa stayed second and Rossi did enough to take third, ahead of Stoner, with Dovizioso fifth. The worst off was Hayden, whose no-score meant that he dropped to seventh, behind Spies, so the rookie also claimed the honour of being top American.

## MOTO2 RACE – 27 laps

The finale of the new class was electrifying: Moto2 at its best, with no major crashes and a pack of five bitterly disput-ing the lead right up to the last lap.

Elias was on pole for his last race in the class, from Bradl, Iannone and Redding; second-race man Sofuoglu was in sixth. But the champion was a little slow off the line, finish-ing lap one fifth in the middle of a huge brawl – all having survived the first lap without any of the usual tangles.

It was Iannone in front, then Bradl and Redding, with So-fuoglu fourth and pushing hard.

For a minute, it looked as if Iannone might run away again, but Sofuoglu wasn't having that. Quickly past Redding, the leaders still all over one another, he was second ahead of Bradl on lap four. The gap was still less than a second, and Sofuoglu closed it by a tenth or so over the next couple of laps. Then as they started the eighth lap, Bradl fought back, diving inside the Turk under braking for the first corner and pushing him wide. Sofuoglu did not give way, even though he was off line, and paid the price, running straight on into the gravel at high speed and bailing out before hitting the barrier.

There were still seven riders in the chase pack, and Si-

mon, ninth on lap one, was moving through steadily. On lap 12, he took second from Bradl, the German falling off before they'd completed the next lap, trying to get back.

The Spaniard was 1.4 seconds behind Iannone, but had the pace to close him down, getting on his tail soon after half-distance. What is more, Abraham, Elias, Redding, Luthi and de Angelis were with him to make a brawl of seven disputing the lead.

Iannone had most of it, Simon pushing ahead frequently here and there, the others all ducking and diving in ultra-close company.

By the time they started the last lap, it was Iannone from Simon, Abraham, Elias and Luthi, with Redding a couple of seconds adrift and de Angelis fading behind him.

Elias was the wild-card, with a crazy attack that determined the race. Diving under Simon to push him wide, he ran into Iannone's rear, sending him off also towards the outer white line. With some justice, Elias himself crashed out.

It was a gift for Abraham. The gap opened wide and he took it, hanging on grimly for the rest of the lap. After labouring under the reputation of being a spoilt rich-man's kid, and following his first rostrum in Japan, the win was welcome: "I think I have proved I can be fast and I am a good rider. But today I was lucky."

Iannone was half a second down, Simon six-hundredths behind him, and Luthi less than two-tenths away. What a nail-biter.

Corsi was a lone seventh; Gadea finally defeated Aegerter for eighth, with Talmacsi leading the next trio for tenth. Cluzel and Kenny Noyes were still close at the end, the American's first points on the lone Harris since Catalunya.

The battle for second overall still went to Simon – it would have been the other way had Iannone won – with Luthi a distant fourth and Corsi fifth. Redding had jumped up to eighth with his strong season finish, the last rider to score 100 points, more than half of them in the final five races.

## 125cc RACE – 24 laps

With the last title in the balance, between two Spaniards, for many this was the race of the day. It was tense, but comparatively tame, as Smith, head well down, led from start to finish, breaking a run of 26 consecutive Spanish 125 wins. The major issue was resolved without tears or any scratching in his wake.

Marquez claimed pole, his 12th in 15 races, from his last title rival, Terol. Smith and Cortese completed the front row; Espargaro led the second.

Smith was first away, and he took a lead he would never relinquish, a second clear by lap 11, and almost three by the end, after an impressive feat of clear concentration. "It's the perfect way to finish with 125s," he said.

Behind him, team-mate Terol gave chase, with Marquez closing up on him after eight laps, setting fastest lap. All he had to do was follow Terol home, although he did make one half-hearted attempt to get ahead.

After five laps, Espargaro emerged from a fierce scrap behind and gradually closed up. By lap 12, he was with the pair, and Marquez found himself sandwiched. After four laps of it, he ran wide out of the first corner to let Espargaro past. By the end, he had dropped back by five seconds for a safe and very sufficient fourth place. The title was won. But Marquez was not the youngest-ever world champion – Loris Capirossi (1990) was also 17, but 98 days younger.

Terol and Espargaro battled to the finish, changing places twice on the last lap, Espargaro ending up fractionally ahead. Cortese broke free from the next gang to take fourth, leaving Rabat, Koyama and Vazquez locked in combat to the flag. Krummenacher narrowly won a race-long battle for ninth from team-mate Salom.

Webb (16th) and wild-card Taylor Mackenzie (21st, and son of Niall) were out of the points.

# GP GENERALI DE LA COMUNITAT VALENCIANA

5-7 November 2010 · FIM WORLD CHAMPIONSHIP ROUND 18

MotoGP | TISSOT OFFICIAL TIMEKEEPER

## CIRCUITO DE LA COMUNITAT VALENCIANA

Key
96/60 kph/mph
Gear

Angel Nieto 96/60
Mick Doohan 69/43
Afición 250/156
Turn 8 96/60
Turn 11 80/50
Turn 13 195/122
Turn 5 102/64
Turn 4 98/61
Adrian Campos 85/53
Champi Herreros 156/97
Turn 1 136/85

## MotoGP

**RACE DISTANCE: 30 laps, 74.658 miles/120.150 km · RACE WEATHER: Dry (air 22°, humidity 33%, track 27°)**

| Pos. | Rider | Nat. | No. | Entrant | Machine | Tyres | Laps | Time & speed |
|---|---|---|---|---|---|---|---|---|
| 1 | **Jorge Lorenzo** | SPA | 99 | Fiat Yamaha Team | Yamaha | B | 30 | 46m 44.622s 95.830mph/ 154.223km/h |
| 2 | **Casey Stoner** | AUS | 27 | Ducati Marlboro Team | Ducati | B | 30 | 46m 49.198s |
| 3 | **Valentino Rossi** | ITA | 46 | Fiat Yamaha Team | Yamaha | B | 30 | 46m 53.620s |
| 4 | **Ben Spies** | USA | 11 | Monster Yamaha Tech 3 | Yamaha | B | 30 | 47m 02.265s |
| 5 | **Andrea Dovizioso** | ITA | 4 | Repsol Honda Team | Honda | B | 30 | 47m 03.782s |
| 6 | **Marco Simoncelli** | ITA | 58 | San Carlo Honda Gresini | Honda | B | 30 | 47m 05.296s |
| 7 | **Dani Pedrosa** | SPA | 26 | Repsol Honda Team | Honda | B | 30 | 47m 11.419s |
| 8 | **Hector Barbera** | SPA | 40 | Paginas Amarillas Aspar | Ducati | B | 30 | 47m 13.910s |
| 9 | **Alvaro Bautista** | SPA | 19 | Rizla Suzuki MotoGP | Suzuki | B | 30 | 47m 14.073s |
| 10 | **Randy de Puniet** | FRA | 14 | LCR Honda MotoGP | Honda | B | 30 | 47m 14.482s |
| 11 | **Aleix Espargaro** | SPA | 41 | Pramac Racing Team | Ducati | B | 30 | 47m 16.383s |
| 12 | **Colin Edwards** | USA | 5 | Monster Yamaha Tech 3 | Yamaha | B | 30 | 47m 18.226s |
| 13 | **Marco Melandri** | ITA | 33 | San Carlo Honda Gresini | Honda | B | 30 | 47m 21.244s |
| 14 | **Hiroshi Aoyama** | JPN | 7 | Interwetten Honda MotoGP | Honda | B | 30 | 47m 23.590s |
| 15 | **Carlos Checa** | SPA | 71 | Pramac Racing Team | Ducati | B | 30 | 47m 40.791s |
| | Loris Capirossi | ITA | 65 | Rizla Suzuki MotoGP | Suzuki | B | 13 | DNF |
| | Nicky Hayden | USA | 69 | Ducati Marlboro Team | Ducati | B | 2 | DNF |

**Fastest lap:** Dani Pedrosa, on lap 5, 1m 32.914s, 96.421mph/155.175km/h.

**Lap record:** Casey Stoner, AUS (Ducati), 1m 32.582s, 96.767mph/155.732km/h (2008).

**Event best maximum speed:** Hector Barbera, 194.5mph/313.0km/h (warm up).

### Qualifying

Weather: Dry
Air Temp: 22° Humidity: 49°
Track Temp: 31°

| | | |
|---|---|---|
| 1 | Stoner | 1m 31.799s |
| 2 | Lorenzo | 1m 32.130s |
| 3 | Simoncelli | 1m 32.244s |
| 4 | Rossi | 1m 32.330s |
| 5 | Hayden | 1m 32.422s |
| 6 | Spies | 1m 32.566s |
| 7 | Edwards | 1m 32.579s |
| 8 | Pedrosa | 1m 32.603s |
| 9 | Dovizioso | 1m 32.886s |
| 10 | Melandri | 1m 32.917s |
| 11 | de Puniet | 1m 32.925s |
| 12 | Espargaro | 1m 33.085s |
| 13 | Barbera | 1m 33.170s |
| 14 | Capirossi | 1m 33.339s |
| 15 | Aoyama | 1m 33.343s |
| 16 | Checa | 1m 33.499s |
| 17 | Bautista | 1m 33.515s |

### Fastest race laps

| | | |
|---|---|---|
| 1 | Pedrosa | 1m 32.914s |
| 2 | Lorenzo | 1m 32.940s |
| 3 | Rossi | 1m 32.970s |
| 4 | Stoner | 1m 33.018s |
| 5 | Simoncelli | 1m 33.245s |
| 6 | Dovizioso | 1m 33.279s |
| 7 | Spies | 1m 33.294s |
| 8 | Hayden | 1m 33.546s |
| 9 | de Puniet | 1m 33.620s |
| 10 | Bautista | 1m 33.675s |
| 11 | Edwards | 1m 33.723s |
| 12 | Barbera | 1m 33.735s |
| 13 | Melandri | 1m 33.784s |
| 14 | Espargaro | 1m 33.784s |
| 15 | Aoyama | 1m 34.087s |
| 16 | Checa | 1m 34.163s |
| 17 | Capirossi | 1m 34.231s |

### Championship Points

| | | |
|---|---|---|
| 1 | Lorenzo | 383 |
| 2 | Pedrosa | 245 |
| 3 | Rossi | 233 |
| 4 | Stoner | 225 |
| 5 | Dovizioso | 206 |
| 6 | Spies | 176 |
| 7 | N. Hayden | 163 |
| 8 | Simoncelli | 125 |
| 9 | de Puniet | 116 |
| 10 | Melandri | 103 |
| 11 | Edwards | 103 |
| 12 | Barbera | 90 |
| 13 | Bautista | 85 |
| 14 | Espargaro | 65 |
| 15 | Aoyama | 53 |
| 16 | Capirossi | 44 |
| 17 | Kallio | 43 |
| 18 | de Angelis | 11 |
| 19 | R. Hayden | 5 |
| 20 | Akiyoshi | 4 |
| 21 | Checa | 1 |
| 22 | Yoshikawa | 1 |

### Grid order / Lap chart

| Grid order | 1 | 2 | 3 | 4 | 5 | 6 | 7 | 8 | 9 | 10 | 11 | 12 | 13 | 14 | 15 | 16 | 17 | 18 | 19 | 20 | 21 | 22 | 23 | 24 | 25 | 26 | 27 | 28 | 29 | 30 | |
|---|---|---|---|---|---|---|---|---|---|---|---|---|---|---|---|---|---|---|---|---|---|---|---|---|---|---|---|---|---|---|---|
| 27 STONER | 27 | 27 | 27 | 27 | 27 | 27 | 27 | 27 | 27 | 27 | 27 | 27 | 27 | 27 | 27 | 27 | 27 | 27 | 27 | 27 | 27 | 27 | 99 | 99 | 99 | 99 | 99 | 99 | 99 | 99 | 1 |
| 99 LORENZO | 69 | 99 | 26 | 26 | 26 | 26 | 26 | 26 | 26 | 26 | 46 | 46 | 99 | 99 | 99 | 99 | 99 | 99 | 99 | 99 | 99 | 99 | 27 | 27 | 27 | 27 | 27 | 27 | 27 | 27 | 2 |
| 58 SIMONCELLI | 26 | 26 | 58 | 58 | 58 | 46 | 46 | 46 | 46 | 46 | 99 | 99 | 46 | 46 | 46 | 46 | 46 | 46 | 46 | 46 | 46 | 46 | 46 | 46 | 46 | 46 | 46 | 46 | 46 | 46 | 3 |
| 46 ROSSI | 58 | 58 | 46 | 46 | 46 | 58 | 99 | 99 | 99 | 26 | 26 | 26 | 26 | 26 | 26 | 26 | 26 | 26 | 58 | 58 | 58 | 58 | 4 | 4 | 4 | 11 | 11 | 11 | 11 | 11 | 4 |
| 69 HAYDEN | 99 | 4 | 4 | 99 | 99 | 99 | 58 | 58 | 58 | 58 | 58 | 58 | 58 | 58 | 58 | 58 | 58 | 58 | 26 | 4 | 4 | 4 | 58 | 58 | 58 | 4 | 4 | 4 | 4 | 5 | 5 |
| 11 SPIES | 4 | 46 | 99 | 4 | 4 | 4 | 4 | 4 | 4 | 4 | 4 | 4 | 4 | 4 | 4 | 4 | 4 | 4 | 4 | 11 | 11 | 11 | 11 | 11 | 11 | 58 | 58 | 58 | 58 | | 6 |
| 5 EDWARDS | 11 | 11 | 11 | 11 | 11 | 11 | 11 | 11 | 11 | 11 | 11 | 11 | 11 | 11 | 11 | 11 | 11 | 11 | 11 | 26 | 26 | 26 | 26 | 26 | 26 | 26 | 26 | 26 | 26 | | 7 |
| 26 PEDROSA | 46 | 99 | 40 | 40 | 40 | 40 | 40 | 40 | 40 | 40 | 40 | 40 | 40 | 40 | 40 | 40 | 40 | 40 | 40 | 40 | 40 | 40 | 40 | 40 | 40 | 19 | 19 | 19 | 40 | | 8 |
| 4 DOVIZIOSO | 33 | 40 | 33 | 33 | 33 | 33 | 33 | 33 | 33 | 33 | 33 | 33 | 33 | 33 | 33 | 33 | 33 | 33 | 19 | 19 | 19 | 40 | 40 | 40 | 19 | | | | | | 9 |
| 33 MELANDRI | 40 | 33 | 41 | 41 | 41 | 41 | 41 | 41 | 41 | 41 | 41 | 41 | 41 | 41 | 41 | 41 | 14 | 14 | 14 | 19 | 33 | 14 | 14 | 14 | 14 | 14 | 14 | | | | 10 |
| 14 de PUNIET | 41 | 41 | 5 | 5 | 5 | 5 | 14 | 14 | 14 | 14 | 14 | 14 | 14 | 14 | 14 | 14 | 41 | 41 | 41 | 14 | 14 | 33 | 33 | 41 | 41 | 41 | 41 | | | | 11 |
| 41 ESPARGARO | 5 | 5 | 14 | 14 | 14 | 14 | 5 | 5 | 5 | 5 | 5 | 5 | 5 | 5 | 5 | 5 | 19 | 19 | 19 | 41 | 41 | 41 | 41 | 33 | 33 | 33 | 5 | | | | 12 |
| 40 BARBERA | 14 | 14 | 71 | 71 | 71 | 19 | 19 | 19 | 19 | 19 | 19 | 19 | 19 | 19 | 19 | 19 | 5 | 5 | 5 | 5 | 5 | 5 | 5 | 5 | 5 | 5 | 33 | | | | 13 |
| 65 CAPIROSSI | 71 | 71 | 19 | 19 | 19 | 71 | 71 | 71 | 71 | 65 | 65 | 65 | 7 | 7 | 7 | 7 | 7 | 7 | 7 | 7 | 7 | 7 | 7 | 7 | 7 | 7 | 7 | | | | 14 |
| 7 AOYAMA | 65 | 65 | 65 | 65 | 65 | 65 | 65 | 65 | 65 | 7 | 7 | 7 | 71 | 71 | 71 | 71 | 71 | 71 | 71 | 71 | 71 | 71 | 71 | 71 | 71 | 71 | 71 | | | | 15 |
| 71 CHECA | 19 | 19 | 7 | 7 | 7 | 7 | 7 | 7 | 7 | 71 | 71 | 71 | 65 | | | | | | | | | | | | | | | | | | |
| 19 BAUTISTA | 7 | 7 | | | | | | | | | | | | | | | | | | | | | | | | | | | | | |

### Team Points

| 1 | Fiat Yamaha Team | 617 |
|---|---|---|
| 2 | Repsol Honda Team | 451 |
| 3 | Ducati Marlboro Team | 388 |
| 4 | Monster Yamaha Tech 3 | 279 |
| 5 | San Carlo Honda Gresini | 228 |
| 6 | Rizla Suzuki MotoGP | 129 |
| 7 | LCR Honda MotoGP | 121 |
| 8 | Pramac Racing Team | 109 |
| 9 | Paginas Amarillas Aspar | 90 |
| 10 | Interwetten Honda MotoGP | 68 |

### Constructor Points

| 1 | Yamaha | 404 |
|---|---|---|
| 2 | Honda | 342 |
| 3 | Ducati | 286 |
| 4 | Suzuki | 108 |

## Moto2

RACE DISTANCE: 27 laps, 67.192 miles/108.135 km · RACE WEATHER: Dry (air 22°, humidity 34%, track 28°)

| Pos. | Rider | Nat. | No. | Entrant | Machine | Laps | Time & Speed |
|---|---|---|---|---|---|---|---|
| 1 | **Karel Abraham** | CZE | 17 | Cardion AB Motoracing | FTR | 27 | 43m 49.499s (mph/km/h) 91.991/148.045 |
| 2 | **Andrea Iannone** | ITA | 29 | Fimmco Speed Up | Speed Up | 27 | 43m 50.021s |
| 3 | **Julian Simon** | SPA | 60 | Mapfre Aspar Team | Suter | 27 | 43m 50.082s |
| 4 | **Thomas Luthi** | SWI | 12 | Interwetten Moriwaki Moto2 | Moriwaki | 27 | 43m 50.259s |
| 5 | **Scott Redding** | GBR | 45 | Marc VDS Racing Team | Suter | 27 | 43m 53.704s |
| 6 | **Alex de Angelis** | RSM | 15 | JIR Moto2 | MotoBI | 27 | 43m 54.884s |
| 7 | **Simone Corsi** | ITA | 3 | JIR Moto2 | MotoBI | 27 | 44m 00.898s |
| 8 | **Sergio Gadea** | SPA | 40 | Tenerife 40 Pons | Pons Kalex | 27 | 44m 10.919s |
| 9 | **Dominique Aegerter** | SWI | 77 | Technomag-CIP | Suter | 27 | 44m 11.938s |
| 10 | **Gabor Talmacsi** | HUN | 2 | Fimmco Speed Up | Speed Up | 27 | 44m 12.411s |
| 11 | **Jules Cluzel** | FRA | 16 | Forward Racing | Suter | 27 | 44m 13.010s |
| 12 | **Kenny Noyes** | USA | 9 | Jack & Jones by A.Banderas | Promoharris | 27 | 44m 14.668s |
| 13 | **Alex Debon** | SPA | 6 | Aeroport de Castello - Ajo | FTR | 27 | 44m 20.070s |
| 14 | **Yonny Hernandez** | COL | 68 | Blusens-STX | BQR-Moto2 | 27 | 44m 20.576s |
| 15 | **Xavier Simeon** | BEL | 19 | Holiday Gym Racing | Moriwaki | 27 | 44m 20.775s |
| 16 | Javier Fores | SPA | 46 | Twelve Motorsport/Motorrad | AJR | 27 | 44m 22.880s |
| 17 | Alex Baldolini | ITA | 25 | Caretta Technology Race Dept. | I.C.P. | 27 | 44m 23.047s |
| 18 | Yuki Takahashi | JPN | 72 | Tech 3 Racing | Tech 3 | 27 | 44m 27.055s |
| 19 | Claudio Corti | ITA | 71 | Forward Racing | Suter | 27 | 44m 28.101s |
| 20 | Michael Ranseder | AUT | 56 | Vector Kiefer Racing | Suter | 27 | 44m 28.262s |
| 21 | Hector Faubel | SPA | 55 | Marc VDS Racing Team | Suter | 27 | 44m 29.039s |
| 22 | Ratthapark Wilairot | THA | 14 | Thai Honda PTT Singha SAG | Bimota | 27 | 44m 29.334s |
| 23 | Roman Ramos | SPA | 43 | Mir Racing | Mir Racing | 27 | 44m 29.348s |
| 24 | Raffaele de Rosa | ITA | 35 | Tech 3 Racing | Tech 3 | 27 | 44m 30.018s |
| 25 | Roberto Rolfo | ITA | 44 | Italtrans S.T.R. | Suter | 27 | 44m 32.302s |
| 26 | Mike di Meglio | FRA | 63 | Mapfre Aspar Team | Suter | 27 | 44m 33.733s |
| 27 | Anthony West | AUS | 8 | MZ Racing Team | MZ-RE Honda | 27 | 44m 51.221s |
| 28 | Joan Olive | SPA | 5 | Jack & Jones by A.Banderas | Promoharris | 27 | 44m 51.530s |
| 29 | Vladimir Ivanov | UKR | 61 | Gresini Racing Moto2 | Moriwaki | 27 | 44m 59.025s |
| 30 | Toni Elias | SPA | 24 | Gresini Racing Moto2 | Moriwaki | 27 | 45m 15.028s |
| 31 | Yannick Guerra | SPA | 88 | Holiday Gym G22 | Moriwaki | 26 | 43m 50.836s |
| 32 | Mashel Al Naimi | QAT | 95 | Blusens-STX | BQR-Moto2 | 26 | 44m 04.606s |
| 33 | Hiromichi Kunikawa | JPN | 66 | Bimota - M Racing | Bimota | 26 | 44m 05.040s |
| | Axel Pons | SPA | 80 | Tenerife 40 Pons | Pons Kalex | 26 | DNF |
| | Robertino Pietri | VEN | 39 | Italtrans S.T.R. | Suter | 22 | DNF |
| | Fonsi Nieto | SPA | 10 | Holiday Gym G22 | Moriwaki | 18 | DNF |
| | Ferruccio Lamborghini | ITA | 70 | Matteoni Racing | Moriwaki | 17 | DNF |
| | Stefan Bradl | GER | 65 | Viessmann Kiefer Racing | Suter | 11 | DNF |
| | Kenan Sofuoglu | TUR | 54 | Technomag-CIP | Suter | 9 | DNF |
| | Carmelo Morales | SPA | 31 | Racing Team Germany | Suter | 7 | DNF |
| | Valentin Debise | FRA | 53 | WTR San Marino Team | ADV | 4 | DNF |
| | Ricard Cardus | SPA | 4 | Maquinza-SAG Team | Bimota | 0 | DNS |

**Fastest lap:** Karel Abraham, on lap 13, 1m 36.611s, 92.732mph/149.237km/h (record).
**Previous lap record:** New category.
**Event best maximum speed:** Alex Debon, 166.8mph/268.4km/h (race).

**Qualifying:** Dry
Air: 23° Humidity 27% Ground: 32°

| | | |
|---|---|---|
| 1 | Elias | 1m 36.141s |
| 2 | Bradl | 1m 36.247s |
| 3 | Iannone | 1m 36.255s |
| 4 | Redding | 1m 36.343s |
| 5 | de Angelis | 1m 36.413s |
| 6 | Sofuoglu | 1m 36.443s |
| 7 | Simon | 1m 36.515s |
| 8 | Morales | 1m 36.572s |
| 9 | Abraham | 1m 36.624s |
| 10 | Luthi | 1m 36.821s |
| 11 | Cluzel | 1m 36.875s |
| 12 | Talmacsi | 1m 36.885s |
| 13 | Noyes | 1m 36.905s |
| 14 | Ramos | 1m 36.956s |
| 15 | Fores | 1m 36.993s |
| 16 | Faubel | 1m 37.006s |
| 17 | Aegerter | 1m 37.011s |
| 18 | Rolfo | 1m 37.047s |
| 19 | Simeon | 1m 37.108s |
| 20 | Corsi | 1m 37.140s |
| 21 | Gadea | 1m 37.237s |
| 22 | Takahashi | 1m 37.252s |
| 23 | Ranseder | 1m 37.262s |
| 24 | Hernandez | 1m 37.277s |
| 25 | Debon | 1m 37.307s |
| 26 | Corti | 1m 37.403s |
| 27 | de Rosa | 1m 37.511s |
| 28 | Baldolini | 1m 37.541s |
| 29 | Pons | 1m 37.551s |
| 30 | di Meglio | 1m 37.567s |
| 31 | Nieto | 1m 37.577s |
| 32 | Ivanov | 1m 37.587s |
| 33 | Wilairot | 1m 37.697s |
| 34 | Cardus | 1m 37.727s |
| 35 | Lamborghini | 1m 37.953s |
| 36 | West | 1m 38.088s |
| 37 | Olive | 1m 38.270s |
| 38 | Pietri | 1m 38.664s |
| 39 | Debise | 1m 39.100s |
| 40 | Al Naimi | 1m 39.182s |
| 41 | Guerra | 1m 39.318s |
| 42 | Kunikawa | 1m 40.686s |

**Fastest race laps**

| | | |
|---|---|---|
| 1 | Abraham | 1m 36.611s |
| 2 | Elias | 1m 36.682s |
| 3 | Simon | 1m 36.686s |
| 4 | Iannone | 1m 36.709s |
| 5 | Sofuoglu | 1m 36.788s |
| 6 | Bradl | 1m 36.788s |
| 7 | Redding | 1m 36.819s |
| 8 | de Angelis | 1m 36.822s |
| 9 | Luthi | 1m 36.895s |
| 10 | Corsi | 1m 36.956s |
| 11 | Morales | 1m 37.079s |
| 12 | Talmacsi | 1m 37.147s |
| 13 | Gadea | 1m 37.278s |
| 14 | Aegerter | 1m 37.333s |
| 15 | Noyes | 1m 37.379s |
| 16 | Cluzel | 1m 37.444s |
| 17 | Pons | 1m 37.486s |
| 18 | Debon | 1m 37.521s |
| 19 | di Meglio | 1m 37.616s |
| 20 | Fores | 1m 37.620s |
| 21 | Simeon | 1m 37.641s |
| 22 | Baldolini | 1m 37.668s |
| 23 | Corti | 1m 37.692s |
| 24 | Hernandez | 1m 37.759s |
| 25 | Takahashi | 1m 37.864s |
| 26 | Faubel | 1m 37.878s |
| 27 | de Rosa | 1m 37.893s |
| 28 | Nieto | 1m 37.957s |
| 29 | Wilairot | 1m 37.966s |
| 30 | Ranseder | 1m 37.980s |
| 31 | Ramos | 1m 38.044s |
| 32 | Rolfo | 1m 38.198s |
| 33 | Pietri | 1m 38.385s |
| 34 | Ivanov | 1m 38.461s |
| 35 | Olive | 1m 38.502s |
| 36 | West | 1m 38.650s |
| 37 | Lamborghini | 1m 38.971s |
| 38 | Guerra | 1m 39.510s |
| 39 | Al Naimi | 1m 39.712s |
| 40 | Debise | 1m 40.323s |
| 41 | Kunikawa | 1m 40.346s |

**Championship Points**

| | | |
|---|---|---|
| 1 | Elias | 271 |
| 2 | Simon | 201 |
| 3 | Iannone | 199 |
| 4 | Luthi | 156 |
| 5 | Corsi | 138 |
| 6 | Talmacsi | 109 |
| 7 | Cluzel | 106 |
| 8 | Redding | 102 |
| 9 | Bradl | 97 |
| 10 | Abraham | 96 |
| 11 | de Angelis | 95 |
| 12 | Y. Takahashi | 86 |
| 13 | Tomizawa | 82 |
| 14 | Rolfo | 75 |
| 15 | Aegerter | 74 |
| 16 | Debon | 73 |
| 17 | Gadea | 67 |
| 18 | Nieto | 45 |
| 19 | Baldolini | 38 |
| 20 | di Meglio | 34 |
| 21 | Y. Hernandez | 32 |
| 22 | Wilairot | 30 |
| 23 | West | 26 |
| 24 | Noyes | 22 |
| 25 | Corti | 20 |
| 26 | Faubel | 18 |
| 27 | de Rosa | 15 |
| 28 | Pasini | 12 |
| 29 | Sofuoglu | 11 |
| 30 | Simeon | 10 |
| 31 | Cudlin | 9 |
| 32 | Di Salvo | 7 |
| 33 | Pons | 7 |
| 34 | Pesek | 5 |
| 35 | Ranseder | 4 |
| 36 | Pirro | 2 |
| 37 | Ivanov | 2 |
| 38 | Tode | 2 |
| 39 | Pietri | 1 |
| 40 | Teshima | 1 |

**Constructors**

| | | |
|---|---|---|
| 1 | Suter | 322 |
| 2 | Moriwaki | 309 |
| 3 | Speed Up | 232 |
| 4 | MotoBI | 194 |
| 5 | FTR | 149 |
| 6 | Tech 3 | 99 |
| 7 | Pons Kalex | 81 |
| 8 | I.C.P. | 38 |
| 9 | BQR-Moto2 | 32 |
| 10 | Bimota | 30 |
| 11 | MZ-RE Honda | 26 |
| 12 | Promoharris | 22 |
| 13 | Force GP210 | 11 |
| 14 | RSV | 10 |

## 125cc

RACE DISTANCE: 24 laps, 59.726 miles/96.120 km · RACE WEATHER: Dry (air 18°, humidity 47%, track 21°)

| Pos. | Rider | Nat. | No. | Entrant | Machine | Laps | Time & Speed |
|---|---|---|---|---|---|---|---|
| 1 | **Bradley Smith** | GBR | 38 | Bancaja Aspar Team | Aprilia | 24 | 40m 25.648s (mph/km/h) 88.642/142.655 |
| 2 | **Pol Espargaro** | SPA | 44 | Tuenti Racing | Derbi | 24 | 40m 28.434s |
| 3 | **Nicolas Terol** | SPA | 40 | Bancaja Aspar Team | Aprilia | 24 | 40m 28.797s |
| 4 | **Marc Marquez** | SPA | 93 | Red Bull Ajo Motorsport | Derbi | 24 | 40m 33.974s |
| 5 | **Sandro Cortese** | GER | 11 | Avant Mitsubishi Ajo | Derbi | 24 | 40m 50.023s |
| 6 | **Esteve Rabat** | SPA | 12 | Blusens-STX | Aprilia | 24 | 40m 52.391s |
| 7 | **Tomoyoshi Koyama** | JPN | 71 | Racing Team Germany | Aprilia | 24 | 40m 52.471s |
| 8 | **Efren Vazquez** | SPA | 7 | Tuenti Racing | Derbi | 24 | 40m 53.282s |
| 9 | **Randy Krummenacher** | SWI | 35 | Stipa-Molenaar Racing GP | Aprilia | 24 | 41m 06.859s |
| 10 | **Luis Salom** | SPA | 39 | Stipa-Molenaar Racing GP | Aprilia | 24 | 41m 06.927s |
| 11 | **Alberto Moncayo** | SPA | 23 | Andalucia Cajasol | Aprilia | 24 | 41m 28.188s |
| 12 | **Marcel Schrotter** | GER | 78 | Interwetten Honda 125 | Honda | 24 | 41m 28.647s |
| 13 | **Isaac Vinales** | SPA | 55 | CBC Corse | Aprilia | 24 | 41m 34.170s |
| 14 | **Simone Grotzkyj** | ITA | 15 | Fontana Racing | Aprilia | 24 | 41m 34.446s |
| 15 | **Jakub Kornfeil** | CZE | 84 | Racing Team Germany | Aprilia | 24 | 41m 50.446s |
| 16 | Danny Webb | GBR | 99 | Andalucia Cajasol | Aprilia | 24 | 41m 53.262s |
| 17 | Peter Sebestyen | HUN | 56 | Ongetta Team | Aprilia | 24 | 42m 04.587s |
| 18 | Joan Perello | SPA | 58 | SAG Castrol | Honda | 24 | 42m 05.004s |
| 19 | Lorenzo Savadori | ITA | 32 | Matteoni Racing | Aprilia | 24 | 42m 06.035s |
| 20 | Zulfahmi Khairuddin | MAL | 63 | AirAsia-Sepang Int. Circuit | Aprilia | 23 | 40m 31.240s |
| 21 | Taylor Mackenzie | GBR | 73 | KRP MMCG | Honda | 23 | 40m 39.965s |
| 22 | John McPhee | GBR | 70 | KRP Bradley Smith Racing | Honda | 23 | 40m 46.807s |
| | Sturla Fagerhaug | NOR | 50 | AirAsia-Sepang Int. Circuit | Aprilia | 23 | DNF |
| | Niklas Ajo | FIN | 31 | Monlau Competicion | Derbi | 21 | DNF |
| | Marco Ravaioli | ITA | 72 | Lambretta Reparto Corse | Lambretta | 20 | DNF |
| | Johann Zarco | FRA | 14 | WTR San Marino Team | Aprilia | 19 | DNF |
| | Johnny Rosell | SPA | 59 | SAG Castrol | Honda | 19 | DNF |
| | Danny Kent | GBR | 52 | Lambretta Reparto Corse | Lambretta | 15 | DNF |
| | Louis Rossi | FRA | 69 | CBC Corse | Aprilia | 12 | DNF |
| | Jonas Folger | GER | 94 | Ongetta Team | Aprilia | 10 | DNF |
| | Tommaso Gabrielli | ITA | 96 | Ongetta Team | Aprilia | 10 | DNF |
| | Adrian Martin | SPA | 26 | Aeroport de Castello - Ajo | Aprilia | 5 | DNF |

**Fastest lap:** Marc Marquez, on lap 6, 1m 40.216s, 89.396mph/143.869km/h.
**Lap record:** Hector Faubel, SPA (Aprilia), 1m 39.380s, 90.148mph/145.079km/h (2007).
**Event best maximum speed:** Pol Espargaro, 142.4mph/229.2km/h (race).

**Qualifying:** Dry
Air: 21° Humidity 41% Ground: 31°

| | | |
|---|---|---|
| 1 | Marquez | 1m 39.564s |
| 2 | Terol | 1m 39.672s |
| 3 | Smith | 1m 39.712s |
| 4 | Cortese | 1m 39.878s |
| 5 | Espargaro | 1m 39.919s |
| 6 | Rabat | 1m 40.459s |
| 7 | Vazquez | 1m 40.615s |
| 8 | Salom | 1m 41.371s |
| 9 | Martin | 1m 41.378s |
| 10 | Krummenacher | 1m 41.451s |
| 11 | Koyama | 1m 41.461s |
| 12 | Folger | 1m 41.805s |
| 13 | Zarco | 1m 41.855s |
| 14 | Webb | 1m 41.910s |
| 15 | Moncayo | 1m 41.950s |
| 16 | Vinales | 1m 42.379s |
| 17 | Schrotter | 1m 42.383s |
| 18 | Grotzkyj | 1m 42.687s |
| 19 | Sebestyen | 1m 42.715s |
| 20 | Kornfeil | 1m 42.733s |
| 21 | Savadori | 1m 42.941s |
| 22 | Kent | 1m 43.083s |
| 23 | Ajo | 1m 43.115s |
| 24 | Khairuddin | 1m 43.247s |
| 25 | Perello | 1m 43.456s |
| 26 | Rosell | 1m 43.657s |
| 27 | Fagerhaug | 1m 44.195s |
| 28 | Rossi | 1m 44.540s |
| 29 | Mackenzie | 1m 44.548s |
| 30 | Ravaioli | 1m 44.681s |
| 31 | McPhee | 1m 45.214s |
| 32 | Gabrielli | 1m 45.593s |

**Fastest race laps**

| | | |
|---|---|---|
| 1 | Marquez | 1m 40.216s |
| 2 | Espargaro | 1m 40.222s |
| 3 | Smith | 1m 40.363s |
| 4 | Terol | 1m 40.506s |
| 5 | Vazquez | 1m 40.927s |
| 6 | Rabat | 1m 41.022s |
| 7 | Cortese | 1m 41.075s |
| 8 | Koyama | 1m 41.275s |
| 9 | Krummenacher | 1m 41.356s |
| 10 | Folger | 1m 41.554s |
| 11 | Salom | 1m 41.613s |
| 12 | Moncayo | 1m 42.479s |
| 13 | Schrotter | 1m 42.514s |
| 14 | Webb | 1m 42.592s |
| 15 | Zarco | 1m 42.611s |
| 16 | Grotzkyj | 1m 42.820s |
| 17 | Kent | 1m 42.864s |
| 18 | Vinales | 1m 42.923s |
| 19 | Ajo | 1m 43.099s |
| 20 | Martin | 1m 43.229s |
| 21 | Kornfeil | 1m 43.546s |
| 22 | Khairuddin | 1m 43.966s |
| 23 | Savadori | 1m 44.165s |
| 24 | Mackenzie | 1m 44.167s |
| 25 | Fagerhaug | 1m 44.246s |
| 26 | Perello | 1m 44.289s |
| 27 | Ravaioli | 1m 44.323s |
| 28 | Sebestyen | 1m 44.390s |
| 29 | McPhee | 1m 44.834s |
| 30 | Gabrielli | 1m 44.842s |
| 31 | Rosell | 1m 44.881s |
| 32 | Rossi | 1m 45.841s |

**Championship Points**

| | | |
|---|---|---|
| 1 | Marquez | 310 |
| 2 | Terol | 296 |
| 3 | Espargaro | 281 |
| 4 | Smith | 223 |
| 5 | Vazquez | 152 |
| 6 | Rabat | 147 |
| 7 | Cortese | 143 |
| 8 | Koyama | 127 |
| 9 | Krummenacher | 113 |
| 10 | Webb | 93 |
| 11 | Zarco | 77 |
| 12 | Salom | 72 |
| 13 | Moncayo | 70 |
| 14 | Folger | 69 |
| 15 | Martin | 35 |
| 16 | Iwema | 34 |
| 17 | Kornfeil | 28 |
| 18 | Schrotter | 27 |
| 19 | Grotzkyj | 26 |
| 20 | Masbou | 20 |
| 21 | Fagerhaug | 12 |
| 22 | Kartheininger | 6 |
| 23 | Savadori | 5 |
| 24 | Khairuddin | 4 |
| 25 | Vinales | 3 |
| 26 | Tonucci | 3 |
| 27 | Morciano | 2 |
| 28 | Rossi | 2 |

**Constructors**

| | | |
|---|---|---|
| 1 | Derbi | 405 |
| 2 | Aprilia | 348 |
| 3 | Honda | 27 |
| 4 | KTM | 6 |
| 5 | Lambretta | 1 |

# WORLD CHAMPIONSHIP POINTS 2010

## Compiled by PETER McLAREN

Photo: Gold & Goose

## MotoGP

| Position | Rider | Nationality | Machine | Qatar | Spain | France | Italy | Great Britain | Netherlands | Catalunya | Germany | United States | Czech Republic | Indianapolis | San Marino | Aragon | Japan | Malaysia | Australia | Portugal | Valencia | Points total |
|---|---|---|---|---|---|---|---|---|---|---|---|---|---|---|---|---|---|---|---|---|---|---|
| 1 | **Jorge Lorenzo** | SPA | Yamaha | 20 | 25 | 25 | 20 | 25 | 25 | 25 | 20 | 25 | 25 | 16 | 20 | 13 | 13 | 16 | 20 | 25 | 25 | **383** |
| 2 | **Dani Pedrosa** | SPA | Honda | 9 | 20 | 11 | 25 | 8 | 20 | 20 | 25 | - | 20 | 25 | 25 | 20 | - | - | - | 8 | 9 | **245** |
| 3 | **Valentino Rossi** | ITA | Yamaha | 25 | 16 | 20 | - | - | - | - | 13 | 16 | 11 | 13 | 16 | 10 | 16 | 25 | 16 | 20 | 16 | **233** |
| 4 | **Casey Stoner** | AUS | Ducati | - | 11 | - | 13 | 11 | 16 | 16 | 16 | 20 | 16 | - | 11 | 25 | 25 | - | 25 | - | 20 | **225** |
| 5 | **Andrea Dovizioso** | ITA | Honda | 16 | 10 | 16 | 16 | 20 | 11 | 2 | 11 | 13 | - | 11 | 13 | - | 20 | 20 | - | 16 | 11 | **206** |
| 6 | **Ben Spies** | USA | Yamaha | 11 | - | - | 9 | 16 | 13 | 10 | 8 | 10 | 13 | 20 | 10 | 11 | 8 | 13 | 11 | - | 13 | **176** |
| 7 | **Nicky Hayden** | USA | Ducati | 13 | 13 | 13 | - | 13 | 9 | 8 | 9 | 11 | 10 | 10 | - | 16 | 4 | 10 | 13 | 11 | - | **163** |
| 8 | **Marco Simoncelli** | ITA | Honda | 5 | 5 | 6 | 7 | 9 | 7 | - | 10 | - | 5 | 9 | 2 | 9 | 10 | 8 | - | 13 | 10 | **125** |
| 9 | **Randy de Puniet** | FRA | Honda | 10 | 7 | 9 | 10 | 10 | 10 | 13 | - | - | 6 | 3 | 3 | - | 7 | 6 | 6 | 10 | 6 | **116** |
| 10 | **Marco Melandri** | ITA | Honda | 3 | 8 | 10 | 11 | - | - | 7 | 6 | 8 | 8 | - | 6 | 7 | 5 | 7 | 7 | 7 | 3 | **103** |
| 11 | **Colin Edwards** | USA | Yamaha | 8 | 4 | 4 | 3 | 7 | 8 | 5 | - | 9 | 9 | - | 9 | 4 | 11 | - | 9 | 9 | 4 | **103** |
| 12 | **Hector Barbera** | SPA | Ducati | 4 | 3 | 8 | 4 | 5 | 4 | 6 | 7 | - | 7 | 6 | 7 | 5 | 3 | 5 | 2 | 6 | 8 | **90** |
| 13 | **Alvaro Bautista** | SPA | Suzuki | - | 6 | - | 2 | 4 | 2 | 11 | - | - | - | 8 | 8 | 8 | 9 | 11 | 4 | 5 | 7 | **85** |
| 14 | **Aleix Espargaro** | SPA | Ducati | - | 1 | 7 | 8 | 6 | 6 | - | - | - | 4 | 7 | 5 | 6 | 2 | - | 8 | - | 5 | **65** |
| 15 | **Hiroshi Aoyama** | JPN | Honda | 6 | 2 | 5 | 5 | - | - | - | - | - | - | 4 | 4 | 3 | 6 | 9 | 3 | 4 | 2 | **53** |
| 16 | **Loris Capirossi** | ITA | Suzuki | 7 | - | - | 6 | - | 3 | 9 | 5 | 6 | - | 5 | - | - | - | - | - | 3 | - | **44** |
| 17 | **Mika Kallio** | FIN | Ducati | - | 9 | 3 | 1 | - | 3 | 5 | 4 | - | 7 | - | - | 2 | 1 | 4 | 6 | - | - | **43** |
| 18 | **Alex de Angelis** | RSM | Honda | - | - | - | - | - | - | - | 4 | 4 | 3 | - | - | - | - | - | - | - | - | **11** |
| 19 | **Roger Lee Hayden** | USA | Honda | - | - | - | - | - | - | - | - | 5 | - | - | - | - | - | - | - | - | - | **5** |
| 20 | **Kousuke Akiyoshi** | JPN | Honda | - | - | - | - | - | - | - | 1 | 3 | - | - | - | - | - | - | - | - | - | **4** |
| 21 | **Carlos Checa** | SPA | Ducati | - | - | - | - | - | - | - | - | - | - | - | - | - | - | - | - | - | 1 | **1** |
| 22 | **Wataru Yoshikawa** | JPN | Yamaha | - | - | - | - | - | - | 1 | - | - | - | - | - | - | - | - | - | - | - | **1** |

# Moto2

| Position | Rider | Nationality | Machine | Qatar | Spain | France | Italy | Catalunya | Great Britain | Netherlands | Germany | Czech Republic | Indianapolis | San Marino | Aragon | Japan | Malaysia | Australia | Portugal | Valencia | Points total |
|---|---|---|---|---|---|---|---|---|---|---|---|---|---|---|---|---|---|---|---|---|---|
| 1 | Toni Elias | SPA | Moriwaki | 13 | 25 | 25 | 11 | 6 | 20 | 11 | 25 | 25 | 25 | 25 | 13 | 25 | 13 | 9 | - | - | 271 |
| 2 | Julian Simon | SPA | RSV/Suter | - | 8 | 20 | 7 | 16 | 10 | 16 | - | 11 | 20 | 20 | 20 | 20 | - | 13 | 4 | 16 | 201 |
| 3 | Andrea Iannone | ITA | Speed Up | - | - | 13 | 25 | 4 | 25 | 3 | 20 | 16 | 13 | - | 25 | 3 | 16 | 16 | - | 20 | 199 |
| 4 | Thomas Luthi | SWI | Moriwaki | 9 | 16 | - | 13 | 20 | 16 | 20 | - | 5 | 9 | 16 | 6 | 8 | - | 5 | - | 13 | 156 |
| 5 | Simone Corsi | ITA | MotoBI | 8 | 11 | 16 | 16 | - | 4 | 10 | - | 8 | 11 | 13 | 11 | 5 | 6 | 8 | 2 | 9 | 138 |
| 6 | Gabor Talmacsi | HUN | Speed Up | 7 | 7 | 11 | 9 | - | 3 | 5 | 10 | 10 | 8 | 9 | 16 | - | - | - | 8 | 6 | 109 |
| 7 | Jules Cluzel | FRA | Suter | 16 | 5 | - | - | 25 | 9 | 2 | 4 | 13 | - | 10 | - | - | 7 | - | - | 5 | 106 |
| 8 | Scott Redding | GBR | Suter | - | - | 5 | - | 13 | 5 | - | - | 16 | - | 8 | 11 | - | 20 | 13 | 11 | | 102 |
| 9 | Stefan Bradl | GER | Suter | - | 2 | 7 | 2 | - | - | 7 | 7 | - | 11 | 7 | 9 | 9 | 11 | 25 | - | | 97 |
| 10 | Karel Abraham | CZE | RSV/FTR | 2 | - | - | - | 7 | 13 | 11 | - | - | - | - | 16 | 10 | 6 | 6 | 25 | | 96 |
| 11 | Alex de Angelis | RSM | FORCE GP210/MotoBI | - | - | - | 5 | - | 6 | - | - | - | - | - | 13 | 25 | 16 | 10 | - | | 95 |
| 12 | Yuki Takahashi | JPN | Tech 3 | - | 13 | - | 8 | - | 6 | 25 | - | 20 | - | - | 4 | 10 | - | - | - | | 86 |
| 13 | Shoya Tomizawa | JPN | Suter | 25 | 20 | - | 10 | 10 | 11 | - | 6 | - | - | - | - | - | - | - | - | | 82 |
| 14 | Roberto Rolfo | ITA | Suter | 11 | 4 | 6 | - | - | - | 16 | - | - | 6 | - | 7 | 25 | - | - | - | | 75 |
| 15 | Dominique Aegerter | SWI | Suter | 5 | 3 | - | - | 7 | - | - | 8 | - | 5 | 8 | 9 | 4 | 8 | 3 | 7 | 7 | 74 |
| 16 | Alex Debon | SPA | FTR | 20 | - | - | 6 | 11 | - | - | - | 9 | - | - | 6 | 11 | 7 | - | 3 | | 73 |
| 17 | Sergio Gadea | SPA | Pons Kalex | 6 | 10 | 10 | 20 | 1 | - | - | - | 2 | 10 | - | - | - | - | - | 8 | | 67 |
| 18 | Fonsi Nieto | SPA | Moriwaki | 3 | - | 8 | 1 | 5 | - | 8 | 13 | 3 | - | - | - | - | 4 | - | - | | 45 |
| 19 | Alex Baldolini | ITA | I.C.P. | 4 | - | 2 | 3 | - | - | - | 5 | - | - | - | 4 | - | 20 | - | - | | 38 |
| 20 | Mike di Meglio | FRA | RSV/Suter | - | - | - | - | 9 | 8 | - | - | 4 | - | 3 | - | - | 10 | - | 2 | | 34 |
| 21 | Yonny Hernandez | COL | BQR-Moto2 | - | 6 | 4 | - | - | 1 | 4 | 6 | - | 1 | 5 | - | 3 | - | - | 2 | | 32 |
| 22 | Ratthapark Wilairot | THA | Bimota | - | - | 9 | - | 3 | 13 | - | - | - | 4 | 1 | - | 9 | - | - | - | | 30 |
| 23 | Anthony West | AUS | MZ-RE Honda | - | 1 | - | - | - | 7 | 3 | - | 6 | - | - | - | 9 | - | 4 | - | | 26 |
| 24 | Kenny Noyes | USA | Promoharris | - | 9 | - | - | - | - | 9 | - | - | - | - | - | - | - | - | - | | 22 |
| 25 | Claudio Corti | ITA | Suter | - | - | 1 | - | - | - | - | 3 | 7 | 5 | 2 | 1 | 1 | - | - | - | | 20 |
| 26 | Hector Faubel | SPA | Suter | - | - | - | 4 | - | - | - | 4 | - | - | - | - | 5 | - | 5 | | 18 |
| 27 | Raffaele de Rosa | ITA | Tech 3 | - | - | - | - | - | - | - | 1 | - | 3 | - | 1 | - | 10 | | 15 |
| 28 | Mattia Pasini | ITA | MotoBI | 10 | - | - | - | 2 | - | - | - | - | - | - | - | - | - | | 12 |
| 29 | Kenan Sofuoglu | TUR | Suter | - | - | - | - | - | - | 1 | - | - | - | - | - | 11 | - | | 11 |
| 30 | Xavier Simeon | BEL | Moriwaki | - | - | - | 8 | - | - | 1 | - | - | - | - | - | - | 1 | | 10 |
| 31 | Damian Cudlin | AUS | Pons Kalex | - | - | - | - | - | 9 | - | - | - | - | - | - | - | | 9 |
| 32 | Jason Di Salvo | USA | FTR | - | - | - | - | 7 | - | - | - | - | - | - | | 7 |
| 33 | Axel Pons | SPA | Pons Kalex | - | - | - | 2 | - | - | - | - | 2 | 3 | - | | 7 |
| 34 | Lukas Pesek | CZE | Moriwaki | 1 | - | 3 | - | - | - | 1 | - | - | - | | 5 |
| 35 | Michael Ranseder | AUT | Suter | - | - | - | - | 2 | - | 2 | - | | 4 |
| 36 | Michele Pirro | ITA | Moriwaki | - | - | 2 | - | | 2 |
| 37 | Vladimir Ivanov | UKR | Moriwaki | - | 2 | - | | 2 |
| 38 | Arne Tode | GER | Suter | - | 2 | - | | 2 |
| 39 | Robertino Pietri | VEN | Suter | - | - | 1 | - | | 1 |
| 40 | Yusuke Teshima | JPN | MotoBI | - | - | 1 | | 1 |

# 125cc

| Position | Rider | Nationality | Machine | Qatar | Spain | France | Italy | Catalunya | Great Britain | Netherlands | Germany | Czech Republic | Indianapolis | San Marino | Aragon | Japan | Malaysia | Australia | Portugal | Valencia | Points total |
|---|---|---|---|---|---|---|---|---|---|---|---|---|---|---|---|---|---|---|---|---|---|
| 1 | Marc Marquez | SPA | Derbi | 16 | - | 16 | 25 | 25 | 25 | 25 | 25 | 9 | 6 | 25 | - | 25 | 25 | 25 | 25 | 13 | 310 |
| 2 | Nicolas Terol | SPA | Aprilia | 25 | 20 | 20 | 20 | 13 | 20 | - | - | 25 | 25 | 20 | 20 | 20 | 16 | 16 | 20 | 16 | 296 |
| 3 | Pol Espargaro | SPA | Derbi | 13 | 25 | 25 | 16 | 20 | 16 | 16 | - | 20 | 16 | 10 | 25 | 13 | 20 | 20 | 6 | 20 | 281 |
| 4 | Bradley Smith | GBR | Aprilia | 8 | 13 | 11 | 13 | 16 | 13 | 20 | 11 | 10 | - | 13 | 16 | 16 | 11 | 13 | 8 | 8 | 223 |
| 5 | Efren Vazquez | SPA | Derbi | 20 | - | 13 | 11 | 5 | - | 11 | 8 | - | 13 | 16 | 13 | 9 | 9 | 10 | - | 10 | 152 |
| 6 | Esteve Rabat | SPA | Aprilia | 9 | 16 | 9 | 9 | 7 | - | 13 | 16 | 11 | 9 | 9 | 10 | 9 | 10 | - | - | 11 | 143 |
| 7 | Sandro Cortese | GER | Derbi | 11 | 5 | 10 | - | 10 | 11 | 13 | 16 | - | 20 | 11 | 11 | 4 | 10 | - | - | 11 | 127 |
| 8 | Tomoyoshi Koyama | JPN | Aprilia | 7 | 11 | 8 | 8 | 11 | 2 | 10 | 20 | 7 | - | 8 | 10 | - | 7 | 9 | - | 9 | 113 |
| 9 | Randy Krummenacher | SWI | Aprilia | 10 | 8 | 2 | 10 | 9 | 10 | 9 | 5 | - | 9 | 7 | - | 5 | 6 | 7 | 9 | 7 | 93 |
| 10 | Danny Webb | GBR | Aprilia | 5 | - | 7 | 6 | 6 | 9 | 8 | 10 | - | 10 | 6 | 7 | 8 | 6 | - | 7 | - | 77 |
| 11 | Johann Zarco | FRA | Aprilia | 4 | 9 | 5 | 7 | 8 | 4 | 8 | 10 | - | 3 | 4 | 6 | 8 | 8 | 11 | 6 | | 72 |
| 12 | Luis Salom | SPA | Lambretta/Aprilia | - | 1 | - | - | - | - | 6 | 4 | 6 | 3 | - | 11 | 4 | - | 10 | 5 | | 70 |
| 13 | Alberto Moncayo | SPA | Aprilia | 3 | 10 | - | 4 | 5 | 3 | - | - | 3 | - | - | - | - | 13 | - | | 69 |
| 14 | Jonas Folger | GER | Aprilia | 1 | - | 3 | 5 | 1 | 6 | 7 | - | 13 | 7 | 5 | 8 | - | - | - | | 35 |
| 15 | Adrian Martin | SPA | Aprilia | - | 3 | 1 | - | - | - | 5 | - | 5 | - | 1 | 5 | 7 | 3 | 5 | | 34 |
| 16 | Jasper Iwema | NED | Aprilia | 2 | 6 | 4 | 2 | 3 | 3 | - | - | - | 8 | 5 | - | 1 | - | - | | 28 |
| 17 | Jakub Kornfeil | CZE | Aprilia | - | 2 | - | - | 1 | - | - | 11 | 2 | - | 2 | 2 | 1 | 3 | - | 4 | 27 |
| 18 | Marcel Schrotter | GER | Honda | - | 4 | - | 3 | 2 | 2 | 3 | - | - | - | 2 | - | 3 | - | 1 | 4 | 2 | 26 |
| 19 | Simone Grotzkyj | ITA | Aprilia | - | - | 1 | 2 | 7 | 4 | - | - | - | - | 2 | - | - | 1 | 4 | 2 | 20 |
| 20 | Alexis Masbou | FRA | Aprilia | 6 | 7 | - | 4 | - | - | 3 | - | - | - | 1 | - | - | 4 | - | | 12 |
| 21 | Sturla Fagerhaug | NOR | Aprilia | - | - | - | - | 6 | - | 7 | - | - | - | - | - | | 6 |
| 22 | Daniel Kartheininger | GER | KTM | - | - | - | - | 4 | 1 | - | - | - | - | | 5 |
| 23 | Lorenzo Savadori | ITA | Aprilia | - | - | - | - | 1 | - | 1 | - | - | 1 | | 4 |
| 24 | Zulfahmi Khairuddin | MAL | Aprilia | - | - | - | - | - | - | 3 | | 3 |
| 25 | Isaac Vinales | SPA | Lambretta/Aprilia | - | - | - | 3 | - | | 3 |
| 26 | Alessandro Tonucci | ITA | Aprilia | - | - | - | 2 | - | | 2 |
| 27 | Luigi Morciano | ITA | Aprilia | - | 2 | - | | 2 |
| 28 | Louis Rossi | FRA | Aprilia | - | - | | 2 |

219

# RIDE
## WITH US!

FIM-**LIVE**.COM     FIM-**STORE**.COM     FIM-**TV**.COM

FÉDÉRATION INTERNATIONALE
DE MOTOCYCLISME

# SUPERBIKE WORLD CHAMPIONSHIP
# REVIEW OF 2010

By GORDON RITCHIE

Photo: Gold & Goose

Results and statistics

By PETER McLAREN

CHAMPION PROFILE: MAX BIAGGI

# FIVE-STAR RATING

By GORDON RITCHIE

THERE can have been fewer more complicated characters in any form of racing than Max Biaggi. Smooth in riding style, sometimes rough in his on-track manners, according to many of his past and present rivals, Biaggi is the racing world's favourite enigma. What other modern-era rider has drawn such extremes of enmity and affection from competitors and race watchers alike?

From the minute he arrived in the upper echelon of the 250GP championship, his career was filled with controversy and glory. For four magic years in 250GP racing, the glory seemed never ending.

His debut win at Suzuka in the 500cc era sealed his reputation as a superstar; his erratic off-track behaviour made sure he was always the subject of publicity. Eventually, inevitably, his GP life went sour. A succession of teams and machines, right through the first few years of four-stroke MotoGP, brought some success and many recriminations. But his soul-deep conflict with new Italian superstar Valentino Rossi will probably define his GP reputation. Sometimes Max beat Valentino, most times he didn't. Other than his hardcore fans, the GP world took against him and he was forced into retirement.

But not for long.

In an Italian run series like WSB, Biaggi's value was gigantic, and with no Italian rider having ever won the title, he could see a chance to add a much desired fifth championship to his collection. Symbiosis with FGSport (now Infront Motorsports) was the driving force over the recent years in the series, but when he agreed to race in 2007 with Alstare Suzuki, he still had some magic left to play with, on track and off.

As in 500GPs, he won his first ever WSB race on the Suzuki at Qatar. He took another couple that year and was in contention for some time. He lasted one year with Suzuki and had to accept a private ride on a Sterilgarda Borciani Ducati in 2008, but he didn't win a single race. Ducati simply refused to sign him as a factory rider that year and the following year. But for the reappearance of Aprilia in WSB racing, it could have been curtains for Biaggi's championship hopes.

He had won three of his four 250 crowns with Aprilia and, indeed, with some of the same technical staff who were involved in making the RSV4 road bike/race bike an all-Italian factory effort. Suddenly Max was standing on the threshold of potential greatness once again.

In year one, 2009, the endlessly complicated RSV4 provided so many challenges that it took techno-perfectionist Luigi Dall'Igna and set-up perfectionist Biaggi until the Brno race to snare the first win. But nine podiums in total showed that they had a real contender.

After a winter of testing, Biaggi finally had a bike, in WSB terms at least, that was infinitely adjustable and tuneable. As a race bike, the narrow V4 had been developed with him in mind. Aprilia and Biaggi chased every technical issue, no matter how small, overcoming them with impressive amounts of effort and expertise.

Suddenly Ducati was no longer the top Italian effort. It is unrealistic to think that Aprilia and Biaggi's joint success did not contribute significantly to Ducati's decision to leave WSB in an official capacity. New champ Biaggi even thanked Ducati for not signing him when the team had the chance. Ouch!

For Biaggi, his fifth world championship was historic, the location impossibly apt, as Imola witnessed the culmination of single-minded effort from man, team and manufacturer that no other team could match. If Haslam and his squad had lacked support from the manufacturer, Biaggi revelled in the attention of riding in the most supportive team imaginable. Sponsors, machine, personnel: it was Team Italia and Team Max in all but name.

Machinery-wise, Biaggi received all he had asked for in 2010, but he also made the most of it most often, with ten wins and 14 podiums in total. Experience, not excess, got Max over the line. In true champion style, however, he won the final race of the year, even though the title had been made safe a week before.

*Above, clockwise from top left:* Racing title rival Haslam; number 3 is Max's trademark; Roman centurion ready for action; the Aprilia team exultant at Magny-Cours.
*Photos:* Gold & Goose

*Above:* Victory at Misano brought the fourth double win in eight races.

*Opposite page:* A jubilant Max Biaggi celebrates his fifth world title.
*Photos:* Gold & Goose

## SUPERBIKE WORLD CHAMPIONSHIP

# 2010 TEAMS AND RIDERS

By GORDON RITCHIE

### APRILIA

#### Aprilia Alitalia Racing
In a more widely competitive season than 2009, winning both the riders' and manufacturers' titles was a major feat. The marriage of Max Biaggi (39) and his machine was most effective most often, and they never made a slip-up all year. Overseeing the success was all-round technical boss, Luigi Dall'Igna.

Alongside Biaggi, although not always on the same level of equipment, was new boy Leon Camier (24), the most convincing BSB champion ever. The physical opposite of Biaggi, he showed plenty of vim and a little too much vigour. Alitalia gave them all wings.

A one-off leased EmTek Racing Aprilia was given to Sheridan Morais (25) at his home round in South Africa. CIV regular Federico Sandi (21) had two outings on his Gabrielli Racing Team Aprilia in 2010. He added variety, if not spice.

#### Team PATA B&G Racing Aprilia/Ducati
Jakub Smrz (27) started out on Ducatis, but ended on Aprilias, and was effective in practice on both. He made more reliable progress in races with the leased RSV4. The new team was an amalgam of the previous Guandalini and Borciani Ducati squads. Pata was a good title sponsor to land.

### BMW

#### BMW Motorrad Motorsport
At season start, the official team was much changed behind the retained rider line-up of Troy Corser (38) and Ruben Xaus (32). The new team manager on the ground was WSB great Davide Tardozzi. Predict-

ably, the fiery Italian and the straight-laced Bavarians parted ways, bizarrely between the final two rounds. Soon after the season finished, Bertie Hauser was also moved on from his overseer's job.

Mid-season Corser looked set for a classy top five, but ended a confused 11th. Xaus offered his skin as sacrifice every time out, but bravery was his undoing, not his redemption. Too many chiefs, too many personality clashes; it was an exercise in self-destruction in the final few rounds.

#### Team Reitwagen BMW
Alfred Inzinger's new guys came to WSB in 2010 as moths to a flame, but were burned by cash shortages and controversy before the European season fully got going. Spain, round three, was the final fling. Andrew Pitt (33) and Roland Resch (25) were regulars; Makoto Tamada (33) was a stand-in when Resch got hurt in Australia.

### DUCATI

#### Ducati Xerox Team
The last in a long line of factory Ducati squads, this one featured Ernesto Marinelli as team boss, as opposed to just engineering boss, after the departure of Tardozzi. Several key engineers had also left, but both 2009 riders, Noriyuki Haga (35) and Michel Fabrizio (26), were retained.

As a result, privateers beat them to the top Ducati slot. The disappointing results probably hastened the demise of the team.

#### Althea Racing Ducati
Proof that a well-tended and funded privateer Ducati is still the best non-factory way to go WSB racing, even

JAMES TOSELAND

SHANE BYRNE

LUCA SCASSA

JAKUB SMRZ

ROGER LEE HAYDEN

CHRIS VERMEULEN

TROY CORSER

LEON CAMIER

MAX NEUKIRCHNER

in the era of handicapping rules, Althea rode a wave with veteran Carlos Checa (38) and a roller coaster with Shane Byrne (33). Checa found a friend in the 1198 and placed third overall, in a championship with 14 full works bikes, even more remarkable now than it appeared at the time. Byrne's year was an enigma.

### DFX Corse Ducati
Swamped early season, somehow Lorenzo Lanzi (28) managed to find a narrow seam of speed in the last two races, which made the last year of the standalone DFX Corse team end in smiles all round.

### Supersonic Racing Team Ducati
A new team, an old Superstock name in Luca Scassa (27), and the results were often fresher than they had any right to be. Scassa scalped many a top rider as the squad ran on a tight yet workable budget.

## HONDA

### Hannspree Ten Kate Honda
An exciting line-up on paper, Jonathan Rea (23) and Max Neukirchner (27), made Ten Kate a team of two halves. Rea continued his sometimes impressive, sometimes luckless progress. Neukirchner, from Suzuki star to injured hero to refugee in one year, could not get his latest bike work as effectively as Rea's, and he finished in near oblivion. Ronald Ten Kate was in charge of the old family firm once more.

Wild-cards in Honda colours included BSB regular HM Plant Honda, with Ryuichi Kiyonari (28) and Josh Brookes (27) out at Silverstone. TYCO Racing Honda rider Tommy Bridewell (22) also made an appearance at the same meeting.

### ECHO CRS Honda
Funded, if not loaded, ECHO CRS started the year with regular rider Broc Parkes (28) suffering from injury, so first the team brought in BSB regular Josh Brookes and then the versatile Sheridan Morais. When Parkes left the team, Fabrizio Lai (31) took the ride. The odd point was hewn from the fringes of the privateer allotment.

### S.C.I. Honda Garvie Image
Money was the problem in 2010, and Vittorio Iannuzzo (28) had a devil of a job reaching even the finish line, never mind any points. Five DNFs in eight individual races, before the financial plug was pulled after Monza, sums it all up.

## KAWASAKI

### Kawasaki Racing Team
Back in WSB racing, Chris Vermeulen (28) was set to give the big green Kawasaki and Paul Bird Motorsports their best season in years, but a serious knee injury pretty much ended his year at the first round. Tom Sykes (25) suffered some bumps and bruises of his own, but he was the man who finally restored pride and points.

Vermeulen's understudies ran to BSB men Simon Andrews (28) and Ian Lowry (24), while at Silverstone former winner Akira Yanagawa (39) flew in. Paul Risbridger was the team manager and Ichiro Yoda the head of operations from KHI.

### Team Pedercini Kawasaki
Although not exactly marking time until the new bike arrives in 2011, it was an uphill struggle all year for Roger Lee Hayden (27) and Matteo Baiocco (26).

Beating any of the top two Kawasakis was a tough target for Lucio Pedercini's team, and points came along sporadically.

## SUZUKI

### Team Suzuki Alstare
Much more Alstare than Suzuki by the end of the season: the lack of eventual home factory support, just as Leon Haslam (27) looked a championship fighter all the way, was as inexplicable as it was self-destructive. The start had been very bright for class rookie Sylvain Guintoli (28) and Haslam, but from then on, the efforts of tech chief Giacomo Guidotti and the Alstare crew were more akin to top privateers than the normal idea of an official squad. Viru beer helped pay for it all.

The Yoshimura Suzuki Racing Team was supposed to take part in three races, but ended up at only one, Monza, with JSB rider Daisaku Sakai (28). Sakai's heavy race-one fall led to pain, then panic and scrapped plans for any more appearances.

## YAMAHA

### Yamaha Sterilgarda Team
Early test and racing crashes for James Toseland (29) injured his hand, and many more no-scores plagued his comeback season. Cal Crutchlow (24) attacked his bike, his rivals, his team and WSB in general with the same terrier-like tendencies that had won him WSS in 2009. His Superpole brilliance and eventual ability to win races did not go unnoticed.

Maio Meregalli was once more team boss, Sterilgarda the new title sponsor.

# THE BIKES OF 2010

By GORDON RITCHIE

## APRILIA RSV4

Aprilia as a factory and Aprilia Racing as co-designers threw the book at the original bike in 2009, hence the cassette gearbox and variable everything, but it took a second winter of testing to get everything to work together properly.

Sometimes a perfect scalpel, never less than a rapier, the complicated Aprilia was not always the best weapon for the job, but the number of circuits it worked at was far greater than of those it had trouble with. As infinitely adjustable as any WSB homologated machine can be, the 999cc 65-degree V4 was almost as narrow as a twin and had more natural tractability from its engine layout than any other four.

Bore and stroke of 78x52.3mm and a compression ratio of 14.5:1 gave it 215bhp at 15,000rpm. More if you believed the opposition.

Variable-height intake ducts, electronic injection with eight injectors and latest-generation ride-by-wire throttle control were all Aprilia's own work. In 2010, the ECU was also fed by inertial-input gyroscopes.

A full gear camshaft drive arrived in 2010, but it was banned by a behind-closed-doors agreement until Miller. The bike really didn't need it, but Aprilia said it helped with top end service life, as well as gaining a couple more horses on top.

A popular Brembo/Öhlins cocktail took care of stopping and bump absorption respectively. Öhlins was in with full-factory kit for Biaggi, the 42mm TRVP25 (through-rod) front forks and RSP40 (TTX40) rear shock. The rear swing-arms were works of art, designed and fabricated by Aprilia.

## BMW S1000RR

Second year, first class; the BMW was a very good bike awaiting greatness in other areas.

The powerful standard motor, complete with finger-style cam followers, was an otherwise modern, but conventional liquid-cooled transverse four, weighing in at 999cc and featuring a radical 80x49.7mm bore and stroke ratio. A 14:1 compression ratio led to a quoted top end of 215bhp at 14,000 rpm.

Another factory team that eschewed the conventional Marelli ignition kit, BMW ran Dell'Orto injection with 48mm throttle bodies, the ride-by-wire system controlled by a BMW RSM5 EFI unit.

BMW opted for a varied braking set-up, with Brembos for Xaus, Nissins for Corser.

The aluminium twin-spar bridge-type chassis cradled the very narrow engine, riding on Öhlins TTX20 or TRVP25 front forks and Öhlins RSP40 or TTX36 rear shocks.

Right on the 162kg weight limit, the BMW went through lot of geometry changes and featured unique rear swing-arms, with the top and bottom halves glued together. The highly-visible machining marks on the surface imparted their own element to the rigidity-versus-flexibility equation.

## DUCATI 1198F10

Largely the same as the 2009 model, the Ducati still featured a 50mm air restrictor by regulation, but the other balancing rules came into force and the minimum weight of the twins dropped from 168kg to 165kg, and finally 162kg – parity with the fours.

The L-shaped, 90-degree V-twin had the same 106x67.9mm bore and stroke as before, but there did

appear to be a lift in top revs, despite the restrictor, thanks in part to exhaust modifications for the works Termignoni system.

The engine electronics were controlled again by a Magneti Marelli Marvel 4 EFI unit, with IWP 162 + IWP 189 twin injectors per cylinder.

The claim from Ducati was for 200bhp at the crank, at 11,000rpm. Maybe a few more bhp could be added if the bike did really rev to 11,500rpm. Even with titanium exhausts fitted as the weight came down, the bike was about 0.8kg over the permitted 162kg.

Factory Öhlins TTX suspension, TRVP25 or TTX25 42mm forks and TTX36 rear shocks were pressed into action. The rear swing-arm, single-sided as usual, was a Ducati production. Brembo radial P4X34-38 calipers and 320mm front discs controlled the power outputs.

## HONDA CBR1000RR

The latest 'Blade looked very similar to the previous one, because it pretty much was the previous one, albeit with the usual mix of new home-made Ten Kate parts and HRC material studded into its body.

The engine was a bit more powerful than it had been in 2009, which took it over 220bhp, at revs that Ten Kate was always reticent about. A reserved bore and stroke ratio of 76x55.1mm came with an undisclosed compression ratio.

An HRC kit airbox was used to feed the 46mm throttle bodies, while PI Research Pectel equipment looked after the EFI functions.

Neo-factory Öhlins TTX25 front forks and TTX36 rear shocks finally showed up, run for Ten Kate by Andreani, not the full factory Öhlins service.

Rea used a beefy KR swing-arm, Neukirchner often the kit HRC version. The individualism of Ten Kate carried on to the PVM forged magnesium wheels, and although Nissin brakes are hardly ubiquitous now, with Ten Kate they were highly visible.

A long winter was spent on the dyno, but week-to-week mapping and electronic controls were the most crucial changes made. In a team that provided its own electronics solutions, this was sometimes a blessing, but maybe not always.

## KAWASAKI ZX-10R

A display of doggedness to succeed before the new bike came along delivered Kawasaki some strong results at the end of the season. The old-tech bike found some new settings in a one-off BSB round, and the powerful Kawasaki engine started finding a chassis balance better matched to it. The DOHC transverse four ran at 999.8cc, and overall it was all right out of the middle of the UJM engine drawing book.

A bore and stroke of 76x55mm was also from the conservative end of the spectrum. New exhausts came from Leo Vince, in titanium.

Over 200bhp was easily found, but the engine itself was big and upright, which made the bike difficult to steer into turns. Smart engine bracketry, hidden behind the existing frame spars, helped move the weight and rigidity closer to the centre.

Magneti Marelli electronics took care of the sparks and fuel, the same type as most other teams used.

Where the Brembo equipped Kawasaki differed from convention most obviously was in the Showa suspension, full factory material at that. The 47mm Big Piston Forks (BPF) were third generation, and featured compres-

sion and rebound adjustment via small screwdriver slots in the top of the fork. The preload was also located on top, making this a visually neat solution. The latest generation of BFR rear shock was used.

The bike was maybe a kilo over the 162kg limit, but the main issue was simply the age of its overall design. It was a mystery why it took so long to find proper settings like those that made it fly in Germany, Imola and, to some extent, France, but the facts are that the old stager was good enough to win BSB races, and take Sykes to Superpole and near podium places in WSB.

## SUZUKI GSX-R1000K10

Factory to start, in-house to finish, the Suzuki was the latest interpretation of the 74.5x57.3mm bore-and-stroke 1000cc engine. The 2010 bike ran a compression ratio of 14.5:1 and delivered around 215bhp at about 14,000rpm.

A new piston design and cam timing mods were matched to the latest Arrow exhaust. Fuelling and injection were taken care of by Keihin injectors and Marelli Marvel 4 engine management. Data acquisition was by both Marelli and 2D, the latter the preferred option of Suzuki in Japan. Different rear swing-arms, made to the team's own design, were tried and chosen from during winter testing.

With so little budget for mid-year testing and with a championship at stake, experimentation with the Öhlins TR25 front forks was limited, so the existing TTX25 units were used most often. An Öhlins RSP40 delivered infinite adjustments, but the Suzuki team could not get the most out of the new generation of Pirelli tyres as quickly as others.

Riders tried both Nissin and Brembo brakes in 2010. Haslam moved to Brembo after Monza; Guintoli persevered with the Nissins.

## YAMAHA YZF-R1

After winning in 2009, no one could accuse the Yamaha Sterilgarda team of resting on its laurels. The proud claim at the 2010 launch was of 228bhp at the crossplane crank, at 15,000 revs, with a smooth power band all the way. Bore and stroke figures of 78x52.2mm made the engine rev, but were not the most radical in the class.

The new Akrapovic exhaust was a 4-2-1-2 unit, and a new camshaft made more use of the liberated power. The sparks and fuel delivery came via a Magneti Marelli MHT unit, Crutchlow and Toseland using different forms of traction control, sometimes even different philosophies, as the year went on.

A narrower radiator and a new rear sub-frame/fuel tank made in carbon fibre were other pre-season mods that nearly took the Yamaha down to 162kg.

The changes on paper seemed just that to the 2010 riding line-up, with chatter a constant companion in the early races, and a hurried re-acquaintance with what 2009 parts they still had available. Changes were made through the year, but the verdict was that the R1 was a fickle flyer still.

Crutchlow, in particular, felt that tyre life was an issue over full race distance, and it took some time to get the package working well in real race conditions. He won three races, when he could get the rubber to hold out almost all the way.

Yamaha used the latest Öhlins kit, a TTX40 rear shock (RSP40) and the TRVP25 front forks. Brembo brakes and calipers completed the cycle parts

Aprilia RSV4

Ducati 1198F10

Kawasaki Ninja ZX-10R

Yamaha YZF-R1

Suzuki GSX-R1000K10

*Above:* Haslam, the young-ish pretender and a real contender.

*Right:* Fabrizio leads team-mate Haga at the start of race one.

*Below right:* Race-one podium, with Fabrizio, Haslam and Haga, after the closest ever WSB race finish.

*Below centre right:* James Toseland, back in World Superbike.

*Below far right:* Race-two winner Checa leads Guintoli.

*Photos:* Gold & Goose

HASLAM would be a formidable force in 2010; that much had been obvious for some time in winter testing. He was the superior in Superpole, and he went on to win the first race, making a bit of history. A sliver of it, in fact, because his winning margin was the narrowest in WSB history, 0.004 second. A last-corner charge from Fabrizio was only just mistimed, the finish so close that the result was given initially to Fabrizio. Closer examination showed that Haslam had a tyre-width advantage after 97.790 intense kilometres, giving the English rider his first ever win in WSB, in his first ever race on a real factory machine.

Third was a hurting Haga, coming back from a grid placing of tenth and a whopper of a crash in warm-up. The top three, covered by only 0.779 second, were ten seconds up on a four-rider inter-marque squabble between Rea, Biaggi, Guintoli and Checa: Honda, Aprilia, Suzuki and Ducati.

It was a horror start for Spies's old Yamaha Sterilgarda team, with first Toseland and then Crutchlow falling. The latter had qualified third and the former eighth. Their pre-season tests of the 'improved' 2010 racebike, just a few days before, had been nothing short of a crisis, and race day was little better.

In the second race, the finish was arguably even more remarkable than the record breaker of the first, as Checa had what he later called, "One of those races that maybe happens one, two or three times in your life." He rode his privateer Ducati (albeit with ride-by-wire wizardry and a factory electronics engineer in the backroom) to a well-judged late charge through the leading bunch.

A decade of GP experience was displayed masterfully and a salient lesson was given on how to conserve tyres. It was Checa's first win in Ducati colours, in his first meeting on a big V-twin. Unpredictable to say the least, but a performance everybody agreed was already a candidate for 'win of the year'.

The top four in the second 22-lap race were covered by 0.837 second, with Haslam second and Fabrizio third. Fourth was a name few would have expected to have done so well until after qualifying and Superpole. Sylvain Guintoli was yet another rider to prove that there is life after MotoGP. He even led for eight laps.

Haga was three seconds back in fifth; Rea ran off track and back on again, and therefore was unable to compete for a podium, despite his fierce pace. He was sixth.

The venerable works Kawasaki had another GP exile, Vermeulen, on board, alongside Yamaha WSB transferee Sykes. A fall in race one for homeboy Vermeulen was followed by a fast tumble and heavy impact to his right knee in race two, and the end to his season before it had really begun.

It was a thrilling start in the best of senses, and a dramatic one in more negative ways, with over 30 crashes during the weekend. The name of Resch was added to Vermeulen's at the more serious end of the injury list, after he fell and broke his collarbone in practice.

Xaus's own works BMW team banned him from riding on race day after he took out Haga at the start of the braking zone for the scary turn one. In total, Xaus fell four times in two days.

*Above:* Biaggi leads at the start of race two.

*Right:* Crutchlow and Sykes.

*Below right:* Shane Byrne took a tumble in practice, but scored two solid finishes.

*Centre right:* Biaggi after completing his first career double.

*Below far right:* Camier leads Sykes, Smrz, Toseland and Co in race one.

Photos: Gold & Goose

*Below, top to bottom:* Haslam, the early championship leader; Vital adjustments for Checa; Aprilia's Francesco Guidotti.

*Below left:* Much to his surprise, Rea was playing second British fiddle.

*Photos:* Gold & Goose

TWO wins for Biaggi and his increasingly perfect Aprilia RSV4 were portents in Portugal and landmarks for the Italian rider. He had never had a swift double in WSB before, just the single measure of champagne. He had to work hard, however, because in each race he had Haslam for close company, while Rea was another aggressive leader in race two.

Races won by 0.200 second and 0.191 second are usually pretty great viewing, but ultimately Biaggi took command of the situation at this roller-coaster for racers, set in the hills of the Algarve.

The two very different riders who were the top championship challengers were on their own at the end of race one. Rea was six seconds back, closely shadowed by Checa and Camier in the final stretch, all of them finishing within 0.7 second.

Race two was even more of a classic confrontation, with the top four being squeezed into 1.015 seconds; Biaggi from Camier, from Crutchlow and Checa.

Crutchlow, who scored his first Superpole, was third in the second race, his first Yamaha podium. The very essence of racing, he made up in determination and ebullience what his Yamaha clearly lacked in traction and sheer usability all race long.

Biaggi set the new lap record of 1m 42.774s in race one, but Crutchlow had secured a new best lap in Superpole, showing how fast he could be in his rookie year. Faster even than Spies, if you compare like for like.

Four races done, three different race winners, seven different podium finishers, and on a diverse mix of Suzuki, Aprilia, Ducati, Honda and now Yamaha machinery. Shame the crowd was so paltry.

Off the podiums, Camier's brace of fifths showed that the Aprilia could be as fast and adept for a rider of six foot plus as it was for one of Biaggi's smaller frame. Checa was fast once more, banging in a brace of fourths.

Toseland, still hurting from a broken right hand sustained at Phillip Island, took a seventh and a sixth, and although not in any way satisfied with these performances, in a championship with 14 works bikes, he was glad of the points.

The BMW Motorrad Motorsport push in the winter had yet to bear its best fruit; thus Corser was ninth and tenth. Qualifying into the final sector of Superpole showed the promise of the fastest bike in the class in stock trim.

Clearly the fastest machine in WSB trim was the Aprilia, up to 10km/h faster than the rest. Biaggi used this to full advantage, but claimed that his ability to hold off Haslam in two runs to the flag had more to do with superior drive on a tighter line out of the long last corner. He had a point, but so did his jealous rivals, who simply could not get past the Aprilia on the straights.

Haslam still left Portugal with the series lead, but with the ex-GP crew from Aprilia really getting into their stride, he would need more help from Japan, and soon.

After all, the competing forces were wide ranging, as four different manufacturers had filled the four top slots in each race. Ducati had to rely on Checa, not works boys Haga and Fabrizio, for the best results again. And not for the last time.

*Above:* Crutchlow, speed to burn in Superpole.

*Top:* Haga takes the lead from Biaggi in race two.

*Right:* Corser leads Checa, Biaggi and Haslam on lap one of race one.

*Above centre right:* BMW's Tardozzi. A love affair that didn't last.

*Centre right:* Toseland leads Guintoli and Crutchlow in a race-two battle.

*Photos:* Gold & Goose

*Left:* Haslam celebrates the win in race one.

*Below:* Vermeulen stand-in Simon Andrews was lucky to escape serious injury after a nasty crash.

*Below centre:* Kawasaki team owner Paul Bird.

*Below right:* Troy Corser debriefs with his BMW crew.

*Photos:* Gold & Goose

HAVING taken his first career pole in WSB at the previous round in Portugal, Crutchlow did it again at Valencia, although he would have swapped it for better final race results than seventh and ninth.

After taking two beatings in Portimao, Haslam reasserted himself at this tight and tricky stadium circuit, winning the first from Biaggi at a venue where the top speed of the Aprilia was not relevant. The RSV4's nimbleness and good corner-exit grunt were very good weapons to have, nonetheless.

Ducati twins, even old Aprilia V-twins it has to be said, have always gone well at Valencia and, in an aggregate race two, Haga exorcised the demons of the end of the 2009 season, if only once and not for all.

His team-mate, Fabrizio, would take 11th in race one, but then his bike failed to finish race two, making Haga's win all the more welcome, especially as it was the first since Tardozzi had left to join BMW.

Tardozzi was still working some magic, however, as BMW had its best result to date. Corser scored fourth in race one, only four seconds from a win.

In the opener, Biaggi was second, 1.7 seconds adrift of a cruising Haslam, but Toseland was plainly relieved to be third on his Yamaha, proving he really was back to try to win, and steadily getting the measure of his sometimes fickle machine.

The astonishing variety of broadly competitive machines for 2010 was underlined by the fact that the top six in race one read like this: Haslam (Suzuki), Biaggi (Aprilia), Toseland (Yamaha), Corser (BMW), Haga (Ducati) and Rea (Honda). Six marques covered by less than ten seconds, five of them by less than five seconds. The Spaniards who had bothered to show up – more than ever it appeared – were entranced by a colourful kinetic palette and aurally stimulated by a symphony of diverse instruments.

Local-ish rider Checa was second behind Haga in the aggregate race two, Biaggi third, but it was an incredibly tight final count after a horrid collision between Vermeulen stand-in Andrews and SCI Honda runner Iannuzzo, after only three laps. Andrews took out several pit boards as he bounced sickeningly down the side of the pit wall; Iannuzzo ended up at the end of the main straight, and a fluid spill from his bike took a long time to mop and dust. Thankfully, broken bones in Andrews's foot and ankle were slight immediate injuries.

Haga was inspired at the restart (which came an hour after the start of the original scheduled version), holding off Checa by 0.025 second and Biaggi by 0.299 second. The combined margins from first to second in all six races so far – 2.484 seconds.

Despite not having an ideal chassis and suspension set-up as yet, Camier led nine laps of race two before falling, asking too much, but proving his pace, as he had in race one. Fabrizio and Byrne crashed out of race one.

Of all the top competitors, Haslam had most reason to be pleased with his race weekend. His relatively easy win in race one was proof that when it all went right, the Suzuki, without much in the way of direct support from Japan, was still a winner – in his committed hands at least.

The BMW also came of age at Valencia, even if race two was a slight disaster for Corser in 12th. The massive effort put in by the Bavarians and their new Italian WSB specialists in the backroom was bearing fruit.

The balance of power in WSB had already started shifting, as MotoGP (Aprilia) and Formula One (BMW) refugees got their heads and bankrolls around production-based racing at last.

# ASSEN
## ROUND 4 · HOLLAND

*Above:* A dynamic Toseland heads Rea in their race-one battle.

*Right:* Toseland, Rea and Camier – the north, Northern Irish and south of it – completed an all-UK podium.

*Photos: Gold & Goose*

*Left:* Race one: Rea leads Toseland, Corser and Camier in front of the usual big Assen crowd.

*Below & below centre:* Suzuki Alstare boss Francis Batta and Yamaha tech chief Silvano Galbusera.

*Bottom:* Yamaha team boss and former rider Maio Meregalli.

*Below right:* British fans make their annual pilgrimage to Assen.

Photos: Gold & Goose

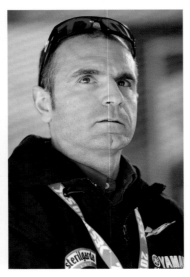

W ITH seven British riders on works or top privateer machinery, there had to be a 1-2-3 of Union flags on a podium somewhere, and it happened at Assen. Twice.

The grandstands may not have been as packed out with British fans as they had been in the heyday of Fogarty's dominance of the North Loop lay-out, but surely even Foggy-time was not like this. On track at least.

What Assen has always provided, however, is a venue that throws up close races, and in that respect, nothing had changed at this frequently altered racetrack.

Rea won his first double at Assen by a second and almost two seconds, but the action was tight and on many occasions very tough, with lines being stolen, bartered and invented all the way. The Ulsterman may have had the edge on race day because he had tested there in an effort to keep his bike on a competitive level, particularly after a hard Valencia race. He moved weight backwards, went radical on his front suspension, and won two races he will be proud to reminisce about decades from now, no matter what other glories may await him.

The latest new winner for the season – joining Haslam, Checa, Biaggi and Haga – Rea looked every inch a contender again.

In the first race, he had renaissance-man Toseland just over a second behind him, heading a tight battle that finally delivered Camier his first ever podium, with Checa in fourth, proving he could still mix it when required. Corser and Biaggi were welded together, fifth and sixth, and only 2.8 seconds from the winner.

The race-two podium men, Rea, Haslam and Toseland, were more spread out, but it was still a cast-iron classic. The intensity in the fight for third was such that Camier fell, while Toseland, Biaggi, Corser, Checa and Smrz were all within 0.7 second as they dashed over the line.

Toseland, overcoming the misfortune that had pulled him down in the early rounds, now had three podiums in the previous four races, his latest achievements thanks to a late change of rear link after qualifying only tenth.

Camier was probably the most satisfied to score a podium, having beaten his team-mate fair and square. He was also possibly the most pugilistic of riders, harrying and trying passes only a first-time visitor to Assen would attempt, never mind pull off.

Assen was another circuit where the WSB boys were fast enough to embarrass the MotoGP lot: Rea's Superpole lap of 1m 34.944s (on Pirelli's not-quite-qualifiers) was good enough to have put him fifth on the GP grid. Haslam's race time was 0.334 second faster than qualifying. Smrz's ancient Ducati was nearly in the 1m 34s region with Rea and took second spot in Superpole.

Corser, third in Superpole, was showing that BMW had reached its latest target, finally mixing it with the other big beasts of Superbike. A brace of fifths was actually better than the final results suggested.

For Ducati, only Checa was a leading light, Fabrizio and Haga being lost in the wilderness again. Haga was only just in the top ten in race one, while Fabrizio was 12th each time.

Haslam suffered a slow puncture in race one, making his 11th a miracle; his second place in race two was a resurrection.

Superstar Vermeulen was back for the KRT Team, if clearly nowhere near fit. He took points in race two, which eased his pain.

*Above:* Biaggi leads Crutchlow, Haslam and Corser in race two.

*Centre right:* Biaggi the victor greets his adoring fans at adorable Monza.

*Below:* Sykes whipped his ageing Kawasaki to an impressive fifth in race two.

Photos: Gold & Goose

*Left:* Sakai and Kato flew the flag in memory of Pops Yoshimura.

*Below:* Troy Corser gained BMW's first ever WSB podium.

*Photos: Gold & Goose*

*Left:* Haga suffered from a lack of top speed on his restricted Ducati.

*Below:* Toseland crashes down in the middle of the pack in an accident that would also take out Rea and Xaus.

*Photos: Gold & Goose*

AT the classic parkland circuit of Monza, and nearly 90 races into his career, Biaggi finally got a first Superpole win. An astounding career statistic for a rider of such obvious prowess, but statistics were very much the order of his day.

At the first of three Italian venues on the calendar, he scored Superpole, set a new absolute WSB top-speed figure of 330.2km/h and took two race wins.

His race-one advantage was slender, as the slipstreaming opportunities offered by Monza ensured he had company: the final podium ranking of Biaggi, Toseland and Crutchlow was covered by only 0.297 second. Haslam's outgunned Suzuki was fourth, but still only 0.958 second adrift of his remorseless nemesis, Biaggi.

With Camier fifth, race one could have been a Brit-fest like Assen had it not been for the astoundingly effective combination of Biaggi, his industrious team and the jewel-like Aprilia V4.

In the second race, the challenge to Biaggi evaporated after a serious lap-one crash at the infamous and recently remodelled first chicane. Toseland, Rea and Xaus clashed and crashed, the first two heavily. Battered and bruised, they were lucky to escape worse injury.

In general, race two was costly, as eight riders failed to finish, including the only man left in the race who could keep the pace of Biaggi – Crutchlow. Before the race, he had said he would do anything to beat Biaggi, and he was making a great job of plotting and planning in the Italian's slipstream, until his bike suffered a holed radiator and then a blown motor, which caused him to crash on the way out of the first chicane with six laps to go.

This spoiled the run of impressively close finishes in WSB, as Biaggi simply outpaced the increasingly finicky Suzuki of Haslam by 4.5 seconds.

After a tough first race in eighth, two places behind team-mate Xaus, Corser gave BMW its first podium finish. It was appropriate that this historic moment occurred at the most historic track in mainland Europe.

Fifth and fourth places for Camier proved again that he really could get his lanky frame squeezed in behind that tiny Aprilia's bodywork.

Tom Sykes gave a new-season highpoint to KRT in race two by finishing fifth. He may have been 15 seconds down on Biaggi after 18 laps, but the old Kawasaki at least still had an engine, going easily over 200mph in full race trim.

The Ducati riders, all of them, demonstrated that their bikes really didn't have the legs any more at tracks like this, amplifying their pleas to change the air restrictor rules for 2011.

There was novelty at Monza in the form of the celebrated eastern entity, Yoshimura Suzuki. Daisaku Sakai represented the all-Japanese squad, dressed in 1970s retro overalls and with a visual tribute to founder Pops Yoshimura overlooking their efforts on the pit garage wall. Sakai qualified 21st of 24, but fell hard in race one, on lap 11, and was ruled out of race two.

Back in the championship fight, Haslam's fourth- and second-place finishes were just enough to keep him in the championship lead. But Biaggi was irresistible at home, and even let some emotion crack his normally controlled and cool demeanour. After the podium ceremonies, he said, "For emotion, this is my best ever win, but if you put in a weight balance of this against winning my first ever GP 500 race at Suzuka, I would have to say that one at Suzuka." Feet on the ground, yet heart in the clouds.

*Above:* A photo opportunity for WSB at World Cup HQ, Soccer City. Back row: Biaggi, ZA soccer star Shaun Bartlett, Corser, Crutchlow, Fabrizio, Sykes. Front row: Haslam, Morais, Rea and Checa.

*Left:* Haslam, race-two winner.

*Far left:* The field settle into place on the first lap, of race one.

*Below left:* Local wild-card Sheridan Morais on a leased Aprilia.

*Below centre left:* Scassa, a new star on the rise.

*Bottom left:* Camier, BSB champ to WSB challenger in one easy bound.

*Below far left:* Rea leads Biaggi, Haslam and Crutchlow in race two.

*Below:* Fabrizio scored a win for Ducati in race one.

Photos: Gold & Goose

MONZA had started off a busy month of May, and only a few days after that the lead riders reconvened in the new Soccer City Stadium, near Soweto, for a pre-Kyalami press conference. South Africa had long since begun its countdown to the start of the World Cup contest.

It was a prestigious start for WSB as it crossed its third continental boundary of the year, the launch being the focus of the first big media event at the astounding new/old stadium. Sadly, Kyalami was just old/old, and it was showing its cracks and wrinkles, particularly in the track surface.

It was great for the best twins, though: a return to a high-altitude track where the fours could not breathe deeply, the straights were short, and the braking and turning ease of the Ducatis could maybe work some magic on the cramped, but characterful circuit.

Ducati rider Fabrizio took race one by just over a second from Checa, and by a whopping five seconds from Haslam. The last finished almost two seconds ahead of Biaggi, who had predicted quite rightly that his precise little Aprilia would be swallowed by the bumps and dips in South Africa.

The real close fights in race one would take place further down the field, however, with Rea and Camier in fifth and sixth; Toseland, Crutchlow and Smrz bashed fairings three seconds back.

A rock-hard midfield saw privateer Scassa take Corser's scalp, and local man Sheridan Morais score points for a 13th place in a one-off ride on a leased Aprilia.

Race two was one of those where determination was the main characteristic on display, Haslam wrestling his way to the win in yet another multi-rider fight that sent the enthusiastic crowd into paroxysms of joy. Four riders in the same second, the fifth only 1.4 seconds behind the winner, and five different makes of bike in the top five places.

Each race winner scored one of the best wins they will ever take, under pressure and with rivals at, literally, every turn. Even Fabrizio demonstrated maturity that some thought he might never find.

With a slender championship lead, Haslam could have opted to play safe in the final laps of the second race. His racer's spirit took over, however, and he risked it all to win. Rea had led more laps, but Haslam would not be denied.

Noriyuki Haga watched his team-mate win race one, 35 seconds behind in 17th. Tenth in race two was marginally better, but for a rider who had been so potent at this track in 2009, something was deeply wrong. He said he had "the fear", but why? Had he not won at Valencia in mid-April?

After race one had been a virtual benefit for the top twins, the fours made up ground in race two, and after the race the FIM's balancing calculations, designed to ensure parity between the 1200cc twins and the rest, finally kicked in after a long period of complete stability. From the next round at Miller, the twins could drop their weight by three kilos.

The main talking point for the riders on their way to the airport was – yet again – inconsistencies in tyre performance, a problem that had been encountered before, but had become chronic in 2010.

Camier went back so far so fast in race two, after a solid sixth in the opener, that he pulled in. Others saw their entire weekends determined by how well or badly their tyres behaved. Not at all the idea in a mono-tyre class.

FULL-ON technical failures at the top level of World Superbike racing are not unheard of, but normally they happen most often to the underfunded privateers, on old bikes. So for Checa, in the relatively flush Althea Ducati team and on ride-by-wire, neo-factory bikes, suffering breakdowns in two races he was well on course to win was a bitter blow in America.

Miller Motorsports Park is Checa's favourite circuit, a high-altitude venue with air as thin as Kyalami's, where he had won both races for Honda in 2008. A second double disappeared after he encountered a fading spark from his electronics package and a transmission issue. Even so, he was admirably dignified in circumstances that would have reduced others to public tears or tantrums.

The fact that sometimes he was 15km/h slower on the long main straight than Biaggi's Aprilia, but more than made up for it in Miller's generally fast corners and frequent elevation changes, showed just how well he and his set-up were rising to the race-day challenges.

Biaggi took a hard earned third double of the year; he was the best of the rest, by nearly five seconds in race one and nearly six in race two. His fast Aprilia and Miller's long straight helped a bit.

To his credit, like the other top riders, he acknowledged that Checa was the real star of the show, and that he had been lucky to take two wins instead of two clear seconds.

The turning point of the season in so many ways, Miller saw Biaggi regain the championship lead, as Haslam could only manage second in race one after a hard struggle, and then he fell in race two while trying to make up for his now troublesome machine, which was showing all the signs of an utter lack of development by the factory, despite hard work from the Alstare team itself.

After all his recent talk of racing fear and loathing, Haga took a third and a fourth – at a circuit where he had smashed his collarbone to kindling only a couple of years before.

The other podium finishers at Miller were Camier (his career best to date, delivering a first 1-2 for Aprilia) and Crutchlow, who had not actually scored Superpole this time around. Checa had scooped that early advantage with a new track best. But a new lap record, plus two Pirelli awards for the fastest laps in each race, proved to be his only race-day rewards. Nothing useful, like points. The ultimate result was slipping back up to fourth overall, following Rea's disappointing 14th (crash and restart) and seventh places.

With only 15 finishers in race two, there were plenty of clearing up for the corner workers to do. Rather than falling, however, Smrz suffered two break-downs with his Ducati.

Camier had been fourth in race one at Miller; Corser was a factor again in America, just not a leading one. He still won a three-way fight for fifth in race one, heading off Byrne and improving Ducati privateer Scassa.

The second race saw Corser fifth again, while Guintoli beat Byrne in a dash across the line for sixth. A painful home race for Roger Lee Hayden saw him 16th in the opener, but he crashed, remounted and retired in the pits in race two. Being a privateer was hard in 2010, as Hayden could have reasonably expected better results than that in most other seasons, even on the least favoured of the fours.

The most favoured was obviously the V4 Aprilia, now with its controversial gear-drive-camshaft engine being allowed for race use for the first time.

*Above:* A tough home weekend for Roger Lee Hayden.

*Top left:* Guintoli leads Rea, Byrne, Fabrizio and Smrz in race two.

*Top:* Haslam tumbles in race two – a pivotal, painful moment.

*Top right:* Cowboy Smrz twice had his old nag go lame under him.

*Above centre:* Race one: Checa is the filling in an Aprilia club sandwich.

*Right:* Crutchlow ploughs on past a field of Stars and Stripes.

*Left:* Dramatic scenery looms as Corser chases Biaggi.

*Photos:* Gold & Goose

*Above:* Biaggi leads away from Corser, Checa, Crutchlow, Fabrizio et al at the start of race two.

*Right:* Fabrizio and Crutchlow rocket down pit-board alley.

Photos: Gold & Goose

*Below:* Bikes on display in the San Marino main piazza.

*Below left:* CIV regular rider Sandi in action on the Aprillia.

*Bottom:* Race-one podium man Corser holds off Biaggi, for a while at least.

*Below right:* Checa loiters outside the 'other' Ducati garage.

Photos: Gold & Goose

THE fates had given Biaggi a couple of early birthday presents at Miller, but a day after his real 39th birthday, he earned a couple more by himself. Two hot 24-lappers by the Adriatic Riviera were thoroughly deserved. But at least we were back to competitive racing again. Biaggi, Checa and Corser finished well within the same second in race one.

Yes, Checa's bike made it all the way this time, while Corser took his and BMW's second top three of the year. At a circuit hardly reminiscent of Monza, scene of the S1000RR's first podium visit, this was good news for those involved in the German manufacturer's bid to push to the top.

The only underlying worry for all concerned was the fact that the average rider age on the podium was 38.

Relative youth Haslam recovered from another bout of problems with his clutch and back torque limiting system under braking by swapping bikes to a different spec. He went from eighth to second, so it was a good, if risky tactic.

Michel Fabrizio reasserted himself for a podium place as well, third in race two and now looking more settled. This result, added to his fourth from race one, showed that he still had speed, and could even deliver consistency.

Biaggi had some barbed comments for him in the post-race media conference, however, when Fabrizio said that he was riding a GP bike while everyone else was on a WSB machine. Biaggi reminded the factory Ducati rider in precise terms which factory used to have a clear cc advantage before the handicapping rules, had always built high-price specials to homologate new racing parts, had pushed the tech envelope as far as it could go and had won piles of titles as a result. Ouch.

Haga, on the other official Ducati, was a subdued seventh and ninth, so there was work still to do.

Race one non-scorer Crutchlow was fourth in the second outing, but even though Haslam, Fabrizio and he were locked together, Biaggi was four seconds up on them all, in a race that was only one second faster than race one. He certainly rode with full commitment in race two, on the grass on the entry to the fast back straight as he attempted, successfully, to get out in front and break any final challenge from behind.

Corser's problems in race two were not blamed on tyres this time, but a small change in the front set-up, which caused him to run on at one corner, losing places. He led the first six laps, only to drop down from fifth to tenth on the final tour. But one podium and a maiden Superpole win in the same weekend were welcome new developments for the Bavarian contingent.

For the Yamaha Sterilgarda team, another home race was a case of one up, one down for each rider. Toseland finished race one (albeit tenth), but fell in race two. Crutchlow fell in race one, but posted a new lap record on the fourth lap of race two, riding what was still a difficult bike to control over full race distance.

The Honda riders, the three left in the running after the demise of Vittorio Iannuzzo's SCI team, had bike chatter problems that threatened their dental health, even their mental health. Rea, the same Rea who had been a double winner in Assen, was down in 13th and 12th, with a self-confessed messed-up head due to his bike's schizophrenic nature: great at one track, terrible at another, with chatter so severe that daylight was evident under the tyre, according to some.

Guintoli rallied once more for Suzuki in Misano, fifth and sixth.

# BRNO

## ROUND 9 · CZECH REPUBLIC

*Above:* Pieter Breddels, Ten Kate team co-ordinator.

*Right:* Xaus showed renewed speed on the BMW before falling.

*Above centre right:* Haslam on the grid, ruing the lack of factory support.

*Centre right:* Rea after his resurgent race-one win.

Photos: Gold & Goose

*Far left:* Rea leads Biaggi, Crutchlow and Guintoli.

*Left:* Smrz had a new bike for his home race, but no luck to go with it.

*Below left:* The crocked Vermeulen called a halt to his injury-ridden season.

*Below:* A spectacular practice crash left Troy Corser a spectator on race day.

*Bottom:* Fabrizio always shines at Brno; he took third place in race two.

*Below right:* Biaggi 'only' managed a single win on his favoured circuit.

Photos: Gold & Goose

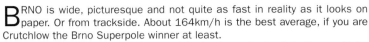

BRNO is wide, picturesque and not quite as fast in reality as it looks on paper. Or from trackside. About 164km/h is the best average, if you are Crutchlow the Brno Superpole winner at least.

Whatever else Brno is, it is certainly the favourite track in the world for Biaggi. He's won on everything here, even taking the nascent Aprilia WSB four to its first win in 2009.

The most remarkable thing about the Brno results in 2010, however, is not that Biaggi won again, but that he didn't win a double, only the second of the two 20-lap races.

Another remarkable thing about Brno was that Rea won that opening race only two weeks after leaving Misano a near broken man, with chatter so extreme it could turn a rider's healthy liver into pâté over a weekend.

The problem had not been solved this time around, but at least tamed, after a test at Assen when most of the rest had been out testing at Imola.

Rea was simply peerless in race one, leading every lap across the line and pulling away in a fabulous display of concentration. He was 2.5 seconds up on Biaggi at the end, with the Yamaha of Crutchlow third, four seconds adrift.

Guintoli continued his steady rise back into contention, fourth and one place ahead of another man who was simply reborn at Brno, Xaus. With the same BMW on which he had injured his thigh at Brno in 2009, his front-running showing in race one was gutsy and assured. After all, the 11-times race winner had to make up for the absence of team-mate Corser.

The Australian had fallen in practice and his bike had hit him hard in the chest. Although he had not suffered any fractures, he was advised not to ride. That was a shame, because Brno was exactly the kind of circuit the adaptable Beemer enjoyed most of all.

The second race podium featured Biaggi on top, Rea second (four seconds and more off) and Fabrizio, another Brnophile, third. Rea had led six laps, Biaggi 14.

Toseland was fourth, Haga fifth and Checa sixth, but for the second time that day the races were relative snooze-fests in terms of entertainment. Unlike most Superbike races, the riders were strung out, with seconds between most of them.

Incidents there were aplenty, however; Xaus fell while fourth, looking good for a podium, then simply pushing too hard when Fabrizio went past. Only 15 riders finished each race.

Toseland was more like himself again, but Crutchlow was a tyre sufferer, setting a new lap record of 1m 59.291s (to go with his new Superpole track best of 1m 58.018s), but only after pulling in to change a rear. The first was so bad that he stopped in the pit lane, punched it, and then his crew changed it for another of the same code, but far superior performance.

The issue of the Pirelli tyres, particularly the newer ones said to be free of the inconsistencies shown by the 625 rears most had been using all year, reached boiling point at Brno.

Haslam felt he had been dealt a bad hand or two with his rubber, having battled to eighth in race one, then tenth in race two. Desperate results for a man chasing a class-leading bike, which clearly was better than his, and a class act like Biaggi, who was not making any mistakes.

Sadly for local hero Smrz, he had little time to try out his newly leased factory Aprilia (late 2009 vintage, it appeared) and he would qualify only 17th. He had fallen shortly before Superpole and then crashed again in each race.

Vermeulen fell in race one, tweaking his never healing knee injury; rider and team called a halt for 2010 to allow for reconstructive surgery.

# SILVERSTONE
## ROUND 10 · GREAT BRITAIN

*Above:* A determined Sykes leads fellow struggler Haga.
*Photo:* Gold & Goose

*Right:* British riders filled the first five places at the end of race two.
*Photo:* Clive Challinor

*Centre right:* Camier laid down a smokescreen only after the race-two battle was over.
*Photo:* Gold & Goose

*Left:* Race two starts under leaden Silverstone skies.

Photo: Clive Challinor

*Below:* BSB wild-card Kiyonari made little impact.

*Below centre:* Haslam leads Toseland, Biaggi, Guintoli and Byrne.

*Bottom:* Rea, Crutchlow and Haslam on the race-one podium.

*Below right:* British young gun Bridewell, beating Kiyo in race one.

Photos: Gold & Goose

ALL-BRITISH podiums in WSB racing are nothing new, and in a class where there are seven British riders on some of the top bikes, we had already seen not one, but two races, each at Assen, where Union flags were omnipresent in 2010.

This time around, the top three in race one, and the top five in race two were all UK riders, a result that the owners of the new-look Silverstone could only have dreamed of when they agreed to add WSB to the F1 and MotoGP races the track had gone after originally.

The fans were pretty happy, although what felt like a good and noisy crowd was simply lost in the expanse of the vast Silverstone complex. As was much of the close-quarter fighting we had hoped for.

Rea had Superpole winner Crutchlow to compete with for the 11 laps he led in race one, but in the end Crutchlow just eased way, slowing up to win by 1.6 seconds. Haslam, having to cool his pace in the final laps, was third and eight seconds from Rea. Fabrizio was fourth, and four seconds from Haslam in his turn.

Biaggi was a whopping 17 seconds from Crutchlow, Camier a whisper behind the Italian on the Italian bike. But the only thing that mattered to the embattled Haslam was that Biaggi was only two places behind him.

It was the same in race two, even though Biaggi was sixth and Haslam fourth this time. A full 60 points adrift going into the long summer break, Haslam had a lot to think about.

Crutchlow had a lot to smile about, the local lad from Coventry finally nailing a set-up that allowed his Yamaha to be fast and his tyres to last. Maybe it was overcast skies and cool track temperatures that helped him most of all. He had said that he did not fancy his chances in the races, simply because his bike used tyres more rapidly than most others. Nobody thought he was sandbagging, as it had been happening more or less all year.

Crutchlow waited until three laps from the end to really pounce on Rea in race two, winning by two seconds this time.

Unleashed from his obvious team orders not to beat Biaggi in race one, Camier was a joyful third, the reigning BSB champion riding at a Silverstone he only partially knew from previous experience. Haslam in fourth and Toseland in fifth completed a perfect UK poker hand.

The lack of action up front was in contrast to the scrap for fourth in race two, as Toseland went wide to avoid a determined Haslam, running over the self-same grass on the outside of the final corner that had delayed proceedings on day one. It had been deemed too soft should a rider have to use it as extra-run-off, so it was repaired.

Biaggi and Guintoli were right in the drafts of the final two top-five Brits, only 0.7 second covering all four of them.

With the big-five Brits up front, privateer Shane Byrne and works KRT rider Tom Sykes toiled for results, but maybe not as much as the fancied wild-cards from the BSB class leading HM Plant Honda team. Ryuichi Kiyonari and Josh Brookes were the highest-class wild-cards imaginable, but 16th and 12th for Brookes, plus 21st (and last), then 16th in race two for Kiyonari were unexpectedly poor showings.

Money and effort from Aprilia and BMW really had moved WSB on in 2010, and now we had a relative measure of just how much, from outside the paddock itself.

And what about rising force BMW in England? Corser was tenth in race one, fuming about his rear tyre, Xaus 17th. Corser crashed on lap two of race two, having just overtaken Biaggi. Xaus took 11th, a day to put behind him also.

*Above, from left:* Althea boss Genesio Bevilacqua; home disappointment for one-point Neukirchner; Corser's day was spoiled by injury; Crutchlow beat Biaggi both times.

*Right:* Leon Haslam grimaces in pain as he holds an ice pack over his dislocated thumb.

*Centre right:* Haslam is down, Toseland (52) and Corser (11) soon to follow; Crutchlow (35) got through.

*Far right:* Camier broke his wrist in practice, ending his season.

*Furthest right:* BMW's top home scorer Xaus heads Shane Byrne.

Photos: Gold & Goose

*Left:* Haga wins race two – only his second victory of the season.

*Far left:* Rea is the spectre, Checa his pursuer, in race one.

*Below left:* BSB's Ian Lowry took Vermeulen's Kawasaki seat.

Photos: Gold & Goose

HAVING spent the previous round chasing a Crutchlow-shaped phantom in the final few laps of each race, Rea made himself the spectre none could catch one weekend later in Germany. He led across the line for all 20 laps of race one, from fourth on the grid. He also set a new lap record, on lap five, of 1m 55.392s.

The first race was restarted, over the full scheduled distance. Two connected falls on the first lap of the first running saw Haslam high-side off, then Corser and Toseland get tangled as they tried to avoid Haslam. They finally hit the deck themselves, Corser hurting his throttle elbow. Haslam was down, in pain, and the red flag was thrown. He got up and was allowed to restart, continuing the battle to keep Biaggi somewhere near him with the rounds counting down just too quickly.

Checa chased Rea to within 1.126 seconds at the end; he never quite gave up hope of finishing third in the championship, ahead of the Ulsterman. Third was Crutchlow, winning a personal battle with Biaggi for the podium place.

Behind, a remarkable result of fifth for Sykes was no flash in the pan, as he had been seventh in qualifying on the big Kawasaki. A race at Brands Hatch in the BSB series had delivered two race wins and some new chassis settings that at least had dipped the bike's Achilles' heel in a balm potent enough for it to reach the top five again. And this time at a circuit where more than straight-line speed is the prerequisite.

Haslam was sixth after his big fall, hurting, but fighting against his injured thumb and left knee ligament. More ground lost to Biaggi, but more evidence of guts and fight, on a bike that now was slightly outmatched, even by the old-school Kawasaki in race one.

Panned as too sterile and modern when it replaced the old Nordschleife in the 1980s, now the 'new' Nürburgring circuit is something of a challenge compared to some newer tracks. One that Haga plainly also rose to, as he had won races there three times in the previous three WSB visits. He took race two, by a clear margin of three seconds from Rea, having overhauled early leader and eventual crasher Checa.

Haslam was a semi-miraculous third, beating Crutchlow across the line, not to mention Biaggi and the reborn Guintoli. Biaggi had been on pole, for only the second time in his entire WSB career, but Guintoli had started from third.

On home tarmac, much was expected from the BMW team, but at the start of a late-season slide, Corser was first on the gravel and then in the pits to retire in the 'real' race one, his sore elbow and fingers preventing him from feeling how hard he was braking. He was only 12th in race two. Corser had pushed Guintoli to the back in his injury induced off-track escapade, and the Frenchman had done well to rally to eighth.

Xaus, a rider who was usually either lukewarm or too hot, scored the best points for BMW. On Haslam's tail in the opener, seventh, he was ninth in race two.

Kawasaki had another new face to replace Vermeulen, a certain BSB rider, Lowry, and he delivered a strong 12th in race one, but fell in race two. In any event, he gained the gig for the rest of the year.

Home ground was a battleground for Neukirchner. He crashed and rejoined in race one, only to retire; in race two, he took away a single point for 15th. It was almost as hideous a day for Toseland, who fell in race one and scrambled to eighth in race two.

Ninth and tenth for Byrne were good results in the end, but for one British rider Germany was a costly campaign. Camier fell in the first qualifying session in Friday and broke his right scaphoid. He missed the German races and the rest of the season.

*Above:* Checa's satellite Ducati notched a double win, beating the works team again.

*Left:* Haga salvaged some pride by taking a double podium for the factory Ducati.

*Far left:* Kawasaki's late revival: Superpole winner Sykes leads away in race one.

*Below far left:* New champion Max Biaggi celebrates with the Aprilia team; technical chief Luigi Dall'Igna is on the right.

*Below:* Haslam's title hopes blew up, along with his Suzuki's engine.

*Bottom:* Lanzi was a surprise second in race one.

Photos: Gold & Goose

FRIGHTENING and compelling, Imola is a race venue of stark contrasts, from the new pits and paddock complex to the ancient track surface and the unique topography.

But it is as unmistakeably Italian as Biaggi and Aprilia Racing and Alitalia, so there was no better place to win the championship, for maximum personal and PR reasons.

Biaggi was clearly nervous, partly because he knew podiums, far less wins, would be very difficult here. The Aprilia is an astounding machine in many regards, but the very characteristics that make it so raceworthy are the same ones that hold it back at places like Imola and Kyalami. It does not like bumps and it prefers a set series of tasks towards which all its various adjustments can be moved. At Imola, there is an infinite variety of bumps and track surfaces, and no two corners that are quite the same in curvature, camber or elevation change.

Biaggi toiled in damp and changeable practice conditions, but turned it around enough to go seventh in qualifying, while chaser Haslam was on the front row, in third, and set to make a bar-room fight of it.

In fact, until Haslam made a brave, but ultimately ill-judged lunge into the braking zone of the first Rivazza corner, on the very last lap of race one, it looked like we would have to go to France to finish it off after all.

But in attempting to pass impressive eventual winner Checa around the outside, Haslam ran off circuit, re-joined, finished fifth and lost a bucket of points. Biaggi was only 11th, so it was a double-dip depression. The third dip, the final chasm, would come in race two.

Elsewhere, the Imola race weekend had been something of a resurrection special, with riders as diverse as former race winner Lanzi (DFX Corse Ducati) finishing only a second away from another win, Haga posting third in a late-season flurry of competitiveness, and Smrz taking his rented Aprilia to a worthy top four.

With his relatively new and extremely effective base settings still on his Kawasaki, Sykes led for eight laps and finished sixth. His cause was helped because he had taken his first Superpole win on Saturday – finally a class leading success for rider and machine. He would go out and finish fourth in race two, a season best, and he would lead yet again. This time, however, Checa was more in control for longer, leading 17 of the 21 laps and taking his first double for Ducati Althea.

Haga was second, Crutchlow an effusive third, but after Haslam's bike suffered a blow-up at half race distance, the usual top story of the race was relegated to sub-plot by the fact that Biaggi did not even have to finish to be awarded the championship. He had been more effective in race two in any case, and would finish fifth after some offset modifications were made to his bike's geometry.

Ducati had an outstanding day in the park, but love was hard to find at the circuit closest to its Borgo Panigale headquarters. Multiple banners criticised Ducati's decision to leave WSB in an official capacity in 2011. Some were vitriolic, some outright abusive, but most of all, they were surprisingly prevalent. On track, a Ducati privateer won both races, and five of the top places were taken by 1198s. But overall, the barrier between the Aprilia and Ducati home camps was clearly defined, on a day when the Ducatis had clearly won the battles, but an Aprilia rider had won the war.

Byrne enjoyed a resurgent weekend, posting an eighth and a sixth, but another British rider was out altogether. Rea, like many others, had fallen in a wet Superpole, but unlike them he had cracked his scaphoid, and snapped a wrist ligament and collarbone (all left); after another big morning warm-up fall, he pulled out of the event. Checa, 50 points closer to him in third, was looking forward to France.

# MAGNY-COURS
## ROUND 13 · FRANCE

*Above:* Rostrum spat after Crutchlow sprayed bubbly into race-two winner Biaggi's face.

*Top:* Smrz heads Toseland (52), Haslam (91), Byrne (67), Checa (7) and the rest in race one.

*Right:* Biaggi and Crutchlow battle for the lead in race two.

Photos: Gold & Goose

E VEN if the all-important riders' championship had been decided the week-end before, Magny-Cours was the kind of end-of-season event that still had a lot to compel the attention.

In fact, everybody either had a target to attack or a position to defend, and for many of the riders, a contract to chase.

This was the race in which Crutchlow would score his sixth pole of 2010, and in race one he would take his WSB win tally to three.

It was also the weekend when Biaggi would raise his win total to ten; a feat he had said was unimportant. Sure.

Crutchlow won the first race by 3.7 seconds. Haslam, pugilistic as ever, provided a last-lap Biaggi smash at the chicane; Checa grabbed his chance, and Max was left off podium by a tenth or two. He had led seven laps, so was less than satisfied. Aprilia staff were quite happy, however, as this finish absolutely guaranteed the manufacturers' championship.

Biaggi made up for race one's disappointment in race two, and no matter what Crutchlow tried, he could not pass Biaggi, losing by only 0.087 second.

Race two also saw a bit of last-chicane mugging, as Guintoli, finishing the season as strongly as he had started it, looked set for a podium at last, only for Fabrizio to be more forceful and take third. Guintoli had led for eight laps. He had also been disqualified from race one, having been penalised when he ran off track and returned in a place deemed inappropriate by race control. He was well in the podium mix, but missed his five chances to take his ride-through penalty and was black-flagged. Even at the end, he was mystified that the spot he had chosen to re-enter the track had been deemed inappropriate.

Now up to speed on his private works Aprilia, Smrz was 'Mr Effective': fifth in race one, sixth in race two.

Rea, who had fallen again pre-race at Magny-Cours, had only been passed fit to ride on Friday morning. His gritted teeth finally parted enough for him to bow to the inevitable after he had ridden to a brave 12th in race one, still beating his out-of-sorts team-mate Neukirchner. Out of action after race one, and with Checa on the first podium, he would lose overall third when Carlos finished ninth in race two.

Crutchlow, first then second, played himself into fifth overall, only eight points behind the gutsy Rea, who had done enough in race one keep the Yamaha rider behind him before he headed off to MotoGP.

Haga was sixth in the table, Guintoli a consistent seventh overall, Fabrizio an inconsistent eighth. Down and out near Paris and Sheffield was James Toseland, ninth overall being the stuff of nightmares for a double champion. An eighth at the Nürburgring was his only score in the previous six races.

Byrne's late-season flourish made him a top-ten man overall, ninth and eighth enough to push one-time podium man Corser to 11th. Corser rivalled Toseland for a poor season finish, and in France he took away no points at all, following two technical retirements.

Sykes and Kawasaki were not quite up to their Nürburgring and Imola standards in France, but eighth and 11th were once dream results in a field of 14 factory bikes, and Kawasaki ended the reign of the old Ninja on a generally positive note.

Camier did not get back to full fitness after his scaphoid op in time to defend his top-ten place in the final stats, and eventually he was 12th.

A season full of incident ended up with some unpleasantness on the podium. Crutchlow sprayed champagne into Biaggi's face, the Italian took exception, and there was some wrestling and invective before calm returned and the final points were allocated. After analysis, consistency as much as ten wins gave Biaggi his 75-point final advantage over Haslam.

Compiled by PETER McLAREN

**Round 1** **PHILLIP ISLAND, Australia** · 28 February 2010 · 2.762mile/4.445km circuit · WEATHER: Race 1 · Dry · Track 25°C · Air 18°C; Race 2 · Dry · Track 31°C · Air 20°C

**Race 1:** 22 laps, 60.764m/97.790km

Time of race: 34m 13.435s · Average speed: 106.529mph/171.442km/h

| Pos. | Rider | Nat. | No. | Entrant | Machine | Tyres | Time & Gap | Laps |
|------|-------|------|-----|---------|---------|-------|-----------|------|
| 1 | **Leon Haslam** | GBR | 91 | Team Suzuki Alstare | Suzuki GSX-R1000 | P | | 22 |
| 2 | **Michel Fabrizio** | ITA | 84 | Ducati Xerox Team | Ducati 1198 | P | 0.004s | 22 |
| 3 | **Noriyuki Haga** | JPN | 41 | Ducati Xerox Team | Ducati 1198 | P | 0.769s | 22 |
| 4 | **Jonathan Rea** | GBR | 65 | HANNspree Ten Kate Honda | Honda CBR1000RR | P | 10.201s | 22 |
| 5 | **Max Biaggi** | ITA | 3 | Aprilia Alitalia Racing | Aprilia RSV4 1000 F | P | 10.782s | 22 |
| 6 | **Sylvain Guintoli** | FRA | 50 | Team Suzuki Alstare | Suzuki GSX-R1000 | P | 11.079s | 22 |
| 7 | **Carlos Checa** | SPA | 7 | Althea Racing | Ducati 1198 | P | 11.208s | 22 |
| 8 | **Jakub Smrz** | CZE | 96 | Team PATA B&G Racing | Ducati 1198 | P | 16.522s | 22 |
| 9 | **Troy Corser** | AUS | 11 | BMW Motorrad Motorsport | BMW S1000RR | P | 20.291s | 22 |
| 10 | **Lorenzo Lanzi** | ITA | 57 | DFX Corse | Ducati 1198 | P | 26.352s | 22 |
| 11 | **Leon Camier** | GBR | 2 | Aprilia Alitalia Racing | Aprilia RSV4 1000 F | P | 29.775s | 22 |
| 12 | **Max Neukirchner** | GER | 76 | HANNspree Ten Kate Honda | Honda CBR1000RR | P | 30.155s | 22 |
| 13 | **Tom Sykes** | GBR | 66 | Kawasaki Racing Team | Kawasaki ZX-10R | P | 31.951s | 22 |
| 14 | **Shane Byrne** | GBR | 67 | Althea Racing | Ducati 1198 | P | 31.957s | 22 |
| 15 | **Andrew Pitt** | AUS | 88 | Team Reitwagen BMW | BMW S1000RR | P | 55.082s | 22 |
| 16 | Vittorio Iannuzzo | ITA | 31 | S.C.I. Honda Garvie Image | Honda CBR1000RR | P | 70.932s | 22 |
| 17 | Matteo Baiocco | ITA | 15 | Team Pedercini | Kawasaki ZX-10R | P | 71.237s | 22 |
| 18 | Roger Lee Hayden | USA | 95 | Team Pedercini | Kawasaki ZX-10R | P | 77.357s | 22 |
| 19 | Joshua Brookes | AUS | 25 | ECHO CRS Honda | Honda CBR1000RR | P | 6 laps | 16 |
| | Cal Crutchlow | GBR | 35 | Yamaha Sterilgarda Team | Yamaha YZF-R1 | P | DNF | 5 |
| | Chris Vermeulen | AUS | 77 | Kawasaki Racing Team | Kawasaki ZX-10R | P | DNF | 3 |
| | James Toseland | GBR | 52 | Yamaha Sterilgarda Team | Yamaha YZF-R1 | P | DNF | 2 |

Fastest race lap: Leon Haslam on lap 2, 1m 32.193s, 107.852mph/173.571km/h.

**Race 2:** 22 laps, 60.763m/97.790km

Time of race: 34m 16.428s · Average speed: 106.374mph/171.192km/h

| Pos. | Rider | Time & Gap | Laps |
|------|-------|-----------|------|
| 1 | **Carlos Checa** | | 22 |
| 2 | **Leon Haslam** | 0.307s | 22 |
| 3 | **Michel Fabrizio** | 0.434s | 22 |
| 4 | **Sylvain Guintoli** | 0.837s | 22 |
| 5 | **Noriyuki Haga** | 3.453s | 22 |
| 6 | **Jonathan Rea** | 11.530s | 22 |
| 7 | **Troy Corser** | 12.026s | 22 |
| 8 | **Max Biaggi** | 13.068s | 22 |
| 9 | **Cal Crutchlow** | 14.401s | 22 |
| 10 | **James Toseland** | 14.707s | 22 |
| 11 | **Leon Camier** | 14.743s | 22 |
| 12 | **Shane Byrne** | 14.851s | 22 |
| 13 | **Lorenzo Lanzi** | 15.143s | 22 |
| 14 | **Joshua Brookes** | 30.947s | 22 |
| 15 | **Andrew Pitt** | 41.855s | 22 |
| 16 | Max Neukirchner | 48.844s | 22 |
| 17 | Vittorio Iannuzzo | 66.866s | 22 |
| 18 | Roger Lee Hayden | 67.751s | 22 |
| | Matteo Baiocco | DNF | 17 |
| | Tom Sykes | DNF | 13 |
| | Chris Vermeulen | DNF | 7 |
| | Jakub Smrz | DNF | 6 |

| Superpole | | |
|-----------|--|--|
| 1 | Haslam | 1m 31.229s |
| 2 | Fabrizio | 1m 31.245s |
| 3 | Crutchlow | 1m 31.642s |
| 4 | Checa | 1m 31.671s |
| 5 | Guintoli | 1m 31.696s |
| 6 | Smrz | 1m 31.757s |
| 7 | Rea | 1m 31.912s |
| 8 | Toseland | 1m 32.019s |
| 9 | Lanzi | 1m 32.205s |
| 10 | Haga | 1m 32.229s |
| 11 | Biaggi | 1m 32.293s |
| 12 | Sykes | 1m 32.398s |
| 13 | Corser | 1m 32.430s |
| 14 | Vermeulen | 1m 32.561s |
| 15 | Xaus | 1m 32.842s |
| 16 | Camier | 1m 32.895s |
| 17 | Neukirchner | 1m 32.782s |
| 18 | Byrne | 1m 32.823s |
| 19 | Pitt | 1m 33.207s |
| 20 | Resch | |

| Points | | |
|--------|--|--|
| 1 | Haslam | 45 |
| 2 | Fabrizio | 36 |
| 3 | Checa | 34 |
| 4 | Haga | 27 |
| 5 | Guintoli | 23 |
| 6 | Rea | 23 |
| 7 | Biaggi | 19 |
| 8 | Corser | 16 |
| 9 | Camier | 10 |
| 10 | Lanzi | 9 |
| 11 | Smrz | 8 |
| 12 | Crutchlow | 7 |
| 13 | Toseland | 6 |
| 14 | Byrne | 6 |
| 15 | Neukirchner | 4 |
| 16 | Sykes | 3 |
| 17 | Brookes | 2 |
| 18 | Pitt | 2 |

Fastest race lap: Sylvain Guintoli on lap 3, 1m 32.236s, 107.802mph/173.490km/h.

Lap record: Troy Corser, AUS (Yamaha), 1m 31.826s, 108.823mph/174.260km/h (2007).

## Round 2 · PORTIMAO, Portugal · 28 March 2010 · 2.853mile/4.592km circuit · WEATHER: Race 1 · Dry · Track 29°C · Air 20°C; Race 2 · Dry · Track 33°C · Air 20°C

**Race 1:** 22 laps, 62.773m/101.024km
**Time of race:** 37m 59.283s · **Average speed:** 99.147mph/159.562km/h

| Pos. | Rider | Nat. | No. | Entrant | Machine | Tyres | Time & Gap | Laps |
|---|---|---|---|---|---|---|---|---|
| 1 | Max Biaggi | ITA | 3 | Aprilia Alitalia Racing | Aprilia RSV4 1000 F | P | | 22 |
| 2 | Leon Haslam | GBR | 91 | Team Suzuki Alstare | Suzuki GSX-R1000 | P | 0.200s | 22 |
| 3 | Jonathan Rea | GBR | 65 | HANNspree Ten Kate Honda | Honda CBR1000RR | P | 6.901s | 22 |
| 4 | Carlos Checa | SPA | 7 | Althea Racing | Ducati 1198 | P | 7.457s | 22 |
| 5 | Leon Camier | GBR | 2 | Aprilia Alitalia Racing | Aprilia RSV4 1000 F | P | 7.564s | 22 |
| 6 | Shane Byrne | GBR | 67 | Althea Racing | Ducati 1198 | P | 11.420s | 22 |
| 7 | James Toseland | GBR | 52 | Yamaha Sterilgarda Team | Yamaha YZF-R1 | P | 18.391s | 22 |
| 8 | Noriyuki Haga | JPN | 41 | Ducati Xerox Team | Ducati 1198 | P | 18.536s | 22 |
| 9 | Troy Corser | AUS | 11 | BMW Motorrad Motorsport | BMW S1000RR | P | 24.514s | 22 |
| 10 | Ruben Xaus | SPA | 111 | BMW Motorrad Motorsport | BMW S1000RR | P | 32.427s | 22 |
| 11 | Michel Fabrizio | ITA | 84 | Ducati Xerox Team | Ducati 1198 | P | 35.045s | 22 |
| 12 | Lorenzo Lanzi | ITA | 57 | DFX Corse | Ducati 1198 | P | 36.816s | 22 |
| 13 | Sylvain Guintoli | FRA | 50 | Team Suzuki Alstare | Suzuki GSX-R1000 | P | 36.841s | 22 |
| 14 | Cal Crutchlow | GBR | 35 | Yamaha Sterilgarda Team | Yamaha YZF-R1 | P | 44.678s | 22 |
| 15 | Tom Sykes | GBR | 66 | Kawasaki Racing Team | Kawasaki ZX-10R | P | 44.942s | 22 |
| 16 | Vittorio Iannuzzo | ITA | 31 | S.C.I. Honda Garvie Image | Honda CBR1000RR | P | 59.135s | 22 |
| 17 | Sheridan Morais | RSA | 32 | ECHO CRS Honda | Honda CBR1000RR | P | 59.852s | 22 |
| 18 | Roger Lee Hayden | USA | 95 | Team Pedercini | Kawasaki ZX-10R | P | 60.097s | 22 |
| 19 | Matteo Baiocco | ITA | 15 | Team Pedercini | Kawasaki ZX-10R | P | 70.151s | 22 |
| 20 | Luca Scassa | ITA | 99 | Supersonic Racing Team | Ducati 1198 | P | 6 laps | 16 |
| | Andrew Pitt | AUS | 88 | Team Reitwagen BMW | BMW S1000RR | P | DNF | 18 |
| | Jakub Smrz | CZE | 96 | Team PATA B&G Racing | Ducati 1198 | P | DNF | 16 |
| | Makoto Tamada | JPN | 49 | Team Reitwagen BMW | BMW S1000RR | P | DNF | 4 |
| | Max Neukirchner | GER | 76 | HANNspree Ten Kate Honda | Honda CBR1000RR | P | DNF | 3 |

**Fastest race lap:** Max Biaggi on lap 4, 1m 42.774s, 99.948mph/160.850km/h (record).

**Race 2:** 22 laps, 62.773m/101.024km
**Time of race:** 38m 06.128s · **Average speed:** 98.850mph/159.084km/h

| Pos. | Rider | Time & Gap | Laps |
|---|---|---|---|
| 1 | Max Biaggi | | 22 |
| 2 | Leon Haslam | 0.191s | 22 |
| 3 | Cal Crutchlow | 0.658s | 22 |
| 4 | Carlos Checa | 1.015s | 22 |
| 5 | Leon Camier | 3.123s | 22 |
| 6 | James Toseland | 9.131s | 22 |
| 7 | Shane Byrne | 11.033s | 22 |
| 8 | Noriyuki Haga | 13.452s | 22 |
| 9 | Sylvain Guintoli | 13.964s | 22 |
| 10 | Troy Corser | 16.377s | 22 |
| 11 | Michel Fabrizio | 26.351s | 22 |
| 12 | Ruben Xaus | 27.964s | 22 |
| 13 | Tom Sykes | 33.566s | 22 |
| 14 | Lorenzo Lanzi | 33.823s | 22 |
| 15 | Max Neukirchner | 37.372s | 22 |
| 16 | Luca Scassa | 45.611s | 22 |
| 17 | Roger Lee Hayden | 56.512s | 22 |
| 18 | Matteo Baiocco | 58.980s | 22 |
| 19 | Makoto Tamada | 75.819s | 22 |
| 20 | Andrew Pitt | 101.672s | 22 |
| | Sheridan Morais | DNF | 12 |
| | Jakub Smrz | DNF | 10 |
| | Jonathan Rea | DNF | 7 |
| | Vittorio Iannuzzo | DNF | 7 |

**Superpole**

| | | |
|---|---|---|
| 1 | Crutchlow | 1m 42.092s |
| 2 | Biaggi | 1m 42.513s |
| 3 | Checa | 1m 42.586s |
| 4 | Haslam | 1m 42.596s |
| 5 | Rea | 1m 42.807s |
| 6 | Smrz | 1m 42.889s |
| 7 | Byrne | 1m 42.960s |
| 8 | Corser | 1m 43.152s |
| 9 | Guintoli | 1m 42.984s |
| 10 | Xaus | 1m 42.999s |
| 11 | Camier | 1m 43.039s |
| 12 | Sykes | 1m 43.199s |
| 13 | Neukirchner | 1m 43.380s |
| 14 | Lanzi | 1m 43.568s |
| 15 | Toseland | 1m 49.401s |
| 16 | Scassa | |
| 17 | Fabrizio | 1m 43.564s |
| 18 | Haga | 1m 43.686s |
| 19 | Pitt | 1m 43.781s |
| 20 | Tamada | 1m 45.142s |

**Points**

| | | |
|---|---|---|
| 1 | Haslam | 85 |
| 2 | Biaggi | 69 |
| 3 | Checa | 60 |
| 4 | Fabrizio | 46 |
| 5 | Haga | 43 |
| 6 | Rea | 39 |
| 7 | Guintoli | 33 |
| 8 | Camier | 32 |
| 9 | Corser | 29 |
| 10 | Crutchlow | 25 |
| 11 | Toseland | 25 |
| 12 | Byrne | 25 |
| 13 | Lanzi | 15 |
| 14 | Xaus | 10 |
| 15 | Smrz | 8 |
| 16 | Sykes | 7 |
| 17 | Neukirchner | 5 |
| 18 | Brookes | 2 |
| 19 | Pitt | 2 |

**Fastest race lap:** Carlo Checa on lap 2, 1m 43.285s, 99.453mph/160.054km/h.
**Lap record:** Michel Fabrizio, ITA (Ducati), 1m 43.529s, 99.221mph/159.680km/h (2009).

## Round 3 · VALENCIA, Spain · 11 April 2010 · 2.489mile/4.005km circuit · WEATHER: Race 1 · Dry · Track 29°C · Air 20°C; Race 2 · Dry · Track 46°C · Air 25°C

**Race 1:** 23 laps, 57.238m/92.115km
**Time of race:** 36m 47.723s · **Average speed:** 93.334mph/150.206km/h

| Pos. | Rider | Nat. | No. | Entrant | Machine | Tyres | Time & Gap | Laps |
|---|---|---|---|---|---|---|---|---|
| 1 | Leon Haslam | GBR | 91 | Team Suzuki Alstare | Suzuki GSX-R1000 | P | | 23 |
| 2 | Max Biaggi | ITA | 3 | Aprilia Alitalia Racing | Aprilia RSV4 1000 F | P | 1.757s | 23 |
| 3 | James Toseland | GBR | 52 | Yamaha Sterilgarda Team | Yamaha YZF-R1 | P | 3.621s | 23 |
| 4 | Troy Corser | AUS | 11 | BMW Motorrad Motorsport | BMW S1000RR | P | 4.209s | 23 |
| 5 | Noriyuki Haga | JPN | 41 | Ducati Xerox Team | Ducati 1198 | P | 4.378s | 23 |
| 6 | Jonathan Rea | GBR | 65 | HANNspree Ten Kate Honda | Honda CBR1000RR | P | 9.834s | 23 |
| 7 | Cal Crutchlow | GBR | 35 | Yamaha Sterilgarda Team | Yamaha YZF-R1 | P | 10.466s | 23 |
| 8 | Lorenzo Lanzi | ITA | 57 | DFX Corse | Ducati 1198 | P | 16.080s | 23 |
| 9 | Sylvain Guintoli | FRA | 50 | Team Suzuki Alstare | Suzuki GSX-R1000 | P | 18.382s | 23 |
| 10 | Jakub Smrz | CZE | 96 | Team PATA B&G Racing | Ducati 1198 | P | 18.589s | 23 |
| 11 | Tom Sykes | GBR | 66 | Kawasaki Racing Team | Kawasaki ZX-10R | P | 22.903s | 23 |
| 12 | Ruben Xaus | SPA | 111 | BMW Motorrad Motorsport | BMW S1000RR | P | 25.203s | 23 |
| 13 | Max Neukirchner | GER | 76 | HANNspree Ten Kate Honda | Honda CBR1000RR | P | 25.676s | 23 |
| 14 | Luca Scassa | ITA | 99 | Supersonic Racing Team | Ducati 1198 | P | 26.606s | 23 |
| 15 | Andrew Pitt | AUS | 88 | Team Reitwagen BMW | BMW S1000RR | P | 43.797s | 23 |
| 16 | Roger Lee Hayden | USA | 95 | Team Pedercini | Kawasaki ZX-10R | P | 48.094s | 23 |
| 17 | Matteo Baiocco | ITA | 15 | Team Pedercini | Kawasaki ZX-10R | P | 48.190s | 23 |
| 18 | Simon Andrews | GBR | 17 | Kawasaki Racing Team | Kawasaki ZX-10R | P | 52.863s | 23 |
| | Vittorio Iannuzzo | ITA | 31 | S.C.I. Honda Garvie Image | Honda CBR1000RR | P | DNF | 12 |
| | Leon Camier | GBR | 2 | Aprilia Alitalia Racing | Aprilia RSV4 1000 F | P | DNF | 7 |
| | Michel Fabrizio | ITA | 84 | Ducati Xerox Team | Ducati 1198 | P | DNF | 5 |
| | Shane Byrne | GBR | 67 | Althea Racing | Ducati 1198 | P | DNF | 5 |
| | Carlos Checa | SPA | 7 | Althea Racing | Ducati 1198 | P | DNF | 2 |
| | Roland Resch | AUT | 123 | Team Reitwagen BMW | BMW S1000RR | P | DNF | 2 |

**Fastest race lap:** Carlos Checa on lap 2, 1m 34.750s, 94.553mph/152.169km/h.

**Race 2 (aggregate):** 3+20 laps, 57.238m/92.115km
**Time of race:** 36m 51.500s · **Average speed:** 92.951mph/149.590km/h

| Pos. | Rider | Time & Gap | Laps |
|---|---|---|---|
| 1 | Noriyuki Haga | | 23 |
| 2 | Carlos Checa | 0.025s | 23 |
| 3 | Max Biaggi | 0.299s | 23 |
| 4 | Leon Haslam | 10.100s | 23 |
| 5 | Jonathan Rea | 12.811s | 23 |
| 6 | Sylvain Guintoli | 13.459s | 23 |
| 7 | James Toseland | 14.845s | 23 |
| 8 | Shane Byrne | 14.861s | 23 |
| 9 | Cal Crutchlow | 15.202s | 23 |
| 10 | Jakub Smrz | 18.071s | 23 |
| 11 | Ruben Xaus | 25.179s | 23 |
| 12 | Troy Corser | 26.116s | 23 |
| 13 | Lorenzo Lanzi | 30.189s | 23 |
| 14 | Luca Scassa | 30.387s | 23 |
| 15 | Tom Sykes | 35.741s | 23 |
| 16 | Andrew Pitt | 43.244s | 23 |
| 17 | Max Neukirchner | 43.540s | 23 |
| 18 | Roland Resch | 47.145s | 23 |
| 19 | Roger Lee Hayden | 48.502s | 23 |
| 20 | Matteo Baiocco | 57.838s | 23 |
| | Michel Fabrizio | DNF | 15 |
| | Leon Camier | DNF | 12 |
| | Simon Andrews | DNF | 3 |
| | Vittorio Iannuzzo | DNF | 3 |

**Superpole**

| | | |
|---|---|---|
| 1 | Crutchlow | 1m 33.615s |
| 2 | Checa | 1m 33.840s |
| 3 | Biaggi | 1m 33.860s |
| 4 | Haslam | 1m 33.961s |
| 5 | Corser | 1m 34.059s |
| 6 | Guintoli | 1m 34.073s |
| 7 | Rea | 1m 34.235s |
| 8 | Lanzi | 1m 34.261s |
| 9 | Toseland | 1m 33.988s |
| 10 | Fabrizio | 1m 34.021s |
| 11 | Haga | 1m 34.100s |
| 12 | Byrne | 1m 34.246s |
| 13 | Camier | 1m 34.273s |
| 14 | Smrz | 1m 34.280s |
| 15 | Scassa | 1m 34.730s |
| 16 | Neukirchner | 1m 34.934s |
| 17 | Xaus | 1m 34.756s |
| 18 | Sykes | 1m 34.894s |
| 19 | Pitt | 1m 36.088s |
| 20 | Morais | |

**Points**

| | | |
|---|---|---|
| 1 | Haslam | 123 |
| 2 | Biaggi | 105 |
| 3 | Checa | 80 |
| 4 | Haga | 79 |
| 5 | Rea | 60 |
| 6 | Toseland | 50 |
| 7 | Guintoli | 50 |
| 8 | Fabrizio | 46 |
| 9 | Corser | 46 |
| 10 | Crutchlow | 41 |
| 11 | Byrne | 33 |
| 12 | Camier | 32 |
| 13 | Lanzi | 26 |
| 14 | Smrz | 20 |
| 15 | Xaus | 19 |
| 16 | Sykes | 13 |
| 17 | Neukirchner | 8 |
| 18 | Scassa | 4 |
| 19 | Pitt | 3 |
| 20 | Brookes | 2 |

**Fastest race lap:** Max Biaggi on lap 8, 1m 34.632s, 94.671mph/152.359km/h.
**Lap record:** Noriyuki Haga, JPN (Ducati), 1m 34.618s, 94.685mph/152.380km/h (2009).

## Round 4 · ASSEN, Holland · 25 April 2010 · 2.822mile/4.542km circuit · WEATHER: Race 1 · Dry · Track 23°C · Air 21°C; Race 2 · Dry · Track 31°C · Air 26°C

**Race 1:** 22 laps, 62.090m/99.924km
Time of race: 35m 38.483s · Average speed: 104.525mph/168.216km/h

| Pos. | Rider | Nat. | No. | Entrant | Machine | Tyres | Time & Gap | Laps |
|---|---|---|---|---|---|---|---|---|
| 1 | **Jonathan Rea** | GBR | 65 | HANNspree Ten Kate Honda | Honda CBR1000RR | P | | 22 |
| 2 | **James Toseland** | GBR | 52 | Yamaha Sterilgarda Team | Yamaha YZF-R1 | P | 1.106s | 22 |
| 3 | **Leon Camier** | GBR | 2 | Aprilia Alitalia Racing | Aprilia RSV4 1000 F | P | 1.249s | 22 |
| 4 | **Carlos Checa** | SPA | 7 | Althea Racing | Ducati 1198 | P | 1.548s | 22 |
| 5 | **Troy Corser** | AUS | 11 | BMW Motorrad Motorsport | BMW S1000RR | P | 2.738s | 22 |
| 6 | **Max Biaggi** | ITA | 3 | Aprilia Alitalia Racing | Aprilia RSV4 1000 F | P | 2.813s | 22 |
| 7 | **Jakub Smrz** | CZE | 96 | Team PATA B&G Racing | Ducati 1198 | P | 6.296s | 22 |
| 8 | **Cal Crutchlow** | GBR | 35 | Yamaha Sterilgarda Team | Yamaha YZF-R1 | P | 12.022s | 22 |
| 9 | **Shane Byrne** | GBR | 67 | Althea Racing | Ducati 1198 | P | 12.146s | 22 |
| 10 | **Noriyuki Haga** | JPN | 41 | Ducati Xerox Team | Ducati 1198 | P | 19.753s | 22 |
| 11 | **Leon Haslam** | GBR | 91 | Team Suzuki Alstare | Suzuki GSX-R1000 | P | 22.204s | 22 |
| 12 | **Tom Sykes** | GBR | 66 | Kawasaki Racing Team | Kawasaki ZX-10R | P | 22.282s | 22 |
| 13 | **Michel Fabrizio** | ITA | 84 | Ducati Xerox Team | Ducati 1198 | P | 22.780s | 22 |
| 14 | **Sylvain Guintoli** | FRA | 50 | Team Suzuki Alstare | Suzuki GSX-R1000 | P | 23.364s | 22 |
| 15 | **Luca Scassa** | ITA | 99 | Supersonic Racing Team | Ducati 1198 | P | 37.097s | 22 |
| 16 | Lorenzo Lanzi | ITA | 57 | DFX Corse | Ducati 1198 | P | 39.467s | 22 |
| 17 | Chris Vermeulen | AUS | 77 | Kawasaki Racing Team | Kawasaki ZX-10R | P | 46.468s | 22 |
| 18 | Matteo Baiocco | ITA | 15 | Team Pedercini | Kawasaki ZX-10R | P | 57.170s | 22 |
| 19 | Roger Lee Hayden | USA | 95 | Team Pedercini | Kawasaki ZX-10R | P | 61.634s | 22 |
| 20 | Max Neukirchner | GER | 76 | HANNspree Ten Kate Honda | Honda CBR1000RR | P | 64.295s | 22 |
| | Broc Parkes | AUS | 23 | ECHO CRS Honda | Honda CBR1000RR | P | DNF | 9 |
| | Ruben Xaus | SPA | 111 | BMW Motorrad Motorsport | BMW S1000RR | P | DNF | 8 |

**Fastest race lap:** Carlos Checa on lap 5, 1m 36.413s, 105.381mph/169.595km/h.

**Race 2:** 22 laps, 62.090m/99.924km
Time of race: : 35m 43.137s · Average speed: 104.297mph/167.850km/h

| Pos. | Rider | Time & Gap | Laps |
|---|---|---|---|
| 1 | **Jonathan Rea** | | 22 |
| 2 | **Leon Haslam** | 1.942s | 22 |
| 3 | **James Toseland** | 3.928s | 22 |
| 4 | **Max Biaggi** | 4.067s | 22 |
| 5 | **Troy Corser** | 4.176s | 22 |
| 6 | **Carlos Checa** | 4.525s | 22 |
| 7 | **Jakub Smrz** | 4.682s | 22 |
| 8 | **Shane Byrne** | 7.698s | 22 |
| 9 | **Max Neukirchner** | 9.903s | 22 |
| 10 | **Ruben Xaus** | 11.465s | 22 |
| 11 | **Luca Scassa** | 15.489s | 22 |
| 12 | **Michel Fabrizio** | 23.604s | 22 |
| 13 | **Sylvain Guintoli** | 29.085s | 22 |
| 14 | **Chris Vermeulen** | 35.401s | 22 |
| 15 | **Matteo Baiocco** | 44.330s | 22 |
| 16 | Roger Lee Hayden | 50.830s | 22 |
| 17 | Broc Parkes | 58.819s | 22 |
| | Leon Camier | DNF | 20 |
| | Cal Crutchlow | DNF | 11 |
| | Noriyuki Haga | DNF | 6 |
| | Lorenzo Lanzi | DNF | 0 |
| | Tom Sykes | DNF | 0 |

| Superpole | | |
|---|---|---|
| 1 | Rea | 1m 34.944s |
| 2 | Smrz | 1m 35.062s |
| 3 | Corser | 1m 35.306s |
| 4 | Haslam | 1m 35.330s |
| 5 | Camier | 1m 35.633s |
| 6 | Checa | 1m 35.892s |
| 7 | Byrne | 1m 35.909s |
| 8 | Fabrizio | 1m 36.405s |
| 9 | Crutchlow | 1m 36.027s |
| 10 | Toseland | 1m 36.061s |
| 11 | Biaggi | 1m 36.069s |
| 12 | Xaus | 1m 36.094s |
| 13 | Guintoli | 1m 36.327s |
| 14 | Sykes | 1m 36.348s |
| 15 | Haga | 1m 36.574s |
| 16 | Neukirchner | 1m 36.581s |
| 17 | Scassa | 1m 36.906s |
| 18 | Lanzi | 1m 36.989s |
| 19 | Vermeulen | 1m 38.378s |
| 20 | Parkes | 1m 38.622s |

| Points | | |
|---|---|---|
| 1 | Haslam | 148 |
| 2 | Biaggi | 128 |
| 3 | Rea | 110 |
| 4 | Checa | 103 |
| 5 | Toseland | 86 |
| 6 | Haga | 85 |
| 7 | Corser | 68 |
| 8 | Guintoli | 55 |
| 9 | Fabrizio | 53 |
| 10 | Crutchlow | 49 |
| 11 | Camier | 48 |
| 12 | Byrne | 48 |
| 13 | Smrz | 38 |
| 14 | Lanzi | 26 |
| 15 | Xaus | 25 |
| 16 | Sykes | 17 |
| 17 | Neukirchner | 15 |
| 18 | Scassa | 10 |
| 19 | Pitt | 3 |
| 20 | Vermeulen | 2 |
| 21 | Brookes | 2 |
| 22 | Baiocco | 1 |

**Fastest race lap:** Jonathan Rea on lap 2, 1m 36.312s, 105.492mph/169.773km/h (record).
**Lap record:** New circuit configuration

## Round 5 · MONZA, Italy · 9 May 2010 · 3.590mile/5.777km circuit · WEATHER: Race 1 · Dry · Track 20°C · Air 18°C; Race 2 · Dry · Track 30°C · Air 21°C

**Race 1:** 18 laps, 64.614m/103.986km
Time of race: 31m 07.044s · Average speed: 124.587mph/200.504km/h

| Pos. | Rider | Nat. | No. | Entrant | Machine | Tyres | Time & Gap | Laps |
|---|---|---|---|---|---|---|---|---|
| 1 | **Max Biaggi** | ITA | 3 | Aprilia Alitalia Racing | Aprilia RSV4 1000 F | P | | 18 |
| 2 | **James Toseland** | GBR | 52 | Yamaha Sterilgarda Team | Yamaha YZF-R1 | P | 0.247s | 18 |
| 3 | **Cal Crutchlow** | GBR | 35 | Yamaha Sterilgarda Team | Yamaha YZF-R1 | P | 0.297s | 18 |
| 4 | **Leon Haslam** | GBR | 91 | Team Suzuki Alstare | Suzuki GSX-R1000 | P | 0.958s | 18 |
| 5 | **Leon Camier** | GBR | 2 | Aprilia Alitalia Racing | Aprilia RSV4 1000 F | P | 4.493s | 18 |
| 6 | **Ruben Xaus** | SPA | 111 | BMW Motorrad Motorsport | BMW S1000RR | P | 7.343s | 18 |
| 7 | **Michel Fabrizio** | ITA | 84 | Ducati Xerox Team | Ducati 1198 | P | 7.369s | 18 |
| 8 | **Troy Corser** | AUS | 11 | BMW Motorrad Motorsport | BMW S1000RR | P | 9.344s | 18 |
| 9 | **Tom Sykes** | GBR | 66 | Kawasaki Racing Team | Kawasaki ZX-10R | P | 15.338s | 18 |
| 10 | **Sylvain Guintoli** | FRA | 50 | Team Suzuki Alstare | Suzuki GSX-R1000 | P | 16.761s | 18 |
| 11 | **Noriyuki Haga** | JPN | 41 | Ducati Xerox Team | Ducati 1198 | P | 16.921s | 18 |
| 12 | **Max Neukirchner** | GER | 76 | HANNspree Ten Kate Honda | Honda CBR1000RR | P | 22.231s | 18 |
| 13 | **Shane Byrne** | GBR | 67 | Althea Racing | Ducati 1198 | P | 22.602s | 18 |
| 14 | **Carlos Checa** | SPA | 7 | Althea Racing | Ducati 1198 | P | 22.742s | 18 |
| 15 | **Jakub Smrz** | CZE | 96 | Team PATA B&G Racing | Ducati 1198 | P | 26.266s | 18 |
| 16 | Luca Scassa | ITA | 99 | Supersonic Racing Team | Ducati 1198 | P | 26.415s | 18 |
| 17 | Lorenzo Lanzi | ITA | 57 | DFX Corse | Ducati 1198 | P | 26.968s | 18 |
| 18 | Chris Vermeulen | AUS | 77 | Kawasaki Racing Team | Kawasaki ZX-10R | P | 36.964s | 18 |
| 19 | Roger Lee Hayden | USA | 95 | Team Pedercini | Kawasaki ZX-10R | P | 51.646s | 18 |
| 20 | Broc Parkes | AUS | 23 | ECHO CRS Honda | Honda CBR1000RR | P | 1 lap | 17 |
| | Daisaku Sakai | JPN | 71 | Yoshimura Suzuki Racing Team | Suzuki GSX-R1000 | P | DNF | 9 |
| | Jonathan Rea | GBR | 65 | HANNspree Ten Kate Honda | Honda CBR1000RR | P | DNF | 8 |
| | Vittorio Iannuzzo | ITA | 31 | S.C.I. Honda Garvie Image | Honda CBR1000RR | P | DNF | 1 |
| | Matteo Baiocco | ITA | 15 | Team Pedercini | Kawasaki ZX-10R | P | DSQ | 8 |

**Fastest race lap:** Jonathan Rea on lap 6, 1m 43.031s, 125.426mph/201.854km/h.

**Race 2:** 18 laps, 64.614m/103.986km
Time of race: 31m 07.122s · Average speed: 124.582mph/200.496km/h

| Pos. | Rider | Time & Gap | Laps |
|---|---|---|---|
| 1 | **Max Biaggi** | | 18 |
| 2 | **Leon Haslam** | 4.547s | 18 |
| 3 | **Troy Corser** | 5.469s | 18 |
| 4 | **Leon Camier** | 10.267s | 18 |
| 5 | **Tom Sykes** | 15.561s | 18 |
| 6 | **Noriyuki Haga** | 15.816s | 18 |
| 7 | **Sylvain Guintoli** | 15.861s | 18 |
| 8 | **Jakub Smrz** | 20.977s | 18 |
| 9 | **Shane Byrne** | 21.920s | 18 |
| 10 | **Luca Scassa** | 21.974s | 18 |
| 11 | **Carlos Checa** | 27.152s | 18 |
| 12 | **Max Neukirchner** | 29.315s | 18 |
| 13 | **Chris Vermeulen** | 30.858s | 18 |
| 14 | **Roger Lee Hayden** | 47.160s | 18 |
| 15 | **Broc Parkes** | 48.824s | 18 |
| | Cal Crutchlow | DNF | 12 |
| | Matteo Baiocco | DNF | 10 |
| | Lorenzo Lanzi | DNF | 9 |
| | Vittorio Iannuzzo | DNF | 6 |
| | Michel Fabrizio | DNF | 1 |
| | James Toseland | DNF | 0 |
| | Ruben Xaus | DNF | 0 |
| | Jonathan Rea | DNF | 0 |

| Superpole | | |
|---|---|---|
| 1 | Biaggi | 1m 42.121s |
| 2 | Crutchlow | 1m 42.154s |
| 3 | Fabrizio | 1m 42.499s |
| 4 | Rea | 1m 42.566s |
| 5 | Haslam | 1m 42.633s |
| 6 | Xaus | 1m 42.725s |
| 7 | Toseland | 1m 42.789s |
| 8 | Sykes | 1m 43.111s |
| 9 | Neukirchner | 1m 43.410s |
| 10 | Scassa | 1m 43.431s |
| 11 | Checa | 1m 43.506s |
| 12 | Corser | 1m 43.508s |
| 13 | Camier | 1m 43.530s |
| 14 | Guintoli | 1m 43.691s |
| 15 | Byrne | 1m 43.813s |
| 16 | Haga | 1m 43.957s |
| 17 | Smrz | 1m 44.291s |
| 18 | Vermeulen | 1m 44.802s |
| 19 | Lanzi | 1m 44.878s |
| 20 | Baiocco | 1m 46.180s |

| Points | | |
|---|---|---|
| 1 | Haslam | 181 |
| 2 | Biaggi | 178 |
| 3 | Rea | 110 |
| 4 | Checa | 110 |
| 5 | Toseland | 106 |
| 6 | Haga | 100 |
| 7 | Corser | 92 |
| 8 | Camier | 72 |
| 9 | Guintoli | 70 |
| 10 | Crutchlow | 65 |
| 11 | Fabrizio | 62 |
| 12 | Byrne | 58 |
| 13 | Smrz | 47 |
| 14 | Sykes | 35 |
| 15 | Xaus | 35 |
| 16 | Lanzi | 26 |
| 17 | Neukirchner | 23 |
| 18 | Scassa | 16 |
| 19 | Vermeulen | 5 |
| 20 | Pitt | 3 |
| 21 | Hayden | 2 |
| 22 | Brookes | 2 |
| 23 | Parkes | 1 |
| 24 | Baiocco | 1 |

**Fastest race lap:** Cal Crutchlow on lap 3, 1m 42.937s, 125.541mph/202.038km/h (record).
**Previous lap record:** New circuit configuration.

**Race 1:** 24 laps, 63.320m/101.904km

Time of race: 39m 48.343s · Average speed: 95.444mph/153.602km/h

| Pos. | Rider | Nat. | No. | Entrant | Machine | Tyres | Time & Gap | Laps |
|---|---|---|---|---|---|---|---|---|
| 1 | **Michel Fabrizio** | ITA | 84 | Ducati Xerox Team | Ducati 1198 | P | | 24 |
| 2 | **Carlos Checa** | SPA | 7 | Althea Racing | Ducati 1198 | P | 1.098s | 24 |
| 3 | **Leon Haslam** | GBR | 91 | Team Suzuki Alstare | Suzuki GSX-R1000 | P | 5.049s | 24 |
| 4 | **Max Biaggi** | ITA | 3 | Aprilia Alitalia Racing | Aprilia RSV4 1000 F | P | 6.974s | 24 |
| 5 | **Jonathan Rea** | GBR | 65 | HANNspree Ten Kate Honda | Honda CBR1000RR | P | 13.71s | 24 |
| 6 | **Leon Camier** | GBR | 2 | Aprilia Alitalia Racing | Aprilia RSV4 1000 F | P | 13.848s | 24 |
| 7 | **James Toseland** | GBR | 52 | Yamaha Sterilgarda Team | Yamaha YZF-R1 | P | 16.064s | 24 |
| 8 | **Cal Crutchlow** | GBR | 35 | Yamaha Sterilgarda Team | Yamaha YZF-R1 | P | 16.231s | 24 |
| 9 | **Jakub Smrz** | CZE | 96 | Team PATA B&G Racing | Ducati 1198 | P | 16.580s | 24 |
| 10 | **Sylvain Guintoli** | FRA | 50 | Team Suzuki Alstare | Suzuki GSX-R1000 | P | 23.100s | 24 |
| 11 | **Luca Scassa** | ITA | 99 | Supersonic Racing Team | Ducati 1198 | P | 24.561s | 24 |
| 12 | **Troy Corser** | AUS | 11 | BMW Motorrad Motorsport | BMW S1000RR | P | 25.504s | 24 |
| 13 | **Sheridan Morais** | RSA | 32 | EmTek Racing | Aprilia RSV4 1000 F | P | 27.073s | 24 |
| 14 | **Ruben Xaus** | SPA | 111 | BMW Motorrad Motorsport | BMW S1000RR | P | 27.273s | 24 |
| 15 | **Shane Byrne** | GBR | 67 | Althea Racing | Ducati 1198 | P | 30.692s | 24 |
| 16 | Tom Sykes | GBR | 66 | Kawasaki Racing Team | Kawasaki ZX-10R | P | 34.008s | 24 |
| 17 | Noriyuki Haga | JPN | 41 | Ducati Xerox Team | Ducati 1198 | P | 35.948s | 24 |
| 18 | Chris Vermeulen | AUS | 77 | Kawasaki Racing Team | Kawasaki ZX-10R | P | 44.030s | 24 |
| 19 | Max Neukirchner | GER | 76 | HANNspree Ten Kate Honda | Honda CBR1000RR | P | 48.382s | 24 |
| | Roger Lee Hayden | USA | 95 | Team Pedercini | Kawasaki ZX-10R | P | DNF | 13 |
| | Broc Parkes | AUS | 23 | ECHO CRS Honda | Honda CBR1000RR | P | DNF | 11 |
| | Matteo Baiocco | ITA | 15 | Team Pedercini | Kawasaki ZX-10R | P | DNF | 6 |

**Fastest race lap:** Michel Fabrizio on lap 3, 1m 38.170s, 96.751mph/155.705km/h (record).

**Race 2:** 24 laps, 63.320m/101.904km

Time of race: 39m 52.870s · Average speed: 95.263mph/153.311km/h

| Pos. | Rider | Time & Gap | Laps | | Superpole | | | Points | | |
|---|---|---|---|---|---|---|---|---|---|---|
| 1 | **Leon Haslam** | | 24 | 1 | Crutchlow | 1m 37.243s | 1 | Haslam | 222 |
| 2 | **Jonathan Rea** | 0.522s | 24 | 2 | Toseland | 1m 37.260s | 2 | Biaggi | 207 |
| 3 | **Max Biaggi** | 0.601s | 24 | 3 | Checa | 1m 37.296s | 3 | Rea | 141 |
| 4 | **Cal Crutchlow** | 0.991s | 24 | 4 | Fabrizio | 1m 37.368s | 4 | Checa | 141 |
| 5 | **Carlos Checa** | 1.479s | 24 | 5 | Haslam | 1m 37.401s | 5 | Toseland | 125 |
| 6 | **James Toseland** | 13.324s | 24 | 6 | Smrz | 1m 37.561s | 6 | Haga | 106 |
| 7 | **Troy Corser** | 13.740s | 24 | 7 | Biaggi | 1m 37.613s | 7 | Corser | 105 |
| 8 | **Michel Fabrizio** | 14.250s | 24 | 8 | Camier | 1m 38.148s | 8 | Fabrizio | 95 |
| 9 | **Jakub Smrz** | 15.190s | 24 | | | | 9 | Crutchlow | 86 |
| 10 | Noriyuki Haga | 16.790s | 24 | 9 | Scassa | 1m 37.756s | 10 | Camier | 82 |
| 11 | Ruben Xaus | 21.101s | 24 | 10 | Guintoli | 1m 37.875s | 11 | Guintoli | 77 |
| 12 | Luca Scassa | 22.670s | 24 | 11 | Rea | 1m 37.953s | 12 | Byrne | 62 |
| 13 | Shane Byrne | 24.506s | 24 | 12 | Sykes | 1m 38.206s | 13 | Smrz | 61 |
| 14 | Tom Sykes | 31.301s | 24 | 13 | Corser | 1m 38.210s | 14 | Xaus | 42 |
| 15 | Sylvain Guintoli | 31.836s | 24 | 14 | Morais | 1m 38.404s | 15 | Sykes | 37 |
| 16 | Chris Vermeulen | 33.710s | 24 | 15 | Xaus | 1m 38.471s | 16 | Lanzi | 26 |
| 17 | Max Neukirchner | 35.203s | 24 | 16 | Haga | 1m 38.496s | 17 | Scassa | 25 |
| 18 | Broc Parkes | 55.929s | 24 | | | | 18 | Neukirchner | 23 |
| 19 | Roger Lee Hayden | 56.074s | 24 | 17 | Neukirchner | 1m 38.917s | 19 | Vermeulen | 5 |
| 20 | Matteo Baiocco | 68.481s | 24 | 18 | Byrne | 1m 39.037s | 20 | Morais | 3 |
| | Leon Camier | DNF | 17 | 19 | Vermeulen | 1m 39.317s | 21 | Pitt | 3 |
| | Sheridan Morais | DNF | 10 | 20 | Parkes | 1m 40.713s | 22 | Hayden | 2 |
| | | | | | | | 23 | Brookes | 2 |
| | | | | | | | 24 | Parkes | 1 |
| | | | | | | | 25 | Baiocco | 1 |

**Fastest race lap:** Jonathan Rea on lap 2, 1m 38.658s, 96.272mph/154.935km/h.

**Previous lap record:** Michel Fabrizio, ITA (Ducati), 1m 38.548s, 96.381mph/155.110km/h (2009).

---

**Race 1:** 21 laps, 64.030m/103.047km

Time of race: 38m 20.442s · Average speed: 100.202mph/161.260km/h

| Pos. | Rider | Nat. | No. | Entrant | Machine | Tyres | Time & Gap | Laps |
|---|---|---|---|---|---|---|---|---|
| 1 | **Max Biaggi** | ITA | 3 | Aprilia Alitalia Racing | Aprilia RSV4 1000 F | P | | 21 |
| 2 | **Leon Haslam** | GBR | 91 | Team Suzuki Alstare | Suzuki GSX-R1000 | P | 4.931s | 21 |
| 3 | **Noriyuki Haga** | JPN | 41 | Ducati Xerox Team | Ducati 1198 | P | 6.432s | 21 |
| 4 | **Leon Camier** | GBR | 2 | Aprilia Alitalia Racing | Aprilia RSV4 1000 F | P | 8.576s | 21 |
| 5 | **Troy Corser** | AUS | 11 | BMW Motorrad Motorsport | BMW S1000RR | P | 11.150s | 21 |
| 6 | **Shane Byrne** | GBR | 67 | Althea Racing | Ducati 1198 | P | 11.243s | 21 |
| 7 | **Luca Scassa** | ITA | 99 | Supersonic Racing Team | Ducati 1198 | P | 12.432s | 21 |
| 8 | **Sylvain Guintoli** | FRA | 50 | Team Suzuki Alstare | Suzuki GSX-R1000 | P | 15.145s | 21 |
| 9 | **James Toseland** | GBR | 52 | Yamaha Sterilgarda Team | Yamaha YZF-R1 | P | 16.091s | 21 |
| 10 | **Ruben Xaus** | SPA | 111 | BMW Motorrad Motorsport | BMW S1000RR | P | 16.502s | 21 |
| 11 | **Cal Crutchlow** | GBR | 35 | Yamaha Sterilgarda Team | Yamaha YZF-R1 | P | 18.719s | 21 |
| 12 | **Max Neukirchner** | GER | 76 | HANNspree Ten Kate Honda | Honda CBR1000RR | P | 24.285s | 21 |
| 13 | **Tom Sykes** | GBR | 66 | Kawasaki Racing Team | Kawasaki ZX-10R | P | 36.479s | 21 |
| 14 | **Jonathan Rea** | GBR | 65 | HANNspree Ten Kate Honda | Honda CBR1000RR | P | 39.700s | 21 |
| 15 | **Chris Vermeulen** | AUS | 77 | Kawasaki Racing Team | Kawasaki ZX-10R | P | 41.253s | 21 |
| 16 | Roger Lee Hayden | USA | 95 | Team Pedercini | Kawasaki ZX-10R | P | 41.661s | 21 |
| 17 | Broc Parkes | AUS | 23 | ECHO CRS Honda | Honda CBR1000RR | P | 60.427s | 21 |
| 18 | Matteo Baiocco | ITA | 15 | Team Pedercini | Kawasaki ZX-10R | P | 4 laps | 17 |
| | Carlos Checa | SPA | 7 | Althea Racing | Ducati 1198 | P | DNF | 18 |
| | Michel Fabrizio | ITA | 84 | Ducati Xerox Team | Ducati 1198 | P | DNF | 1 |
| | Jakub Smrz | CZE | 96 | Team PATA B&G Racing | Ducati 1198 | P | DNF | 0 |

**Fastest race lap:** Carlos Checa on lap 4, 1m 48.045s, 101.594mph/163.499km/h (record).

**Race 2:** 21 laps, 64.030m/103.047km

Time of race: 38m 17.842s · Average speed: 100.315mph/161.442km/h

| Pos. | Rider | Time & Gap | Laps | | Superpole | | | Points | | |
|---|---|---|---|---|---|---|---|---|---|---|
| 1 | **Max Biaggi** | | 21 | 1 | Checa | 1m 47.081s | 1 | Biaggi | 257 |
| 2 | **Leon Camier** | 5.899s | 21 | 2 | Biaggi | 1m 47.414s | 2 | Haslam | 242 |
| 3 | **Cal Crutchlow** | 7.363s | 21 | 3 | Crutchlow | 1m 47.648s | 3 | Rea | 151 |
| 4 | **Noriyuki Haga** | 8.842s | 21 | 4 | Smrz | 1m 47.662s | 4 | Checa | 141 |
| 5 | **Troy Corser** | 9.473s | 21 | 5 | Haslam | 1m 48.006s | 5 | Haga | 135 |
| 6 | **Sylvain Guintoli** | 12.293s | 21 | 6 | Haga | 1m 48.035s | 6 | Toseland | 132 |
| 7 | **Shane Byrne** | 12.483s | 21 | 7 | Rea | 1m 48.378s | 7 | Corser | 127 |
| 8 | **Jonathan Rea** | 15.959s | 21 | 8 | Camier | 1m 48.621s | 8 | Camier | 115 |
| 9 | **Michel Fabrizio** | 18.897s | 21 | | | | 9 | Crutchlow | 107 |
| 10 | **Luca Scassa** | 20.372s | 21 | 9 | Xaus | 1m 48.141s | 10 | Fabrizio | 102 |
| 11 | **Ruben Xaus** | 26.823s | 21 | 10 | Fabrizio | 1m 48.154s | 11 | Guintoli | 95 |
| 12 | **Max Neukirchner** | 30.344s | 21 | 11 | Byrne | 1m 48.159s | 12 | Byrne | 81 |
| 13 | **Chris Vermeulen** | 33.337s | 21 | 12 | Guintoli | 1m 48.162s | 13 | Smrz | 61 |
| 14 | **Tom Sykes** | 38.772s | 21 | 13 | Scassa | 1m 48.274s | 14 | Xaus | 53 |
| 15 | **Broc Parkes** | 44.994s | 21 | 14 | Toseland | 1m 48.640s | 15 | Sykes | 42 |
| | Jakub Smrz | DNF | 18 | 15 | Corser | 1m 48.706s | 16 | Scassa | 40 |
| | Matteo Baiocco | DNF | 15 | 16 | Neukirchner | 1m 48.964s | 17 | Neukirchner | 31 |
| | James Toseland | DNF | 14 | | | | 18 | Lanzi | 26 |
| | Roger Lee Hayden | DNF | 12 | 17 | Vermeulen | 1m 49.635s | 19 | Vermeulen | 9 |
| | Carlos Checa | DNF | 7 | 18 | Sykes | 1m 50.135s | 20 | Morais | 3 |
| | Leon Haslam | DNF | 7 | 19 | Parkes | 1m 50.479s | 21 | Pitt | 3 |
| | | | | 20 | Hayden | 1m 50.596s | 22 | Hayden | 2 |
| | | | | | | | 23 | Brookes | 2 |
| | | | | | | | 24 | Parkes | 1 |
| | | | | | | | 25 | Baiocco | 1 |

**Fastest race lap:** Carlos Checa on lap 2, 1m 48.148s, 101.509mph/163.363km/h.

**Previous lap record:** Ben Spies, USA (Yamaha), 1m 48.768s, 100.917mph/162.410km/h (2009).

## Round 8 — MISANO, Italy · 27 June 2010 · 2.626mile/4.226km circuit · WEATHER: Race 1 · Dry · Track 40°C · Air 27°C; Race 2 · Dry · Track 47°C · Air 29°C

**Race 1:** 24 laps, 63.022m/101.424km
Time of race: 38m 59.319s · Average speed: 96.985mph/156.082km/h

| Pos. | Rider | Nat. | No. | Entrant | Machine | Tyres | Time & Gap | Laps |
|---|---|---|---|---|---|---|---|---|
| 1 | **Max Biaggi** | ITA | 3 | Aprilia Alitalia Racing | Aprilia RSV4 1000 F | P | | 24 |
| 2 | **Carlos Checa** | SPA | 7 | Althea Racing | Ducati 1198 | P | 0.387s | 24 |
| 3 | **Troy Corser** | AUS | 11 | BMW Motorrad Motorsport | BMW S1000RR | P | 0.822s | 24 |
| 4 | **Michel Fabrizio** | ITA | 84 | Ducati Xerox Team | Ducati 1198 | P | 4.911s | 24 |
| 5 | **Sylvain Guintoli** | FRA | 50 | Team Suzuki Alstare | Suzuki GSX-R1000 | P | 5.916s | 24 |
| 6 | **Leon Camier** | GBR | 2 | Aprilia Alitalia Racing | Aprilia RSV4 1000 F | P | 8.658s | 24 |
| 7 | **Noriyuki Haga** | JPN | 41 | Ducati Xerox Team | Ducati 1198 | P | 11.872s | 24 |
| 8 | **Leon Haslam** | GBR | 91 | Team Suzuki Alstare | Suzuki GSX-R1000 | P | 11.907s | 24 |
| 9 | **Shane Byrne** | GBR | 67 | Althea Racing | Ducati 1198 | P | 16.490s | 24 |
| 10 | **James Toseland** | GBR | 52 | Yamaha Sterilgarda Team | Yamaha YZF-R1 | P | 18.458s | 24 |
| 11 | **Luca Scassa** | ITA | 99 | Supersonic Racing Team | Ducati 1198 | P | 18.646s | 24 |
| 12 | **Lorenzo Lanzi** | ITA | 57 | DFX Corse | Ducati 1198 | P | 19.315s | 24 |
| 13 | **Jonathan Rea** | GBR | 65 | HANNspree Ten Kate Honda | Honda CBR1000RR | P | 25.405s | 24 |
| 14 | **Max Neukirchner** | GER | 76 | HANNspree Ten Kate Honda | Honda CBR1000RR | P | 31.671s | 24 |
| 15 | **Tom Sykes** | GBR | 66 | Kawasaki Racing Team | Kawasaki ZX-10R | P | 39.658s | 24 |
| 16 | Chris Vermeulen | AUS | 77 | Kawasaki Racing Team | Kawasaki ZX-10R | P | 48.137s | 24 |
| 17 | Roger Lee Hayden | USA | 95 | Team Pedercini | Kawasaki ZX-10R | P | 56.316s | 24 |
| 18 | Federico Sandi | ITA | 90 | Gabrielli Racing Team | Aprilia RSV4 1000 F | P | 56.667s | 24 |
| 19 | Matteo Baiocco | ITA | 15 | Team Pedercini | Kawasaki ZX-10R | P | 57.218s | 24 |
| | Ruben Xaus | SPA | 111 | BMW Motorrad Motorsport | BMW S1000RR | P | DNF | 8 |
| | Cal Crutchlow | GBR | 35 | Yamaha Sterilgarda Team | Yamaha YZF-R1 | P | DNF | 4 |
| | Jakub Smrz | CZE | 96 | Team PATA B&G Racing | Ducati 1198 | P | DNF | 1 |
| | Broc Parkes | AUS | 23 | ECHO CRS Honda | Honda CBR1000RR | P | DSQ | 10 |

**Fastest race lap:** Carlos Checa on lap 2, 1m 36.670s, 97.790mph/157.377km/h.

**Race 2:** 24 laps, 63.022m/101.424km
Time of race: 38m 58.149s · Average speed: 97.033mph/156.160km/h

| Pos. | Rider | Time & Gap | Laps | | Superpole | |
|---|---|---|---|---|---|---|
| 1 | **Max Biaggi** | | 24 | 1 | Corser | 1m 35.001s |
| 2 | **Leon Haslam** | 4.095s | 24 | 2 | Biaggi | 1m 35.502s |
| 3 | **Michel Fabrizio** | 4.631s | 24 | 3 | Fabrizio | 1m 35.680s |
| 4 | **Cal Crutchlow** | 5.014s | 24 | 4 | Crutchlow | 1m 35.683s |
| 5 | **Carlos Checa** | 6.256s | 24 | 5 | Checa | 1m 35.851s |
| 6 | **Sylvain Guintoli** | 7.677s | 24 | 6 | Guintoli | 1m 36.096s |
| 7 | **Shane Byrne** | 10.144s | 24 | 7 | Haslam | 1m 36.302s |
| 8 | **Luca Scassa** | 10.942s | 24 | 8 | Scassa | 1m 36.607s |
| 9 | **Noriyuki Haga** | 13.640s | 24 | | | |
| 10 | **Troy Corser** | 16.279s | 24 | 9 | Haga | 1m 36.093s |
| 11 | **Leon Camier** | 17.799s | 24 | 10 | Smrz | 1m 36.170s |
| 12 | **Jonathan Rea** | 22.793s | 24 | 11 | Lanzi | 1m 36.200s |
| 13 | **Lorenzo Lanzi** | 24.131s | 24 | 12 | Xaus | 1m 36.204s |
| 14 | **Max Neukirchner** | 28.212s | 24 | 13 | Toseland | 1m 36.216s |
| 15 | **Chris Vermeulen** | 36.551s | 24 | 14 | Camier | 1m 36.245s |
| 16 | Tom Sykes | 49.636s | 24 | 15 | Byrne | 1m 36.376s |
| 17 | Broc Parkes | 50.041s | 24 | 16 | Rea | 1m 36.561s |
| 18 | Roger Lee Hayden | 51.246s | 24 | | | |
| 19 | Matteo Baiocco | 58.174s | 24 | 17 | Neukirchner | 1m 36.889s |
| 20 | Federico Sandi | 70.588s | 24 | 18 | Sykes | 1m 36.928s |
| | James Toseland | DNF | 10 | 19 | Parkes | 1m 37.574s |
| | Ruben Xaus | DNF | 7 | 20 | Hayden | 1m 37.986s |
| | Jakub Smrz | DNF | 2 | | | |

**Points**

| Pos | Rider | Pts |
|---|---|---|
| 1 | Biaggi | 307 |
| 2 | Haslam | 270 |
| 3 | Checa | 172 |
| 4 | Rea | 158 |
| 5 | Haga | 151 |
| 6 | Corser | 149 |
| 7 | Toseland | 138 |
| 8 | Fabrizio | 131 |
| 9 | Camier | 130 |
| 10 | Crutchlow | 120 |
| 11 | Guintoli | 116 |
| 12 | Byrne | 97 |
| 13 | Smrz | 61 |
| 14 | Xaus | 53 |
| 15 | Scassa | 53 |
| 16 | Sykes | 43 |
| 17 | Neukirchner | 35 |
| 18 | Lanzi | 33 |
| 19 | Vermeulen | 10 |
| 20 | Morais | 3 |
| 21 | Pitt | 3 |
| 22 | Hayden | 2 |
| 23 | Brookes | 2 |
| 24 | Parkes | 2 |
| 25 | Baiocco | 1 |

**Fastest race lap:** Cal Crutchlow on lap 4, 1m 36.546s, 97.915mph/157.579km/h (record).
**Previous lap record:** Noriyuki Haga, JPN (Ducati), 1m 37.135s, 97.319mph/156.620km/h (2009).

## Round 9 — BRNO, Czech Republic · 11 July 2010 · 3.357mile/5.403km circuit · WEATHER: Race 1 · Dry · Track 48°C · Air 29°C; Race 2 · Dry · Track 57°C · Air 31°C

**Race 1:** 20 laps, 67.145m/108.060km
Time of race: 40m 16.037s · Average speed: 100.049mph/161.014km/h

| Pos. | Rider | Nat. | No. | Entrant | Machine | Tyres | Time & Gap | Laps |
|---|---|---|---|---|---|---|---|---|
| 1 | **Jonathan Rea** | GBR | 65 | HANNspree Ten Kate Honda | Honda CBR1000RR | P | | 20 |
| 2 | **Max Biaggi** | ITA | 3 | Aprilia Alitalia Racing | Aprilia RSV4 1000 F | P | 2.518s | 20 |
| 3 | **Cal Crutchlow** | GBR | 35 | Yamaha Sterilgarda Team | Yamaha YZF-R1 | P | 4.071s | 20 |
| 4 | **Sylvain Guintoli** | FRA | 50 | Team Suzuki Alstare | Suzuki GSX-R1000 | P | 7.160s | 20 |
| 5 | **Ruben Xaus** | SPA | 111 | BMW Motorrad Motorsport | BMW S1000RR | P | 8.602s | 20 |
| 6 | **Noriyuki Haga** | JPN | 41 | Ducati Xerox Team | Ducati 1198 | P | 11.379s | 20 |
| 7 | **James Toseland** | GBR | 52 | Yamaha Sterilgarda Team | Yamaha YZF-R1 | P | 11.513s | 20 |
| 8 | **Leon Haslam** | GBR | 91 | Team Suzuki Alstare | Suzuki GSX-R1000 | P | 16.487s | 20 |
| 9 | **Carlos Checa** | SPA | 7 | Althea Racing | Ducati 1198 | P | 20.829s | 20 |
| 10 | **Lorenzo Lanzi** | ITA | 57 | DFX Corse | Ducati 1198 | P | 25.164s | 20 |
| 11 | **Tom Sykes** | GBR | 66 | Kawasaki Racing Team | Kawasaki ZX-10R | P | 32.602s | 20 |
| 12 | **Shane Byrne** | GBR | 67 | Althea Racing | Ducati 1198 | P | 36.748s | 20 |
| 13 | **Broc Parkes** | AUS | 23 | ECHO CRS Honda | Honda CBR1000RR | P | 39.183s | 20 |
| 14 | **Roger Lee Hayden** | USA | 95 | Team Pedercini | Kawasaki ZX-10R | P | 59.889s | 20 |
| 15 | **Matteo Baiocco** | ITA | 15 | Team Pedercini | Kawasaki ZX-10R | P | 65.329s | 20 |
| | Michel Fabrizio | ITA | 84 | Ducati Xerox Team | Ducati 1198 | P | DNF | 12 |
| | Luca Scassa | ITA | 99 | Supersonic Racing Team | Ducati 1198 | P | DNF | 4 |
| | Leon Camier | GBR | 2 | Aprilia Alitalia Racing | Aprilia RSV4 1000 F | P | DNF | 4 |
| | Chris Vermeulen | AUS | 77 | Kawasaki Racing Team | Kawasaki ZX-10R | P | DNF | 0 |
| | Jakub Smrz | CZE | 96 | Team PATA B&G Racing | Aprilia RSV4 1000 F | P | DNF | 0 |
| | Max Neukirchner | GER | 76 | HANNspree Ten Kate Honda | Honda CBR1000RR | P | DNF | 0 |

**Fastest race lap:** Cal Crutchlow on lap 3, 1m 59.964s, 100.749mph/162.139km/h.

**Race 2:** 20 laps, 67.145m/108.060km
Time of race: 40m 12.236s · Average speed: 100.207mph/161.268km/h

| Pos. | Rider | Time & Gap | Laps | | Superpole | |
|---|---|---|---|---|---|---|
| 1 | **Max Biaggi** | | 20 | 1 | Crutchlow | 1m 58.018s |
| 2 | **Jonathan Rea** | 4.627s | 20 | 2 | Biaggi | 1m 58.743s |
| 3 | **Michel Fabrizio** | 13.600s | 20 | 3 | Rea | 1m 59.094s |
| 4 | **James Toseland** | 16.372s | 20 | 4 | Xaus | 1m 59.135s |
| 5 | **Noriyuki Haga** | 17.530s | 20 | 5 | Guintoli | 1m 59.179s |
| 6 | **Carlos Checa** | 21.704s | 20 | 6 | Scassa | 1m 59.393s |
| 7 | **Sylvain Guintoli** | 23.769s | 20 | 7 | Fabrizio | 1m 59.451s |
| 8 | **Leon Camier** | 25.875s | 20 | 8 | Checa | 1m 59.571s |
| 9 | **Shane Byrne** | 30.374s | 20 | | | |
| 10 | **Leon Haslam** | 34.002s | 20 | 9 | Lanzi | 1m 59.699s |
| 11 | **Lorenzo Lanzi** | 34.691s | 20 | 10 | Toseland | 1m 59.699s |
| 12 | **Broc Parkes** | 49.270s | 20 | 11 | Neukirchner | 1m 59.829s |
| 13 | **Roger Lee Hayden** | 63.258s | 20 | 12 | Sykes | 1m 59.830s |
| 14 | **Cal Crutchlow** | 1 lap | 19 | 13 | Camier | 1m 59.841s |
| 15 | **Matteo Baiocco** | 1 lap | 19 | 14 | Haslam | 1m 59.995s |
| | Jakub Smrz | DNF | 15 | 15 | Haga | 2m 00.258s |
| | Ruben Xaus | DNF | 14 | 16 | Byrne | 2m 00.564s |
| | Chris Vermeulen | DNF | 2 | | | |
| | Tom Sykes | DNF | 0 | 17 | Smrz | 2m 00.341s |
| | Max Neukirchner | DNF | 0 | 18 | Vermeulen | 2m 01.167s |
| | | | | 19 | Baiocco | 2m 01.523s |

**Points**

| Pos | Rider | Pts |
|---|---|---|
| 1 | Biaggi | 352 |
| 2 | Haslam | 284 |
| 3 | Rea | 203 |
| 4 | Checa | 189 |
| 5 | Haga | 172 |
| 6 | Toseland | 160 |
| 7 | Corser | 149 |
| 8 | Fabrizio | 147 |
| 9 | Camier | 138 |
| 10 | Crutchlow | 138 |
| 11 | Guintoli | 138 |
| 12 | Byrne | 108 |
| 13 | Xaus | 64 |
| 14 | Smrz | 61 |
| 15 | Scassa | 53 |
| 16 | Sykes | 48 |
| 17 | Lanzi | 44 |
| 18 | Neukirchner | 35 |
| 19 | Vermeulen | 10 |
| 20 | Parkes | 9 |
| 21 | Hayden | 7 |
| 22 | Morais | 3 |
| 23 | Baiocco | 3 |
| 24 | Pitt | 3 |
| 25 | Brookes | 2 |

**Fastest race lap:** Cal Crutchlow on lap 12, 1m 59.291s, 101.316mph/163.053km/h (record).
**Previous lap record:** Max Biaggi, ITA (Aprilia), 1m 59.961s, 100.749mph/162.140km/h (2009).

**Race 1:** 18 laps, 66.012m/106.236km
**Time of race:** 37m 47.851s · **Average speed:** 104.788mph/168.640km/h

| Pos. | Rider | Nat. | No. | Entrant | Machine | Tyres | Time & Gap | Laps |
|---|---|---|---|---|---|---|---|---|
| 1 | Cal Crutchlow | GBR | 35 | Yamaha Sterilgarda Team | Yamaha YZF-R1 | P | | 18 |
| 2 | Jonathan Rea | GBR | 65 | HANNspree Ten Kate Honda | Honda CBR1000RR | P | 1.621s | 18 |
| 3 | Leon Haslam | GBR | 91 | Team Suzuki Alstare | Suzuki GSX-R1000 | P | 11.433s | 18 |
| 4 | Michel Fabrizio | ITA | 84 | Ducati Xerox Team | Ducati 1198 | P | 15.874s | 18 |
| 5 | Max Biaggi | ITA | 3 | Aprilia Alitalia Racing | Aprilia RSV4 1000 F | P | 17.085s | 18 |
| 6 | Leon Camier | GBR | 2 | Aprilia Alitalia Racing | Aprilia RSV4 1000 F | P | 17.532s | 18 |
| 7 | Carlos Checa | SPA | 7 | Althea Racing | Ducati 1198 | P | 18.250s | 18 |
| 8 | James Toseland | GBR | 52 | Yamaha Sterilgarda Team | Yamaha YZF-R1 | P | 18.938s | 18 |
| 9 | Shane Byrne | GBR | 67 | Althea Racing | Ducati 1198 | P | 22.997s | 18 |
| 10 | Troy Corser | AUS | 11 | BMW Motorrad Motorsport | BMW S1000RR | P | 25.830s | 18 |
| 11 | Max Neukirchner | GER | 76 | HANNspree Ten Kate Honda | Honda CBR1000RR | P | 30.972s | 18 |
| 12 | Sylvain Guintoli | FRA | 50 | Team Suzuki Alstare | Suzuki GSX-R1000 | P | 31.808s | 18 |
| 13 | Jakub Smrz | CZE | 96 | Team PATA B&G Racing | Aprilia RSV4 1000 F | P | 32.193s | 18 |
| 14 | Noriyuki Haga | JPN | 41 | Ducati Xerox Team | Ducati 1198 | P | 33.206s | 18 |
| 15 | Lorenzo Lanzi | ITA | 57 | DFX Corse | Ducati 1198 | P | 34.207s | 18 |
| 16 | Joshua Brookes | AUS | 25 | HM Plant Honda | Honda CBR1000RR | P | 35.939s | 18 |
| 17 | Ruben Xaus | SPA | 111 | BMW Motorrad Motorsport | BMW S1000RR | P | 38.282s | 18 |
| 18 | Tom Sykes | GBR | 66 | Kawasaki Racing Team | Kawasaki ZX-10R | P | 39.923s | 18 |
| 19 | Akira Yanagawa | JPN | 87 | Kawasaki Racing Team | Kawasaki ZX-10R | P | 81.620s | 18 |
| 20 | Tommy Bridewell | GBR | 46 | TYCO Racing | Honda CBR1000RR | P | 81.678s | 18 |
| 21 | Ryuichi Kiyonari | JPN | 8 | HM Plant Honda | Honda CBR1000RR | P | 81.793s | 18 |
| | Matteo Baiocco | ITA | 15 | Team Pedercini | Kawasaki ZX-10R | P | DNF | 13 |
| | Roger Lee Hayden | USA | 95 | Team Pedercini | Kawasaki ZX-10R | P | DNF | 0 |
| | Broc Parkes | AUS | 23 | ECHO CRS Honda | Honda CBR1000RR | P | DNF | 0 |

**Race 2:** 18 laps, 66.012m/106.236km
**Time of race:** 37m 48.348s · **Average speed:** 104.765mph/168.603km/h

| Pos. | Rider | Time & Gap | Laps |
|---|---|---|---|
| 1 | Cal Crutchlow | | 18 |
| 2 | Jonathan Rea | 2.070s | 18 |
| 3 | Leon Camier | 8.834s | 18 |
| 4 | Leon Haslam | 13.232s | 18 |
| 5 | James Toseland | 13.258s | 18 |
| 6 | Max Biaggi | 13.568s | 18 |
| 7 | Sylvain Guintoli | 13.963s | 18 |
| 8 | Shane Byrne | 14.432s | 18 |
| 9 | Jakub Smrz | 16.399s | 18 |
| 10 | Carlos Checa | 19.874s | 18 |
| 11 | Ruben Xaus | 26.268s | 18 |
| 12 | Joshua Brookes | 28.003s | 18 |
| 13 | Noriyuki Haga | 28.550s | 18 |
| 14 | Tom Sykes | 30.117s | 18 |
| 15 | Lorenzo Lanzi | 30.415s | 18 |
| 16 | Ryuichi Kiyonari | 58.607s | 18 |
| 17 | Roger Lee Hayden | 63.157s | 18 |
| 18 | Tommy Bridewell | 63.298s | 18 |
| 19 | Akira Yanagawa | 80.285s | 18 |
| 20 | Matteo Baiocco | 80.419s | 18 |
| | Michel Fabrizio | DNF | 14 |
| | Broc Parkes | DNF | 7 |
| | Max Neukirchner | DNF | 6 |
| | Troy Corser | DNF | 1 |

**Superpole**

| | | |
|---|---|---|
| 1 | Crutchlow | 2m 04.091s |
| 2 | Rea | 2m 04.763s |
| 3 | Fabrizio | 2m 05.083s |
| 4 | Smrz | 2m 05.168s |
| 5 | Haslam | 2m 05.595s |
| 6 | Biaggi | 2m 05.682s |
| 7 | Corser | 2m 05.740s |
| 8 | Xaus | 2m 06.787s |
| 9 | Byrne | 2m 05.026s |
| 10 | Checa | 2m 05.035s |
| 11 | Guintoli | 2m 05.066s |
| 12 | Toseland | 2m 05.397s |
| 13 | Sykes | 2m 05.564s |
| 14 | Lanzi | 2m 05.903s |
| 15 | Haga | 2m 06.425s |
| 16 | Camier | 2m 10.663s |
| 17 | Brookes | 2m 06.271s |
| 18 | Neukirchner | 2m 07.041s |
| 19 | Parkes | 2m 07.636s |
| 20 | Scassa | |

**Points**

| | | |
|---|---|---|
| 1 | Biaggi | 373 |
| 2 | Haslam | 313 |
| 3 | Rea | 243 |
| 4 | Checa | 204 |
| 5 | Crutchlow | 188 |
| 6 | Toseland | 179 |
| 7 | Haga | 177 |
| 8 | Camier | 164 |
| 9 | Fabrizio | 160 |
| 10 | Corser | 155 |
| 11 | Guintoli | 151 |
| 12 | Byrne | 123 |
| 13 | Smrz | 71 |
| 14 | Xaus | 69 |
| 15 | Scassa | 53 |
| 16 | Sykes | 50 |
| 17 | Lanzi | 46 |
| 18 | Neukirchner | 40 |
| 19 | Vermeulen | 10 |
| 20 | Parkes | 9 |
| 21 | Hayden | 7 |
| 22 | Brookes | 6 |
| 23 | Morais | 3 |
| 24 | Baiocco | 3 |
| 25 | Pitt | 3 |

**Fastest race lap:** Cal Crutchlow on lap 13, 2m 05.259s, 105.401mph/169.626km/h (record).

**Fastest race lap:** Cal Crutchlow on lap 17, 2m 05.421s, 105.265mph/169.407km/h.
**Previous lap record:** New circuit.

---

**Race 1:** 20 laps, 63.840m/102.740km
**Time of race:** 38m 42.640s · **Average speed:** 98.949mph/159.243km/h

| Pos. | Rider | Nat. | No. | Entrant | Machine | Tyres | Time & Gap | Laps |
|---|---|---|---|---|---|---|---|---|
| 1 | Jonathan Rea | GBR | 65 | HANNspree Ten Kate Honda | Honda CBR1000RR | P | | 20 |
| 2 | Carlos Checa | SPA | 7 | Althea Racing | Ducati 1198 | P | 1.126s | 20 |
| 3 | Cal Crutchlow | GBR | 35 | Yamaha Sterilgarda Team | Yamaha YZF-R1 | P | 10.006s | 20 |
| 4 | Max Biaggi | ITA | 3 | Aprilia Alitalia Racing | Aprilia RSV4 1000 F | P | 10.716s | 20 |
| 5 | Tom Sykes | GBR | 66 | Kawasaki Racing Team | Kawasaki ZX-10R | P | 17.391s | 20 |
| 6 | Leon Haslam | GBR | 91 | Team Suzuki Alstare | Suzuki GSX-R1000 | P | 19.301s | 20 |
| 7 | Ruben Xaus | SPA | 111 | BMW Motorrad Motorsport | BMW S1000RR | P | 19.613s | 20 |
| 8 | Sylvain Guintoli | FRA | 50 | Team Suzuki Alstare | Suzuki GSX-R1000 | P | 19.880s | 20 |
| 9 | Shane Byrne | GBR | 67 | Althea Racing | Ducati 1198 | P | 21.176s | 20 |
| 10 | Luca Scassa | ITA | 99 | Supersonic Racing Team | Ducati 1198 | P | 29.752s | 20 |
| 11 | Lorenzo Lanzi | ITA | 57 | DFX Corse | Ducati 1198 | P | 30.156s | 20 |
| 12 | Ian Lowry | GBR | 5 | Kawasaki Racing Team | Kawasaki ZX-10R | P | 53.622s | 20 |
| 13 | Roger Lee Hayden | USA | 95 | Team Pedercini | Kawasaki ZX-10R | P | 58.82s | 20 |
| 14 | Matteo Baiocco | ITA | 15 | Team Pedercini | Kawasaki ZX-10R | P | 85.906s | 20 |
| | Fabrizio Lai | ITA | 33 | ECHO CRS Honda | Honda CBR1000RR | P | DNF | 19 |
| | Michel Fabrizio | ITA | 84 | Ducati Xerox Team | Ducati 1198 | P | DNF | 12 |
| | Noriyuki Haga | JPN | 41 | Ducati Xerox Team | Ducati 1198 | P | DNF | 8 |
| | Jakub Smrz | CZE | 96 | Team PATA B&G Racing | Aprilia RSV4 1000 F | P | DNF | 6 |
| | Troy Corser | AUS | 11 | BMW Motorrad Motorsport | BMW S1000RR | P | DNF | 6 |
| | Max Neukirchner | GER | 76 | HANNspree Ten Kate Honda | Honda CBR1000RR | P | DNF | 6 |
| | James Toseland | GBR | 52 | Yamaha Sterilgarda Team | Yamaha YZF-R1 | P | DNF | 1 |

**Race 2:** 20 laps, 63.840m/102.740km
**Time of race:** 38m 43.565s · **Average speed:** 98.910mph/159.180km/h

| Pos. | Rider | Time & Gap | Laps |
|---|---|---|---|
| 1 | Noriyuki Haga | | 20 |
| 2 | Jonathan Rea | 3.061s | 20 |
| 3 | Leon Haslam | 8.060s | 20 |
| 4 | Cal Crutchlow | 8.457s | 20 |
| 5 | Max Biaggi | 9.392s | 20 |
| 6 | Sylvain Guintoli | 9.556s | 20 |
| 7 | Tom Sykes | 16.819s | 20 |
| 8 | James Toseland | 20.564s | 20 |
| 9 | Ruben Xaus | 21.040s | 20 |
| 10 | Shane Byrne | 21.168s | 20 |
| 11 | Jakub Smrz | 21.734s | 20 |
| 12 | Troy Corser | 22.746s | 20 |
| 13 | Lorenzo Lanzi | 24.526s | 20 |
| 14 | Luca Scassa | 28.218s | 20 |
| 15 | Max Neukirchner | 38.406s | 20 |
| 16 | Roger Lee Hayden | 68.039s | 20 |
| 17 | Matteo Baiocco | 81.294s | 20 |
| 18 | Fabrizio Lai | 81.362s | 20 |
| 19 | Michel Fabrizio | 98.427s | 20 |
| | Ian Lowry | DNF | 11 |
| | Carlos Checa | DNF | 9 |

**Superpole**

| | | |
|---|---|---|
| 1 | Biaggi | 1m 54.595s |
| 2 | Checa | 1m 54.621s |
| 3 | Guintoli | 1m 54.934s |
| 4 | Rea | 1m 55.138s |
| 5 | Haslam | 1m 55.161s |
| 6 | Haga | 1m 55.276s |
| 7 | Sykes | 1m 55.378s |
| 8 | Toseland | 1m 54.909s* |
| *penalty | | |
| 9 | Fabrizio | 1m 55.264s |
| 10 | Crutchlow | 1m 55.295s |
| 11 | Xaus | 1m 55.375s |
| 12 | Lanzi | 1m 55.524s |
| 13 | Smrz | 1m 55.577s |
| 14 | Corser | 1m 55.599s |
| 15 | Neukirchner | 1m 55.735s |
| 16 | Scassa | 1m 55.908s |
| 17 | Byrne | 1m 56.457s |
| 18 | Hayden | 1m 57.613s |
| 19 | Lowry | 1m 57.669s |

**Points**

| | | |
|---|---|---|
| 1 | Biaggi | 397 |
| 2 | Haslam | 339 |
| 3 | Rea | 288 |
| 4 | Checa | 224 |
| 5 | Crutchlow | 217 |
| 6 | Haga | 202 |
| 7 | Toseland | 187 |
| 8 | Guintoli | 169 |
| 9 | Camier | 164 |
| 10 | Fabrizio | 160 |
| 11 | Corser | 159 |
| 12 | Byrne | 136 |
| 13 | Xaus | 85 |
| 14 | Smrz | 76 |
| 15 | Sykes | 70 |
| 16 | Scassa | 61 |
| 17 | Lanzi | 54 |
| 18 | Neukirchner | 41 |
| 19 | Hayden | 10 |
| 20 | Vermeulen | 10 |
| 21 | Parkes | 9 |
| 22 | Brookes | 6 |
| 23 | Baiocco | 5 |
| 24 | Lowry | 4 |
| 25 | Morais | 3 |
| 26 | Pitt | 3 |

**Fastest race lap:** : Jonathan Rea on lap 5, 1m 55.392s, 99.583mph/160.264km/h (record).

**Fastest race lap:** Jonathan Rea on lap 2, 1m 55.502s, 99.489mph/160.112km/h.
**Previous lap record:** Jonathan Rea, GBR (Honda), 1m 56.234s, 98.860mph/159.100km/h (2009).

# 2010 WORLD SUPERBIKE CHAMPIONSHIP RESULTS

## Round 12 · IMOLA, Italy · 26 September 2010 · 3.067mile/4.936km circuit · WEATHER: Race 1 · Dry · Track 28°C · Air 21°C; Race 2 · Dry · Track 41°C · Air 25°C

**Race 1:** 21 laps, 64.409m/103.656km
Time of race: 38m 27.631s · Average speed: 100.481mph/161.708km/h

| Pos. | Rider | Nat. | No. | Entrant | Machine | Tyres | Time & Gap | Laps |
|---|---|---|---|---|---|---|---|---|
| 1 | **Carlos Checa** | SPA | 7 | Althea Racing | Ducati 1198 | P | | 21 |
| 2 | **Lorenzo Lanzi** | ITA | 57 | DFX Corse | Ducati 1198 | P | 1.171s | 21 |
| 3 | **Noriyuki Haga** | JPN | 41 | Ducati Xerox Team | Ducati 1198 | P | 1.472s | 21 |
| 4 | **Jakub Smrz** | CZE | 96 | Team PATA B&G Racing | Aprilia RSV4 1000 F | P | 6.691s | 21 |
| 5 | **Leon Haslam** | GBR | 91 | Team Suzuki Alstare | Suzuki GSX-R1000 | P | 9.584s | 21 |
| 6 | **Tom Sykes** | GBR | 66 | Kawasaki Racing Team | Kawasaki ZX-10R | P | 10.979s | 21 |
| 7 | **Michel Fabrizio** | ITA | 84 | Ducati Xerox Team | Ducati 1198 | P | 15.023s | 21 |
| 8 | **Shane Byrne** | GBR | 67 | Althea Racing | Ducati 1198 | P | 15.913s | 21 |
| 9 | **Sylvain Guintoli** | FRA | 50 | Team Suzuki Alstare | Suzuki GSX-R1000 | P | 17.025s | 21 |
| 10 | **Cal Crutchlow** | GBR | 35 | Yamaha Sterilgarda Team | Yamaha YZF-R1 | P | 20.795s | 21 |
| 11 | **Max Biaggi** | ITA | 3 | Aprilia Alitalia Racing | Aprilia RSV4 1000 F | P | 21.243s | 21 |
| 12 | **Ruben Xaus** | SPA | 111 | BMW Motorrad Motorsport | BMW S1000RR | P | 25.860s | 21 |
| 13 | **Luca Scassa** | ITA | 99 | Supersonic Racing Team | Ducati 1198 | P | 31.551s | 21 |
| 14 | **Max Neukirchner** | GER | 76 | HANNspree Ten Kate Honda | Honda CBR1000RR | P | 31.689s | 21 |
| 15 | **Troy Corser** | AUS | 11 | BMW Motorrad Motorsport | BMW S1000RR | P | 44.349s | 21 |
| 16 | Federico Sandi | ITA | 90 | Gabrielli Racing Team | Aprilia RSV4 1000 F | P | 58.693s | 21 |
| 17 | Ian Lowry | GBR | 5 | Kawasaki Racing Team | Kawasaki ZX-10R | P | 70.388s | 21 |
| 18 | Matteo Baiocco | ITA | 15 | Team Pedercini | Kawasaki ZX-10R | P | 73.648s | 21 |
| 19 | Fabrizio Lai | ITA | 33 | ECHO CRS Honda | Honda CBR1000RR | P | 75.939s | 21 |
| | James Toseland | GBR | 52 | Yamaha Sterilgarda Team | Yamaha YZF-R1 | P | DNF | 7 |
| | Roger Lee Hayden | USA | 95 | Team Pedercini | Kawasaki ZX-10R | P | DNF | 1 |

**Fastest race lap:** Leon Haslam on lap 13, 1m 48.966s, 101.330mph/163.075km/h.

**Race 2:** 21 laps, 64.409m/103.656km
Time of race: 38m 24.452s · Average speed: 100.619mph/161.931km/h

| Pos. | Rider | Time & Gap | Laps |
|---|---|---|---|
| 1 | **Carlos Checa** | | 21 |
| 2 | **Noriyuki Haga** | 2.129s | 21 |
| 3 | **Cal Crutchlow** | 3.926s | 21 |
| 4 | **Tom Sykes** | 5.762s | 21 |
| 5 | **Max Biaggi** | 7.025s | 21 |
| 6 | **Shane Byrne** | 12.147s | 21 |
| 7 | **Lorenzo Lanzi** | 14.212s | 21 |
| 8 | **Sylvain Guintoli** | 18.029s | 21 |
| 9 | **Ruben Xaus** | 18.249s | 21 |
| 10 | **Luca Scassa** | 19.446s | 21 |
| 11 | **Troy Corser** | 23.674s | 21 |
| 12 | **Max Neukirchner** | 34.804s | 21 |
| 13 | **Federico Sandi** | 53.540s | 21 |
| 14 | **Fabrizio Lai** | 63.102s | 21 |
| 15 | **Matteo Baiocco** | 67.185s | 21 |
| 16 | Ian Lowry | 68.926s | 21 |
| | Michel Fabrizio | DNF | 13 |
| | Leon Haslam | DNF | 10 |
| | Jakub Smrz | DNF | 9 |
| | Roger Lee Hayden | DNF | 9 |
| | James Toseland | DNF | 3 |

| Superpole | |
|---|---|
| 1 Sykes | 2m 07.341s |
| 2 Smrz | 2m 07.392s |
| 3 Haslam | 2m 08.273s |
| 4 Scassa | 2m 08.427s |
| 5 Lanzi | 2m 08.490s |
| 6 Corser | 2m 09.842s |
| 7 Biaggi | 2m 09.924s |
| 8 Xaus | 2m 10.482s |
| 9 Checa | 2m 11.117s |
| 10 Fabrizio | 2m 11.130s |
| 11 Neukirchner | 2m 11.150s |
| 12 Crutchlow | 2m 11.271s |
| 13 Byrne | 2m 11.395s |
| 14 Rea | 2m 11.558s |
| 15 Haga | 2m 11.601s |
| 16 Guintoli | 2m 11.706s |
| 17 Toseland | 2m 13.823s |
| 18 Hayden | 2m 15.026s |
| 19 Lai | 2m 15.268s |
| 20 Sandi | 2m 20.464s |

| Points | | |
|---|---|---|
| 1 | Biaggi | 413 |
| 2 | Haslam | 350 |
| 3 | Rea | 288 |
| 4 | Checa | 274 |
| 5 | Crutchlow | 239 |
| 6 | Haga | 238 |
| 7 | Toseland | 187 |
| 8 | Guintoli | 184 |
| 9 | Fabrizio | 169 |
| 10 | Corser | 165 |
| 11 | Camier | 164 |
| 12 | Byrne | 154 |
| 13 | Xaus | 96 |
| 14 | Sykes | 93 |
| 15 | Smrz | 89 |
| 16 | Lanzi | 83 |
| 17 | Scassa | 70 |
| 18 | Neukirchner | 47 |
| 19 | Hayden | 10 |
| 20 | Vermeulen | 10 |
| 21 | Parkes | 9 |
| 22 | Brookes | 6 |
| 23 | Baiocco | 6 |
| 24 | Lowry | 4 |
| 25 | Sandi | 3 |
| 26 | Morais | 3 |
| 27 | Pitt | 3 |
| 28 | Lai | 2 |

**Fastest race lap:** Carlos Checa on lap 7, 1m 48.877s, 101.413mph/163.208km/h (record).
**Previous lap record:** Noriyuki Haga, JPN (Ducati), 1m 48.982s, 101.315mph/163.050km/h (2009).

## Round 13 · MAGNY-COURS, France · 3 October 2010 · 2.741mile/4.411km circuit · WEATHER: Race 1 · Dry · Track 28°C · Air 23°C; Race 2 · Dry · Track 35°C · Air 25°C

**Race 1:** 23 laps, 63.040m/101.453km
Time of race: 38m 15.586s · Average speed: 98.861mph/159.101km/h

| Pos. | Rider | Nat. | No. | Entrant | Machine | Tyres | Time & Gap | Laps |
|---|---|---|---|---|---|---|---|---|
| 1 | **Cal Crutchlow** | GBR | 35 | Yamaha Sterilgarda Team | Yamaha YZF-R1 | P | | 23 |
| 2 | **Leon Haslam** | GBR | 91 | Team Suzuki Alstare | Suzuki GSX-R1000 | P | 3.779s | 23 |
| 3 | **Carlos Checa** | SPA | 7 | Althea Racing | Ducati 1198 | P | 4.261s | 23 |
| 4 | **Max Biaggi** | ITA | 3 | Aprilia Alitalia Racing | Aprilia RSV4 1000 F | P | 4.416s | 23 |
| 5 | **Jakub Smrz** | CZE | 96 | Team PATA B&G Racing | Aprilia RSV4 1000 F | P | 7.476s | 23 |
| 6 | **Michel Fabrizio** | ITA | 84 | Ducati Xerox Team | Ducati 1198 | P | 11.866s | 23 |
| 7 | **Noriyuki Haga** | JPN | 41 | Ducati Xerox Team | Ducati 1198 | P | 16.390s | 23 |
| 8 | **Tom Sykes** | GBR | 66 | Kawasaki Racing Team | Kawasaki ZX-10R | P | 21.669s | 23 |
| 9 | **Shane Byrne** | GBR | 67 | Althea Racing | Ducati 1198 | P | 22.065s | 23 |
| 10 | **Luca Scassa** | ITA | 99 | Supersonic Racing Team | Ducati 1198 | P | 22.281s | 23 |
| 11 | **Lorenzo Lanzi** | ITA | 57 | DFX Corse | Ducati 1198 | P | 26.748s | 23 |
| 12 | **Jonathan Rea** | GBR | 65 | HANNspree Ten Kate Honda | Honda CBR1000RR | P | 35.608s | 23 |
| 13 | **Max Neukirchner** | GER | 76 | HANNspree Ten Kate Honda | Honda CBR1000RR | P | 39.929s | 23 |
| 14 | **Ian Lowry** | GBR | 5 | Kawasaki Racing Team | Kawasaki ZX-10R | P | 54.836s | 23 |
| 15 | **Matteo Baiocco** | ITA | 15 | Team Pedercini | Kawasaki ZX-10R | P | 67.191s | 23 |
| 16 | Fabrizio Lai | ITA | 33 | ECHO CRS Honda | Honda CBR1000RR | P | 74.632s | 23 |
| | Roger Lee Hayden | USA | 95 | Team Pedercini | Kawasaki ZX-10R | P | DNF | 20 |
| | Troy Corser | AUS | 11 | BMW Motorrad Motorsport | BMW S1000RR | P | DNF | 7 |
| | James Toseland | GBR | 52 | Yamaha Sterilgarda Team | Yamaha YZF-R1 | P | DNF | 3 |
| | Ruben Xaus | SPA | 111 | BMW Motorrad Motorsport | BMW S1000-RR | P | DNF | 3 |
| | Sylvain Guintoli | FRA | 50 | Team Suzuki Alstare | Suzuki GSX-R1000 | P | DSQ | 23 |

**Fastest race lap:** Cal Crutchlow on lap 3, 1m 38.781s, 99.889mph/160.756km/h.

**Race 2:** 23 laps, 63.040m/101.453km
Time of race: 38m 11.343s · Average speed: 99.044mph/159.396km/h

| Pos. | Rider | Time & Gap | Laps |
|---|---|---|---|
| 1 | **Max Biaggi** | | 23 |
| 2 | **Cal Crutchlow** | 0.087s | 23 |
| 3 | **Michel Fabrizio** | 3.715s | 23 |
| 4 | **Sylvain Guintoli** | 4.004s | 23 |
| 5 | **Noriyuki Haga** | 15.471s | 23 |
| 6 | **Jakub Smrz** | 18.378s | 23 |
| 7 | **Luca Scassa** | 21.180s | 23 |
| 8 | **Shane Byrne** | 23.055s | 23 |
| 9 | **Carlos Checa** | 25.657s | 23 |
| 10 | **Leon Haslam** | 27.781s | 23 |
| 11 | **Tom Sykes** | 28.206s | 23 |
| 12 | **Max Neukirchner** | 44.634s | 23 |
| 13 | **Ian Lowry** | 64.181s | 23 |
| 14 | **Matteo Baiocco** | 76.446s | 23 |
| | Lorenzo Lanzi | DNF | 17 |
| | Roger Lee Hayden | DNF | 9 |
| | James Toseland | DNF | 4 |
| | Troy Corser | DNF | 4 |
| | Fabrizio Lai | DNF | 4 |
| | Jonathan Rea | DNS | |
| | Ruben Xaus | DNS | |

| Superpole | |
|---|---|
| 1 Crutchlow | 1m 37.699s |
| 2 Guintoli | 1m 37.768s |
| 3 Smrz | 1m 37.784s |
| 4 Biaggi | 1m 38.039s |
| 5 Fabrizio | 1m 38.082s |
| 6 Rea | 1m 38.155s |
| 7 Checa | 1m 38.252s |
| 8 Haga | 1m 38.421s |
| 9 Corser | 1m 38.250s |
| 10 Haslam | 1m 38.327s |
| 11 Xaus | 1m 38.364s |
| 12 Sykes | 1m 38.370s |
| 13 Lanzi | 1m 38.519s |
| 14 Byrne | 1m 38.538s |
| 15 Toseland | 1m 38.551s |
| 16 Scassa | 1m 38.585s |
| 17 Neukirchner | 1m 39.341s |
| 18 Lowry | 1m 40.278s |
| 19 Baiocco | 1m 40.890s |
| 20 Lai | 1m 41.471s |

| Points | | |
|---|---|---|
| 1 | Biaggi | 451 |
| 2 | Haslam | 376 |
| 3 | Checa | 297 |
| 4 | Rea | 292 |
| 5 | Crutchlow | 284 |
| 6 | Haga | 258 |
| 7 | Guintoli | 197 |
| 8 | Fabrizio | 195 |
| 9 | Toseland | 187 |
| 10 | Byrne | 169 |
| 11 | Corser | 165 |
| 12 | Camier | 164 |
| 13 | Smrz | 110 |
| 14 | Sykes | 106 |
| 15 | Xaus | 96 |
| 16 | Lanzi | 88 |
| 17 | Scassa | 85 |
| 18 | Neukirchner | 54 |
| 19 | Hayden | 10 |
| 20 | Vermeulen | 10 |
| 21 | Lowry | 9 |
| 22 | Parkes | 9 |
| 23 | Baiocco | 9 |
| 24 | Brookes | 6 |
| 25 | Sandi | 3 |
| 26 | Morais | 3 |
| 27 | Pitt | 3 |
| 28 | Lai | 2 |

**Fastest race lap:** Cal Crutchlow on lap 5, 1m 38.879s, 99.790mph/160.596km/h.
**Lap record:** Noriyuki Haga, JPN (Ducati), 1m 38.619s, 100.053mph/161.020km/h (2009).

| Position | Rider | Nationality | Machine | Phillip Island/1 | Phillip Island/2 | Portimão/1 | Portimão/2 | Valencia/1 | Valencia/2 | Assen/1 | Assen/2 | Monza/1 | Monza/2 | Kyalami/1 | Kyalami/2 | Utah/1 | Utah/2 | Misano/1 | Misano/2 | Brno/1 | Brno/2 | Silverstone/1 | Silverstone/2 | Nürburgring/1 | Nürburgring/2 | Imola/1 | Imola/2 | Magny-Cours/1 | Magny-Cours/2 | Total Points |
|---|---|---|---|---|---|---|---|---|---|---|---|---|---|---|---|---|---|---|---|---|---|---|---|---|---|---|---|---|---|---|
| 1 | **Max Biaggi** | ITA | Aprilia | 11 | 8 | 25 | 25 | 20 | 16 | 10 | 13 | 25 | 25 | 13 | 16 | 25 | 25 | 25 | 25 | 20 | 25 | 11 | 10 | 13 | 11 | 5 | 11 | 13 | 25 | **451** |
| 2 | **Leon Haslam** | GBR | Suzuki | 25 | 20 | 20 | 20 | 25 | 13 | 5 | 20 | 13 | 20 | 16 | 25 | 20 | – | 8 | 20 | 8 | 6 | 16 | 13 | 10 | 16 | 11 | – | 20 | 6 | **376** |
| 3 | **Carlos Checa** | SPA | Ducati | 9 | 25 | 13 | 13 | – | 20 | 13 | 10 | 2 | 5 | 20 | 11 | – | – | 20 | 11 | 7 | 10 | 9 | 6 | 20 | – | 25 | 25 | 16 | 7 | **297** |
| 4 | **Jonathan Rea** | GBR | Honda | 13 | 10 | 16 | – | 10 | 11 | 25 | 25 | – | – | 11 | 20 | 2 | 8 | 3 | 4 | 25 | 20 | 20 | 20 | 25 | 20 | – | – | 4 | – | **292** |
| 5 | **Cal Crutchlow** | GBR | Yamaha | – | 7 | 2 | 16 | 9 | 7 | 8 | – | 16 | – | 8 | 13 | 5 | 16 | – | 13 | 16 | 2 | 25 | 25 | 16 | 13 | 6 | 16 | 25 | 20 | **284** |
| 6 | **Noriyuki Haga** | JPN | Ducati | 16 | 11 | 8 | 8 | 11 | 25 | 6 | – | 5 | 10 | – | 6 | 13 | 9 | 7 | 10 | 11 | 2 | 3 | – | 25 | 16 | 20 | 9 | 16 | 11 | **258** |
| 7 | **Sylvain Guintoli** | FRA | Suzuki | 10 | 13 | 3 | 7 | 7 | 10 | 2 | 3 | 6 | 9 | 6 | 1 | 8 | 10 | 11 | 10 | 13 | 9 | 4 | 9 | 8 | 10 | 7 | 8 | – | 13 | **197** |
| 8 | **Michel Fabrizio** | ITA | Ducati | 20 | 16 | 5 | 5 | – | – | 3 | 4 | 9 | – | 25 | 8 | – | 7 | 13 | 16 | – | 16 | 13 | – | – | – | 9 | – | 10 | 16 | **195** |
| 9 | **James Toseland** | GBR | Yamaha | – | 6 | 9 | 10 | 16 | 9 | 20 | 16 | 20 | – | 9 | 10 | 7 | – | 6 | – | 9 | 13 | 8 | 11 | – | 8 | – | – | – | – | **187** |
| 10 | **Shane Byrne** | GBR | Ducati | 2 | 4 | 10 | 9 | – | 8 | 7 | 8 | 3 | 7 | 1 | 3 | 10 | 9 | 7 | 9 | 4 | 7 | 8 | 7 | 6 | 8 | 8 | 10 | 7 | 8 | **169** |
| 11 | **Troy Corser** | AUS | BMW | 7 | 9 | 7 | 6 | 13 | 4 | 11 | 11 | 8 | 16 | 4 | 9 | 11 | 11 | 16 | 6 | – | – | 6 | – | 4 | 1 | 5 | – | – | – | **165** |
| 12 | **Leon Camier** | GBR | Aprilia | 5 | 5 | 11 | 11 | – | – | 16 | – | 11 | 13 | 10 | – | 13 | 20 | 10 | 5 | – | 8 | 10 | 16 | – | – | – | – | – | – | **164** |
| 13 | **Jakub Smrz** | CZE | Ducati Aprilia | 8 | – | – | – | 6 | 6 | 9 | 9 | 1 | 8 | 7 | 7 | – | – | – | – | – | – | 3 | 7 | – | 5 | 13 | – | 11 | 10 | **110** |
| 14 | **Tom Sykes** | GBR | Kawasaki | 3 | – | 1 | 3 | 5 | 1 | 4 | – | 7 | 11 | – | 2 | 3 | 2 | 1 | – | 5 | – | – | 2 | 11 | 9 | 10 | 13 | 8 | 5 | **106** |
| 15 | **Ruben Xaus** | SPA | BMW | – | – | 6 | 4 | 4 | 5 | – | 6 | 10 | – | 2 | 5 | 6 | 5 | – | – | 11 | – | 5 | 9 | 7 | 4 | 7 | – | – | – | **96** |
| 16 | **Lorenzo Lanzi** | ITA | Ducati | 6 | 3 | 4 | 2 | 8 | 3 | – | – | – | – | – | – | – | – | 4 | 3 | 6 | 5 | 1 | 1 | 5 | 3 | 20 | 9 | 5 | – | **88** |
| 17 | **Luca Scassa** | ITA | Ducati | – | – | – | – | 2 | 2 | 1 | 5 | – | 6 | 5 | 4 | 9 | 6 | 5 | 8 | – | – | – | – | 6 | 2 | 3 | 6 | 6 | 9 | **85** |
| 18 | **Max Neukirchner** | GER | Honda | 4 | – | – | 1 | 3 | – | – | 7 | 4 | 4 | – | 4 | 4 | 2 | 2 | – | – | – | 5 | – | – | 1 | 2 | 4 | 3 | 4 | **54** |
| 19 | **Roger Lee Hayden** | USA | Kawasaki | – | – | – | – | – | – | – | – | – | 2 | – | – | – | – | – | – | 2 | 3 | – | 3 | – | – | – | – | – | – | **10** |
| 20 | **Chris Vermeulen** | AUS | Kawasaki | – | – | – | – | – | – | 2 | – | 3 | – | 1 | 3 | – | 1 | – | – | – | – | – | – | – | – | – | – | – | – | **10** |
| 21 | **Ian Lowry** | GBR | Kawasaki | – | – | – | – | – | – | – | – | – | – | – | – | – | – | – | – | – | – | – | 4 | – | – | – | – | 2 | 3 | **9** |
| 22 | **Broc Parkes** | AUS | Honda | – | – | – | – | – | – | – | – | – | 1 | – | – | – | 1 | – | – | 3 | 4 | – | – | – | – | – | – | – | – | **9** |
| 23 | **Matteo Baiocco** | ITA | Kawasaki | – | – | – | – | – | – | – | 1 | – | – | – | – | – | – | – | – | 1 | 1 | – | – | 2 | – | – | 1 | 1 | 2 | **9** |
| 24 | **Josh Brookes** | AUS | Honda | – | 2 | – | – | – | – | – | – | – | – | – | – | – | – | – | – | – | – | – | 4 | – | – | – | – | – | – | **6** |
| 25 | **Federico Sandi** | ITA | Aprilia | – | – | – | – | – | – | – | – | – | – | – | – | – | – | – | – | – | – | – | – | – | – | – | 3 | – | – | **3** |
| 26 | **Sheridan Morais** | RSA | Aprilia | – | – | – | – | – | – | – | – | – | – | 3 | – | – | – | – | – | – | – | – | – | – | – | – | – | – | – | **3** |
| 27 | **Andrew Pitt** | AUS | BMW | 1 | 1 | – | – | 1 | – | – | – | – | – | – | – | – | – | – | – | – | – | – | – | – | – | – | – | – | – | **3** |
| 28 | **Fabrizio Lai** | ITA | Honda | – | – | – | – | – | – | – | – | – | – | – | – | – | – | – | – | – | – | – | – | – | – | – | 2 | – | – | **2** |

# CONSISTENCY TRUMPS VELOCITY

By GORDON RITCHIE

*Above:* At full lean, Laverty and Sofuoglu trade paint.

*Above right, clockwise from top:* Chaz Davies found his feet on the Triumph; Ulsterman Eugene Laverty won the most races; Spaniard Joan Lascorz had his season ruined by injury; victorious Turk Sofuoglu ice-packs his wrist.

*Right:* Pirro took a win at Imola after Laverty and Sofuoglu clashed.

*Below right:* Runaway Superstock 1000 FIM Cup winner Ayrton Badovini.
*Photos:* Gold & Goose

IT'S difficult to see how eventual World Supersport champion Kenan Sofuoglu (Hannspree Ten Kate Honda) could have missed out on the title, having scored a podium finish in every race of the 2010 season.

It's also difficult for a rider who wins eight of 13 rounds not to be crowned champion, but that's what happened to overall second-place man Eugene Laverty (Parkalgar Honda).

It's unusual, too, for a rider who scored no points at all in the last four rounds of a championsip to take third, but that was the bitter-sweet experience of Joan Lascorz (Provec Motocard.com Kawasaki).

In 2009, there was a clear big two in the final championship fight. For the 2010 season, it was a trio from the outset. But for a horrible accident involving Lascorz, it was still shaping up for a three-rider sort-out at the final round in France.

Even though other riders took podium finishes, and Sofuoglu's team-mate, Michele Pirro, was gifted a whole race win at Imola, the real story of 2010 was a trilogy, scripted in three distinct languages.

Triumph's Italian-based BE1 squad brought four regular machines and a host of irregular rider line-ups to the party, the best pairing being Chaz Davies and a ParkinGO Triumph BE-1 Daytona 675.

Elsewhere, there were no regular top-line Suzukis or Yamahas. Despite this, there were some solid efforts from such old stagers as Fabien Foret (Lorenzini by Leoni Kawasaki), Robbin Harms (Harms Benjan Racing Honda) and Katsuaki Fujiwara, team-mate to Lascorz. Names, famous and less so, came and went, particularly in the vast Triumph encampment.

In Australia, at the first of 13 rounds, the suspected big three drew themselves up to their full height, but Laverty cast the longest shadow. Lascorz, who had been on pole, was second, taking an early advantage against Sofuoglu, who was 0.141 second back in third.

Triumph's expected finishing order was upset by the supposed second string, with David Salom (ParkinGO BE-1 Triumph) fourth, his team-mate Jason DiSalvo eighth. The lead ParkinGO Triumph BE-1 duo of Chaz Davies and surprise comeback legend Sébastien Charpentier were only 12th and 13th. Charpentier, realising a return had maybe not been his best idea, left soon after, making way for fellow Frenchman, Matthieu Lagrive.

Round two was a home event for Laverty's Parkalgar team. It started well, with Laverty on pole, but he would fall after clipping a kerb, restarting to finish 11th. Front-row men Sofuoglu and Lascorz squeezed themselves across the line within 0.031 second of each other, Sofuoglu the victor. Michele Pirro (Hannspree Ten Kate Honda), who had been forced out by a tyre woe in Phillip Island, went third. Davies was fourth, Foret fifth and Fujiwara sixth.

Home advantage worked for Lascorz in Spain, where he beat Sofuoglu by over three seconds, with Laverty fifth. Davies was third, by no means his last trip to the top steps. Only 12 riders finished, showing the lack of depth in the middle to lower orders in particular.

The polar opposite of Valencia in general track design, Assen delivered a demonstration of just how far the big three were ahead, with Laverty out front, Lascorz second and Sofuoglu a shadow in third across the famous old finish line. Davies, now a fully fledged WSS rider it appeared, was fourth, but 23 seconds from the win.

At Monza, it was the same tearaway top three again, by some distance. Laverty from Sofuoglu and Lascorz.

By some miracle, the triangle was broken at Kyalami: Laverty won again, by 4.1 seconds, with Sofuoglu the same distance ahead of Davies. Lascorz was a disappointed fifth, just not finding a strong race set-up.

America provided a great WSS race for the watching fans, as Sofuoglu motivated himself to the win by just over a sec-

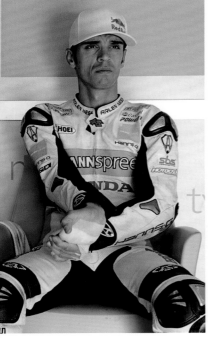

When the Silverstone race was finally run, Laverty was the victor by a squeaking 0.220 second, from Sofuoglu. Third for Rea was a career best and would be a season best. Davies was fourth, Harms fifth.

The loss of Lascorz had an immediate effect on the outcome of the championship. The fight was now between Sofuoglu and Laverty.

The issue for Laverty was no longer having any potential buffer between himself and Sofuoglu, to rob the former champion of more than five points each round. Laverty looked capable of winning every race now, but even taking all three remaining victories, with Sofuoglu second each time, would not deliver the Parkalgar rider the title. What he needed was another top-level rider to take the role left vacant by Lascorz.

Initially, Rea stepped forward, taking a very close second at the very next round, with Laverty winning and Sofuoglu five seconds adrift. However, a technical inspection after the race relegated Rea out of the running altogether, when it was discovered that his bike had an illegal modification that reduced crankcase pressure.

WSB refugee Broc Parkes had replaced Lascorz in the official Kawasaki squad, and had started well; his fourth in Germany became a podium finish after Rea's exclusion, although he had not stood on it. Maybe Broc would be the rider who would split Sofuoglu from Laverty, thought the Parkalgar crew.

He would not, and that fact contributed to what Eugene did at the next round.

A bizarre Imola race was not just noteworthy because Pirro, still nursing an injured wrist from his high-speed crash in Brno, won his first ever race in this category.

The strongest memory will not even be that Davies was cruelly robbed of the win, simply because he ran out of gas almost within sight of the flag, while ahead of eventual winner Pirro.

No, the most unforgettable sight of a sometimes-classic man-to-man fight was unveiled at the very last chicane, within spitting distance of the finish. Sofuoglu had taken a narrow lead that Laverty could not do anything about, entering the final flip-flop a few bike lengths back. Laverty, fatefully, went for the pass anyway. He lost the front mid-corner and skittled Sofuoglu; both went into the gravel unhurt. Sofuoglu recovered both composure and handlebars first, crossing the line second, Laverty third.

The finale to the season could only have been an anti-climax after that, with ten-lap leader Sofuoglu eventually content to finish behind race winner Laverty, as the title went to Turkey by 11-points. It was Kenan's second crown, and well deserved, after his and his team's unerring ability to podium, no matter what the circuit.

Lascorz was a remarkable third, despite missing four rounds. Davies was fourth overall, well clear of Pirro.

Ayrton Badovini (BMW Motorrad Italia STK) had the most remarkable season imaginable in the Superstock 1000 FIM Cup, winning nine out of ten races, only losing the final one to French rider Maxime Berger (Ten Kate Race Junior Honda) after he suffered pain from a few uncharacteristic pre-race crashes. Badovini was still second in the Magny-Cours race, finishing five points from perfection in a stunning first official year for the BMW S1000RR in this class.

Berger was second overall; Michele Magnoni fought off the blues caused by the early demise of his original Honda team by finishing third, after a final series of ostensibly one-off rides.

In the Superstock 600 European Championship, 17-year-old Frenchman Jeremy Guarnoni (MRS Racing Yamaha) took the title in Imola, after nine of ten rounds. He had won five races. Second-place Florian Marino (Ten Kate Race Junior Honda) won three, with wild-cards Luke Mossey and Jed Metcher taking the glory at Silverstone and Magny-Cours respectively.

ond. Laverty was runner-up, Lascorz third; only 1.6 seconds covered them all. Davies, at one of his old AMA hunting grounds, was fourth, 13 seconds adrift of the top step.

Misano, hot rather than outright blistering, was Laverty country; Lascorz was 3.8 seconds behind in second, Sofuoglu an off-form third, but still well ahead of Davies. Wild-card Roberto Tamburini (Bike Service RT Yamaha) was a good fifth.

If Portugal had been a reversal, Brno was a disaster for Laverty and his Parkalgar crew. Starting off the front row, he was in for the win until his engine gave out. Sofuoglu, utterly determined to take full points (despite a horridly deep gash in his elbow from a moped crash) held off Lascorz by only 0.124 second. He was lucky to be allowed to ride, but his fight against pain was utterly justified by 25 points. Davies won his private battle of Britain for the last podium place against reigning Superstock 600 European champion Gino Rea (Intermoto Czech Honda).

Rea, no relation to Jonathan, would go one better at Silverstone, finishing third in what was a pivotal race, for lots of the wrong reasons.

Off the start, Laverty and Lascorz tangled. The Spaniard's brake lever was pushed by the Honda's tail and he fell, sliding towards the run-off on the exit of Turn One in a sitting position. But the pack behind had been scattered, and the unfortunate Roberto Tamburini was unable to avoid Lascorz. The impact on the latter's back, neck and head was as hideous as it was obvious to all onlookers. Clearly, he was badly injured. Tamburini would suffer his own sickening impact, on the trackside wall, injuring a shoulder. Everyone feared the worst, but both riders 'escaped' to walk another day.

Lascorz's season ended abruptly as his injury tally became longer/shorter/longer in the hours and weeks that followed. Stretched nerves and ligaments in his left arm and upper torso were the longest lasting legacies of the day.

# BIG MONEY MAKES THE TT TASTIER

Ian Hutchinson, the 'Bingley Bullet', swept the record books with five wins in one TT week. MARK FORSYTH reports on how risk assessment has changed on the fast roads past the bankers' backyards.

IT'S a funny thing, crisis. The meltdown of the global economy and the knock-back effect on bike sales has actually changed racers' perceptions of risk. It's made them question what they do, how they do it and what they expect to earn. The golden days of short-circuit racing have clearly disappeared, with many top riders having to ride for little or no pay just to keep their abilities and names in the spotlight.

The TT is well placed to capitalise on this seismic shift of economic austerity. It's situated on a large rock equidistant between Ireland, Lancashire, Cumbria and the Galloway peninsular. Even though it's tied to the Crown, it governs itself. It has also established itself as a tax-efficient banking maverick and, as such, has become a mecca for offshore investment and tax avoidance, a haven for those looking to minimise their capital-gains tax exposure. The place is awash with money.

Racers on the mainland, doing battle in the once prestigious British Superbike series, are understandably feeling the pinch. They look to the TT and its enormous pay packets with wistful eyes.

On a good fortnight, a good race week, top TT riders can earn in excess of £100,000. "You only have to read the programme and work it out for yourself," said 2010's dominant force, Ian Hutchinson. He was, of course, referring to the prize money structure offered by the governing body: money paid for laps led, fastest lap and for the win. All information in the public domain.

What isn't publicised, however, are riders' private bonus structures: cash bonuses from their tyre company, helmet firm, leathers company, lubricant backer, motorhome pro-

vider, etc. There's a bumper payday for a successful TT racer, that's for sure. Let's guess – and it's a wild stab in the dark – that Hutchinson banked between £150,000 and £175,000 from his fortnight's endeavours on the Island in June. It might be too far north of the truth, but there's a whole load of impoverished BSB riders doing the same cack-handed sums and working out that once they've got 'the knowledge', they'll be enjoying mortgage-free futures – if they survive the apprenticeship.

After all, let's not skirt about the main issue: the TT is an extreme sport that makes others look pedestrian and a trifle silly. If you make a mistake, the chances are you'll be going home in a box, to quote a well-used Dave Jefferies phrase.

Again in 2010, North One TV did a fantastic job of reporting the comings and goings of race week with amazing action clips and incredible slo-mo coverage of the event. It went out on ITV4 as a slickly edited package and globally across the satellite channels. Manx firm Duke Marketing also did a remarkable job with its free-to-listen internet TT radio coverage and live data stream. The UK's top newspapers may completely ignore this massive event, but in all other forms of media, the TT enjoys far-reaching exposure.

A host of big-name sponsors have cashed in, too. The event was marginalised just ten years ago, but the organisers have lured global companies like Monster Energy, Dainese and Poker Stars to participate.

It's taken over 100 years, but at last the TT has realised its worth, capitalised on it and begun to reap the rewards. All racers know the risks of racing between the walls and telegraph poles, but the rewards are likely to attract some even bigger names in 2011.

*Above:* Record breaking five-times winner Ian Hutchinson heads out into the country from Union Mills.

*Right:* TT grand master John McGuinness had a week to forget.

*Below right:* Keith Amor en route to sixth on the HM Plant Honda Superbike.
*Photos:* Gavan Caldwell

## SUPERBIKE TT

In a weird quirk of Manx weather, the first race of the week was repeatedly delayed due to heavy mist in the Douglas area. For the spectators sitting eagerly around the rest of the circuit in brilliant sunshine and clear blue skies, it was a mystifying decision.

The three-and-a-half-hour delay can't have helped Hutchinson's confidence. The night before, during his first practice run on the 1000cc Superstock Fireblade, he'd suffered one of those moments that every road rider dreads. Entering the four blindingly fast rights of the Verandah, he'd tucked the front tyre. "It was like I'd hit a patch of oil, it went so fast. I really thought that was it," he said. Thankfully, the tyre gripped again and disaster was avoided. The cause was a front tyre puncture, but it's the last thing a rider wants the night before the first big race. So even though Hutchinson had set the pace in practice, there was a nagging thought that his confidence could have been shattered.

HM Plant Honda's John McGuinness set the early pace on lap one, and by Glen Helen he held a slender 0.08-second lead over hard charging Conor Cummins on his McAdoo Kawasaki from Hutchinson in third and Cameron Donald in fourth. But that initial hard work was in vain for McGuinness: he was reported to be touring at Sulby, his efforts thwarted by a faulty crank sensor.

Cummins's stunning opening lap of 131.511mph gave him a lead of over eight seconds from Hutchinson by the time they blasted across the line at the Grandstand. Donald overshot the tricky Nook section at the end of the lap and dropped from third to 13th place as he paddled his Relentless Suzuki out of the slip road. His mistake donated third to Guy Martin.

Cummins's second lap was also in excess of 131mph, a speed Hutchinson couldn't seem to match, the gap stretching between the leading pair. The former seemed to be reading his boards around the circuit well and looked to have the race in control, but his advantage would almost disappear at the second pit stop, when his McAdoo Kawasaki ZX-10 was reluctant to fire up. By the time it did, his hard-earned lead was down to four seconds from Hutchinson. Martin was also in the pit-stop wars. He broke the new pit-lane speed limit and was awarded a 30-second penalty, which demoted him from third place to fifth.

Then, just a few miles into the fourth lap, Cummins broke down with reported clutch trouble at Laurel Bank. This gave the lead to Hutchinson who, in turn, had a comfortable 50-second cushion over Michael Dunlop, Donald and Keith Amor, locked together in a titanic short-circuit-style scrap for the lower steps of the podium.

Hutchinson kept his pace to the flag to take win number one of the week. Michael Dunlop on his Robinson's Concrete/Street Sweep Honda took a brilliant second, with Donald third – a momentous ride back from the lower ranks. Martin hauled himself up to fourth, while Adrian Archibald and Amor – the fastest man on the last lap at 129.6mph – rounded out the top six. TT stalwart Ian Lougher placed seventh on his Kawasaki; Michael Rutter was eighth on his Superstock-spec Bathams Fireblade; Dan Stewart was ninth; and Ryan Farquhar rounded out the top ten on his MSS Kawasaki.

## SIDECAR TT – Race One

Klaus Klaffenbock became the first Austrian to win at the TT since 1954 when he clinched honours in the first sidecar race of the week with Manx passenger Dan Sayle. Compatriot Rupert Hollaus had won the ultra-lightweight event 46 years before.

Klaffenbock didn't have it easy, though. Just five seconds separated the top five by the end of the first lap, but his initial threat came from John Holden and Andy Winkle, with practice pace-setters Dave Molyneux and Patrick Farrance taking their time to build up to speed in third. Simon Neary and Paul

Knapton held fourth against immense pressure from sidecar world champions Tim Reeves and Dipash Chauhan.

Molyneux hunted down Holden and Winkle to take second, but even third wasn't safe for the pair, as their machine coasted to a halt at Sulby. Now with no pressure from behind, Molyneux piled on the coals in an attempt to cut the time deficit on Klaffenbock.

On the last lap at Glen Helen, the gap was ten seconds; by Ramsey, it was eight-and-a-half; and by the time they rattled over the tramlines at the Bungalow, it was down to a nail-biting five. Everything hung on the mountain descent.

As number one on the road, it was Molyneux who took the flag first. Klaffenbock crossed the line 2.63 seconds in front to take his first ever win on the TT circuit since his 2004 debut. Reeves and Chauhan filled the final podium spot, ahead of Neary and Knapton.

## SUPERSPORT TT – Race One

After his pit-lane speeding infringement in Saturday's Superbike race, Martin was obviously on a mission to right what he saw as wrongs. The hirsute North Lincs rider pulled the pin from the start and built up a slender 1.7-second lead from Hutchinson by Glen Helen. By Ramsey, he'd stretched it by another tenth of a second, but Hutchinson pegged him back in the dash over the mountain to take the lead by the time they crossed the line on the first flying lap. Manxman Dan Kneen was doing a terrific job in third, with a whole host of Supersport celebrities behind him.

Martin clawed back the lead on the run to Glen Helen, but, as on the previous lap, Hutchinson was the quicker man over the remainder of the lap, posting a speed of over 126mph to take the lead as they pitted. Michael Dunlop also matched Hutchinson's speed to take third away from Kneen.

Some slick pit work by Clive Padgett's crew stretched Hutchinson's lead over Martin to four seconds as they screamed off for the final two laps. Michael Dunlop was closing in on Martin's second place – six seconds adrift. But, yet again, the latter's run through the first nine miles was stellar and he pegged back Hutchinson's advantage to just under half a second. Hutchinson responded and by the end of lap three had gapped Martin to the tune of five seconds with just one lap remaining.

Martin rode the lap of his life to smash the record on his final attack on the lead. His speed of 126.555mph was impressive, but the record was short lived, as Amor went one better with a stunning last lap of 126.909mph to claim fifth from Kneen.

Martin's flyer wasn't quite enough, and Hutchinson took win number two by just 3.03 seconds. Martin didn't come into the winner's circle. When he did eventually return, he said, confusingly referring to the previous Saturday's events, "I've been to see a man about a dog and get a brew on. How fast was I going in the pits? 60.112mph? I'll do what I want at my speed. I'm doing this for Wilson and the boys."

Michael Dunlop was a miserable third: "I'm disappointed. That was a waste of time," he said. Amor was fourth and Kneen an incredible fifth, while William Dunlop, McGuinness, Cummins, Farquhar and Donald completed the top ten.

## SUPERSTOCK TT

Monday was a hectic, but profitable day for Ian Hutchinson. The 'Bingley Bullet' had always known that the Superstock race would be tough, but with the guarantee of air in his front tyre, he knew he'd be there or thereabouts.

There were some remarkable Superstock times in practice, to the point where many began to question the logic of multi-thousand-pound Superbikes. Michael Dunlop, Amor and Farquhar all posted 128mph laps on their Superstockers in the final practice session, while the best Superbike lap of the week was only 2mph faster. Even more telling was Amor's

*Above:* Guy Martin, who was lucky to escape serious injury after a crash in the Senior TT.

*Above centre:* Klaus Kaffenblock celebrates his first IOM TT win with passenger Dan Sayle.

*Top:* Bruce Anstey and Hutchinson battle in the Supersport race.

*Photos: Gavan Caldwell*

Sulby speed-trap figure on his very standard S1000RR BMW – just 4mph down on Hutchinson's full-blown Superbike.

Perhaps more important than the negligible disparity between Superbike and Superstock speeds, was that the practice times promised a great race, with four manufacturers and at least seven riders all in the hunt for race honours.

The opening lap did not disappoint. Farquhar blasted his KMR ZX-10R Kawasaki into an early lead, holding a slender advantage over the pursuing pack. Slender is probably an understatement. At Glen Helen, just 4.5 seconds separated the top ten riders, with just over a second splitting the top five. Dunlop, Amor, Hutchinson, Cummins and Donald filled the top six.

But Farquhar was pushing hard. An opening lap of 129.648mph increased his leading margin to 6.78 seconds over Dunlop at the line.

On lap two – the first flying lap – Farquhar broke the existing record with a 129.816mph lap speed. Hutchinson had moved up into second place, but by the time they pitted for fuel at the end of the second lap, Farquhar was 8.8 seconds ahead. Michael Dunlop elected to change a rear tyre, and the extra time dropped him from fourth to 11th.

Hutchinson's pit stop was a blinder, and as they rocketed off towards St Ninians, the Yorkshireman had overhauled all of Farquhar's advantage to lead on time. But by the leafy glades of Glen Helen, Farquhar had put his Kawasaki back in front to the tune of 1.4 seconds. Cummins lay eight seconds adrift of Hutchinson, with McGuinness, Amor and Martin rounding out the top six. Farquhar continued his charge on the third lap to pull four seconds clear by Ramsey, and five-and-a-half seconds ahead by the start of the final lap. It looked like a foregone conclusion.

But Hutchinson was just getting into his stride. By Ballaugh, he'd halved Farquhar's lead, and by Ramsey hairpin that cushion was down to under two seconds, leaving the blast over the mountain to decide the outcome.

Hutchinson's staggering final lap of 130.741mph was not only a new lap record and the first time a Superstock machine had officially cracked the 130mph barrier, but also enough to beat Farquhar to the win by a slender 1.32 seconds. Kawasaki's disappointment was buoyed, however, by Cummins, who brought his McAdoo ZX-10 home in third to make it two on the podium.

McGuinness was fourth, with Martin just squeezing Amor's BMW back into sixth. Lougher placed seventh, with a charging Michael Dunlop eighth, Rutter ninth and Archibald tenth.

### SIDECAR TT – Race Two

The good weather that had blessed the 2010 TT had to break sooner or later – it's the law – and Wednesday dawned foggy and damp. The situation worsened, and the low cloud

and rain was enough for the organisers to postpone activities to the following day.

The sidecars were first away. Neary and Knapton pushed hard from the start to build up a slender lead over Molyneux and Farrance by Glen Helen. Holden and Klaffenbock were having their own tussle over third place. But just a mile later, local man Molyneux was out with machine problems on the long, bumpy straight at Cronk-y-Voddy. Reeves had already retired just four miles in at the Highlander.

Neary piled on the coals to overhaul Holden on the road, and by Ramsey his lead was a healthy ten seconds. But it would be short lived. He also succumbed to machine problems, coasting to a halt just after Mountain Box, thus handing the lead to Holden.

At the end of an action packed first lap, Holden led by eight seconds from Klaffenbock, who held a comfortable 22-second advantage over Conrad Harrison. Gary Bryan, Greg Lambert and Dave Wallis rounded out the top six.

Holden put in a blistering 113.569mph second lap to stretch his lead over Klaffenbock to ten seconds, but the Austrian responded to the pressure by winding up his speed on the third and final lap. The gap came down to eight seconds by Glen Helen, five by Ramsey and three by the Bungalow. By the time the crews hammered into the bumpy braking zone of the Nook, Klaffenbock held a slim advantage, which he stretched to 1.12 seconds by the chequered flag with a blistering lap of 114.157mph.

Harrison and Kerry Williams placed third to record their first ever TT podium. Gary Bryan finished fourth with 19-year-old passenger Jason Slous, while, at the opposite end of the age spectrum, 62-year-young Roy Hanks took sixth.

### SUPERSPORT TT – Race Two

Warm, dry, but mildly blustery weather offered near-perfect conditions for the second Supersport race of the week. The rev-happy 600s are popular among the competitors. With considerably less physical bulk and power, the smaller-capacity bikes are easier to muscle around the TT circuit. Data traces prove that over 70 per cent of a racing lap is spent with the throttle wide open on a 600, as opposed to just 20 per cent for the Superbikes, a startling difference.

With three wins already under his belt, it would have taken a foolhardy punter to bet against on-form Hutchinson to take the honours again. From the very beginning of the first lap, the softly spoken Yorkshireman led the field by the very smallest of margins. In a mirror image of the first lap of the Superstock race, just four-and-a-half seconds covered the top ten. Michael Dunlop deposed Martin for second, and although he clawed Hutchinson's lead down to just half a second by Ramsey Hairpin, The latter proved yet again that

SPORTMAX
GP RACER D211

# WE RACE, YOU WIN

DERIVED FROM THE RACE DOMINATING D211 GP, THE GP RACER D211
SETS A NEW REFERENCE FOR TRACK DAY TYRES *

SPORTMAX
GP RACER D211

/ NTEC SYSTEM ALLOWS RIDERS TO LOWER TYRE PRESSURES FOR ULTIMATE GRIP IN TRACK DAY CONDITIONS

/ MULTI-TREAD (MT) COMPOUND GUARANTEES RAPID WARM-UP, HIGH STABILITY UNDER BRAKING AND TOTALLY FOCUSED FEEDBACK OVER A HIGH MILEAGE IN ALL CONDITIONS

/ BELT-TO-CARCASS ANGLES ARE ENGINEERED TO STABILISE SIDEWALLS FOR SMOOTH, RESPONSIVE TRANSITIONS BETWEEN MAXIMUM LEAN ANGLES

/ NYLON BREAKER BELTS AND CONTINUOUSLY-WOUND ARAMID-FIBRE TREAD BELT ELIMINATE CIRCUMFERENTIAL GROWTH FOR COOLER RUNNING AND PREDICTABLE PERFORMANCE UNDER HEAVY USE

MT MULTI TREAD COMPOUND TECHNOLOGY    NTec JLB

* IN 2010 DUNLOP D211 GP RACE
TYRES AND NTEC SLICKS DELIVERED
A CLEAN SWEEP OF FIVE RACE WINS,
TEN PODIUM FINISHES AND TWO LAP
RECORDS AT THE I.O.M TT .

DUNLOP

RIDE WITH CONFIDENCE

WWW.DUNLOPMOTORCYCLE.EU

*Above:* Hutchinson's Senior victory made him the first in history with five in a week.

Photo: Dave Purves

*Centre, top to bottom:* A jump and a stone wall at Barregarrow – Ramsey resident Conor Cummins's TT week ended with a serious crash in the Senior; Ryan Farquhar was second in the Senior TT; TT Zero winner Mark Miller clocked a whispering 130mph and a 96mph lap on the impressive MotoCzysz E1PC; Ian Hutchinson celebrates his Senior win with a pint of the black stuff.

Photos: David Collister/photocycles.com

*Far right:* Close friends of Japanese rider Jun Maeda, killed in 2006, visit the TT's ever growing memorial wall.

Photo: Gavan Caldwell

he was the best Mountain scratcher, and by the time they crossed the line for the first time, that gap had stretched to 5.4 seconds with a lap from Hutchinson of 126.652mph. Michael Dunlop had a similar gap over Martin, with Amor, McGuinness and Bruce Anstey completing the top six.

Controversy unfolded on the second lap. Just a few miles into the lap, at Ballagarey, a fatal accident involving popular Kiwi rider Paul Dobbs resulted in yellow flags being waved. Witnesses claimed that the leading riders didn't slow down, but that accusation was hotly contested by the riders concerned. Whatever the situation, Michael Dunlop had clawed back Hutchinson's lead by Ramsey, only for him to stretch it again on the run over the Mountain.

At the end of the second lap, the refuelling session saw Michael Dunlop make a quicker pit stop than Hutchinson. By Ramsey, the gap was a mere 1.8 seconds. Martin was also under immense pressure from the hard charging Amor, and less than a second split this battle for third place. As Hutchinson and Michael Dunlop flashed across the line on their fourth and final lap, the former had eked a 3.19-second lead. Cummins held fifth, while McGuinness had worked his way up to sixth.

As the leaders leapt Ballaugh Bridge, spirited riding from Dunlop saw him take the lead by the slimmest of margins. By Ramsey, he had stretched the advantage to 1.8 seconds, but could he hold it to the line?

Hutchinson's performance, both up and back down the mountain, looked to be unbeatable. By the Bungalow, he had squeezed back ahead by just under half a second. He flashed across the line with an incredible record-breaking lap of 127.611mph. Michael Dunlop went even quicker, at 127.836mph, but still it wasn't enough, and Hutchinson took his record equalling fourth win of the week.

Amor's last lap was also in the 126mph bracket – enough to depose Martin from third place, while McGuinness's last-lap circuit was strong enough to squeeze Cummins from fifth. William Dunlop had a solid ride to seventh, and the final three top-ten positions went to Anstey, Farquhar and Kneen.

## TT ZERO

From the moment the battery-powered racers took to the TT course, the result looked entirely predictable. While the majority of the machines looked like conventional motorcycles fitted with electric motors and huge amounts of battery power, only one bike appeared to have been designed from the ground up.

Once a few technical hiccups had been sorted, the beautifully engineered MotoCzysz E1PC, ridden by American Mark Miller, appeared to be in a different class. Clocking a whisperingly fast 130mph through the Sulby speed trap – a full 30mph faster than Rob Barber's Team AGNI bike – the MotoCzysz lapped at an impressive 94.664mph during the class's brief practice. To put that in perspective, Miller's best lap time was just under 23 minutes faster than sixth-placed Mark Buckley's lap – a slight difference to the close racing the fans had enjoyed all week.

While the winner of the TT Zero race was a safe bet, the £10,000 prize, put up by the Manx government for the first electric bike to lap at more than 100mph, didn't look as safe.

In the end, however, the ten grand remained in the public purse. Miller won the one-lap race in 23 minutes, 22.89 seconds, an average speed of 96.820mph.

Despite being almost 30mph down on the top speed, Rob Barber finished second at an average of 89.290mph – an impressive feat – and James McBride employed every ounce of his vast track knowledge to finish third, at 88.653mph, seven seconds ahead of Jenny Tinmouth on the second of Team AGNI's bikes.

Looks like the £10,000 could be converted into US dollars in 2011.

## SENIOR TT

A lot rested on the final event of TT week. The Senior race was the last chance to right wrongs, break records, regain faith.

McGuinness, previously the undisputed Mountain King, had

suffered a lousy TT and hadn't stood on the podium once. Martin also felt robbed, with speeding penalties and a healthy dose of bad luck. Both TAS Suzuki riders, Donald and Anstey, weren't having the best of weeks, and local sensation Cummins had looked set to win his first big race on the Saturday, only to be cruelly robbed of any chance by a minor mechanical failure.

Then, there was Hutchinson. He'd won every race he'd entered and had a tally of four wins to rival the record set by Philip McCallen. One more win would be another record for the Padgetts rider.

In almost perfect sun-kissed conditions, the battle was on. For the first two laps, Hutchinson, Martin, Cummins and McGuinness slugged it out at the front, all four lapping in excess of 130mph. After they took on fuel at the end of the second lap, less than six seconds separated the top four. McGuinness led from Martin, Cummins and Hutchinson.

On lap three, the Glen Helen commentator counted the leaders through and noted, with an audible wobble in his voice, that Martin had gone missing. News filtered through with painful delay of an 'incident' at Ballagarey, the corner that had cost Paul Dobbs his life the day before. The race was red-flagged to "allow fire engines to attend". Everyone feared the worst. The commentator said, "We can't say any more at this point, other than the fire engines have been deployed to the area."

But even though his bike had exploded into flames after the 160mph impact with a wall, Guy Martin was conscious and, miraculously, not too seriously hurt.

After a major clean-up operation, a four-lap re-start got under way at 3pm. At the front of the pack, the action was just as furious. Hutchinson held a narrow lead from McGuinness who, in turn, was being hounded by Cummins. Donald, Michael Dunlop and Farquhar rounded out the top six.

By the end of lap one, despite a lap in excess of 131mph from a standing start, Hutchinson's lead over McGuinness had stretched to an almost inconsequential 0.6 second. Cummins was still in touch, too, with Amor battling his way up to fourth place on the second HM Plant Honda.

Hutchinson gapped McGuinness slightly on the run to Glen Helen, but more drama unfolded when, for the second time that week, the latter coasted to a silent halt on the steep hill coming out of the wooded section of Glen Helen. Another faulty crank sensor was reported as the culprit.

Cummins found himself three seconds behind the leader in second by the time they braked into Ramsey hairpin towards the end of the second lap. Amor, Farquhar and Anstey placed third, fourth and fifth.

Just a few miles later, though, at the super-fast four-bend Verandah section, Cummins crashed out of second place. In an accident too horrific to broadcast (even though the helicopter had captured it all), the Ramsey resident cartwheeled down the steep banking and over a dry-stone wall, suffering serious arm and leg injuries in the process.

Hutchinson now held a commanding 27-second lead as they approached their one and only pit stop. By the time he'd refuelled and blasted his way to Glen Helen, the gap had extended to 31 seconds, but soon it would increase, as Amor coasted to a halt exactly where his team-mate had retired a lap earlier, posing the question: who supplied the crank sensors? Farquhar and Anstey now found themselves in podium positions.

For the remainder of the race, Hutchinson watched his pit boards closely and controlled the race from the front. He crossed the line stood on the footrests, both hands punching the air, to break TT history with five wins in one week. Farquhar took second and Anstey filled the last podium step. Veteran Lougher completed a strong week with fourth, while Rutter took fifth on his Superstock-spec Honda Fireblade.

## DEATH TOLL REACHES 229

A second rider lost his life in the second Supersport race, Austrian Martin Loicht succumbing to injuries sustained at Quarry Bends. New Zealander Paul Dobbs had already died when he crashed on the second lap of the same race. Each rider left a widow and two children.

This brought one estimate of the Mountain Circuit's death toll since 1911 to 229, including the Manx GP.

Welsh rider Paul Owen, who had been following his close friend, Dobbs, on the track, was awarded the inaugural PokerStars Spirit of the TT award after he stopped to help at the crash scene, sacrificing his own race chances.

*Inset above:* John McGuinness on his HM Plant Honda, first Superbike winner, leads Guy Martin (Wilson Craig Honda).

*Inset above right:* Ian Hutchinson was on top form, with three Ulster GP wins.

*Photos: Gavan Caldwell*

NORTH WEST 200 & ULSTER GRAND PRIX

# DOUBLE HUTCH

By GARY PINCHIN

*Main photo:* Massed start between the kerbs – the North West 200 Superbike race winners John McGuinness (4) and Alastair Seeley (34) tuck in behind early leader Keith Amor (37).

*Inset above left:* Bruce Anstey, the world's fastest road racer at an average of 133.97mph.

*Inset above right:* Local boy Alastair Seeley crosses the line on his TAS Suzuki to take his first Superbike race win.

*Photos: Gavan Caldwell*

*Above:* Slipstreaming battles down long straights – William Dunlop follows Ian Lougher in the 125cc race.
Photo: Gavan Caldwell

*Top:* Swan Honda rider Stuart Easton was a welcome attraction at the North West 200.
Photo: Swan Honda

*Above right:* At the Ulster Grand Prix, Bruce Anstey made a surprise move on the last lap of the second Superbike race to win, ahead of Hutchinson and Amor.
Photo: Gavan Caldwell

WHEN Ian Hutchinson won the final race of the 2010 North West 200, he could have had no idea of what success would follow. Hot on the heels of his Supersport win in Ireland, the Padgetts Honda rider went on to chalk up an incredible record breaking five TT race wins in a week and then added three more victories at the Ulster Grand Prix to establish himself as the man of the moment on the roads.

The North West and Ulster might both be massed-start races on Irish public roads, but they could not be more different events.

The North West 200 in May has become a huge corporate show, backed by the government and shown live on local TV. The attendance is said to be around 150,000, and it's certainly packed around the 8.9-mile triangle of public roads that links Portstewart, Coleraine and Portrush, on the beautiful Causeway Coast, North Antrim.

The racing is a high-speed game of slipstreaming down long fast straights with some serious short-circuit-style scratching around the tight corners that link them. Close-run dramas are usually resolved in the final two corners: the chicane at Junipers and the tight left-hander coming off the coast road into the start/finish loop.

The Ulster GP has tradition. There's been a grand prix on the Dundrod course since 1953, and up to 1971 it enjoyed world championship status. These days, it's a stand-alone event, starting on Thursday with the Dundrod 150 (formerly a national race run at a different time of the year) and culminating with the grand prix on the Saturday, which attracts 20–25,000 fans.

Its rural location in County Antrim is only five miles from Belfast International Airport, but it doesn't attract the same massive crowds as the North West 200 –neither does it receive the same government backing. But it certainly is the most spectacular of road races.

The rolling 7.4-mile course is far more of a traditional road race in style – and more technical than the North West – while the open, flowing bends make it the fastest road race in the world.

## NORTH WEST 200

Practice for the North West was marred by Steve Plater's horrific looking 120mph crash late in Thursday's practice as rain was beginning to be felt in the air. Plater – an eight-times winner at the event and the man to beat going into it – lost the front as he tipped into the left-hander in sight of the start/finish chute and sustained what initially was thought to be a badly broken left arm, which required two plates and 13 screws to stabilise, and which also left him with some nerve damage.

Worse was to follow later, however, when doctors discovered that he had also broken vertebrae in his neck, which would require surgery and metalwork to stabilise. Thankfully, he made a complete recovery and was able to return to race in the National Superstock championship towards the end of the season.

Alastair Seeley was the star of the show. He finished in third place in the first Superbike race, and had rain not shortened the event by two laps, he might have been able to

challenge eventual winner John McGuinness and runner-up Conor Cummins.

The second Superbike race was also cut short to four laps, but Seeley came out on top after a dogfight with Stuart Easton, passing the Swan Honda into Church on the last lap. Seeley's other win came on the unlikeliest machine, the long-in-the-tooth GSX-R600, when he beat Padgetts Honda rider Ian Hutchinson in the first Supersport race by 0.72 second.

While Seeley did the business for the Relentless by TAS team, his more acknowledged 'roads specialist' team-mates, Bruce Anstey and Cameron Donald, struggled. Anstey's only real result was beating Seeley to third in the second Supersport race and the final race of the day, which was won by Hutchinson.

Cameron Donald, who returned from the massive shoulder injury sustained in practice for the 2009 TT, never got into the top six all day.

Scot Keith Amor won the Superstock race on his BMW S1000RR, and finished fourth and sixth in the two Superbike races on a similar machine. He also took fourth and second in the two Supersport races on his Ten Kate-built Honda. His superb all-round day earned the privateer a ride at the TT with the HM Plant Honda team, where he replaced Plater.

## ULSTER GRAND PRIX

After his amazing record breaking TT, all eyes were on Hutchinson to see what he could do at the Ulster Grand Prix, the final of the three major international road races in 2010. And

he didn't disappoint, winning three of the day's big races on the Dundrod road course – which gave him nine international road race wins on the trot – and finishing second in two others.

Hutchinson's first win came in the Superstock race, which was red-flagged on the sixth of seven laps, giving him the victory by 0.2 second in front of Amor – now back on his own BMW. Hutchinson also set a new lap record of 132.163mph.

Win number two came in the first Supersport race, another close-fought scrap with Amor that he won by 0.176 second, while Michael Dunlop was only 0.424 second behind the winner.

The third came in the opening Superbike race, by 0.106 second from Bruce Anstey, with Amor only four-tenths adrift of the winner.

Close racing and split-second victories characterised the entire day. Amor finally chalked up his first ever Ulster GP race win, beating Ian Hutchinson by 0.21 second in the second Supersport race of the day on his Kojak Honda.

The second Superbike race produced an epic finish, however, to bring down the curtain on what people were calling the 'greatest day ever in the history of motorcycle racing'.

Kiwi Bruce Anstey – after a typically quiet day in the saddle – pulled out one of his equally typical brilliant performances on the Relentless by TAS Suzuki. He rode the perfect last lap from third to first to beat Hutchinson and Amor to the line, and established a stunning new lap record of 133.977mph.

It was a fitting end to an incredible day, underlining just how competitive, and downright exciting, racing on the roads has become in the modern era.

# 2010 MCE Insurance British Superbike Championship

**2010 BSB CHAMPION**
Ryuichi Kiyonari

**2010 BSB RUNNER-UP**
Josh Brookes

**2010 BSB MANUFACTURERS' CHAMPIONSHIP**
HM Plant Honda

**1 Ryuichi Kiyonari**

**2 Josh Brookes**

**3 years 0% APR TYPICAL finance**

Honda Contact Centre: 0845 200 8000

www.honda.co.uk

# BACK TO THE FRONT

By GARY PINCHIN

A champion returns. Back from World
Superbikes, Kiyonari rides his HM
Plant Honda to victory – and the title
– at the Oulton Park finale.
*Photo: Clive Challinor Motorsport Photography*

*Above:* BSB blast-off at Thruxton. The front row comprises (*l to r*) Kagayama (Suzuki), Easton (Honda), Rutter (Ducati) and Hill (Suzuki).

Photo: Clive Challinor Motorsport Photography

AFTER two years in WSB, Ryuichi Kiyonari returned to his old BSB stamping ground with HM Plant Honda for the 2010 MCE British Superbike Championship and claimed his third title, adding to his previous victories of 2006 and 2007.

Kiyo clinched it with a truly awesome performance at Oulton Park, winning all three races in the final leg of the all-new three-round Showdown decider. Three rides worthy of a champion.

And to cap the team's great season, Josh Brookes shook off the bad-boy tag he had unjustly earned in 2009 to make it a resounding one-two for the Louth-based Honda team, which had started the season anything but favourite.

Tommy Hill set the pace most of the season on the Worx Suzuki, but his bid for the title crumbled in the final two Showdown rounds; his double crash in race two at Oulton Park will remain a talking point for years to come.

The Showdown was the biggest change to the series since 2001 and brought a complete revamp of the championship points system. Interest in the series had plummeted drastically with Leon Camier's domination of the 2009 campaign. Now organiser MotorSports Vision Racing (MSVR) introduced an innovative structure that split the season into two separate parts: a nine-round Regular Season, followed by the three-round Showdown. Riders scored points as usual in the Regular Season, but also accrued podium credits, points awarded three to a win, two for second and one for third.

At the end of the first nine rounds (after the second Cadwell meeting on August Bank Holiday), the top six riders qualified as 'Title Fighters' for the Showdown and were awarded a starting total of 500 points – plus the podium credits they had earned.

From the moment the new structure was announced, riders talked up the need for consistent results, but while that was the case, they also needed to grab as many podium finishes as possible, for points to take into the Showdown.

Ironically, 2010 was the most open BSB season for some time, with any one of eight to ten riders capable of winning races. This made the Showdown concept largely superfluous, although in fairness to MSVR, it couldn't have predicted that at the start of the year.

The real effect of the split season was to take the excitement off the last couple of rounds of the Regular Season. By then, it was pretty evident who was going to make the top six – Kiyonari, Brookes, Hill, Michael Laverty, the rejuvenated Michael Rutter and Alastair Seeley – and the focus switched to what turned out to be a rather lacklustre scrabble for seventh, between James Ellison, John Laverty and Stuart Easton.

## Evolution of the series

That wasn't the only change though. With one eye on the future, BSB series director Stuart Higgs's introduction of BSB Evo in 2009 – persuading the Relentless by TAS Suzuki team to run a bike for Superstock champion Seeley at Silverstone – had been astute.

Seeley proved the bike competitive out of the box, and for 2010 Evo was introduced as a lower-cost replacement class for the BSB Privateer Cup – with the intention of adopting

the class rules across the entire championship for 2011. The bikes ran Superstock-spec engines with a control Motec ECU, but retained a full FIM-spec Superbike chassis. This kept all the aftermarket suppliers in business, and race fans interested in the technical aspects.

The lower-spec engines would be cheaper to maintain, and a stock ECU meant that organisers could control electronic rider aids and even impose rpm limits if need be. In addition, smaller teams would not have the burden of employing staff to analyse the confusing masses of data modern motorcycle systems can provide.

Initially, some top BSB teams suggested that they would run a third bike in Evo, but the hard facts of the recession scuppered such folly. Even so, the new initiative brought Aprilia, BMW and KTM to the class, as well as privateers running bikes from Japanese manufacturers.

John Dimbylow's new Splitlath team (so called because his line of business is renovating old churches and other historic buildings using traditional methods) opted to run a pair of Aprilias, initially for brothers Chris and Joe Burns, the latter eventually running his own BMW in Superstock. He was replaced by South African Hudson Kennaugh, and immediately the team became a title contender.

Kennaugh had been competitive on a no-frills ZX-10 Kawasaki run by Malcolm Ashley. He demonstrated the worth of the Evo class by buying a spare motor from a scrap yard to keep going, but in the end he didn't have sufficient funds to complete the season.

Jentin Racing – long-time Yamaha privateer – hooked up with BMW to run an S1000RR for Steve Brogan. Team owner Bernie Toleman is a committed Superbike man, but BMW's main thrust was a Superstock entry for Richard Cooper. It was only running the Superbike, however, that gave BMW the kind of paddock presence (i.e., pit garage allocation) it was looking for.

KTM dealer Redline ran an RC8R for James Edmeades with the backing of not only the UK KTM importer, but also the KTM factory in Austria, which ensured top-level technical support from the official team in the German IDM Superbike championship.

Other top runners included AIM Suzuki with roads star Gary Johnson on a Suzuki GSX-R1000, and Pauli Pekkanen, who came all the way from Finland every race weekend with his Suzuki.

Evo, along with BSB proper, was hit by another rule change, which prohibited teams from having two bikes in the garage. They were allowed a spare bike, but it had to be in component form in the truck; while frames could be changed, the work could only be done with the permission of the scrutineers – and each frame carried a bar-code so its legality could be checked easily.

The idea was to cut costs, but it didn't stop teams from building complete spare bikes, even if they did keep them stripped down in their trucks.

What it did add was an edge to practice and qualifying that the teams could probably have done without. One slip meant that a rider could miss the entire qualifying session, and several times in the year there was feverish activity in the pit boxes, with mechanics desperately trying to repair crashed bikes to get their riders back on track.

*Above and right:* James Ellison's season started badly, with serious injury.
Photo: Clive Challinor Motorsport Photography

*Top:* Stuart Easton flies at Cadwell.
Photo: Swan Honda

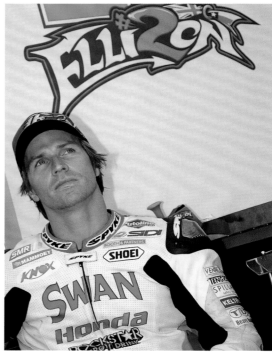

## Honda: Swan starts favourite

Following the mass exodus of top riders to WSB, BSB took another big hit when the title winning Airwaves Yamaha team shut up shop. Team owner Darrell Healey was unable to secure a major title sponsor and, rather than mothball the team for a season, as he'd done in the past, everything was sold.

By that time, BSB champion Leon Camier had secured an Aprilia WSB ride, while BSB number two, James Ellison, had signed for Swan Honda. That teamed Ellison with number-three plate holder Stuart Easton, and the Guisborough-based outfit arguably had the strongest team going into the season.

Its Hondas probably had better specs than the official HM Plant CBR1000RRs in 2009, with their Pectel electronics and KR swing-arms against more basic HRC kit equipment. Improving the electronics even further over the winter and switching to the K-Tech DDS suspension during testing appeared to ensure that both riders went into the season as favourites for the title.

Easton's season started to go off the rails when he crashed in a final pre-season test at Cadwell and lacerated the back of his leg. He still scored solid points in the first two rounds, winning the first race at Oulton, but slipping off in the second, then crashing in almost identical circumstances in the opening race of Cadwell's round four.

He seemed to lose confidence, and some niggling technical issues left him bemoaning the fact that the Honda just didn't give him the same feel as the 2009 bike. He missed the cut for the Showdown.

Ellison's tale of woe was even worse. He was third and first in the Brands opener, but then crashed at Thruxton and broke his femur, which sidelined him until late June. Even though he could run the lap times, his comeback was jinxed by bike problems (including, can you believe, a puncture at Croft?) and a Snetterton crash (where he was taken out by Seeley). Only at the penultimate round did things run smoothly – he took fourth, then won the second race.

HM Plant Honda had a busy winter. Realising the short-

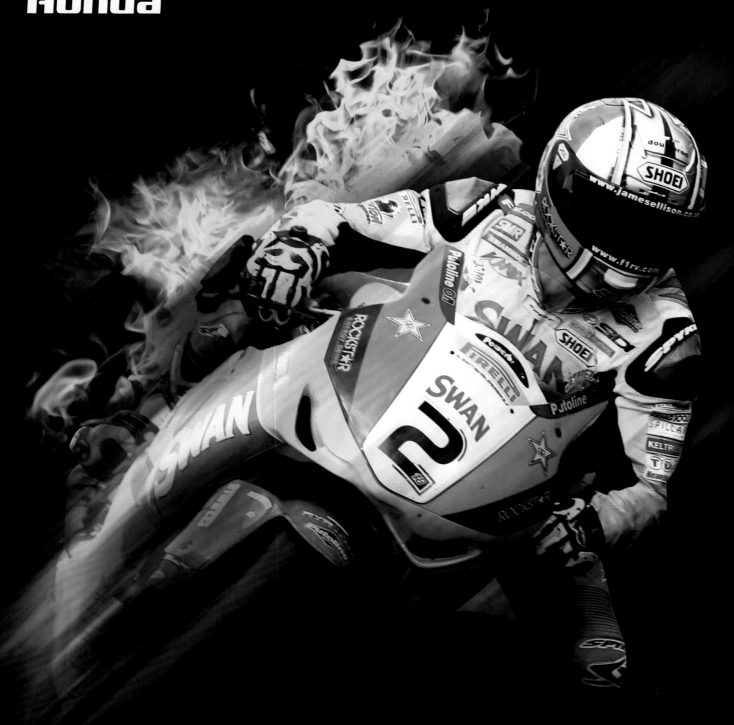

ROLL WITH SWAN

ASK FOR SWAN COMBI - 50 FILTERS & 50 PAPERS

*Above:* Josh Brookes redeemed his bad-boy reputation.

*Top right:* Tommy Bridewell, wild child on a Honda.

*Above right:* Alastair Seeley impressed in his debut season.

*Right:* Tommy Hill came close to taking the title for Suzuki. Here he leads Ellison at Oulton Park just before his costly crash.

*Photos: Clive Challinor Motorsport Photography*

comings of the HRC kit electronics, it made a radical (for the team) decision to upgrade to a Motec M800 electronics package, switched from Showa to Öhlins and brought former two-time BSB champion Kiyonari back to the fold to run alongside Brookes.

Although the team had previously run HRC electronics on its official bikes, Motec was nothing new for the Louth-based squad, which had operated similar systems on its satellite Red Bull and Dunlop backed teams with Jonathan Rea and Karl Harris, and on its Supersport bikes.

Brookes had gained a bad-boy tag early in 2009, but as the season progressed, his mistakes were being overlooked as he emerged as one of the great characters of the series – as well as a fiercely competitive rider.

Kiyonari, on the other hand, came back to BSB a broken man after two fruitless seasons in WSB with Ten Kate. All hoped that the HM Plant 'family' atmosphere he had relished during his four years in Louth would help him restore his lost confidence.

Both riders figured strongly in the Regular Season. Brookes finished three points adrift of Tommy Hill, but chalked up the most wins (five to Kiyonari's four and Hill's three). His only real disappointment in the first nine rounds was the August Brands meeting, where his tally was a sixth, a crash and a fourth in a meeting dominated by Kawasaki WSB wild-card Tom Sykes. Kiyonari was blindingly quick, but inconsistent, sometimes due to his bike, sometimes down to him.

Pre-season, another Honda team emerged as a potential threat: the small privateer Quay Garage squad. It stuck to its tried-and-tested 2007 ex-Gregorio Lavilla Honda that team boss Ian Woollacott had bought from Paul Bird Motorsport and used to win the BSB Cup with Gary Mason. The big difference for 2010 was the decision to run popular 'wild-child' Tommy Bridewell in the main Superbike competition.

Most thought that this ageing war-horse of a motorcycle had seen better times. But in truth this was probably one of the best-spec'ed Superbikes in the competition. Its Magneti Marelli electronics incorporated a blipper box, traction con-

trol, anti-wheelie and launch control. The chassis sported a KR swing-arm and had top-grade Öhlins, so it was no surprise that Bridewell put in some impressive times during Spanish testing. He still had some massive crashes, but his strongest performance came at the first Cadwell round, where he finished fourth and sixth.

The other Honda team of note was the one-man SMT outfit, owned by Robin Croft – with close business ties to Swan Honda boss Shaun Muir as well as technical support from SMR in the racing paddock. The SMT Honda was virtually a Swan Honda minus the electronics, and Croft pulled something of a shock, signing Supermoto star Christian Iddon – with virtually no experience on a Superbike and very little in any form of road racing.

While Iddon was often quick and showed potential, not surprisingly, he also crashed a lot. Eventually, Croft tired of the costly exercise and replaced him with Chris Walker, who did a thoroughly efficient job.

Walker had ridden for a new team in the paddock, run by Ray Stringer. He had signed Walker and Alex Lowes to ride Suzukis in BSB, plus Luke Mossey to run in Supersport on a Triumph and Tristan Palmer to compete in Superstock on a BMW. The money came from businessman Dave Copley, who previously had joined with Stringer to run a BSB race team, but the funds to see out the season arrived late, and never in full.

That meant the plan to buy two 2009 ex-Alstare Suzukis came to naught. Stringer bought the K9 Suzuki, built by Crescent, that Michael Rutter had used at the TT, so Walker, Mossey and Palmer were able to start the season, although Lowes was not. Walker rode the ex-Rutter bike, built for the roads with a kit Yoshimura ECU, without traction control, anti-wheelie or launch control.

In the end, Walker went to MSS Kawasaki as a replacement for injured Simon Andrews, then to SMT; Palmer replaced injured Richard Cooper in Superstock, and the impressive Lowes had a brief run on the BSB Evo Redline KTM, then joined the Seton Yamaha Supersport outfit.

## Suzuki wars

After losing Sylvain Guintoli to the WSB Alstare Suzuki team, Worx Suzuki regrouped to sign Tommy Hill, who had substituted for the injured Guintoli in 2009, and reverted to two riders, with former BSB favourite Yukio Kagayama as part of the Guintoli trade.

Winter testing in Spain and in the UK proved frustrating, with many glitches in the new Motec M800 system. But Hill was a model of professionalism and never let the problems get to him. Each time he sat patiently, waiting for the bike to be fixed, when others might have thrown toys out of the pram. And he seemed to jump straight on to lap-record pace once the bike was running, as if to prove to himself and his rivals that actually the team was well on the money.

While Kagayama lived up to his reputation as a spectacular crasher, Hill tried to live up to his pre-season message that "consistency will win the championship." In the first six races (three rounds), he won two, and finished second three times and third once, but then he failed to finish at the first Cadwell. He bounced back to take second in race two, but seemed to lose confidence in the front end for a lean patch, including a terrible triple-header at Brands, where he scored just 24 points from the three rides.

The team worked hard and helped him recover at Cadwell, where he won race one and finished second to end the Regular Season at the top of the table – and take 25 podium credits (equal top with Kiyo) into the Showdown.

There were plenty of raised eyebrows when Relentless by TAS Suzuki brought Michael Laverty back to its team for 2010 at the expense of Ian Lowry, fifth in 2009, his rookie Superbike season.

Laverty, by contrast, had won the 2007 British Supersport title for the team and had moved with them to BSB the following year, but the team's first tentative steps in the top flight had proved difficult. Laverty had disappeared to enter occasional races in the States and in Europe in 2009, but that may have helped give him a new hunger. That's what team boss Philip Neill saw in him for 2010.

Also in the line-up was Alastair Seeley, who had dominated the National Superstock title in 2009 for TAS. The Relentless backed outfit had run him on a Superbike at the end of the season, and the wee man had impressed everyone, so he was always assured a place in 2010.

Seeley started the season strong enough – fourth and third in the Brands opener, a fourth at Oulton and third at Snetterton, while his first-race Brands win showed what a brilliant talent he is. But the wheels came off after a super-successful North West, and his first full year of BSB was marred by inconsistency, although he managed to make the Showdown – an impressive result considering that essentially it was his rookie BSB season.

Laverty's season came alive with a win in the damp at Oulton, and from there on he was both fast and consistent to finish fifth in the Regular Season.

## The Ducati threat

No one really gave Bridgwater based Riders Motorcycle much credit after team owner Phil Jessop announced that it would be running the same Ducati 1098s that Michael Rutter had raced in North West 200 colours in 2008, and in the latter half of 2009 to keep himself in the frame.

What no one realised was that they would be upgraded

*Above:* Michael Rutter, reunited with Ducati, found some of his old form.

*Centre right:* Neil Hodgson announced his retirement after the season finale.

*Right:* Michael Laverty impressed on the Relentless Suzuki.

*Below right:* A tearful Tommy Hill after his season ended disastrously at Oulton Park.

*Photos:* Clive Challinor Motorsport Photography

*Bottom right:* Kiyonari celebrates his third BSB championship.

*Photo:* Gavan Caldwell

with new engines and electronics to turn them into effectively the same 1198-spec bikes that were being raced by Shane Byrne's Althea Ducati in WSB.

Rutter's potential as a front-runner, his team-mate Martin Jessopp and the team's ability to get the best from the bikes and riders were completely underestimated by his rivals. They had overlooked Rutter's Ducati experience, how well Jessopp had ridden a 748 Ducati in British Supersport, and that the team had a wealth of Magneti Marelli electronics experience on its previous Honda Superbike.

The final part of the equation was ex-Airwaves engine builder 'Desmo' Dave Allenby, who worked magic as Rutter's crew chief.

Rutter was a sensation. He was obviously happy to be back on a Ducati and, where once he'd spend more time in the pit box searching for the ultimate set-up, now he spent it doing laps, building confidence with the bike. With that came a newfound aggression, and not only did he make the Showdown comfortably, but also he won at Knockhill and finished in the top four 11 times in the 19 races.

Jessopp wasn't so fortunate. He had a really good Thruxton (sixth and fifth), but suffered a compound break to his tibia and fibula after being involved with a Dan Linfoot crash at Mallory.

## Kawasaki's struggle

It was always going to be a difficult final season with the old-style ZX-10 Kawasaki, with its long-frame/short-swing-arm geometry that gave teams so many headaches. MSS Kawasaki was tied in ever closer to the Kawasaki factory and during 2010 enjoyed a growing bond with Paul Bird's Penrith-based factory backed WSB Kawasaki team, which ensured a good flow of technical support that benefited both teams.

MSS continued to develop its bikes around the Magneti Marelli electronics, and signed BSB Cup champion Gary Mason from Quay Garage and former Jentin Yamaha rider Simon Andrews.

Mason endured small technical issues and never enjoyed the consistency he'd shown in 2009. Andrews suffered a massive ankle injury while guesting for the factory WSB Kawasaki team at Valencia. He missed three BSB rounds as a result – and took a lot longer to get back to fitness than most realised. But fourth at Croft in the first round of the Showdown indicated its potential, along with that of the much maligned ZX-10.

The Buildbase Kawasaki team, run by Stuart Hicken of Hawk Racing, continued to develop its ZX-10s in-house,

switching to Pectel electronics and forging links with Cosworth to develop new engine internals, something MSS had started in 2009.

Buildbase retained John Laverty for a second year and signed Superstock rider Adam Jenkinson, who had impressed previously in a brief BSB flirtation with SMT Honda until badly injured at Thruxton in early 2008, returning only in 2009. Jenkinson, to be frank, struggled to come to terms with the ZX-10, but Laverty was impressive, being fast and consistent (until he crashed at Brands in the second of the three August races). Chatter problems spoiled his bid to make the Showdown, but a third at Oulton in May, and three fifth places in the Regular Season gave the team plenty to be pleased about.

## Yamaha's problems

Motorpoint Yamaha pulled off a massive coup, signing former WSB and BSB champion, and now AMA Superbike racer, Neil Hodgson. He'd injured his shoulder badly in a motocross accident in 2009, but was certain he'd be 100-per-cent fit for the start of the year to give the beleaguered Rob McElnea owned team a boost.

Alongside him was Dan Linfoot, again bringing Stonebaker funds to boost the team's coffers for a second successive year. Linfoot had started 2009 in Supersport, but was promoted to BSB mid-term and now had a chance of a full year on the R1.

Initially, McElnea's crew planned to run in-house R1s, but after initial testing persuaded Yamaha UK to let it have the ex-Airwaves factory bikes that had dominated the previous season.

McElnea couldn't afford to go the full factory engine/Marelli route (the engines were at the end of their life anyway after the cash strapped Airwaves team had run them to the absolute maximum mileage) and instead used the factory rolling chassis with engines developed in-house (but with similar horsepower) and their existing Motec electronics.

Hodgson crashed in practice for the first round at Brands Hatch, re-injuring his shoulder so badly that it forced him to call time on his career. McElnea was in dire need of results, but Ian Lowry, Andrew Pitt and Linfoot all struggled with the bike. And it wasn't until after the team hooked up with the Yamaha Italia crew, that it finally got the bike going well.

That was at Croft in the Showdown, when French 17-year-old Loris Baz made such an impressive debut for the team. He finished seventh, while Linfoot scored his best result of the year with fifth.

## The Showdown

The final three-round Showdown produced the epic kind of action that MSVR had hoped for. Michael Laverty proved the sensation at Croft, showing a new kind of aggression. Hill beat him in the first race by 0.155 second, but Laverty slammed straight back to win the second by 0.202 second and jump to second in the championship.

The HM Plant Hondas struggled. Kiyo's team had fitted the front-wheel speed sensor incorrectly, so he rode the first race without any electronic aids and finished down in 11th. He battled back to sixth from the lowly grid slot in race two.

Brookes was also off-colour, taking sixth and eighth places, his worst weekend since Oulton back in May.

Rutter was out of luck, too. He slipped off the Ducati in race one, but finished fifth in the second race, while Seeley, also a crasher in race one, was 15th in the second. His title hopes were gone.

Hill led on 570, from Laverty 554, Kiyonari 543, Brookes 542, Rutter 521 and Seeley 501.

Rutter took the first race at Silverstone, 1.2 seconds ahead of a rejuvenated Brookes, with Laverty third. Kiyonari could only finish fifth, behind James Ellison, while Hill struggled in eighth, complaining of a lack of front-end feel.

Race two spun even more intrigue as 'rain-master' Rutter crashed on lap three in the wet to kiss goodbye to his hopes.

Ellison had no regard for Title Fighters and scored his first win since his comeback from injury, leading by a massive (in BSB terms) 5.85 seconds from Kiyonari, with Brookes an even more distant third.

Laverty, having finished a strong third in race one, took a tumble in the first corner on the opening lap of race two. The team said that he had had only ten-per-cent throttle when the rear tyre inexplicably lost traction. The only possible explanation was that he had gone in tight to defend his line, run out wider than usual and hit a slick spot on the track.

Seeley finished fourth, taking a couple of valuable points off fifth-placed Hill, who was now only 11 points clear of Brookes going into the final triple-header at Oulton.

Now Hill's lead had shrunk: on 589 to Brookes 578, Kiyonari 574, Laverty 570, Rutter 548 and Seeley 529.

Oulton was officially billed as Judgement Day, and certainly fire and brimstone was served up in front of a massive 40,000 crowd on Sunday.

Hill qualified on pole from Kiyonari, with Ellison playing the spoiler role again, third from Laverty. Brookes was a distant ninth, struggling to find a set-up, having set the pace in Friday's first free practice.

Kiyonari won the first encounter – held on Saturday afternoon – by 0.821 second from Hill, with Ellison completing the podium. Laverty was fourth from Brookes. Hill's lead from Kiyonari was now down to ten points.

Sunday's first race brought not one, but two defining moments in the championship. Ellison was leading from Kiyonari going into Lodge on the fifth lap, and Hill – in third – tried to outbrake the HM Plant Honda, but got out of shape on the bumps. He just about got the bike straightened up, but by then he was deep into the corner and nailed the luckless Ellison, who was just turning in and had no idea that Hill was there.

Both riders went down, but Hill dragged his bike out of the gravel and remounted – only to crash in exactly the same corner a lap later, when his brakes failed as a result of the first crash. He actually bailed off when he realised he wasn't going to stop, and the bike cartwheeled to the gravel, dumping fluids all over the track, which brought four other riders down. The red flag came out as the Worx bike lay against the safety barrier, flames licking its battered carcase.

Thanks to the one-bike rule, Hill never made the restart, which was won by Kiyonari from another non-Title Fighter, Stuart Easton. Brookes was third from Rutter and Seeley.

Kiyonari went into the final race with a 15-point lead from Hill, but while the Worx team had somehow totally rebuilt the Suzuki from the bare frame up between races, Hill never figured in the final.

Instead it was a scrap between the two HM Plant Hondas, Kiyonari crossing the line 0.63 second ahead of Brookes to complete a title winning treble. And with Hill only fifth, Brookes overtook him in the final standings to claim a 1-2 for Honda.

The final standings were Kiyonari 649, Brookes 625, Hill 620, Laverty 604, Rutter 559, Seeley 550.

It was an astounding finish to a season when no one rider had taken the championship by the scruff of the neck until it really mattered, in the final showdown. And in dominating Oulton to claim his third BSB title, Kiyonari had finally proved to everyone that not only was he back to his very best, but also a very worthy champion.

*Above:* BMW burn-out: Brogan celebrates his 2010 Evo title win.

*Above centre:* Sam Lowes swept to Supersport honours.
*Photos:* Clive Challinor Motorsport Photography

*Top left:* National Superstock champion John Kirkham.
*Photo:* Gavan Caldwell

*Top centre:* Superstock 600cc champion by just a single point, Josh Day on his Yamaha.
*Photo:* Clive Challinor Motorsport Photography

*Top right:* James Lodge claimed the 125cc championship.
*Photo:* Gavan Caldwell

## Mirror.co.uk BSB Evo

Even without the contrived Showdown formula of the main championship, the Mirror.co.uk BSB Evo class went all the way to the wire, with Jentin BMW's Steve Brogan winning one race and finishing second twice at Oulton to secure the title by three points from Aprilia mounted Kennaugh (431–428, Kennaugh having scored 198 of his points on a Kawasaki in the first half of the year).

Gary Johnson finished third overall on the AIM Suzuki after an impressive second half of the season, while Finnish rider Pauli Pekkanen enjoyed a consistent season on his 777 RR Motorsport Suzuki. He scored in all but one race and finished fourth overall.

## British Supersport

Sam Lowes wrapped up the Fuchs-Silkolene British Supersport title in the penultimate round at Silverstone with a third straight win on Gary Stubbington's GNS Honda CBR600RR.

Lowes, 20 years old from Lincoln, finished on the podium in ten of the 12 races, winning five of them to finish 33 points clear of nearest challenger James Westmorland. Shortly after the final round, Lowes joined the Louth-based Parkalgar Honda team to race in World Supersport.

Twenty-two-year-old Westmoreland, from Wyton, East Yorkshire, also put a strong season together, taking two of his ten podium finishes on the ex-World Supersport Came Yamaha R6.

Westmoreland's team-mate, Billy McConnell, won back-to-back races at Cadwell and Mallory, but crashes ruined his title bid and he slipped to fifth in the standings, behind all-action Gearlink Kawasaki rider Ben Wilson and the highly promising 22-year-old from Dublin, Jack Kennedy, on a Colin Appleyard/Macadam Racing Yamaha.

## Metzeler National Superstock

It seemed like every weekend there was one more BMW S1000RR on the Metzeler National Superstock grid, and many riders gave up the ghost trying to compete with the superfast German superbikes.

Jon Kirkham made the best use of his, winning five races and scoring in every round to take the title by a whopping 89 points from closest rival Glen Richards. The veteran Aussie was injured at Brands at the start of the year, but finished with a strong run on the Padgetts Honda, with seven straight podium finishes to beat another BMW rider, Tristan Palmer, to second overall by just two points.

Twenty-three-year-old Howie Mainwaring matured into a class act, manhandling the MSS Kawasaki ZX-10 – not the sweetest race bike in the class – to fourth in the points, ahead of another BMW ridden by Luke Quigley.

While the new BMWs were still being sorted early in the season, Steve Plater set a raging pace on the HM Plant Honda. He looked set to run away with the series after two wins and a second in the first three races, but a crash at the North West left him with a broken neck and nerve damage to his left arm. Despite two major operations on his neck to stabilise the injury, and an inordinate time for the nerve damage to heal, Plater was back for the last four races, finishing fourth in the final round at Oulton.

## Metzeler National Superstock 600

Josh Day – 22, from Cirencester – clinched the Metzeler National Superstock 600 title by a single point from 19-year-old Luke Stapleford in the final round at Oulton. Stapleford won the race on his Bournemouth Kawasaki by 0.342 second from John Simpson's Trickbits Triumph, but Day's eighth place on the AIR Racing Yamaha was just enough to give him the title.

Seventeen-year-old Danny Buchan finished third on an MSS Kawasaki, just four points down on Day, and Simpson was fourth.

## SpeedyRetail.com British 125

RS Racing/Earnshaws Motorcycle Honda rider James Lodge, 21, won the SpeedyRetail.com British 125 by four points from Rob Guiver on the SP125 Honda. Colin Appleyard/Macadam Racing's Dean Brown finished equal on points with Guiver, but lost out on count-back, with Guiver scoring two wins to 17-year-old Brown's one.

Taylor Mackenzie (17-year-old son of former GP star and three-times British Superbike champion Niall) took his third win of the year when he beat Brown by 2.9 seconds in the final round at Oulton.

Mackenzie finished fourth overall on the KRP Node 4 bike, while another son of a famous racer, Dakota Mamola (Randy's 15-year-old offspring), also competed in selected rounds of the championship, with second place at Snetterton his best result for KRP Monster Energy Honda.

## Henderson Harley-Davidson XR1200 Trophy

Former MotoGP rider Jeremy McWilliam (46) beat fellow veteran racer Mike Edwards (48) to the Henderson Harley-Davidson XR1200 Trophy, which was held at selected rounds of the BSB championship.

Riding for Kings Road, London dealer Warrs, McWilliams won five of the seven races (held at four circuits) and finished second in the other two. Edwards – on the Riders of Bridgwater entry – won one, and finished second four times and third once, with one dnf.

The only other rider to claim a race win was Lea Gourlay at Mallory, but he suffered serious injuries in a crash at the Ulster Grand Prix.

# SIDECAR WORLD CHAMPIONSHIP
# FINN BOUNCES BACK
By JOHN McKENZIE

AFTER the financial failure of the German management company that had run the Sidecar World Championship under the Superside banner for the last few years, it briefly looked as though the class might finally expire. But sidecars have a history of survival against the odds. The FIM stepped in immediately to manage and maintain the continuity of the series that has run uninterrupted since the inception of the world championship in 1949.

The calendar was revised, with planned visits to Knockhill, Carthegena and the Slovakiaring cancelled. The well-received day with the MotoGP series at the Sachsenring survived on the five-round schedule.

Once under way, it was another varied season of diverse venues, ranging from MotoGP to endurance racing, and it was the usual contenders in the spotlight – reigning champions Tom and Ben Birchall, three-times champion Tim Reeves, passengered by Greg Cluze, and 2008 champion Pekka Paivarinta, in his second season with the seemingly ageless Swiss Adolf Haenni in the chair.

Added to the mix was a new face (albeit 50 years old) in Kurt Hock, who was delighted to win his first world championship race in front of his home crowd at the Sachsenring; he finished fourth overall.

Mansfield brothers Ben and Tom Birchall began their title defence with a new LCR chassis and a change of motive power from the widely used Suzuki GSX-R1000 to a Yamaha R1.

## Round 1 – April 17, Le Mans, France

The 2010 championship opened where it had finished seven months before, at Le Mans, with 18 laps scheduled for noon on the Saturday prior to the 24-hour race.

Paivarinta claimed the first pole, with a 1m 43.643s, while Gary and Dan Knight were second, just ahead of the Birchalls, who were hampered by niggling steering problems.

The Finn took full advantage and led into the first corner, but just as Birchall moved into second on lap two, the race was stopped after Knight's engine blew, dumping oil on the track.

The restart was for 15 laps, and once more Paivarinta and Birchall shot away to set the pace. The Finn was able to find the quicker way through some back-markers, but the Birchalls closed up again, posting fastest lap (1m 43.058s) on the ninth, but they were unable to pass. In the end, Paivarinta claimed a clear win. Making up the rostrum for a best ever finish were Germans Hock and Rico Becker.

Ben Birchall was pleased to get some points. "We are happy with second today," he said. "We didn't have much luck passing the back-markers because there were yellow flags out…"

## Round 2 – May 8/9, Schleiz, Germany

The 3.805-mile Schleiz circuit in Germany hosted the first two-race weekend of the year, with 19 outfits from 11 countries participating. Birchall's qualifying time of 1m 29.542s secured pole from Paivarinta, with Reeves third.

Saturday's 11-lap sprint race saw Birchall swiftly establish a lead, closely followed by Paivarinta, who succumbed to determined home-race rider Hock on the second lap. The German got to within a couple of seconds of Birchall, but dropped to 4.030 seconds at the flag. Another best result for the fast-improving driver. Paivarinta and Reeves were left scrapping for third, the Finn prevailing.

Birchall had a four-point lead heading into Sunday's 22-lap Gold Race.

Paivarinta led away, but the English driver dropped to fourth on the first lap, and had to overcome both Reeves and Hock before he was able to tag on to the leader. Birchall claimed fastest lap, at 1m 28.856s, on the sixth, only to run into brake problems, which caused him to settle for a safe second. Reeves won his battle with Hock to gain his first rostrum place of the year; Paivarinta established a one-point overall lead.

## Round 3 – June 19/20, Rijeka, Croatia

In retrospect, every season seems to have a fulcrum, the point at which the outcome is sealed. The 2010 title was decided in Friday's free practice, when Ben and Tom Birchall hit a kerb and crashed heavily, flipping the outfit. Tom was thrown clear, but driver Ben was trapped under the skidding

upturned outfit, suffering a badly grazed back that required brief hospitalisation.

Despite his injuries, the pair continued and with a truly heroic effort picked up 21 points. It could have been more like 40 or so had Ben been fit. The return to his winning ways by Reeves put further pressure on the defenders.

Paivarinta took pole, seven-tenths in front of Reeves. Birchall qualified sixth.

Saturday afternoon's 11-lap sprint saw a mid-race battle between Paivarinta and Reeves, before the Team Suzuki Finland outfit finally broke clear to win by four seconds. Josef Moser and Manfred Wechselberger took their first rostrum 25 seconds behind in third. Battered and on the wrong tyre, Birchall battled to 11th. Now Paivarinta was 21 points clear and looking confident.

Changeable weather before Sunday's 20-lap Gold race made tyre choice a lottery. Paivarinta started on slicks, while Reeves picked an intermediate front, which proved to be a wise choice.

Reeves led early on, with Paivarinta chasing and then taking his turn at leading. Into the final lap, the Finn was on Reeves's tail, but was unable to make the move when they got among back-markers.

Reeves won by just under three seconds, his first victory since winning here in August, 2009. It was also his 25th world championship win.

Hero of the day was a desperately sore and patched-up Ben Birchall in third, wearing borrowed leathers – his own had been destroyed.

The outcome left Paivarinta and Haenni 25 points clear with 50 to go. A measured approach and conclusion to the season would see the 2008 champion regain the title.

Reeves moved into second, one point in front of Birchall, whose flayed back required skin grafts and weeks of treatment on his return home.

## Round 4 – July 17/18, Sachsenring, Germany

The second visit to Germany was in front of a huge MotoGP crowd at the Sachsenring. With Ben Birchall still recovering and Tim Reeves back on form, there was a surprise result when Hock popped up again to take his first world championship win.

Reeves took pole, from Birchall and Hock. Paivarinta, heading row two, was suffering tyre problems, and he made a mid-meeting switch from Yokohama to Avon rubber.

Reeves set an early lead, but couldn't meet Hock's challenge, and the German won by 4.3 seconds.

Paivarinta's safe third place kept him on target for the title. The Birchall brothers were now battling for second. "Before the accident in Croatia, we were positive we could win the title again," said Ben.

## Round 5 – September 11, Magny-Cours, France

The sidecars returned to Magny-Cours for the first time since October 2003, supporting the Bol D'Or endurance race.

After scoring 111 points over the previous six races, Paivarinta and Haenni needed just one more to take the title. Keeping out of trouble would do it. There was still a runner-up spot to battle for, though, with triple champion Tim Reeves leading Ben Birchall by just one point. Pride was at stake.

Swiss pair Markus Schlosser and Thomas Hofer were early leaders, but their progress was halted by the red flag after just two laps. The race was restarted, but another incident brought a second stoppage. With the clock ticking towards the start of the biggest event in the French racing calendar, circuit officials cut the race to a five-lap dash.

Reeves and Schlosser set the pace again. Birchall was third, but with only five laps was unable to make an impression. Reeves took his second win of the year by 0.287 second and so sealed the runner-up spot in the championship.

The title went to fifth-placed Paivarinta and Haenni. It was the Finn's second title, but the entire paddock was pleased with Adolf Haenni's success after 21 years in the sport. After passengering at the top level with the likes of Steve Webster, Klaus Klaffenbock, Jorg Steinhausen, Markus Schlosser, Derek Brindley, Hans Hugli and Mike Roscher, finally he had realised his dream.

In 2009, Tom Birchall had been the youngest world champion; in 2010, it was Haenni who set a new record at the other end of the scale, at 55 years and 3 months.

# JOURNEY TO THE TOP

By PAUL CARRUTHERS

I F a journeyman is truly a craftsman who has fully learned his trade and has earned money, but is not yet a master, then Josh Hayes was most definitely a journeyman racer. But not any more. After earning his first championship in the premier class of AMA road racing, he has reached master status, his work as the 2010 AMA American Superbike champion definitely being deemed worthy by those making such judgements.

Looking back at the former AMA Superbike champions, the roads they followed to the title are far different from the one that Hayes travelled. Take Nicky Hayden for example: quick rise through the Supersport ranks to a factory Honda Superbike ride, an AMA Superbike title, and then off to MotoGP and a world championship. Mat Mladin? Whisked off to Europe at too young an age to dabble in GPs, a return to Australia and then off to America with factory rides beckoning; retires with seven AMA Superbike titles. Ben Spies? Another rocket-ship ride to stardom in the support classes, factory Suzukis for Superbike, AMA titles and then off to conquer the world.

Not so for Hayes. Despite a hot start that saw him win the opening 750cc Superstock race at Daytona in 1999 on a Valvoline Suzuki, his career didn't magically take flight. His rides that year attracted the attention of team owner Kevin Erion, and Hayes joined the Honda backed team for 2000. A big crash at Daytona left him with injuries that hampered his entire season and he went winless. Ditto for the following year. In 2002, Hayes was back in the Valvoline backed Suzuki support team, but again he was winless in Supersport and Formula Xtreme.

In 2003, Hayes won his first title, taking Superstock on an Attack Suzuki with two wins. Still the factories didn't take the bait, and the following year saw him in the Superbike class

on a privateer Kawasaki. He showed well with some fifth-place finishes, and that led to a better effort the following year, with his first Superbike podium on the Attack Kawasaki at Road America.

But still no factory Superbike offers. Instead he went back to Erion Honda where he earned the Formula Xtreme title in 2006 – an effort he hoped would lead to a promotion to the American Honda Superbike team. But nothing came of that. So he was back to Erion in 2007, coming away with another title and seven wins in Formula Xtreme, and four wins in Supersport. But that still wasn't enough. And it didn't help matters when the factory Honda team was disbanded. Still, Hayes didn't get the call to ride a CBR1000RR for the Corona team; that 'factory' spot went to Neil Hodgson.

So Hayes returned to Erion Honda in 2008 and started off the season by winning the Daytona 200 – only to lose it shortly thereafter when it was discovered that his CBR600RR had an illegal crankshaft. Damn the black cloud. He bravely fought back, however, and ended up second in the title chase. Then, finally, the reward came. From Yamaha.

Hayes was a full-on Yamaha factory Superbike rider in 2009, and he made the most of it, winning seven races en route to finishing second in the title chase to the master himself – Mladin. He'd finally arrived – at the ripe young age of 34. And he entered the 2010 season as the man to beat, often a surefire lead-in to disaster. Not this time.

But the new year didn't start well for Hayes, who never seems to find the easy road to success. Instead he began at Daytona with a 13th and a sixth. Not the start he was looking for, especially with National Guard Suzuki's Jake Zemke winning both races and looking virtually unbeatable.

Zemke's reign at the top didn't last long, however, and it

*Above:* Tommy Hayden came close to emulating younger brother Nicky's AMA title.
Photo: Gold & Goose

*Top:* Josh Hayes took a long awaited Superbike crown, his Yamaha ending a long reign by Suzuki.
Photo: AMA Pro Series

*Above left:* Hayes leads rivals Zemke and Pegram.

*Left:* Privateer Ducati rider Larry Pegram enjoys his hard earned win at Fontana.

*Right* Jake Zemke started well, but his reign did not last.
Photo: Photos: AMA Pro Series

turned out that Daytona would be the highlight of his season. Though he would end up third in the title chase, the Michael Jordan Motorsports rider would only finish on the podium three more times, and he never won another race in his first season on the Suzuki GSX-R1000.

But Hayes was also soldiering on without a victory. After fourth- and second-place finishes in the second round at Auto Club Speedway in Southern California, and sixth and second at Road Atlanta in Georgia, he finally won his first of the season at Infineon Raceway in Northern California's wine country. Infineon was the site of his first win on a Superbike in 2009, and he went in confident and ready. In turn, he won and he won big, sweeping the two races to show that the series favourite wasn't done yet.

A win and a second at the next two rounds at Road America and Mid-Ohio put him where he needed to be to make a run at his first Superbike title. He came up against teammate Ben Bostrom's buzz-saw at Laguna Seca and finished second (just one race is held there, supporting MotoGP), but bounced back with third and a victory at Virginia International Raceway. A perfect two races at New Jersey Motorsports Park left him with a handy points lead going into the series finale at Barber Motorsports Park, and after a second place and a steady seventh, he was crowned as the champion. It also earned him job security, as Yamaha signed him up for two more years.

After the early part of the season, this was a championship about only two men, as Yoshimura Suzuki's Tommy Hayden stepped up as the only one capable of competing with Hayes week in and week out. The races, though, often were close and featured more than those two. It was just that they were far more consistent than the rest.

Suzuki went into the season hopeful that the oldest of the three Hayden brothers could deliver its eighth straight title in the class, and he came close. Hayden won his first ever AMA Superbike race at California Speedway in April and took four more along the way. He would end up with five wins and ten other podium finishes, just 14 points behind Hayes. After winning the first race at Virginia International Raceway, Hay-

den was just a single point behind Hayes in the fight for the title, but the latter fired back with three wins in a row, giving him a 22-point lead going into the season finale.

Still, if it weren't for Hayes, this story would be about Hayden finally having the breakthrough season many have predicted for years.

With Zemke ending the series third after his red-hot start burned out, fourth went to Larry Pegram on his self-run Ducati with backing from Foremost Insurance. Pegram won the first race at Auto Club Speedway, but never repeated that effort and didn't finish better than third in posting just four more podium finishes. It was the same place he'd finished in 2009, but that year saw him win three times, so this was far less fulfilling.

Ben Bostrom's season in the well-funded Pat Clark Motorsports team started slowly, hit its stride mid-season with an impressive victory in front of the year's largest crowd at Laguna Seca, and continued strong until injuries at the end cost him an easy fourth overall. The Laguna round was the highlight of the season for Bostrom and the team as the likeable Californian ended a six-year winless drought in AMA Superbike racing with a hard-fought victory over Hayes. Laguna Seca has always been good to Bostrom, this latest win there being his second AMA Superbike victory on the Monterey Peninsula; three of his career World Superbike wins also came at Laguna. The 2010 win was also the first ever in AMA Superbike racing at Laguna Seca for Yamaha.

Despite missing the final two races of the season with broken ribs, Bostrom only came up two points short of fourth in the title chase.

Sixth went to Blake Young, the second Yoshimura Suzuki rider bouncing back after suffering a broken neck at a test at Barber Motorsports Park and missing five races. Young had won his career-first AMA Superbike race at Road Atlanta (and backed it up with a double-header sweep the next day) prior to the accident, and anyone who thought the crash and recovery would slow the Wisconsinite was mistaken, as he returned with three fourth places and a win in the very last race. He was hoping he would be remembered when it came

*Above:* Ben Bostrom scored a high-profile victory at Laguna Seca.
Photo: Gold & Goose

*Top:* Suzuki-mounted Blake Young (22) and John Hopkins (21) battled for victory in the season finale at Barber Motorsports Park. Young won.

*Centre right:* Daytona Sportbike champion Martin Cardenas.
Photos: AMA Pro Series

time for Suzuki to name its line-up for 2011.

Privateer Taylor Knapp was seventh, with three fifth places highlighting his season on the ex-Mat Mladin 2009 Suzuki GSX-R100. Knapp ended up ahead of Monster Suzuki's Chris Ulrich, Canadian Brett McCormick (filling in for Aaron Yates, who had suffered a season ending broken leg at the second round at Auto Club Speedway) and Ulrich's team-mate, John Hopkins, back from GP and World Superbike racing for his first foray in AMA Superbike racing.

Hopkins's season was rough as he battled through the early part with three fifth-place finishes before finally opting to have his oft-injured right wrist surgically repaired. Close to being forced into retirement, his last grasp at saving his career worked and he came back from the surgery to post a fifth, two thirds and a second as the season came to a close. If he stays healthy through the off-season, Hopkins could end up being a major threat in 2011.

Jake Holden, the man everyone calls as the first choice for fill-in rides, did well in replacing Hopkins on the Monster Suzuki, a pair of fifths and a fourth highlighting his tenure.

## DAYTONA SPORTBIKE

Although the Daytona SportBike Championship won't be remembered for how it started, it definitely will be remembered for how it ended. And the road to get there was pretty damn exciting as well.

While five different riders won on four different brands of motorcycle in 2009, only four men on three brands took victories in 2010, but the racing was just as competitive, if not more so.

For most of the season, it was Graves Yamaha's Josh Herrin vs Geico Insurance Suzuki's Danny Eslick, who took the title in 2009 on the controversial Buell. Herrin won five races and Eslick three, and they both went into the final round with a chance to lift the title. The two of them went at it with a vengeance, the battle between them ultimately ending with Eslick – without remorse or shouts of "not-guilty" – simply punting Herrin off the track and into the gravel trap in the

final race. No love lost there, and it's an on-track, off-track hatred that will surely spill over to 2011's series.

But a funny thing happened to those two as they battled away to the title – Martin Cardenas came along and pulled the rug out from under both their preoccupied feet.

Cardenas is the Columbian import who won seven times in 2009, but ended up suffering a broken hand late in the season that ruined his title chances. He was well up to the task in 2010. Again he had a few crashes – something you wouldn't expect from a rider seemingly so immaculate in his riding style – and the first was on the opening lap of the all-important Daytona 200, a race ultimately won by Herrin.

Cardenas crashed out of race two at Auto Club Speedway after winning the first race, then he crashed out of race two at Infineon Raceway after winning race one. From there, he was nearly picture perfect, and he ended up with nine victories – four more than Herrin and six more than Eslick – and the title was his by eight points. And a worthy champion he was. He didn't get caught up in the Eslick/Herrin scrum, he minded his own business, kept his mouth shut, and went out and won on the racetrack.

Eslick took second, while Herrin was third. Then came the first non-Japanese machine, with veteran Steve Rapp fourth on his Latus Motors backed Ducati. Rapp nearly had started the season without a ride, but Latus, long-time sponsor of dirt-tracker Joe Kopp, decided it wanted to try road racing, and Rapp was rescued. He repaid that faith ten-fold with a season that featured seven podium finishes.

Project 1 Yamaha's Dane Westby was fifth, the Oklahoman's best results coming in the first and last races of the season – second in the Daytona 200 and third in the series finale at Barber. Next came another fast young rider from Oklahoma, Cory West, giving the Sooner State three riders in the top ten.

Much was expected of Herrin's young Yamaha team-mate, Tommy Aquino, after the Californian had ended 2009 with four podium finishes. For 2010, the youngster was on the podium only twice, and he finished the year seventh.

The only other rider to win a race in 2010, other than

Cardenas, Herrin and Eslick, was another of the rising group of racers, Bobby Fong. The Californian made up for crashing out of the lead at Laguna Seca to finally earn his first victory at Virginia International Raceway a month later.

South African Clinton Seller also made a name for himself in 2010, the Project 1 Yamaha team-mate of Westby finishing a career best second in the first race at the season finale in Alabama. Former two-time AMA Supermoto champion Chris Fillmore was tenth in the series on his Vesrah Suzuki.

## MAJOR IMPROVEMENT

The upheavals of 2009 had meant a year of turmoil, controversy and complaint, as well as some good racing. In the second year of the DMG regime in AMA racing, during which there was a change of leadership, it didn't take long for 2009's season-long bickering to be forgotten.

The season started with a smoothly run Daytona Bike Week and no sign of the calamities that had wrecked the previous season's race and most of the season. The revised categories had become familiar, and by and large the teams had resettled and got on with the racing. It was a warm and fuzzy paddock for most of the season.

There was some significant and welcome fine tuning, most significantly the return to clutch starts rather than rolling starts, and the abandonment of pace cars joining the track mid-race: henceforth, they would be used only in red-flag situations, rather than on a 'hot' racetrack, one on which bikes were travelling at racing speed.

There was a new requirement, also on safety grounds, for riders in some categories to be equipped with 'ship-to-shore' radios to communicate with their pits. These were introduced

under the management of Roger Edmondson late in 2009, but the former czar's era in AMA road racing ended when he was tossed out for a second time. The new leader was his former right-hand man, David Atlas, a lawyer who could actually be seen at the races – even mingling with team owners, riders and crew. Yes, things were definitely different, although the series is far from perfect. Still, there seems to be hope. A lot more hope than what the 2009 season ended with.

As for 2011, a bleak economy continues to wreak havoc. Hayes has a contract with Yamaha. Ditto Herrin with the Chuck Graves run team, but he will stick with the Daytona SportBike class. And class champion Cardenas has signed again with Monster Suzuki, presumably for a move up to the Superbike series, although that has yet to be announced.

Will Yoshimura have both Hayden and Young back for more? At press time, neither had been signed, although one would expect that at least one, if not both, would return. Will Pegram get enough support to bring his Ducatis back?

There are still no factory Kawasakis in the paddock, although there's talk of Eric Bostrom returning to the series full time on a new ZX-10 with Attack Racing. And there's still no sign of Honda, although rumours of it also returning are always being spun. We'll believe it when we see it. Most are optimistic that the Pat Clark Yamaha team will return with Bostrom and Pat Clark's racing son, Chris.

Again, more questions than answers. But the on-track action during the 2010 season was epic, and there's hope that the economy will continue to improve and the big teams will return. One thing is certain, it won't be easy for them when they do, because the journeyman racer Hayes will be a serious foe to anyone trying to take away what has taken him so long to make his own.

*Above:* Josh Herrin (Yamaha) had a feisty run to third in the Daytona Sportbike class.
*Photo:* AMA Pro Series

*Above:* Picture perfect: Columbian import Martin Cardenas took a narrow title victory in the Sportbike class on his Monster Suzuki.

*Left:* Danny Eslick – his bitter battle with Herrin was a season highlight.
*Photos:* Tom Hnatiw/Flick Of The Wrist

# MAJOR RESULTS

## OTHER CHAMPIONSHIP RACING SERIES WORLDWIDE

Compiled by PETER McLAREN

## AMA Championship Road Race Series (Superbike)

**DAYTONA INTERNATIONAL SPEEDWAY, Daytona Beach, Florida, 4–5 March, 44.300 miles/70.006km**
**Race 1**
**1** Jake Zemke (Suzuki); **2** Tommy Hayden (Suzuki); **3** Larry Pegram (Ducati); **4** Aaron Yates (Suzuki); **5.** Blake Young (Suzuki); **6** Chris Urlich (Suzuki); **7** Taylor Knapp (Suzuki); **8** Shawn Higbee (Buell); **9** Shane Narbone (Suzuki); **10** Barrett Long (Ducati)

**Race 2**
**1** Jake Zemke (Suzuki); **2** Tommy Hayden (Suzuki); **3** Ben Bostrom (Yamaha); **4** Aaron Yates (Suzuki); **5** Larry Pegram (Ducati); **6** Josh Hayes (Yamaha); **7** Blake Young (Suzuki); **8** Brett McCormick (Suzuki); **9** David Anthony (Suzuki); **10** Taylor Knapp (Suzuki).

**AUTO CLUB SPEEDWAY, Fontana, California, 27–28 March, 43.700 miles/70.328km**
**Race 1**
**1** Larry Pegram (Ducati); **2** Jake Zemke (Suzuki); **3** Aaron Yates (Suzuki); **4** Josh Hayes (Yamaha); **5** Blake Young (Suzuki); **6** Tommy Hayden (Suzuki); **7** John Hopkins (Suzuki); **8** Ben Bostrom (Yamaha); **9** Chris Ulrich (Suzuki); **10** David Anthony (Suzuki).

**Race 2**
**1** Tommy Hayden (Suzuki); **2** Josh Hayes (Yamaha); **3** Blake Young (Suzuki); **4** Jake Zemke (Suzuki); **5** John Hopkins (Suzuki); **6** Ben Bostrom (Yamaha); **7** Brett McCormick (Suzuki); **8** Chris Ulrich (Suzuki); **9** Taylor Knapp (Suzuki); **10** David Anthony (Suzuki).

**ROAD ATLANTA, Braselton, Georgia, 17–18 April, 51.000 miles/82.077km**
**Race 1**
**1** Blake Young (Suzuki); **2** Tommy Hayden (Suzuki); **3** Jake Zemke (Suzuki); **4** Ben Bostrom (Yamaha); **5** John Hopkins (Suzuki); **6** Josh Hayes (Yamaha); **7** Chris Ulrich (Suzuki); **8** Taylor Knapp (Suzuki); **9** Chris Clark (Yamaha); **10** Barrett Long (Ducati).

**Race 2**
**1** Blake Young (Suzuki); **2** Josh Hayes (Yamaha); **3** Tommy Hayden (Suzuki); **4** Jake Zemke (Suzuki); **5** John Hopkins (Suzuki); **6** Larry Pegram (Ducati); **7** Taylor Knapp (Suzuki); **8** Chris Ulrich (Suzuki); **9** Chris Clark (Yamaha); **10** Barrett Long (Ducati).

**INFINEON RACEWAY, Sonoma, California, 15–16 May, 51.040 miles/82.141km**
**Race 1**
**1** Josh Hayes (Yamaha); **2** Ben Bostrom (Yamaha); **3** Larry Pegram (Ducati); **4** Jake Zemke (Suzuki); **5** Blake Young (Suzuki); **6** Tommy Hayden (Suzuki); **7** Jake Holden (Suzuki); **8** Chris Ulrich (Suzuki); **9** David Anthony (Suzuki); **10** Chris Peris (BMW).

**Race 2**
**1** Josh Hayes (Yamaha); **2** Ben Bostrom (Yamaha); **3** Larry Pegram (Ducati); **4** Tommy Hayden (Suzuki); **5** Blake Young (Suzuki); **6** Jake Zemke (Suzuki); **7** Jake Holden (Suzuki); **8** Chris Ulrich (Suzuki); **9** Taylor Knapp (Suzuki); **10** Geoff May (Buell).

**ROAD AMERICA, Elkhart Lake, Wisconsin, 5–6 June, 52.000 miles/83.686km**
**Race 1**
**1** Josh Hayes (Yamaha); **2** Tommy Hayden (Suzuki); **3** Blake Young (Suzuki); **4** Larry Pegram (Ducati); **5** Jake Zemke (Suzuki); **6** Jake Holden (Suzuki); **7** Ben Bostrom (Yamaha); **8** Taylor Knapp (Suzuki); **9** Brett McCormick (Suzuki); **10** Chris Ulrich (Suzuki)

**Race 2**
**1** Tommy Hayden (Suzuki); **2** Josh Hayes (Yamaha); **3** Jake Zemke (Suzuki); **4** Larry Pegram (Ducati); **5** Jake Holden (Suzuki); **6** Ben Bostrom (Yamaha); **7** Blake Young (Suzuki); **8** Brett McCormick (Suzuki); **9** Chris Ulrich (Suzuki); **10** Geoff May (Buell).

**MID-OHIO, Lexington, Ohio, 17–18 July, 50.400 miles/81.110km**
**Race 1**
**1** Josh Hayes (Yamaha); **2** Ben Bostrom (Yamaha); **3** Tommy Hayden (Suzuki); **4** Larry Pegram (Ducati); **5** Jake Holden (Suzuki); **6** Jake Zemke (Suzuki); **7** Brett McCormick (Suzuki); **8** Eric Bostrom (Suzuki); **9** Chris Ulrich (Suzuki); **10** Jordan Szoke (Honda).

**Race 2**
**1** Tommy Hayden (Suzuki); **2** Josh Hayes (Yamaha); **3** Larry Pegram (Ducati); **4** Ben Bostrom (Yamaha); **5** Brett McCormick (Suzuki); **6** Jake Zemke (Suzuki); **7** Taylor Knapp (Suzuki); **8** Chris Ulrich (Suzuki); **9** Geoff May (Buell); **10** Kurtis Roberts (Yamaha).

**MAZDA RACEWAY LAGUNA SECA, Monterey, California, 25 July, 41.400 miles/66.627km**
**1** Ben Bostrom (Yamaha); **2** Josh Hayes (Yamaha); **3** Tommy Hayden (Suzuki); **4** Jake Holden (Suzuki); **5** Larry Pegram (Ducati); **6** Jake Zemke (Suzuki); **7** Eric Bostrom (Suzuki); **8** Brett McCormick (Suzuki); **9** Chris Peris (BMW); **10** Geoff May (Buell).

**VIRGINIA INTERNATIONAL RACEWAY, Alton, Virginia, 14–15 August, 51.750 miles/83.248km**
**Race 1**
**1** Tommy Hayden (Suzuki); **2** Ben Bostrom (Yamaha); **3** Josh Hayes (Yamaha); **4** Larry Pegram (Ducati); **5** Taylor Knapp (Suzuki); **6** Brett McCormick (Suzuki); **7** Eric Bostrom (Suzuki); **8** Jake Zemke (Suzuki); **9** Chris Ulrich (Suzuki); **10** Jordan Szoke (Honda).

**Race 2**
**1** Josh Hayes (Yamaha); **2** Ben Bostrom (Yamaha); **3** Tommy Hayden (Suzuki); **4** Brett McCormick (Suzuki); **5** Taylor Knapp (Suzuki); **6** Geoff May (Buell); **7** Chris Ulrich (Suzuki); **8** Jake Zemke (Suzuki); **9** Larry Pegram (Ducati); **10** Jordan Szoke (Honda).

**NEW JERSEY MOTORSPORTS PARK, Millville, New Jersey, 4–5 September, 51.750 miles/82.284km**
**Race 1**
**1** Josh Hayes (Yamaha); **2** Tommy Hayden (Suzuki); **3** Ben Bostrom (Yamaha); **4** Blake Young (Suzuki); **5** John Hopkins (Suzuki); **6** Jake Zemke (Suzuki); **7** Larry Pegram (Ducati); **8** Geoff May (Buell); **9** Taylor Knapp (Suzuki); **10** Chris Peris (BMW)

**Race 2**
**1** Josh Hayes (Yamaha); **2** Tommy Hayden (Suzuki); **3** John Hopkins (Suzuki); **4** Blake Young (Suzuki); **5** Brett McCormick (Suzuki); **6** Jake Zemke (Suzuki); **7** Geoff May (Buell); **8** Taylor Knapp (Suzuki); **9** Chris Ulrich (Suzuki); **10** Shane Narobonne (Suzuki).

**BARBER MOTORSPORTS PARK, Leeds, Alabama, 25–26 September, 49.890 miles/80.435km**
**Race 1**
**1** Tommy Hayden (Suzuki); **2** Josh Hayes (Yamaha); **3** John Hopkins (Suzuki); **4** Blake Young (Suzuki); **5** Taylor Knapp (Suzuki); **6** Geoff May (Buell); **7** Jake Holden (Yamaha); **8** Jeff Wood (Suzuki); **9** Shane Narobonne (Suzuki); **10** Brett McCormick (Suzuki).

**Race 2**
**1** Blake Young (Suzuki); **2** John Hopkins (Suzuki); **3** Larry Pegram (Ducati); **4** Tommy Hayden (Suzuki); **5** Jake Zemke (Suzuki); **6** Geoff May (Buell); **7** Josh Hayes (Yamaha); **8** Taylor Knapp (Suzuki); **9** Trent Gibson (Suzuki); **10** Jeff Wood (Suzuki).

**Final Championship Points**

| | | |
|---|---|---|
| 1 | Josh Hayes | 466 |
| 2 | Tommy Hayden | 452 |
| 3 | Jake Zemke | 332 |
| 4 | Larry Pegram | 297 |
| 5 | Ben Bostrom | 295 |
| 6 | Blake Young | 283 |
| 7 | Taylor Knapp | 227 |
| 8 | Chris Ulrich | 188 |
| 9 | Brett McCormick | 180 |
| 10 | John Hopkins | 151 |

## Endurance World Championship

**24 HEURES DU MANS, Le Mans Bugatti Circuit, France, 17–18 April.**
**Endurance World Championship, Round 1.**
**828 laps of the 2.600-mile/4.185km circuit, 2152.800 miles/3465.180km**
**1** GSR-Kawasaki, FRA: Julien da Costa/Olivier Four/Gregory Lablanc (Kawasaki), 24h 0m 47.253s, 89.66mph/144.30km/h.
**2** Yamaha Austria Racing Team, AUT: Igor Jerman/Steve Martin/Gwen Giabbani (Yamaha), 817 laps; **3** RAC 41 - City Bike, FRA: Greg Junod/Gregg Black/Olivier Deporter (Suzuki), 813 laps; **4** Yamaha France GMT 94 Ipone, FRA: David Checa/Gregorio Lavilla/Kenny Foray (Yamaha), 808 laps; **5** RT Moto Virus Racing, ITA: William Grarre/Eric Mizera/Frédéric Jond (Suzuki), 803 laps; **6** Bolliger Team Switzerland, SWI: Saiger Horst/Frederic Chabosseau/Roman Stamm (Kawasaki), 802 laps; **7** Qatar Endurance Racing Team I, QAT: Anthony Delhalle/Alex Cudlin/Rashid Al Mannai (Suzuki), 801 laps; **8** Team Motors Events, FRA: Vincent Bocquet/Emilien Humeau/Gérald Muteau (Suzuki), 797 laps; **9** Infini Power Bike Troyes, FRA: Etienne Dupuis/Kevin Hiernaux/Fabrice Holub (Kawasaki), 793 laps; **10** Metiss JLC Moto, FRA: Christophe Michel/Cyril Huvier/Emmanuel Cheron (Metiss), 793 laps; **11** Colexon Racing Team, BEL: Florian Kresse/Marc Wildisen/Udo Reichmann (BMW), 790 laps; **12** TRT27/Bazar 2 La Becane FRA: Dylan Buisson/Etienne Masson/Vincent Houssin (Suzuki), 789 laps; **13** 3D Endurance Moto Center, FRA: Jero Danton/Charles Geers/Emmanuel Labussiere (Kawasaki), 785 laps; **14** Atomic Moto Sport, FRA: Josetxo Sainz Zozaya/Olivier Ulmann/Pierrot Lerat Vanstaen (Suzuki), 782 laps; **15** BMP Elf 99 Racing Team, BEL: Matthieu Lagrive/Werner Daemen/Damian Cudlin (Honda), 780 laps;
**Fastest lap:** BMW Michelin, 1m 38.425s, 95.114mph/153.071km/h, on lap 122.
**Championship points: 1** GSR-Kawasaki, 35; **2** Yamaha Austria Racing Team, 28; **3** RAC 41 - City Bike, 22; **4** Yamaha France GMT 94 Ipone, 18; **5** RT Moto Virus Racing, 15; **6** Bolliger Team Switzerland, 14.

**8 HOURS OF ALBACETE, Albacete, Spain, 22 May.**
**Endurance World Championship, Round 2.**
**295 laps of the 2.199-mile/3.539km circuit, 648.705 miles/1044.005km**
**1** Suzuki Endurance Racing Team, FRA: Vincent Philippe/Freddy Foray/Daisaku Sakai (Suzuki), 8h 1m 23.339s, 80.85mph/130.12km/h.
**2** Bolliger Team Switzerland, SWI: Saiger Horst/Patric Muff/Roman Stamm (Kawasaki), 294 laps; **3** National Moto Honda, FRA: Emeric Jonchiere/David Morillon (Honda), 293 laps; **4** YMES Folch Endurance, SPA: Pedro Vallcaneras/Jose Manuel Luis Rita/Jordi Almeda (Yamaha), 292 laps; **5** RT Moto Virus Racing, ITA: Lucas de Carolis/Eric Mizera/William Grarre (Suzuki), 291 laps; **6** AM Moto Racing Competition, FRA: Raphaël Chèvre/Anthony Dos Santos/Julien Millet (Suzuki), 290 laps; **7** BMP Elf 99 Racing Team, BEL: Matthieu Lagrive/Werner Daemen/Damian Cudlin (Honda), 289 laps; **8** Team X-One ITA: Vittorio Iannuzzo/Emiliano Bellucci/Luca Bono (Yamaha), 287 laps; **9** Andalucia BMW, SPA: Alvaro Molina/Camille Hedelin/Augustin Rosivall (BMW), 286 laps; **10** Boening Penz 13 Racing, GER: Jure Stibilj/Rico Penzkofer/Steve Mizera (BMW), 286 laps; **11** Atomic Moto Sport, FRA: Josetxo Sainz Zozaya/Emmanuel Thuillier/Michael Lalevee (Suzuki), 286 laps; **12** MCS Racing Ipone ITA: Janez Prosenic/Ricardo Saseta/Bostjan Pintar (Suzuki), 285 laps; **13** Qatar Endurance Racing Team I, QAT: Anthony Delhalle/Alex Cudlin/Rashid Al Mannai (Suzuki), 285 laps; **14** No Limits Motor Team, ITA: Alessio Aldrovandi/Victor Casas/Ferrán Casas (Suzuki), 284 laps; **15** Cordoba Patrimonio De La Humanidad, SPA: Dailos Sainz/Javi Valera/Santi Sanz (Kawasaki), 283 laps.
**Fastest lap:** BMP Elf 99 Racing Team, 1m 32.844s, 85.26mph/137.22km/h, on lap 251.
**Championship points: 1** Bolliger Team Switzerland, 38; **2** Yamaha Austria Racing Team, 36; **3** GSR-Kawasaki, 35; **4** Suzuki Endurance Racing Team, 30; **5** RT Moto Virus Racing, 28; **6** RAC 41 - City Bike, 22.

**8 HOURS OF SUZUKA, Suzuka, Japan, 25 July.**
**Endurance World Championship, Round 3.**
**215 laps of the 3.618-mile/5.821km circuit, 777.870 miles/1251.515km**
**1** MuSashi RT Harc Pro, JPN: Ryuichi Kiyonari/Takaaki Nakagami/Takumi Takahashi (Honda), 8h 1m 13.428s, 96.96mph/156.04km/h.
**2** Keihin Kohara RT, JPN: Shinichi Ito/Makoto Tamada (Honda), 214 laps; **3** FCC TSR Honda, JPN: Kousuke Akiyoshi/Jonathan Rea/Yuki Takahashi (Honda), 213 laps; **4** Plot Faro Panthera, JPN: Osamu Deguchi/Takashi Yasuda (Suzuki), 212 laps; **5** Team Plus One, JPN: Satoru Iwata/Yusuke Teshima (Honda), 211 laps; **6** Yoshimura Suzuki with Eneos, JPN: Yukio Kagayama/Daisaku Sakai/Nobuatsu Aoki (Suzuki), 211 laps; **7** Teluru Honey Bee, JPN: Hiroki Noda/Taro Sekiguchi (Honda), 210 laps; **8** Beet Racing, JPN: Hidemichi Takahashi/Yuki Hatano/Osamu Nishijima (Kawasaki), 208 laps; **9** Bolliger Team Switzerland, SWI: Saiger Horst/Patric Muff/Roman Stamm (Kawasaki), 206 laps; **10** Honda Escargot & PGR, JPN: Masao Kuboyama/Naohiro Nakatsuhara (Honda), 206 laps; **11** Honda Suzuka Racing Team, JPN: Taketsuna Morii/Yusuke Masuda/Tomomasa Nakamura (Honda), 205 laps; **12** Motobum and Ishigaki Island Uminchu, JPN: Takaomi Takahashi/Takayuki Oki/Ikumi Shimizu (Honda), 204 laps; **13** RS Itoh & Asia, JPN: Isami Higashimura/Tetsuro Iwasaki/Akihiro Ioda (Kawasaki), 204 laps; **14** Team Frontier Clever-Wolf Racing, JPN: Mitsuo Saito/Takahiro Fukami/Magali Langlois (Yamaha), 203 laps; **15** Evangelio RT & Trick Star, JPN: Sinya Takeishi/Tamaki Serizawa/Yoshihiro Konno (Kawasaki), 203 laps.
**Fastest lap:** FCC TSR Honda, 2m 8.705s, 101.17mph/162.82km/h, on lap 113.
**Championship points: 1** Bolliger Team Switzerland, 46; **2** Yamaha Austria Racing Team, 36; **3** GSR-Kawasaki, 35; **4** MuSashi RT Harc Pro, 30; **5** Suzuki Endurance Racing Team, 30; **6** RT Moto Virus Racing, 28.

**24 HOURS BOL D'OR, Magny-Cours, France, 11–12 September.**
**Endurance World Championship, Round 4.**
**781 laps of the 2.741-mile/4.411km circuit, 2140.721 miles/3444.991km**
**1** Suzuki Endurance Racing Team, FRA: Vincent Philippe/Freddy Foray/Guillaume Dietrich (Suzuki), 24h 0m 17.682s, 89.17mph/143.51km/h.
**2** Bolliger Team Switzerland, SWI: Saiger Horst/Patric Muff/Roman Stamm (Kawasaki), 767 laps; **3** YMES Folch Endurance, SPA: Pedro Vallcaneras/Jose Manuel Luis Rita/Jordi Almeda (Yamaha), 766 laps; **4** RAC 41 - City Bike, FRA: Mathieu Gines/Gregg Black/Olivier Depoorter (Suzuki), 765 laps; **5** Yamaha France GMT 94 Ipone, FRA: David Checa/Gregory Junod/Kenny Foray (Yamaha), 759 laps; **6** Team Biker's Day, SWI: Gregory Fastre/Ray Schouten/Marc Fissette (Yamaha), 756 laps; **7** Metiss JLC Moto, FRA: Christophe Michel/Cyril Huvier/Emmanuel Cheron (Metiss), 755 laps; **8** LTG 57, FRA: Kevin Denis/Bastien Mackels/David Perret (Yamaha), 752 laps; **9** BK Maco Racing, SK: Jason Pridmore/Dani Ribalta/ Pawel Szkopek (Yamaha), 752 laps; **10** RT Moto Virus Racing, ITA: Frederic Jond/Cyril Brivet/William Grarre (Suzuki), 746 laps; **11** Endurance Moto 45, FRA: Frederic Bernon/Julien Diguet/Alexandre Lagrive (Suzuki), 745 laps; **12** Andalucia BMW, SPA: Alvaro Molina/Camille Hedelin/Augustin Rosivall (BMW), 736 laps; **13** Motobox Kremer Shell Advance, GER: Martin Scherrer/Franck Gaziello/Timo Paavalainen (Suzuki), 736 laps; **14** 3D Endurance Moto Center, FRA: Lionel Braun/Charles Geers/Emmanuel Labussiere (Kawasaki), 733 laps; **15** Racing Team Sarazin, FRA: Chistophe Guerouah/Xavier Barbancon/Jeran Philippe Genetay (Kawasaki), 731 laps.
**Fastest lap:** BMP Elf 99 Racing Team, 1m 42.195s, 96.55mph/155.39km/h, on lap 12.
**Championship points: 1** Bolliger Team Switzerland, 74; **2** Suzuki Endurance Racing Team, 65; **3** RT Moto Virus Racing, 41; **4** RAC 41 - City Bike, 40; **5** YMES Folch Endurance, 38; **6** Yamaha Austria Racing Team, 36.

**8 HOURS OF DOHA, Losail, Qatar, 13 November.**
**Endurance World Championship, Round 5.**
**231 laps of the 3.343-mile/5.380km circuit, 772.233 miles/1242.780km**
**1** Suzuki Endurance Racing Team, FRA: Vincent Philippe/Freddy Foray/Sylvain Guintoli (Suzuki), 8h 1m 39.174s, 96.19mph/154.81km/h.
**2** Yamaha Austria Racing Team, AUT: Igor Jerman/Steve Martin/Gwen Giabbani (Yamaha), 227 laps; **3** RMT 21 Racing Germany, GER: Viktor Kispataki/ Didier Van Keymeulen/Arie Vos (Honda), 226 laps; **4** Bolliger Team Switzerland, SWI: Saiger Horst/Patric Muff/Roman Stamm (Kawasaki), 225 laps; **5** AM Moto Racing Competition, FRA: Fabrice Auger/ Etienne Masson/ Louis Bulle (Suzuki), 224 laps; **6** BMP Elf 99 Racing Team, BEL: Sebastien Gimbert/ Erwan Nigon//Damian Cudlin (BMW), 224 laps; **7** RAC 41 - City Bike, FRA: Greg Junod/Gregg Black/ Olivier Depoorter (Suzuki), 223 laps; **8** Qatar Endurance Racing Team I, QAT: Anthony Delhalle/Alex Cudlin/Mashel Al Naimi (Suzuki), 223 laps; **9** Team Motors Events, FRA: Vincent Bocquet/Emilien Humeau/Baptiste Guittet (Suzuki), 222 laps; **10** RT Moto Virus Racing, ITA: Frederic Jond/Cyril Brivet/Lucas Carolis (Suzuki), 219 laps; **11** Boening Penz 13 Racing, GER: Jure Stibilj/Matti Seidel/Steve Mizera (BMW), 217 laps; **12** Motobox Kremer Shell Advance, GER: Martin Scherrer/Franck Gaziello/Timo Paavalainen (Suzuki), 217 laps; **13** Cordoba Patrimonio De La Humanidad, SPA: Dailos Sainz/Javi Valera/Luis Castro (Kawasaki), 216 laps; **14** Qatar Endurance Racing Team II, QAT: Nasser Al Malki/ Yousef Al Malki/Sultan Al Kuwari (Suzuki), 215 laps; **15** SP Racing, FRA: Cyril Huvier/David La Bail/Philippe Le Pecheur (Honda), 214 laps;
**Fastest lap:** BMP Elf 99 Racing Team, 2m 1.483s, 99.07mph/159.43km/h, on lap 96.

**Final Endurance World Championship (EWC) points:**

| | | |
|---|---|---|
| **1** | Suzuki Endurance Racing Team, FRA | 95 |
| **2** | Bolliger Team Switzerland, SUI | 90 |
| **3** | Yamaha Austria Racing Team, AUT | 60 |
| **4** | RAC 41 - City Bike, FRA | 51 |
| **5** | RT Moto Virus Racing, ITA | 51 |
| **6** | Motobox Kremer Shell Advance, GER | 39 |

**7** YMES Folch Endurance, SPA 38; **8** GSR-Kawasaki, FRA 35; **9** Yamaha France GMT 94 Ipone, FRA 35; **10** BMP Elf 99 Racing Team, BEL 34; **11** MuSashi RT Harc Pro, JPN 30; **12** Team FMA Assurances, FRA 27; **13** AM Moto Racing Competition, FRA 25; **14** Keihin Kohara RT, JPN 24; **15** National Moto Honda, FRA 22.

## Isle of Man Tourist Trophy Races

**ISLE OF MAN TOURIST TROPHY COURSE, 5–11 June, 37.730-mile/60.720km circuit.**
**PokerStars Superbike TT (6 laps, 226.380 miles/ 364.320km)**
**1** Ian Hutchinson (1000cc Honda), 1h 46m 31.82s, 127.502mph/205.195km/h.
**2** Michael Dunlop (1000cc Honda), 1h 47m 05.75s; **3** Cameron Donald (1000cc Suzuki), 1h 47m 15.40s; **4** Guy Martin (1000cc Honda), 1h 47m 18.05s; **5** Adrian Archibald (1000cc Suzuki), 1h 47m 21.72s; **6** Keith Amor (1000cc Honda), 1h 47m 24.11s; **7** Ian Lougher (1000cc Kawasaki), 1h 48m 45.20s; **8** Michael Rutter (1000cc Honda), 1h 49m 32.47s; **9** Daniel Stewart (1000cc Honda), 1h 50m 02.24s; **10** Ryan Farquhar (1000cc Kawasaki), 1h 50m 02.81s; **11** Bruce Anstey (1000cc Suzuki), 1h 50m 07.67s; **12** Dan Kneen (1000cc Suzuki), 1h 51m 15.26s; **13** Ian Mackman (1000cc Suzuki), 1h 51m 22.28s; **14** Davy Morgan (1000cc Suzuki), 1h 51m 31.16s; **15** Stephen Oates (1000cc Suzuki), 1h 51m 39.72s.
**Fastest lap:** Conor Cummins (1000cc Kawasaki), 17m 12.83s, 131.511mph/211.646km/h, on lap 1 (record).
**Previous Superbike TT lap record:** John McGuinness (1000cc Honda), 17m 21.29s, 130.442mph/209.926km/h (2009).

**Sure Sidecar Race A (3 laps, 113.190 miles/ 182.160km)**
**1** Klaus Klaffenbock/Dan Sayle (600cc LCR Honda), 59m 21.61s, 114.410mph/184.125km/h.
**2** Dave Molyneux/Patrick Farrance (600cc DMR Kawasaki), 59m 24.24s; **3** Tim Reeves/Dipash Chauhan (600cc Honda), 1h 00m 16.41s; **4** Simon Neary/Paul Knapton (600cc LCR Honda), 1h 00m 27.12s; **5** Tony Elmer/Darren Marshall (600cc Ireson Yamaha), 1h 01m 38.41s; **6** Gary Bryan/Gary Partridge (600cc Baker Honda), 1h 01m 43.49s; **7** Gregory Lambert/Jason Slous (600cc GLR Honda), 1h 02m 19.07s; **8** Bill Currie/Robert Biggs (600cc LCR Yamaha), 1h 02m 54.96s; **9** David Kimberley/Robert Bell (600cc Ireson Honda), 1h 03m 27.37s; **10** Gordon Shand/Stuart Graham (600cc Shand F2 Suzuki), 1h 03m 45.92s; **11** Robert Handcock/ Mike Aylott (600cc Shelbourne Honda), 1h 03m 51.75s; **12** Wayne Lockey/Ken Edwards (600cc Ireson Honda), 1h 04m 02.58s; **13** Mike Cookson/Kris Hibberd (600cc Shelbourne Honda), 1h 04m 14.79s; **14** Dean Banks/Pete Alton (600cc LCR), 1h 04m 26.07s; **15** Francois Leblond/Sylvie Leblond (600cc Shelbourne Suzuki), 1h 04m 47.55s.
**Fastest lap:** Molyneux/Farrance, 19m 38.20s, 115.284mph/185.532km/h, on lap 3.
**Sidecar lap record:** Nick Crowe/Dan Sayle (600cc LCR Honda), 19m 24.24s, 116.667mph/187.757km/h (2007).

**Monster Energy Supersport TT Race 1 (4 laps, 150.920 miles/242.880km)**
**1** Ian Hutchinson (600cc Honda), 1h 12m 37.75s, 124.677mph/200.648km/h.
**2** Guy Martin (600cc Honda), 1h 12m 40.78s; **3** Michael Dunlop (600cc Yamaha), 1h 12m 52.24s; **4** Keith Amor (600cc Honda), 1h 13m 09.59s; **5** Dan Kneen (600cc Yamaha), 1h 13m 25.92s; **6** William Dunlop (600cc Yamaha), 1h 13m 34.81s; **7** John McGuinness (600cc Honda), 1h 13m 42.17s; **8** Conor Cummins (600cc Kawasaki), 1h 13m 48.51s; **9** Ryan Farquhar (600cc Kawasaki), 1h 13m 54.95s; **10** Cameron Donald (600cc Suzuki), 1h 14m 30.99s; **11** Gary Johnson (600cc Yamaha), 1h 14m 36.49s; **12** Ian Lougher (600cc Kawasaki), 1h 14m 59.09s; **13** Derek Brien (600cc Yamaha), 1h 15m 03.92s; **14** James Hillier (600cc Kawasaki), 1h 15m 25.56s; **15** Ben Wylie (600cc Yamaha), 1h 15m 35.02s.
**Fastest lap:** Amor, 17m 50.28s, 126.909mph/ 204.240km/h, on lap 4 (record, beaten Race 2).
**Previous Supersport lap record:** Bruce Anstey (600cc Suzuki), 17m 53.32s, 126.549mph/ 203.661km/h (2009).

**Royal London 360 Superstock TT (4 laps, 150.920 miles/242.880km)**
**1** Ian Hutchinson (1000cc Honda), 1h 10m 41.31s, 128.100mph/206.157km/h.
**2** Ryan Farquhar (1000cc Kawasaki), 1h 10m 42.63s; **3** Conor Cummins (1000cc Kawasaki), 1h 11m 14.12s; **4** John McGuinness (1000cc Honda), 1h 11m 35.92s; **5** Guy Martin (1000cc Honda), 1h 11m 50.06s; **6** Keith Amor (1000cc BMW), 1h 11m 50.25s; **7** Ian Lougher (1000cc Kawasaki), 1h 12m 10.97s; **8** Michael Dunlop (1000cc Honda), 1h 12m 28.63s; **9** Michael Rutter (1000cc Honda), 1h 12m 32.78s; **10** Adrian Archibald (1000cc Suzuki), 1h 12m 43.08s; **11** Cameron Donald (1000cc Suzuki), 1h 13m 17.09s; **12** James Hillier (1000cc Kawasaki), 1h 13m 20.45s; **13** Gary Johnson (1000cc Suzuki), 1h 13m 28.43s; **14** James McBride (1000cc Yamaha), 1h 13m 31.47s; **15** Dan Kneen (1000cc Suzuki), 1h 13m 35.76s.
**Fastest lap:** Hutchinson, 17m 18.91s, 130.741mph/210.407km/h, on lap 4 (record).
**Previous Superstock lap record:** Ian Hutchinson (1000cc Honda), 17m 26.88s, 129.746mph/208.806km/h (2009).

**Sure Sidecar Race B (3 laps, 113.190 miles/ 182.160km)**
**1** Klaus Klaffenbock/Dan Sayle (600cc LCR Honda), 59m 52.35s, 113.431mph/182.549km/h.
**2** John Holden/Andrew Winkle (600cc LCR Suzuki), 59m 53.47s; **3** Conrad Harrison/Kerry Williams (600cc Shelbourne Honda), 1h 01m 12.29s; **4** Gary Bryan/Gary Partridge (600cc Baker Honda), 1h 02m 14.77s; **5** Gregory Lambert/Jason Slous (600cc GLR Honda), 1h 02m 40.38s; **6** Roy Hanks/Dave Wells (600cc Molyneux Rose Suzuki), 1h 02m 44.03s; **7** Robert Handcock/Mike Aylott (600cc Shelbourne Honda), 1h 03m 17.92s; **8** David Kimberley/Robert Bell (600cc Ireson Honda), 1h 03m 28.39s; **9** Gordon Shand/Stuart Graham (600cc Shand F2 Suzuki), 1h 03m 48.42s; **10** Brian Kelly/Dicky Gale (600cc DMR Honda), 1h 04m 35.68s; **11** Wayne Lockey/Ken Edwards (600cc Ireson Honda), 1h 04m 59.78s; **12** Karl Bennett/Lee Cain (600cc MREquipe), 1h 05m 06.33s; **13** Tony Thirkell/Nigel Barlow (600cc MR Equipe Honda), 1h 05m 10.57s; **14** Mike Roscher/Gregory Cluze (600cc LCR Suzuki), 1h 05m 13.36s; **15** Francois Leblond/Sylvie Leblond (600cc Shelbourne Suzuki), 1h 05m 43.48s.
**Fastest lap:** Klaffenbock/Sayle, 19m 49.84s, 114.157mph/183.718km/h, on lap 3.
**Sidecar lap record:** Nick Crowe/Dan Sayle (600cc LCR Honda), 19m 24.24s, 116.667mph/187.757km/h (2007).

**Monster Energy Supersport TT Race 2 (4 laps, 150.920 miles/242.880km)**
**1** Ian Hutchinson (600cc Honda), 1h 12m 20.89s, 125.161mph/201.427km/h.
**2** Michael Dunlop (600cc Yamaha), 1h 12m 22.34s; **3** Keith Amor (600cc Honda), 1h 12m 55.19s; **4** Guy Martin (600cc Honda), 1h 13m 00.31s; **5** John McGuinness (600cc Honda), 1h 13m 33.64s; **6** Conor Cummins (600cc Kawasaki), 1h 13m 33.87s; **7** William Dunlop (600cc Yamaha), 1h 13m 46.12s; **8** Bruce Anstey (600cc Suzuki), 1h 14m 12.26s; **9** Ryan Farquhar (600cc Kawasaki), 1h 14m 15.97s; **10** Dan Kneen (600cc Yamaha), 1h 14m 26.04s; **11** Gary Johnson (600cc Yamaha), 1h 14m 28.43s; **12** Adrian Archibald (600cc Yamaha), 1h 14m 37.62s; **13** Cameron Donald (600cc Suzuki), 1h 14m 47.59s; **14** Ian Lougher (600cc Kawasaki), 1h 14m 56.95s; **15** Jimmy Moore (600cc Yamaha), 1h 15m 17.26s.
**Fastest lap:** M. Dunlop, 17m 42.52s, 127.836mph/205.732km/h, on lap **4** (record).
**Previous Supersport lap record:** Keith Amor (600cc Honda), 17m 50.28s, 126.909mph/ 204.240km/h, (2010 Race 1).

**TT Zero (1 lap, 37.730 miles/60.720km)**
**1** Mark Miller (MotoCzysz E1PC), 23m 22.89s, 96.820mph/155.817km/h.
**2** Robert Barber (Agni), 25m 21.19s; **3** James McBride (Man TTX), 25m 32.13s; **4** Jennifer Tinmouth (Agni), 25m 39.50s; **5** George Spence (Peter Williams), 34m 59.19s.

**Dainese Senior TT (4 laps, 150.920 miles/ 242.880km)**
**1** Ian Hutchinson (1000cc Honda), 1h 10m 24.59s, 128.607mph/206.973km/h.
**2** Ryan Farquhar (1000cc Kawasaki), 1h 11m 02.36s; **3** Bruce Anstey (1000cc Suzuki), 1h 11m 38.08s; **4** Ian Lougher (1000cc Kawasaki), 1h 12s 01.57s; **5** Michael Rutter (1000cc Honda), 1h 12m 10.74s; **6** Daniel Stewart (1000cc Honda), 1h 12m 33.57s; **7** Adrian Archibald (1000cc Suzuki), 1h 12m 37.82s; **8** Dan Kneen (1000cc Suzuki), 1h 13m 29.30s; **9** Davy Morgan (1000cc Suzuki), 1h 13m 40.98s; **10** James McBride (1000cc Yamaha), 1h 13m 50.69s; **11** Jimmy Moore (1000cc Yamaha), 1h 13m 53.09s; **12** Rico Penzkofer (1000cc BMW), 1h 14m 05.81s; **13** Ian Mackman (1000cc Suzuki), 1h 14m 08.49s; **14** Gary Johnson (1000cc Suzuki), 1h 14m 20.72s; **15** John Burrows (1000cc Suzuki), 1h 14m 21.74s.
**Fastest lap:** Hutchinson, 17m 13.01s, 131.487mph/211.608km/h, on lap 1.
**Senior TT and Outright lap record:** John McGuinness (1000cc Honda), 17m 12.30s, 131.578mph/211.754km/h (2009).

## British Championships

**BRANDS HATCH INDY, 5 April, 1.199-mile/ 1.929km circuit.**
**MCE Insurance British Superbike Championship, Rounds 1 and 2 (2 x 30 laps, 35.970 miles/ 57.870km)**
**Race 1**
**1** Tommy Hill (Suzuki), 23m 10.296s, 93.11mph/ 149.85km/h.
**2** Ryuichi Kiyonari (Honda); **3** James Ellison (Honda); **4** Alastair Seeley (Suzuki); **5** Josh Brookes (Honda); **6** Stuart Easton (Honda); **7** Michael Rutter (Ducati); **8** Dan Linfoot (Yamaha); **9** Chris Walker (Suzuki); **10** John Laverty (Kawasaki); **11** Martin Jessopp (Ducati); **12** Yukio Kagayama (Suzuki); **13** Gary Mason (Kawasaki); **14** Steve Brogan (BMW); **15** Peter Hickman (Yamaha).
**Fastest lap:** Brookes, 45.879s, 94.05mph/ 151.36km/h.

**Race 2**
**1** James Ellison (Honda), 23m 3.278s, 93.58mph/150.60km/h.
**2** Tommy Hill (Suzuki); **3** Alastair Seeley (Suzuki); **4** Michael Laverty (Suzuki); **5** Stuart Easton (Honda); **6** Michael Rutter (Ducati); **7** John Laverty (Kawasaki); **8** Simon Andrews (Kawasaki); **9** Martin Jessopp (Ducati); **10** Steve Brogan (BMW); **11** Adam Jenkinson (Kawasaki); **12** Luke Jones (Yamaha); **13** Christian Iddon (Honda); **14** Steve Mercer (Yamaha); **15** Hudson Kennaugh (Kawasaki).
**Fastest lap:** Seeley, 45.671s, 94.48mph/ 152.05km/h.
**Championship points: 1** Hill, 45; **2** Ellison, 41; **3** Seeley, 29; **4** Easton, 21; **5** Kiyonari, 20; **6** Rutter, 19.

**Fuchs-Silkolene British Supersport Championship, Round 1 (21 laps, 25.179 miles/ 40.522km)**
**1** Sam Lowes (Honda), 16m 39.683s, 90.64mph/ 145.87km/h.
**2** James Westmoreland (Yamaha); **3** Billy McConnell (Yamaha); **4** Jason O'Halloran (Triumph); **5** Graeme Gowland (Honda); **6** Daniel Cooper (Triumph): **7** Paul Young (Triumph): **8** Ian Hutchinson (Honda); **9** Tom Grant (Yamaha); **10** Allan Jon Venter (Triumph): **11** Jack Kennedy (Yamaha); **12** Marty Nutt (Yamaha); **13** Luke Mossey (Triumph): **14** Lee Johnston (Kawasaki): **15** David Jones (Triumph).
**Fastest lap:** S. Lowes, 46.808s, 92.18mph/ 148.35km/h.
**Championship points: 1** S. Lowes, 25; **2** Westmoreland, 20; **3** McConnell, 16; **4** O'Halloran, 13; **5** Gowland, 11; **6** Cooper, 10.

**SpeedyRetail.com British 125GP Championship, Round 1 (22 laps, 26.378 miles/ 42.451km)**
**1** James Lodge (Honda), 18m 37.247s, 84.96mph/136.73km/h.
**2** Rob Guiver (Honda); **3** Fraser Rogers (Honda); **4** John McPhee (Honda); **5** Danny Kent (Honda); **6** William Dunlop (Honda); **7** Wayne Ryan (Honda); **8** James Ford (Honda); **9** Philip Wakefield (Honda); **10** Jon Vincent (Honda); **11** Sam Hornsey (Cougar); **12** Tom Weeden (Honda); **13** Andrew Reid (Honda); **14** Lee Jackson (Honda); **15** Simon Low (Honda).
**Fastest lap:** Lodge, 49.729s, 86.77mph/ 139.64km/h.
**Championship points: 1** Lodge, 25; **2** Guiver, 20; **3** Rogers, 16; **4** McPhee, 13; **5** Kent, 11; **6** Dunlop, 10.

**THRUXTON, 18 April, 2.356-mile/3.792km circuit.**
**MCE Insurance British Superbike Championship, Rounds 3 and 4 (2 x 20 laps, 47.120 miles/ 75.840km)**
**Race 1**
**1** Tommy Hill (Suzuki), 25m 27.870s, 111.02mph/ 178.67km/h.
**2** Josh Brookes (Honda); **3** Yukio Kagayama (Suzuki); **4** Stuart Easton (Honda); **5** Michael Rutter (Ducati); **6** Martin Jessopp (Ducati); **7** John Laverty (Kawasaki); **8** Gary Mason (Kawasaki); **9** Ryuichi Kiyonari (Honda); **10** Michael Laverty (Suzuki); **11** Peter Hickman (Yamaha); **12** Alastair Seeley (Suzuki); **13** David Anthony (Suzuki); **14** Gary Johnson (Suzuki); **15** Craig Fitzpatrick (Honda).
**Fastest lap:** Jessopp, 1m 15.738s, 111.98mph/ 180.22km/h.

**Race 2**
**1** Josh Brookes (Honda), 25m 23.986s, 111.30mph/179.12km/h.
**2** Tommy Hill (Suzuki); **3** Stuart Easton (Honda); **4** Ryuichi Kiyonari (Honda); **5** Martin Jessopp (Ducati); **6** Michael Laverty (Suzuki); **7** Michael Rutter (Ducati); **8** John Laverty (Kawasaki); **9** Alastair Seeley (Suzuki); **10** Gary Mason (Kawasaki); **11** Yukio Kagayama (Suzuki); **12** Dan Linfoot (Yamaha); **13** Peter Hickman (Yamaha); **14**

Steve Brogan (BMW); **15** Chris Walker (Suzuki).
**Fastest lap:** Hill, 1m 14.976s, 113.12mph/182.05km/h.
**Championship points:** **1** Hill, 90; **2** Brookes, 56; **3** Easton, 50; **4** Ellison, 41; **5** Seeley, 40; **6** Kiyonari, 40.

**Fuchs-Silkolene British Supersport Championship, Round 2 (18 laps, 42.408 miles/68.249km)**
**1** James Westmoreland (Yamaha), 23m 23.215s, 108.79mph/175.08km/h.
**2** Graeme Gowland (Honda); **3** Tom Grant (Yamaha); **4** Billy McConnell (Yamaha); **5** Jack Kennedy (Yamaha); **6** Ian Hutchinson (Honda); **7** Ben Wilson (Kawasaki); **8** Chris Martin (Kawasaki); **9** Lee Johnston (Kawasaki): **10** Jason O'Halloran (Triumph); **11** Daniel Keen (Yamaha); **12** Guy Martin (Honda); **13** Paul Jordan (Honda); **14** Allan Jon Venter (Triumph); **15** David Jones (Triumph).
**Fastest lap:** S. Lowes, 1m 16.908s, 110.28mph/177.48km/h.
**Championship points:** **1** Westmoreland, 45; **2** Gowland, 31; **3** McConnell, 29; **4** S. Lowes, 25; **5** Grant, 23; **6** O'Halloran, 19.

**SpeedyRetail.com British 125GP Championship, Round 2 (14 laps, 32.984 miles/53.083km)**
**1** James Lodge (Seel/Honda), 19m 23.494s, 102.05mph/164.23km/h.
**2** Brian Clark (Honda); **3** James Ford (Honda); **4** Taylor Mackenzie (Honda); **5** William Dunlop (Honda); **6** Fraser Rogers (Honda); **7** Andrew Reid (Honda); **8** Edward Rendell (Honda); **9** Philip Wakefield (Honda); **10** John McPhee (Honda); **11** Tom Weeden (Honda); **12** Matthew Paulo (Honda); **13** Lee Jackson (Honda); **14** Jon Vincent (Honda); **15** Matthew Davies (Honda).
**Fastest lap:** Lodge, 1m 21.853s, 103.61mph/166.75km/h.
**Championship points:** **1** Lodge, 50; **2** Rogers, 26; **3** Ford, 24; **4** Dunlop, 21; **5** Guiver, 20; **6** Clark, 20.

**OULTON PARK, 3 May, 2.692-mile/4.332km circuit.**
**MCE Insurance British Superbike Championship, Rounds 5 and 6**
**Race 1 (18 laps, 48.456 miles/77.976km)**
**1** Stuart Easton (Honda), 28m 55.815s, 100.49mph/161.72km/h.
**2** Tommy Hill (Suzuki); **3** John Laverty (Kawasaki); **4** Alastair Seeley (Suzuki); **5** Michael Laverty (Suzuki); **6** Josh Brookes (Honda); **7** Gary Mason (Kawasaki); **8** Chris Walker (Kawasaki); **9** Dan Linfoot (Yamaha); **10** Tommy Bridewell (Honda); **11** Martin Jessopp (Ducati); **12** Peter Hickman (Yamaha); **13** Adam Jenkinson (Kawasaki); **14** Hudson Kennaugh (Kawasaki); **15** Steve Brogan (BMW).
**Fastest lap:** Kiyonari, 1m 35.859s, 101.09mph/162.70km/h.

**Race 2 (15 laps, 40.380 miles/64.985km)**
**1** Michael Laverty (Suzuki), 27m 26.150s, 88.30mph/142.11km/h.
**2** Michael Rutter (Ducati); **3** Tommy Hill (Suzuki); **4** Ryuichi Kiyonari (Honda); **5** John Laverty (Kawasaki); **6** Alastair Seeley (Suzuki); **7** Tommy Bridewell (Honda); **8** Josh Brookes (Honda); **9** Hudson Kennaugh (Kawasaki); **10** Adam Jenkinson (Kawasaki); **11** Chris Walker (Kawasaki); **12** Martin Jessopp (Ducati); **13** Aaron Zanotti (Suzuki); **14** Dan Linfoot (Yamaha);15 Steve Brogan (BMW).
**Fastest lap:** M. Laverty, 1m 48.173s, 89.59mph/144.18km/h.
**Championship points:** **1** Hill, 126; **2** Easton, 75; **3** Brookes, 74; **4** M. Laverty, 65; **5** Seeley, 63; **6** J. Laverty, 59.

**Fuchs-Silkolene British Supersport Championship, Round 3 (12 laps, 32.304 miles/51.988km)**
**1** Ben Wilson (Kawasaki), 23m 24.023s, 82.83mph/133.30km/h.
**2** Sam Lowes (Honda); **3** Jack Kennedy (Yamaha); **4** Daniel Cooper (Triumph): **5** Glen Richards (Honda); **6** Tom Grant (Yamaha); **7** Patrick McDougall (Yamaha); **8** Jesse Trayler (Kawasaki); **9** Jenny Tinmouth (Honda); **10** Mark Cringle (Triumph); **11** Chris Martin (Kawasaki); **12** Marty Nutt (Yamaha); **13** Max Hunt (Yamaha); **14** Craig Sproston (Yamaha); **15** Rikki Owen (Triumph).
**Fastest lap:** Hutchinson, 1m 48.952s, 88.95mph/143.15km/h.
**Championship points:** **1** Westmoreland, 45; **2** S. Lowes, 45; **3** Wilson, 34; **4** Grant, 33; **5** Kennedy, 32; **6** Gowland, 31.

**SpeedyRetail.com British 125GP Championship, Round 3 (14 laps, 37.688 miles/60.653km)**
**1** James Lodge (Seel/Honda), 25m 13.703s, 89.63mph/144.25km/h.
**2** Deane Brown (Honda); **3** Rob Guiver (Honda); **4** Taylor Mackenzie (Honda); **5** Matthew Davies (Honda); **6** Wayne Ryan (Honda); **7** Dakota Mamola (Honda); **8** Edward Rendell (Honda); **9** Danny Kent (Honda); **10** William Dunlop (Honda); **11** Philip Wakefield (Honda); **12** Sam Hornsey (Cougar); **13** Jon Vincent (Honda); **14** Lee Jackson (Honda); **15** Peter Sutherland (Honda).
**Fastest lap:** Lodge, 1m 47.084s, 90.50mph/145.64km/h.
**Championship points:** **1** Lodge, 75; **2** Guiver, 36; **3** Dunlop, 27; **4** Rogers, 26; **5** Mackenzie, 26; **6** Ford, 24.

**CADWELL PARK, 23 May, 2.180-mile/3.508km circuit.**
**MCE Insurance British Superbike Championship, Rounds 7 and 8**
**Race 1 (18 laps, 39.240 miles/63.144km)**
**1** Ryuichi Kiyonari (Honda), 27m 35.356s, 85.33mph/137.33km/h.
**2** Michael Laverty (Suzuki); **3** Michael Rutter (Ducati); **4** Tommy Bridewell (Honda); **5** Josh Brookes (Honda); **6** John Laverty (Kawasaki); **7** Chris Walker (Kawasaki); **8** Martin Jessopp (Ducati); **9** Alastair Seeley (Suzuki); **10** Dan Linfoot (Yamaha); **11** Ian Lowry (Yamaha); **12** Adam Jenkinson (Kawasaki); **13** Peter Hickman (Yamaha); **14** Steve Brogan (BMW); **15** Tom Tunstall (Honda);
**Fastest lap:** Kiyonari, 1m 28.288s, 88.89mph/143.05km/h.

**Race 2 (15 laps, 32.700 miles/52.626km)**
**1** Josh Brookes (Honda), 22m 15.411s, 88.15mph/141.86km/h.
**2** Tommy Hill (Suzuki); **3** Michael Laverty (Suzuki); **4** Michael Rutter (Ducati); **5** John Laverty (Kawasaki); **6** Tommy Bridewell (Honda); **7** Alastair Seeley (Suzuki); **8** Chris Walker (Kawasaki); **9** Martin Jessopp (Ducati); **10** Stuart Easton (Honda); **11** Adam Jenkinson (Kawasaki); **12** Ian Lowry (Yamaha); **13** Peter Hickman (Yamaha); **14** Steve Brogan (BMW); **15** Alex Lowes (KTM).
**Fastest lap:** Brookes, 1m 28.166s, 89.01mph/143.25km/h.
**Championship points:** **1** Hill, 146; **2** Brookes, 110; **3** M. Laverty, 101; **4** Rutter, 88; **5** Easton, 81; **6** J. Laverty, 80.

**Fuchs-Silkolene British Supersport Championship, Round 4 (16 laps, 34.880 miles/56.134km)**
**1** Billy McConnell (Yamaha), 24m 15.161s, 86.29mph/138.87km/h.
**2** James Westmoreland (Yamaha); **3** Sam Lowes (Honda); **4** Graeme Gowland (Honda); **5** Ian Hutchinson (Honda); **6** Jack Kennedy (Yamaha); **7** Glen Richards (Honda); **8** Allan Jon Venter (Triumph): **9** Joe Dickinson (Honda); **10** Jason O'Halloran (Triumph); **11** Daniel Cooper (Triumph): **12** Chris Martin (Kawasaki); **13** Marty Nutt (Yamaha); **14** Lee Johnston (Kawasaki): **15** Patrick McDougall (Yamaha).
**Fastest lap:** McConnell, 1m 29.868s, 87.32mph/140.54km/h.
**Championship points:** **1** Westmoreland, 65; **2** S. Lowes, 61; **3** McConnell, 54; **4** Gowland, 44; **5** Kennedy, 42; **6** Wilson, 34.

**SpeedyRetail.com British 125GP Championship, Round 4 (14 laps, 30.520 miles/49.117km)**
**1** Taylor Mackenzie (Honda), 22m 56.167s, 79.83mph/128.47km/h.
**2** Deane Brown (Honda); **3** Rob Guiver (Honda); **4** Fraser Rogers (Honda); **5** Brian Clark (Honda); **6** John McPhee (Honda); **7** William Dunlop (Honda); **8** Philip Wakefield (Honda); **9** Jon Vincent (Honda); **10** Shaun Horsman (Honda); **11** Lee Jackson (Honda); **12** Arnie Shelton (Honda); **13** Ross Walker (Honda); **14** Matthew Paulo (Honda); **15** Sam Hornsey (Cougar).
**Fastest lap:** Guiver, 1, 34.516s, 83.03mph/133.63km/h.
**Championship points:** **1** Lodge, 75; **2** Guiver, 52; **3** Mackenzie, 51; **4** Brown, 40; **5** Rogers, 39; **6** Dunlop, 36.

**MALLORY PARK, 27 June, 1.410-mile/2.269km circuit.**
**MCE Insurance British Superbike Championship, Rounds 9 and 10**
**Race 1 (25 laps, 21.150 miles/34.038km)**
**1** Ryuichi Kiyonari (Honda), 23m 42.274s, 89.22mph/143.59km/h.
**2** Josh Brookes (Honda); **3** Michael Laverty (Suzuki); **4** Michael Rutter (Ducati); **5** Stuart Easton (Honda); **6** Chris Walker (Suzuki); **7** Simon Andrews (Kawasaki); **8** John Laverty (Kawasaki); **9** Andrew Pitt (Yamaha); **10** Alastair Seeley (Suzuki); **11** Tommy Bridewell (Honda); **12** Gary Mason (Kawasaki); **13** James Ellison (Honda); **14** Steve Brogan (BMW); **15** Tom Tunstall (Honda).
**Fastest lap:** Kiyonari, 56.327s, 90.11mph/145.03km/h.

**Race 2 (30 laps, 42.300 miles/68.075km)**
**1** Ryuichi Kiyonari (Honda), 28m 20.065s, 89.57mph/144.15km/h.
**2** Josh Brookes (Honda); **3** Michael Laverty (Suzuki); **4** Michael Rutter (Ducati); **5** Chris Walker (Suzuki); **6** John Laverty (Kawasaki); **7** Simon Andrews (Kawasaki); **8** Tommy Hill (Suzuki); **9** Tommy Bridewell (Honda); **10** Andrew Pitt (Yamaha); **11** Alastair Seeley (Suzuki); **12** James Ellison (Honda); **13** Gary Mason (Kawasaki); **14** Dan Linfoot (Yamaha); **15** Peter Hickman (Yamaha).
**Fastest lap:** Kiyonari, 56.071s, 90.52mph/145.69km/h.
**Championship points:** **1** Hill, 154; **2** Brookes, 150; **3** M. Laverty, 133; **4** Kiyonari, 128; **5** Rutter, 114; **6** J. Laverty, 98.

**Fuchs-Silkolene British Supersport Championship, Round 5 (25 laps, 35.250 miles/56.729km)**
**1** Billy McConnell (Yamaha), 24m 30.058s, 86.32mph/138.92km/h.
**2** Sam Lowes (Honda); **3** James Westmoreland (Yamaha); **4** Glen Richards (Honda); **5** Jack Kennedy (Yamaha); **6** Graeme Gowland (Honda); **7** Ben Wilson (Kawasaki); **8** Allan Jon Venter (Triumph); **9** Luke Mossey (Triumph); **10** Joe Dickinson (Honda); **11** Dean Hipwell (Yamaha); **12** Chris Martin (Kawasaki); **13** Daniel Cooper (Triumph); **14** Jamie Hamilton (Kawasaki); **15** Paul Jordan (Honda).
**Fastest lap:** Westmoreland, 56.858s, 89.27mph/143.67km/h.
**Championship points:** **1** S. Lowes, 81; **2** Westmoreland, 81; **3** McConnell, 79; **4** Gowland, 54; **5** Kennedy, 53; **6** Wilson, 43.

**SpeedyRetail.com British 125GP Championship, Round 5 (22 laps, 31.020 miles/49.922km)**
**1** Ross Walker (Honda), 23m 11.675s, 80.24mph/129.13km/h.
**2** Deane Brown (Honda); **3** James Lodge (Seel/Honda); **4** Sam Hornsey (Honda); **5** Lee Jackson (Honda); **6** Philip Wakefield (Honda); **7** Taylor Mackenzie (Honda); **8** Jon Vincent (Honda); **9** John McPhee (Honda); **10** Matthew Paulo (Honda); **11** Tom Weeden (Honda); **12** Ben Barratt (Honda); **13** Edward Rendell (Honda); **14** Wayne Ryan (Honda); **15** Andrew Reid (Honda).
**Fastest lap:** Davies, 1m 0.143s, 84.39mph/135.82km/h.
**Championship points:** **1** Lodge, 91; **2** Mackenzie, 60; **3** Brown, 60; **4** Guiver, 52; **5** Rogers, 39; **6** Wakefield, 37.

**KNOCKHILL, 4 July, 1.271-mile/2.046km circuit.**
**MCE Insurance British Superbike Championship, Round 11**
**Race 1 (15 laps, 19.065 miles/30.682km)**
**1** Michael Rutter (Ducati), 13m 32.658s, 84.47mph/135.94km/h.
**2** Ryuichi Kiyonari (Honda); **3** Josh Brookes (Honda); **4** Michael Laverty (Suzuki); **5** Alastair Seeley (Suzuki); **6** John Laverty (Kawasaki); **7** Simon Andrews (Kawasaki); **8** Tommy Hill (Suzuki); **9** Gary Mason (Kawasaki); **10** Chris Walker (Suzuki); **11** Andrew Pitt (Yamaha); **12** Gary Johnson (Suzuki); **13** David Johnson (Kawasaki); **14** Christian Iddon (Honda); **15** Tom Tunstall (Honda).
**Fastest lap:** Rutter, 53.533s, 85.49mph/137.58km/h.
**Championship points:** **1** Brookes, 166; **2** Hill, 162; **3** Kiyonari, 148; **4** M. Laverty, 146; **5** Rutter, 139; **6** J. Laverty, 108.

**Race 2**
*Postponed until Snetterton due to weather.*

**Fuchs-Silkolene British Supersport Championship, Round 6 (13 laps, 16.523 miles/26.591km)**
**1** Sam Lowes (Honda), 12m 24.995s, 79.86mph/128.52km/h.
**2** Ben Wilson (Kawasaki); **3** Daniel Cooper (Triumph): **4** Ian Hutchinson (Honda); **5** Alex Lowes (Yamaha); **6** James Westmoreland (Yamaha); **7** Glen Richards (Honda); **8** Graeme Gowland (Honda); **9** Jack Kennedy (Yamaha); **10** Jason O'Halloran (Yamaha); **11** Luke Mossey (Triumph): **12** Billy McConnell (Yamaha); **13** Marty Nutt (Yamaha); **14** Dean Hipwell (Yamaha); **15** Joe Dickinson (Honda).
**Fastest lap:** S. Lowes, 54.353s, 84.20mph/135.51km/h.
**Championship points:** **1** S. Lowes, 106; **2** Westmoreland, 91; **3** McConnell, 83; **4** Wilson, 63; **5** Gowland, 62; **6** Kennedy, 60.

**SpeedyRetail.com British 125GP Championship**
*Postponed until Croft.*

**SNETTERTON, 17/18 July, 1.952-mile/3.141km circuit.**
**MCE Insurance British Superbike Championship, Rounds 12, 13 and 14**
**Race 1 (18 laps, 35.136 miles/56.538km)**
**1** Josh Brookes (Honda), 19m 41.650s, 107.04mph/172.26km/h.
**2** Ryuichi Kiyonari (Honda); **3** Tommy Hill (Suzuki); **4** Michael Rutter (Ducati); **5** Alastair Seeley (Suzuki); **6** Michael Laverty (Suzuki); **7** James Ellison (Honda); **8** Simon Andrews (Kawasaki); **9** Gary Mason (Kawasaki); **10** Tommy Bridewell (Honda); **11** Chris Walker (Honda); **12** John Laverty (Kawasaki); **13** Dan Linfoot (Yamaha); **14** Andrew Pitt (Yamaha); **15** Peter Hickman (Yamaha).
**Fastest lap:** Brookes, 1m 4.878s, 108.31mph/174.31km/h.

**Race 2 (22 laps, 42.944 miles/69.102km)**
**1** Josh Brookes (Honda), 24m 13.327s, 106.37mph/171.19km/h.
**2** Tommy Hill (Suzuki); **3** Alastair Seeley (Suzuki); **4** James Ellison (Honda); **5** Michael Laverty (Suzuki); **6** Tommy Bridewell (Honda); **7** Chris Walker (Honda); **8** Stuart Easton (Honda); **9** Simon Andrews (Kawasaki); **10** John Laverty (Kawasaki); **11** Gary Mason (Kawasaki); **12** Andrew Pitt (Yamaha); **13** Steve Brogan (BMW); **14** Gary Johnson (Suzuki); **15** Tom Tunstall (Honda).
**Fastest lap:** Brookes, 1m 5.195s, 107.78mph/173.46km/h.

**Race 3 (24 laps, 46.848 miles/75.395km)**
**1** Ryuichi Kiyonari (Honda), 26m 52.964s, 104.55mph/168.26km/h.
**2** Tommy Hill (Suzuki); **3** Michael Laverty (Suzuki); **4** Michael Rutter (Ducati); **5** John Laverty (Kawasaki); **6** Simon Andrews (Kawasaki); **7** Chris Walker (Honda); **8** Andrew Pitt (Yamaha); **9** Gary Mason (Kawasaki); **10** Yukio Kagayama (Suzuki); **11** Peter Hickman (Yamaha); **12** Dan Linfoot (Yamaha); **13** Steve Brogan (BMW); **14** Gary Johnson (Suzuki); **15** Hudson Kennaugh (Aprilia).
**Fastest lap:** Kiyonari, 1m 4.991s, 108.12mph/174.00km/h.
**Championship points:** **1** Hill, 218; **2** Brookes, 216; **3** Kiyonari, 193; **4** M. Laverty, 183; **5** Rutter, 165; **6** J. Laverty, 129.

**Fuchs-Silkolene British Supersport Championship, Round 7 (20 laps, 39.040 miles/62.829km)**
**1** Graeme Gowland (Honda), 22m 44.806s, 102.97mph/165.71km/h.
**2** Sam Lowes (Honda); **3** Daniel Cooper (Triumph): **4** Glen Richards (Honda); **5** Ben Wilson (Kawasaki); **6** Jason O'Halloran (Yamaha); **7** Marty Nutt (Yamaha); **8** Billy McConnell (Yamaha); **9** Jack Kennedy (Yamaha); **10** Alex Lowes (Yamaha); **11** Ian Hutchinson (Honda); **12** Lee Johnston (Triumph): **13** Dean Hipwell (Yamaha); **14** Chris Martin (Kawasaki); **15** Allan Jon Venter (Triumph).
**Fastest lap:** Wilson, 1m 7.598s, 103.95mph/167.29km/h.
**Championship points:** **1** S. Lowes, 126; **2** McConnell, 91; **3** Westmoreland, 91; **4** Gowland, 87; **5** Wilson, 74; **6** Kennedy, 67.

**SpeedyRetail.com British 125GP Championship, Round 6 (15 laps, 29.280 miles/47.122km)**
**1** Rob Guiver (Honda), 18m 48.387s, 93.41mph/150.33km/h.
**2** Dakota Mamola (Honda); **3** Sam Hornsey (Honda); **4** Wayne Ryan (Honda); **5** Philip Wakefield (Honda); **6** Jon Vincent (Honda); **7** Peter Sutherland (Honda); **8** Lee Jackson (Honda); **9** Andrew Reid (Honda); **10** Simon Low (Honda);

**11** Matthew Paulo (Honda); **12** Shaun Horsman (Honda); **13** Bradley Hughes (Honda); **14** Nigel Percy (Honda); **15** Catherine Green (Honda).
**Fastest lap:** Mamola, 1m 13.890s, 95.10mph/153.05km/h.
**Championship points: 1** Lodge, 91; **2** Guiver, 77; **3** Mackenzie, 60; **4** Brown, 60; **5** Wakefield, 48; **6** Rogers, 39.

**BRANDS HATCH GP, 7/8 August, 2.301-mile/3.703km circuit.**
**MCE Insurance British Superbike Championship, Rounds 15, 16 and 17 Race 1 (10 laps, 23.010 miles/37.031km)**
**1** Alastair Seeley (Suzuki), 16m 22.271s, 84.32mph/135.70km/h.
**2** Michael Rutter (Ducati); **3** Ryuichi Kiyonari (Honda); **4** Josh Brookes (Honda); **5** Tom Sykes (Kawasaki); **6** Michael Laverty (Suzuki); **7** James Ellison (Honda); **8** Yukio Kagayama (Suzuki); **9** John Laverty (Kawasaki); **10** Ian Lowry (Kawasaki); **11** Andrew Pitt (Yamaha); **12** Tommy Bridewell (Honda); **13** Dan Linfoot (Yamaha); **14** Chris Burns (Aprilia); **15** Tommy Hill (Suzuki).
**Fastest lap:** Seeley, 1m 36.665s, 85.68mph/137.90km/h.

**Race 2 (14 laps, 32.214 miles/51.843km)**
**1** Tom Sykes (Kawasaki), 20m 19.948s, 95.05mph/152.97km/h.
**2** Ryuichi Kiyonari (Honda); **3** Michael Rutter (Ducati); **4** Michael Laverty (Suzuki); **5** James Ellison (Honda); **6** Tommy Hill (Suzuki); **7** Stuart Easton (Honda); **8** Yukio Kagayama (Suzuki); **9** Dan Linfoot (Yamaha); **10** Gary Mason (Kawasaki); **11** Ian Lowry (Kawasaki); **12** Simon Andrews (Kawasaki); **13** Peter Hickman (Yamaha); **14** Steve Brogan (BMW); **15** Adam Jenkinson (Kawasaki).
**Fastest lap:** M. Laverty, 1m 26.467s, 95.79mph/154.16km/h.

**Race 3 (20 laps, 46.020 miles/74.060km)**
**1** Tom Sykes (Kawasaki), 28m 56.799s, 95.38mph/153.50km/h.
**2** Ryuichi Kiyonari (Honda); **3** Michael Rutter (Ducati); **4** Tommy Hill (Suzuki); **5** James Ellison (Honda); **6** Josh Brookes (Honda); **7** Yukio Kagayama (Suzuki); **8** Stuart Easton (Honda); **9** John Laverty (Kawasaki); **10** Simon Andrews (Kawasaki); **11** Ian Lowry (Kawasaki); **12** Tommy Bridewell (Honda); **13** Chris Walker (Honda); **14** Peter Hickman (Yamaha); **15** Tom Tunstall (Honda).
**Fastest lap:** Rutter, 1m 26.059s, 96.24mph/154.89km/h.
**Championship points: 1** Kiyonari, 249; **2** Hill, 242; **3** Brookes, 239; **4** Rutter, 217; **5** M. Laverty, 206; **6** Seeley, 153.

**Fuchs-Silkolene British Supersport Championship, Round 8 (16 laps, 36.816 miles/59.250km)**
**1** James Westmoreland (Yamaha), 24m 44.545s, 89.27mph/143.67km/h.
**2** Sam Lowes (Honda); **3** Graeme Gowland (Honda); **4** Jason O'Halloran (Yamaha); **5** Ian Hutchinson (Honda); **6** Ben Wilson (Kawasaki); **7** Glen Richards (Honda); **8** Billy McConnell (Yamaha); **9** Joe Dickinson (Honda); **10** Patrick McDougall (Yamaha); **11** Jesse Trayler (Kawasaki); **12** Max Hunt (Yamaha); **13** Tom Grant (Kawasaki); **14** Daniel Keen (Yamaha); **15** Matthew Hoyle (Kawasaki).
**Fastest lap:** Westmoreland, 1m 28.691s, 93.39mph/150.30km/h.
**Championship points: 1** S. Lowes, 146; **2** Westmoreland, 116; **3** Gowland, 103; **4** McConnell, 99; **5** Wilson, 84; **6** Kennedy, 67.

**SpeedyRetail.com British 125GP Championship, Round 7 (13 laps, 29.913 miles/48.140km)**
**1** James Lodge (Seel/Honda), 20m 41.075s, 86.76mph/139.63km/h.
**2** Taylor Mackenzie (Honda); **3** John McPhee (Honda); **4** Fraser Rogers (Honda); **5** Dakota Mamola (Honda); **6** Deane Brown (Honda); **7** Danny Kent (Honda); **8** Rob Guiver (Honda); **9** Sam Hornsey (Honda); **10** Matthew Davies (Honda); **11** Philip Wakefield (Honda); **12** Wayne Ryan (Honda); **13** Kyle Ryde (Honda); **14** Nigel Percy (Honda); **15** Lee Jackson (Honda).
**Fastest lap:** Lodge, 1m 33.989s, 88.12mph/141.82km/h.
**Championship points: 1** Lodge, 116; **2** Guiver, 85; **3** Mackenzie, 80; **4** Brown, 70; **5** Wakefield, 53; **6** McPhee, 52.

**CADWELL PARK, 30 August, 2.180-mile/3.508km circuit.**
**MCE Insurance British Superbike Championship, Rounds 18 and 19**
**Race 1 (18 laps, 39.240 miles/63.144km)**
**1** Tommy Hill (Suzuki), 26m 25.609s, 89.09mph/143.38km/h.
**2** Josh Brookes (Honda); **3** Ryuichi Kiyonari (Honda); **4** Michael Laverty (Suzuki); **5** Michael Rutter (Ducati); **6** James Ellison (Honda); **7** Yukio Kagayama (Suzuki); **8** Alastair Seeley (Suzuki); **9** Dan Linfoot (Yamaha); **10** Stuart Easton (Honda); **11** Chris Walker (Honda); **12** Adam Jenkinson (Kawasaki); **13** Steve Brogan (BMW); **14** Gary Johnson (Suzuki); **15** Tom Tunstall (Honda).
**Fastest lap:** Brookes, 1m 27.398s, 89.79mph/144.51km/h.

**Race 2 (13 laps, 28.340 miles/45.609km)**
**1** Josh Brookes (Honda), 19m 0.530s, 89.45mph/143.96km/h.
**2** Tommy Hill (Suzuki); **3** Ryuichi Kiyonari (Honda); **4** Michael Laverty (Suzuki); **5** Michael Rutter (Ducati); **6** James Ellison (Honda); **7** Yukio Kagayama (Suzuki); **8** Tommy Bridewell (Honda); **9** Alastair Seeley (Suzuki); **10** Gary Mason (Kawasaki); **11** Stuart Easton (Honda); **12** John Laverty (Kawasaki); **13** Dan Linfoot (Yamaha); **14** Adam Jenkinson (Kawasaki); **15** Chris Walker (Honda).
**Fastest lap:** Kiyonari, 1m 26.848s, 90.36mph/145.42km/h.
*The top six BSB riders in points after Cadwell Park qualified for 'The Showdown', to decide the championship over the last three rounds. These six 'Title Fighters' had their points equalised at 500 and then individual podium credits added (3 points for each 1st place, 2 points for 2nd, 1 point for 3rd).*
**Championship points for start of Showdown: 1** Kiyonari, 525; **2** Hill, 525; **3** Brookes, 524; **4** Rutter, 510; **5** M. Laverty, 509; **6** Seeley, 505.

**Fuchs-Silkolene British Supersport Championship, Round 9 (14 laps, 30.520 miles/49.117km)**
**1** Sam Lowes (Honda), 21m 9.055s, 86.57mph/139.32km/h.
**2** James Westmoreland (Yamaha); **3** Ben Wilson (Kawasaki); **4** Jason O'Halloran (Yamaha); **5** Ian Hutchinson (Honda); **6** Glen Richards (Honda); **7** Jack Kennedy (Yamaha); **8** Daniel Cooper (Triumph): **9** Karl Harris (Triumph): **10** Marty Nutt (Yamaha); **11** Allan Jon Venter (Triumph): **12** Luke Mossey (Triumph): **13** Guy Martin (Honda); **14** Daniel Keen (Yamaha); **15** Jesse Trayler (Kawasaki).
**Fastest lap:** McConnell, 1m 29.287s, 87.89mph/141.45km/h.
**Championship points: 1** S. Lowes, 171; **2** Westmoreland, 136; **3** Gowland, 103; **4** Wilson, 100; **5** McConnell, 99; **6** Kennedy, 76.

**SpeedyRetail.com British 125GP Championship, Round 8 (14 laps, 30.520 miles/49.117km)**
**1** Rob Guiver (Honda), 22m 52.848s, 80.03mph/128.80km/h.
**2** John McPhee (Honda); **3** Andrew Reid (Honda); **4** Shaun Horsman (Honda); **5** Edward Rendell (Honda); **6** Sam Hornsey (Honda); **7** Lee Jackson (Honda); **8** Nigel Percy (Honda); **9** Matthew Paulo (Honda); **10** Tom Weeden (Honda); **11** Jon Vincent (Honda); **12** Ben Barratt (Honda); **13** Simon Low (Honda); **14** Kyle Ryde (Honda); **15** Wayne Ryan (Honda);.
**Fastest lap:** Guiver, 1m 34.371s, 83.16mph/133.83km/h.
**Championship points: 1** Lodge, 116; **2** Guiver, 110; **3** Mackenzie, 80; **4** McPhee, 72; **5** Brown, 70; **6** Hornsey, 56.

**CROFT, 12 September, 2.125-mile/3.420km circuit.**
**MCE Insurance British Superbike Championship, Rounds 20 and 21**
**Race 1 (20 laps, 42.500 miles/68.400km)**
**1** Tommy Hill (Suzuki), 27m 43.359s, 91.98mph/148.03km/h.
**2** Michael Laverty (Suzuki); **3** Stuart Easton (Honda); **4** Simon Andrews (Kawasaki); **5** Dan Linfoot (Yamaha); **6** Josh Brookes (Honda); **7** Loris Baz (Yamaha); **8** John Laverty (Kawasaki); **9** Chris Walker (Honda); **10** Gary Mason (Kawasaki); **11** Ryuichi Kiyonari (Honda); **12** Peter Hickman (Yamaha); **13** Adam Jenkinson (Kawasaki); **14** Tom Tunstall (Honda); **15** Hudson Kennaugh (Aprilia).
**Fastest lap:** Hill, 1m 20.798s, 94.68mph/152.37km/h.

**Race 2 (19 laps, 40.375 miles/64.980km)**
**1** Michael Laverty (Suzuki), 25m 42.670s, 94.22mph/151.63km/h.
**2** Tommy Hill (Suzuki); **3** Stuart Easton (Honda); **4** Ryuichi Kiyonari (Honda); **5** Michael Rutter (Ducati); **6** James Ellison (Honda); **7** Tommy Bridewell (Honda); **8** Josh Brookes (Honda); **9** Dan Linfoot (Yamaha); **10** Simon Andrews (Kawasaki); **11** Gary Mason (Kawasaki); **12** Chris Walker (Honda); **13** John Laverty (Kawasaki); **14** Yukio Kagayama (Suzuki); **15** Alastair Seeley (Suzuki).
**Fastest lap:** Hill, 1m 20.484s, 95.05mph/152.97km/h.
**Championship points: 1** Hill, 570; **2** M. Laverty, 554; **3** Kiyonari, 543; **4** Brookes, 542; **5** Rutter, 521; **6** Seeley, 506.

**Fuchs-Silkolene British Supersport Championship, Round 10 (14 laps, 29.750 miles/47.880km)**
**1** Sam Lowes (Honda), 20m 3.072s, 89.02mph/143.26km/h.
**2** James Westmoreland (Yamaha); **3** Jack Kennedy (Yamaha); **4** Alex Lowes (Yamaha); **5** Jason O'Halloran (Yamaha); **6** Daniel Cooper (Triumph): **7** Lee Johnston (Triumph): **8** Allan Jon Venter (Triumph): **9** Glen Richards (Honda); **10** Chris Martin (Kawasaki); **11** Jesse Trayler (Kawasaki); **12** Dean Hipwell (Yamaha); **13** Jamie Hamilton (Kawasaki); **14** Daniel Keen (Yamaha); **15** Jenny Tinmouth (Honda).
**Fastest lap:** A. Lowes, 1m 22.043s, 93.24mph/150.06km/h.
**Championship points: 1** S. Lowes, 196; **2** Westmoreland, 156; **3** Gowland, 103; **4** Wilson, 100; **5** McConnell, 99; **6** Kennedy, 92.

**SpeedyRetail.com British 125GP Championship, Round 9 (3 laps, 6.375 miles/10.260km)**
**Round postponed from Knockhill, half points awarded due to early stoppage.**
**1** John McPhee (Honda), 5m 3.624s, 75.58mph/121.63km/h.
**2** Deane Brown (Honda); **3** Rob Guiver (Honda); **4** Nigel Percy (Honda); **5** Matthew Davies (Honda); **6** Matthew Paulo (Honda); **7** Sam Hornsey (Honda); **8** Peter Sutherland (Honda); **9** Edward Rendell (Honda); **10** Fraser Rogers (Honda); **11** Harry Stafford (Honda); **12** Lee Jackson (Honda); **13** Jon Vincent (Honda); **14** Taylor Mackenzie (Honda); **15** Ben Barratt (Honda).
**Fastest lap:** Percy, 1m 37.696s, 78.30mph/126.01km/h.

**SpeedyRetail.com British 125GP Championship, Round 10 (14 laps, 29.750 miles/47.880km)**
**1** Taylor Mackenzie (Honda), 20m 31.118s, 86.99mph/140.00km/h.
**2** Deane Brown (Honda); **3** John McPhee (Honda); **4** Edward Rendell (Honda); **5** Rob Guiver (Honda); **6** Jon Vincent (Honda); **7** Andrew Reid (Honda); **8** Lee Jackson (Honda); **9** Shaun Horsman (Honda); **10** Matthew Davies (Honda); **11** Fraser Rogers (Honda); **12** Nigel Percy (Honda); **13** Peter Sutherland (Honda); **14** Kyle Ryde (Honda); **15** Ben Barratt (Honda).
**Fastest lap:** Brown, 1m 27.062s, 87.86mph/141.40km/h.
**Championship points: 1** Guiver, 129; **2** Lodge, 116; **3** Mackenzie, 106; **4** McPhee, 100.5; **5** Brown, 100; **6** Hornsey, 60.5.

**SILVERSTONE, 26 September, 3.667-mile/5.902km circuit.**
**MCE Insurance British Superbike Championship, Rounds 22 and 23 (2 x 10 laps, 36.670 miles/59.020km)**
**Race 1**
**1** Michael Rutter (Ducati), 24m 5.289s, 91.34mph/147.00km/h.
**2** Josh Brookes (Honda); **3** Michael Laverty (Suzuki); **4** James Ellison (Honda); **5** Ryuichi Kiyonari (Honda); **6** Alastair Seeley (Suzuki); **7** Simon Andrews (Kawasaki); **8** Tommy Hill (Suzuki); **9** Chris Walker (Honda); **10** Dan Linfoot (Yamaha); **11** Loris Baz (Yamaha); **12** Chris Burns (Aprilia); **13** Yukio Kagayama (Suzuki); **14** Gary Mason (Kawasaki); **15** Tom Tunstall (Honda).
**Fastest lap:** Rutter, 2m 22.448s, 92.68mph/149.15km/h.

**Race 2**
**1** James Ellison (Honda), 23m 58.750s, 91.76mph/147.67km/h.
**2** Ryuichi Kiyonari (Honda); **3** Josh Brookes (Honda); **4** Alastair Seeley (Suzuki); **5** Tommy Hill (Suzuki); **6** Dan Linfoot (Yamaha); **7** Gary Mason (Kawasaki); **8** Chris Walker (Honda); **9** John Laverty (Kawasaki); **10** Peter Hickman (Yamaha); **11** Gary Johnson (Suzuki); **12** Tommy Bridewell (Honda); **13** Pauli Pekkanen (Suzuki); **14** Yukio Kagayama (Suzuki); **15** Hudson Kennaugh (Aprilia).
**Fastest lap:** Ellison, 2m 21.670s, 93.19mph/149.98km/h.
**Championship points: 1** Hill, 589; **2** Brookes, 578; **3** Kiyonari, 574; **4** M. Laverty, 570; **5** Rutter, 546; **6** Seeley, 529.

**Fuchs-Silkolene British Supersport Championship, Round 11 (8 laps, 29.336 miles/47.216km)**
**1** Sam Lowes (Honda), 19m 46.063s, 89.05mph/143.31km/h.
**2** James Westmoreland (Yamaha); **3** Jason O'Halloran (Yamaha); **4** Jack Kennedy (Yamaha); **5** Glen Richards (Honda); **6** Ben Wilson (Kawasaki); **7** Alex Lowes (Yamaha); **8** Marty Nutt (Yamaha); **9** Lee Johnston (Triumph): **10** Dean Hipwell (Yamaha); **11** Billy McConnell (Yamaha); **12** Paul Young (Triumph): **13** Daniel Cooper (Triumph); **14** Graeme Gowland (Honda); **15** Adam Blacklock (Yamaha).
**Fastest lap:** S. Lowes, 2m 25.662s, 90.63mph/145.86km/h.
**Championship points: 1** S. Lowes, 221; **2** Westmoreland, 176; **3** Wilson, 110; **4** Gowland, 105; **5** Kennedy, 105; **6** McConnell, 104.

**SpeedyRetail.com British 125GP Championship, Round 11 (9 laps, 33.003 miles/53.118km)**
**1** Deane Brown (Honda), 24m 37.249s, 80.43mph/129.44km/h.
**2** James Lodge (Honda); **3** Edward Rendell (Honda); **4** Fraser Rogers (Honda); **5** Shaun Horsman (Honda); **6** Kyle Ryde (Honda); **7** Philip Wakefield (Honda); **8** Harry Stafford (Honda); **9** James Ford (Honda); **10** Andrew Reid (Honda); **11** Dan Moreton (Honda); **12** Bradley Hughes (Honda); **13** Simon Low (Honda); **14** Elliot Lodge (Honda); **15** Ben Barratt (Honda).
**Fastest lap:** Guiver, 2m 42.718s, 81.13mph/130.57km/h.
**Championship points: 1** J. Lodge, 136; **2** Guiver, 129; **3** Brown, 125; **4** Mackenzie, 106; **5** McPhee, 100.5; **6** Rogers, 73.

**OULTON PARK, 9/10 October, 2.692-mile/4.332km circuit.**
**MCE Insurance British Superbike Championship, Rounds 24, 25 and 26**
**Race 1 (16 laps, 43.072 miles/69.318km)**
**1** Ryuichi Kiyonari (Honda), 25m 43.282s, 100.47mph/161.69km/h.
**2** Tommy Hill (Suzuki); **3** James Ellison (Honda); **4** Michael Laverty (Suzuki); **5** Josh Brookes (Honda); **6** Tommy Bridewell (Honda); **7** Stuart Easton (Honda); **8** Gary Mason (Kawasaki); **9** John Laverty (Kawasaki); **10** Loris Baz (Yamaha); **11** Dan Linfoot (Yamaha); **12** Simon Andrews (Kawasaki); **13** Yukio Kagayama (Suzuki); **14** Peter Hickman (Yamaha); **15** Alastair Seeley (Suzuki).
**Fastest lap:** Hill, 1m 35.680s, 101.28mph/162.99km/h.

**Race 2 (7 laps, 18.844 miles/30.326km)**
**1** Ryuichi Kiyonari (Honda), 11m 16.253s, 100.31mph/161.43km/h.
**2** Stuart Easton (Honda); **3** Josh Brookes (Honda); **4** Michael Rutter (Ducati); **5** Alastair Seeley (Suzuki); **6** John Laverty (Kawasaki); **7** James Ellison (Honda); **8** Michael Laverty (Suzuki); **9** Loris Baz (Yamaha); **10** Adam Jenkinson (Kawasaki); **11** Steve Brogan (BMW); **12** Tom Tunstall (Honda); **13** Yukio Kagayama (Suzuki); **14** Gary Mason (Kawasaki); **15** Hudson Kennaugh (Aprilia).
**Fastest lap:** Kiyonari, 1m 35.808s, 101.15mph/162.79km/h.

**Race 3 (16 laps, 43.072 miles/69.318km)**
**1** Ryuichi Kiyonari (Honda), 26m 7.496s, 98.92mph/159.20km/h.
**2** Josh Brookes (Honda); **3** James Ellison (Honda); **4** Michael Laverty (Suzuki); **5** Tommy Hill (Suzuki); **6** Loris Baz (Yamaha); **7** Alastair Seeley (Suzuki); **8** John Laverty (Kawasaki); **9** Chris Walker (Honda); **10** Dan Linfoot (Yamaha); **11** Yukio Kagayama (Suzuki); **12** Adam Jenkinson (Kawasaki); **13** Tom Tunstall (Honda); **14** Hudson Kennaugh (Aprilia); **15** Simon Andrews (Kawasaki).
**Fastest lap:** Ellison, 1m 35.848s, 101.11mph/162.72km/h.

**Fuchs-Silkolene British Supersport Championship, Round 12 (12 laps, 32.304 miles/51.988km)**
**1** Ben Wilson (Kawasaki), 19m 57.002s, 97.15mph/156.35km/h.
**2** James Westmoreland (Yamaha); **3** Jack Kennedy (Yamaha); **4** Glen Richards (Honda); **5** Billy McConnell (Yamaha); **6** Paul Young (Triumph): **7** Marshal Neill (Honda); **8** Sam Lowes (Honda); **9** Lee Johnston (Triumph): **10** Luke Mossey (Triumph): **11** Jesse Trayler (Kawasaki); **12** Allan Jon Venter (Triumph): **13** Christian Iddon (Honda); **14** Alex Lowes (Yamaha); **15** Matthew Hoyle (Kawasaki).
**Fastest lap:** Westmoreland, 1m 38.715s, 98.17mph/157.99km/h.

**SpeedyRetail.com British 125GP Championship, Round 12 (10 laps, 26.920 miles/43.320km)**
**1** Taylor Mackenzie (Honda), 17m 52.421s, 90.36mph/145.42km/h.
**2** Deane Brown (Honda); **3** Rob Guiver (Honda); **4** James Lodge (Honda); **5** Fraser Rogers (Honda); **6** Wayne Ryan (Honda); **7** Sam Hornsey (Honda); **8** Matthew Davies (Honda); **9** Lee Jackson (Honda); **10** Harry Stafford (Honda); **11** Nigel Percy (Honda); **12** Shaun Horsman (Honda); **13** Ben Barratt (Honda); **14** Tom Weeden (Honda); **15** Peter Sutherland (Honda).
**Fastest lap:** Mackenzie, 1m 45.637s, 91.74mph/147.64km/h.

**Final British Superbike Championship points:**
**Final Championship Points**

| | | |
|---|---|---|
| **1** | Ryuichi Kiyonari | 649 |
| **2** | Josh Brookes | 625 |
| **3** | Tommy Hill | 620 |
| **4** | Michael Laverty | 604 |
| **5** | Michael Rutter | 559 |
| **6** | Alastair Seeley | 550 |

**7** James Ellison, 210; **8** John Laverty, 190; **9** Stuart Easton, 189; **10** Chris Walker, 130; **11** Tommy Bridewell, 105; **12** Gary Mason, 104; **13** Simon Andrews, 103; **14** Dan Linfoot, 101; **15** Yukio Kagayama, 92.

**Final British Supersport Championship points:**

| | | |
|---|---|---|
| **1** | Sam Lowes | 229 |
| **2** | James Westmoreland | 196 |
| **3** | Ben Wilson | 135 |
| **4** | Jack Kennedy | 121 |
| **5** | Billy McConnell | 115 |
| **6** | Graeme Gowland | 105 |

**7** Glen Richards, 105; **8** Jason O'Halloran, 94; **9** Daniel Cooper, 84; **10** Ian Hutchinson, 69; **11** Allan Jon Venter, 42; **12** Alex Lowes, 41; **13** Lee Johnston, 38; **14** Marty Nutt, 37; **15** Tom Grant, 36.

**Final British 125GP Championship points:**

| | | |
|---|---|---|
| **1** | James Lodge | 149 |
| **2** | Rob Guiver | 145 |
| **3** | Deane Brown | 145 |
| **4** | Taylor Mackenzie | 131 |
| **5** | John McPhee | 100.5 |
| **6** | Fraser Rogers | 84 |

**7** Sam Hornsey, 69.5; **8** Edward Rendell, 62.5; **9** Philip Wakefield, 62; **10** Lee Jackson, 58; **11** Jon Vincent, 52.5; **12** Andrew Reid, 51; **13** Wayne Ryan, 49; **14** Shaun Horsman, 45; **15** Dakota Mamola, 40.

# Supersport World Championship

**PHILLIP ISLAND, Australia, 28 February, 2.762-mile/4.445km circuit.**
**Supersport World Championship, Round 1 (21 laps, 58.002 miles/93.345km)**
**1** Eugene Laverty, IRL (Honda), 33m 37.836s, 103.481mph/166.536km/h.
**2** Joan Lascorz, SPA (Kawasaki); **3** Kenan Sofuoglu, TUR (Honda); **4** David Salom, SPA (Triumph); **5** Fabien Foret, FRA (Kawasaki); **6** Massimo Roccoli, ITA (Honda); **7** Robbin Harms, DEN (Honda); **8** Jason DiSalvo, USA (Triumph); **9** Miguel Praia, POR (Honda); **10** Gino Rea, GBR (Honda); **11** Katsuaki Fujiwara, JPN (Kawasaki); **12** Chaz Davies, GBR (Triumph); **13** Sebastien Charpentier, FRA (Triumph); **14** Paola Cazzola, ITA (Honda); **15** Danilo Dell'Omo, ITA (Honda).

**Fastest lap:** Eugene Laverty, IRL (Honda), 1m 35.204s, 104.441mph/168.081km/h.
**Championship points: 1** Laverty, 25; **2** Lascorz, 20; **3** Sofuoglu, 16; **4** Salom, 13; **5** Foret, 11; **6** Roccoli, 10.

**PORTIMAO, Portugal, 28 March, 2.853-mile/4.592km circuit.**
**Supersport World Championship, Round 2 (20 laps, 57.067 miles/91.840km)**
**1** Kenan Sofuoglu, TUR (Honda), 35m 21.143s, 96.854mph/155.871km/h.
**2** Joan Lascorz, SPA (Kawasaki); **3** Michele Pirro, ITA (Honda); **4** Chaz Davies, GBR (Triumph); **5** Fabien Foret, FRA (Kawasaki); 6 Katsuaki Fujiwara, JPN (Kawasaki); **7** Robbin Harms, DEN (Honda); **8** Gino Rea, GBR (Honda); **9** Massimo Roccoli, ITA (Honda); 10 David Salom, SPA (Triumph); **11** Eugene Laverty, IRL (Honda); **12** Jason DiSalvo, USA (Triumph); **13** Alexander Lundh, SWE (Honda); **14** Bastien Chesaux SUI (Honda); **15** Danilo Dell'Omo, ITA (Honda).
**Fastest lap:** Michele Pirro, ITA (Honda), 1m 45.180s, 97.662mph/157.171km/h (record).
**Championship points: 1** Sofuoglu, 41; **2** Lascorz, 40; **3** Laverty, 30; **4** Foret, 22; **5** Salom, 19; **6** Harms, 18.

**VALENCIA, Spain, 11 April, 2.489-mile/4.005km circuit.**
**Supersport World Championship, Round 3 (23 laps, 57.238 miles/92.115km)**
**1** Joan Lascorz, SPA (Kawasaki); 37m 32.610s, 91.474mph/147.213km/h.
**2** Kenan Sofuoglu, TUR (Honda); **3** Chaz Davies, GBR (Triumph); **4** David Salom, SPA (Triumph); **5** Eugene Laverty, IRL (Honda); **6** Gino Rea, GBR (Honda); **7** Matthieu Lagrive, FRA (Triumph); **8** Alexander Lundh, SWE (Honda); **9** Robbin Harms, DEN (Honda); **10** Fabien Foret, FRA (Kawasaki); **11** Michele Pirro, ITA (Honda); **12** Miguel Praia, POR (Honda).
**Fastest lap:** Joan Lascorz, SPA (Kawasaki); 1m 37.049s, 92.313mph/148.564km/h.
**Championship points: 1** Lascorz, 65; **2** Sofuoglu, 61; **3** Laverty, 41; **4** Davies, 33; **5** Salom, 32; **6** Foret, 28.

**ASSEN, Holland, 25 April, 2.822-mile/4.542km circuit.**
**Supersport World Championship, Round 4 (21 laps, 59.268 miles/95.382km)**
**1** Eugene Laverty, IRL (Honda), 34m 45.753s, 102.296mph/164.629km/h.
**2** Joan Lascorz, SPA (Kawasaki); **3** Kenan Sofuoglu, TUR (Honda); **4** Chaz Davies, GBR (Triumph); **5** Matthieu Lagrive, FRA (Triumph); 6 Robbin Harms, DEN (Honda); **7** Gino Rea, GBR (Honda); **8** Katsuaki Fujiwara, JPN (Kawasaki); **9** Massimo Roccoli, ITA (Honda); **10** Miguel Praia, POR (Honda); **11** Alexander Lundh, SWE (Honda); **12** Jason DiSalvo, USA (Triumph); **13** Danilo Dell'Omo, ITA (Honda); **14** Bastien Chesaux SUI (Honda); **15** Paola Cazzola, ITA (Honda).
**Fastest lap:** Kenan Sofuoglu, TUR (Honda), 1m 38.608s, 103.036mph/165.820km/h (new circuit layout).
**Championship points: 1** Lascorz, 85; **2** Sofuoglu, 77; **3** Laverty, 66; **4** Davies, 46; **5** Harms, 35; **6** Rea, 33.

**MONZA, Italy, 9 May, 3.590-mile/5.777km circuit.**
**Supersport World Championship, Round 5 (16 laps, 57.435 miles/92.432km)**
**1** Eugene Laverty, IRL (Honda), 28m 51.936s, 119.383mph/192.129km/h.
**2** Kenan Sofuoglu, TUR (Honda); **3** Joan Lascorz, SPA (Kawasaki); **4** Michele Pirro, ITA (Honda); **5** Katsuaki Fujiwara, JPN (Kawasaki); **6** Matthieu Lagrive, FRA (Triumph); **7** Chaz Davies, GBR (Triumph); **8** David Salom, SPA (Triumph); **9** Gino Rea, GBR (Honda); **10** Miguel Praia, POR (Honda); **11** Massimo Roccoli, ITA (Honda); **12** Gianluca Vizziello, ITA (Honda); **13** Alexander Lundh, SWE (Honda); **14** Andrea Boscoscuro, ITA (Honda); **15** Bastien Chesaux SUI (Honda).
**Fastest lap:** Eugene Laverty, IRL (Honda), 1m 47.767s, 119.914mph/192.983km/h (new circuit layout).
**Championship points: 1** Lascorz, 101; **2** Sofuoglu, 97; **3** Laverty, 91; **4** Davies, 55; **5** Salom, 40; **6** Rea, 40.

**KYALAMI, South Africa, 16 May, 2.638-mile/4.246km circuit.**
**Supersport World Championship, Round 6 (23 laps, 60.682 miles/97.658km)**
**1** Eugene Laverty, IRL (Honda), 39m 13.215s, 92.832mph/149.399km/h.
**2** Kenan Sofuoglu, TUR (Honda); **3** Chaz Davies, GBR (Triumph); **4** Michele Pirro, ITA (Honda); **5** Joan Lascorz, SPA (Kawasaki); **6** Matthieu Lagrive, FRA (Triumph); **7** David Salom, SPA (Triumph); **8** Robbin Harms, DEN (Honda); **9** Gino Rea, GBR (Honda); **10** Miguel Praia, POR (Honda); **11** Lance Isaacs, RSA (Honda); **12** Katsuaki Fujiwara, JPN (Kawasaki); **13** Alexander Lundh, SWE (Honda); **14** Bastien Chesaux SUI (Honda); **15** Andrea Boscoscuro, ITA (Honda).
**Fastest lap:** Kenan Sofuoglu, TUR (Honda), 1m 41.054s, 93.990mph/151.262km/h.
**Championship points: 1** Sofuoglu, 117; **2** Laverty, 116; **3** Lascorz, 112; **4** Davies, 71; **5** Salom, 49; **6** Pirro, 47.

**MILLER, USA, 31 May, 3.049-mile/4.907km circuit.**
**Supersport World Championship, Round 7 (18 laps, 54.883 miles/88.326km)**
**1** Kenan Sofuoglu, TUR (Honda), 33m 45.278s, 97.557mph/157.002km/h.
**2** Eugene Laverty, IRL (Honda); **3** Joan Lascorz, SPA (Kawasaki); **4** Chaz Davies, GBR (Triumph); **5** Michele Pirro, ITA (Honda); **6** Katsuaki Fujiwara, JPN (Kawasaki); **7** David Salom, SPA (Triumph); **8** Robbin Harms, DEN (Honda); **9** Gino Rea, GBR (Honda); **10** Fabien Foret, FRA (Kawasaki); **11** Jason DiSalvo, USA (Triumph); **12** Matthieu Lagrive, FRA (Triumph); **13** Massimo Roccoli, ITA (Honda); **14** Miguel Praia, POR (Honda); **15** Alexander Lundh, SWE (Honda).
**Fastest lap:** Kenan Sofuoglu, TUR (Honda), 1m 51.702s, 98.167mph/158.146km/h (record).
**Championship points: 1** Sofuoglu, 142; **2** Laverty, 136; **3** Lascorz, 128; **4** Davies, 84; **5** Pirro, 58; **6** Salom, 58.

**MISANO, Italy, 27 June, 2.623-mile/4.226km circuit.**
**Supersport World Championship, Round 8 (22 laps, 57.770 miles/92.972km)**
**1** Eugene Laverty, IRL (Honda), 36m 46.369s, 94.260mph/151.697km/h.
**2** Joan Lascorz, SPA (Kawasaki); **3** Kenan Sofuoglu, TUR (Honda); **4** Chaz Davies, GBR (Triumph); **5** Roberto Tamburini, ITA (Yamaha); **6** Robbin Harms, DEN (Honda); **7** Massimo Roccoli, ITA (Honda); **8** Fabien Foret, FRA (Kawasaki); **9** Miguel Praia, POR (Honda); **10** David Salom, SPA (Triumph); **11** Matthieu Lagrive, FRA (Triumph); **12** Vittorio Iannuzzo, ITA (Triumph); **13** Alessio Palumbo, ITA (Kawasaki); **14** Danilo Dell'Omo, ITA (Honda); **15** Bastien Chesaux SUI (Honda).
**Fastest lap:** Kenan Sofuoglu, TUR (Honda), 1m 39.239s, 95.258mph/153.303km/h.
**Championship points: 1** Laverty, 161; **2** Sofuoglu, 158; **3** Lascorz, 148; **4** Davies, 97; **5** Salom, 64; **6** Harms, 61.

**BRNO, Czech Republic, 11 July, 3.357-mile/5.403km circuit.**
**Supersport World Championship, Round 9 (18 laps, 60.431 miles/97.254km)**
**1** Kenan Sofuoglu, TUR (Honda), 37m 25.108s, 96.900mph/155.945km/h.
**2** Joan Lascorz, SPA (Kawasaki); **3** Chaz Davies, GBR (Triumph); **4** Gino Rea, GBR (Honda); **5** Katsuaki Fujiwara, JPN (Kawasaki); **6** Robbin Harms, DEN (Honda); **7** Miguel Praia, POR (Honda); **8** David Salom, SPA (Triumph); **9** Matthieu Lagrive, FRA (Triumph); **10** Fabien Foret, FRA (Kawasaki); **11** Vittorio Iannuzzo, ITA (Triumph); **12** Massimo Roccoli, ITA (Honda); **13** Daniel Bukowski, POL (Honda); **14** Alessio Palumbo, ITA (Kawasaki); **15** Tomas Holubec, CZE (Honda).
**Fastest lap:** Joan Lascorz, SPA (Kawasaki), 2m 03.998s, 97.471mph/156.864km/h.
**Championship points: 1** Sofuoglu, 183; **2** Lascorz, 168; **3** Laverty, 161; **4** Davies, 113; **5** Salom, 72; **6** Harms, 71.

**SILVERSTONE, Great Britain, 1 August, 3.667-mile/5.902km circuit.**
**Supersport World Championship, Round 10 (16 laps, 58.677 miles/94.432km)**
**1** Eugene Laverty, IRL (Honda), 34m 35.068s, 101.798mph/163.828km/h.

**2** Kenan Sofuoglu, TUR (Honda); **3** Gino Rea, GBR (Honda); **4** Chaz Davies, GBR (Triumph); **5** Robbin Harms, DEN (Honda); **6** Miguel Praia, POR (Honda); **7** Matthieu Lagrive, FRA (Triumph); **8** David Salom, SPA (Triumph); **9** Massimo Roccoli, ITA (Honda); **10** Sam Lowes, GBR (Honda); **11** James Westmoreland, GBR (Yamaha); **12** Fabien Foret, FRA (Kawasaki); **13** Billy McConnell, AUS (Yamaha); **14** Vittorio Iannuzzo, ITA (Triumph); **15** Katsuaki Fujiwara, JPN (Kawasaki).
**Fastest lap:** Kenan Sofuoglu, TUR (Honda), 2m 08.717s, 102.569mph/165.069km/h (new circuit).
**Championship points: 1** Sofuoglu, 203; **2** Laverty, 186; **3** Lascorz, 168; **4** Davies, 126; **5** Rea, 83; **6** Harms, 82.

**NÜRBURGRING, Germany, 5 September, 3.192-mile/5.137km circuit.**
**Supersport World Championship, Round 11 (19 laps, 60.648 miles/97.603km)**
**1** Eugene Laverty, IRL (Honda), 37m 52.893s, 96.059mph/154.592km/h.
**2** Kenan Sofuoglu, TUR (Honda); **3** Broc Parkes, AUS (Kawasaki); **4** Fabien Foret, FRA (Kawasaki); **5** Chaz Davies, GBR (Triumph); **6** David Salom, SPA (Triumph); **7** Massimo Roccoli, ITA (Honda); **8** Michele Pirro, ITA (Honda); **9** Roberto Tamburini, ITA (Yamaha); **10** Danilo Dell'Omo, ITA (Honda); **11** Robbin Harms, DEN (Honda); **12** Christian Iddon, GBR (Honda); **13** Miguel Praia, POR (Honda); **14** Imre Toth, CZE (Honda).
**Fastest lap:** Eugene Laverty, IRL (Honda), 1m 59.027s, 96.542mph/155.370km/h.
**Championship points: 1** Sofuoglu, 223; **2** Laverty, 211; **3** Lascorz, 168; **4** Davies, 137; **5** Salom, 90; **6** Harms, 87.

**IMOLA, Italy, 26 September, 3.067-mile/4.936km circuit.**
**Supersport World Championship, Round 12 (19 laps, 58.275 miles/93.784km)**
**1** Michele Pirro, ITA (Honda), 36m 07.906s, 96.770mph/155.737km/h.
**2** Kenan Sofuoglu, TUR (Honda); **3** Eugene Laverty, IRL (Honda); **4** Broc Parkes, AUS (Kawasaki); **5** Katsuaki Fujiwara, JPN (Kawasaki); **6** Massimo Roccoli, ITA (Honda); **7** Mark Aitchison, AUS (Honda); **8** Cristiano Migliorati, ITA (Kawasaki); **9** Roberto Tamburini, ITA (Yamaha); **10** Gianluca Vizziello, ITA (Honda); **11** Matthieu Lagrive, FRA (Triumph); **12** Vittorio Iannuzzo, ITA (Triumph); **13** Alessio Palumbo, ITA (Kawasaki); **14** Giuseppe Barone, ITA (Yamaha); **15** Alexander Lundh, SWE (Honda).
**Fastest lap:** Eugene Laverty, IRL (Honda), 1m 52.198s, 98.411mph/158.377km/h.
**Championship points: 1** Sofuoglu, 243; **2** Laverty, 227; **3** Lascorz, 168; **4** Davies, 137; **5** Pirro, 91; **6** Salom, 90.

**MAGNY-COURS, France, 3 October, 2.741-mile/4.411km circuit.**
**Supersport World Championship, Round 13 (22 laps, 60.299 miles/97.042km)**
**1** Eugene Laverty, IRL (Honda), 37m 46.575s, 95.773mph/154.132km/h.
**2** Kenan Sofuoglu, TUR (Honda); **3** Chaz Davies, GBR (Triumph); **4** Massimo Roccoli, ITA (Honda); **5** Robbin Harms, DEN (Honda); **6** Katsuaki Fujiwara, JPN (Kawasaki); **7** David Salom, SPA (Triumph); **8** Michele Pirro, ITA (Honda); **9** Roberto Tamburini, ITA (Yamaha); **10** Miguel Praia, POR (Honda); **11** Axel Maurin, FRA (Yamaha); **12** Florian Marino, FRA (Honda).
**Fastest lap:** Eugene Laverty, IRL (Honda), 1m 42.295s, 96.457mph/155.233km/h.

**Final World Supersport Championship points:**

| | | |
|---|---|---|
| **1** | Kenan Sofuoglu, TUR | 263 |
| **2** | Eugene Laverty, IRL | 252 |
| **3** | Joan Lascorz, SPA | 168 |
| **4** | Chaz Davies, GBR | 153 |
| **5** | Michele Pirro, ITA | 99 |
| **6** | David Salom, SPA | 99 |

**7** Robbin Harms, DEN, 98; **8** Massimo Roccoli, ITA, 84; **9** Gino Rea, GBR, 83; **10** Katsuaki Fujiwara, JPN, 81; **11** Matthieu Lagrive, FRA, 70; **12** Miguel Praia, POR, 66; **13** Fabien Foret, FRA, 65; **14** Roberto Tamburini, ITA, 32; **15** Broc Parkes, AUS, 29.